GENERAL MOTORS

SPECTRUM/STORM
1985-93 REPAIR MANUAL

CHILTON'S

Senior Vice President	Ronald A. Hoxter
Publisher and Editor-In-Chief	Kerry A. Freeman, S.A.E.
Executive Editors	Dean F. Morgantini, S.A.E., W. Calvin Settle, Jr., S.A.E.
Managing Editor	Nick D'Andrea
Special Products Manager	Ken Grabowski, A.S.E., S.A.E.
Senior Editors	Jacques Gordon, Michael L. Grady, Debra McCall, Kevin M. G. Maher, Richard J. Rivele, S.A.E., Richard T. Smith, Jim Taylor, Ron Webb
Project Managers	Martin J. Gunther, Will Kessler, A.S.E., Richard Schwartz
Production Manager	Andrea Steiger
Product Systems Manager	Robert Maxey
Director of Manufacturing	Mike D'Imperio
Editors	Sam Fiorani, Kevin M. G. Maher, Anthony Tortorici

CHILTON BOOK COMPANY

Manufactured in USA
© 1993 Chilton Book Company
Chilton Way, Radnor, PA 19089
ISBN 0-8019-8425-4
Library of Congress Catalog Card No. 92-054900
456789012   5432109876

Contents

Contents

SAFETY NOTICE

Proper service and repair procedures are vital to the safe, reliable operation of all motor vehicles, as well as the personal safety of those performing repairs. This manual outlines procedures for servicing and repairing vehicles using safe, effective methods. The procedures contain many NOTES, CAUTIONS, and WARNINGS which should be followed along with standard procedures to eliminate the possibility of personal injury or improper service which could damage the vehicle or compromise its safety.

It is important to note that the repair procedures and techniques, tools and parts for servicing motor vehicles, as well as the skill and experience of the individual performing the work vary widely. It is not possible to anticipate all of the conceivable ways or conditions under which vehicles may be serviced, or to provide cautions as to all of the possible hazards that may result. Standard and accepted safety precautions and equipment should be used when handling toxic or flammable fluids, and safety goggles or other protection should be used during cutting, grinding, chiseling, prying,or any other process that can cause material removal or projectiles.

Some procedures require the use of tools specially designed for a specific purpose. Before substituting another tool or procedure, you must be completely satisfied that neither your personal safety, nor the performance of the vehicle will be endangered.

Although information in this manual is based on industry sources and is complete as possible at the time of publication, the possibility exists that some car manufacturers made later changes which could not be included here. While striving for total accuracy, Chilton Book Company cannot assume responsibility for any errors, changes or omissions that may occur in the compilation of this data.

PART NUMBERS

Part numbers listed in this reference are not recommendation by Chilton for any product by brand name. They are references that can be used with interchange manuals and aftermarket supplier catalogs to locate each brand supplier's discrete part number.

SPECIAL TOOLS

Special tools are recommended by the vehicle manufacturer to perform their specific job. Use has been kept to a minimum, but where absolutely necessary, they are referred to in the text by the part number of the tool manufacturer. These tools can be purchased, under the appropriate part number, from your Honda dealer or regional distributor, or an equivalent tool can be purchased locally from a tool supplier or parts outlet. Before substituting any tool for the one recommended, read the SAFETY NOTICE at the top of this page.

ACKNOWLEDGMENTS

The Chilton Book Company expresses appreciation to the General Motors Corp. for their generous assistance.

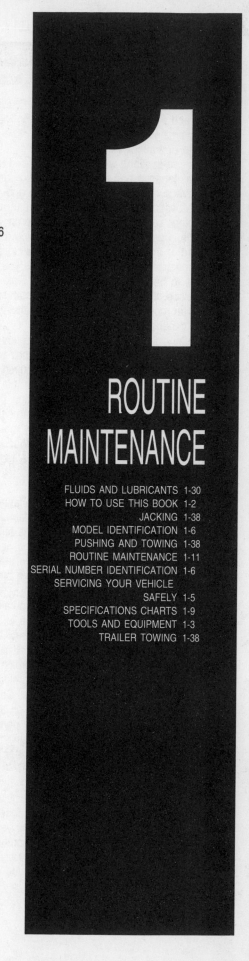

1
ROUTINE
MAINTENANCE

HOW TO USE THIS BOOK

Chilton's Total Car Care Manual for the Chevrolet/Geo Spectrum and Storm is intended to help you learn more about the inner workings of your vehicle and save you money on its upkeep and operation.

The first two sections will be the most used, since they contain maintenance and tune-up information and procedures. Studies have shown that a properly tuned and maintained car can get at least 10% better gas mileage than an out-of-tune car. The other sections deal with the more complex systems of your vehicle. Operating systems from engine through brakes are covered to the extent that the average do-it-yourselfer becomes mechanically involved. It will give you detailed instructions to help you change your own brake pads and shoes, replace spark plugs, and perform many more jobs that will save you money, give you personal satisfaction, and help you avoid expensive problems.

A secondary purpose of this book is a reference for owners who want to understand their car and/or their mechanics better. In this case, no tools at all are required.

Before removing any bolts, read through the entire procedure. This will give you the overall view of what tools and supplies will be required. There is nothing more frustrating than having to walk to the bus stop on Monday morning because you were short one bolt on Sunday afternoon. So read ahead and plan ahead. Each operation should be approached logically and all procedures thoroughly understood before attempting any work.

All sections contain adjustments, maintenance, removal and installation procedures and repair or overhaul procedures. When repair is not considered practical, we tell you how to remove the part and then how to install the new or rebuilt replacement. In this way, you at least save the labor costs. Backyard repair of such components as the alternator is just not practical.

Two basic mechanic's rules should be mentioned here. One, whenever the left side of the car or engine is referred to, it is meant to specify the driver's side of the car. Conversely, the right side of the car means the passenger's side. Secondly, most screws and bolts are removed by turning counterclockwise, and tightened by turning clockwise.

Safety is always the most important rule. Constantly be aware of the dangers involved in working on an automobile and take the proper precautions. (See the portion of this section on Servicing Your Vehicle Safely and the SAFETY NOTICE on the acknowledgment page.)

Pay attention to the instructions provided. There are 3 common mistakes in mechanical work:

1. Incorrect order of assembly, disassembly or adjustment. When taking something apart or putting it together, doing things in the wrong order usually just costs you extra time; however in some cases it CAN damage components. Read the entire procedure before beginning disassembly. Do everything in the order in which the instructions say you should do it,

even if you can't immediately see a reason for it. When you're taking apart something that is very intricate, you might want to draw a picture of how it looks when assembled at one or more points in order to assure you get everything back in its proper position. (We will supply exploded views whenever possible). When making adjustments, especially tune-up adjustments, do them in order; often, one adjustment affects another, and you cannot expect even satisfactory results unless each adjustment is made only when it cannot be changed by any other.

2. Overtorquing (or undertorquing): While it is more common for overtorquing to cause damage, undertorquing can cause a fastener to vibrate loose causing serious damage. Especially when dealing with aluminum parts, pay attention to torque specifications and utilize a torque wrench in assembly. If a torque figure is not available, remember that if you are using the right tool to do the job, you will probably not have to strain yourself to get a fastener tight enough. The pitch of most threads is so slight that the tension you put on the wrench will be multiplied many, many times in actual force on what you are tightening. A good example of how critical torque is can be seen in the case of spark plug installation, especially where you are putting the plug into an aluminum cylinder head. Too little torque can fail to crush the gasket, causing leakage of combustion gases and consequent overheating of the plug and engine parts. Too much torque can damage the threads or distort the plug, which changes the sp ark gap.

There are many commercial products available for ensuring the fasteners won't come loose, even if they are not torqued just right (a very common brand is Loctite®). If you're worried about getting something together tight enough to hold, but loose enough to avoid mechanical damage during assembly, one of these products might offer substantial insurance. Read the label on the package and make sure the product is compatible with the materials, fluids, etc. involved.

3. Crossthreading. This occurs when a part such as a bolt is screwed into a nut or casting at the wrong angle and forced. Crossthreading is more likely to occur if access is difficult. It helps to clean and lubricate fasteners, and to begin threading with the part to be installed going straight inward. Then, start the bolt, spark plug, etc. with your fingers. If you encounter resistance, unscrew the part and start over again at a different angle until it can be inserted and turned several turns without much effort. Keep in mind that many parts, especially spark plugs, use tapered threads so that gentle turning will automatically bring the part you're threading to the proper angle if you don't force it or resist a change in angle. Don't put a wrench on the part until it's been turned a couple of turns by hand. If you suddenly encounter resistance, and the part has not seated fully, don't force it. Screw it back out and make sure it's clean and threading properly.

Always take your time and be patient; once you have some experience, working on your car will become an enjoyable hobby.

TOOLS AND EQUIPMENT

◆ **See Figures 1, 2 and 3**

Naturally, without the proper tools and equipment it is impossible to properly service your vehicle. It would be impossible to catalog each tool that you would need to perform each or any operation in this book. It would also be unwise for the amateur to rush out and buy an expensive set of tools on the theory that he may need one or more of them at sometime.

The best approach is to proceed slowly, gathering together a good quality set of those tools that are used most frequently. Don't be misled by the low cost of bargain tools. It is far better to spend a little more for better quality. Forged wrenches, 6 or 12-point sockets and fine tooth ratchets are by far preferable than their less expensive counterparts. As any good mechanic can tell you, there are few worse experiences than trying to work on a car with bad tools. Your monetary savings will be far outweighed by frustration and mangled knuckles.

Begin accumulating those tools that are used most frequently; those associated with routine maintenance and tune-up.

In addition to the normal assortment of pliers and screwdrivers, you should have the following tools for routine maintenance jobs:

1. Metric and SAE wrenches, sockets and combination open end/box end wrenches in sizes from 3mm to 19mm, 1/8 in. to 3/4 in. and a spark plug socket (13/16 in. or 5/8 in. depending on plug type). With Spectrum and Storm vehicles, you will most likely find that Metric tools are usually sufficient or required for your purposes.

If possible, buy various length socket drive extensions. One break in this department is that the metric sockets available in the U.S. will all fit the ratchet handles and extensions you may already have (1/4 in., 3/8 in., and 1/2 in. drive).

2. Jackstands for support.
3. Oil filter wrench.
4. Oil filler spout or funnel.
5. Grease gun for lubrication.
6. Hydrometer for checking the battery.
7. A container for draining oil.
8. Many rags for wiping up the inevitable mess.

In addition to the above items there are several other tools that are not absolutely necessary, but handy to have around. These include oil dry, a transmission funnel and the usual supply of lubricants, antifreeze and fluids, although these can be purchased as needed. This is a basic list for routine maintenance, but only your personal needs and desire can accurately determine your list of tools.

The second list of tools is for tune-ups. While the tools involved here are slightly more sophisticated, they need not be outrageously expensive. There are several inexpensive tachometers on the market that are every bit as good for the average mechanic as a $100.00 professional model. Just be sure that the meter goes to at least 1500 rpm on the scale and that it can be used on 4, 6, or 8 cylinder engines. A basic list of tune-up equipment could include:

9. Tachometer.
10. Spark plug wrench.
11. Wire spark plug gauge/adjusting tools.

In addition to these basic tune-up tools there are several other tools and gauges you may find useful. These include:

12. A compression gauge. The screw in type is slower to use but it eliminates the possibility of a faulty reading due to escaping pressure.
13. A manifold vacuum gauge.
14. A 12V test light.
15. An induction meter. This is used for determining whether or not there is current in a wire. These are handy for use if a wire is broken somewhere in a wiring harness.

As a final note, you will probably find a torque wrench necessary for all but the most basic work. The beam type models are perfectly adequate although the newer click types are more precise.

Special Tools

Normally, the use of special factory tools is avoided for repair procedures, since these are not readily available for the do-it-yourself mechanic. When it is possible to perform the job with more commonly available tools, it will be pointed out, but occasionally, a special tool was designed to perform a specific function and should be used. Before substituting another tool, you should be convinced that neither your safety nor the performance of the vehicle will be compromised.

Some special tools are available commercially from major tool manufacturers. Others can be purchased from your Chevrolet/Geo dealer or from the Kent-Moore SPX Corporation, 29784 Little Mack, Roseville, MI 48066-2298. For fast service call the toll-free order line at 1-800-345-2233 Mon.-Fri. 8:00 A.M-8:00 P.M. EST or Fax your order to 313-578-7375.

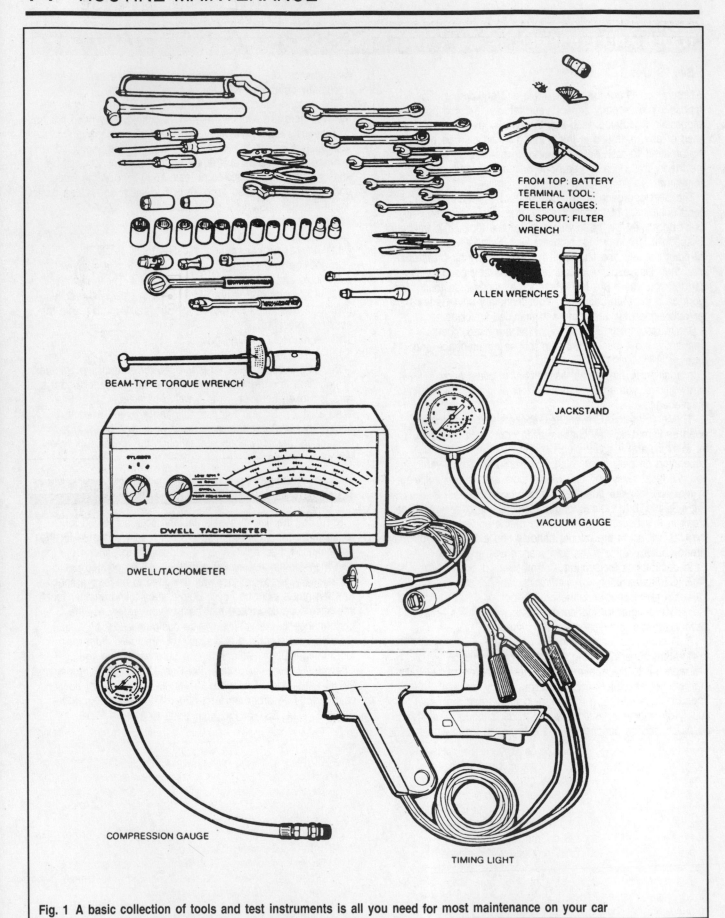

FROM TOP: BATTERY
TERMINAL TOOL;
FEELER GAUGES;
OIL SPOUT; FILTER
WRENCH

ALLEN WRENCHES

JACKSTAND

BEAM-TYPE TORQUE WRENCH

DWELL TACHOMETER

DWELL/TACHOMETER

VACUUM GAUGE

COMPRESSION GAUGE

TIMING LIGHT

Fig. 1 A basic collection of tools and test instruments is all you need for most maintenance on your car

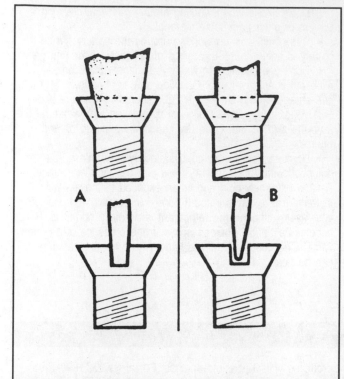

Fig. 2 Keep screwdrivers in good shape. They should fit the slot as shown in 'A'. If they look like those shown in 'B', they need grinding or replacing

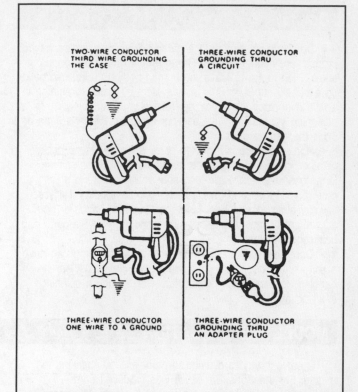

Fig. 3 When using electric tools, make sure they are properly grounded

SERVICING YOUR VEHICLE SAFELY

It is virtually impossible to anticipate all of the hazards involved with automotive maintenance and service, but care and common sense will prevent most accidents.

The rules of safety for mechanics range from 'don't smoke around gasoline' to 'use the proper tool for the job.' The trick to avoiding injuries is to develop safe work habits and take every possible precaution.

Do's

• Do keep a fire extinguisher and first aid kit within easy reach.

• Do wear safety glasses or goggles when cutting, drilling, grinding or prying, even if you have 20/20 vision. If you wear glasses for the sake of vision, then they should be made of hardened glass that can serve also as safety glasses, or wear safety goggles over your regular glasses.

• Do shield your eyes whenever you work around the battery. Batteries contain sulfuric acid; in case of contact with the eyes or skin, flush the area with water or a mixture of water and baking soda and get medical attention immediately.

• Do use safety stands for any under-car service. Jacks are for raising vehicles; safety stands are for making sure the vehicle stays raised until you want it to come down. Whenever the vehicle is raised, block the wheels remaining on the ground and set the parking brake.

• Do use adequate ventilation when working with any chemicals. Just like carbon monoxide, the asbestos dust resulting from brake lining wear can be poisonous in sufficient quantities.

• Do disconnect the negative battery cable when working on the electrical system. The primary ignition system can contain up to 40,000 volts.

• Do follow manufacturer's directions whenever working with potentially hazardous materials. Both brake fluid and antifreeze are poisonous if taken internally.

• Do properly maintain your tools. Loose hammerheads, mushroomed punches and chisels, frayed or poorly grounded electrical cords, excessively worn screwdrivers, spread wrenches (open end), cracked sockets, slipping ratchets, or faulty droplight sockets can cause accidents.

• Do use the proper size and type of tool for the job being done.

• Do when possible, pull on a wrench handle rather than push on it, and adjust your stance to prevent a fall.

• Do be sure that adjustable wrenches are tightly adjusted on the nut or bolt and pulled so that the face is on the side of the fixed jaw.

• Do select a wrench or socket that fits the nut or bolt. The wrench or socket should sit straight, not cocked.

• Do strike squarely with a hammer. Avoid glancing blows.

• Do set the parking brake and block the drive wheels if the work requires that the engine be running.

Don'ts

• Don't run an engine in a garage or anywhere else without proper ventilation — EVER! Carbon monoxide is poisonous; it takes a long time to leave the human body and you can build up a deadly supply of it in your system by simply breathing in a little every day. You may not realize you are slowly poisoning yourself. Always use power vents, windows, fans or open the garage door.

• Don't work around moving parts while wearing a necktie or other loose clothing. Short sleeves are much safer than long, loose sleeves. Hard-toed shoes with neoprene soles protect your toes and give a better grip on slippery surfaces. Jewelry such as watches, fancy belt buckles, beads or body adornment of any kind is not safe working around a car. Long hair should be hidden under a hat or cap.

• Don't use pockets for toolboxes. A fall or bump can drive a screwdriver deep into your body. Even a wiping cloth hanging from the back pocket can wrap around a spinning shaft or fan.

• Don't smoke when working around gasoline, cleaning solvent or other flammable material.

• Don't smoke when working around the battery. When the battery is being charged, it gives off explosive hydrogen gas.

• Don't use gasoline to wash your hands; there are excellent soaps available. Gasoline may contain lead, and lead can enter the body through a cut, accumulating in the body until you are very ill. Gasoline also removes all the natural oils from the skin so that bone dry hands will suck up oil and grease.

• Don't service the air conditioning system unless you are equipped with the necessary tools and training. The refrigerant, R-12 is extremely cold and when exposed to the air, will instantly freeze any surface it comes in contact with, including your eyes. Although the refrigerant is normally non-toxic, R-12 becomes a deadly poisonous gas in the presence of an open flame. One good whiff of the vapors from burning refrigerant can be fatal.

MODEL IDENTIFICATION

The easiest way to distinguish models is by checking the engine. For the Spectrum which was produced from 1985-1989, only 2 engines were ever available. Most models were equipped with a 2 barrel carbureted 1.5L engine, thought a few produced in 1987 and 1988 came with a turbocharged, fuel injected version of the same engine. The Storm was produced with 3 possible engines. For all years, 1990-1993, the base model was equipped with a 1.6L SOHC fuel injected engine. For 1990 and 1991, the GSI performance model was equipped with a DOHC version of the same engine. For 1992 and 1993, a larger 1.8L DOHC engine was provided for the GSI models.

SERIAL NUMBER IDENTIFICATION

Vehicle

▶ See Figures 4, 5 and 6

The Vehicle Identification Number (VIN) is stamped on a metal plate that is attached to the instrument panel adjacent to the windshield. It can be seen by looking through the lower corner of the windshield on the driver's side of the vehicle. The VIN is also located on various identification stickers throughout the vehicle and on certain metal parts such as the engine or transaxle.

The VIN is a 17 digit combination of numbers and letters. The 1st digit represents the country of manufacture, this is a 'J' for all Spectrum and Storm models and means the vehicle was built in Japan. The 2nd and 3rd digits are '81", which represent Isuzu and Chevrolet, respectively. The 4th digit, 'R' represents the car line while the 5th digit is for the particular sales code of the vehicle. For example, sales codes for the Spectrum will the 'F' or 'G' depending on the year. The Storm sales code should either be 'F' for the base model or 'T' for the GSI. For the Spectrum, the 6th and 7th digits identify the vehicle's body style, in other words whether it is a 2 door hatchback or 4 door notchback. For the Storm, the 6th digit represents the body style while the 7th digit represents the safety restraint features with which that particular car was produced. The 8th number tells with what engine the vehicle was equipped. The 9th digit is a check digit for all vehicles. The 10th dig it indicates the model year. The 11th digit should be a '7' or '8' indicating the vehicle was built in the Fujisawa plant. The 12th through 17th digits indicate the production sequence number.

Vehicle Certification Label

▶ See Figure 7

The Vehicle Certification Label is attached to the left door jamb, below the latch striker. The upper half of the label contains the date of manufacture and vehicle weight information. The lower half of the label contains a statement that the vehicle conforms to U.S. federal standards in effect at

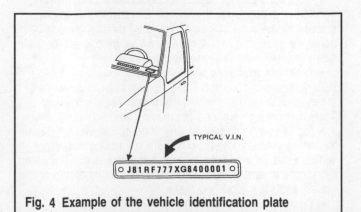

TYPICAL V.I.N.

J81RF777XG8400001

Fig. 4 Example of the vehicle identification plate

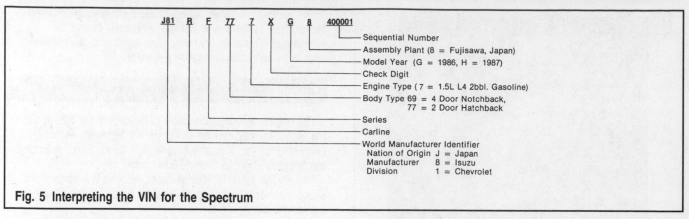

Fig. 5 Interpreting the VIN for the Spectrum

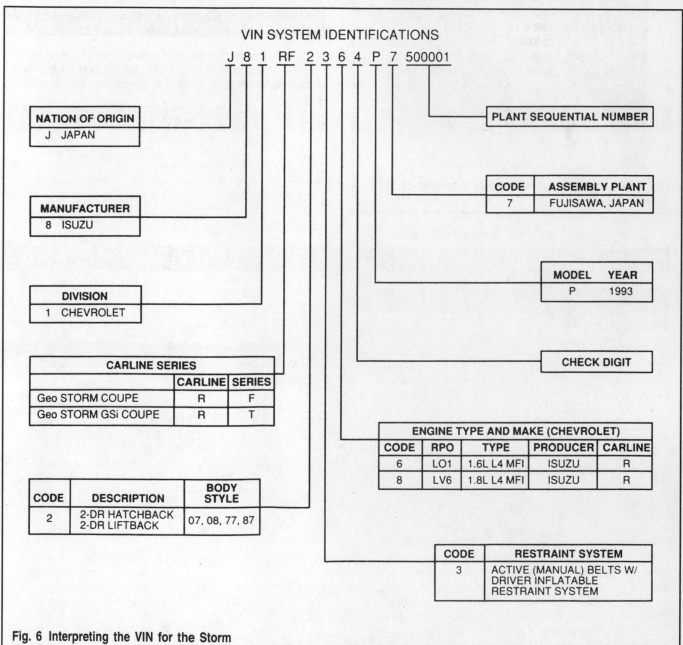

Fig. 6 Interpreting the VIN for the Storm

Fig. 7 The vehicle certification label is located on the driver's door jamb

the time of production. The VIN is listed at the bottom of the label

The certification label is part of the Federal Vehicle Theft Prevention Standard and like the VIN label, cannot be removed or altered in any way. The label must be masked prior to painting the surrounding surface.

Engine

The engine identification code is located in the VIN at the 8th digit. The VIN can be found on the Vehicle Certification Label and on the instrument panel VIN plate. See the Engine Identification chart for engine VIN codes.

The engine block is also stamped with an engine production sequence number. This code may be found on the front or side of the block.

Transaxle

The transaxle is stamped with a production sequence code. This is normally located on the transmission towards the front of the vehicle, either on or directly behind the clutch/converter housing.

VEHICLE IDENTIFICATION CHART

It is important for servicing and ordering parts to be certain of the vehicle and engine identification. The VIN (vehicle identification number) is a 17 digit number visible through the windshield on the driver's side of the dash and contains the vehicle and engine identification codes. The tenth digit indicates model year and the eighth digit indicates engine code. It can be interpreted as follows:

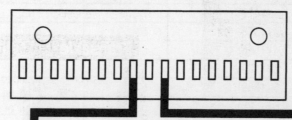

	Engine Code				
Code	Liters	Cu. In. (cc)	Cyl.	Fuel Sys.	Eng. Mfg.
7	1.5	90 (1472)	4	2 bbl	Isuzu
9	1.5	90 (1472)	4	MFI Turbo	Isuzu
6	1.6	97 (1588)	4	MFI	Isuzu
5	1.6	97 (1588)	4	MFI	Isuzu
8	1.8	110 (1810)	4	MFI	Isuzu

Model Year	
Code	Year
F	1985
G	1986
H	1987
J	1988
K	1989
L	1990
M	1991
N	1992
P	1993

2 bbl—2 Barrel Carburetor
MFI—Multi-Port Fuel Injection

ENGINE IDENTIFICATION

Year	Model	Engine Displacement Liters (cc)	Engine Series (ID/VIN)	Fuel System	No. of Cylinders	Engine Type
1985	Spectrum	1.5 (1472)	7	2 bbl	4	SOHC
1986	Spectrum	1.5 (1472)	7	2 bbl	4	SOHC
1987	Spectrum	1.5 (1472)	7	2 bbl	4	SOHC
	Spectrum	1.5 (1472)	9	MFI Turbo	4	SOHC
1988	Spectrum	1.5 (1472)	7	2 bbl	4	SOHC
	Spectrum	1.5 (1472)	9	MFI Turbo	4	SOHC
1989	Spectrum	1.5 (1472)	7	2 bbl	4	SOHC
1990	Storm	1.6 (1588)	6	MFI	4	SOHC
	Storm GSi	1.6 (1588)	5	MFI	4	DOHC
1991	Storm	1.6 (1588)	6	MFI	4	SOHC
	Storm GSi	1.6 (1588)	5	MFI	4	DOHC
1992	Storm	1.6 (1588)	6	MFI	4	SOHC
	Storm GSi	1.8 (1810)	8	MFI	4	DOHC
1993	Storm	1.6 (1588)	6	MFI	4	SOHC
	Storm GSi	1.8 (1810)	8	MFI	4	DOHC

2 bbl—2 Barrel Carburetor
MFI—Multi-Port Fuel Injection
SOHC—Single Overhead Camshaft
DOHC—Dual Overhead Camshaft

TRANSAXLE IDENTIFICATION

Year	Model	Type	(ID)	No. of [1] Gears
1985	Spectrum	Man.	75 mm	5
	Spectrum	Auto	KF100	3
1986	Spectrum	Man.	75 mm	5
	Spectrum	Auto	KF100	3
1987	Spectrum	Man.	75 mm	5
	Spectrum	Auto	KF100	3
1988	Spectrum	Man.	75 mm	5
	Spectrum	Auto	KF100	3
1989	Spectrum	Man.	75 mm	5
	Spectrum	Auto	KF100	3
1990	Storm/Storm GSi	Man.	75mm	5
	Storm	Auto.	KF100	3
	Storm GSi	Auto.	JF403E	4
1991	Storm/Storm GSi	Man.	75mm	5
	Storm	Auto.	KF100	3
	Storm GSi	Auto.	JF403E	4
1992	Storm/Storm GSi	Man.	75mm	5
	Storm	Auto.	KF100	3
	Storm GSi	Auto.	JF403E	4
1993	Storm/Storm GSi	Man.	75mm	5
	Storm	Auto.	KF100	3
	Storm GSi	Auto.	JF403E	4

Auto.—Automatic
Man.—Manual
[1] Forward Gears

ROUTINE MAINTENANCE

▶ **See Figures 8 and 9**

Air Cleaner

The air cleaner is a paper element contained in a housing located either on the left side of the engine compartment (fuel injected vehicles) or over the carburetor. The air filter element should be inspected at each oil change and replaced, at least every 30,000 miles or 36 months, whichever comes first.

The air cleaner serves a dual purpose. It removes dust and dirt particles from incoming air in order to protect the internal engine parts. But it also acts as a flame arrestor in the event of an engine backfire. For this reason, the engine should never be started with the air cleaner removed from the housing or an engine fire could occur in the event of a backfire.

➡**Check the air filter element more often if the vehicle is operated under severe dusty conditions and replace, as necessary.**

REMOVAL & INSTALLATION

▶ **See Figures 10, 11 and 12**

1. Loosen the clamp, then separate the air duct from the air cleaner housing.

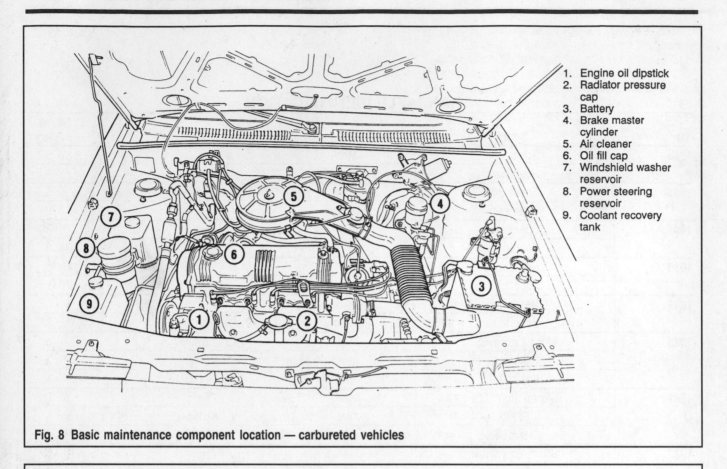

1. Engine oil dipstick
2. Radiator pressure cap
3. Battery
4. Brake master cylinder
5. Air cleaner
6. Oil fill cap
7. Windshield washer reservoir
8. Power steering reservoir
9. Coolant recovery tank

Fig. 8 Basic maintenance component location — carbureted vehicles

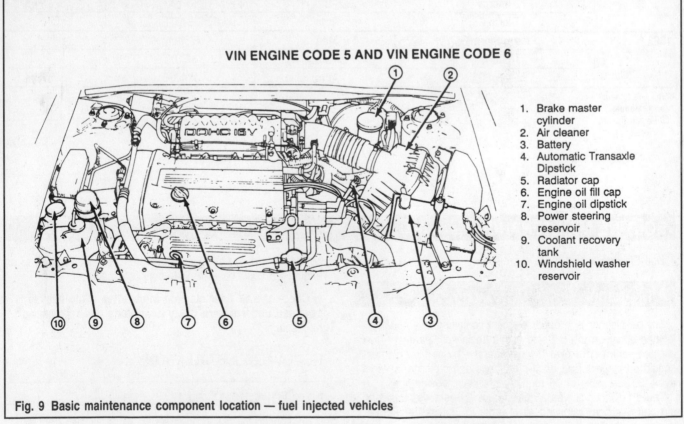

VIN ENGINE CODE 5 AND VIN ENGINE CODE 6

1. Brake master cylinder
2. Air cleaner
3. Battery
4. Automatic Transaxle Dipstick
5. Radiator cap
6. Engine oil fill cap
7. Engine oil dipstick
8. Power steering reservoir
9. Coolant recovery tank
10. Windshield washer reservoir

Fig. 9 Basic maintenance component location — fuel injected vehicles

2. For carbureted vehicles, remove the wing nut from the top center of the air cleaner housing assembly.

3. Release the air cleaner housing hold-down tabs.

4. Either lift the housing cover or separate the housing, then remove the air cleaner element and replace if dirty. If the element is only slightly dusty it can be cleaned by blowing compressed air through the element from the clean side.

To install:

5. Wipe all dust from the inside of the housing using a clean rag or cloth.

6. Install the element into the housing, then position the cover over the element.

7. Secure the cover using the fasteners and, if applicable, the wing nut.

8. Attach the air duct and secure using the clamp.

Fig. 10 Loosen the clamp on the air duct — Storm

Fig. 11 Separate the air duct from the housing — Storm

Fig. 12 With the housing cover removed, the air filter may accessed for replacement or cleaning — Storm

Fuel Filter

The fuel filter is located under the power brake booster for the Spectrum or under the brake booster, near the strut tower for the Storm.

REMOVAL & INSTALLATION

Spectrum

▶ See Figures 13 and 14

1. Relieve the pressure in the fuel system; remove the fuel filler cap.

2. Note the routing of inlet and outlet lines and the direction of flow as marked by the arrow on the filter. With a pair of pliers, shift the clips on the inlet and outlet hoses back and well away from the connections on the filter.

3. Disconnect the fuel lines, using a slight twisting motion to break them loose. Pull the filter out of its retaining clip. Plug the lines immediately to prevent excessive fuel spillage or system contamination.

To install:

4. Install the filter in the holder. When reconnecting the fuel lines, make sure the hoses are connected to the correct ports on the filter. The arrow on the filter indicates direction of flow and points towards the carburetor.

5. Install the hose clips to the inside of the bulged sections of the fuel filter connections, and not right at the ends of the fuel lines. Start the engine and check for leaks.

6. Install the fuel filler cap.

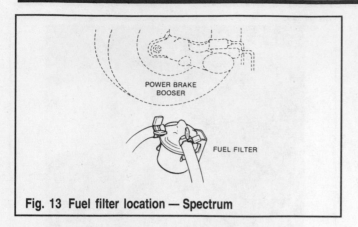

Fig. 13 Fuel filter location — Spectrum

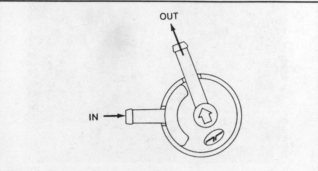

Fig. 14 Make sure the lines are connected to the proper ports on the filter — Spectrum

Storm

▶ **See Figure 15**

1. Relieve the pressure in the fuel system.
2. Disconnect the negative battery cable.
3. Except for 1993 vehicles, remove the air intake duct.
4. Disconnect the fuel filter outlet pipe from the fuel filter upper fitting. Be sure to cap the ends of the fuel pipe fittings to prevent both the entry of dirt and the spillage of fuel.
5. Raise the front of the vehicle and support safely.
6. Disconnect the fuel filter inlet pipe from the fuel filter lower fitting. Be sure to cap the ends of the fuel pipe fittings to prevent both the entry of dirt and the spillage of fuel.
7. For 1993 vehicles, remove the 2 bracket mounting bolts, then remove the filter and bracket assembly from the vehicle.
8. Loosen the fuel filter bracket clamp bolt, then remove the filter from the bracket.
   To install:
9. For 1993 vehicles, position the fuel filter into the bracket, then install the bracket clamp bolt and tighten to 21 ft. lbs. (28 Nm).
10. Position the filter and bracket assembly (1993 vehicles) or the filter (1990-1992 vehicles) into the vehicle, with the flow line pointing upward toward the fuel outlet pipe. Install the retaining bolt(s) and tighten to 25 ft. lbs. (34 Nm).
11. Remove the cap from the fuel inlet line, then connect the line to the lower filter fitting. Tighten the fitting nut to 25 ft. lbs. (34 Nm).
12. Remove the supports and carefully lower the vehicle.

13. Remove the cap from the fuel outlet line, then connect the line to the upper filter fitting. Tighten the fitting nut to 25 ft. lbs. (34 Nm).
14. If removed, install the air intake duct.
15. Connect the negative battery cable, then cycle the ignition switch **ON** and **OFF** to build system pressure. Check the fittings for leaks.

PCV Valve

In most cases, the PCV valve is located in a grommet attached to the top of the rocker or camshaft cover. On carbureted vehicles, the regulating orifice may be located in the rocker cover underneath the snorkle of the air cleaner assembly or in the side of the intake manifold facing the cylinder head and directly below the carburetor mounting plate. For crankcase ventilation system testing, refer to Section 4.

REMOVAL & INSTALLATION

▶ **See Figures 16, 17 and 18**

1. For carbureted engines, remove the air cleaner for access.
2. Loosen the clamp and disconnect the hose from the PCV valve.
3. Remove the PCV valve from the mounting grommet. Check the PCV valve for deposits and clogging. The valve should rattle when shaken. If the valve does not rattle, clean the valve with solvent until the plunger is free or replace the valve.
4. Check the PCV hose(s) and the grommet for clogging and signs of wear or deterioration. Replace, as necessary.
   To install:
5. Install the PCV valve into the grommet.
6. Connect the PCV hose to the PCV valve.
7. If removed, install the air cleaner assembly.

Evaporative Canister

The vapor or carbon canister is part of the evaporative emission control system. It is located in the left rear of the engine compartment for the Spectrum or the right rear of the engine compartment for the Storm.

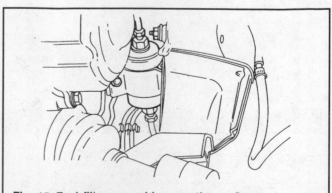

Fig. 15 Fuel filter assembly mounting — Storm

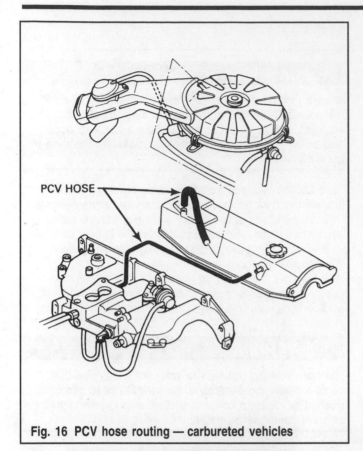

Fig. 16 PCV hose routing — carbureted vehicles

Fig. 17 Loosen the clamp and disconnect the hose from the PCV valve — Storm SOHC engine

SERVICING

Servicing the carbon canister is only necessary if it is clogged, cracked or contains liquid fuel, indicated by odor or by excessive weight. For evaporative emission control system testing, refer to Section 4.

Battery

GENERAL MAINTENANCE

Corrosion of the battery and cable terminals interferes with both the flow of power out of the battery and the charge

Fig. 18 Remove the PCV valve from the rubber grommet — Storm SOHC engine

flowing into the battery from the charging system. This can result in a 'no start' condition. If the battery becomes completely discharged, battery life may be shortened. In some cases, a totally discharged battery may not readily accept a charge.

To reduce the need for service and to extend battery life, keep the battery and cable terminals clean and free of corrosion. Make sure the cable clamps are tightly fastened to the battery terminals. If corrosion is found, disconnect the cables and clean the terminals with a wire brush. Neutralize the corrosion with a solution of baking soda and water. After installing the cables, apply a light coating of petroleum jelly to the cable terminals to help prevent corrosion.

Parasitic loads are small current drains which are constantly drawing current from the battery. Normal parasitic loads may drain a battery on a vehicle that is in storage and not used for 6-8 weeks. Vehicles that have additional accessories such as a cellular phone, an alarm system or other devices that increase parasitic load may discharge a battery sooner. If the vehicle is to be stored for 6-8 weeks or longer in a secure area and an alarm system, if present, is not necessary, the negative battery cable should be disconnected at the onset of storage to protect the battery charge.

Remember that constantly discharging and recharging a battery will shorten battery life. Take care not to allow a battery to be needlessly discharged.

FLUID LEVEL CHECK

With Built-in Hydrometer
▶ See Figure 19

All Spectrum and Storm vehicles are equipped with sealed maintenance free batteries. The battery is equipped with 6 vents at the top or side of the battery to allow a small amount of gas produced in the battery to escape. A built-in hydrometer is provided in the top of the battery to determine if the battery is charged, in need of a charge or must be replaced. The hydrometer eye consists of a floating blue or green hydrometer ball which controls what is visible through the window depending on the current electrolyte level. When any blue or green is visible through the hydrometer eye in the top of the battery, there is a sufficient electrolyte level and the battery may be jumped or tested. If the entire window is blue or green, then battery is in good condition. If the eye is clear or light yellow, electrolyte level is low and the battery is need of a charge. If the window is dark, but not blue or green, the electrolyte fluid level is below the hydrometer and is too low for charging and must be rep laced.

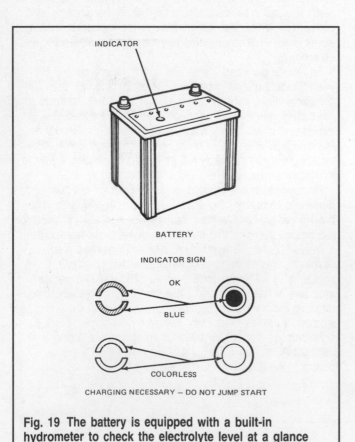

INDICATOR

BATTERY

INDICATOR SIGN

OK

BLUE

COLORLESS

CHARGING NECESSARY – DO NOT JUMP START

Fig. 19 The battery is equipped with a built-in hydrometer to check the electrolyte level at a glance

CABLE INSPECTION

✳✳CAUTION

Always remove the negative battery cable first, to avoid the possibility of grounding the car's electrical system by accident. Failure to do so could allow a spark to occur and cause battery gases to explode, possibly resulting in personal injury.

1. Loosen the negative battery cable bolt using a socket or box wrench, then remove the cable from the battery terminal.
2. Loosen the positive battery cable bolt using a socket or box wrench, then remove the cable from the battery terminal.
3. Clean both battery terminals using standard battery terminal cleaning tools.
4. Remove the remaining corrosion deposits from the battery and cables by flushing with a baking soda-water solution comprised of 2 teaspoons of baking soda and 1 cup of water.

✳✳WARNING

Do not allow the solution to enter the battery as this could weaken the electrolyte. Be careful not to allow the flushed deposits to come in contact with painted surfaces as paint damage may result.

5. Follow the negative battery cable to the transaxle bracket in order to check the connection. If it is loose or corroded, remove the cable and clean the cable end and contact with sandpaper, then reconnect the cable.
6. Follow the positive cable to the starter solenoid, then clean and tighten, if necessary.
7. Apply a small amount of petroleum jelly around the base of each battery terminal to help reduce the possibility of corrosion. Do not thoroughly coat the terminal.
8. Install the positive battery cable to the positive battery terminal and tighten the fastener to 11 ft. lbs. (15 Nm).
9. Install the negative battery cable to the negative battery terminal and tighten the fastener to 11 ft. lbs. (15 Nm).
10. After the cables are installed, coat the top of each terminal lightly with petroleum jelly

CAPACITY TESTING

▶ See Figure 20

A voltmeter and a battery load tester is used for this test.
1. Connect the battery tester and voltmeter cables to the battery terminals, according to the tester manufacturer's instructions. If the battery is installed in the vehicle, be careful not to touch any surrounding metal on the vehicle.
2. Remove the surface charge from the battery by applying a 300 amp load across the battery terminals for 15 seconds using the tester. Turn the load **OFF** for 15 seconds to allow the battery to recover.
3. Estimate the battery temperature from the battery's surrounding temperature from the past few hours proceeding the test.

4. Find the label on top of the battery that specifies the proper 'Load Test' for this battery, then using the tester, apply this load across the terminals for 15 seconds. The load will likely be around 260 amps. With the load still applied, observe the minimum voltage on the voltmeter, then turn the load **OFF**.

5. Compare the battery voltage to the estimated temperature to determine if the battery is good. The desired minimum readings should be as follows:

   a. Temperature above 70°F (21°C) — minimum voltage is 9.6V

   b. Temperature of 50°-70°F (10°-21°C) — minimum voltage is 9.4V

   c. Temperature of 30°-50°F (0°-10°C) — minimum voltage is 9.1V

   d. Temperature of 15°-30°F (-10°-0°C) — minimum voltage is 8.8V

   e. Temperature of 0°-15°F (-18°--10°C) — minimum voltage is 8.5V

   f. Temperature below 0°F (-18°C) — minimum voltage is 8.0V

6. A battery which fails this test should be replaced.

CHARGING

✳✳CAUTION

Keep flame or sparks away from the battery. The battery emits explosive hydrogen gas, especially when being charged. Battery electrolyte contains sulfuric acid. If electrolyte accidentally comes in contact with your skin or eyes, flush with plenty of clear water. If it lands in your eyes, get medical help immediately.

When the battery voltage is below 11 volts, the weakened electrolyte becomes very resistant to accepting charger current. A battery in this condition may only draw a few millamps of current. At this rate, it may take a long time before the current flow is high enough to read on all but the most sensitive ammeters.

If after the recommended time, the current is measurable, then the battery is good and will charge normally. Be sure to charge a completely discharged battery until the blue or green eye appears. Follow the charging procedure closely to prevent replacing a good battery.

1. Using a Digital Volt/Ohm Meter (DVOM) measure the voltage across the battery terminals. If the voltage is below 11 volts, the current draw is likely to be very slow.

2. Set the battery charger's rate at the highest applicable setting for a 12 volt battery. If the charger is equipped with a timer, set the timer for 30 minutes.

3. Check the battery every 30 minutes for a blue or green eye indicating proper charge. Also check the battery for temperatures in excess of 125°F (52°C) and, if necessary, pause the charging procedure until the battery cools.

4. Always make sure the charger is properly connected to the battery. Some chargers have a polarity protection circuit built into the charger and will prevent charging until the circuit is properly connected. A completely discharged battery may not be able to activate such a circuit, thereby appearing not to accept a charge regardless of whether the charger is properly connected or not. If this is suspected, consult the charger manufacturer's instructions on bypassing this feature so the discharged battery may be charged.

5. Because battery chargers will vary in the amount of current supplied to the battery and as stated previously, battery condition will also affect the rate of charge, the time necessary to charge a battery will also vary. The time necessary for a battery to begin accepting a charge should be approximately as follows:

High boost of 16.0 volts or more — up to 4 hours.
Medium boost of 14.0-15.9 volts — up to 8 hours
Low boost of 13.9 volts or less — up to 16 hours.

REPLACEMENT

▶ **See Figure 21**

1. Disconnect the negative battery cable from the battery terminal.

2. Disconnect the positive battery cable from the battery terminal.

3. Remove the battery retainer nut from one end and bolt from the other, then remove the retainer from the top of the battery.

4. Carefully lift the battery out of the vehicle and place in a safe location.

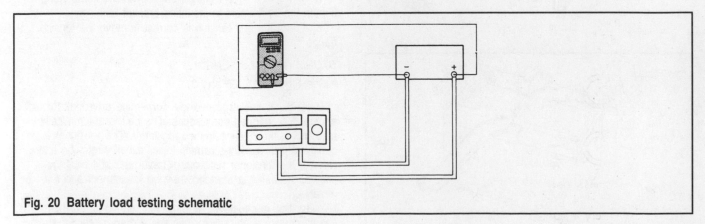

Fig. 20 Battery load testing schematic

To install:

5. Inspect and, if necessary, clean the battery tray and the battery cables of all corrosion. Make sure the battery and terminals are free of cracks or damage and that the terminals are also free of corrosion.

6. Carefully lower the battery into position in the battery tray. Do not allow the terminals to short to any bare metal during installation.

7. Position the retainer over the battery and install the fasteners. Tighten the nut and bolt to 71 inch lbs. (8 Nm).

8. Connect the positive battery cable and tighten to 11 ft. lbs. (15 Nm).

9. Connect the negative battery cable and tighten to 11 inch lbs. (15 Nm).

Accessory Drive Belt(s)

INSPECTION & ADJUSTMENT

Belt Tension

SPECTRUM

▶ **See Figure 22**

➡The following procedures require the use of GM belt tension gauge No. BT-33-95-ACBN (regular V-belts) or BT-33-97M (poly V-belts).

1. If the belt is cold, operate the engine (at idle speed) for 15 minutes; the belt will seat itself in the pulleys allowing the belt fibers to relax or stretch. If the belt is hot, allow it to cool, until it is warm to the touch.

2. Loosen the component-to-mounting bracket bolts.

3. Using a GM belt tension gauge No. BT-33-95-ACBN (standard V-belts) or BT-33-97M (poly V-belts), place the tension gauge at the center of the belt between the longest span.

4. Applying belt tension pressure on the component, adjust the drive belt tension to 70-110 inch lbs.

5. While holding the correct tension on the component, tighten the component-to-mounting bracket bolt.

6. When the belt tension is correct, remove the tension gauge.

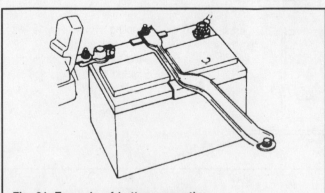

Fig. 21 Example of battery mounting

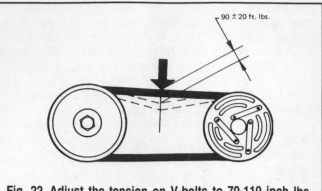

Fig. 22 Adjust the tension on V-belts to 70-110 inch lbs.

STORM (EXCEPT 1.8L ENGINE)

▶ **See Figures 23 and 24**

1. If the belt is cold, operate the engine, at idle speed, for 15 minutes; the belt will seat itself in the pulleys allowing the belt fibers to relax or stretch. If the belt is hot, allow it to cool, until it is warm to touch.

➡**A used belt is one that has been rotated at least 1 complete revolution on the pulleys. This begins the belt seating process and it must never be tensioned to the new belt specifications.**

2. Loosen the component-to-mounting bracket bolts.

3. Use a belt tension gauge (J-23600-B or equivalent) to determine proper belt adjustment; place the gauge at the center of the belt between the longest span.

4. Applying belt tension pressure on the component, adjust the drive belt tension to the correct specification:

  a. For 1990 and 1991 vehicles, adjust the power steering pump belt to 145 lbs on vehicles with A/C or to 90 lbs on vehicles without A/C.

  b. For 1990 — 1992 vehicles, adjust a new alternator belt to 140-180 lbs or a used belt to 110-150 lbs.

  c. For 1992 power steering pump belts and 1993 vehicles, adjust the belt so that 22 lbs of thumb pressure produces the specified belt deflection at the center of the belt, between 2 pulleys. Under proper belt tension a new belt should deflect about 0.31-0.47 in. (8-12mm) or a used belt about 0.28-0.43 in. (7-11mm).

5. While holding the correct tension on the component, tighten the component-to-mounting bracket bolt.

6. When the belt tension is correct, remove the tension gauge.

STORM (WITH 1.8L ENGINE)

▶ **See Figures 25, 26 and 27**

The 1.8L engine uses a single serpentine drive belt for all engine belt operated accessories. The belt is automatically adjusted using a spring loaded tensioner. The tensioner is equipped with markings to help indicate belt stretching and wear. If the tensioner runs out of travel and belt slippage occurs, the belt has stretched beyond adjustment and must be replaced.

In addition to checking the tensioner markings, the belt should check periodically for damage. When inspecting the belt, cracks in the belt ribs are normal and should not require belt replacement. However, the belt should be replaced if

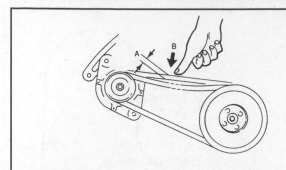

Fig. 23 Adjusting an alternator belt using deflection — 1993 vehicles

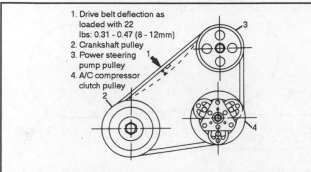

1. Drive belt deflection as loaded with 22 lbs: 0.31 - 0.47 (8 - 12mm)
2. Crankshaft pulley
3. Power steering pump pulley
4. A/C compressor clutch pulley

Fig. 24 Adjusting the power steering belt — 1992 and 1993 vehicles

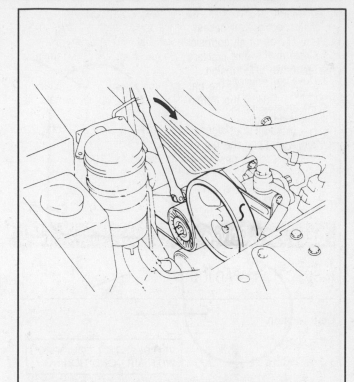

Fig. 25 To remove the serpentine drive, use a ⅜ in. breaker bar or ratchet to rotate the tensioner and loosen the belt — 1.8L engine

sections of the belt ribs are missing. Belt fraying may be an indication that the belt is not properly aligned in the pulleys and if severe could require belt replacement. If a whining noise is heard around the tensioner or idle pulley assemblies, even after the vehicle is warmed on a cold morning, check for possible bearing failure.

REMOVAL & INSTALLATION

1. Except for the 1.8L engine, loosen the pivot and anchor bolts on 1 of the belt's components, then pivot the component sufficiently to release belt tension and remove belt.

2. For the 1.8L engine, use a ⅜ in. breaker bar or ratchet to pivot the belt tensioner and release the serpentine drive belt, then remove the belt from the pulleys and the vehicle.

To install:

3. Position the belt over the pulleys.

4. For the 1.8L engine, pivot the tensioner and install the serpentine belt. Make sure the belt is properly aligned in all of the pulley grooves, then gently pivot the tensioner into contact with the belt. Do not allow the tensioner to snap into position or damage could occur.

5. Except for the 1.8L engine, adjust the belt tension and tighten the accessory mounting bolts.

Hoses

✳✳CAUTION

Disconnect the negative battery cable or fan motor wiring harness connector before replacing any radiator/heater hose. The fan may come ON, under certain circumstances, even though the ignition is OFF.

INSPECTION

Inspect the condition of the radiator and heater hoses periodically. Early spring and at the beginning of the fall or winter when you are performing other maintenance, are good times. Make sure the engine and cooling system is cold. Visually inspect for cracking, rotting or collapsed hoses, replace as necessary. Run your hand along the length of the hose. If a weak or swollen spot is noted when squeezing the hose wall, replace the hose.

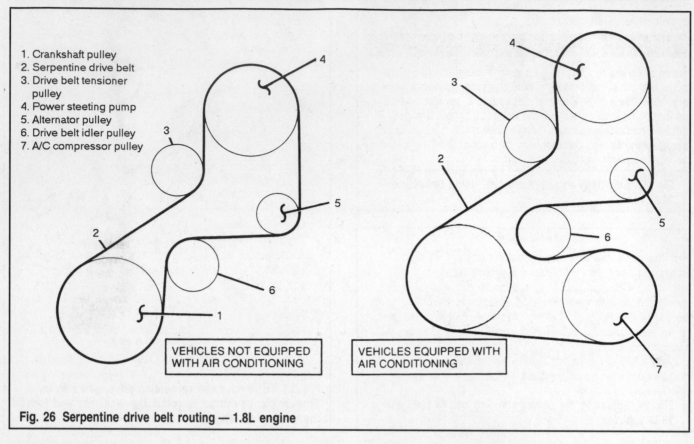

1. Crankshaft pulley
2. Serpentine drive belt
3. Drive belt tensioner pulley
4. Power steeting pump
5. Alternator pulley
6. Drive belt idler pulley
7. A/C compressor pulley

VEHICLES NOT EQUIPPED WITH AIR CONDITIONING

VEHICLES EQUIPPED WITH AIR CONDITIONING

Fig. 26 Serpentine drive belt routing — 1.8L engine

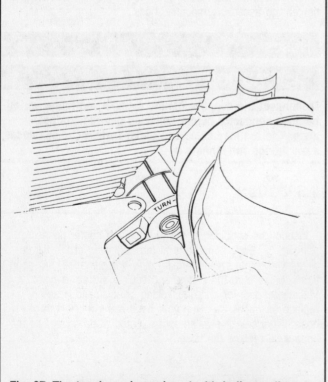

Fig. 27 The tensioner is equipped with indicator lines to provide belt wear information — 1.8L engine

REMOVAL & INSTALLATION

▶ See Figures 28, 29 and 30

1. Remove the radiator pressure cap.

❋❋CAUTION

Never remove the pressure cap while the engine is running or personal injury from scalding hot coolant or steam may result. If possible, wait until the engine has cooled to remove the pressure cap. If this is not possible, wrap a thick cloth around the pressure cap and turn it slowly to the stop. Step back while the pressure is released from the cooling system. When you are sure all the pressure has been released, still using the cloth, turn and remove the cap.

2. Position a clean container under the radiator drain plug, then open the drain and allow the cooling system to drain to an appropriate level. For some upper hoses only a little coolant must be drained, to remove hoses positioned lower on

the engine, such as the lower radiator hose, the entire cooling system must be drained.

❄❄CAUTION

When draining the coolant, keep in mind that cats and dogs are attracted by the ethylene glycol antifreeze, and are quite likely to drink any that is left in an uncovered container or in puddles on the ground. This will prove fatal in sufficient quantity. Always drain the coolant into a sealable container. Coolant may be reused unless it is contaminated or several years old.

3. Loosen the hose clamps at each end of the hose requiring replacement. Pull the clamps back on the hose away from the connection.

4. Twist, pull and slide the hose off the fitting.

➡**If the hose is stuck at the connection, do not try to insert a screwdriver or other sharp tool under the hose end in an effort to free it, as the connection and/or hose may become damaged. Heater connections especially may be easily damaged by such a procedure. If the hose is not to be reused, use a single-edged razor blade to make a slice at the end of the hose, perpendicular to the end of the hose. Do not cut deep so as not to damage the connection. The hose can then be peeled from the connection.**

5. Clean both hose mounting connections. Inspect the condition of the hose clamps and replace them, if necessary.

To install:

6. Dip the ends of the new hose into clean engine coolant to ease installation.

7. Slide the hose clamps over the replacement hose and slide the hose ends over the connections into position.

8. Position and secure the hose clamps. Make sure they are located inside the raised bead of the connector.

9. If available, install a pressure tester to the bottle and check for leaks.

10. Close the radiator drainplug and fill the cooling system with the clean drained engine coolant or a suitable 50-70 percent mixture of ethylene glycol coolant and water.

11. Leave the radiator cap off, then start and run the engine to normal operating temperature. When the engine is at operating temperature and the thermostat has opened, continue to fill the radiator until the level stabilizes just below the filler neck.

12. Install the radiator pressure cap and check the clamped hose ends for leaks.

13. Shut the engine **OFF** and allow the engine to cool. Once the engine has cooled, check the surge tank for proper coolant level and add, as necessary.

Air Conditioning System

SAFETY WARNINGS

1. Avoid contact with a charged refrigeration system, even when working on another part of the air conditioning system or vehicle. If a heavy tool comes into contact with a section of air conditioning line, it can easily cause the relatively soft material to rupture.

2. When it is necessary to apply force to a fitting which contains refrigerant, as when checking that all system couplings are securely tightened, use a wrench on both parts of the fitting involved, if possible. This will avoid putting torque on the refrigerant tubing. (It is advisable, when possible, to use tube or line wrenches when tightening these flare nut fittings.)

3. Do not attempt to discharge the system by merely loosening a fitting, or removing the service valve caps and cracking these valves. Precise control is possible only when using the appropriate service gauges and a suitable recovery system. Place a rag under the open end of the charging hose while discharging the system to catch any drops of liquid that might escape. Wear protective gloves when connecting or disconnecting service gauge hoses.

4. Discharge the system only in a well ventilated area, as high concentrations of the gas can exclude oxygen and act as an anesthetic. When leak testing or soldering this is particularly important, as toxic gas is formed when R-12 contacts any flame.

5. Never start a system without first verifying that all service valves are properly installed and that all fittings throughout the system are snugly connected.

6. Avoid applying heat to any refrigerant line or storage vessel. Charging may be aided by using water heated to less than +125°F (+51°C) to warm the refrigerant container. Never allow a refrigerant storage container to sit out in the sun or near any other source of heat, such as a radiator.

7. Always wear goggles when working on a system to protect the eyes. If refrigerant contacts the eye, it is advisable in all cases to see a physician as soon as possible.

8. Frostbite from liquid refrigerant should be treated by first gradually warming the area with cool water, and then gently applying petroleum jelly. A physician should be consulted.

9. Always keep refrigerant can fittings capped when not in use. If the container is equipped with a safety cap to protect the valve, make sure the cap is in place when the can is not being used. Avoid sudden shock to the can which might occur from dropping it, or from banging a heavy tool against it. Never carry a can in the passenger compartment of a car.

10. Always completely discharge the system into a suitable recovery unit before painting the vehicle (if the paint is to be baked on), or before welding anywhere near the refrigerant lines.

11. When servicing the system, minimize the time that any refrigerant line or fitting is open to the air to prevent moisture or dirt which can damage the internal system components. Always replace O-rings on lines or fittings which are removed. Prior to installation coat, but do not soak, replacement O-rings with a suitable compressor oil.

SYSTEM INSPECTION

The easiest and often most important check for the air conditioning system consists of a visual inspection of the system components. Visually inspect the air conditioning system for refrigerant leaks, damaged compressor clutch, compressor drive belt tension and condition, plugged evaporator drain tube, blocked condenser fins, disconnected or

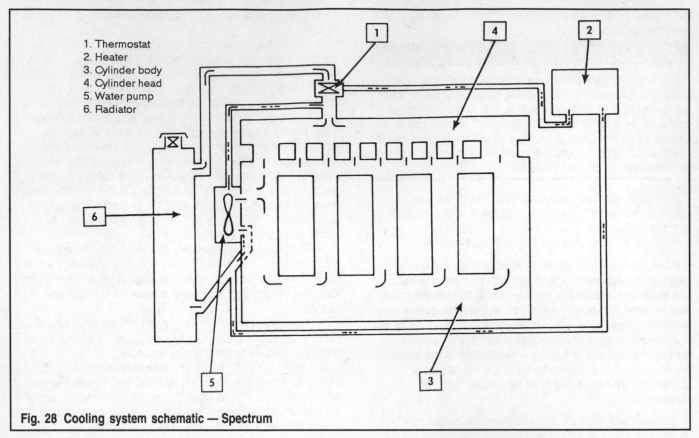

1. Thermostat
2. Heater
3. Cylinder body
4. Cylinder head
5. Water pump
6. Radiator

Fig. 28 Cooling system schematic — Spectrum

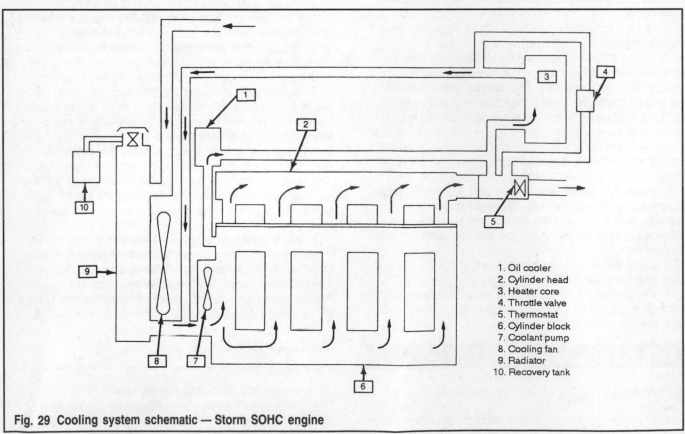

1. Oil cooler
2. Cylinder head
3. Heater core
4. Throttle valve
5. Thermostat
6. Cylinder block
7. Coolant pump
8. Cooling fan
9. Radiator
10. Recovery tank

Fig. 29 Cooling system schematic — Storm SOHC engine

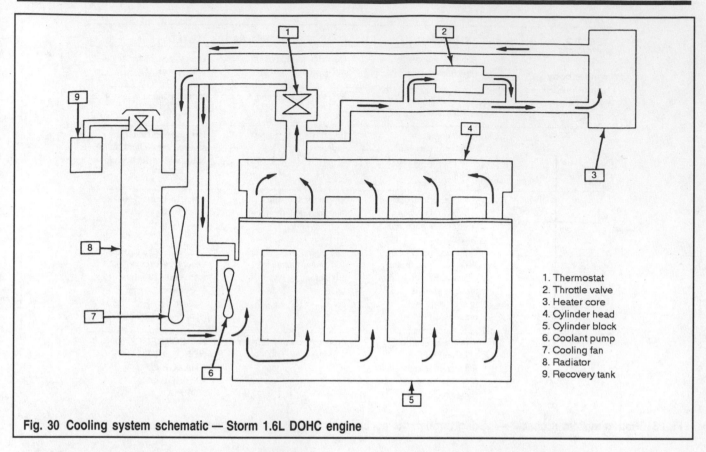

Fig. 30 Cooling system schematic — Storm 1.6L DOHC engine

1. Thermostat
2. Throttle valve
3. Heater core
4. Cylinder head
5. Cylinder block
6. Coolant pump
7. Cooling fan
8. Radiator
9. Recovery tank

broken wires, blown fuses, corroded connections and poor insulation.

A refrigerant leak will usually appear as an oily residue at the leakage point in the system. The oily residue soon picks up dust or dirt particles from the surrounding air and appears greasy. Through time, this will build up and appear to be a heavy dirt impregnated grease. Most leaks are caused by damaged or missing O-ring seals at the component connections, damaged charging valve cores or missing service gauge port caps.

For a thorough visual and operational inspection, check the following:

1. Inspect the air inlet duct and air deflector for missing or damaged parts which might affect air flow.
2. Check the surface of the radiator and condenser for dirt, leaves or other material which might block air flow.
3. Check for kinks in hoses and lines. Check the system for leaks.
4. Make sure the drive belt is under the proper tension. When the air conditioning is operating, make sure the drive belt is free of noise or slippage.
5. Make sure the blower motor operates at all appropriate, then check for equal distribution of the air from all outlets with the blower on **HIGH**.

➡**Keep in mind that under conditions of high humidity, air discharged from the A/C vents may not feel as cold as expected, even if the system is working properly. This is because the vaporized moisture in humid air retains heat more effectively than does dry air, making the humid air more difficult to cool.**

6. Make sure the air passage selection lever is operating correctly. Start the engine and warm it to normal operating temperature, then make sure the hot/cold selection lever is operating correctly.

REFRIGERANT LEVEL CHECK

Spectrum and 1990-1991 Storm
▶ **See Figure 31**

1. Start the engine and run at fast idle, about 1500 rpm.
2. Operate the A/C at maximum cooling for several minutes.
3. Check the refrigerant level by looking through the sight glass provided on the top of the accumulator/dehydrator. To locate the accumulator, follow the refrigerant line from the condenser to the accumulator/dehydrator assembly. The other condenser line runs from the compressor.
4. Compare the symptoms visible through the sight glass to the conditions in the appropriate illustration, in order to determine coolant charge.

1992 and 1993 Storm
▶ **See Figure 32**

1. Install a suitable manifold gauge set.
2. Install a thermometer in the passenger compartment right center air outlet, then open the vehicle doors and windows to stabilize the vehicle interior with the ambient air temperature.
3. Ground the coolant fan check connector (the connector is on a WHITE wire and is located in the left rear of the

ITEM NO.	SYMPTOM	CHARGE OF REFRIGERANT	REMEDY
1	Bubbles observed in sight glass.	Insufficient charge of refrigerant in system.	Check system for leaks with a leak tester.
2	No bubbles observed in sight glass.	Refer to Items 3 and 4.	Refer to Items 3 and 4.
3	No temperature difference between compressor inlet and outlet.	Empty or near empty system.	Evacuate and charge system, then check it for leaks with a leak tester.
4	Noticeable temperature difference between compressor inlet and outlet.	Proper or too much charge of refrigerant in system.	Refer to Items 5 and 6.
5	When air conditioner is turned OFF, refrigerant in sight glass is clear immediately and remains clear.	Too much charge of refrigerant in system.	Discharge excess refrigerant to adjust it to a specified charge.
6	When air conditioner is turned OFF, refrigerant in sight glass produces foam and then remains clear.	Proper charge of refrigerant in system.	NO CORRECTION NEEDED BECAUSE CHARGE OF REFRIGERANT IS NORMAL.

Fig. 31 Refrigerant level check — looking through the accumulator/dehydrator sight glass

engine compartment, above the power brake booster), then start the engine and allow it to idle.

4. Depress the A/C switch to the **ON** position, move the air source lever to the recirculation position, set the temperature lever to full cold and select the 3rd blower speed.

5. When the engine is fully warmed, run the engine at 2000 rpm. Continue to run the engine until the system pressure and outlet temperature stabilize. This should take about 5 minutes.

6. Record the pressure and temperature readings, then compare them to the specifications in the appropriate illustration. Remember that humidity can greatly affect A/C performance. System pressures and outlet temperatures can be expected to increase 5-10 percent under humidity conditions of 70 percent or higher.

GAUGE SETS

▶ **See Figures 33, 34 and 35**

Most of the service work performed in air conditioning requires the use of a set of two gauges, one for the high pressure side of the system and the other for the low pressure side of the system.

The low side gauge records both pressure and vacuum. Vacuum readings are calibrated from 0 to 30 in. Hg and the pressure graduations read from 0 to no less than 60 psi (414kpa). The high side gauge measures pressure from 0 to at least 600 psi (4140kpa).

Both gauges are threaded into a manifold that contains two hand shut-off valves. Proper manipulation of these valves, and

AMBIENT TEMPERATURE	LOW SIDE PRESSURE	HIGH SIDE PRESSURE	OUTLET TEMPERATURE
21°C (70°F)	103 – 138 kPa (15 – 20 psi)	1034 – 1240 kPa (150 – 180 psi)	3 – 7°C (38 – 45°F)
27°C (80°F)	124 – 158 kPa (18 – 23 psi)	1171 – 1447 kPa (170 – 210 psi)	6 – 9°C (42 – 48°F)
32°C (90°F)	152 – 186 kPa (22 – 27 psi)	1309 – 1585 kPa (190 – 230 psi)	6 – 12°C (43 – 53°F)
38°C (100°F)	165 – 207 kPa (24 – 30 psi)	1516 – 1861 kPa (220 – 270 psi)	8 – 14°C (47 – 58°F)

Fig. 32 A/C performance test — 1992 and 1993 Storm

the use of the attached hoses allow the user to perform the following services:

1. Test high and low side pressures.
2. Remove air, moisture, and contaminated refrigerant.
3. Purge the system (of refrigerant).
4. Charge the system (with refrigerant).

The manifold valves are designed so they have no direct affect on gauge readings, but serve only to provide for, or cut off, flow of refrigerant through the manifold. During all testing and hook-up operations, the valves are kept in the closed position to avoid disturbing the refrigeration system. The valves are opened only to purge the system or to charge it.

Connect the manifold gauge set as follows:

5. Make sure that both gauges read '0″, then close both valves.

6. Connect the low pressure gauge hose to the compressor suction port located on the suction hose (between the evaporator and compressor), then hand-tighten the hose nut.

7. Connect the high pressure gauge hose to the discharge service port located on the compressor discharge hose (between the compressor and condenser), then hand-tighten the hose nut.

DISCHARGING THE SYSTEM

➡ **R-12 refrigerant is a chlorofluorocarbon which, when released into the atmosphere, can contribute to the depletion of the ozone layer in the upper atmosphere. Ozone filters out harmful radiation from the sun.**

Consult the laws in your area before servicing the air conditioning system. In some states it is illegal to perform repairs involving refrigerant unless the work is done by a certified technician.

The use of refrigerant recovery systems and recycling stations makes possible the recovery and reuse of refrigerant after contaminants and moisture have been removed. If a recovery system or recycling station is available, the following general procedures should be observed, in addition to the operating instructions provided by the equipment manufacturer.

1. Check the system for pressure using the manifold gauge set. Take note, if a recovery system is used to draw refrigerant from a system that is already ruptured and open to the atmosphere, only air may be pulled into the tank.

2. Connect the refrigerant recycling station hose(s) to the vehicle air conditioning service ports and the recovery station inlet fitting.

➡ **Hoses should have shut off devices or check valves within 12 in. (305mm) of the hose end to minimize the introduction of air into the recycling station and to minimize the amount of refrigerant released when the hose(s) is disconnected.**

3. Turn the power to the recycling station **ON** to start the recovery process. Allow the recycling station to pump the refrigerant from the system until the station pressure goes into a vacuum. On some stations the pump will be shut off automatically by a low pressure switch in the electrical system. On other units it may be necessary to manually turn off the pump.

4. Once the recycling station has evacuated the vehicle air conditioning system, close the station inlet valve, if equipped. Then switch **OFF** the electrical power.

5. Allow the vehicle air conditioning system to remain closed for about 2 minutes. Observe the system vacuum level as shown on the gauge. If the pressure does not rise, disconnect the recycling station hose(s).

6. If the system pressure rises, repeat Steps 3, 4 and 5 until the vacuum level remains stable for 2 minutes.

7. If A/C oil is expelled during the discharge procedure, save the oil in order to measure the proper quantity which must be added to the system during charging.

EVACUATING/CHARGING

Evacuating and charging the air conditioning system is a combined procedure in which the lines are purged, then refrigerant is added to the system in proper quantity. Charging is always conducted through the low pressure fitting in the pipe behind the compressor. NEVER attempt to charge the air conditioning through the high pressure side of the system.

1. Properly connect a manifold gauge set, then connect the manifold to a vacuum pump.

2. Turn the vacuum pump **ON** and slowly open the high and low side valves to the pump. Allow the system to evacuate for 20-30 minutes, then note the gauge reading.

3. Close the gauge high and low side valves, then shut the pump **OFF**.

4. Watch the low side gauge for vacuum loss. If vacuum loss is in excess of 1 in. Hg (3.38 kPa), then leak test the system, repair the leaks and return to Step 1. Before leak testing, remember to disconnect the gauge high side connector from the service port.

5. If after 1-3 minutes, the loss is less than 1 in. Hg (3.38 kPa), then proceed with the system charging.

6. Disconnect the gauge high side connection from the service port and the gauge manifold from the vacuum pump.

7. If components were replaced, such as the compressor, add the amount of A/C oil recovered from the component to that expelled during the discharge procedure in order to arrive at the total amount of fresh A/C oil which must be added to the system. Be sure to use only the proper A/C oil that is specified for your vehicle's system. Place the appropriate amount of fresh oil in a clean container and submerge the center gauge manifold hose. Slowly open the low-side manifold valve and allow the vacuum to draw in the oil from the container, then quickly close the valve.

8. Connect the manifold connection (which was attached used to draw in the fresh oil) to an R-12 source. If you are using a refrigerant drum instead of a charging station, place the drum on a scale to determine the amount of refrigerant being used.

9. Open the source and low side gauge valve, then monitor the weight of the drum or the rate at which the charging system is introducing R-12 into the system.

10. When 0.5 lbs. (227 g) of R-12 has been added to the system, start the engine and turn the air conditioning system **ON**. Set the temperature lever to full cold, the blower speed on high and the selector lever to the upper outlets. Under this condition, slowly draw in the remainder of the R-12 charge.

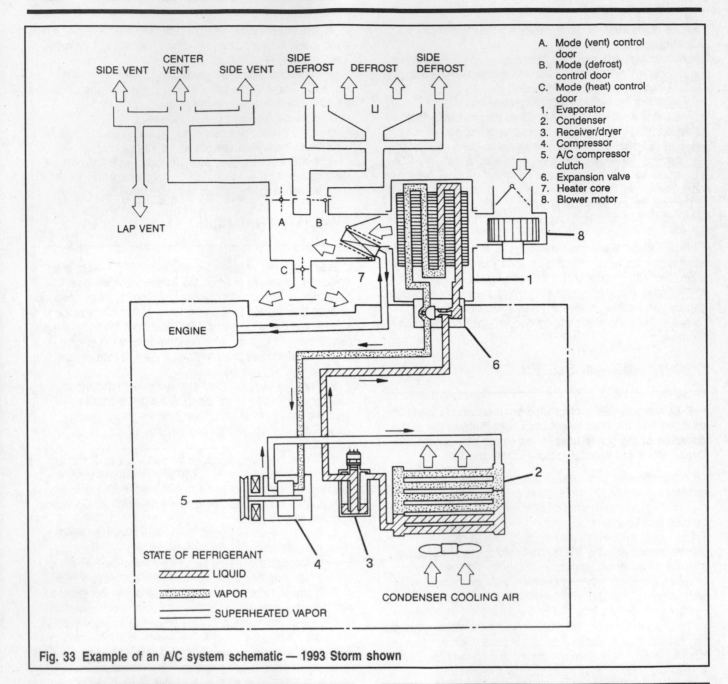

A. Mode (vent) control door
B. Mode (defrost) control door
C. Mode (heat) control door
1. Evaporator
2. Condenser
3. Receiver/dryer
4. Compressor
5. A/C compressor clutch
6. Expansion valve
7. Heater core
8. Blower motor

SIDE VENT   CENTER VENT   SIDE VENT   SIDE DEFROST   DEFROST   SIDE DEFROST

LAP VENT

ENGINE

STATE OF REFRIGERANT

LIQUID

VAPOR

SUPERHEATED VAPOR

CONDENSER COOLING AIR

Fig. 33 Example of an A/C system schematic — 1993 Storm shown

Fig. 34 The high pressure hose service port — 1990 Storm

Fig. 35 Low pressure hose service port — 1990 Storm

The total charge should range between 1.2-1.7 lbs depending on the model.

11. When the system is charged, turn the source valve **OFF** and continue to run the engine for 30 seconds in order to clear the gauges and lines.

12. With the engine still running, carefully remove the gauge low side hose from the suction pipe service fitting. Unscrew the connection rapidly to avoid excess refrigerant loss.

❈❈CAUTION

If the hoses of the manifold gauge set disconnect from the gauge, NEVER remove a hose from the gauge while the other end of the hose is still connected to an air conditioning system service fitting. Because the service fitting check valve is depressed by the hose connection, this would cause a complete and uncontrolled discharge of the system. Serious personal injury could be caused by the escaping R-12

13. Install the protective service fitting caps and hand-tighten.

14. Turn the engine **OFF**.

15. If an electronic leak tester is available, test the system for leaks.

16. If there are no leaks, perform the refrigerant level test to verify proper system charging.

LEAK TESTING

▶ **See Figure 36**

Whenever a refrigerant leak is suspected, begin by checking for leaks at the fittings and valves. Use of an electronic leak detector, if available is preferable. Follow the manufacturer's instructions carefully. Move the detector probe at approximately 1 in. per second in the suspected leak area. When escaping refrigerant gas is located, the ticking/beeping signal from the detector will increase in ticks/beeps per second. If the gas is relatively concentrated, the signal will be increasingly shrill.

If a tester is not available, perform a visual inspection and apply a soap solution to the questionable fitting or area. Bubbles will form to indicate a leak. Make sure to rinse the solution from the fitting before attempting repairs.

Windshield Wipers

▶ **See Figure 37**

For maximum effectiveness and longest element life, the windshield and wiper blades should be kept clean. Dirt, tree sap, road tar and so on will cause streaking, smearing and blade deterioration if left on the glass. It is advisable to wash the windshield carefully with a commercial glass cleaner at least once a month. Wipe off the rubber blades with the wet rag afterwards. Do not attempt to move the wipers by hand; damage to the motor and drive mechanism will result.

To inspect and/or replace the wiper blades, place the wiper switch in the **LOW** speed position and the ignition switch in the **ACC** position. When the wiper blades are approximately vertical on the windshield, turn the ignition switch to **OFF**.

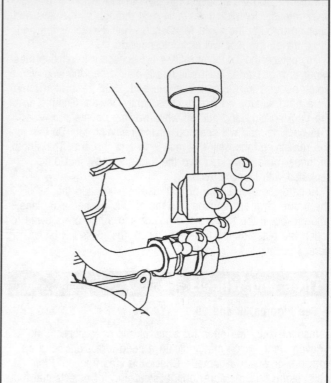

Fig. 36 A soap solution applied to the suspected area or fitting can be helpful in pinpointing a refrigerant leak

Examine the wiper blades. If they are found to be cracked, broken or torn, they should be replaced immediately. Replacement intervals will vary with usage, although ozone deterioration usually limits blade life to about one year. If the wiper pattern is smeared or streaked, or if the blade chatters across the glass, the elements should be replaced. It is easiest and most sensible to replace the elements in pairs.

Most original wiper blades found on the Spectrum and Storm are easily replaceable. The wiper blade slides from the arm assembly once the catch is released. If your vehicle is equipped with aftermarket blades, there are several different types of refills and your vehicle might have any kind. Aftermarket blades and arms rarely use the exact same type blade or refill as the original equipment. Here are some typical aftermarket blades, not all may be available for your car.

The Anco® type uses a release button that is pushed down to allow the refill to slide out of the yoke jaws. The new refill slides back into the frame and locks in place.

Some Trico® refills are removed by locating where the metal backing strip or the refill is wider. Insert a small screwdriver blade between the frame and metal backing strip. Press down to release the refill from the retaining tab.

Other types of Trico® refills have two metal tabs which are unlocked by squeezing them together. The rubber filler can then be withdrawn from the frame jaws. A new refill is installed by inserting the refill into the front frame jaws and sliding it rearward to engage the remaining frame jaws. There are usually four jaws; be certain when installing, that the refill is engaged in all of them. At the end of its travel, the tabs will lock into place on the front jaws of the wiper blade frame.

Another type of refill is made from polycarbonate. The refill has a simple locking device at one end which flexes downward out of the groove into which the jaws of the holder fit, allowing easy release. By sliding the new refill through all the jaws and pushing through the slight resistance when it reaches the end of its travel, the refill will lock into position.

To replace the Tridon® refill, it is necessary to remove the wiper arm or blade. This refill has a plastic backing strip with a notch about 1 in. (25mm) from the end. Hold the blade (frame) on a hard surface so the frame is tightly bowed. Grip the tip of the backing strip and pull up while twisting counterclockwise. The backing strip will snap out of the retaining tab. Do this for the remaining tabs until the refill is free of the arm. The length of these refills is molded into the end and they should be replaced with identical types.

Regardless of the type of refill used, make sure that all of the frame jaws are engaged as the refill is pushed into place and locked. If the metal blade holder and frame are allowed to touch the glass during wiper operation, the glass will be scratched.

Tires and Wheels

▶ **See Figures 38 and 39**

Inspect your tires often for signs of improper inflation and uneven wear, which may indicate a need for balancing, rotation, or wheel alignment. Check the tires frequently for cuts, stone bruises, abrasions, blisters and for objects that may have become embedded in the tread. More frequent inspections are recommended when rapid or extreme temperature changes occur or where road surfaces are rough or occasionally littered with debris. Check the condition of the wheels and replace any that are bent, cracked, severely dented or have excessive run-out.

The tires on your car have built-in wear indicators molded into the bottom of the tread grooves. The indicators will begin to appear as the tire approaches replacement tread depth. Once the indicators are visible across 2 or more adjacent grooves and at 3 or more locations, the tires should be replaced.

Wear that occurs only on certain portions of the tire may indicate a particular problem, which when corrected or avoided, may significantly extend tire life. Wear that occurs only in the center of the tire indicates either overinflation or heavy acceleration on a drive wheel. Wear occurring at the outer edges of the tire and not at the center may indicate underinflation, excessively hard cornering or a lack of rotation. If wear occurs at only the outer edge of the tire, there may be

a problem with the wheel alignment or the tire, when constructed, contained a non-uniformity defect.

TIRE ROTATION

▶ **See Figures 40 and 41**

Your tires should be rotated at the intervals recommended in the Maintenance Interval chart at the end of this section. Rotate them according to either of the tire rotation diagrams. The spare should not be included in the rotation.

TIRE DESIGN

▶ **See Figure 42**

Your Spectrum or Storm was originally equipped with metric-sized radial tires. Radial tires get their name from their construction, because the carcass plies on a radial tire run at an angle of 90° to the tire bead, as opposed to a conventional bias ply tire where the carcass plies run at an angle of 90° to each another. The radial tire's construction gives the tread a great deal of rigidity and the side wall a great deal of flexibility.

When replacing your tires, use only the size, load range and construction type (radial) originally installed on the car. This information can be found on the tire-loading information decal, which is located on the top right underside of the trunk lid and is also located on the tire sidewall. The use of any other size or type may affect ride, handling, speedometer/odometer calibration, vehicle ground clearance, and tire to body clearance.

Do not mix tires of different construction (radial, bias ply or bias belted) on the same vehicle unless it is an emergency. Mixing types may seriously affect handling and possibly cause a loss of vehicle control.

TIRE INFLATION

At least once a month, check the inflation pressure on all tires, including the spare. Use an accurate tire pressure gauge. Do not trust the gauges on service station air pumps, as they are not always accurate. The inflation specifications are listed on the tire-loading information decal usually affixed to the driver's door jamb, immediately below the vehicle certification label. Check and adjust inflation pressures only when the tires are cold, as pressures can increase as much as 4 psi (28kpa) due to heat. Tires are considered 'warmed-up' once they are driven for more than 1 mile.

Inflation pressures that are higher than recommended can cause a hard ride, tire bruising, carcass damage and rapid tread wear at the center of the tire. Inflation pressures that are lower than recommended can cause tire squeal, hard steering, rim dents, high temperatures and rapid wear on the outer edges of the tires. Unequal tire pressures can compromise handling and cause uneven braking.

As previously stated, radial tires have a highly flexible sidewall and this accounts for the characteristic sidewall bulge that makes the tire appear underinflated. This is normal for a radial tire, so you should not attempt to reduce this bulge by overinflating the tire.

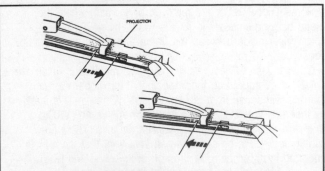

Fig. 37 Removing and installing the original wiper blades — Storm shown

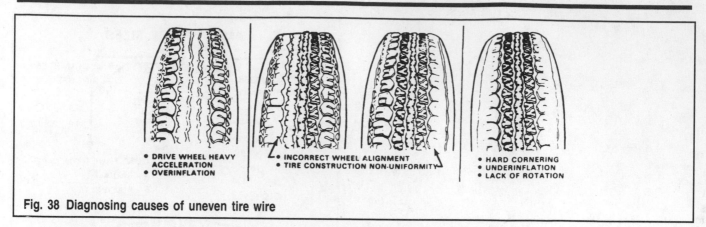

Fig. 38 Diagnosing causes of uneven tire wire

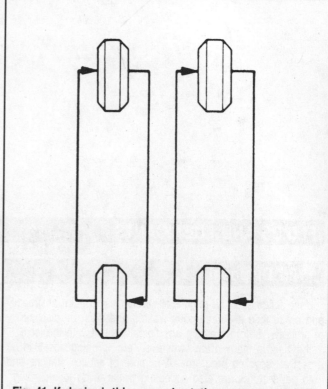

WEAR INDICATOR

WEAR INDICATOR

Fig. 39 Wear indicators are built into the tires to inform you when they are in need of replacement

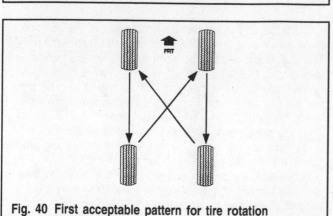

Fig. 41 If desired, this second rotation pattern may be substituted for the first

The tire valve caps are installed on the tire valve to prevent the entrance of dirt and moisture. Be sure to always replace the cap after checking or adjusting the tire pressure.

CARE OF ALUMINUM WHEELS

If your car is equipped with aluminum wheels, they are normally coated to preserve their appearance. To clean the aluminum wheels, use a mild soap and water solution and rinse thoroughly with clean water. If you want to use one of the commercially available wheel cleaners, make sure the label indicates that the cleaner is safe for coated wheels. Never use steel wool or any cleaner that contains an abrasive, or use strong detergents that contain high alkaline or caustic agents, as this will damage your wheels.

Fig. 40 First acceptable pattern for tire rotation

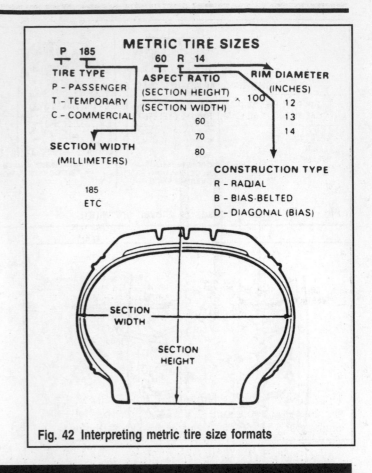

Fig. 42 Interpreting metric tire size formats

FLUIDS AND LUBRICANTS

Fluid Disposal

Used fluids such as engine oil, transmission fluid, antifreeze and brake fluid are hazardous wastes and must be disposed of properly. Before draining any fluids, consult with the local authorities; in many areas, waste oil, etc. is being accepted as a part of recycling programs. A number of service stations and auto parts stores are also accepting waste fluids for recycling.

Be sure of the recycling center's policies before draining any fluids, as many will not accept different fluids that have been mixed together, such as oil and antifreeze.

Fuel and Engine Oil Recommendations

▶ See Figure 43

All Spectrum and Storms are equipped with a catalytic converter, necessitating the use of unleaded gasoline. The use of leaded gasoline will damage the catalytic converter. Both the SOHC and DOHC engines are designed to use unleaded gasoline with a minimum octane rating of 87, which usually means regular unleaded.

Oil must be selected with regard to the anticipated temperatures during the period before the next oil change. Using the chart, select the oil viscosity for the lowest expected temperature and you will be assured of easy cold starting and sufficient engine protection. The oil you pour into your engine should have the designation SG marked on the container. For maximum fuel economy benefits, use an oil with the Roman Numeral II next to the words Energy Conserving in the API Service Symbol.

Engine

OIL LEVEL CHECK

▶ See Figures 44 and 45

Check the engine oil level every time you fill the gas tank. Make sure the oil level is between the **FULL** and **ADD** marks. The engine and oil must be warm and the vehicle parked on level ground to get an accurate reading. Always allow a few minutes after turning the engine OFF for the oil to drain back into the pan before checking, or an inaccurate reading will result. Check the engine oil level as follows:

1. Open the hood and locate the engine oil dipstick.
2. If the engine is hot, you may want to wrap a rag around the dipstick handle before removing it.
3. Remove the dipstick and wipe it with a clean, lint-free rag, then reinsert it into the dipstick tube. Make sure it is inserted all the way to avoid and inaccurate reading.
4. Pull out the dipstick and note the oil level. It should be between the marks, as stated above.

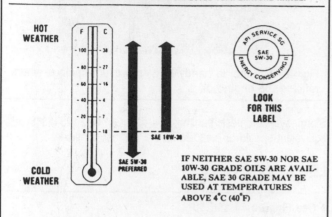

RECOMMENDED SAE VISCOSITY GRADE ENGINE OILS

FOR BEST FUEL ECONOMY AND COLD STARTING, SELECT THE LOWEST SAE VISCOSITY GRADE OIL FOR THE EXPECTED TEMPERATURE RANGE.

HOT WEATHER

COLD WEATHER

SAE 5W-30 PREFERRED

SAE 10W-30

API SERVICE SG SAE 5W-30 ENERGY CONSERVING II

LOOK FOR THIS LABEL

IF NEITHER SAE 5W-30 NOR SAE 10W-30 GRADE OILS ARE AVAILABLE, SAE 30 GRADE MAY BE USED AT TEMPERATURES ABOVE 4°C (40°F)

Fig. 43 Select an engine oil of the proper viscosity for the ambient temperature — 5W-30 is preferred for SOHC engines and 10W-30 is preferred for DOHC engines

5. If the oil level is below the lower mark, replace the dipstick and add fresh oil to bring the level within the proper range. Do not overfill.

6. Recheck the oil level and close the hood.

OIL AND FILTER CHANGE

▶ See Figures 46, 47 and 48

The engine oil and oil filter should be changed together, at the recommended interval on the Maintenance Intervals Chart. The oil should be changed more frequently if the vehicle is being operated in very dusty areas. Before draining the oil,

Fig. 44 After the dipstick is wiped, fully inserted and removed again from the guide tube, an accurate level reading may be performed

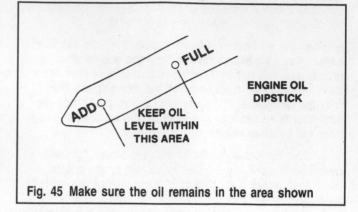

FULL

ADD

ENGINE OIL DIPSTICK

KEEP OIL LEVEL WITHIN THIS AREA

Fig. 45 Make sure the oil remains in the area shown

make sure the engine is at operating temperature. Hot oil will hold more impurities in suspension and will flow better, allowing the removal of more oil and dirt.

As noted earlier, used oil has been classified as a hazardous waste and must be disposed of properly. Before draining any oil from the engine crankcase, make sure you are aware of the proper disposal procedures for your area.

Change the oil and filter as follows:

1. Run the engine until it reaches the normal operating temperature, then shut off the engine and remove the oil filler cap.

2. Raise and safely support the front of the car. If possible, make sure the engine drain plug is lower than the rest of the oil pan. Position a drain pan under the plug.

✳✳CAUTION

The EPA warns that prolonged contact with used engine oil may cause a number of skin disorders, including cancer! You should make every effort to minimize your exposure to used engine oil. Protective gloves should be worn when changing the oil. Wash your hands and any other exposed skin areas as soon as possible after exposure to used engine oil. Soap and water, or waterless hand cleaner should be used.

3. Wipe the drain plug and the surrounding area clean. Loosen the drain plug with a socket or box wrench, then remove it by hand using a rag to shield your fingers from the heat. Push in on the plug as you turn it out, so that no oil escapes until the plug is completely removed.

4. Allow the oil to drain into the pan. Be careful; if the engine is at operating temperature, as the oil is hot enough to burn you.

5. Clean and install the drain plug, making sure that the gasket or washer is still on the plug. Use a new drain plug gasket whenever possible, but if the gasket is damaged, a new gasket MUST be installed. Tighten the drain plug until snug, but be careful not to overtighten and strip the plug.

6. The oil filter is on the rear right side of the block protruding towards the firewall. Slide the drain pan under the oil filter. Slip an oil filter wrench onto the filter and turn counterclockwise to loosen the filter. Wrap a rag around the

filter and unscrew it the rest of the way by hand. Be careful of hot oil which may run down the side of the filter.

➡When the oil filter is removed, make sure the old filter gasket has also been removed from the engine or a proper seal will not be achieved with the new filter. More than a few people have installed the replacement filter with the old gasket still partially in place, preventing the new filter from sealing, and have wound up with a garage floor full of clean engine oil.

7. Coat the rubber gasket on the replacement filter with clean engine oil. Place the filter in position on the adapter fitting, then thread it and tighten by hand, do not use a filter wrench or the replacement filter may be overtightened.

8. Pull the drain pan from under the vehicle, remove the supports and lower the vehicle to the ground.

9. Fill the crankcase with the proper type and quantity of engine oil right away. If the engine is started and run without oil in the crankcase, serious damage may occur almost immediately.

10. Run the engine and check for leaks. Stop the engine and check the oil level.

Manual Transaxle

FLUID RECOMMENDATIONS

For all Spectrum vehicles, the manual transaxle should be filled using SAE 5W-30 SF/CC or SF/CD engine oil. For the

Fig. 46 Loosen the drainplug using a suitable sized socket or box wrench

Fig. 47 The oil filter is usually threaded to an adapter on the rear side of the block, facing the firewall — 1990 Storm SOHC engine shown

Fig. 48 A funnel is handy to help prevent spillage when refilling the engine oil

Storm, sycnchromesh transmission fluid GM No. 12345348 or equivalent should be used to fill the manual transaxle.

LEVEL CHECK

▶ See Figures 49 and 50

1. The manual transaxle fluid should be checked when the transaxle is cool enough so that your fingers may comfortably rest on the transaxle housing.

2. If necessary, move the car to a level spot and allow the powertrain to cool.

3. For the Spectrum, loosen the fastener and remove the speedometer driven gear bushing. Make sure the lubricant is between the L and H markings.

4. For the Storm, remove the filler plug located in the side of the transaxle case and check that lubricant is even with the bottom of the filler plug hole.

5. If necessary, add sufficient lubricant to bring the fluid level either up to the L mark or even with the bottom of the filler plug hole, as applicable.

DRAIN AND REFILL

For fluid replacement and other transaxle service procedures, refer to Section 7 of this manual.

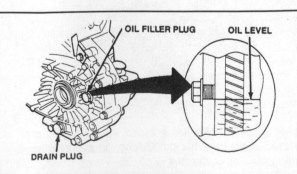

Fig. 49 Manual transaxle fluid should be even with the bottom of the filler plug hole on the Storm

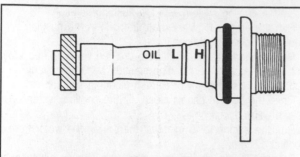

Fig. 50 For the Spectrum, make sure the manual transaxle fluid is at least up to the L marking on the speedometer driven gear bushing assembly

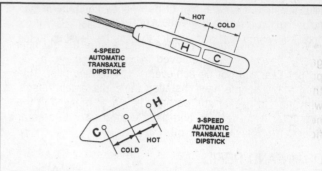

Fig. 51 Make sure the level is in the appropriate range for fluid temperature

Automatic Transaxle

FLUID RECOMMENDATIONS

DEXRON®II automatic transmission/transaxle fluid must be used in the Spectrum and Storm automatic transaxles.

LEVEL CHECK

♦ **See Figure 51**

The fluid level should be checked at least with every engine oil change. Operating your vehicle with too much or too little automatic transaxle fluid could seriously damage the transaxle.

1. Start the engine and operate the vehicle for a few minutes or until the transaxle fluid reaches room temperature. An incorrect level reading will be obtained if the vehicle is operated under the following conditions immediately before checking the dipstick:

At sustained highway speeds.
In heavy city traffic, during hot weather.
Used as a towing vehicle.

2. Park the vehicle on a level surface and apply the parking brake.
3. Move the gear selector through all gears, then position the selector in **P**.
4. If the engine was cold to being with, turn all accessories **OFF** and allow the vehicle to idle for about 2 minutes in order to properly warm the fluid.
5. Withdraw the dipstick and check for proper fluid level as compared with the picture. If the fluid is cool (between 68°F-86°F) the level should be between the center marking and the **C** mark. If the fluid is hot (between 158°F-176°F) the level should be between the center marking and the **H** mark.
6. Check the fluid color and condition; fluid should be smooth, transparent and red. If fluid is not transparent or if it is a dark brown, the fluid is contaminated or overheated and must be replaced.
7. If necessary, change the fluid or add fluid to bring the amount to the proper level. Add fluid slowly as it takes only 1 pint to raise the level from range mark-to-range mark on the dipstick.

FLUID AND FILTER CHANGE

For fluid and filter replacement or other transaxle service procedures, refer to Section 7 of this manual.

Cooling System

Check the cooling system at the interval specified in the Maintenance Intervals chart at the end of this section.

If necessary, hose clamps should be checked and soft or cracked hoses replaced. Damp spots or accumulations of rust or dye near hoses, the water pump or other areas indicate areas of possible leakage. Check the radiator pressure cap for a worn or cracked gasket. If the cap doesn't seal properly, fluid will be lost and the engine will overheat. A worn cap should be replaced with a new one. The radiator should be free of rust and the coolant should be free from oil. If oil is found in the coolant, the engine thermostat may not function correctly, therefore the system must be flushed and filled with fresh coolant.

Periodically clean any debris such as leaves, paper, insects, etc. from the radiator fins. Pick the large pieces off by hand. The smaller pieces can be washed away with water pressure from a hose.

Carefully straighten any bent radiator fins with a pair of needle nose pliers. Be careful — the fins are very soft. Don't wiggle the fins back and forth too much. Straighten them once and try not to move them again.

FLUID RECOMMENDATIONS

The recommended fluid is a 50/50 mixture of a ethylene glycol antifreeze and water for year round use. Make sure the solution is never less than 50 percent or more than 70 percent antifreeze. Use a good quality antifreeze with rust and other corrosion inhibitors, along with acid neutralizers.

LEVEL CHECK

♦ **See Figure 52**

To check the coolant level, simply raise the hood and locate the 'see-through' radiator surge tank. The tank has a MAX fill line to which the coolant level should always be raised, whether the engine is hot or cold. If necessary, remove the surge tank cap (NOT THE RADIATOR CAP, especially if the engine is warm) and add coolant to raise the level up to the MAX line.

Under certain conditions, air trapped in the system may adversely affect the surge tank and radiator's ability to obtain a proper level. If this is suspected, allow the engine too cool, then follow the 'fill' portion of the Drain and Refill procedure later in this section.

DRAIN AND REFILL

1. Make sure the engine is cool and the vehicle is parked on a level surface, then remove the radiator pressure cap.
2. Position a large drain pan under the radiator drain plug, then open the radiator drain and allow the coolant to drain from the system.
3. Close the radiator plug, then fill the system through the radiator using a suitable solution of water and a glycol antifreeze.
4. Once the coolant level reaches the base of the radiator filler neck, leave the pressure cap OFF and start the engine.
5. When the engine reaches normal operating temperature, the thermostat will open allowing coolant to flow into the engine and trapped air to escape from the coolant passages. At this point, more coolant will be necessary to bring the system up to full capacity.
6. Continue to add coolant until the level stabilizes just below the radiator filler neck, then install the pressure cap. Make sure the arrows on the pressure cap, if present, line up with the overflow tube on the radiator filler neck.
7. After the engine has run for another 2 or 3 minutes, check to make sure the coolant has reached the MAX fill line in the surge tank. If necessary add coolant to the surge tank.

FLUSHING AND CLEANING THE SYSTEM

1. Prepare 2 gallons of a flushing solution consisting of 4 ounces of Calgon®, or an equivalent automatic dishwasher detergent.
2. Run the engine until normal operating temperature is reached and the thermostat opens; this will allow the cleaning solution to circulate through the entire cooling system.
3. Carefully drain the engine cooling system.

Fig. 52 Whether the engine is hot or cold, the coolant level should always be even with the surge tank MAX fill line

4. Fill the cooling system with the flushing solution.
5. Run the engine for 5 minutes, then drain the flushing solution into a clean container.
6. Repeat Steps 4 and 5 until the drained water is free of coolant and/or rust. If the cleaning solution becomes overly dirty, substitute clean water or a fresh cleaning solution.
7. Once the system seems clean, fill the cooling system with clean water 1 last time.
8. Run the engine for 5 minutes, then drain the water from the cooling system.
9. Properly fill the engine cooling system with an ethylene glycol antifreeze.

Master Cylinder

FLUID RECOMMENDATIONS

The brake fluid reservoir is located on top of the master cylinder. The master cylinder and brake system requires brake fluid that meets DOT 3 standards. DO NOT use DOT 5 silicone fluid or any fluid that contains a mineral or paraffin base oil or system damage could occur.

LEVEL CHECK

▶ See Figures 53 and 54

The reservoir is translucent, with lines indicating the proper fluid fill level. It is normal for the brake fluid level to decrease slightly as the brake pads wear, so it is necessary to check the reservoir periodically in order to maintain a proper level of brake fluid. If the reservoir requires constant filling, a serious mechanical problem may be the cause and the entire brake system must be inspected for leaks and proper operation.

If it is necessary to add fluid, first wipe away any accumulated dirt or grease from the reservoir and cap. Then remove the reservoir cap by twisting counterclockwise. Add fluid to the proper level. Avoid spilling brake fluid on any painted surface as it will harm the finish. Replace the reservoir cap.

Power Steering Pump

FLUID RECOMMENDATIONS

GM power steering fluid specification No. 9985010, No. 1050017 or equivalent must be used. Failure to use a fluid which meets these specifications may cause damage and fluid leaks.

LEVEL CHECK

▶ See Figures 55, 56 and 57

The power steering pump reservoir is translucent so the level may be checked without removing the cap. The level is best checked after the vehicle has been driven a short

Fig. 53 Always keep the brake fluid level near the MAX fill line

Fig. 54 The cap must be cleaned prior to removal in order to prevent brake fluid contamination

Fig. 56 Always clean the cap before removal to prevent system contamination

oil for automatic transaxles. Also annually or whenever squeaking should occur, the clutch pedal bushing, clevis pin

Fig. 55 The power steering fluid reservoir is located next to the radiator surge tank at the right front of the engine compartment

distance with the engine at normal operating temperature. The warmed level should be between the MIN and MAX lines on the side of the reservoir. If fluid must be added, always clean the cap and surrounding area before removing the cap in order to prevent system contamination.

Chassis Greasing

For most vehicles covered by this manual, the steering and suspension joints are sealed at the factory and do not require any form of periodic lubrication. Some earlier models may contain joints with grease fittings. If present, a grease fitting should be lubed once a year using a suitable chassis grease and grease gun.

At least annually, the transaxle shift linkage may be lubricated with chassis grease for manual transaxles or engine

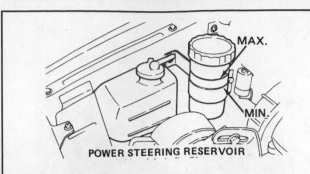

Fig. 57 With the system warm, make sure the power steering fluid is between the MIN and MAX lines

and clutch control cable ends should be lubricated using chassis grease.

For all Spectrums and 1990 Storms, the parking brake cable guides should be lubricated annually using chassis grease. Do not lubricate the parking brake cables on 1991 and later Storm vehicles as this will destroy the protective plastic coating on the cables.

Body Lubrication and Maintenance

At least once a year, use a multi-purpose grease to lubricate the body door hinges, including the hood, fuel door and trunk or liftgate hinges and latches. The glovebox, console doors and folding seat hardware should also be lightly lubricated. Be careful not to stain the interior fabrics with the grease.

The door and window weather-stripping should be lubricated with silicone lubricant. Flush the underbody using plain water to remove any corrosive materials picked up from the road and used for ice, snow or dust control. Make sure you thoroughly clean areas where mud and dirt may collect. If necessary, loosen sediment packed in closed areas before flushing.

To preserve the appearance of your car, it should be washed periodically with a mild soap or detergent and water solution. A liquid dishwashing detergent that DOES NOT contain any abrasives may be useful in loosening dirt or grease from the vehicle, while not endangering the finish. Only wash the vehicle when the metal feels cool and the vehicle is in the shade. Rinse the entire vehicle with cold water, then wash and rinse one panel at a time, beginning with the roof and upper areas. After washing is complete, rinse the vehicle one final time and dry with a soft cloth or chamois. Air drying a vehicle, by driving at highway speeds for a few miles, may quickly and easily dry a vehicle without the need for excessive elbow grease.

Periodic waxing will remove harmful deposits from the vehicles surface and protect the finish. If the finish has dulled due to age or neglect, polishing may be necessary to restore the original gloss.

There are many specialized products available at your local auto parts store to care for the appearance of painted metal surfaces, plastic, chrome, wheels and tires as well as the interior upholstery and carpeting. Be sure to follow the manufacturers instructions before using them.

Rear Wheel Bearings

REMOVAL, PACKING & INSTALLATION

Spectrum

▶ **See Figures 58, 59 and 60**

The rear wheel bearings of the Spectrum should be cleaned, inspected and repacked every 15,000 miles or at each brake relining if you are following maintenance schedule I. If primary use of your vehicle allows you to follow schedule II, the bearings should be serviced every 30,000 miles or at each brake relining, whichever comes first.

1. Raise and support the vehicle safely.
2. Remove the rear tire and wheel assemblies.
3. Remove the hub cap, cotter pin, hub nut, washer and outer bearing.
4. Remove the hub and drum assembly.
5. Using a slide hammer puller and attachment, pull the oil seal from the hub. Remove the inner bearing.
6. Using a brass drift and a hammer, drive both bearing races from the hub.
7. Thoroughly clean the grease from all parts, then inspect and/or replace parts as necessary. New bearings require the use of new races, do not use an old race when a new bearing is installed.
8. To install, pack the bearings with grease, coat the oil seal lips with grease and reverse the removal procedures. Always use a properly sized driver to install the races or seals in order to avoid cocking and damaging components. Torque the hub nut to 22 ft. lbs. (29 Nm).

➡**If the cotter pin holes are out of alignment upon reassembly, use a wrench to tighten the nut until the hole in the shaft and a slot of the nut align. Do not back off the designated torque in order to insert the cotter pin.**

Storm

▶ **See Figures 61 and 62**

1. Raise and safely support the vehicle.
2. Remove the tire and wheel assemblies.
3. Before removing the hub assembly, check the end-play as follows:
    a. Using a suitable dial indicator tool (J-8001 or equivalent) along with the magnetic base (J-26900-1 or equivalent) measure the hub assembly end-play.
    b. If the end-play exceeds 0.020 in. (0.05mm), the axle hub bearing must be replaced.
4. Remove the 4 retaining bolts holding the hub assembly to the knuckle.
5. Remove the hub assembly from the knuckle.
6. Press the axle hub bearing out of the hub assembly or if possible use a brass drift and a hammer and drive the rear wheel bearings from the axle hub.
7. Thoroughly clean the grease from all parts, then inspect and/or replace parts as necessary. New bearings require the use of new races, do not use an old race when a new bearing is installed.

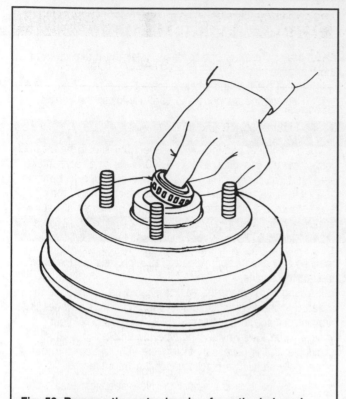

Fig. 58 Remove the outer bearing from the hub and drum assembly

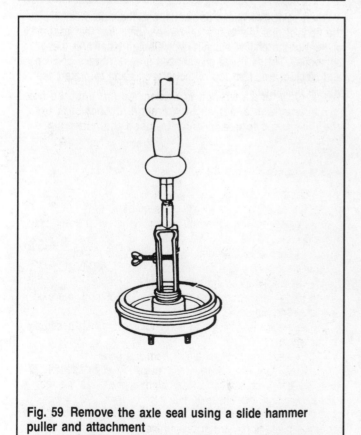

Fig. 59 Remove the axle seal using a slide hammer puller and attachment

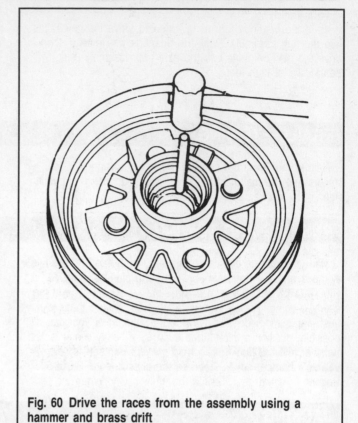

Fig. 60 Drive the races from the assembly using a hammer and brass drift

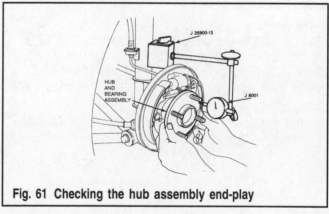

Fig. 61 Checking the hub assembly end-play

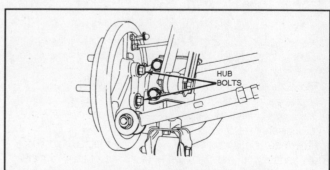

Fig. 62 The hub bolts are located in the knuckle assembly at the rear of the brake backing plate

To install:

8. If the bearings are being replaced, drive the new races into the hub assembly. Pack the bearings with grease, then drive the new bearings into the axle hub assembly using a bearing installation tool.

9. Install the hub assembly to the brake backing plate and the knuckle. Install the retaining bolts and torque them to 49 ft. lbs. (66 Nm).

10. Adjust the drum brakes, then install the brake drum to the hub assembly.

11. Install the tire and wheel assemblies.

12. Remove the supports and carefully lower the vehicle.

TRAILER TOWING

Neither the Spectrum nor the Storm are designed to tow trailers and the manufacturer does not recommend that you attempt to tow using your vehicle.

PUSHING AND TOWING

Manual transaxle equipped cars may be started by pushing, in the event of a dead battery. But push starting IS NOT RECOMMENDED because of possible severe damage to the catalytic converter. If you must push start, ensure that the push car bumper doesn't override the bumper of your car. If possible, position a thick fabric such as a heavy winter jacket between the car bumpers to help prevent damage to your vehicle's bumper cover. Depress the clutch pedal. Select Second or Third gear. Switch the ignition ON. When the car reaches a speed of approximately 10 mph, release the clutch to start the engine.

If towing is required, the vehicle should be flat bedded or towed with the front wheels off of the ground on a wheel lift to prevent damage to the transaxle. DO NOT ALLOW your vehicle to be towed by a sling type tow truck, if it is at all avoidable. If it is necessary to tow the vehicle from the rear, a wheel dolly should be placed under the front tires.

JACKING

▶ **See Figures 63, 64 and 65**

The vehicle is supplied with a scissors jack for emergency road repairs. The scissors jack may be used to raise the car via the notches on either side at the front and rear of the doors. Do not attempt to use the jack in any other places. Always block the diagonally opposite wheel when using a jack.

When using floor jacks or stands, use the side members at the front or rear, the center of the rear crossmember assembly or front of the engine support center beam (shown in the appropriate illustration as the shaded areas). Always position and block of wood on top of the jack or stand to protect the vehicle during jacking and supporting.

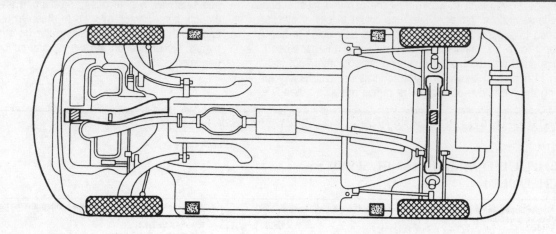

 FLOOR JACK
FRONT: ENGINE LOWER CROSSMEMBER
REAR : REAR SUBFRAME

 FRAME CONTACT HOIST/SAFETY STAND

 SUSPENSION CONTACT HOIST

Fig. 63 Jacks or jackstands may be used at the shaded areas

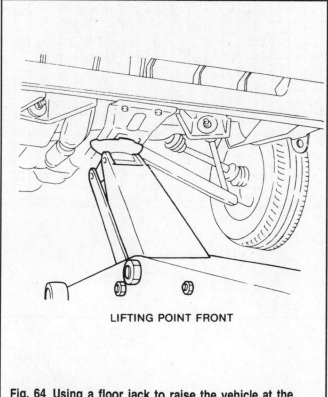

LIFTING POINT FRONT

Fig. 64 Using a floor jack to raise the vehicle at the engine support center beam

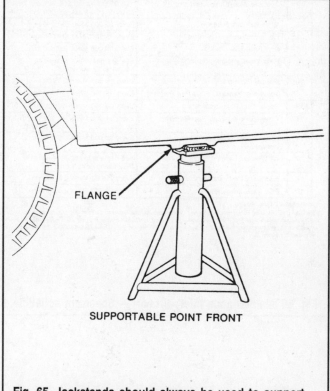

FLANGE

SUPPORTABLE POINT FRONT

Fig. 65 Jackstands should always be used to support the vehicle while work is performed

Whenever you plan to work under the car, you must support it on jackstands or ramps. Never use cinder blocks or stacks of wood to support the car, even if you're only going to be under it for a few minutes. Never crawl under the car when it is supported only by the tire-changing jack or other floor jack.

Small hydraulic, screw, or scissors jacks are satisfactory for raising the car. Drive-on trestles or ramps are also a handy and safe way to both raise and support the car. Be careful though, some ramps may be to steep to drive your Spectrum and Storm onto without scraping the front bottom plastic panels. Never support the car on any suspension member or underbody panel.

SCHEDULED MAINTENANCE SERVICES
SCHEDULE I

Follow Schedule I if your car is MAINLY operated under one or more of the following conditions:
- When most trips are less than 4 miles (6 kilometers).
- When most trips are less than 10 miles (16 kilometers) and outside temperatures remain below freezing.

- When most trips include extended idling and/or frequent low-speed operation as in stop-and-go traffic.
- Towing a trailer.‡
- Operating in dusty areas.
Schedule I should also be followed if the car is used for delivery service, police, taxi or other commercial applications.

The services shown in this schedule up to 60 000 miles (96 000 km) are to be performed after 60 000 miles at the same intervals.

ITEM NO.	TO BE SERVICED	WHEN TO PERFORM Miles (kilometers) or Months, Whichever Occurs First	MILES (000) 3	6	9	12	15	18	21	24	27	30	33	36	39	42	45	48	51	54	57	60
			KILOMETERS (000) 5	10	15	20	25	30	35	40	45	50	55	60	65	70	75	80	85	90	95	100
1	Engine Oil Replacement*	Every 3 000 Miles (5 000 km) or 3 Months	•	•	•	•	•	•	•	•	•	•	•	•	•	•	•	•	•	•	•	•
	Oil Filter Replacement*	At First and Then Every Other Oil Change	•		•		•		•		•		•		•		•		•		•	
2	Chassis and Body Lubrication	Every Other Oil Change		•		•		•		•		•		•		•		•		•		•
3	Carburetor Choke Inspection*‡	Every 30 000 Miles (50 000 km)										•										
4	Valve Clearance Adjustment*	Every 15 000 Miles (25 000 km)					•					•					•					•
5	Timing Belt Replacement	Every 60 000 Miles (96 000 km)																				•
6	Engine Idle Speed Adjustment*	At 3 000 Miles (5 000 km) Only	•																			
7	Tire and Wheel Inspection and Rotation	At 6 000 Miles (10 000 km) and Then Every 15 000 Miles (25 000 km)		•					•					•					•			
8	Drive Belt Inspection*	Every 30 000 Miles (50 000 km)										•										
9	Cooling System Inspection*	Every 15 000 Miles (25 000 km)					•					•					•					•
	Cooling System Refill*	Every 30 000 Miles (50 000 km)										•										
10	Rear Wheel Bearing Repack	See Explanation of Scheduled Maintenance Services																				
11	Manual Transaxle Fluid Replacement	Every 15 000 Miles (25 000 km)					•					•					•					•
	Automatic Transaxle Fluid Replacement	Every 15 000 Miles (25 000 km)					•					•					•					•
12	Spark Plug Replacement*	Every 30 000 Miles (50 000 km)										•										
13	Power Steering Fluid Replacement	Every 21 000 Miles (35 000 km) or 24 Months							•							•						
14	Power Steering Rubber Hose Inspection	Every 42 000 Miles (70 000 km)														•						
15	Air Cleaner Element Replacement*	See Explanation of Scheduled Maintenance Services										•										
16	Fuel Cap, Lines and Tank Inspection*‡	Every 15 000 Miles (25 000 km)					•					•					•					•
17	PCV Valve Inspection*‡	Every 30 000 Miles (50 000 km)										•										•

* An Emission Control Service.

‡The U.S. Environmental Protection Agency has determined that the failure to perform this maintenance item will not nullify the emission warranty or limit recall liability prior to the completion of vehicle useful life. General Motors, however, urges that all recommended maintenance services be performed at the indicated intervals and the maintenance be recorded in Section C.

‡ Trailering is not recommended for some models. See your Owner's Manual for details.

Fig. 66 Maintenance interval chart — Spectrum schedule 1

SCHEDULED MAINTENANCE SERVICES
SCHEDULE II

Follow Schedule II only if none of the driving conditions specified in Schedule I apply.

The services shown in this schedule up to 60 000 miles (96 000 km) are to be performed after 60 000 miles at the same intervals.

ITEM NO.	TO BE SERVICED	WHEN TO PERFORM Miles (kilometers) or Months, Whichever Occurs First	MILES (000) 3 / KM 5	6 / 10	7.5 / 12.5	9 / 15	12 / 20	15 / 25	18 / 30	21 / 35	22.5 / 37.5	24 / 40	27 / 45	30 / 50	33 / 55	36 / 60	37.5 / 62.5	39 / 65	42 / 70	45 / 75	48 / 80	51 / 85	52.5 / 87.5	54 / 90	57 / 95	60 / 100
1	Engine Oil Replacement*	Every 7 500 Miles (12 500 km) or 12 Months			•			•			•			•			•			•			•			•
	Oil Filter Replacement*	At First and Then Every Other Oil Change			•						•						•						•			
2	Chassis and Body Lubrication	Every 7 500 Miles (12 500 km) or 12 Months			•			•			•			•			•			•			•			•
3	Carburetor Choke Inspection*‡	Every 30 000 Miles (50 000 km)												•												•
4	Valve Clearance Adjustment*	Every 15 000 Miles (25 000 km)						•						•						•						•
5	Timing Belt Replacement	Every 60 000 Miles (96 000 km)																								•
6	Engine Idle Speed Adjustment*	At 5 000 Miles (8 000 km) Only		•																						
7	Tire and Wheel Inspection and Rotation	At 7 500 Miles (12 500 km) and Then Every 15 000 Miles (25 000 km)			•						•						•						•			
8	Drive Belt Inspection*	Every 30 000 Miles (50 000 km)												•												•
9	Cooling System Inspection*	Every 15 000 Miles (25 000 km)						•						•						•						•
	Cooling System Refill*	Every 30 000 Miles (50 000 km)												•												•
10	Rear Wheel Bearing Repack	Every 30 000 Miles (50 000 km)												•												•
11	Manual Transaxle Fluid Replacement	Every 30 000 Miles (50 000 km)			•									•												•
	Automatic Transaxle Fluid Replacement	Every 30 000 Miles (50 000 km)												•												•
12	Spark Plug Replacement*	Every 30 000 Miles (50 000 km)												•												•
13	Power Steering Fluid Replacement	Every 22 500 Miles (37 500 km) or 24 Months									•									•						
14	Power Steering Rubber Hose Replacement	Every 45 000 Miles (75 000 km)																		•						
15	Air Cleaner Element Replacement*	Every 30 000 Miles (50 000 km)												•												•
16	Fuel Cap, Lines and Tank Inspection*‡	Every 15 000 Miles (25 000 km)						•						•						•						•
17	PCV Valve Inspection*‡	Every 30 000 Miles (50 000 km)												•												•

* An Emission Control Service.

‡ The U.S. Environmental Protection Agency has determined that the failure to perform this maintenance item will not nullify the emission warranty, or limit recall liability prior to the completion of vehicle useful life. General Motors, however, urges that all recommended maintenance services be performed at the indicated intervals and the maintenance be recorded in Section C.

Fig. 67 Maintenance interval chart — Spectrum schedule 2

SCHEDULED MAINTENANCE SERVICES
SCHEDULE I

Follow Schedule I if your car is MAINLY operated under one or more of the following conditions:
- When most trips are less than 4 miles (6 kilometers).
- When most trips are less than 10 miles (16 kilometers) and outside temperatures remain below freezing.
- When most trips include extended idling and/or frequent low-speed operation as in stop-and-go traffic.
- Towing a trailer.#
- Operating in dusty areas.

Schedule I should also be followed if the car is used for delivery service, police, taxi or other commercial applications.

The services shown in this schedule up to 60 000 miles (100 000 km) are to be performed after 60 000 miles at the same intervals.

	TO BE SERVICED	WHEN TO PERFORM — Miles (kilometers) or Months, Whichever Occurs First	MILES (000) 3 / KM 5	6 / 10	9 / 15	12 / 20	15 / 25	18 / 30	21 / 35	24 / 40	27 / 45	30 / 50	33 / 55	36 / 60	39 / 65	42 / 70	45 / 75	48 / 80	51 / 85	54 / 90	57 / 95	60 / 100
1	Engine Oil Replacement*	Every 3 000 Miles (5 000 km) or 3 Months	●	●	●	●	●	●	●	●	●	●	●	●	●	●	●	●	●	●	●	●
	Oil Filter Replacement*	At First and Then Every Other Oil Change	●		●		●		●		●		●		●		●		●		●	
2	Chassis and Body Lubrication	Every Other Oil Change		●		●		●		●		●		●		●		●		●		●
3	Valve Clearance Adjustment* VIN 6	Every 15 000 Miles (25 000 km)					●					●					●					●
	VIN 5	Every 60 000 Miles (100 000 km)																				●
4	Timing Belt Replacement	Every 60 000 Miles (100 000 km)																				●
5	Tire and Wheel Inspection and Rotation	At 6 000 Miles (10 000 km) and Then Every 15 000 Miles (25 000 km)		●					●					●					●			
6	Drive Belt Inspection*	Every 30 000 Miles (50 000 km)										●										●
7	Cooling System Inspection*	Every 15 000 Miles (25 000 km)					●					●					●					●
	Cooling System Refill*	Every 30 000 Miles (50 000 km)										●										●
8	Manual Transaxle Fluid Replacement	Every 15 000 Miles (25 000 km)					●					●					●					●
	Automatic Transaxle Fluid Replacement	Every 15 000 Miles (25 000 km)					●					●					●					●
9	Spark Plug Replacement*	Every 30 000 Miles (50 000 km)										●										●
10	Power Steering Fluid Replacement	Every 21 000 Miles (35 000 km) or 24 Months							●							●						
11	Power Steering Hose Inspection	Every 42 000 Miles (70 000 km)														●						
12	Air Cleaner Element Replacement*	See Explanation of Scheduled Maintenance Services										●										●
13	Fuel Cap, Lines and Tank Inspection*‡	Every 15 000 Miles (25 000 km)					●					●					●					●
14	PCV Valve Inspection*‡	Every 30 000 Miles (50 000 km)										●										●

Trailering is not recommended for some models. See your Owner's Manual for details.

* An Emission Control Service.

‡The U.S. Environmental Protection Agency has determined that the failure to perform this maintenance item will not nullify the emission warranty or limit recall liability prior to the completion of vehicle useful life. General Motors, however, urges that all recommended maintenance services be performed at the indicated intervals and the maintenance be recorded in Section C of the Owner's Maintenance Schedule.

Fig. 68 Maintenance interval chart — Storm schedule 1

SCHEDULED MAINTENANCE SERVICES
SCHEDULE II

Follow Schedule II only if none of the driving conditions specified in Schedule I apply.

The services shown in this schedule up to 60 000 miles (96 000 km) are to be performed after 60 000 miles at the same intervals.

	TO BE SERVICED	WHEN TO PERFORM — Miles (kilometers) or Months, Whichever Occurs First
1	Engine Oil Replacement*	Every 7 500 Miles (12 500 km) or 12 Months
	Oil Filter Replacement*	At First and Then Every Other Oil Change
2	Chassis and Body Lubrication	Every 7 500 Miles (12 500 km) or 12 Months
3	Valve Clearance Adjustment* VIN 6	Every 15 000 Miles (25 000 km)
	VIN 5	Every 60 000 Miles (100 000 km)
4	Timing Belt Replacement	Every 60 000 Miles (100 000 km)
5	Tire and Wheel Inspection and Rotation	At 7 500 Miles (12 500 km) and Then Every 15 000 Miles (25 000 km)
6	Drive Belt Inspection*	Every 30 000 Miles (50 000 km)
7	Cooling System Inspection*	Every 15 000 Miles (25 000 km)
	Cooling System Refill*	Every 30 000 Miles (50 000 km)
8	Manual Transaxle Fluid Replacement	Every 30 000 Miles (50 000 km)
	Automatic Transaxle Fluid Replacement	Every 30 000 Miles (50 000 km)
9	Spark Plug Replacement*	Every 30 000 Miles (50 000 km)
10	Power Steering Fluid Replacement	Every 22 500 Miles (37 500 km) or 24 Months
11	Power Steering Hose Inspection	Every 45 000 Miles (75 000 km)
12	Air Cleaner Element Replacement*	Every 30 000 Miles (50 000 km)
13	Fuel Cap, Lines and Tank Inspection*‡	Every 15 000 Miles (25 000 km)
14	PCV Valve Inspection*‡	Every 30 000 Miles (50 000 km)

* An Emission Control Service.

‡The U.S. Environmental Protection Agency has determined that the failure to perform this maintenance item will not nullify the emission warranty or limit recall liability prior to the completion of vehicle useful life. General Motors, however, urges that all recommended maintenance services be performed at the indicated intervals and the maintenance be recorded in Section C of the Owner's Maintenance Schedule.

Fig. 69 Maintenance interval chart — Storm schedule 2

CAPACITIES

Year	Model	Engine ID/VIN	Engine Displacement Liters (cc)	Engine Crankcase with Filter	Transmission (pts.) 4-Spd	5-Spd	Auto.	Drive Axle	Fuel Tank (gal.)	Cooling System (qts.)
1985	Spectrum	7	1.5 (1472)	3.4	—	5.6	13.4	—	11.0	6.7
1986	Spectrum	7	1.5 (1472)	3.4	—	5.6	13.4	—	11.0	6.7
1987	Spectrum	7	1.5 (1472)	3.4	—	5.6	13.4	—	11.0	6.7
	Spectrum	9	1.5 (1472)	3.4	—	5.6	13.4	—	11.0	6.7
1988	Spectrum	7	1.5 (1472)	3.4	—	5.6	13.4	—	11.0	6.7
	Spectrum	9	1.5 (1472)	3.4	—	5.6	13.4	—	11.0	6.7
1989	Spectrum	7	1.5 (1472)	3.4	—	4.0	13.8	—	11.0	6.8
1990	Storm	6	1.6 (1588)	3.5	—	4.0	13.8	—	12.4	7.8
	Storm GSi	5	1.6 (1588)	4.2	—	4.0	13.8	—	12.4	7.8
1991	Storm	6	1.6 (1588)	3.2	—	4.0	13.8	—	12.4	7.8
	Storm GSi	5	1.6 (1588)	4.0	—	4.0	13.8	—	12.4	7.8
1992	Storm	6	1.6 (1588)	3.2	—	4.0	13.8	—	12.4	7.8
	Storm GSi	8	1.8 (1810)	4.0	—	4.0	13.8	—	12.4	7.8
1993	Storm	6	1.6 (1588)	3.2	—	4.0	13.8	—	12.4	7.8
	Storm GSi	8	1.8 (1810)	4.0	—	4.0	13.8	—	12.4	7.8

TORQUE SPECIFICATIONS

Component	U.S.	Metric
Battery cable terminal fastener	11 ft. lbs.	15 Nm
Battery retainer nut and bolt	71 inch lbs.	8 Nm
Fuel filter bracket clamp bolt (1993 Storm)	21 ft. lbs.	28 Nm
Fuel filter bracket retaining bolt	25 ft. lbs.	34 Nm
Fuel line fitting nut	25 ft. lbs.	34 Nm
Rear axle hub nut (Spectrum)	22 ft. lbs.	29 Nm
Rear hub assembly retaining bolts (Storm)	49 ft. lbs.	66 Nm

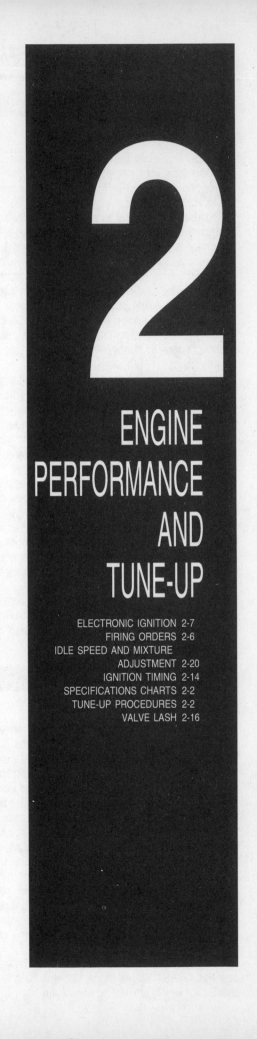

2

ENGINE PERFORMANCE AND TUNE-UP

TUNE-UP PROCEDURES

▶ See Figure 1

In order to extract the full measure of performance and economy from your engine, it is essential that it be properly maintained and tuned. A tuned engine is extremely important to the control of tailpipe emissions.

Because of the more durable components and computer controlled systems on modern vehicles, the annual tune-up of yesterday is gone. The most important thing you may do for your vehicle, to optimize performance and help prevent vehicle breakdown, is to follow the Maintenance Intervals Chart in Section 1. The next most important way to assure your vehicle is tuned and running properly is to thoroughly familiarize yourself with the ignition system and other engine control systems. Understanding the ignition will help you to detect subtle changes in the system which might require repair or maintenance.

A vehicle should be thoroughly inspected and tuned at least every 30,000 miles, though as you can tell from Section 1 of this manual, there are many components which need more frequent attention. Also, this time frame should be halved if the vehicle is operated under severe conditions such as trailer towing, prolonged idling, start-and-stop driving, or if starting or running problems are noticed.

As stated earlier, it is helpful to understand the system and know how it should be operating so that you can detect symptoms before problems develop. Your car's idle speed is noted in the Tune-Up Specification Chart, but can also be found on the emission information label in the engine compartment. If your Spectrum or Storm is equipped with a tachometer, you can easily check for the proper idle speed whenever you are in the car.

The emission information label often reflects changes made during the model year. If any of the specifications on the label disagree with the Tune-Up Specification chart or text in this Section, use the figures on the label.

Spark Plugs

▶ See Figure 2

A typical spark plug consists of a metal shell surrounding a ceramic insulator. A metal electrode extends downward through the center of the insulator and protrudes a small distance. Located at the end of the plug and attached to the side of the outer metal shell is the side electrode. The side electrode bends in at a 90° angle so that its tip is just past and parallel to the tip of the center electrode. The distance between these two electrodes (measured in thousandths of an inch or hundredths of a millimeter) is called the spark plug gap. The spark plug does not produce a spark but instead provides a gap across which the current can arc. The coil produces anywhere from 20,000 to 40,000 volts which travels through the wires to the spark plugs. The current passes along the center electrode and jumps the gap to the side electrode, and in doing so, ignites the fuel/air mixture in the combustion chamber.

Normally, a set of spark plugs requires replacement about every 20,000-30,000 miles, on vehicles such as the Spectrum and Storm which are equipped with an High Energy Ignition

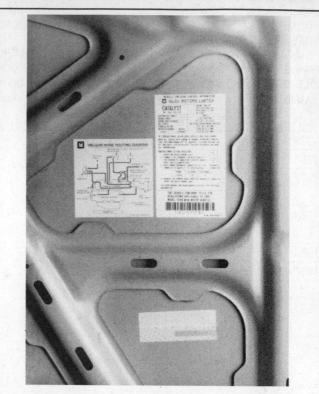

Fig. 1 For the Storm, the vehicle emission label is found under the hood

(HEI) system. Any vehicle which is subjected to severe conditions will need more frequent plug replacement.

Under normal operation, the plug gap increases about 0.001″ (0.0254mm) for every 1,000-2,000 miles. As the gap increases, the plug's voltage requirement also increases. It requires a greater voltage to jump the wider gap and about 2-3 times as much voltage to fire a plug at high speeds than at idle.

SPARK PLUG HEAT RANGE

▶ See Figure 3

Spark plug heat range is the ability of the plug to dissipate heat. The longer the insulator (or the farther it extends into the engine), the hotter the plug will operate; the shorter the insulator (the closer the electrode is to the block's cooling passages) the cooler it will operate. A plug that absorbs little heat and remains too cool will quickly accumulate deposits of oil and carbon since it is not hot enough to burn them off. This leads to plug fouling and consequently to misfiring. A plug that absorbs too much heat will have no deposits but, due to the excessive heat, the electrodes will burn away quickly and possibly lead to preignition. Pre-ignition takes place when plug tips get so hot that they glow sufficiently to ignite the fuel/air mixture before the actual spark occurs. This early ignition will usually cause a pinging during low speeds and heavy loads.

The general rule of thumb for choosing the correct heat range when picking a spark plug is: if most of your driving is

GASOLINE ENGINE TUNE-UP SPECIFICATIONS

Year	Engine ID/VIN	Engine Displacement Liters (cc)	Spark Plugs Gap (in.)	Ignition Timing (deg.)		Fuel Pump (psi)	Idle Speed (rpm)		Valve Clearance	
				MT	AT		MT	AT	In.	Ex.
1985	7	1.5 (1472)	0.040	15B①	10B②	3.8–4.7	750	1000	0.006	0.010
1986	7	1.5 (1472)	0.040	15B①	10B②	3.8–4.7	750	1000	0.006	0.010
1987	7	1.5 (1472)	0.040	15B①	10B②	3.8–4.7	750	1000	0.006	0.010
	9	1.5 (1472)	0.040	15B①	10B②	24.5③	750	1000	0.006	0.010
1988	7	1.5 (1472)	0.040	15B①	10B②	3.8–4.7	750	1000	0.006	0.010
	9	1.5 (1472)	0.042	15B①	10B②	24.5	750	1000	0.006	0.010
1989	7	1.5 (1472)	0.040	15B①	10B②	3.8–4.7	750	1000	0.006	0.010
1990	6	1.6 (1588)	0.041	10B	10B	35–42	700	700	0.006	0.010
	5	1.6 (1588)	0.041	10B	10B	35–42	700	700	0.006	0.010
1991	6	1.6 (1588)	0.041	10B	10B	35–42	700	700	0.006	0.010
	5	1.6 (1588)	0.041	10B	10B	35–42	700	700	0.006	0.010
1992	6	1.6 (1588)	0.041	10B	10B	41–47	700	700	0.006	0.010
	8	1.8 (1810)	0.041	10B	10B	41–47	700	700	Hyd.	Hyd.
1993	6	1.6 (1588)	0.041	10B	10B	30–36	700	700	0.006	0.010
	8	1.8 (1810)	0.041	10B	10B	41–47	700	700	Hyd.	Hyd.

NOTE: The lowest cylinder pressure should be within 75% of the highest cylinder pressure reading. For example, if the highest cylinder is 134 psi, the lowest should be 101. Engine should be at normal operating temperature with throttle valve in the wide open position.
The underhood specifications sticker often reflects tune-up specification changes in production. Sticker figures must be used if they disagree with those in this chart.
B—Before Top Dead Center
Hyd.—Hydraulic
① 750 rpm
② 1000 rpm
③ @ 900 rpm with pressure regulator connected

long distance, high speed travel, use a colder plug; if most of your driving is stop and go, use a hotter plug. Original equipment plugs are generally a good compromise between the 2 styles and most people never have the need to change their plugs from the factory-recommended heat range.

REMOVAL & INSTALLATION

▶ See Figures 4, 5 and 6

When removing the spark plugs, work on one at a time. Don't start by removing the plug wires all at once because unless you number them, they're going to get mixed up. On some models, it will be more convenient for you to remove all of the wires before you start to work on the plugs. If this is necessary, take a minute before you begin and number the

wires with tape before you take them off. The time you spend here will pay off later on.

✳✳WARNING

The Storm's cylinder head is made of aluminum. Damage to the cylinder head and/or spark plug threads may occur if the engine is not allowed to cool before removing the spark plugs.

1. Disconnect the negative battery cable, and if the car has been run recently, allow the engine to thoroughly cool.
2. For the Storm 1.8L engine, remove the 6 Allen® head screws and the spark plug cover from the cylinder head cover.
3. Using compressed air, blow any water or debris from the spark plug well to assure that no harmful contaminants are

Tracking Arc
High voltage arcs between a fouling deposit on the insulator tip and spark plug shell. This ignites the fuel/air mixture at some point along the insulator tip, retarding the ignition timing which causes a power and fuel loss.

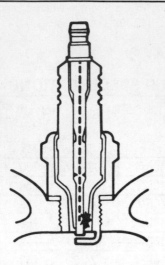

Wide Gap
Spark plug electrodes are worn so that the high voltage charge cannot arc across the electrodes. Improper gapping of electrodes on new or "cleaned" spark plugs could cause a similar condition. Fuel remains unburned and a power loss results.

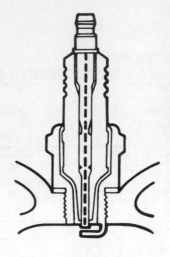

Flashover
A damaged spark plug boot, along with dirt and moisture, could permit the high voltage charge to short over the insulator to the spark plug shell or the engine. AC's buttress insulator design helps prevent high voltage flashover.

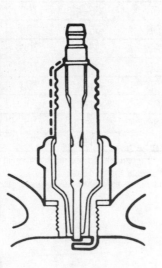

Fouled Spark Plug
Deposits that have formed on the insulator tip may become conductive and provide a "shunt" path to the shell. This prevents the high voltage from arcing between the electrodes. A power and fuel loss is the result.

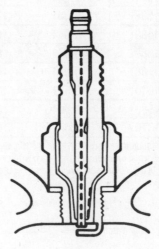

Bridged Electrodes
Fouling deposits between the electrodes "ground out" the high voltage needed to fire the spark plug. The arc between the electrodes does not occur and the fuel air mixture is not ignited. This causes a power loss and exhausting of raw fuel.

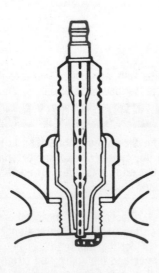

Cracked Insulator
A crack in the spark plug insulator could cause the high voltage charge to "ground out." Here, the spark does not jump the electrode gap and the fuel air mixture is not ignited. This causes a power loss and raw fuel is exhausted.

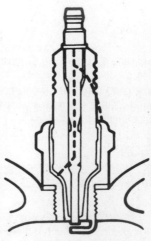

Fig. 2 Spark plug diagnosis

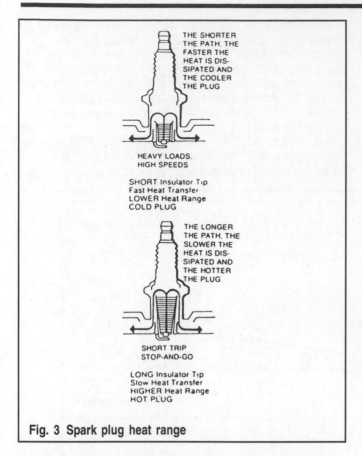

THE SHORTER THE PATH, THE FASTER THE HEAT IS DISSIPATED AND THE COOLER THE PLUG

HEAVY LOADS, HIGH SPEEDS

SHORT Insulator Tip
Fast Heat Transfer
LOWER Heat Range
COLD PLUG

THE LONGER THE PATH, THE SLOWER THE HEAT IS DISSIPATED AND THE HOTTER THE PLUG

SHORT TRIP
STOP-AND-GO

LONG Insulator Tip
Slow Heat Transfer
HIGHER Heat Range
HOT PLUG

Fig. 3 Spark plug heat range

allowed to enter the combustion chamber when the spark plug is removed.

4. Carefully twist the spark plug wire boot to loosen it, then pull upward and remove the boot from the plug. Be sure to pull on the boot and not on the wire, otherwise the connector located inside the boot may become separated.

5. Using a spark plug socket that is equipped with a rubber insert to properly hold the plug, turn the spark plug counterclockwise to loosen and remove the spark plug from the bore. If at all possible, try not to use a flexible extension on the socket. Use of a flexible extension could damage the spark plug insulator.

To install:

6. Inspect the spark plugs and clean or replace, as necessary. Inspect the spark plug boot for tears or damage. If a damaged boot is found, the spark plug wire must be replaced.

7. Using a feeler gauge, check and adjust the spark plug gap to 0.041 in. (1.05mm). When using a gauge, the proper size should pass between the electrodes with a slight drag. The next larger size should not be able to pass while the next smaller size should pass freely.

❋❋CAUTION

Do not use the spark plug socket to thread the plugs. Always thread the plug by hand to prevent the possibility of cross-threading and damaging the cylinder head bore.

8. Carefully start the spark plugs by hand and tighten a few turns until a tool is needed to continue tightening the spark

plug. Using a torque wrench, tighten the spark plug to 14 ft. lbs. (19 Nm).

9. Apply a small amount of silicone dielectric compound to the end of the spark plug lead or inside the spark plug boot to prevent sticking, then install the boot to the spark plug and push until it clicks into place. The click may be felt or heard, then gently pull back on the boot to assure proper contact.

10. For the Storm 1.8L engine, install the spark plug cover and tighten the 6 Allen® head screws to 124 inch lbs. (14 Nm).

11. Connect the negative battery cable.

Fig. 4 Don't remove the boot from the spark plug by pulling on the wire or the boot's connector may be damaged

Fig. 5 In most cases, the spark plugs can be removed using a socket, straight extension and ratchet

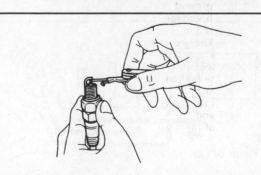

Fig. 6 Use a feeler gauge to check and adjust the spark plug gap before installation

Spark Plug Wires

▶ **See Figure 7**

Visually inspect the spark plug wires for burns, cuts or breaks in the insulation. Check the spark plug boots and the distributor tower connectors. Replace any damaged wiring. Using an ohmmeter, check the resistance of the wires with no spark present. Wire resistance should be below 15,000 Ohms. For the Spectrum, refer to the figure for wire resistance specifications.

When installing a new set of spark plug wires, replace the wires one at a time so there will be no mix-up. Start by replacing the longest cable first. Install the boot firmly over the spark plug. Route the wire exactly the same as the original. Connect the wire tower connector to the distributor. Repeat the process for each wire. Be sure to apply silicone dielectric compound to the spark plug wire boots and tower connectors prior to installation.

If at any time all of the wires must be disconnected from the spark plugs or from the distributor at the same time, be sure to tag the wires to assure proper reconnection.

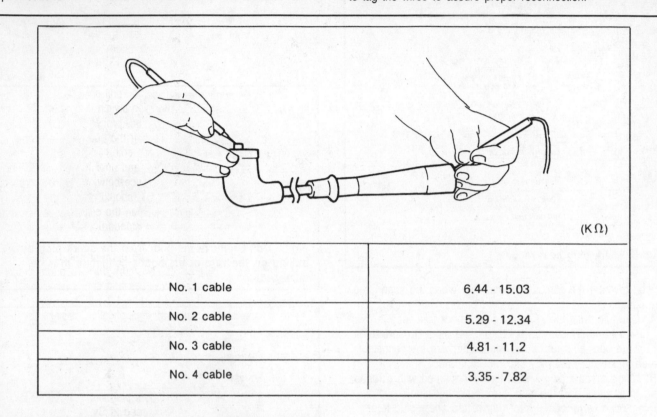

(K Ω)

No. 1 cable	6.44 - 15.03
No. 2 cable	5.29 - 12.34
No. 3 cable	4.81 - 11.2
No. 4 cable	3.35 - 7.82

Fig. 7 Spark plug wire resistance specifications — Spectrum

FIRING ORDERS

➡**To avoid confusion, remove and tag the wires one at a time, for replacement.**

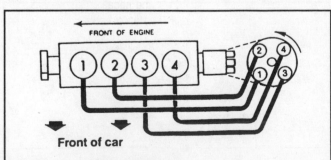

Fig. 8 1.5L Engine — Spectrum
Engine firing order: 1-3-4-2
Distributor rotation: Counterclockwise

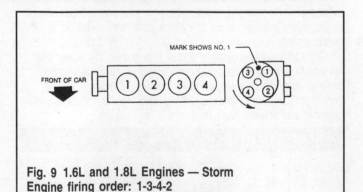

Fig. 9 1.6L and 1.8L Engines — Storm
Engine firing order: 1-3-4-2
Distributor rotation: Counterclockwise

ELECTRONIC IGNITION

Description and Operation

CONVENTIONAL SPARK CONTROL IGNITION SYSTEM

▶ See Figure 10

A conventional electronic ignition system with vacuum/centrifugal spark control is used on the carbureted Spectrum vehicles.

The basic components of this ignition system are the ignition coil, the distributor, the spark plugs and spark plug wiring. The distributor consists of a signal generator (signal rotor and pickup coil), igniter, rotor, ignition module, vacuum advancer and centrifugal advancer.

When the distributor shaft rotates, a fluctuating magnetic field is generated due to changes in the air gap between the pickup coil and signal rotor. As a result, an alternating current (AC) voltage is induced in the pickup coil. This induced AC voltage peaks when a ridge on the signal rotor is adjacent to the ridge on the pickup coil. When the voltage peaks, the igniter breaks the circuit to ground from the negative side of the coil primary winding. With the circuit broken, the magnetic field in the ignition coil, which has been generated by the electrical current passing through it, collapses. The high voltage induced by the collapsing field is then forced to find a ground through the secondary coil wire, the distributor cap, the rotor, the spark plug wire and finally across the spark plug air gap to the engine block.

Spark timing is mechanically controlled by a vacuum advance system which uses engine manifold vacuum and a centrifugal advance mechanism.

ELECTRONIC SPARK CONTROL (ESC) IGNITION SYSTEM

▶ See Figure 11

An electronic spark control ignition system is used on turbocharged 1987-88 Spectrum vehicles and on all Storms.

The ignition circuit consists of the battery, distributor, ignition coil, relay, ignition switch, spark plugs, primary and secondary wiring. The ESC system is monitored and controlled by the Engine Control Module (ECM). The distributor used in this system consists of a signal generator (signal rotor and camshaft position sensor), and rotor. The igniter function is filled by the ECM.

All spark timing changes in the distributor are performed electronically by the ECM. After receiving signals indicating engine speed, manifold vacuum, coolant temperature and other engine functions, the ECM selects the most appropriate timing setting from memory and signals the distributor to alter the base timing accordingly. No vacuum or mechanical advance mechanisms are used.

Diagnosis and Testing

IGNITION COIL

Conventional Spark System
▶ See Figures 12, 13 and 14

1. Check for spark at each spark plug with a spark plug tester. If no spark is detected, proceed to Step 2. If spark is only detected on some spark plugs, check for a faulty distributor cap or rotor. Also check the spark plugs and wires. Replace as needed.

2. Check for voltage at the ignition coil positive terminal with a voltmeter and with the ignition switch in the **ON** position. If battery voltage is detected, proceed to Step 3. If battery voltage is not detected, repair the open in the wiring between the battery and the ignition coil.

3. Turn the ignition switch **OFF** and unplug the ignition coil terminal. Check primary coil resistance between the positive and negative terminals of the coil; it should be 1.2-1.5 ohms.

4. Measure the resistance between the coil positive terminal and the high voltage terminal. The standard value should be 10.2-13.8 Kilo-ohms.

5. Check the insulation resistance between the positive terminal and the body, it should be more than 10 ohms.

6. Unplug the coil resistor terminal and check resistance, the standard value should be between 1.3-1.5 ohms.

7. If resistances are not within specification, replace the coil.

Electronic Spark Control System
▶ See Figures 15 and 16

1. Check for spark at each spark plug with a spark plug tester. If no spark is detected, proceed to Step 2. If spark is only detected on some spark plugs, check for a faulty distributor cap or rotor. Also check the spark plugs and wires. Replace as needed.

2. Check for voltage at the ignition coil positive terminal with a voltmeter. If battery voltage is detected, proceed to Step 3. If battery voltage is not detected, repair the open in the wiring between the battery and the ignition coil.

3. Disconnect the connector on the negative coil wire. Check ignition coil resistance. If resistance is not within specification, replace the coil.

   a. Measure the primary ignition coil resistance; it should be 1.3-1.6 ohms.

   b. Measure the secondary ignition coil resistance, it should be 10.4-14.0 kilo-ohms.

CENTRIFUGAL ADVANCE

1. Remove the distributor cap.
2. Rotate the rotor counter-clockwise.
3. Release rotor, it should spring back.

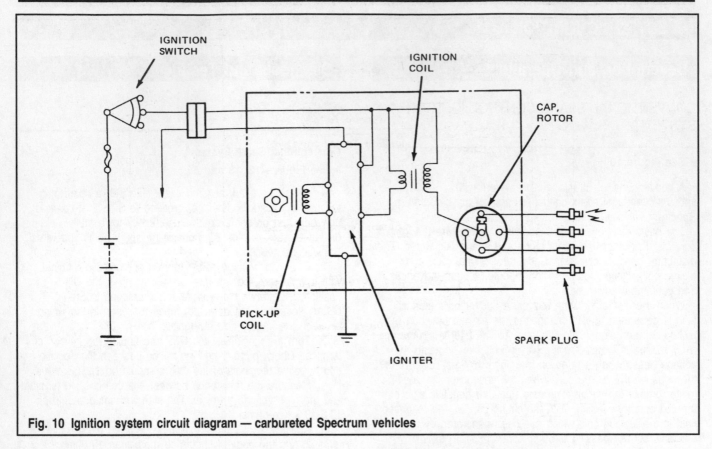

Fig. 10 Ignition system circuit diagram — carbureted Spectrum vehicles

4. Replace the distributor if the centrifugal advance fails this test.

VACUUM ADVANCE

1. Remove the distributor cap.
2. Remove the vacuum hoses.
3. Connect a vacuum pump to the outside vacuum hose on the distributor.
4. Apply 15 in. Hg of vacuum using a hand pump, the pick-up coil should move.
5. Repeat the same test with the inside vacuum hose.
6. If the pick-up coil does not move replace the vacuum advance unit.

PICKUP COIL

Conventional Spark System

1. Turn the ignition switch **OFF**, then remove distributor cap and the dust cover from the module.
2. Disconnect the red and white wires from the module.
3. Connect an ohmmeter to the red and white wires and measure the resistance.
4. Pickup coil resistance should be within 140-180 ohms; if not within specification, replace the pickup coil.

Electronic Spark Control System
▶ See Figures 17 and 18

1. Unplug the pickup coil connector and check resistance between either terminal and case ground. If resistance is not infinite, replace the distributor.
2. Measure the resistance between the pickup coil terminals; it should be 500-1500 ohms. If resistance is not within specification, replace the distributor.

Adjustments

PICKUP COIL AIR GAP

▶ See Figure 19

1. Remove the distributor cap and rotor.
2. Using a nonmagnetic thickness gauge, measure the air gap between the pole piece tooth and pickup coil.
3. Air gap should be 0.008-0.016 in. (0.2-0.4 mm). If the gap is out of specification, it must be adjusted until the proper gap is achieved or the signal generator must be replaced.
4. Remove the module and loosen the screws securing pickup coil. Using a screw driver, move the generator pickup coil and adjust the gap to specification.
5. After adjustment tighten screws and recheck gap. Install module, rotor and distributor cap.

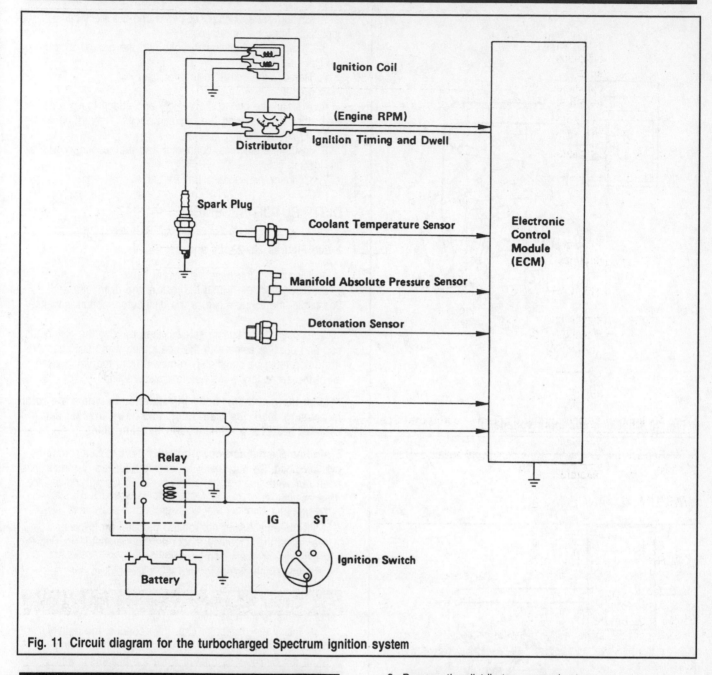

Fig. 11 Circuit diagram for the turbocharged Spectrum ignition system

Component Replacement

IGNITION COIL

Conventional Spark System

▶ See Figure 20

The coil for the conventional spark system is located under the distributor cap, inside the distributor assembly. If the coil retainers are accessible, it may be possible to remove the coil from the distributor without removing the distributor assembly. Check to see if this is possible before remove the assembly.

1. Disconnect the negative battery cable.
2. If necessary, remove the distributor assembly from the vehicle.

3. Remove the distributor cap and rotor.
4. Remove the dust cover, then remove the retainers and the separate the ignition coil from the distributor assembly.
   To install:
5. Position the coil to the distributor, then install the retainers and the dust cover.
6. Install the rotor and the distributor cap.
7. If removed, install the distributor assembly.
8. Connect the negative battery cable, and if the distributor was removed, adjust the ignition timing.

Electronic Spark Control System

▶ See Figure 21

The coil for the electronic spark control system is mounted externally from the distributor.

1. Disconnect the negative battery cable.

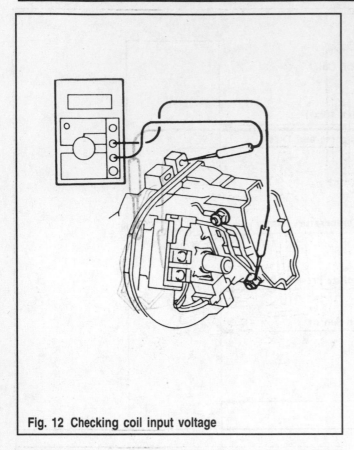

Fig. 12 Checking coil input voltage

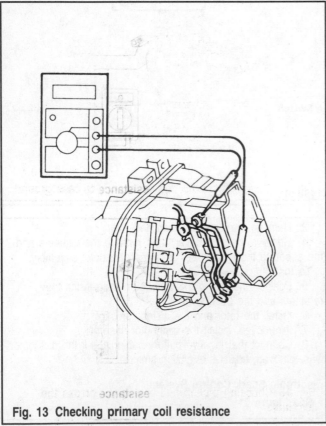

Fig. 13 Checking primary coil resistance

2. Unplug the secondary coil wire and the electrical connector from the ignition coil.

3. Remove the 2 mounting bolts and the ground strap from the coil.

4. Remove the coil from the vehicle.

To install:

5. Position the coil to the vehicle and attach the ground strap, then secure using the mounting bolts. Tighten the bolts to 15 ft. lbs. (20 Nm).

6. Install the electrical connector and the secondary wire to the ignition coil.

7. Connect the negative battery cable.

DISTRIBUTOR ASSEMBLY

▶ **See Figures 22, 23, 24 and 25**

1. Disconnect the negative battery cable.

2. Disconnect the wiring harness at the distributor and, if applicable, the vacuum line at the distributor vacuum advance unit.

3. Loosen the retaining screws, then remove the distributor cap and position aside with the spark plug wires still attached. If the cap must be completely removed from the vehicle, tag all of the secondary wires before disconnecting.

➡ **Mark the distributor body in reference to where the rotor is pointing. Mark the distributor hold-down bracket and cylinder head for a reinstallation location point.**

4. Remove the hold-down bolt and the distributor from the cylinder head. Do not rotate the engine after the distributor has been removed. Inspect the distributor shaft O-ring and replace, if necessary.

To install:

5. If the engine was not rotated proceed as follows:

a. Align the reference marks on the distributor housing to the distributor hold-down bracket.

b. Install the distributor into the offset slot in the camshaft, then loosely install the hold-down bolt.

c. Connect vacuum hoses, if applicable, and the electrical connectors to the distributor.

d. Install the distributor cap, then connect the battery negative cable. Check and/or adjust the ignition timing.

6. If the engine was rotated while the distributor was removed, place the engine on TDC of the compression stroke to obtain the proper ignition timing.

a. Remove the No. 1 spark plug.

b. Place thumb over the spark plug hole. Crank the engine slowly until compression is felt. It will be easier to have someone rotate the engine by hand, using a wrench on the crankshaft pulley.

c. Align the timing mark on the crankshaft pulley with the **0** degrees mark on the timing scale attached to the front of the engine. This places the engine at TDC of the compression stroke.

d. Turn the distributor shaft until the rotor points to the No. 1 spark plug tower on the cap.

e. Install the distributor into the engine. Be sure to align the distributor-to-engine block mark made earlier.

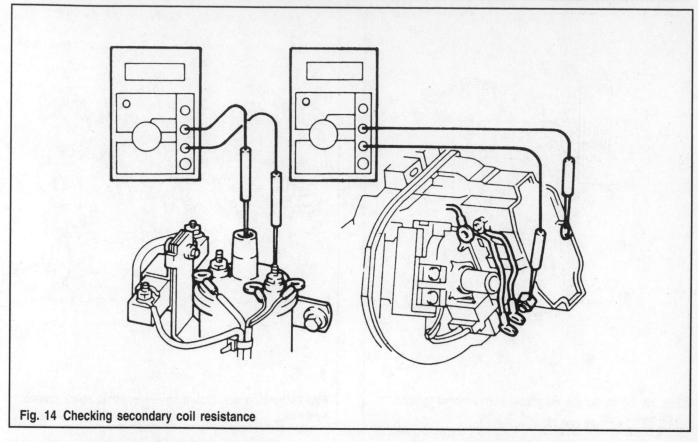

Fig. 14 Checking secondary coil resistance

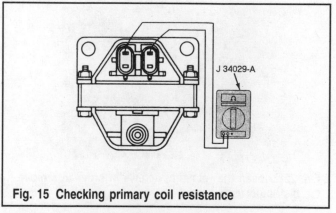

Fig. 15 Checking primary coil resistance

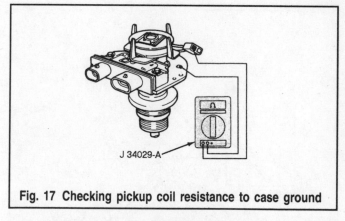

Fig. 17 Checking pickup coil resistance to case ground

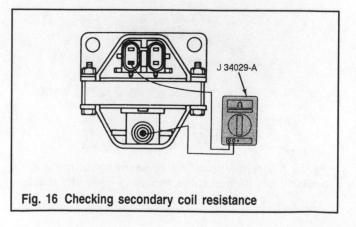

Fig. 16 Checking secondary coil resistance

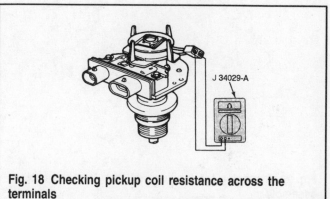

Fig. 18 Checking pickup coil resistance across the terminals

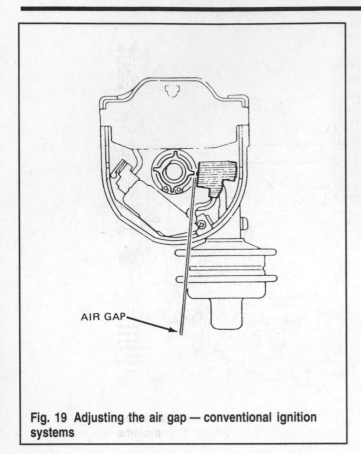

AIR GAP

Fig. 19 Adjusting the air gap — conventional ignition systems

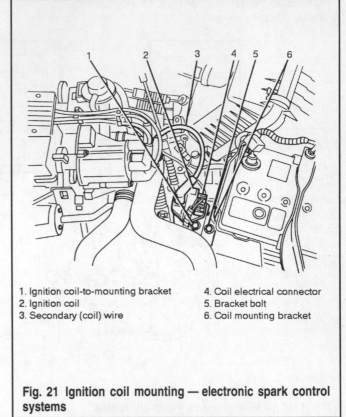

1. Ignition coil-to-mounting bracket
2. Ignition coil
3. Secondary (coil) wire
4. Coil electrical connector
5. Bracket bolt
6. Coil mounting bracket

Fig. 21 Ignition coil mounting — electronic spark control systems

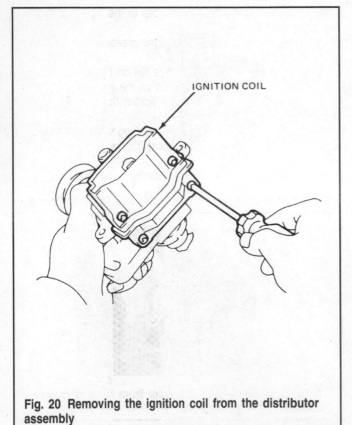

IGNITION COIL

Fig. 20 Removing the ignition coil from the distributor assembly

Fig. 22 Loosen the retaining screws in order to remove the distributor cap

Fig. 23 If possible, save time by removing the cap and positioning it aside with the secondary wires still attach

f. Install the No. 1 spark plug. Connect all vacuum hoses, if applicable, and electrical connectors to the distributor.

g. Install distributor cap, then connect the battery negative cable.

h. Check and/or adjust ignition timing.

CAP AND ROTOR

▶ **See Figures 26 and 27**

1. Disconnect the negative battery cable.

2. Tag and remove the spark plug cables from the distributor cap. For the electronic spark control systems, disconnect the ignition coil high tension wire from the distributor cap.

3. Loosen and remove the 2 distributor cap attaching screws.

4. Remove the distributor cap, taking care not to damage the rotor.

5. Carefully remove the rotor by pulling with a slight twist.

To Install:

6. Inspect the condition of the distributor cap. If the cap shows signs of cracks, broken pieces, carbon tracking, charred or eroded terminals, or a worn or damaged rotor button, replace it.

7. Inspect the condition of the distributor rotor. If the rotor shows signs of cracks, broken pieces, a charred or eroded tip,

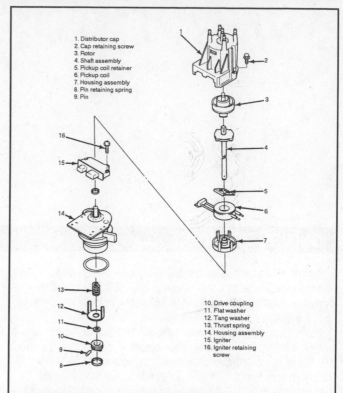

1. Distributor cap
2. Cap retaining screw
3. Rotor
4. Shaft assembly
5. Pickup coil retainer
6. Pickup coil
7. Housing assembly
8. Pin retaining spring
9. Pin

10. Drive coupling
11. Flat washer
12. Tang washer
13. Thrust spring
14. Housing assembly
15. Igniter
16. Igniter retaining screw

Fig. 25 Exploded view of the distributor assembly — electronic spark control ignition systems

physical contact of the tip with the cap or insufficient spring tension, replace it.

8. Apply a light coating of dielectric grease to the distributor cap terminals and rotor tip.

9. Install the rotor by aligning the flat on the rotor and shaft. Push the rotor until it bottoms on the shaft.

10. Install the distributor cap and tighten the attaching screws securely.

11. Connect the spark plug wires as tagged during removal and, if applicable, connect the external coil wire to the distributor cap.

12. Connect the negative battery cable.

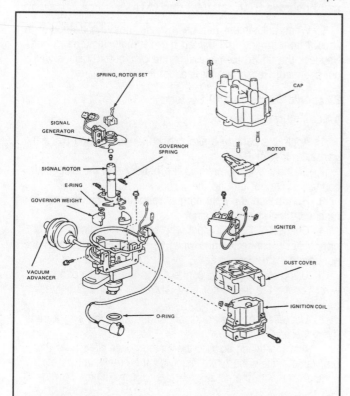

Fig. 24 Exploded view of the distributor assembly — conventional spark systems

Fig. 26 Carefully remove the rotor from the distributor assembly

Fig. 27 Check the distributor cap for corrosion and clean or replace, as necessary

IGNITION TIMING

Before connecting a tachometer to your vehicle, be sure that the tachometer being used is compatible with the ignition system. Installing incompatible equipment could cause damage to the system.

Before setting timing, make sure the headlights, heater fan, engine cooling fan and any other electrical equipment is turned off. If any current drawing systems are operating, vehicle's which are equipped with idle up systems, will operate the systems causing the idle speed to be higher than normal. An incorrect ignition timing will be set if the adjustment is made under these conditions.

✳✳WARNING

When connecting the tachometer in the following procedures, be sure not to ground the tachometer terminal. Grounding the tachometer could result in damage to the igniter or ignition coil.

Timing

ADJUSTMENT

Conventional Spark Control Ignition
▶ See Figure 28

1. Set the parking brake and block the wheels.
2. Place the manual transaxle in **N** or the automatic transaxle in the **P** detent.
3. Allow the engine to reach normal operating temperature. Make sure that the choke valve is open. Turn off all of the accessories.
4. If equipped with power steering, place the front wheels in a straight line.
5. Disconnect and plug the distributor vacuum line, the canister purge line, the EGR vacuum line and the ITC valve vacuum line at the intake manifold.

6. Connect a timing light to the No. 1 spark plug wire and a tachometer to the tachometer filter connector on the coil, tachometer filter is mounted near distributor hold down bolt.

➡**Check the idle speed and adjust as needed.**

7. Loosen the distributor flange bolt.
8. Using the timing light, align the notch on the crankshaft pulley with the mark on the timing cover by turning the distributor.

➡**Adjust the timing to 15 degrees BTDC at 750 rpm (MT) or 10 degrees BTDC at 1000 rpm (AT).**

9. When adjustment has been made, hold the distributor to keep it from turning and tighten the distributor hold-down bolt. Recheck the timing to make sure the distributor position was not changed. Reconnect all vacuum lines.

Electronic Spark Control System
▶ See Figures 29 and 30

1. Apply the parking brake, block the wheels and place the transaxle in **N** or **P**.
2. Connect a tachometer to the battery and the diagnostic connector. Do not ground the tachometer terminal.
3. Run the engine until normal operating temperatures are reached, then stop the engine.
4. Connect a fused jumper wire between terminals 1 and 3 on the ALDL connector (the white connector located under the right hand instrument panel).
5. Using a timing light, connect it to the No. 1 spark plug wire. Loosen the distributor hold-down bolt until it is only finger tight.
6. Depress the accelerator pedal and start the engine, and allow the engine to idle.
7. Aim the timing light at the timing cover plate near the crankshaft pulley; the white notch on the crankshaft pulley should align with the 10 degree mark on the timing cover scale.
8. To adjust the engine timing, turn the distributor slightly to align the marks as specified. When properly adjusted, hold the distributor to keep it from turning and tighten the distributor hold-down bolt to 14 ft. lbs. (20 Nm). Recheck the timing to

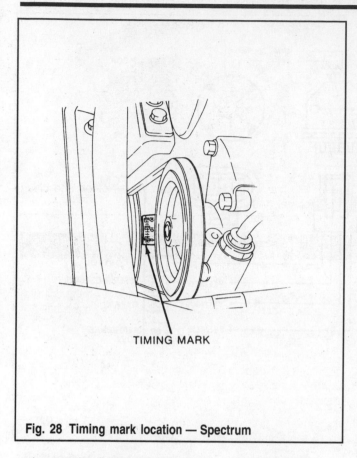

Fig. 28 Timing mark location — Spectrum

make sure the distributor position was not changed while tightening the distributor flange bolt.

9. When the adjustment is correct, remove the jumper wire from the ALDL connector and turn the ignition **OFF**.

10. Disconnect the timing light and the tachometer.

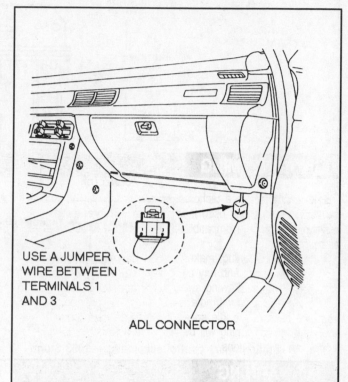

USE A JUMPER
WIRE BETWEEN
TERMINALS 1
AND 3

ADL CONNECTOR

Fig. 29 Terminals 1 and 3 of the ALDL connector must be jumpered in order to disable the ECM controlled spark advance system

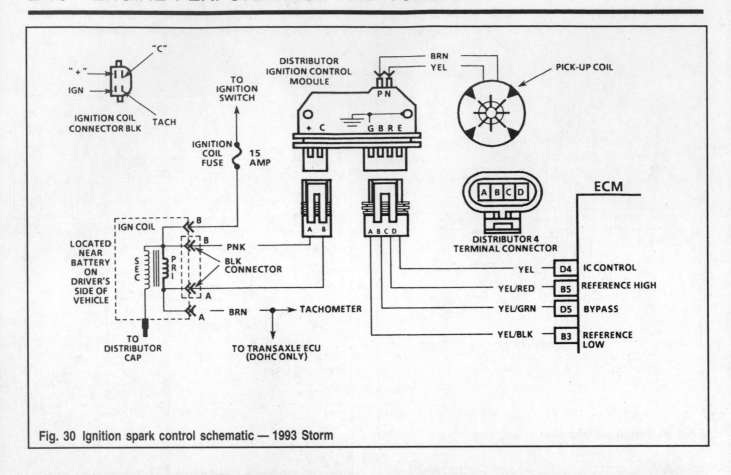

Fig. 30 Ignition spark control schematic — 1993 Storm

VALVE LASH

Valve Lash

ADJUSTMENT

Except Twin Camshaft Engine

▶ See Figures 31 and 32

1. Remove the cylinder head or valve cover; refer to Section 3 of this manual.

2. Rotate the engine in its normal direction of rotation until the notched line on the crankshaft pulley aligns with the **0** degree mark on the timing gear case. The position of the No. 1 piston should be at TDC of the compression stroke.

➡The notch on the crankshaft pulley should align with the 0 degrees mark on the timing gear case. Make sure the rocker arms on the No. 1 cylinder are loose and the rockers on the No. 4 cylinder are tight. If not, turn the crankshaft one complete revolution and align the marks again.

3. Check the valve lash between the rocker arm and valve stem on both the intake and exhaust valves on the number 1 cylinder, the intake valve(s) on the number 2 cylinder and the exhaust valve on the number 3 cylinder. If the valve lash on the intake valves is not 0.006 in. (0.15mm), adjust the valve lash. If the valve lash on the exhaust valve is not 0.010 in. (0.25mm), adjust the valve lash.

4. Adjust the valve lash by loosening the adjusting screw locknut and turning the adjusting screw until the proper specification is obtained. Tighten the adjusting screw locknut.

5. Set the intake valve to 0.006 in. (cold) for No. 1 and 2 cylinders; exhaust valves to 0.010 in. (cold) for No. 1 and 3 cylinders.

6. When the specified valves are adjusted, rotate the crankshaft 1 full revolution until the piston in the No. 4 cylinder is at TDC on compression stroke. (The No. 4 cylinder rockers will now be loose and the No. 1 rockers will be tight) set the intake valves to 0.006 in. (cold) for No. 3 and 4 cylinders; exhaust valves to 0.010 in. (cold) for No. 2 and 4 cylinders.

7. After the adjustment has been completed, install the head cover.

1.6L Twin Camshaft Engine

▶ See Figures 33, 34, 35 and 36

1. Disconnect the negative battery cable.
2. Remove the cylinder head or valve cover.

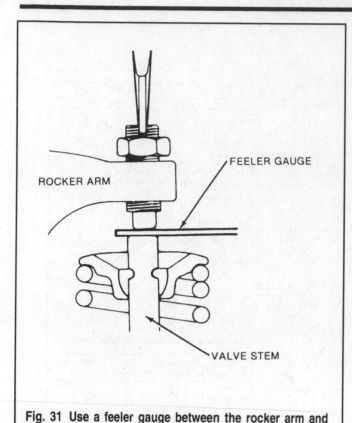

Fig. 31 Use a feeler gauge between the rocker arm and valve stem to properly adjust valve lash

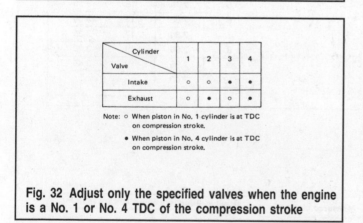

Cylinder Valve	1	2	3	4
Intake	○	○	●	●
Exhaust	○	●	○	●

Note: ○ When piston in No. 1 cylinder is at TDC on compression stroke.

● When piston in No. 4 cylinder is at TDC on compression stroke.

Fig. 32 Adjust only the specified valves when the engine is a No. 1 or No. 4 TDC of the compression stroke

3. Position the No. 1 cylinder at TDC on its compression stroke.

→The notch on the crankshaft pulley should align with the 0 degrees mark on the timing gear case. Make sure the rocker arms on the No. 1 cylinder are loose and the rockers on the No. 4 cylinder are tight. If not, turn the crankshaft one complete revolution and align the marks again.

4. Using a feeler gauge, measure the clearance between the cam lobe and the selective shim on the intake and exhaust valves on the No. 1 cylinder, then the intake valves on the No. 2 cylinder and the exhaust valves on the No. 3 cylinder. Note readings.

5. Rotate the crankshaft 360 degrees. Using a feeler gauge, measure the clearance between the cam lobe and the selective shim on the intake and exhaust valves on the No. 4 cylinder, then the intake valves on the No. 3 cylinder and the exhaust valves on the No. 2 cylinder. Note readings.

6. The valve clearance obtained on the exhaust valves should be between 0.008-0.012 in. (0.20-0.30mm). If not, replace the selective shim by turning the camshaft lobe downward and installing tool J-38413-2 or J-38413-3 (valve lash spring spacer) between the camshaft journal and the cam lobe next to the selective shim. Turn cam lobe upward and remove the selective shim. Install new shim using the selective shim chart.

→The rear camshaft bearing caps must be removed to remove the selective shim.

7. The valve clearance obtained on the intake valves should be between 0.004-0.008 in. (0.10-0.20mm). If not, replace the selective shim by turning the camshaft lobe downward and installing tool J-38413-2 or J-38413-3 between the camshaft journal and the cam lobe next to the selective shim. Turn cam lobe upward and remove the selective shim. Install new shim using the selective shim chart.

8. When the adjustment is completed, install the cylinder head covers and connect the battery negative cable. Start the engine and check for leaks.

1.8L Twincam Engine

The 1992 and 1993 1.8L Storm engine is equipped hydraulic lifters which require no valve lash adjustment. If a tapping noise is noticed at idle, inspect the valve train components for excessive wear.

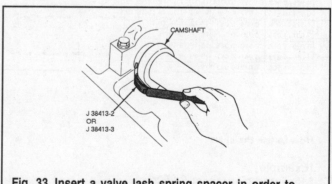

Fig. 33 Insert a valve lash spring spacer in order to remove the selective shim

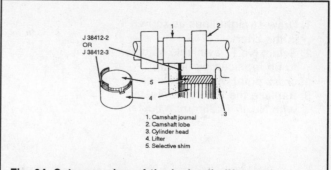

Fig. 34 Cut-away view of the hydraulic lifter and selective shim mounting

Size selection table — intake shim

Measured clearance		Original Adjuster (Shim) Thickness (mm)
mm	inch	2.52 · 2.54 · 2.56 · 2.58 · 2.60 · 2.62 · 2.64 · 2.66 · 2.68 · 2.70 · 2.72 · 2.74 · 2.76 · 2.78 · 2.80 · 2.82 · 2.84 · 2.86 · 2.88 · 2.90 · 2.92 · 2.94 · 2.96 · 2.98 · 3.00 · 3.02 · 3.04 · 3.06 · 3.08 · 3.10 · 3.12 · 3.14 · 3.16 · 3.18 · 3.20 · 3.22 · 3.24 · 3.26 · 3.28 · 3.30 · 3.32 · 3.34 · 3.36 · 3.38 · 3.40 · 3.42 · 3.44 · 3.46 · 3.48
0.000–0.025	0.000–0.001	1 1 2 2 2 3 3 4 4 5 5 6 6 6 7 7 8 8 9 9 10 10 11 11 12 12 13 13 14 14 15 15 16 16 17
0.026–0.050	0.001–0.002	1 1 1 2 2 3 3 3 4 4 5 5 5 6 6 7 7 7 8 8 9 9 9 10 10 11 11 11 12 12 13 13 13 14 14 15 15 15 16 16 17 17 17
0.051–0.075	0.002–0.003	1 1 1 2 2 3 3 3 4 4 5 5 5 6 6 7 7 7 8 8 9 9 9 10 10 11 11 11 12 12 13 13 13 14 14 15 15 15 16 16 17 17 17 18
0.076–0.100	0.003–0.004	1 1 2 2 2 3 3 4 4 4 5 5 5 6 6 6 7 7 7 8 8 8 9 9 9 10 10 10 11 11 11 12 12 13 13 13 14 14 14 15 15 16 16 16 17 17 18 18 18
0.101–0.200	0.004–0.008	Replacement not to be required
0.201–0.225	0.008–0.009	2 2 2 3 3 4 4 4 5 5 6 6 6 6 7 7 8 8 8 9 9 9 10 10 10 11 11 12 12 12 13 13 14 14 14 15 15 16 16 16 17 17 17 18 18 18 19 19
0.226–0.250	0.009–0.010	2 3 3 3 4 4 5 5 5 6 6 7 7 7 8 8 8 9 9 9 10 10 11 11 11 12 12 13 13 13 14 14 14 15 15 16 16 17 17 17 18 18 19 19 19 19
0.251–0.275	0.010–0.011	3 3 3 4 4 5 5 5 6 6 7 7 7 8 8 9 9 9 10 10 11 11 11 12 12 13 13 13 14 14 15 15 15 16 16 17 17 17 18 18 19 19 19
0.276–0.300	0.011–0.012	3 4 4 4 5 5 6 6 6 7 7 8 8 8 9 9 10 10 10 11 11 11 12 12 12 13 13 14 14 14 15 15 15 16 16 17 17 18 18 18 19 19 19
0.301–0.325	0.012–0.013	4 4 4 5 5 6 6 6 7 7 8 8 8 9 9 10 10 10 11 11 12 12 12 13 13 14 14 14 15 15 16 16 16 17 17 18 18 18 19 19 19
0.326–0.350	0.013–0.014	4 5 5 5 6 6 7 7 7 8 8 9 9 10 10 11 11 11 12 12 13 13 13 14 14 14 15 15 16 16 17 17 17 18 18 19 19 19
0.351–0.375	0.014–0.015	5 5 5 6 6 7 7 7 8 8 9 9 9 10 10 11 11 11 12 12 13 13 13 14 14 15 15 15 16 16 17 17 17 18 18 19 19 19 19
0.376–0.400	0.015–0.016	5 6 6 6 7 7 8 8 9 9 9 10 10 11 11 11 12 12 13 13 13 14 14 14 15 15 16 16 16 17 17 18 18 18 19 19
0.401–0.425	0.016–0.017	6 6 6 7 7 8 8 9 9 9 10 10 11 11 11 12 12 13 13 13 14 14 14 15 15 16 16 16 17 17 18 18 19 19 19
0.426–0.450	0.017–0.018	6 7 7 7 8 8 9 9 10 10 11 11 11 12 12 13 13 13 14 14 14 15 15 16 16 16 17 17 18 18 19 19 19 19
0.451–0.475	0.018–0.019	7 7 7 8 8 9 9 9 10 10 11 11 12 12 12 13 13 14 14 14 15 15 16 16 17 17 18 18 19 19 19
0.476–0.500	0.019–0.020	7 8 8 8 9 9 10 10 10 11 11 12 12 12 13 13 14 14 14 15 15 16 16 17 17 18 18 18 19 19
0.501–0.525	0.020–0.021	8 8 8 9 9 10 10 10 11 11 12 12 12 13 13 14 14 15 15 16 16 17 17 17 18 18 19 19
0.526–0.550	0.021–0.022	8 9 9 9 10 10 11 11 12 12 13 13 13 14 14 15 15 15 16 16 17 17 17 18 18 19 19
0.551–0.575	0.022–0.023	9 9 9 10 10 11 11 12 12 13 13 13 14 14 15 15 16 16 17 17 17 18 18 19 19 19
0.576–0.600	0.023–0.024	9 10 10 10 11 11 12 12 13 13 14 14 15 15 16 16 16 17 17 18 18 18 19 19
0.601–0.625	0.024–0.025	10 10 10 11 11 12 12 13 13 14 14 14 15 15 16 16 17 17 18 18 18 19 19
0.626–0.650	0.025–0.026	10 11 11 11 12 12 13 13 14 14 15 15 16 16 16 17 17 18 18 19 19 19
0.651–0.675	0.026–0.027	11 11 11 12 12 13 13 14 14 14 15 15 16 16 17 17 18 18 18 19 19
0.676–0.700	0.027–0.028	11 12 12 12 13 13 14 14 15 15 16 16 16 17 17 18 18 18 19 19
0.701–0.725	0.028–0.029	12 12 12 13 13 14 14 15 15 16 16 16 17 17 18 18 18 19 19
0.726–0.750	0.029–0.030	12 13 13 13 14 14 15 15 15 16 16 17 17 17 18 18 19 19 19 19
0.751–0.775	0.030–0.031	12 13 13 14 14 14 15 15 16 16 17 17 17 18 18 19 19 19
0.776–0.800	0.031–0.032	13 14 14 14 15 15 16 16 17 17 18 18 18 19 19
0.801–0.825	0.032–0.033	14 14 14 15 15 16 16 16 17 17 18 18 18 19 19
0.826–0.850	0.033–0.034	14 15 15 15 16 16 17 17 17 18 18 19 19 19
0.851–0.875	0.034–0.035	15 15 15 16 16 17 17 17 18 18 19 19 19
0.876–0.900	0.035–0.036	15 16 16 16 17 17 18 18 18 19 19
0.901–0.925	0.036–0.037	16 16 16 17 17 18 18 19 19
0.926–0.950	0.0365–0.0374	16 17 17 17 18 18 19 19 19
0.951–0.975	0.037–0.038	17 17 17 18 18 19 19 19
0.976–1.000	0.038–0.039	17 18 18 18 19 19
1.001–1.025	0.039–0.040	18 18 18 19 19
1.026–1.050	0.040–0.041	18 19 19 19
1.051–1.075	0.041–0.042	19 19 19
1.076–1.100	0.042–0.043	19

Thickness of available adjuster (Shim)

NO in Chart	Thickness (mm)	NO in Chart	Thickness (mm)
1	2.55	11	3.05
2	2.60	12	3.10
3	2.65	13	3.15
4	2.70	14	3.20
5	2.75	15	3.25
6	2.80	16	3.30
7	2.85	17	3.35
8	2.90	18	3.40
9	2.95	19	3.45
10	3.00		

How to use the chart

[Example]
Measured clearance; 0.550mm
Original adjuster thickness; 2.96mm
(Thickness mark (2.96) is printed
on the adjuster surface)

1. Draw straight lines as shown
   in the chart.
2. Select No.17 available adjuster
   to be replaced by finding
   cross point of straight lines.
3. Replace the 2.96mm adjuster
   with No.17 (3.35mm) adjuster.

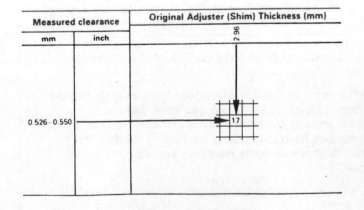

Measured clearance		Original Adjuster (Shim) Thickness (mm)
mm	inch	2.96
0.526–0.550		→ 17

Fig. 35 Size selection table — intake shim

Measured clearance mm	inch	2.52	2.54	2.56	2.58	2.60	2.62	2.64	2.66	2.68	2.70	2.72	2.74	2.76	2.78	2.80	2.82	2.84	2.86	2.88	2.90	2.92	2.94	2.96	2.98	3.00	3.02	3.04	3.06	3.08	3.10	3.12	3.14	3.16	3.18	3.20	3.22	3.24	3.26	3.28	3.30	3.32	3.34	3.36	3.38	3.40	3.42	3.44	3.46	3.48
0.000-0.025	0.000-0.001														1	1	2	2	2	3	3	4	4	4	5	5	6	6	6	7	7	8	8	8	9	9	10	10	10	11	11	12	12	12	13	13	14	14	14	15
0.026-0.050	0.001-0.002												1	1	1	2	2	3	3	3	4	4	5	5	5	6	6	7	7	7	8	8	9	9	9	10	10	11	11	11	12	12	13	13	13	14	14	15	15	15
0.051-0.075	0.002-0.003											1	1	1	2	2	3	3	3	4	4	5	5	5	6	6	7	7	7	8	8	9	9	9	10	10	11	11	11	12	12	13	13	13	14	14	15	15	15	16
0.076-0.100	0.003-0.004										1	1	2	2	2	3	3	4	4	4	5	5	6	6	6	7	7	8	8	8	9	9	10	10	10	11	11	12	12	12	13	13	14	14	14	15	15	16	16	16
0.101-0.125	0.004-0.005									1	1	2	2	2	3	3	4	4	4	5	5	6	6	6	7	7	8	8	8	9	9	10	10	10	11	11	12	12	12	13	13	14	14	14	15	15	16	16	16	17
0.126-0.150	0.005-0.006							1	1	1	2	2	3	3	3	4	4	5	5	5	6	6	7	7	7	8	8	9	9	9	10	10	11	11	11	12	12	13	13	13	14	14	15	15	15	16	16	17	17	17
0.151-0.175	0.006-0.007						1	1	1	2	2	3	3	3	4	4	5	5	5	6	6	7	7	7	8	8	9	9	9	10	10	11	11	11	12	12	13	13	13	14	14	15	15	15	16	16	17	17	17	18
0.176-0.200	0.007-0.008					1	1	2	2	2	3	3	4	4	4	5	5	6	6	6	7	7	8	8	8	9	9	10	10	10	11	11	12	12	12	13	13	14	14	14	15	15	16	16	16	17	17	18	18	18
0.201-0.300	0.008-0.012	Replacement not to be required																																																
0.301-0.325	0.012-0.013	2	2	2	3	3	4	4	4	5	5	6	6	6	7	7	8	8	8	9	9	10	10	10	11	11	12	12	12	13	13	14	14	14	15	15	16	16	16	17	17	18	18	18	19	19				
0.326-0.350	0.013-0.014	2	3	3	3	4	4	5	5	5	6	6	7	7	7	8	8	9	9	9	10	10	11	11	11	12	12	13	13	13	14	14	15	15	15	16	16	17	17	17	18	18	19	19	19					
0.351-0.375	0.014-0.015	3	3	3	4	4	5	5	5	6	6	7	7	7	8	8	9	9	9	10	10	11	11	11	12	12	13	13	13	14	14	15	15	15	16	16	17	17	17	18	18	19	19	19						
0.376-0.400	0.015-0.016	3	4	4	4	5	5	6	6	6	7	7	8	8	8	9	9	10	10	10	11	11	12	12	12	13	13	14	14	14	15	15	16	16	16	17	17	18	18	18	19	19								
0.401-0.425	0.016-0.017	4	4	4	5	5	6	6	6	7	7	8	8	8	9	9	10	10	10	11	11	12	12	12	13	13	14	14	14	15	15	16	16	16	17	17	18	18	18	19	19									
0.426-0.450	0.017-0.018	4	5	5	5	6	6	7	7	7	8	8	9	9	9	10	10	11	11	11	12	12	13	13	13	14	14	15	15	15	16	16	17	17	17	18	18	19	19	19										
0.451-0.475	0.018-0.019	5	5	5	6	6	7	7	7	8	8	9	9	9	10	10	11	11	11	12	12	13	13	13	14	14	15	15	15	16	16	17	17	17	18	18	19	19	19											
0.476-0.500	0.019-0.020	5	6	6	6	7	7	8	8	8	9	9	10	10	10	11	11	12	12	12	13	13	14	14	14	15	15	16	16	16	17	17	18	18	18	19	19													
0.501-0.525	0.020-0.021	6	6	6	7	7	8	8	8	9	9	10	10	10	11	11	12	12	12	13	13	14	14	14	15	15	16	16	16	17	17	18	18	18	19	19														
0.526-0.550	0.021-0.022	6	7	7	7	8	8	9	9	9	10	10	11	11	11	12	12	13	13	13	14	14	15	15	15	16	16	17	17	17	18	18	19	19	19															
0.551-0.575	0.022-0.023	7	7	7	8	8	9	9	9	10	10	11	11	11	12	12	13	13	13	14	14	15	15	15	16	16	17	17	17	18	18	19	19	19																
0.576-0.600	0.023-0.024	7	8	8	8	9	9	10	10	10	11	11	12	12	12	13	13	14	14	14	15	15	16	16	16	17	17	18	18	18	19	19																		
0.601-0.625	0.024-0.025	8	8	8	9	9	10	10	10	11	11	12	12	12	13	13	14	14	14	15	15	16	16	16	17	17	18	18	18	19	19																			
0.626-0.650	0.025-0.026	8	9	9	9	10	10	11	11	11	12	12	13	13	13	14	14	15	15	15	16	16	17	17	17	18	18	19	19	19																				
0.651-0.675	0.026-0.027	9	9	9	10	10	11	11	11	12	12	13	13	13	14	14	15	15	15	16	16	17	17	17	18	18	19	19	19																					
0.676-0.700	0.027-0.028	9	10	10	10	11	11	12	12	12	13	13	14	14	14	15	15	16	16	16	17	17	18	18	18	19	19																							
0.701-0.725	0.028-0.029	10	10	10	11	11	12	12	12	13	13	14	14	14	15	15	16	16	16	17	17	18	18	18	19	19																								
0.726-0.750	0.029-0.030	10	11	11	11	12	12	13	13	13	14	14	15	15	15	16	16	17	17	17	18	18	19	19	19																									
0.751-0.775	0.030-0.031	11	11	11	12	12	13	13	13	14	14	15	15	15	16	16	17	17	17	18	18	19	19	19																										
0.776-0.800	0.031-0.032	11	12	12	12	13	13	14	14	14	15	15	16	16	16	17	17	18	18	18	19	19																												
0.801-0.825	0.032-0.033	12	12	12	13	13	14	14	14	15	15	16	16	16	17	17	18	18	18	19	19																													
0.826-0.850	0.033-0.034	12	13	13	13	14	14	15	15	15	16	16	17	17	17	18	18	19	19	19																														
0.851-0.875	0.034-0.035	13	13	13	14	14	15	15	15	16	16	17	17	17	18	18	19	19	19																															
0.876-0.900	0.035-0.036	13	14	14	14	15	15	16	16	16	17	17	18	18	18	19	19																																	
0.901-0.925	0.036-0.037	14	14	14	15	15	16	16	16	17	17	18	18	18	19	19																																		
0.926-0.950	0.0365-0.0374	14	15	15	15	16	16	17	17	17	18	18	19	19	19																																			
0.951-0.975	0.037-0.038	15	15	15	16	16	17	17	17	18	18	19	19	19																																				
0.976-1.000	0.038-0.039	15	16	16	16	17	17	18	18	18	19	19																																						
1.001-1.025	0.039-0.040	16	16	16	17	17	18	18	18	19	19																																							
1.026-1.050	0.040-0.041	16	17	17	17	18	18	19	19	19																																								
1.051-1.075	0.041-0.042	17	17	17	18	18	19	19	19																																									
1.076-1.100	0.042-0.043	17	18	18	18	19	19																																											
1.101-1.125	0.043-0.044	18	18	18	19	19																																												
1.126-1.150	0.044-0.045	18	19	19	19																																													
1.151-1.175	0.045-0.046	19	19	19																																														
1.176-1.200	0.046-0.047	19																																																

Original Adjuster (Shim) Thickness (mm)

Thickness of available adjuster (Shim)

NO in Chart	Thickness (mm)	NO in Chart	Thickness (mm)
1	2.55	11	3.05
2	2.60	12	3.10
3	2.65	13	3.15
4	2.70	14	3.20
5	2.75	15	3.25
6	2.80	16	3.30
7	2.85	17	3.35
8	2.90	18	3.40
9	2.95	19	3.45
10	3.00		

Note; Thickness mark is printed on the surface to be contacted with tappet.

How to use the chart

[Example]
Measured clearance; 0.550mm
Original adjuster thickness; 2.96mm
(Thickness mark (2.96) is printed on the adjuster surface)

1. Draw straight lines as shown in the chart.
2. Select No.15 available adjuster to be replaced by finding cross point of straight lines.
3. Replace the 2.96mm adjuster with No.15 (3.25mm) adjuster.

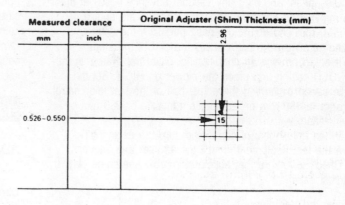

Measured clearance mm	inch	Original Adjuster (Shim) Thickness (mm) 2.96
0.526-0.550		15

Fig. 36 Size selection table — exhaust shim

IDLE SPEED AND MIXTURE ADJUSTMENT

Idle Speed

ADJUSTMENT

Carbureted Vehicles

▶ **See Figures 37 and 38**

The cooling fan runs and stops automatically according to the coolant temperature. For this reason, make sure that the cooling fan is not running while performing the idle speed check and adjustment. If the fan comes on, wait until it stops before continuing.

1. Confirm the following prior to checking or adjusting the idle speed.
   a. Check that the lead wires and hoses of the engine emission control system are connected correctly.
   b. Check that the accelerator cable has 0.12-0.20 in. (3-5 mm) free-play when engine is at operating temperature.
   c. Check that the ignition timing is within specification.
   d. Check that the valve lash is adjusted to specification.
2. Place transaxle gear shift lever in **N** or **P** position, block the wheels and set the parking brake.
3. Check the float level through the sight glass in the side of the carburetor, then start and warm the engine to normal operating temperature.
4. Ensure that the lights, heater fan, rear defogger, cooling fan and air conditioner are **OFF**. If equipped with power steering, place the wheels in the straight forward position.
5. Disconnect and plug the distributor vacuum line, canister purge line, EGR vacuum line and ITC valve vacuum line.
6. Connect a tachometer to the coil tachometer connector and a timing light to the No. 1 spark plug wire. Check the timing and idle speed.
7. If the idle speed needs adjusting, turn the idle speed adjusting screw. Adjust the speed with the choke valve fully opened and the air cleaner in position.
8. Disconnect and plug any vacuum advance hoses at the intake manifold (if not done already), then run the engine at 1900-2100 rpm and adjust the dash pot. Turn the dash pot adjusting screw until it just touches the end of the shaft.
9. If equipped with air conditioning, place the system in the **MAX/COLD** setting and place the blower on **HIGH**. Set the fast idle speed by turning the adjust bolt of the fast idle control diaphragm to 850 rpm on automatic transaxle or 980 rpm on manual transaxle.
10. When adjustment is completed, turn the engine off, remove the test equipment, install the air filter and vacuum lines. Check to ensure that accelerator cable has some play. If not, adjust cable.

Fuel Injected Vehicles

Unlike carbureted vehicles which may occasionally need an idle speed adjustment, fuel injected vehicles use electrical devices (run by the ECM), in order to control idle speed. Although there is a throttle stop screw which may be adjusted,

the manufacturer warns that it is EXTREMELY UNLIKELY that this adjustment will ever be necessary on a throttle body that has not been tampered with after production.

The throttle stop screw is sealed at the factory to prevent unnecessary tampering. Before removing the seal and adjusting the screw, eliminate all other possible causes of an incorrect or erratic idle. For more information, refer to Section 4 of this manual for electronic engine controls.

If a scan tool is available, the throttle stop position may be checked by monitoring the IAC valve:

1. Block the wheels and apply the parking brake.
2. Connect the scan tool the ALDL connector.
3. Start the engine and allow it to warm to normal operating temperature and enter Closed Loop operation. For more information regarding engine controls, refer to Section 4 or 5 of this manual.
4. If equipped with an automatic transaxle, shift into **D** and then back to **N**.
5. Using the scan tool, select the power steering pressure switch input. With the A/C and all accessories **OFF**, the scan tool should rear OFF or NORMAL. If not, repair the power steering pressure switch circuit.
6. Allow the idle to stabilize, then select IAC valve display on the tool and read the valve counts. If counts are between 5-45, then the throttle valve position is acceptable.

➡ **If the idle speed is not allowed to sufficiently stabilize, an incorrect count reading might result in unnecessary tampering or adjustment with the throttle stop screw.**

7. If counts are too low, check for intake vacuum leaks at hoses, the throttle body or intake. Check for a damaged throttle lever. If no other causes are found, remove the seal and adjust the screw to obtain the proper counts. Turn the screw in very small increments and allow the idle to stabilize each time.
8. If counts are too high, check for a damaged throttle lever or an airflow restriction by the throttle valve. If no problem is found, clean the air intake duct and remove residue from the throttle body bore and throttle valve using a carburetor cleaner (which DOES NOT contain methyl ethyl ketone) and check the count again. If counts are still incorrect, remove the seal and adjust the screw to obtain the proper counts. Turn the screw in very small increments and allow the idle to stabilize each time.

Idle Mixture

ADJUSTMENT

Carbureted Vehicles

The carburetor has been calibrated at the factory and should not normally need adjustment. For this reason, the mixture adjustment should never be changed from original factory setting. However if during diagnosis, the check indicates the carburetor to be the cause of a performance complaint or

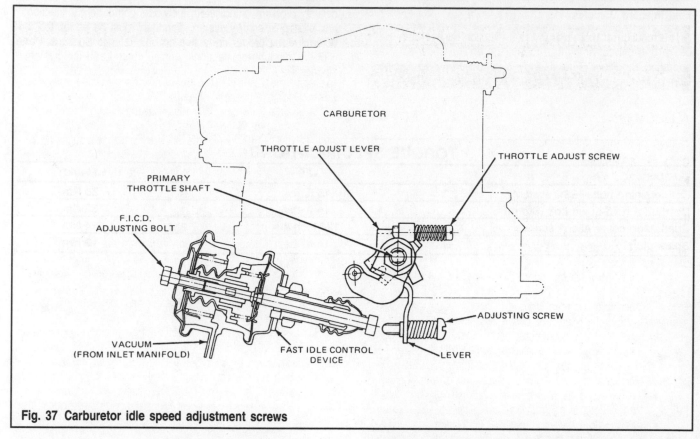

Fig. 37 Carburetor idle speed adjustment screws

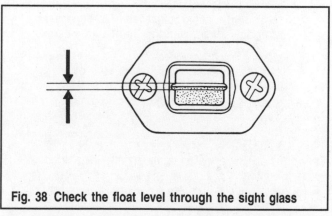

Fig. 38 Check the float level through the sight glass

emission failure, or if the carburetor is being overhauled, the idle mixture can be adjusted using the following procedure:

1. Confirm the following prior to checking or adjusting the idle speed.

  a. Check that the lead wires and hoses of the engine emission control system are connected correctly.

  b. Check that the accelerator cable has some play.

  c. Check that the ignition timing is within specification.

  d. Check that the valve lash is adjusted to specification.

  e. Check that the fast-idle actuator does not operate.

  f. Check that the cooling fan is not operating.

2. If not already done, remove the carburetor from the intake manifold and remove the mixture adjusting screw cover pin. This can be done center punching, then drilling the center

of the pin using a 4-4.5mm drill bit. The drill depth should be less than 10mm. A punch may be used to remove the pin.

❊❊WARNING

When drilling the idle mixture screw plug from the carburetor, always cover the primary and secondary bores along with any other ports to prevent chips or other debris from entering the carburetor.

3. Remove and inspect the idle mixture adjusting screw. Use compressed air (while wearing safety glasses) to blow chips from the screw bore. Inspect the screw and replace if warped or if damaged by the drill.

4. Install the screw and seat it lightly in the bore, then carefully back the screw out 3 turns from fully closed for manual transaxles or 2 turns from fully closed for automatic transaxles.

5. Reinstall the carburetor and air cleaner.

6. Place gear shift lever in **N** (MT) or **P** (AT) position, set the parking brake and block the drive wheels.

7. Start the engine and allow it to reach operating temperature.

8. Check and, if necessary, adjust the ignition timing.

9. Using a dwell meter, connect the positive lead to the duty monitor and the negative lead to ground. Place the meter dial on the 4 cylinder scale. Turn the idle mixture screw until the dwell meter reads 45 degrees (4 cylinder scale).

10. Check idle speed and adjust to specification as necessary.

11. Install a new mixture adjusting screw pin and remove the tachometer.

Fuel Injected Vehicles

The function of the electronic fuel injection system is to deliver the correct amount of fuel to the engine under all operating conditions. Fuel delivery is controlled by the Engine Control Module (ECM) and can not be adjusted. If a fuel delivery problem is indicated, individual component inspection and electronic control system diagnosis must be performed to determine the proper corrective action. Refer to Sections 4 and 5 of this manual for electronic engine control and fuel system diagnosis.

TORQUE SPECIFICATIONS

Component	U.S.	Metric
Coil retaining bolts (ESC system)	15 ft. lbs.	20 Nm
Distributor hold-down bolt (Storm)	14 ft. lbs.	20 Nm
Spark plug cover Allen® screws	124 inch lbs.	14 Nm
Spark plug	14 ft. lbs.	19 Nm

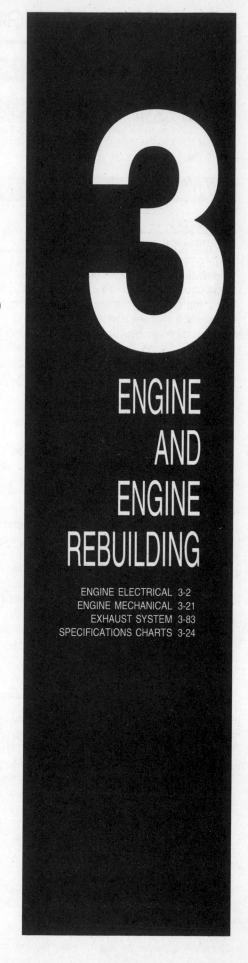

3

ENGINE AND ENGINE REBUILDING

ENGINE ELECTRICAL

Ignition Components

For testing and repair of ignition components, see Section 2 of this manual (Electronic Ignition).

Alternator

ALTERNATOR PRECAUTIONS

Several precautions must be observed with alternator equipped vehicles to avoid damage to the unit.

• If the battery is removed for any reason, make sure it is reconnected with the correct polarity. Reversing the battery connections may result in damage to the one-way rectifiers.

• When utilizing a booster battery as a starting aid, always connect the positive to positive terminals and the negative terminal from the booster battery to a good engine ground on the vehicle being started.

• Never use a fast charger as a booster to start vehicles.

• Disconnect the battery cables when charging the battery with a fast charger.

• Never attempt to polarize the alternator.

• Do not use test lights of more than 12 volts when checking diode continuity.

• Do not short across or ground any of the alternator terminals.

• The polarity of the battery, alternator and regulator must be matched and considered before making any electrical connections within the system.

• Never separate the alternator on an open circuit. Make sure all connections within the circuit are clean and tight.

• Disconnect the battery ground terminal when performing any service on electrical components.

• Disconnect the battery if arc welding is to be done on the vehicle.

DIAGNOSIS & TESTING

Whenever troubleshooting the charging system, always check for obvious problems before proceeding, such as loose belts, bad electrical or battery connections, blown fuses, broken wires, etc.. The battery must be in good condition and in the proper state of charge. When performing tests, make sure the ignition is **OFF** before connecting or disconnecting test equipment.

Spectrum

▶ **See Figures 1, 2 and 3**

The following procedure requires the use of a special alternator/charging system tester which should be available from your dealer. An equivalent tester may be available from aftermarket sources, but be sure the tester is compatible with your vehicle before attempting to use it. When using an equivalent aftermarket tester, follow the tool manufacturer's

instructions for installation and diagnosis. Incorrect diagnosis could lead to unnecessary repairs.

1. Turn the ignition **OFF**.
2. Set the checker switch to 12V.
3. Install the checker harness connector (black, red, white/red wires in the 4-pole connector) to the checker.
4. Install the extension harness (white/red wire, single female connector) to the checker harness.
5. Install the other end of the extension harness to the alternator L-lead wire (white/red).
6. Connect the black alligator clip to the negative battery terminal, then connect the red alligator clip to the positive battery terminal.
7. Check the condition of the alternator, refer to appropriate figures as a guide.

Storm

1990-1992 VEHICLES

▶ **See Figures 4 and 5**

The following procedure requires the use of an Digital Volt/Ohm Meter (DVOM) or multimeter and a battery tester (carbon pile load tester). The alternator in the Storm uses 2 terminals; the battery positive and the L terminal (to the charge indicator). There are other, optional terminals, which may exist on some models. If present, each terminal (P, I and S) is connected to a specific position; the stator (P) and internal positive field (I) or serves a specific function; is available for connecting an external voltage source (S).

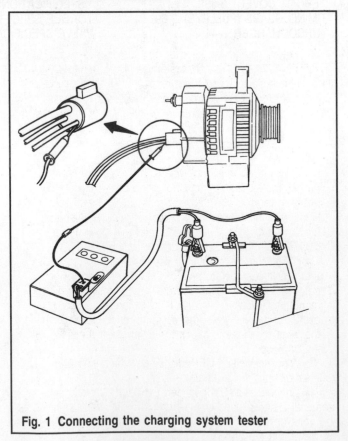

Fig. 1 Connecting the charging system tester

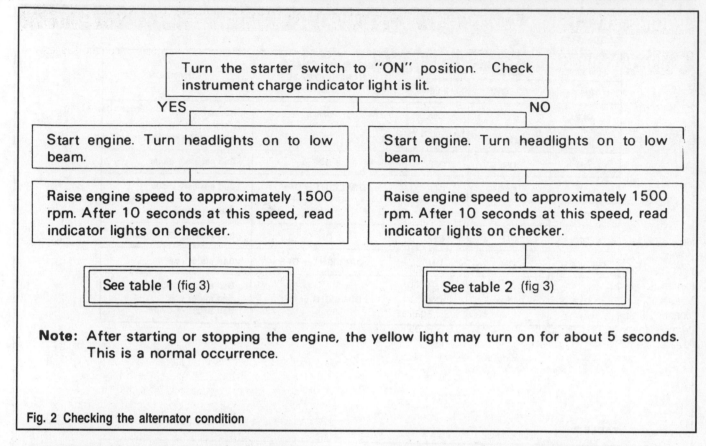

Fig. 2 Checking the alternator condition

Flowchart:

Turn the starter switch to "ON" position. Check instrument charge indicator light is lit.

YES → Start engine. Turn headlights on to low beam. → Raise engine speed to approximately 1500 rpm. After 10 seconds at this speed, read indicator lights on checker. → See table 1 (fig 3)

NO → Start engine. Turn headlights on to low beam. → Raise engine speed to approximately 1500 rpm. After 10 seconds at this speed, read indicator lights on checker. → See table 2 (fig 3)

Note: After starting or stopping the engine, the yellow light may turn on for about 5 seconds. This is a normal occurrence.

The possible problems which may exist in the charging system are; a faulty charge indicator circuit, a battery undercharge condition (indicated by slow cranking or by the hydrometer eye) or a battery overcharge condition (indicated by electrolyte spewing from the battery vents).

1. Before proceeding look for obvious causes of charging system problems. Check all system wiring for improper or loose connections. Inspect belt tension and condition. Inspect the battery for proper charge. Refer to Section 1 of this manual for appropriate procedures.

2. If the vehicle is equipped with a battery charge light in the instrument cluster, proceed as follows:

a. Turn the ignition system to the **RUN** position, but do not start the engine. If the charging lamp does not illuminate, unplug the alternator connector, then attach a fused jumper between terminal L and a good chassis ground. If the lamp lights with the jumper in position, replace the alternator. If the lamp does not illuminate, locate and repair the open between the alternator and ignition switch.

b. With the charging lamp illuminated, start the engine and run at a moderate speed; the lamp should extinguish. If not, carefully unplug the alternator connector for a few moments. A faulty alternator is indicated, if the lamp extinguishes only when the wiring harness is disconnected. If the lamp remains on, check for a grounded terminal wire in the harness.

3. With the ignition **OFF**, disconnect the wiring harness connector from the alternator.

4. Connect a DVOM between the alternator connector terminal L and a good chassis ground. The reading should be 10 volts or more; if not check and repair the open between the terminal and the battery.

5. Install the wiring harness connector to the alternator.

6. Connect the DVOM across the battery terminals, then start and run the engine. Make sure ALL accessories turned **OFF** and, if equipped with power steering, the wheels are pointed to the straight-ahead position. The reading should be less than 16 volts; if not, replace the alternator.

7. Remove the DVOM from the battery terminals and switch it to the amperage setting, then connect it to the alternator output terminal and the battery negative terminal.

8. Turn on all accessories and load the battery using a carbon pile tester; refer to the battery sticker for proper load requirements.

9. Maintain voltage at 13 volts or higher and check the alternator amperage using the DVOM. If amperage is between 60-90 amps the alternator is good. If a problem is still suspected and the alternator tests properly, refer to Section 1 of this manual for battery checking procedures.

1993 VEHICLES
▶ See Figure 6

The following procedure requires the use of an Digital Volt/Ohm Meter (DVOM) and an ammeter. The alternator in the Storm vehicles uses 2 terminals; the battery positive and the L terminal (to the charge indicator). There are other, optional terminals, which may exist on some models. If present, each terminal (P, I and S) is connected to a specific position; the stator (P) and internal positive field (I) or serves a specific function; is available for connecting an external voltage source (S).

1. Before proceeding look for obvious causes of charging system problems. Check all system wiring for improper or loose connections. Inspect belt tension and condition. Inspect

TABLE 1

CHECKER LIGHTS			INSTRUMENT PANEL CHARGE INDICATOR LIGHT	CONDITION
RED	YELLOW	GREEN		
OFF	OFF	ON	OFF	Normal.
ON	ON	OFF	ON	Bad positive diode.
ON	ON	OFF	OFF	Bad negative diode.
ON	ON	OFF	DIM LIGHT or OFF	Bad auxiliary diode.
ON	OFF	OFF	ON	Bad rotor coil.
ON	OFF	OFF	OFF	Bad internal (IC) regulator.
ON or OFF	ON	ON	DIM LIGHT or OFF	Bad stator coil.
OFF	ON	ON	DIM LIGHT or OFF	Bad auxiliary diode. Bad stator coil. Bad negative diode.

TABLE 2

CHECKER LIGHTS			INSTRUMENT PANEL CHARGE INDICATOR LIGHT	CONDITION
RED	YELLOW	GREEN		
OFF	OFF	ON	OFF	Bad positive diode. Bad charge indicator light.
ON	OFF	OFF	OFF	Bad rotor coil Bad internal (IC) regulator Poor or no brush contact

Fig. 3 Diagnosing tester results

the battery for proper charge. Refer to Section 1 of this manual for appropriate procedures.

2. With the engine and all accessories turned **OFF**, connect a DVOM across the battery terminals.

3. Start the engine and run it at a moderate speed, then check battery voltage.

➡**When testing voltage, give consideration to the affect temperature will have on the regulator. As the temperature of the regulator case (mounted in the alternator) increases, voltage output will decrease.**

4. The standard setting for the regulator is 14.2-14.8 volts at 77°F(-25°C). Under normal operating conditions, the reading should be at least 13.5 volts.

5. If the previous tests do not reveal the trouble, turn the engine **OFF** and disconnect the negative battery cable.

6. Remove the rubber protector, nut and the alternator positive wire from the alternator positive terminal.

7. Install an ammeter between the alternator and the disconnected wire. Connect the ammeter negative lead (black wire) to the wire and the red lead (positive wire) to the alternator battery terminal.

8. Install a DVOM between the alternator positive battery terminal and a good chassis ground.

9. Start the engine and run it at 2000 rpm, then turn all accessories and the headlight high-beams ON. Make sure the heating and ventilating blower motor is the maximum position.

10. Adjust the engine speed, as necessary, to obtain the maximum current output. With the voltage between 13.5-16.0 volts, the alternator output should be 45-65 amps. If not, the alternator is faulty.

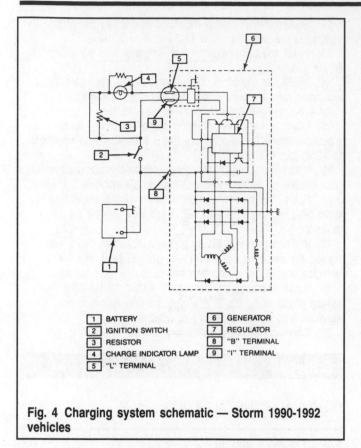

Fig. 4 Charging system schematic — Storm 1990-1992 vehicles

1	BATTERY	6	GENERATOR
2	IGNITION SWITCH	7	REGULATOR
3	RESISTOR	8	"B" TERMINAL
4	CHARGE INDICATOR LAMP	9	"I" TERMINAL
5	"L" TERMINAL		

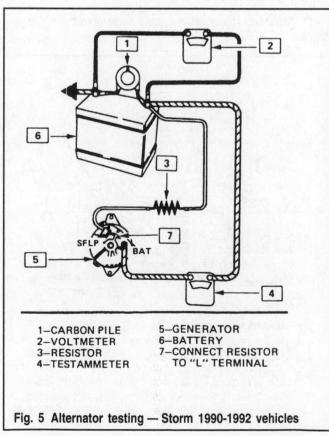

1—CARBON PILE
2—VOLTMETER
3—RESISTOR
4—TESTAMMETER
5—GENERATOR
6—BATTERY
7—CONNECT RESISTOR TO "L" TERMINAL

Fig. 5 Alternator testing — Storm 1990-1992 vehicles

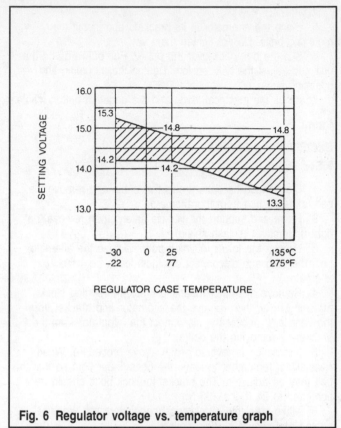

Fig. 6 Regulator voltage vs. temperature graph

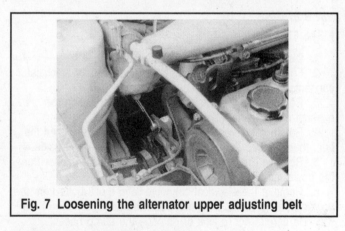

Fig. 7 Loosening the alternator upper adjusting belt

REMOVAL & INSTALLATION

Spectrum

1. Disconnect the negative battery terminal from the battery.

➡**Failure to disconnect the negative cable may result in injury from the positive battery lead at the alternator and may short the alternator and regulator during the removal process.**

2. Disconnect and label the terminal plug and the battery lead from the rear of the alternator.

3. Loosen the mounting bolts. Push the alternator inwards and slip the drive belt off the pulley.

4. Remove the mounting bolts and remove the alternator.

To install:

5. Place the alternator in its brackets and install the mounting bolts. Do not tighten them yet.

6. Slip the belt back over the pulley. Pull outwards on the unit and adjust the belt tension. Tighten the mounting and adjusting bolts.

7. Install the electrical leads and the negative battery cable.

Storm

EXCEPT VIN 8 ENGINE

▶ See Figure 7

1. Disconnect the battery negative cable and remove the belt adjusting bolt from the alternator.

2. Raise and support the vehicle safely, then remove the right undercover (splash shield).

3. Loosen the lower retaining bolt. Remove the alternator belt, then tag and disconnect electrical leads from the alternator.

4. Remove alternator mounting bracket-to-engine block attaching bolts, then remove the alternator and bracket from the vehicle. If necessary, disconnect the alternator from the bracket by removing the bolt(s).

5. Installation is reverse of the above procedure. When reinstalling, remember to leave the bolts finger tight so that the belt may be adjusted. The bracket-to-block bolts should be tightened to 24 ft. lbs. (33 Nm).

6. Make sure that all electrical connectors are properly seated and secure in their mounts.

VIN 8 ENGINE

▶ See Figure 8

1. Disconnect the negative battery cable.

2. For 1993 vehicles, unplug the oxygen sensor electrical connector.

3. Remove the five retaining bolts, then reposition the exhaust manifold heat shield out of the way.

4. Rotate the serpentine drive belt tensioner to loosen the belt, then remove the belt from the tensioner and set aside.

5. Remove the 2 nuts and the wiring harness retainer from the power steering pump.

6. Remove the electrical connector and the 3 bolts from the power steering pump, then reposition the assembly out of the way. Be careful not to kink or damage the pump hoses.

7. Tag and disconnect the electrical connections from the alternator.

8. Raise and support the vehicle safely. Remove the seven screws and the right splash shield, then remove the lower bolt and nut from the alternator.

9. Remove the supports and carefully lower the vehicle, then remove the upper alternator bolt and the 2 upper mounting bracket bolts. Remove the alternator and mounting bracket from the vehicle.

To install:

10. Position the alternator in the vehicle and loosely install a fastener to retain it while the vehicle is raised. Raise and support the vehicle safely.

11. Install the lower bolt and nut to the alternator, but do not fully tighten at this time. Remove the supports and carefully lower the vehicle.

12. Secure the alternator mounting bracket to the engine by tightening the retaining bolts to 24 ft. lbs. (33 Nm).

13. Install the upper bolt to the alternator and tighten to 24 ft. lbs. (33 Nm).

14. Install the electrical connections to the alternator. If equipped with a retaining nut (as opposed to a snap-connector), tighten the nut to 11 ft. lbs. (15 Nm).

15. Position the power steering pump assembly, install the electrical connector and tighten the 3 assembly retaining bolts to 22 ft. lbs. (30 Nm).

16. Install the wiring harness retainer to the pump assembly, then secure by tightening the 2 nuts to 89 inch lbs. (10 Nm).

17. Rotate the belt tensioner, then install the serpentine drive belt, making sure the belt is properly aligned on all pulleys.

18. Position the heat shield to the exhaust manifold and tighten the retaining bolts to 11 ft. lbs. (15 Nm). For 1993 vehicles, install the wiring harness to the oxygen sensor.

19. Raise and support the vehicle safely, then install the splash shield using the 7 retaining screws. Remove the supports and carefully lower the vehicle.

20. Connect the negative battery cable.

Battery

REMOVAL & INSTALLATION

▶ See Figures 9 and 10

1. Disconnect the negative battery cable from the battery terminal.

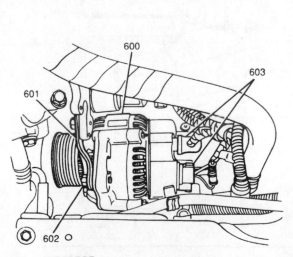

600 GENERATOR
601 GENERATOR MOUNTING BRACKET
602 GENERATOR MOUNTING BRACKET BOLTS
603 GENERATOR ELECTRICAL CONNECTORS

Fig. 8 Alternator mounting — Storm VIN 8 engine

2. Disconnect the positive battery cable from the battery terminal.

3. Remove the hold down retaining nut and/or screw, then remove the retainer from the top of the battery.

4. Carefully lift the battery out of the vehicle and place in a safe location. Be careful not to tilt the battery to more than a 40 degree angle and if the battery is open or cracked, make sure not to spill acid on yourself or the vehicle.

To install:

5. Inspect and, if necessary, clean the battery tray and the battery cables of all corrosion. Make sure the battery and terminals are free of cracks or damage and that the terminals are also free of corrosion.

6. Carefully lower the battery into position in the battery tray. Do not allow the terminals to short to any bare metal during installation.

7. Position the hold down retainer and install the fasteners. Tighten the nut to 72 inch lbs. (8 Nm) and/or screws to 44 inch lbs. (5 Nm).

8. Connect the positive battery cable, then connect the negative battery cable.

Starter

DIAGNOSIS & TESTING

▶ **See Figures 11, 12, 13 and 14**

Before testing the starting system perform a preliminary visual check. Inspect the wiring and connections for the battery cable and the starter solenoid, then check the ignition switch for proper operation. When the switch is turned **ON** the instrument cluster lights should illuminate and accessories such as the radio may be operated. If the accessories do not operate, check the fuse box for a blown ignition fuse.

All vehicles are equipped with a safety switch to prevent the vehicle from being started in gear. This prevents the possibility of sudden and unexpected motion of the vehicle when the ignition switch is turned to **START**. On vehicles equipped with automatic transaxles, the switch prevents the starter from operating unless the transaxle is in **N** or **P**. For vehicles with manual transaxles, a clutch safety switch prevents the starter from operating unless the clutch pedal is depressed.

If a quick visual inspection does not reveal the problem, make sure the safety switch is operating properly and not in need of adjustment. Refer to Section 7 of this manual for more information on these switches.

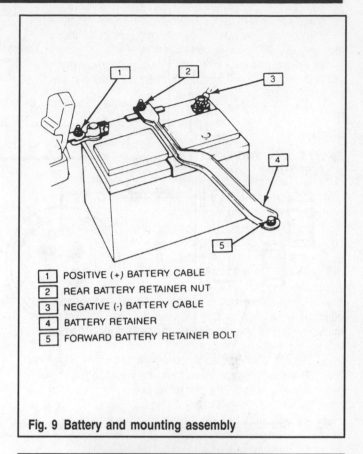

1	POSITIVE (+) BATTERY CABLE
2	REAR BATTERY RETAINER NUT
3	NEGATIVE (-) BATTERY CABLE
4	BATTERY RETAINER
5	FORWARD BATTERY RETAINER BOLT

Fig. 9 Battery and mounting assembly

Fig. 10 Make sure the battery is clean and free of corrosion or acid (as shown) or wear protective gloves when removing the battery from the vehicle

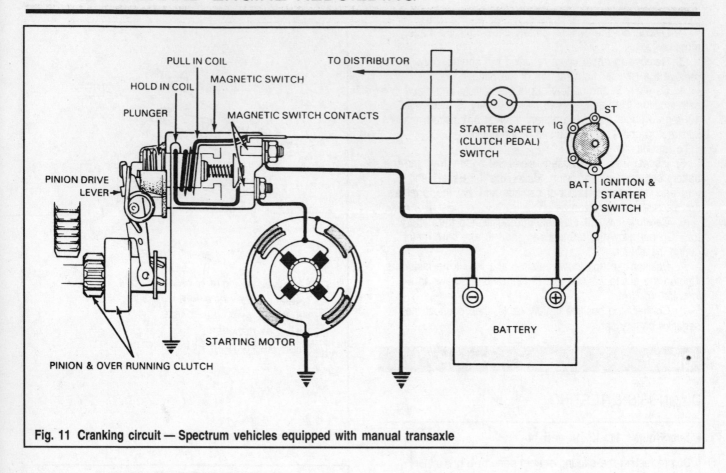

Fig. 11 Cranking circuit — Spectrum vehicles equipped with manual transaxle

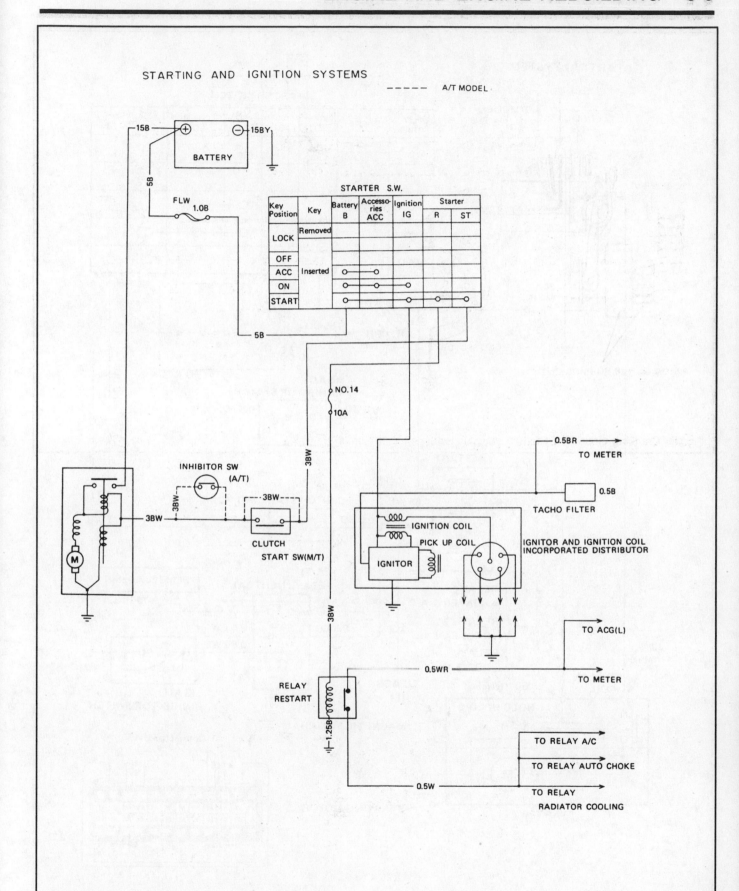

STARTING AND IGNITION SYSTEMS

- - - - - A/T MODEL

STARTER S.W.

Key Position	Key	Battery B	Accessories ACC	Ignition IG	Starter	
					R	ST
LOCK	Removed					
OFF						
ACC	Inserted	o	o			
ON		o	o	o		
START		o		o	o	o

Fig. 12 Ignition circuit — Spectrum

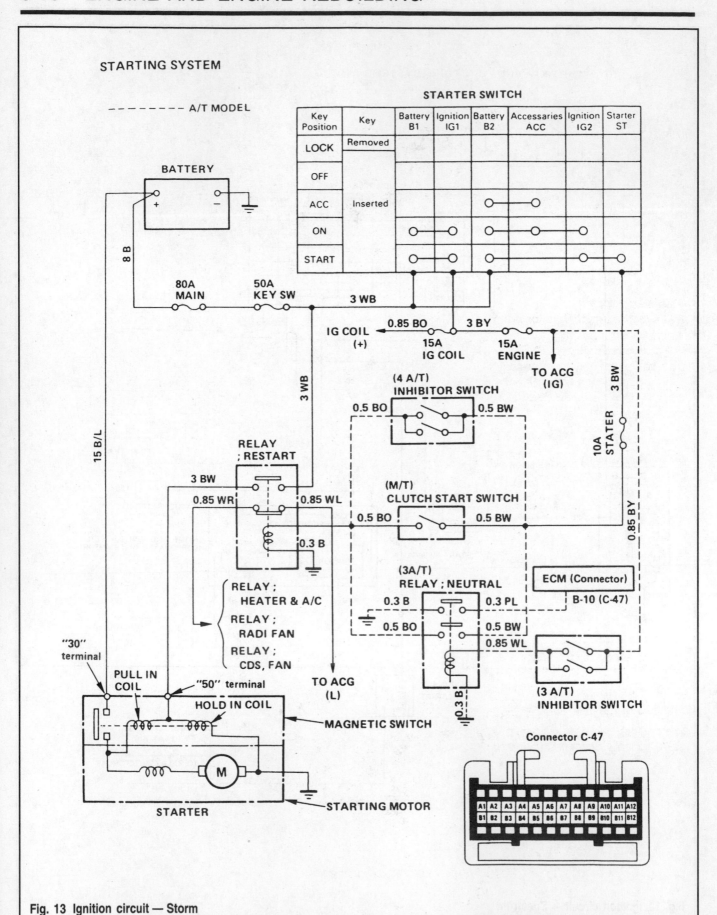

Fig. 13 Ignition circuit — Storm

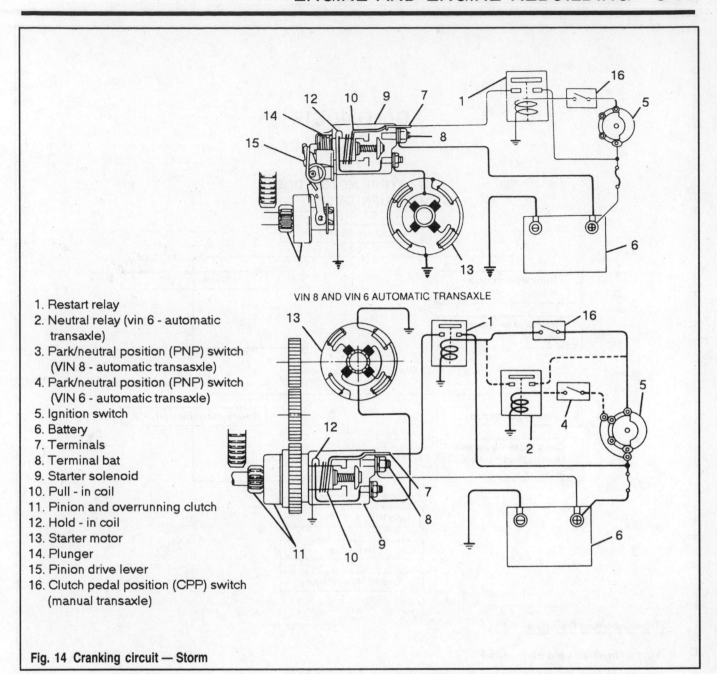

VIN 8 AND VIN 6 AUTOMATIC TRANSAXLE

1. Restart relay
2. Neutral relay (vin 6 - automatic transaxle)
3. Park/neutral position (PNP) switch (VIN 8 - automatic transasxle)
4. Park/neutral position (PNP) switch (VIN 6 - automatic transaxle)
5. Ignition switch
6. Battery
7. Terminals
8. Terminal bat
9. Starter solenoid
10. Pull - in coil
11. Pinion and overrunning clutch
12. Hold - in coil
13. Starter motor
14. Plunger
15. Pinion drive lever
16. Clutch pedal position (CPP) switch (manual transaxle)

Fig. 14 Cranking circuit — Storm

Starting System Diagnostic Charts

The following diagnostic charts may be used to trouble-shoot the Spectrum and Storm engine starting systems. When using the charts for a Storm cranking system, note that terminal C (Spectrum) has been changed to terminal 50 on the Storm circuit diagrams.

DIAGNOSIS

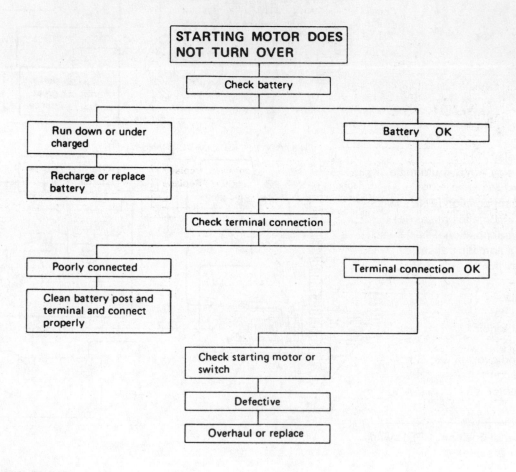

Troubleshooting Procedure

Turn on headlights and starter switch.

Headlights go out or dim considerably.	a) Battery undercharged. b) Starting motor coil circuit shorted. c) Starting motor parts defective.
Headlights stay bright	a) Starting motor circuit open. b) Starting motor coil open. c) Starting switch defective.

Fig. 15 Starting system diagnosis

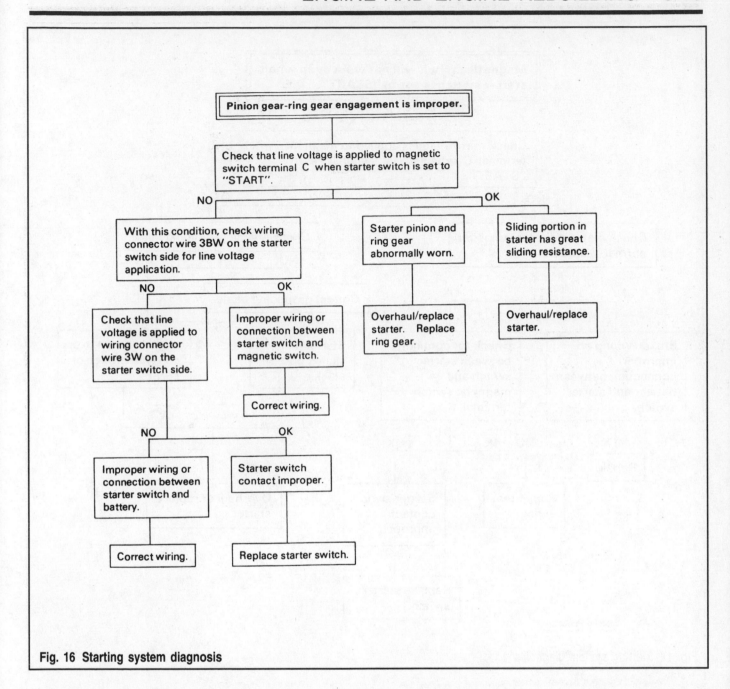

Fig. 16 Starting system diagnosis

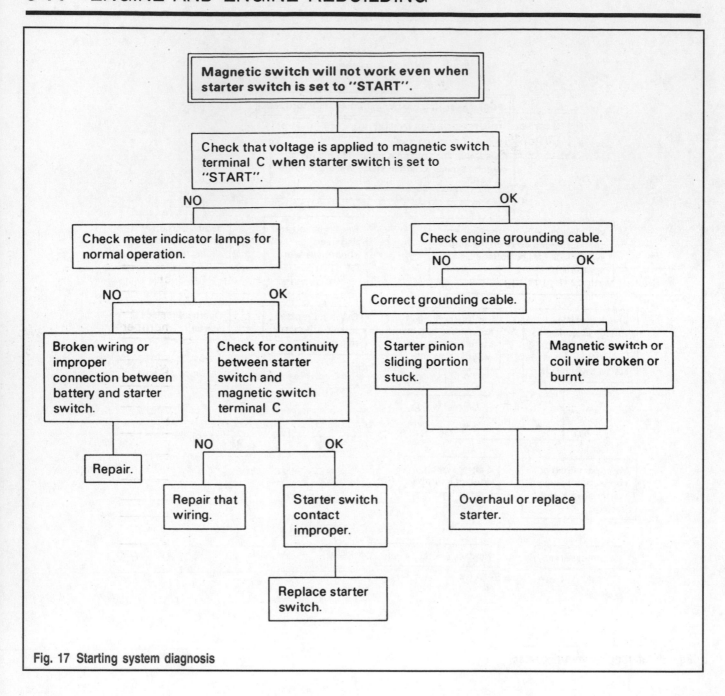

Fig. 17 Starting system diagnosis

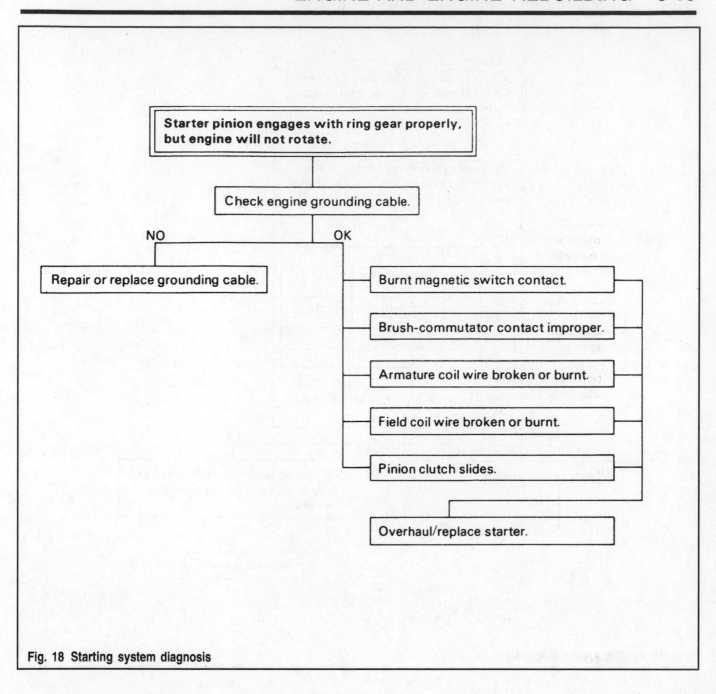

Fig. 18 Starting system diagnosis

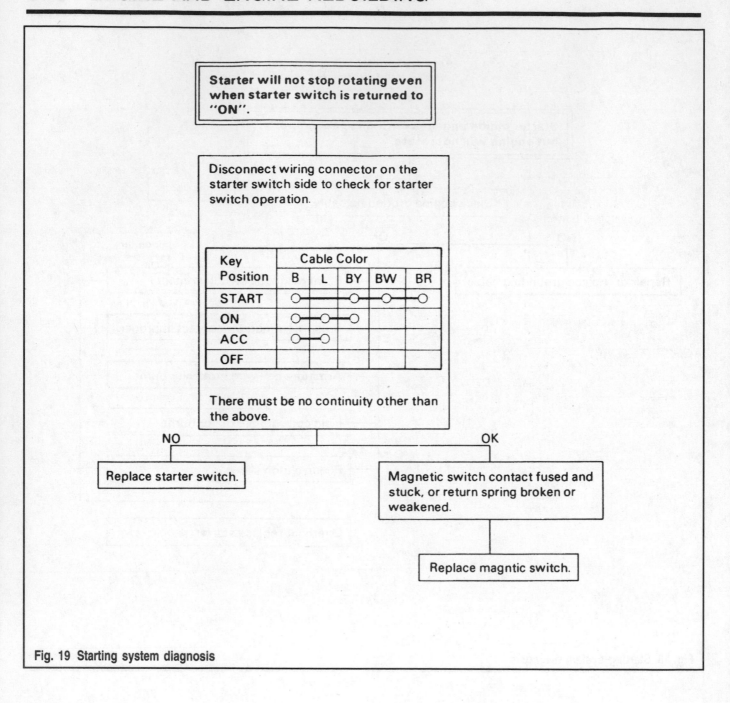

Fig. 19 Starting system diagnosis

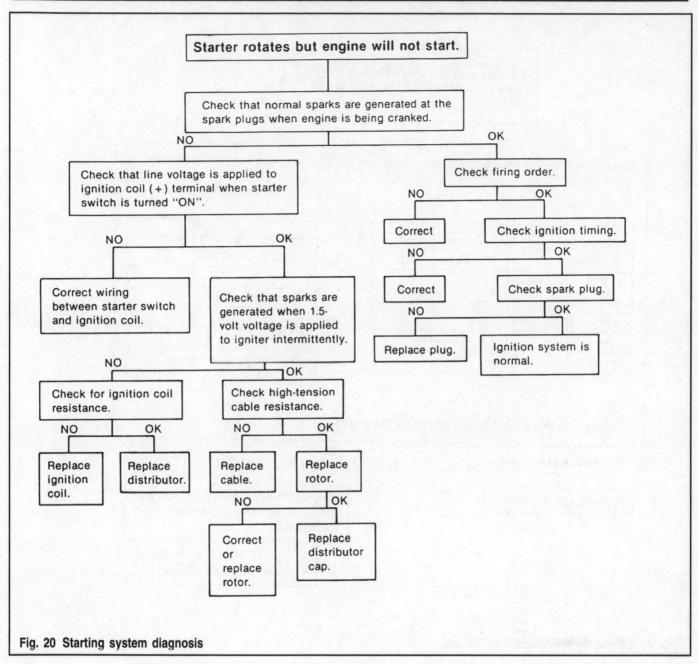

Fig. 20 Starting system diagnosis

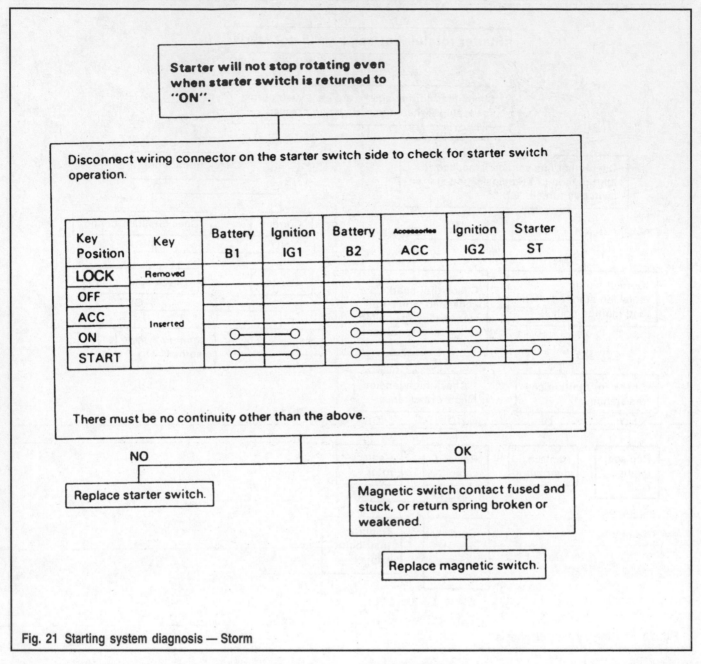

Fig. 21 Starting system diagnosis — Storm

If the diagnostic procedures suggest the problem is in the starter, remove the starter from the vehicle for testing; refer to the procedure found later in this section. The following tests may be performed to determine if the starter is indeed the problem and is in need of repairs or replacement.

❊❊WARNING

In order to protect the starter solenoid coil from damage, limit each of the following tests to 5 seconds or less. Any of the tests may be repeated, as necessary, but leave a few seconds between tests in order to cool the energized coil before applying current again.

PULL-IN TEST

▶ See Figure 22

1. For the Storm, disconnect the field coil lead wire from the starter solenoid.

2. Connect the test leads from the battery as shown in the figure. For the Spectrum, connections should be made at point A.

3. The pinion should extend both quickly and fully. If not, replace the starter solenoid.

HOLD-IN TEST

▶ See Figure 22

1. With the wiring connected as needed for the pull-in test, remove the negative lead from the field coil lead wire terminal.

2. When the negative lead is removed, the pinion should remain in the energized position. A pinion that retracts when

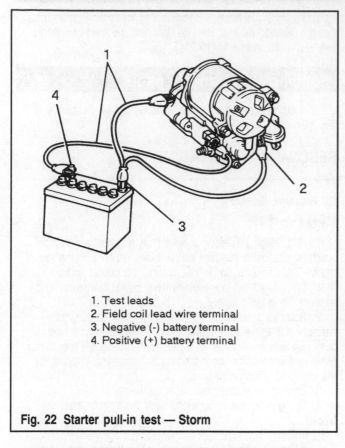

1. Test leads
2. Field coil lead wire terminal
3. Negative (-) battery terminal
4. Positive (+) battery terminal

Fig. 22 Starter pull-in test — Storm

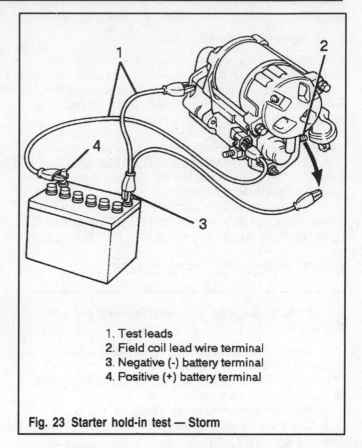

1. Test leads
2. Field coil lead wire terminal
3. Negative (-) battery terminal
4. Positive (+) battery terminal

Fig. 23 Starter hold-in test — Storm

the proper negative test lead is removed indicates a faulty solenoid.

3. If the pinion remained energized, proceed with the Pinion Return Test.

PINION RETURN TEST

▶ See Figure 24

1. Perform the starter hold-in test. Disconnect the negative battery lead from the starter body as shown.

2. The pinion should return quickly and fully to the de-energized position. If the pinion does not perform properly, the cause is likely the starter solenoid return spring. Replace the solenoid and re-test.

3. If the pinion does not perform properly using a new solenoid, the starter must be overhauled or replaced.

REMOVAL & INSTALLATION

Spectrum

1. Disconnect the negative battery cable.

2. Disconnect the ignition switch lead wire and the positive battery cable from the starter motor terminal. Note the position of the wires for installation purposes.

3. Remove the 2 mounting bolts from the starter and carefully remove the starter from the vehicle. Starters tend to be heavy, if working under the vehicle, DO NOT drop it on your head.

4. To install, reverse the removal procedures.

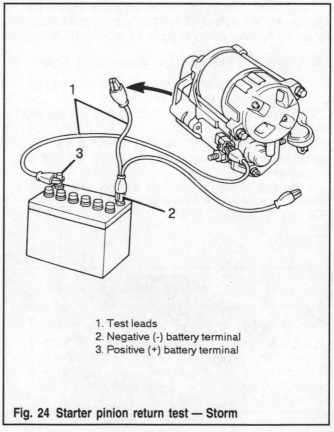

1. Test leads
2. Negative (-) battery terminal
3. Positive (+) battery terminal

Fig. 24 Starter pinion return test — Storm

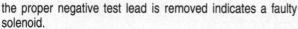

Storm

▶ **See Figure 25**

1. Disconnect the negative battery cable, then raise and support the vehicle safely.

2. Disconnect the positive battery cable and the ignition switch lead from the solenoid terminals. Before removal, note the wire locations for installation purposes.

3. For 1993 vehicles, remove the bolt, nut and frame support bracket from the underbody.

4. Remove the 2 starter-to-engine bolts (1990-1992 vehicles) or the retaining bolt and nut (1993 vehicles), then remove the starter from the vehicle.

5. To install, reverse the removal procedures. Torque the starter retainers to 29 ft. lbs. (39 Nm). For 1993 vehicles, tighten the frame support retainers to 26 ft. lbs. (35 Nm).

STARTER SOLENOID REPLACEMENT

Except 1.6L Engine With Automatic Transaxle and 1.8L Engine

1. Remove the starter from the vehicle, refer to the procedure earlier in this Section.

2. For the Storm, remove the nut and disconnect the field coil lead wire from the solenoid.

3. Remove the solenoid retaining nuts.

4. Carefully separate the solenoid from the pinion drive lever and the drive housing.

5. To install, reverse the removal procedure. Tighten the solenoid retaining nuts to 15 ft. lbs. (20 Nm). For the Storm, tighten the field coil lead wire nut to 89 inch lbs. (10 Nm).

1.6L Engine With Automatic Transaxle and 1.8L Engine

1. Remove the starter from the vehicle, refer to the appropriate procedure earlier in this section.

2. Remove the nut and disconnect the field coil lead wire from the solenoid.

3. Remove the 2 through bolts and the starter mounting bracket, separating the starter motor frame with armature from the solenoid.

4. Remove the starter pinion ball and spring from the solenoid, then remove the driveshaft retainer and pinion clutch gear from the solenoid.

5. To install, reverse the removal procedure. Tighten the through bolts to 80 inch lbs. (9 Nm) and the field coil lead wire nut to 89 inch lbs. (10 Nm).

Sending Units and Sensors

For additional sensors not covered here, see Section 4 of this manual.

REMOVAL & INSTALLATION

Oil Pressure Sensor

▶ **See Figure 26**

The 1.8L engine is equipped with an oil pressure sensor, which is located in the rear of the block, directly to the left of the oil filter. The sensor is just behind the starter motor.

1. Disconnect the negative battery cable, then raise and support the vehicle safely.

2. Remove 1 bolt and 1 nut retaining the starter, then carefully pull the starter motor away from the engine and position aside for access to the sensor. Do not let the starter hang by the electrical connections, if necessary, support the starter using a length of wire.

3. Unplug the sensor electrical connector.

4. Using a socket or wrench, back the sensor from the block.

To install:

5. Wrap the sensor threads with sealing tape, then install the sensor into the block and tighten to 10 ft. lbs. (14 Nm).

6. Install the wiring harness to the sensor connector.

7. Remove the support, then position the starter motor to the engine. If any shims were removed with the starter, make sure they are replaced in their original locations. Install the starter retainers and tighten to 29 ft. lbs. (39 Nm).

8. Remove the supports and carefully lower the vehicle.

9. Connect the negative battery cable and verify proper sensor operation.

Power Steering Pressure Switch

▶ **See Figure 27**

Some Storm models utilize a pressure switch which is mounted to the power steering pump and is designed to monitor hydraulic system pressure. The switch will signal the ECM when pressure becomes to great for the current engine

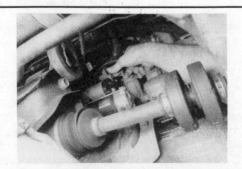

Fig. 25 The starter solenoid wiring is usually protected from moisture and dirt by a rubber boot

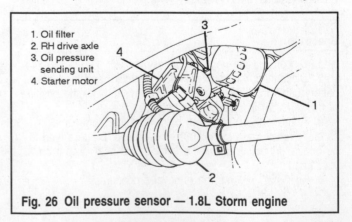

1. Oil filter
2. RH drive axle
3. Oil pressure sending unit
4. Starter motor

Fig. 26 Oil pressure sensor — 1.8L Storm engine

speed. The switch will communicate to the ECM that idle speed must be increased, and if applicable, that the air conditioning compressor must be temporarily be shut OFF, to compensate for the high power steering pump load. This action will help protect the engine from overloading at low speeds.

1. Disconnect the negative battery cable, then place a drain pan below the vehicle to catch any escaping power steering fluid.

2. For vehicles equipped with V-belts, loosen the power steering pump pivot bolt and adjuster bolts, then pivot the steering pump to release belt tension. Remove the belt from the pump pulley, then remove the pump pivot and adjusting bolts.

3. For the 1.8L engine, use a ⅜ in. drive socket wrench to rotate the tensioner pulley clockwise, releasing tension from the serpentine belt, then remove the belt from the pump pulley. Remove the 3 bolts retaining the power steering pump.

4. Position the pump for access to the pressure switch, but be careful not to kink or damage the fluid lines.

5. Unplug the switch electrical connector, then back the switch out from the pump assembly.

To install:

6. Install the switch into the pump and tighten to 124 inch lbs. (14 Nm). Connect the wiring harness to the switch, then reposition the power steering pump to the bracket.

7. For the 1.8L engine, install the 3 retaining bolts and tighten to 15 ft. lbs. (20 Nm). Loosen the serpentine belt by

pivoting the tensioner using a ratchet and reposition the belt over the pump pulley. Make sure the belt is properly routed and seated in all its pulleys, then carefully rotate the tensioner back into contact with the belt.

8. For vehicles equipped with V-belts, install the pump retainers, but do not tighten fully. Position the belt over the pulley and properly adjust belt tension; refer to Section 1 of this manual. Once the belt has been properly tensioned, tighten the pivot and adjuster bolts to 11 ft. lbs. (15 Nm).

9. Connect the negative battery cable and remove the drain pan, then properly bleed the power steering system, refer to Section 8 of this manual.

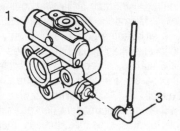

1. Power steering pump assembly
2. Power steering fluid pressure switch
3. Power steering fluid pressure switch electrical connector

Fig. 27 Power steering hydraulic pressure switch — Storm

ENGINE MECHANICAL

Engine Overhaul Tips

Most engine overhaul procedures are fairly standard. In addition to specific parts replacement procedures and complete specifications for your individual engine, this section also is a guide to accepted rebuilding procedures. Examples of standard rebuilding practice are shown and should be used along with specific details concerning your particular engine.

Competent and accurate machine shop services will ensure maximum performance, reliability and engine life. In most instances it is more profitable for the do-it-yourself mechanic to remove, clean and inspect the component, buy the necessary parts and deliver these to a shop for actual machine work.

On the other hand, much of the rebuilding work (crankshaft, block, bearings, piston, rods, and other components) is still within the scope of the do-it-yourself mechanic.

TOOLS

The tools required for an engine overhaul or parts replacement will depend on the depth of your involvement. With a few exceptions, they will be the tools found in a mechanic's tool kit (see Section 1). More in-depth work will require any or all of the following:
• Dial indicator (reading in thousandths) mounted on a universal base.
• Micrometers and telescope gauges.
• Jaw and screw-type pullers.

• Scraper.
• Valve spring compressor.
• Ring groove cleaner.
• Piston ring expander and compressor.
• Ridge reamer.
• Cylinder hone or glaze breaker.
• Plastigage®.
• Engine stand.

The use of most of these tools is illustrated in this section. Many can be rented for a one-time use from a local parts jobber or tool supply house specializing in automotive work.

Occasionally, the use of special tools is called for. See the information on Special Tools and the Safety Notice in the front of this book before substituting another tool.

INSPECTION TECHNIQUES

Procedures and specifications are given in this section for inspecting, cleaning and assessing the wear limits of most major components. Other procedures such as Magnaflux® and Zyglo® can be used to locate material flaws and stress cracks. Magnaflux® is a magnetic process applicable only to ferrous materials. The Zyglo® process coats the material with a fluorescent dye penetrant and can be used on any material. A check for suspected surface cracks can be more readily made using spot check dye. The dye is sprayed onto the suspected area, wiped off and area sprayed with a developer. Cracks will show up brightly.

OVERHAUL TIPS

Aluminum has become extremely popular for use in engines, due to its low weight. Observe the following precautions when handling aluminum parts:

Never hot tank aluminum parts (the caustic hot-tank solution will eat the aluminum).

Remove all aluminum parts (identification tag, etc.) from engine parts prior to hot-tanking.

Always coat threads lightly with engine oil or anti-seize compounds before installation, to prevent seizure.

Never over-torque bolts or spark plugs, especially in aluminum threads. Stripped threads in any component can be repaired using any of several commercial repair kits (Heli-Coil®, Microdot®, Keenserts®, etc..)

When assembling the engine, any parts that will be in frictional contact must be pre-lubed to provide lubrication at initial startup. Any product specifically formulated for this purpose can be used, but engine oil is not recommended as a pre-lube.

When semi-permanent (locked, but removable) installation of bolts or nuts is desired, threads should be cleaned and coated with Loctite® or other similar, commercial non-hardening sealant.

REPAIRING DAMAGED THREADS

▶ **See Figures 28, 29, 30, 31 and 32**

Several methods of repairing damaged threads are available. Heli-Coil® (shown here), Keenserts® and Microdot® are among the most widely used. All involve basically the same principle — drilling out stripped threads, tapping the hole and installing pre-wound insert — making welding, plugging and oversize fasteners unnecessary.

Two types of thread repair inserts are usually supplied: a standard type for most Inch Coarse, Inch Fine, Metric Coarse and Metric Fine thread sizes and a spark plug type to fit most spark plug port sizes. Consult the individual manufacturer's catalog to determine exact applications. Typical thread repair kits will contain a selection of pre-wound threaded inserts, a tap (corresponding to the outside diameter threads of the insert) and an installation tool. Spark plug inserts usually differ because they require a tap equipped with pilot threads and combined reamer/tap section. Most manufacturers also supply blister-packed thread repair inserts separately in addition to a master kit containing a variety of taps and inserts plus installation tools.

Before effecting a repair to a threaded hole, remove any snapped, broken or damaged bolts or studs. Penetrating oil can be used to free frozen threads; the offending item can be removed with locking pliers or with a screw or stud extractor. After the hole is clear, the thread can be repaired, as shown in the illustrations.

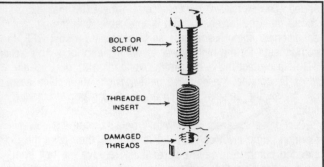

Fig. 28 Damaged bolt hole threads can be replaced with repair thread inserts

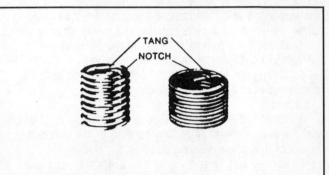

Fig. 29 Standard thread repair insert (left), and spark plug thread insert

Fig. 30 Drill out the damaged threads using the specified size drill. Drill completely through the hole or to the bottom of a blind hole

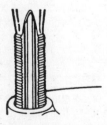

Fig. 31 Using the tap supplied, tap the hole to receive the thread insert. Keep the tap well oiled and back it out frequently to avoid clogging the threads

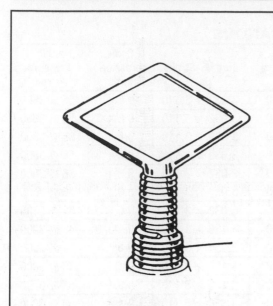

Fig. 32 Screw the threaded insert onto the installer tool until the tang engages the slot. Screw the insert into the tapped hole until it is ¼ or ½ turn below the top surface. After installation break off the tang using a hammer and punch

CHECKING ENGINE COMPRESSION

▶ See Figure 33

A noticeable lack of engine power, excessive oil consumption and/or poor fuel mileage measured over an extended period are all indicators of internal engine wear. Worn piston rings, scored or worn cylinder inserts, blown head gaskets, sticking or burnt valves and worn valve seats are all possible culprits here. A check of each cylinder's compression will help you locate the problems.

As mentioned earlier, a screw-in type compression gauge is more accurate than the type you simply hold against the spark plug hole. Although it takes slightly longer to use, it's worth it to obtain a more accurate reading. Check engine compression as follows:

1. Warm up the engine to normal operating temperature, the stop the engine and turn the ignition **OFF**.

2. Blow dirt from the top of the rocker/camshaft cover to protect the combustion chambers, then remove all spark plugs.

3. Disconnect the wiring harness and connectors from the distributor.

4. For the Storm, unplug the cold start injector and fuel injector connections.

5. Screw the compression gauge into the No. 1 spark plug hole until the fitting is snug.

➡**Be careful not to crossthread the plug hole. On aluminum cylinder heads use extra care, as the threads in these heads are easily ruined.**

6. Ask an assistant to depress the clutch pedal fully, if equipped with a manual transaxle (this will lighted the engine load) and depress the accelerator pedal fully (to the wide open throttle position). Then, while you read the compression gauge, ask the assistant to crank the engine two or three times in short bursts using the ignition switch.

7. Read the compression gauge at the end of each series of cranks, and record the highest of these readings. Repeat this procedure for each of the engine's cylinders. Compare the highest reading to the reading in each cylinder.

8. A cylinder's compression pressure is usually acceptable if it is not less than 80% of the highest reading. For example, if the highest reading is 150 psi, the lowest should be no lower than 120 psi. No cylinder should have a reading below 100 psi. The Spectrum engines should show readings of 128-179 psi (883-1226 kPa). The Storm 1.6L engine should have compression pressure of about 142-191 psi (979-1317 kPa) while the 1.8L engine should read about 170 psi (1177 kPa).

9. If a cylinder is unusually low, pour a tablespoon of clean engine oil into the cylinder through the spark plug hole and repeat the compression test. If the compression comes up after adding the oil, it is likely that the cylinder's piston rings and/or insert are damaged or worn. If the pressure remains low, the valves may not be seating properly (a valve job is needed), or the head gasket may be blown near that cylinder. If compression in any two adjacent cylinders is low, and if the addition of oil doesn't help the compression, there is leakage past the head gasket. Oil and coolant water in the combustion chamber can result from this problem. There may be evidence of water droplets on the engine dipstick when a head gasket has blown.

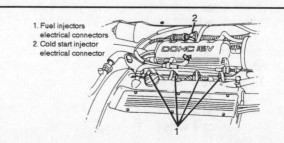

1. Fuel injectors electrical connectors
2. Cold start injector electrical connector

Fig. 33 For the Storm, be sure the cold start injector and all of the fuel injector connectors are removed before checking compression — 1.8L engine shown (1.6L engine similar)

GENERAL ENGINE SPECIFICATIONS

Year	Engine ID/VIN	Engine Displacement Liters (cc)	Fuel System Type	Net Horsepower @ rpm	Net Torque @ rpm (ft. lbs.)	Bore × Stroke (in.)	Compression Ratio	Oil Pressure @ rpm
1985	7	1.5 (1472)	2 bbl	70 @ 5400	87 @ 3400	3.032 × 3.110	9.6:1	56 @ 3800
1986	7	1.5 (1472)	2 bbl	70 @ 5400	87 @ 3400	3.032 × 3.110	9.6:1	56 @ 3800
1987	7	1.5 (1472)	2 bbl	70 @ 5400	87 @ 3400	3.032 × 3.110	9.6:1	56 @ 3800
	9	1.5 (1472)	MFI Turbo	110 @ 5400	120 @ 3400	3.032 × 3.110	8.0:1	56 @ 3800
1988	7	1.5 (1472)	2 bbl	70 @ 5400	87 @ 3400	3.032 × 3.110	9.6:1	56 @ 3800
	9	1.5 (1472)	MFI Turbo	110 @ 5400	120 @ 3400	3.032 × 3.110	8.0:1	56 @ 3800
1989	7	1.5 (1472)	2 bbl	70 @ 5400	87 @ 3400	3.032 × 3.110	9.6:1	56 @ 3800
1990	6	1.6 (1588)	MFI	95 @ 5800	97 @ 4800	3.150 × 3.110	9.1:1	43 @ 3000
	5	1.6 (1588)	MFI	130 @ 7000	102 @ 5800	3.150 × 3.110	9.8:1	51 @ 3000
1991	6	1.6 (1588)	MFI	95 @ 5800	97 @ 4800	3.150 × 3.110	9.1:1	43 @ 3000
	5	1.6 (1588)	MFI	130 @ 7000	102 @ 5800	3.150 × 3.110	9.8:1	51 @ 3000
1992	6	1.6 (1588)	MFI	95 @ 5800	97 @ 4800	3.150 × 3.110	9.1:1	58 @ 3000
	8	1.8 (1810)	MFI	140 @ 6400	120 @ 4600	3.150 × 3.540	9.7:1	71 @ 3000
1993	6	1.6 (1588)	MFI	95 @ 5800	97 @ 4800	3.150 × 3.110	9.1:1	58 @ 3000
	8	1.8 (1810)	MFI	140 @ 6400	120 @ 4600	3.150 × 3.540	9.7:1	71 @ 3000

NOTE: Horsepower and torque are SAE net figures. They are measured at the rear of the transmission with all accessories installed and operating. Since the figures vary when a given engine is installed in different models, some are representative rather than exact.

2 bbl—2 Barrel Carburetor
MFI—Multi-Port Fuel Injection

VALVE SPECIFICATIONS

Year	Engine ID/VIN	Engine Displacement Liters (cc)	Seat Angle (deg.)	Face Angle (deg.)	Spring Test Pressure (lbs. @ in.)	Spring Installed Height (in.)	Stem-to-Guide Clearance (in.) Intake	Exhaust	Stem Diameter (in.) Intake	Exhaust
1985	7	1.5 (1472)	45	45	47 @ 1.57	1.57	0.0009–0.0022	0.0012–0.0025	0.2740–0.2750	0.2740–0.2744
1986	7	1.5 (1472)	45	45	47 @ 1.57	1.57	0.0009–0.0022	0.0012–0.0025	0.2740–0.2750	0.2740–0.2744
1987	7	1.5 (1472)	45	45	47 @ 1.57	1.57	0.0009–0.0022	0.0012–0.0025	0.2740–0.2750	0.2740–0.2744
	9	1.5 (1472)	45	45	47 @ 1.57	1.57	0.0009–0.0022	0.0012–0.0025	0.2740–0.2750	0.2740–0.2744
1988	7	1.5 (1472)	45	45	47 @ 1.57	1.57	0.0009–0.0022	0.0012–0.0025	0.2740–0.2750	0.2740–0.2744
	9	1.5 (1472)	45	45	47 @ 1.57	1.57	0.0009–0.0022	0.0012–0.0025	0.2740–0.2750	0.2740–0.2744
1989	7	1.5 (1472)	45	45	47 @ 1.57	1.57	0.0009–0.0022	0.0012–0.0025	0.2740–0.2750	0.2740–0.2744
1990	6	1.6 (1588)	45	45.5	—	—	0.0009	0.0012	0.2335	0.2335
	5	1.6 (1588)	45	45.5	—	—	0.0009	0.0012	0.2335	0.2335
1991	6	1.6 (1588)	45	45.5	—	—	0.0009	0.0012	0.2335	0.2335
	5	1.6 (1588)	45	45.5	—	—	0.0009	0.0012	0.2335	0.2335
1992	6	1.6 (1588)	45	45.5	—	—	0.0009	0.0012	0.2335	0.2335
	8	1.8 (1810)	45	45.5	—	—	0.0009	0.0012	0.2320	0.2320
1993	6	1.6 (1588)	45	45.5	—	—	0.0009	0.0012	0.2335	0.2335
	8	1.8 (1810)	45	45.5	—	—	0.0009	0.0012	0.2320	0.2320

CAMSHAFT SPECIFICATIONS

All measurements given in inches.

Year	Engine ID/VIN	Engine Displacement Liters (cc)	Journal Diameter 1	2	3	4	5	Elevation In.	Ex.	Bearing Clearance	Camshaft End Play
1985	7	1.5 (1472)	1.0210–1.0220	1.0210–1.0220	1.0210–1.0220	1.0210–1.0220	1.0210–1.0220	1.426	1.426	0.0024–0.0044	0.0039–0.0071
1986	7	1.5 (1472)	1.0210–1.0220	1.0210–1.0220	1.0210–1.0220	1.0210–1.0220	1.0210–1.0220	1.426	1.426	0.0024–0.0044	0.0039–0.0071
1987	7	1.5 (1472)	1.0210–1.0220	1.0210–1.0220	1.0210–1.0220	1.0210–1.0220	1.0210–1.0220	1.426	1.426	0.0024–0.0044	0.0039–0.0071
	9	1.5 (1472)	1.0210–1.0220	1.0210–1.0220	1.0210–1.0220	1.0210–1.0220	1.0210–1.0220	1.426	1.426	0.0024–0.0044	0.0039–0.0071
1988	7	1.5 (1472)	1.0210–1.0220	1.0210–1.0220	1.0210–1.0220	1.0210–1.0220	1.0210–1.0220	1.426	1.426	0.0024–0.0044	0.0039–0.0071
	9	1.5 (1472)	1.0210–1.0220	1.0210–1.0220	1.0210–1.0220	1.0210–1.0220	1.0210–1.0220	1.426	1.426	0.0024–0.0044	0.0039–0.0071
1989	7	1.5 (1472)	1.0210–1.0220	1.0210–1.0220	1.0210–1.0220	1.0210–1.0220	1.0210–1.0220	1.426	1.426	0.0024–0.0044	0.0039–0.0071
1990	6	1.6 (1588)	1.0157	1.0157	1.0157	1.0157	1.0157	1.426	1.426	0.0059	0.0080
	5	1.6 (1588)	1.0157	1.0157	1.0157	1.0157	1.0157	1.503	1.503	0.0059	0.0080
1991	6	1.6 (1588)	1.0157	1.0157	1.0157	1.0157	1.0157	1.426	1.426	0.0059	0.0080
	5	1.6 (1588)	1.0157	1.0157	1.0157	1.0157	1.0157	1.503	1.503	0.0059	0.0080
1992	6	1.6 (1588)	1.0157	1.0157	1.0157	1.0157	1.0157	1.426	1.426	0.0059	0.0080
	8	1.8 (1810)	1.0157	1.0157	1.0157	1.0157	1.0157	1.531	1.531	0.0059	0.0080
1993	6	1.6 (1588)	1.0157	1.0157	1.0157	1.0157	1.0157	1.399	1.413	0.0059	0.0080
	8	1.8 (1810)	1.0157	1.0157	1.0157	1.0157	1.0157	1.531	1.531	0.0059	0.0080

CRANKSHAFT AND CONNECTING ROD SPECIFICATIONS
All measurements are given in inches.

Year	Engine ID/VIN	Engine Displacement Liters (cc)	Crankshaft				Connecting Rod		
			Main Brg. Journal Dia.	Main Brg. Oil Clearance	Shaft End-play	Thrust on No.	Journal Diameter	Oil Clearance	Side Clearance
1985	7	1.5 (1472)	1.8865–1.8873	0.0008–0.0020	0.0024–0.0095	2	1.5720–1.5726	0.0010–0.0034	0.0079–0.0138
1986	7	1.5 (1472)	1.8865–1.8873	0.0008–0.0020	0.0024–0.0095	2	1.5720–1.5726	0.0010–0.0034	0.0079–0.0138
1987	7	1.5 (1472)	1.8865–1.8873	0.0008–0.0020	0.0024–0.0095	2	1.5720–1.5726	0.0010–0.0034	0.0079–0.0138
	9	1.5 (1472)	1.8865–1.8873	0.0008–0.0020	0.0024–0.0095	2	1.5720–1.5726	0.0010–0.0034	0.0079–0.0138
1988	7	1.5 (1472)	1.8865–1.8873	0.0008–0.0020	0.0024–0.0095	2	1.5720–1.5726	0.0010–0.0034	0.0079–0.0138
	9	1.5 (1472)	1.8865–1.8873	0.0008–0.0020	0.0024–0.0095	2	1.5720–1.5726	0.0010–0.0034	0.0079–0.0138
1989	7	1.5 (1472)	1.8865–1.8873	0.0008–0.0020	0.0024–0.0095	2	1.5720–1.5726	0.0010–0.0034	0.0079–0.0138
1990	6	1.6 (1588)	2.0440–2.0448	0.0008–0.0020	0.0024–0.0095	2	1.5724–1.5728	0.0008–0.0019	0.0079–0.0138
	5	1.6 (1588)	2.0440–2.0448	0.0008–0.0020	0.0024–0.0095	2	1.5722–1.5728	0.0010–0.0034	0.0079–0.0138
1991	6	1.6 (1588)	2.0440–2.0448	0.0008–0.0020	0.0024–0.0095	2	1.5724–1.5728	0.0008–0.0019	0.0079–0.0138
	5	1.6 (1588)	2.0440–2.0448	0.0008–0.0020	0.0024–0.0095	2	1.5722–1.5728	0.0010–0.0034	0.0079–0.0138
1992	6	1.6 (1588)	2.0440–2.0448	0.0008–0.0020	0.0024–0.0095	2	1.5724–1.5728	0.0008–0.0019	0.0079–0.0138
	8	1.8 (1810)	2.0440–2.0448	0.0008–0.0020	0.0024–0.0095	2	1.8083–1.8089	0.0010–0.0023	0.0079–0.0138
1993	6	1.6 (1588)	2.0440–2.0448	0.0008–0.0020	0.0024–0.0095	2	1.5724–1.5728	0.0008–0.0019	0.0079–0.0138
	8	1.8 (1810)	2.0440–2.0448	0.0008–0.0020	0.0024–0.0095	2	1.8083–1.8089	0.0010–0.0023	0.0079–0.0138

PISTON AND RING SPECIFICATIONS

All measurements are given in inches.

Year	Engine ID/VIN	Engine Displacement Liters (cc)	Piston Clearance	Ring Gap			Ring Side Clearance		
				Top Compression	Bottom Compression	Oil Control	Top Compression	Bottom Compression	Oil Control
1985	7	1.5 (1472)	0.0011–0.0019	0.0098–0.0138	—	0.0039–0.0236	0.0010–0.0026	—	—
1986	7	1.5 (1472)	0.0011–0.0019	0.0098–0.0138	—	0.0039–0.0236	0.0010–0.0026	—	—
1987	7	1.5 (1472)	0.0011–0.0019	0.0098–0.0138	—	0.0039–0.0236	0.0010–0.0026	—	—
	9	1.5 (1472)	0.0011–0.0019	0.0098–0.0138	—	0.0039–0.0236	0.0010–0.0026	—	—
1988	7	1.5 (1472)	0.0011–0.0019	0.0098–0.0138	—	0.0039–0.0236	0.0010–0.0026	—	—
	9	1.5 (1472)	0.0011–0.0019	0.0098–0.0138	—	0.0039–0.0236	0.0010–0.0026	—	—
1989	7	1.5 (1472)	0.0011–0.0019	0.0098–0.0138	—	0.0039–0.0236	0.0010–0.0026	—	—
1990	6	1.6 (1588)	0.0011–0.0019	0.0110–0.0157	0.0177–0.0236	0.0039–0.0236	0.0012–0.0032	0.0008–0.0024	—
	5	1.6 (1588)	0.0019–0.0027	0.0110–0.0157	0.0177–0.0236	0.0039–0.0236	0.0012–0.0032	0.0008–0.0024	—
1991	6	1.6 (1588)	0.0011–0.0019	0.0110–0.0157	0.0177–0.0236	0.0039–0.0236	0.0012–0.0032	0.0008–0.0024	—
	5	1.6 (1588)	0.0019–0.0027	0.0110–0.0157	0.0177–0.0236	0.0039–0.0236	0.0012–0.0032	0.0008–0.0024	—
1992	6	1.6 (1588)	0.0011–0.0019	0.0110–0.0157	0.0177–0.0236	0.0039–0.0236	0.0012–0.0032	0.0008–0.0024	—
	8	1.8 (1810)	0.0019–0.0027	0.0110–0.0157	0.0177–0.0236	0.0039–0.0236	0.0018–0.0032	0.0008–0.0024	—
1993	6	1.6 (1588)	0.0011–0.0019	0.0110–0.0157	0.0177–0.0236	0.0039–0.0236	0.0012–0.0032	0.0008–0.0024	—
	8	1.8 (1810)	0.0019–0.0027	0.0110–0.0157	0.0177–0.0236	0.0039–0.0236	0.0018–0.0032	0.0008–0.0024	—

TORQUE SPECIFICATIONS
All readings in ft. lbs.

Year	Engine ID/VIN	Engine Displacement Liters (cc)	Cylinder Head Bolts	Main Bearing Bolts	Rod Bearing Bolts	Crankshaft Damper Bolts	Flywheel Bolts	Manifold Intake	Manifold Exhaust	Spark Plugs	Lug Nut
1985	7	1.5 (1472)	①	65	25	108	22	17	17	14	65
1986	7	1.5 (1472)	①	65	25	108	22	17	17	14	65
1987	7	1.5 (1472)	①	65	25	108	22	17	17	14	65
	9	1.5 (1472)	①	65	25	108	22	17	17	14	65
1988	7	1.5 (1472)	①	65	25	108	22	17	17	14	65
	9	1.5 (1472)	①	65	25	108	22	17	17	14	65
1989	7	1.5 (1472)	①	65	25	108	22	17	17	14	65
1990	6	1.6 (1588)	①	44	36	87	47②	17	30	14	76
	5	1.6 (1588)	①	44	36	87	47②	17	30	14	76
1991	6	1.6 (1588)	①	44	11③	87	22③	17	30	14	76
	5	1.6 (1588)	①	44	11③	87	22③	17	30	14	76
1992	6	1.6 (1588)	①	44	11③	87	22③	17	30	14	87
	8	1.8 (1810)	①	65	18⑤	108	22	17	29④	14	87
1993	6	1.6 (1588)	①	44	11③	87	22③	17	30	14	87
	8	1.8 (1810)	①	65	18⑤	108	22	17	29④	14	87

① 1st pass: 29 ft. lbs.
  2nd pass: 58 ft. lbs.
② Specification is for Automatic Transaxle
  Manual Transaxle: 58 ft. lbs.
③ Plus 45-60 degrees
④ Specification is for nuts
  Tighten bolts to 15 ft. lbs.
⑤ Plus 100 degrees

Engine Assembly

REMOVAL & INSTALLATION

Spectrum

1. Remove the hood, relieve the fuel system pressure and disconnect the negative battery cable.
2. Drain the cooling system.
3. If equipped with carburetor, remove the air cleaner and the throttle cable at the carburetor.
4. Disconnect the heater hoses at the intake manifold, the coolant hose at the thermostat housing and the thermostat housing at the cylinder head.
5. Remove the distributor from the cylinder head.
6. Unplug the oxygen sensor electrical connector.
7. Support the engine using a vertical lift to prevent it from dropping suddenly and remove the right motor mount.
8. Disconnect the necessary electrical connectors and vacuum hoses.
9. Disconnect the flex hose at the exhaust manifold and the lower radiator hose at the block.
10. Remove the upper air conditioning compressor bolt and remove the belt.
11. Disconnect the power steering bracket at the block and remove the belt.
12. Disconnect the fuel lines from the fuel pump and the electrical connectors from under the carburetor, if equipped.
13. Remove the upper starter bolt. Raise and support the vehicle safely.
14. Drain the oil from the crankcase and remove the oil filter.

15. Unplug the oil temperature switch connector.

16. Disconnect the exhaust pipe bracket at the block and the exhaust pipe at the manifold.

17. Remove the air conditioning compressor and move to one side. Do not disconnect the air conditioning refrigerant lines. Remove the alternator wires.

18. Disconnect the starter wires and remove the starter.

19. Remove the flywheel cover and the converter bolts, then install a flywheel holding tool J-35271 or equivalent.

20. Remove the front right wheel and inner splash shield.

21. Lower the engine by lowering the crossmember enough to gain access to the crankshaft pulley bolts, then remove the pulley.

22. Raise the engine and crossmember. Remove the engine support.

23. Lower the vehicle and support the transaxle.

24. Remove the transaxle to engine bolts. Remove the engine. Lift the engine only partly out at first and check to make sure that all wires and hoses are free of the engine or vehicle before proceeding.

To install:

25. Carefully lower the engine into position and secure using the transaxle bolts.

26. Remove the transaxle support, then raise and support the vehicle safely.

27. Install the engine support. If necessary, raise the engine and crossmember slightly for access.

28. Lower the engine sufficiently to install the crankshaft pulley and retaining bolts.

29. Install the right front splash shield and wheel.

30. If installed, remove the flywheel holding tool, then install the converter bolts and flywheel cover.

31. Connect the wiring and install the starter motor.

32. Reconnect the alternator wiring, then reposition the A/C compressor and secure using the fasteners. Make sure the refrigerant lines have not been damaged.

33. Connect the exhaust pipe to the manifold and the bracket to the block.

34. Install the wiring harness connector to the oil temperature switch.

35. Install a new oil filter, then lower the vehicle and immediately fill the engine crankcase. It is too easy to forget the oil at the end of the procedure and risk severe engine damage.

36. If not done already, install the upper starter bolt.

37. If equipped, install the electrical connectors under the carburetor, then connect the fuel lines to the pump.

38. Connect the power steering bracket and install the belt.

39. Install the belt and the upper A/C compressor bolt.

40. Connect the lower radiator hose to the block, then connect the flex hose to the exhaust manifold.

41. Install all electrical connectors and vacuum hoses, as tagged during removal.

42. Install the right motor mount, then remove the engine support.

43. Install the wiring harness connector to the oxygen sensor.

44. Install the distributor to the cylinder head.

45. Install the thermostat housing at the cylinder head, then connect the coolant hose to the thermostat housing and the heater hoses to the intake manifold.

46. For carbureted vehicles, connect the throttle cable to the carburetor, then install the air cleaner.

47. Install the hood to the vehicle, then fill then engine cooling system.

48. Connect the negative battery cable.

49. Check and adjust the accessory drive belts.

50. Start the engine and check for leaks. Check all fluids and top-off, as necessary.

Storm

▶ **See Figures 34 and 35**

1.6L ENGINE

1. Properly relieve the fuel system pressure.

2. Disconnect the battery cables, then remove battery and battery tray from vehicle.

3. Scribe match marks between the hood hinge and hood, then remove the hood from the vehicle.

4. Drain cooling system, then disconnect the accelerator cable from the throttle valve.

5. Disconnect the breather hose from the intake air duct, then remove the intake air duct from the throttle valve.

6. Remove the air cleaner cover, filter and the body from the vehicle.

7. Remove the MAP sensor hose from the MAP sensor, then the brake booster vacuum hose.

8. Disconnect the 2 canister hoses from the pipes on the intake manifold (common chamber). If equipped with twincam engine, remove the canister pipe support bracket.

9. Disconnect the 2 cable harness connectors, located near the left shock tower.

10. Disconnect the ignition coil ground cable from the terminal on the thermostat housing flange.

11. Disconnect the ignition coil-to-distributor wire, the 2 primary wires from the ignition coil, then remove the ignition coil and bracket from the vehicle.

12. Disconnect the engine harness ground cable from the left inner fender.

13. Disconnect the harness terminal from the relay and fuse box.

14. Disconnect the cooling fan electrical connector and the 2 battery cable connectors.

15. Disconnect the oxygen sensor electrical connector, then the ground cable terminals from the left front side of the common chamber and/or the rear of the cylinder head cover.

16. If equipped with automatic transaxle, disconnect the electrical connectors from transaxle.

17. If equipped with manual transaxle, loosen the tow adjusting nuts and disconnect the clutch cable. Disconnect the 2 transaxle shaft cables by removing the cotter pin and clip from the shaft cable bracket.

18. If equipped with automatic transaxle, disconnect the shift cable by removing the cotter pin from the shaft cable lever.

19. On all vehicles, remove the 2 heater hoses from the engine.

20. Disconnect the speedometer from the transaxle, then the upper radiator hose from the radiator.

21. Disconnect the fuel feed line and fuel return hose, near the filter, then the coolant recovery tank with bracket.

22. Remove the power steering belt, power steering pump and bracket from the vehicle.

23. Remove the cooling fan and shroud, then raise and support the vehicle safely.

24. Remove the right and left under covers and the lower radiator hose from the engine.

25. If equipped with automatic transaxle, disconnect the oil cooler, lines from the transaxle.

26. Remove the air conditioning compressor bracket bolts and position compressor aside. Be careful not to damage or rupture the compressor lines.

27. Remove the front tire and wheel assemblies, then the halfshafts.

28. Remove the front exhaust pipe from the exhaust manifold.

29. Lower the vehicle and install a suitable engine hoist onto the lifting brackets on the engine.

30. Remove the engine mounts and transaxle mounts, then lift the engine and transaxle assembly out from the vehicle. Lift the assembly only partly out at first and double check to make sure all hoses and wiring are free of the engine or vehicle before proceeding. Separate the transaxle from the engine and place the engine on a suitable stand.

To install:

31. Install the transaxle to the engine, then a suitable hoist onto the engine lifting brackets.

32. Install engine and transaxle into vehicle, then the transaxle mounts and engine mounts.

33. Remove the engine hoist from the vehicle, then raise and support vehicle safely.

34. Install the front exhaust pipe to the exhaust manifold, then the install the halfshafts.

35. Install the tire and wheel assemblies, then the 2 air conditioning bracket mounting bolts.

36. If equipped with automatic transaxle, connect the 2 cooler lines to the transaxle.

37. Install the lower radiator hose, then the right and left undercovers. Lower the vehicle.

38. Install the cooling fan and shroud, then the power steering pump and belt onto the engine.

39. Install the coolant recovery tank with bracket, then connect the fuel feed line and fuel return hose.

40. Install the upper radiator hose, then connect the speedometer cable to the transaxle.

41. Connect the 2 heater hoses to the engine, then the transaxle shift cables, if equipped.

42. If equipped with manual transaxle, connect the clutch cable and adjust.

43. If equipped with automatic transaxle, connect the electrical connectors to the transaxle.

44. Connect the ground cable terminal to the rear of the cylinder head cover.

45. Connect the 2 ground terminals to the right side of the intake manifold (common chamber). If equipped with twincam engine, install the canister pipe support bracket.

46. Connect the oxygen sensor electrical connector and the 2 battery cable harness connectors.

47. Connect the cooling fan harness connector, then the chassis harness terminal connector to the relay and fuse box.

48. Connect the engine ground cable to the left inner fender, then install the ignition coil and bracket.

49. Connect the 2 primary wires to the ignition coil and the ignition coil-to-distributor wire.

50. Connect the ignition coil ground wire to the terminal at the thermostat housing.

51. Connect the 2 cable harness connectors, located near the left shock tower.

52. Connect the 2 canister hoses to the intake manifold (common chamber).

53. Connect the brake booster vacuum hose, then the MAP sensor hose to the MAP sensor.

54. Install the air cleaner body, air cleaner filter and the cover.

55. Connect the air intake duct to the throttle body and the breather hose to the air intake duct.

56. Connect the accelerator cable to the throttle valve.

57. Fill the cooling system, engine oil and transaxle with suitable fluids. Install the battery tray and battery.

58. Align the match marks on the hood hinge scribed during removal, and install the hood. Connect the battery cables. Start the engine and check for leaks.

1.8L ENGINE

1. Properly relieve the fuel system pressure.

2. Disconnect the battery cables, then remove battery and battery tray from vehicle.

3. Scribe match marks between the hood hinge and hood, disconnect the wiper washer hoses and then remove the hood from the vehicle.

4. Drain cooling system, the crankcase oil and the transaxle fluid/oil, then disconnect the accelerator cable from the throttle valve and common chamber.

5. Remove the intake air duct from the air cleaner and the throttle valve.

6. Remove the air cleaner cover, filter and the body from the vehicle.

7. Disconnect all vacuum hoses from the common chamber.

8. Unplug the engine wiring harness-to-chassis wiring harness electrical connectors.

9. Unplug the secondary (coil) wire from the distributor cap and the ground wire from the ignition coil bracket, then remove the 2 screws and position the coil aside.

10. If equipped with an automatic transaxle, disconnect the shift cable by removing the cotter pin, then removing the cable from the shaft cable lever on the transaxle.

11. If equipped with manual transaxle, loosen the 2 adjusting nuts and disconnect the clutch cable. Disconnect the 2 transaxle shift cables by removing the cotter pin and separating the cables from the transaxle.

Fig. 34 When removing the engine, the hood must be removed to provide room for the engine hoist, but it also makes engine compartment access easier throughout the procedure

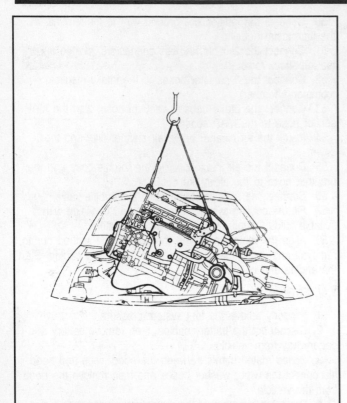

Fig. 35 Carefully raise the engine and transaxle from the vehicle as an assembly — Storm

12. Remove the ground bolt and negative battery cable from the transaxle.

13. If equipped with an automatic transaxle, unplug the 4 electrical connectors from the transaxle.

14. Loosen the hose clamps, then remove the upper and lower radiator hoses from the radiator and the 2 heater hoses from the engine.

15. Disconnect the fuel feed and return pipes near the fuel filter.

16. Disconnect the speedometer cable from the transaxle, then remove the ground bolts and wires from the common chamber.

17. Remove the upper and lower radiator hoses from the engine.

18. Unplug the oxygen sensor and the alternator electrical connectors.

19. If equipped, unplug the A/C compressor electrical connector.

20. Position a drain pan to catch any escaping fluid, then remove the union bolt and the power steering pressure pipe from the pump. Loosen the hose clamp and remove the return hose from the pump.

21. Remove the serpentine drive belt from the engine.

22. Remove the 5 retaining bolts and the heat shield from the exhaust manifold.

23. Remove the 3 mounting bolts and the power steering pump from the bracket. Remove the alternator from the engine.

24. Remove the ground strap from the front of the engine, then remove the cooling fan.

25. If equipped, remove the A/C compressor upper mounting bolt.

26. Install J-28467-A, or an equivalent engine support fixture using a suitable adapter kit, then raise and safely support the vehicle sufficiently for under vehicle access.

27. Remove the left and right splash shields, then if equipped, loosen the hose clamps and disconnect the automatic transaxle fluid cooler lines from the radiator.

28. Remove the A/C compressor lower mounting bolt, then support the compressor aside. Be careful not to kink or rupture the refrigerant lines. Remove the compressor mounting bracket from the engine.

29. Remove the front wheels, then remove the halfshafts.

30. Remove the attaching nuts, then separate the forward exhaust pipe from the exhaust manifold. Remove the forward exhaust pipe bracket.

31. Unplug the starter motor electrical connectors, then remove 1 bolt, 1 nut and the suspension-to-rear engine brace.

32. Remove the rear engine mount through-bolt. Remove the torque rod-to-center crossmember through bolt and nut. Remove the 4 bolts and the center crossmember from the frame.

33. If necessary, remove the supports and lower the vehicle for underhood access. Support the engine/transaxle assembly using a floor jack.

34. Remove the engine support assembly and attach a suitable engine hoist to the lift brackets on the engine, then unclip the wiring harness from the transaxle and position aside.

35. Remove the left transaxle mount. Remove the bolt and nut from the right engine mount bracket. Remove the through bolt and the right engine mount from the vehicle.

36. Carefully lift the engine and transaxle assembly out of the vehicle. Only lift the assembly part way at first and make sure that all wires or hoses are free of the vehicle or engine before proceeding. Remove the assembly from the vehicle.

To install:

37. Connect the hoist to the engine lifting brackets, raise the engine and carefully lower it into position in the vehicle.

38. Install the right engine mount to the vehicle and secure using the through-bolt, but do not fully tighten at this time.

39. Install the bolt and nut to the right engine mount bracket. Tighten the nut and bolt to 30 ft. lbs. (40 Nm), then tighten the through bolt to 50 ft. lbs. (68 Nm).

40. Install the left transaxle mount, then reposition and secure the transaxle wiring harness to the transaxle.

41. Support the engine and transaxle assembly using a floor jack, then remove the engine hoist and chain. Install the engine support assembly.

42. Remove the floor jack, then raise and safely support the vehicle sufficiently for under vehicle access.

43. Install the center crossmember to the frame and tighten the 4 retaining bolts to 45 ft. lbs. (61 Nm). Install the torque rod-to-center crossmember through bolt and nut, tighten the fasteners to 51 ft. lbs. (69 Nm).

44. Install the rear engine mount through bolt and tighten to 37 ft. lbs. (50 Nm). Install the suspension-to-rear engine mount brace, secure using the bolt and nut, then tighten to 15 ft. lbs. (20 Nm).

45. Install the starter motor electrical connections.

46. Install the forward exhaust pipe bracket, then connect the pipe to the exhaust manifold using a new gasket. Tighten the retaining nuts to 29 ft. lbs. (39 Nm).

47. Install the halfshafts, then install the front wheels.

48. If equipped, install the A/C compressor bracket and tighten the retaining bolts to 15 ft. lbs. (20 Nm). Reposition the compressor and tighten the lower mounting bolt to 30 ft. lbs. (40 Nm).

49. If equipped, connect the automatic transaxle fluid cooler lines to the radiator and secure using hose clamps.

50. Install the left and right splash shields, remove the supports and carefully lower the vehicle. Remove the engine support fixture.

51. If equipped, install the A/C compressor upper mounting bolt and tighten to 30 ft. lbs. (40 Nm).

52. Install the cooling fan assembly. Connect the ground strap to the front of the engine.

53. Install the alternator, then install the power steering pump. Tighten the pump mounting bolts to 15 ft. lbs. (20 Nm).

54. Install the heat shield to the exhaust manifold and tighten the retaining bolts to 11 ft. lbs. (15 Nm).

55. Install the serpentine drive belt.

56. Connect the fluid return hose to the power steering pump and secure using a hose clamp. Connect the fluid pressure pipe to the pump and tighten the union bolt to 15 ft. lbs. (20 Nm).

57. If equipped, install the wiring harness to the A/C compressor.

58. Install the alternator and the oxygen sensor electrical connections.

59. Install the upper and lower radiator hoses to the engine using hose clamps.

60. Connect the ground wires to the common chamber and tighten the bolts to 71 inch lbs. (8 Nm).

61. Connect the TP sensor electrical connector, then install the speedometer cable to the transaxle.

62. Connect the fuel feed and return pipes near the fuel filter.

63. Install the 2 heater hoses to the engine and the upper and lower radiator hoses to the radiator. Secure all hoses using clamps.

64. If equipped, install the 4 electrical connectors to the automatic transaxle.

65. Connect the negative battery cable and the transaxle shift cables to the transaxle.

66. If applicable, install and adjust the clutch cable to the manual transaxle.

67. Reposition the ignition coil and secure using the 2 screws. Connect the secondary wire to the distributor cap and the ground wire to the ignition coil bracket.

68. Install the engine wiring harness-to-chassis wiring harness electrical connectors. Connect the vacuum hoses to the common chamber.

69. Install the air cleaner body, filter and element. Connect the air intake duct to the air cleaner and the throttle valve. Connect the accelerator cable to the throttle valve and common chamber.

70. Install the battery tray, then install the battery to the vehicle. Connect only the positive battery cable at this time.

71. Align the marks made earlier and install the hood to the vehicle. Tighten the retaining bolts to 15 ft. lbs. (20 Nm). Connect the washer hoses to the hood.

72. Refill the engine crankcase oil, then connect the negative battery cable.

73. Refill the power steering fluid, the engine coolant and the transaxle fluid/oil.

74. Start the engine and check for leaks.

Valve (Rocker/Camshaft) Cover

REMOVAL & INSTALLATION

Spectrum

▶ See Figures 36, 37 and 38

1. Disconnect the negative battery cable

2. Disconnect the PCV hoses, then remove the spark plug wires from the retaining clip or the clip from the valve cover.

3. Remove the ground wire from the end of the valve cover, near the oil fill.

4. Remove the right side engine mounting rubber and support the engine.

5. Remove the bolts and plate from the side of the engine. Remove the bolt and mounting rubber.

6. Remove the bracket on the timing cover, then remove the 4 bolts securing the timing cover.

7. Remove the 2 valve cover bolts.

8. Loosen the timing cover and remove the valve cover from the cylinder head. If the cover is difficult to remove, loosen it with blows from a rubber mallet to the end of the cover; this should shear it free. A small blunt prytool may also be used to free the cover, but be very careful not to distort the sealing flange.

To install:

9. Thoroughly clean the gasket mating surfaces, making sure that all sealant, gasket material and oils have been completely removed.

10. Apply a coat of TB-1207B, or an equivalent sealant, to the cylinder head mating surface, then apply a thin bead to the arched areas of the No. 1 and No. 5 rocker brackets, as shown in the illustration.

11. Loosen the timing cover sufficiently, then position the valve cover to the cylinder head. Install and tighten the valve cover bolts to 7 ft. lbs. (10 Nm).

12. Make sure the timing cover is properly positioned, then install and tighten the retaining bolts to 7 ft. lbs. (10 Nm).

13. Install the right side engine mount bracket to the timing cover and tighten the retaining bolts to 17 ft. lbs. (23 Nm), then install the mounting rubber.

14. Install the ground wire, the spark plug wires/clip and the connect the PCV hoses.

15. Connect the negative battery cable, start the engine and check for leaks.

Storm

▶ See Figures 39, 40 and 41

1. Disconnect the negative battery cable.

2. Remove the PCV hoses from the valve cover. For the 1.6L DOHC engine, remove the accelerator cable from the 2 cylinder head clips.

3. Remove the spark plug wires from the clips for the SOHC engine or remove the center cover, then tag and disconnect the spark plug wires (from the plugs and clips) for the 1.6L DOHC engine.

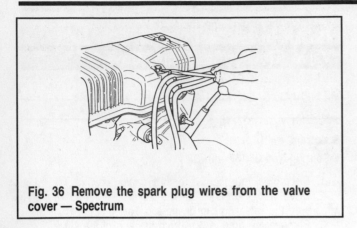

Fig. 36 Remove the spark plug wires from the valve cover — Spectrum

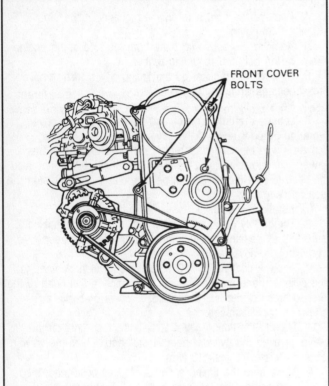

Fig. 37 Remove the 4 timing (front) cover bolts — Spectrum

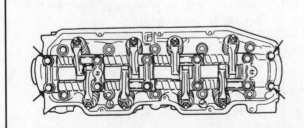

Fig. 38 Place a thin bead of sealant on the No. 1 and No. 5 rocker arches — Spectrum

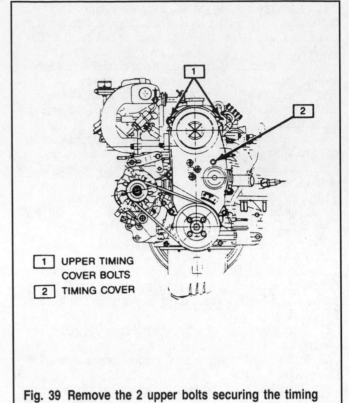

| 1 | UPPER TIMING COVER BOLTS |
| 2 | TIMING COVER |

Fig. 39 Remove the 2 upper bolts securing the timing cover — SOHC engine

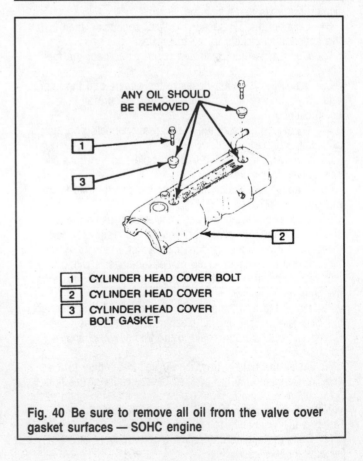

1	CYLINDER HEAD COVER BOLT
2	CYLINDER HEAD COVER
3	CYLINDER HEAD COVER BOLT GASKET

Fig. 40 Be sure to remove all oil from the valve cover gasket surfaces — SOHC engine

4. For the 1.8L engine, remove the 6 retaining screws and the spark plug cover, the tag and disconnect the wires from the spark plugs.

5. For the 1.8L engine, remove the retaining bolt, then reposition the engine wiring harness conduit from the timing belt cover.

6. Remove the 2 top (SOHC engine) or 3 top (1.8L engine) bolts securing the timing cover. For the SOHC engine, loosen but do not remove the lower bolt from the timing cover.

7. Remove the 2 valve cover (SOHC engine) or 12 valve cover (DOHC engines) bolts, then remove the valve cover from the cylinder head. If the cover is difficult to remove, use blows from a rubber mallet on the end of the cover the shear the sealing material and loosen the cover. If the cover must be pried free, be very careful not to damage the sealing surfaces.

To install:

8. Thoroughly clean the gasket mating surfaces, making sure that all sealant, gasket material and oils have been completely removed.

9. Apply a thin bead of GM 1052917, or an equivalent sealant, to the arched areas of the No. 1 and No. 5 camshaft bearing caps.

10. Install the valve cover and tighten the retaining bolts to 89 inch lbs for the SOHC and 1.8L engines or to 29 inch lbs (3 Nm) for the 1.6L DOHC engine.

11. If removed, install and/or tighten the timing cover bolts to 89 inch lbs.

12. For the 1.8L engine, reposition the wiring harness conduit to the timing belt cover and tighten the retaining bolt to 53 inch lbs. (6 Nm).

13. If removed, connect the spark plug wires to the plugs.

14. Fasten the spark plug wires in the retaining clips.

15. For DOHC engines, install the spark plug or center cover.

16. For the 1.6L DOHC engine, install the accelerator cable in the clips.

17. Connect the PCV hoses.

18. Connect the negative battery cable, then start the engine and check for leaks.

1. Cylinder head cover
2. Secondary (spark plug) wires

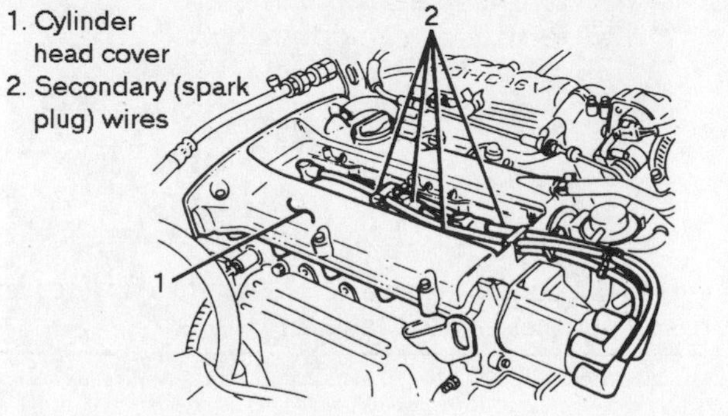

Fig. 41 Valve cover — DOHC engine

Rocker Arms/Shafts

REMOVAL & INSTALLATION

Spectrum

▶ **See Figure 42**

1. Disconnect the negative battery cable.
2. Remove the valve cover from the cylinder head.
3. Remove the rocker arm bracket bolts in sequence, working from both ends equally, toward the middle. Refer to Fig 36.
4. Remove the rocker arm shafts and then the rocker arms from the shafts. Be sure to label or arrange all parts in groups so that they may be reinstalled in their original positions.

To install:

5. Apply a light coat of clean engine oil to the rocker arms/shafts and assemble them for installation.

➡ **The intake and exhaust rocker arm shafts are different from each other, make sure they are installed in the same position that they were removed. Install the rocker arms with the identification marks toward the front of the engine.**

6. Install the rocker arm and shaft assemblies to the cylinder head, making sure the identification marks are facing the front of the engine.
7. Remove oil from the surfaces of the No. 1 and No. 5 (front and rear rocker) brackets, then apply sealant to the bracket and cylinder head mating surfaces of the brackets.
8. Make sure the rocker shaft assemblies are securely mounted on the head dowel pins, then tighten the retaining bolts in the reverse sequence of removal to 16 ft. lbs. (22 Nm).
9. Install the valve cover.
10. Connect the negative battery cable, then start the engine and check for leaks.

Storm

▶ **See Figure 43**

Of the Storm engines, the 1.6L SOHC is the only engine that utilizes rocker arms and shafts.

1. Disconnect the battery negative cable.
2. Remove the valve cover.
3. Remove the rocker arm bracket bolts in the proper sequence, working from both ends equally, toward the middle. Refer to the appropriate illustration.
4. Remove the rocker shaft/arm assembly from the vehicle.
5. Remove the rocker arms from the rocker shaft. Be sure to label or arrange all parts in groups so that they may be reinstalled in their original positions.

To install:

6. Apply a light coat of engine oil to the rocker arms and brackets.
7. Install the rocker arms on the rocker arm shafts.
8. Install the rocker arm shafts on the engine with the ID marks toward the front of the engine.
9. Apply a suitable silicone sealant to the number 1 and number 5 rocker brackets.

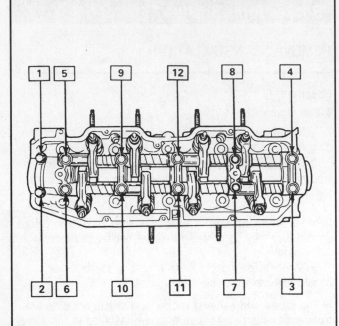

Fig. 42 Rocker arm bracket bolt removal sequence — Spectrum

10. Install the rocker arm brackets. Torque the rocker arm bracket bolts in the reverse sequence of removal to 16 ft. lbs. (22 Nm).

11. Adjust the valves, as necessary, then and install the valve cover.

12. Connect the battery negative cable, then start the engine and check for leaks.

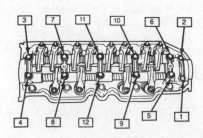

Fig. 43 Rocker arm bracket bolt removal sequence — Storm

Thermostat

REMOVAL & INSTALLATION

Except 1.8L Engine
▶ See Figures 44, 45 and 46

1. Disconnect the battery negative cable and drain cooling system.

2. Remove the top radiator hose from the thermostat housing outlet pipe.

3. Remove the outlet pipe bolts, outlet pipe, gasket and thermostat from the thermostat housing.

4. Reverse procedure to install and tighten the housing bolts to 17 ft. lbs. (24 Nm).

5. Refill cooling system and connect battery negative cable, then start the engine and check for leaks.

1.8L Engine
▶ See Figures 47, 48 and 49

1. Disconnect the negative battery cable, then drain the engine cooling system.

2. Remove the ignition wire from the distributor coil, then remove the distributor cap from the engine for access to the thermostat housing located below the distributor.

3. Loosen the clamp screws, then remove the lower radiator hose from the thermostat housing cap.

4. Loosen the EGR pipe nut at the intake manifold, then remove the EGR pipe bracket from the thermostat housing.

Fig. 44 Thermostat housing assembly — 1.6L engine

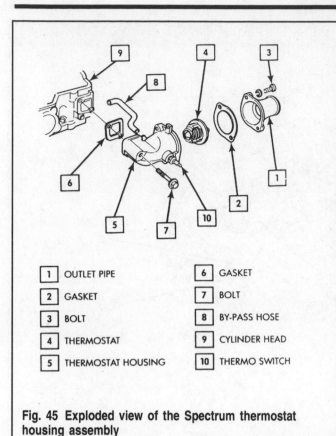

1	OUTLET PIPE		6	GASKET
2	GASKET		7	BOLT
3	BOLT		8	BY-PASS HOSE
4	THERMOSTAT		9	CYLINDER HEAD
5	THERMOSTAT HOUSING		10	THERMO SWITCH

Fig. 45 Exploded view of the Spectrum thermostat housing assembly

Remove the 2 retaining bolts, then remove the EGR pipe from the exhaust manifold.

5. Loosen the clamp, then separate the upper radiator house from the thermostat housing.

6. Remove the 2 short and 1 long thermostat housing cap bolts, then remove the cap and gasket from the housing.

7. Remove the thermostat from the housing.

To install:

8. Install the thermostat into the housing.

9. Position a new cap gasket, then install the cap and tighten the retaining bolts to 18 ft. lbs. (24 Nm).

10. Connect the upper radiator hose to the thermostat housing and secure using a hose clamp.

11. Secure the EGR pipe to the exhaust manifold and tighten the retaining bolts to 18 ft. lbs. (24 Nm). Tighten the EGR pipe-to-intake manifold pipe nut to 32 ft. lbs. (44 Nm). Connect the EGR pipe bracket to the thermostat housing.

12. Connect the lower radiator hose to the thermostat cap and secure using a hose clamp.

13. Install the distributor cap and secure with the cap screws. Connect the ignition wire to the coil.

14. Fill the cooling system.

15. Start the engine and check for leaks.

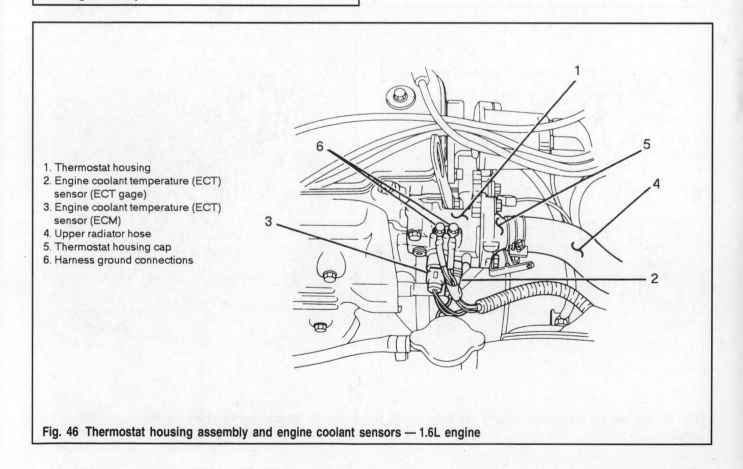

1. Thermostat housing
2. Engine coolant temperature (ECT) sensor (ECT gage)
3. Engine coolant temperature (ECT) sensor (ECM)
4. Upper radiator hose
5. Thermostat housing cap
6. Harness ground connections

Fig. 46 Thermostat housing assembly and engine coolant sensors — 1.6L engine

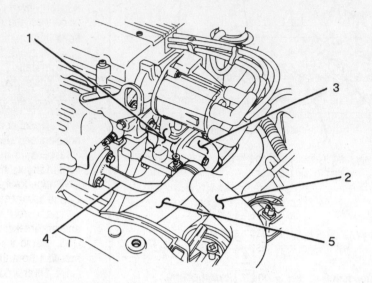

1. Thermostat housing
2. Upper radiator hose
3. Thermostat housing cap
4. Exhaust gas recirculation (EGR) pipe
5. Lower radiator hose

Fig. 47 Thermostat housing assembly — 1.8L engine

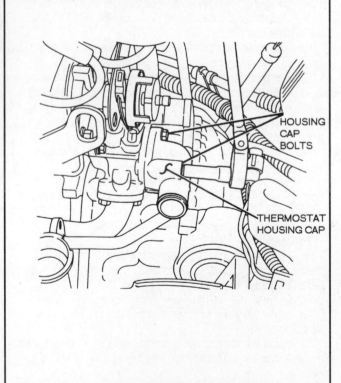

Fig. 48 Remove the thermostat housing cap bolts — 1.8L engine

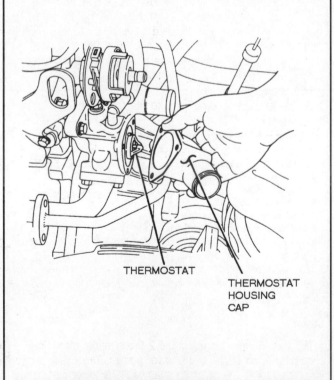

Fig. 49 Remove the cap from the housing to access the thermostat assembly — 1.8L engine

Intake Manifold

REMOVAL & INSTALLATION

Spectrum

▶ See Figure 50

1. Disconnect the negative battery terminal from the battery and drain the cooling system.
2. Remove the bolt securing the alternator adjusting plate to the engine.
3. Disconnect and label all of the hoses attached to the air cleaner and remove the air cleaner.
4. Unplug the intake air temperature switch wiring connector. Remove the clamps for the AI hose, then remove the air cleaner.
5. Disconnect and label the hoses and electrical connectors attached to the carburetor, then disconnect the accelerator control cable
6. If equipped with air conditioning, disconnect the FICD vacuum hose, the pressure tank control valve hose, the distributor 3-way connector hose and the VSV wiring connector.
7. Remove the carburetor attaching bolts, located beneath the intake manifold, then remove the carburetor and the EFE heater.
8. At the intake manifold, remove the PCV hose, the water bypass hose, the heater hoses, the EGR valve/canister hose, the distributor vacuum advance hose and the ground wires.
9. Unplug the thermometer unit switch wiring connector.
10. Remove the intake manifold attaching nuts/bolts and the intake manifold.
11. Thoroughly clean the intake manifold and cylinder head sealing surfaces.

To install:

12. Install the intake manifold to the cylinder head using a new gasket.
13. Tighten the intake manifold fasteners to 17 ft. lbs. (23 Nm).
14. Attach new gaskets to the top and bottom of the EFE heater and install the carburetor.
15. Install the remaining components in the reverse order of removal.
16. Adjust the accelerator control cable.
17. Install the alternator and, if equipped, A/C compressor belts and adjust belt tension.
18. Refill the engine with coolant.
19. Connect the negative battery cable, start the engine and check for leaks.

Storm

The Geo Storm engines utilize 2 piece intake manifolds consisting of an upper and a lower portion. The upper portion is referred to as the common chamber. The lower portion is known as the induction port.

EXCEPT TWINCAM ENGINE

▶ See Figure 51

1. Properly relieve the fuel system pressure, then disconnect the battery negative cable and drain the cooling system.

➡ The cooling system must be drained if the entire manifold assembly, common chamber and induction port, is to be removed. If only the common chamber is being removed, the cooling system may remain filled.

2. Disconnect the ignition coil wire, then remove the accelerator cable from the throttle valve and the common chamber.
3. Unplug the 2 cable harness connectors, located near the left shock tower.
4. Disconnect the cable harness from the Intake Air Temperature (IAT) sensor, the Throttle Position (TP) sensor and the Intake Air Control (IAC) valve.
5. Remove the breather hose from the intake air duct and the duct from the throttle body, then the PCV hose from the valve cover.
6. Tag and disconnect the EGR valve and EVAP canister vacuum hoses from the throttle valve.
7. Disconnect the EGR pipe from the EGR valve and the exhaust manifold.
8. Remove the common chamber bracket bolt, then the throttle body assembly bolts and the throttle body.
9. Remove the coolant bypass pipe clip bolt, then disconnect the MAP sensor from the common chamber.
10. Disconnect the brake booster vacuum hose, then the EVAP canister vacuum hose from the common chamber and the throttle body.
11. Disconnect the pressure regulator vacuum hose from the common chamber, then the EGR vacuum hose.
12. Remove the engine hanger bolt, then remove 2 nuts and 6 bolts attaching the common chamber. Remove the common chamber from the vehicle.
13. Unplug the 2 cable harness connectors from the distributor.
14. Disconnect the fuel feed hose from the engine side and the fuel return hose from the chassis side.
15. Remove the 2 nuts and 8 bolts retaining the induction port to the cylinder, then remove the induction port from the engine.
16. Thoroughly clean all gasket mating surfaces.

To install:

17. Position the induction port to the engine, using a new gasket. Install the port nuts and bolts, then tighten the fasteners to 17 ft. lbs. (23 Nm).
18. Connect the fuel feed and return lines.
19. Install the 2 cable wiring harness connectors to the distributor.
20. Install the common chamber, using a new gasket, onto the induction port. Torque nuts and bolts to 17 ft. lbs. (23 Nm).
21. Install the coolant bypass pipe clip bolts.
22. Install the throttle body with a new gasket. Torque throttle valve bolts to 17 ft. lbs. (23 Nm).
23. Connect the EGR pipe flange to the exhaust manifold. Torque flange bolts to 17 ft. lbs. (23 Nm).

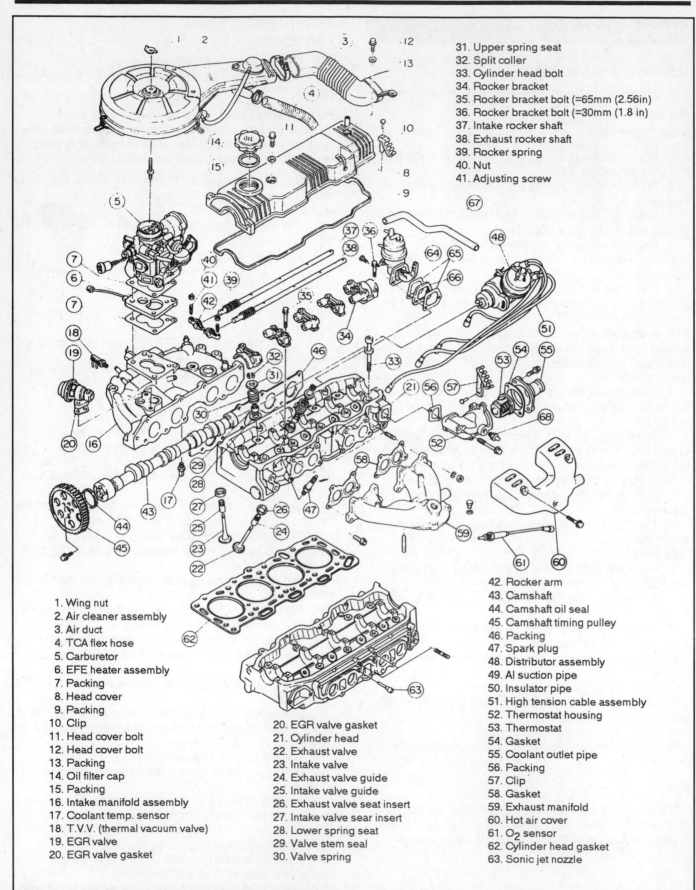

31. Upper spring seat
32. Split coller
33. Cylinder head bolt
34. Rocker bracket
35. Rocker bracket bolt (=65mm (2.56in)
36. Rocker bracket bolt (=30mm (1.8 in)
37. Intake rocker shaft
38. Exhaust rocker shaft
39. Rocker spring
40. Nut
41. Adjusting screw

1. Wing nut
2. Air cleaner assembly
3. Air duct
4. TCA flex hose
5. Carburetor
6. EFE heater assembly
7. Packing
8. Head cover
9. Packing
10. Clip
11. Head cover bolt
12. Head cover bolt
13. Packing
14. Oil filter cap
15. Packing
16. Intake manifold assembly
17. Coolant temp. sensor
18. T.V.V. (thermal vacuum valve)
19. EGR valve
20. EGR valve gasket

20. EGR valve gasket
21. Cylinder head
22. Exhaust valve
23. Intake valve
24. Exhaust valve guide
25. Intake valve guide
26. Exhaust valve seat insert
27. Intake valve sear insert
28. Lower spring seat
29. Valve stem seal
30. Valve spring

42. Rocker arm
43. Camshaft
44. Camshaft oil seal
45. Camshaft timing pulley
46. Packing
47. Spark plug
48. Distributor assembly
49. AI suction pipe
50. Insulator pipe
51. High tension cable assembly
52. Thermostat housing
53. Thermostat
54. Gasket
55. Coolant outlet pipe
56. Packing
57. Clip
58. Gasket
59. Exhaust manifold
60. Hot air cover
61. O_2 sensor
62. Cylinder head gasket
63. Sonic jet nozzle

Fig. 50 Exploded view of the top end engine components — 1.5L engine

24. Connect the EGR vacuum hose, then the pressure regulator vacuum hose to the intake manifold (common chamber).

25. Connect the EVAP canister vacuum hose to the common chamber and the throttle body.

26. Connect the brake booster vacuum hose, install the MAP sensor to the common chamber and connect the PCV hose to the valve cover.

27. Connect the intake air duct to the throttle body, then connect the breather hose to the intake air duct.

28. Connect the cable harness to the IAT sensor, TP sensor and the IAC valve.

29. Connect the 2 cable harness connectors, located near the left shock tower.

30. Connect the accelerator cable to the throttle body and to the intake manifold (common chamber).

31. Connect the ignition coil wire, then connect the battery negative cable.

32. Fill cooling system, then start engine and check for leaks.

1.6L TWINCAM ENGINE
▶ See Figure 52

1. Properly relieve the fuel system pressure. Disconnect the battery negative cable, then remove the ground cable terminal from the common chamber.

2. Remove the PCV hose and the air intake duct, then disconnect the accelerator cable from the intake air duct.

3. Disconnect the accelerator cable from the throttle valve.

4. Disconnect the MAP sensor hose from the MAP sensor, then the vacuum hose from the brake vacuum booster.

5. Tag and disconnect the 2 canister hoses from the pipes located on the common chamber.

6. Remove the canister pipe bracket from the common chamber.

7. Disconnect the vacuum hose from the fuel pressure regulator, then the vacuum hose from the induction control valve port.

8. Remove the throttle valve from the common chamber.

9. Remove the alternator harness clip, then the 3 fuel injector harness cable clips.

10. Loosen the EGR pipe bracket on the exhaust manifold, then loosen the EGR clip from the thermostat housing.

11. Remove the 2 common chamber bracket attaching bolts, located on the left side of the engine and the engine hanger bolt, located on the right side of the common chamber.

12. Remove the 10 bolts and 2 nuts attaching the common chamber to the induction port, then remove the common chamber from the engine.

13. Remove the 2 oil cooler pipe nuts from the studs under the induction port.

14. Disconnect the fuel feed and return lines, then remove the 2 fuel rail retaining bolts. Remove the fuel injector harness bracket retaining bolts.

15. Remove the fuel injector harness, fuel rail and fuel injector assembly from the induction port.

16. Remove the VSV harness connector from the induction port.

17. Remove the 7 bolts and 2 nuts attaching the induction port to the cylinder head, then remove the induction port assembly from the vehicle.

To install:

18. Thoroughly clean all gasket mating surfaces.

19. Install the induction port using a new gasket. Tighten the retainers to 17 ft. lbs. (23 Nm).

20. Install the VSV harness, then install the fuel injector harness, fuel rail and injectors assembly.

21. Install the fuel injector harness bracket bolts and the fuel rail retaining bolts.

22. Connect the fuel feed and return lines, then install the 2 oil cooler pipe clip bolts to the studs under the induction port.

23. Install the common chamber with a new gasket onto the induction port assembly. Torque nuts and bolts to 17 ft. lbs. (23 Nm).

24. Install the common chamber bracket bolts, located on the left side of the engine and the hanger bolt, located on the right side of the engine.

25. Install the EGR pipe bracket bolts on the exhaust manifold and the EGR clip on the thermostat housing. Torque EGR bracket bolts to 32 ft. lbs. (44 Nm).

26. Install the alternator harness cable clip, then the 3 fuel injector harness cable clips.

27. Install the throttle valve onto the common chamber, then connect the induction control valve vacuum hose.

28. Connect the fuel pressure regulator vacuum hose to the common chamber.

29. Connect the canister pipe bracket onto the common chamber, then connect the canister hoses to the pipes on the common chamber.

30. Connect the brake booster vacuum hose, then the MAP sensor hose to the MAP sensor.

31. Connect the accelerator cable to the throttle valve. Install the PCV hose and the intake air duct. Connect the cable ground terminal to the common chamber.

32. Connect the battery negative cable and fill cooling system, then start the engine and check for leaks.

1.8L TWINCAM ENGINE
▶ See Figure 53

1. Properly relieve the fuel system pressure. Disconnect the battery negative cable, then remove the ground cable bolts from the common chamber.

2. Remove the ventilation hose from the intake air duct.

3. Unplug the Throttle Position (TP) sensor, Intake Air Control (IAC) valve and the cold start injector electrical connectors.

4. Remove the air intake duct and the air cleaner from the throttle body.

5. Remove the 2 retaining bolts and the accelerator cable bracket from the common chamber. Disconnect the accelerator cable from the throttle lever.

6. Remove the PCV hose and the Manifold Absolute Pressure (MAP) sensor hose from the common chamber.

7. Remove the pressure regulator hose from the common camber, then remove the 2 retaining bolts and the solenoid vacuum valve assembly from the chamber.

8. Remove the Intake Air Temperature (IAT) sensor from the common chamber.

9. Position and drain pan and a rag to catch any escaping fluid, then remove the 2 coolant hoses from the throttle body.

10. Tag and disconnect the vacuum hoses from the common chamber.

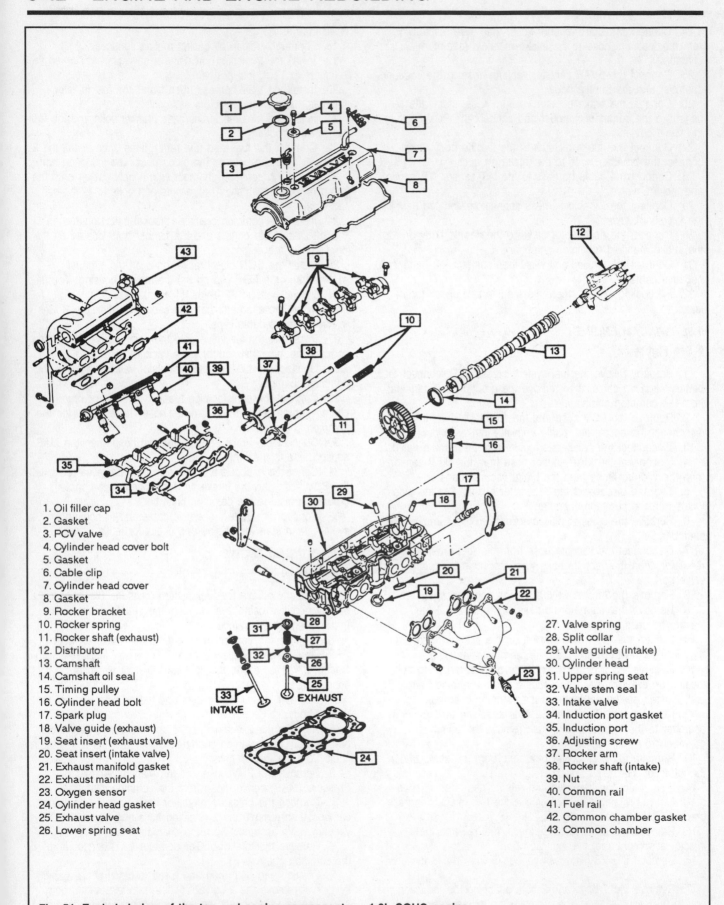

1. Oil filler cap
2. Gasket
3. PCV valve
4. Cylinder head cover bolt
5. Gasket
6. Cable clip
7. Cylinder head cover
8. Gasket
9. Rocker bracket
10. Rocker spring
11. Rocker shaft (exhaust)
12. Distributor
13. Camshaft
14. Camshaft oil seal
15. Timing pulley
16. Cylinder head bolt
17. Spark plug
18. Valve guide (exhaust)
19. Seat insert (exhaust valve)
20. Seat insert (intake valve)
21. Exhaust manifold gasket
22. Exhaust manifold
23. Oxygen sensor
24. Cylinder head gasket
25. Exhaust valve
26. Lower spring seat

27. Valve spring
28. Split collar
29. Valve guide (intake)
30. Cylinder head
31. Upper spring seat
32. Valve stem seal
33. Intake valve
34. Induction port gasket
35. Induction port
36. Adjusting screw
37. Rocker arm
38. Rocker shaft (intake)
39. Nut
40. Common rail
41. Fuel rail
42. Common chamber gasket
43. Common chamber

Fig. 51 Exploded view of the top end engine components — 1.6L SOHC engine

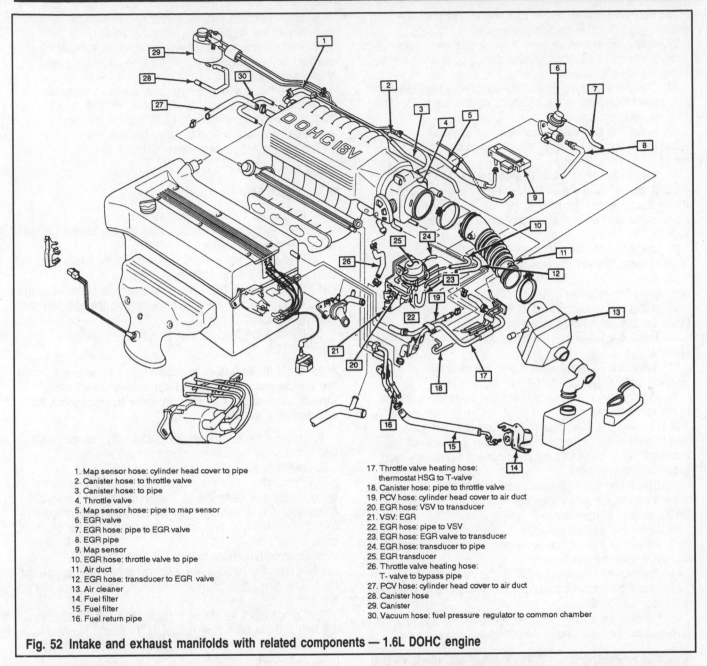

1. Map sensor hose: cylinder head cover to pipe
2. Canister hose: to throttle valve
3. Canister hose: to pipe
4. Throttle valve
5. Map sensor hose: pipe to map sensor
6. EGR valve
7. EGR hose: pipe to EGR valve
8. EGR pipe
9. Map sensor
10. EGR hose: throttle valve to pipe
11. Air duct
12. EGR hose: transducer to EGR valve
13. Air cleaner
14. Fuel filter
15. Fuel filter
16. Fuel return pipe
17. Throttle valve heating hose:
    thermostat HSG to T-valve
18. Canister hose: pipe to throttle valve
19. PCV hose: cylinder head cover to air duct
20. EGR hose: VSV to transducer
21. VSV: EGR
22. EGR hose: pipe to VSV
23. EGR hose: EGR valve to transducer
24. EGR hose: transducer to pipe
25. EGR transducer
26. Throttle valve heating hose:
    T- valve to bypass pipe
27. PCV hose: cylinder head cover to air duct
28. Canister hose
29. Canister
30. Vacuum hose: fuel pressure regulator to common chamber

Fig. 52 Intake and exhaust manifolds with related components — 1.6L DOHC engine

11. Remove the 2 bolts and the engine lift bracket from the common chamber.

12. Remove the 3 bolts and 2 nuts attaching the common chamber to the intake manifold (known as the induction port on earlier engines).

13. Remove 1 bolt from the fuel pipe bracket, then remove 2 bolts and the EGR pipe from the exhaust manifold.

14. Remove 1 bolts from the EGR pipe bracket. Remove the EGR pipe nut and pipe from the EGR valve.

15. Unplug the fuel injector electrical connectors, then remove the ground cable from the intake manifold.

16. Remove the brake booster vacuum hose, then raise and support the vehicle safely.

17. Loosen the hose clamp, then disconnect the fuel return hose from the intake manifold.

18. Remove 1 bolt and set the oil cooler pipe aside, then remove the 2 bolts and the left intake manifold brace,

19. Remove 1 bolt, 1 nut and the right side intake manifold brace.

20. Remove the 4 lower intake manifold retaining bolts, then remove the supports and carefully lower the vehicle for underhood access.

21. Remove the 2 upper intake manifold retaining nuts and the 3 upper bolts, then remove the intake from the cylinder head.

To install:

22. Thoroughly clean all gasket mating surfaces.

23. Install the intake manifold to the cylinder head using a new gasket. Tighten the upper retainers to 17 ft. lbs. (23 Nm), then raise and support the vehicle safely.

24. Install the lower manifold retaining bolts and tighten to 17 ft. lbs. (23 Nm).

25. Install the right, then left manifold braces and tighten the retainers to 15 ft. lbs. (20 Nm).

26. Reposition the oil cooler pipe and secure using the retaining bolt. Tighten the bolt to 89 inch lbs. (10 Nm).

27. Install the fuel return hose to the intake and secure using the hose clamp, then remove the supports and carefully lower the vehicle.

28. Connect the brake booster vacuum hose, then connect the ground cable bolt to the manifold. Tighten the bolt to 71 inch lbs. (8 Nm).

29. Install the fuel injector electrical connectors.

30. Install the EGR pipe to the valve and tighten the pipe nut to 11 ft. lbs. (15 Nm).

31. Install the bolt to the EGR pipe bracket and tighten to 89 inch lbs. (10 Nm). Install the EGR pipe to the exhaust manifold and tighten the bolts to 89 inch lbs. (10 Nm).

32. Install the bolt to the fuel pipe bracket and tighten to 89 inch lbs. (10 Nm).

33. Install the common chamber to the intake manifold using a new gasket. Tighten the retainers to 17 ft. lbs. (23 Nm).

34. Install the engine lift bracket to the common chamber and tighten the retaining bolts to 18 ft. lbs. (25 Nm).

35. Install the vacuum hoses to the common chamber, then install the 2 coolant hoses to the throttle valve.

36. Install the IAT sensor electrical connector to the chamber.

37. Install the SV valve assembly to the chamber using the retaining bolts and tighten to 89 inch lbs. (10 Nm).

38. Connect the pressure regulator and MAP sensor hoses to the common chamber.

39. Connect the PCV hose to the common chamber.

40. Connect the accelerator cable to the throttle lever, then install the cable bracket to the chamber and tighten the bolts to 89 inch lbs. (10 Nm).

41. Check and adjust the accelerator cable, as necessary. Make sure that the cable does not hold the throttle open when the accelerator is released.

42. Install the air intake duct to the throttle body.

43. Install the wiring harness connectors to the TP sensor, IAC valve and cold start injector.

44. Connect the ventilation hose to the intake air duct.

45. Install the ground cable bolts to the chamber and tighten to 71 inch lbs. (8 Nm).

46. Connect the battery negative cable and fill cooling system, then start the engine and check for leaks.

Exhaust Manifold

REMOVAL & INSTALLATION

Spectrum

▶ See Figure 54

1. Disconnect the negative battery cable, then unplug the oxygen sensor wiring connector.

2. Disconnect the Thermostatic Air Cleaner (TAC) flex hose, then remove the suction pipe and clips.

3. Remove the hot air cover, then raise and support the vehicle safely.

4. Disconnect the exhaust pipe from the exhaust manifold, then remove the supports and lower the vehicle.

5. Remove the nuts and bolts securing the exhaust manifold to the cylinder head. Thoroughly clean the gasket mounting surfaces.

6. To install, use new gaskets and reverse the removal procedures. Torque the exhaust manifold to 17 ft. lbs. (23 Nm), the exhaust pipe bolts to 42 ft. lbs. (56 Nm) and, if applicable, the suction pipe to 32 ft. lbs. (44 Nm).

7. Start the engine and check for leaks.

Storm

▶ See Figure 55

1. Disconnect the battery negative cable.

2. Remove the heat protector, then disconnect the oxygen sensor electrical connector.

3. If equipped with the 1.6L twincam engine, disconnect the EGR pipe clip from the thermostat housing.

4. Disconnect the EGR pipe from the exhaust manifold and the EGR valve. For the 1.8L engine, remove the bolt from the EGR pipe bracket.

5. Remove the front exhaust pipe from the exhaust manifold.

➡For the 1.8L engine, it is necessary to raise and support the vehicle, then remove the right splash shield and forward exhaust pipe bracket, in order to disconnect the pipe from the manifold.

6. Remove the exhaust manifold attaching nuts and bolts, then remove the exhaust manifold from the engine.

To install:

7. Thoroughly clean the gasket mating surfaces. Using a straight edge and feeler gauge, inspect the exhaust manifold for damage and/or warpage; maximum allowable warpage is 0.0157 in. (0.4mm), if the warpage is greater, replace the exhaust manifold.

8. Reverse procedure to install. Tighten the exhaust manifold retainers to 30 ft. lbs. (32 Nm) on all engines, except the 1.8L engine which should be tightened to 29 ft. lbs. (39 Nm).

9. Tighten the 1.8L engine exhaust pipe nuts to 46 ft. lbs. (62 Nm) and the EGR pipe nut/bolt to 11 ft. lbs. (15 Nm).

10. Except for the 1.8L engine, tighten the EGR pipe bolts to 32 ft. lbs. (44 Nm).

Turbocharger

REMOVAL & INSTALLATION

1. Disconnect the negative battery terminal from the battery.

2. Remove lower and upper heat protector shield covering turbocharger assembly.

3. Remove manifold heat protector and unplug the oxygen sensor connector.

4. Disconnect vacuum pipe from wastegate and position out of the way.

5. Disconnect water lines.

6. Disconnect oil lines return and delivery.

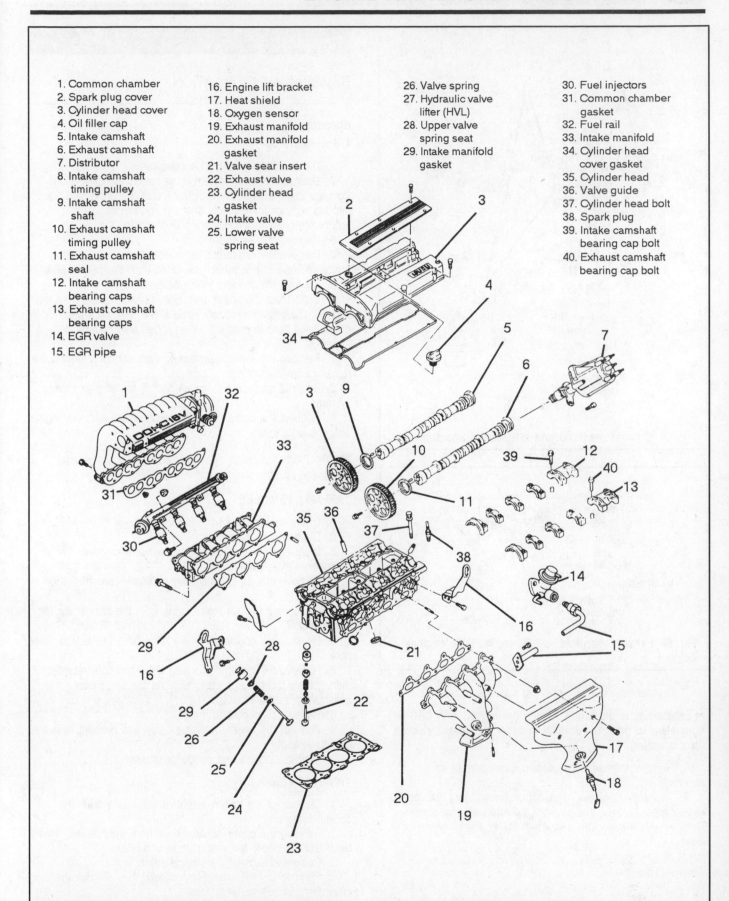

1. Common chamber
2. Spark plug cover
3. Cylinder head cover
4. Oil filler cap
5. Intake camshaft
6. Exhaust camshaft
7. Distributor
8. Intake camshaft timing pulley
9. Intake camshaft shaft
10. Exhaust camshaft timing pulley
11. Exhaust camshaft seal
12. Intake camshaft bearing caps
13. Exhaust camshaft bearing caps
14. EGR valve
15. EGR pipe
16. Engine lift bracket
17. Heat shield
18. Oxygen sensor
19. Exhaust manifold
20. Exhaust manifold gasket
21. Valve sear insert
22. Exhaust valve
23. Cylinder head gasket
24. Intake valve
25. Lower valve spring seat
26. Valve spring
27. Hydraulic valve lifter (HVL)
28. Upper valve spring seat
29. Intake manifold gasket
30. Fuel injectors
31. Common chamber gasket
32. Fuel rail
33. Intake manifold
34. Cylinder head cover gasket
35. Cylinder head
36. Valve guide
37. Cylinder head bolt
38. Spark plug
39. Intake camshaft bearing cap bolt
40. Exhaust camshaft bearing cap bolt

Fig. 53 Exploded view of the top end engine components — 1.8L engine (1.6L DOHC engine similar)

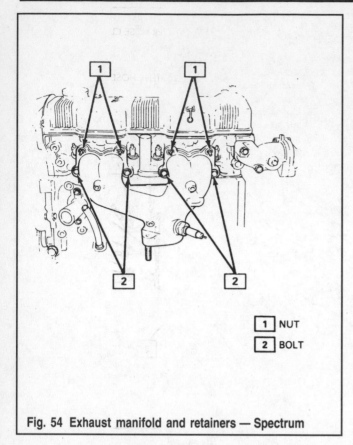

Fig. 54 Exhaust manifold and retainers — Spectrum

| 1 | NUT |
| 2 | BOLT |

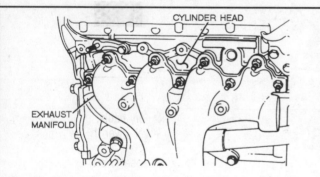

Fig. 55 Exhaust manifold — 1.8L engine (1.6L engines similar)

7. Disconnect exhaust pipe from wastegate manifold.

➡**Exhaust manifold studs should be soaked with CRC or equivalent to prior to removal in order to prevent studs from breaking.**

8. Remove the turbocharger and wastegate as an assembly.

9. To install, use new a gasket on the exhaust manifold to turbocharger housing and reverse the removal procedures. Refill all fluid levels, start and warm the engine to check for leaks.

Radiator

REMOVAL & INSTALLATION

Spectrum

➡ **See Figure 56**

1. Disconnect the battery negative cable.
2. Drain the cooling system by removing the drain plug from the lower side of the radiator. Install the drain plug back into the radiator immediately after the system has been emptied in order to avoid loosing or forgetting the plug.
3. Remove the air intake duct.
4. Remove the fan motor cable from the rear of the fan motor socket and disconnect the cable from the thermo-switch.
5. Remove the fan and motor assembly.
6. Disconnect the upper and lower radiator hoses from the radiator, the coolant recovery hose at the filler neck and the oil cooler lines from the radiator, if equipped with automatic transaxle.
7. Remove the radiator fasteners, then carefully remove the radiator from the vehicle.
8. Reverse procedure to install and fill the engine cooling system.
9. Connect the battery negative cable, then start the engine and check for leaks.

Storm

➡ **See Figure 57**

1990-1991 VEHICLES

1. Disconnect the battery negative cable.
2. Drain cooling system.
3. If equipped with automatic transaxle, disconnect the oil cooler lines from the radiator.
4. Remove the upper and lower radiator hoses from the radiator.
5. Disconnect the fan motor cable from the rear of the fan motor socket.
6. Remove the coolant recovery hose from the radiator filler neck.
7. Remove the radiator attaching bolts and core retainer, then remove the radiator along with the fan and motor assembly from the vehicle.
8. Reverse procedure to install.
9. Connect the battery negative cable and properly refill the cooling system.
10. Start the engine and check for leaks.

1992-1993 VEHICLES

1. Disconnect the battery negative cable and drain the cooling system.
2. Remove the upper radiator hose from the radiator, then remove the 2 upper fan shroud mounting bolts.
3. Raise and support the vehicle safely.
4. Remove the left side splash shield, then remove the lower fan shroud mounting bolts.

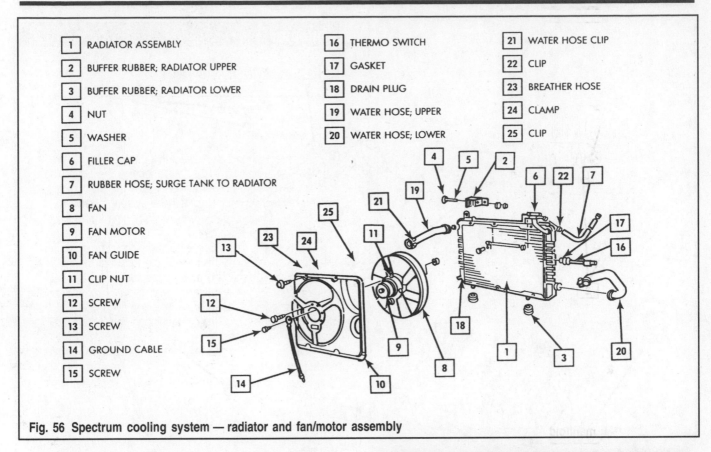

1	RADIATOR ASSEMBLY	16	THERMO SWITCH	21	WATER HOSE CLIP
2	BUFFER RUBBER; RADIATOR UPPER	17	GASKET	22	CLIP
3	BUFFER RUBBER; RADIATOR LOWER	18	DRAIN PLUG	23	BREATHER HOSE
4	NUT	19	WATER HOSE; UPPER	24	CLAMP
5	WASHER	20	WATER HOSE; LOWER	25	CLIP
6	FILLER CAP				
7	RUBBER HOSE; SURGE TANK TO RADIATOR				
8	FAN				
9	FAN MOTOR				
10	FAN GUIDE				
11	CLIP NUT				
12	SCREW				
13	SCREW				
14	GROUND CABLE				
15	SCREW				

Fig. 56 Spectrum cooling system — radiator and fan/motor assembly

5. Disconnect the lower radiator hose and, if applicable, the automatic transaxle fluid cooler lines from the radiator. Cap the transaxle lines to prevent excess fluid loss or contamination.

6. Remove the supports, then carefully lower the vehicle.

7. Unplug the radiator fan and thermo switch electrical connectors, then remove the fan assembly from the vehicle.

8. Remove the 7 radiator core support bolts, then remove the support from the vehicle.

9. Remove the radiator from the vehicle, and if it is being replaced, remove the thermo switch from the radiator.

To install:

10. If removed, install the thermo switch in the base of the radiator.

11. Install the radiator and support to the vehicle, then tighten the support retainers to 89 inch lbs. (10 Nm).

12. Install the radiator fan assembly to the vehicle and tighten the mounting bolts to 89 inch lbs. (10 Nm).

13. Install the wiring harness connectors to the fan and the radiator thermo switch.

14. Raise and support the vehicle safely, then connect the lower radiator hose, and if applicable, the automatic transaxle fluid cooler hoses.

15. Install the lower fan shroud and tighten the mounting bolts to 89 inch lbs. (10 Nm).

16. Install the left splash shield, then remove the supports and carefully lower the vehicle.

17. Connect the upper radiator hose, then refill the engine cooling system.

18. Connect the negative battery cable, then start the engine and check for leaks.

Electric Fan

REMOVAL & INSTALLATION

▶ See Figure 58

1. Disconnect the negative battery cable, then partially drain the engine cooling system to a level lower than the upper radiator hose.

2. Remove the upper radiator hose to provide access for fan and motor assembly removal.

3. Unplug the electrical connector(s) from the cooling fan motor. If multiple connectors are used, be sure to tag the wires before disconnecting.

4. Remove the fan shroud mounting, then remove the fan/shroud assembly from the vehicle.

5. If necessary, disassemble the fan and motor for repair or replacement.

   a. Remove the fan blade-to-motor nut, then separate the fan blade and washer from the motor.

   b. Remove the motor-to-shroud bolts, then remove the the motor from the shroud.

6. Test the fan motor and replace it, if necessary. Make sure the fan blades are free of damage or warpage and, replace if damaged.

✷✷CAUTION

A fan that is damaged must be replaced to prevent possible failure and damage or injury.

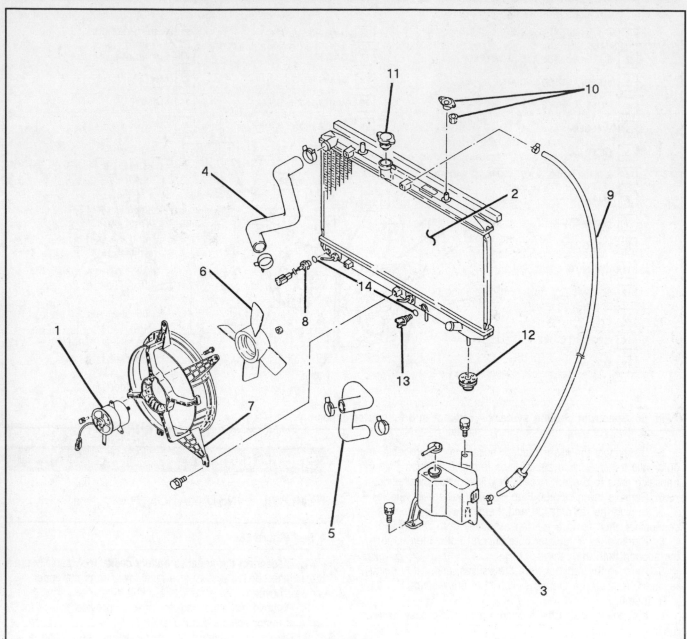

1. Electric cooling fan motor
2. Radiator
3. Coolant recovery reservoir
4. Upper radiator hose
5. Lower radiator hose
6. Radiator fan blade
7. Radiator fan shroud
8. Radiator fan thermo switch
9. Coolant recovery reservoir hose
10. Upper radiator damper
11. Radiator cap
12. Lower radiator damper
13. Radiator drain plug
14. O-ring

Fig. 57 Storm cooling system — radiator and fan/motor assembly

7. To install, reverse the removal procedures.

8. Connect the negative battery cable and refill the cooling system, then start the engine and check for leaks and proper fan operation.

FAN TESTING

Spectrum

1. Unplug the electrical wiring connector from the electric cooling fan.

2. Using a 14 gauge wire, connect it between the fan and the positive terminal; the fan should run.

➡**If the fan does not run while connected to the electrical wiring connector with the engine warm and running, inspect for a defective coolant temperature switch or air conditioning relay, if equipped.**

3. If the fan does not run when connected to the jumper wire, replace the fan assembly.

Storm
▶ **See Figure 59**

1. Unplug the wiring harness electrical connector from the cooling fan.

2. Using an ammeter and jumper wires, connect the fan motor in series with the battery and ammeter. With the fan running, check the ammeter reading, it should be 5.8-7.4A, if the amp readings are not within specifications, replace the motor.

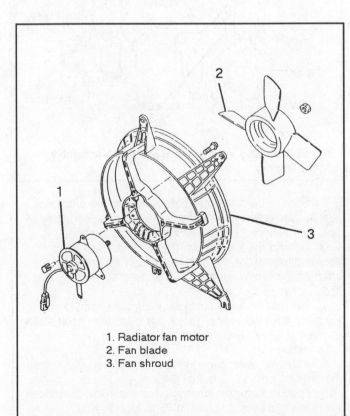

1. Radiator fan motor
2. Fan blade
3. Fan shroud

Fig. 58 Exploded view of the fan and motor assembly

3. Reconnect the wiring harness to the fan's electrical connector. Start the engine, allow it to reach temperatures above 194°F and confirm that the fan runs. If the fan doesn't run, test and/or replace the temperature switch.

THERMO SWITCH TESTING

▶ **See Figure 60**

1. Disconnect the negative battery cable and drain the engine cooling system. For the Spectrum, the system need only be drained to a level ½ way down the radiator, just below thermo switch mounted in the side of the radiator.

2. Unplug the electrical connector and remove the thermo switch from the side or base of the radiator, as applicable.

3. Suspend the a thermometer and the thermo switch in a pan containing a 50/50 mixture of ethylene glycol antifreeze and water. Do not let the switch or thermometer touch the bottom or sides of the pan to assure proper temperature readings.

4. Place the pan on a burner and raise the temperature above 179°F (82°C). As the temperature rises, use an ohm meter to check switch continuity. The switch should close providing continuity only after the specified temperature has been reached.

5. Replace the switch if it closes either too soon or too early.

Water Pump

REMOVAL & INSTALLATION

Except Twincam Engines
▶ **See Figures 61 and 62**

1. Disconnect the negative battery cable and drain the cooling system.

2. Loosen the power steering pump adjustment bolts and remove the drive belt.

3. Remove the timing belt; refer to the procedure later in this section.

4. Remove the tension pulley and spring.

5. Remove the water pump mounting bolts, water pump and gasket. Clean the mounting surfaces of all remaining gasket material.

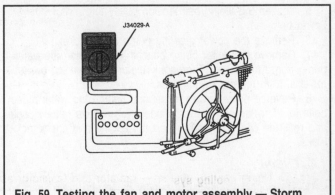

Fig. 59 Testing the fan and motor assembly — Storm

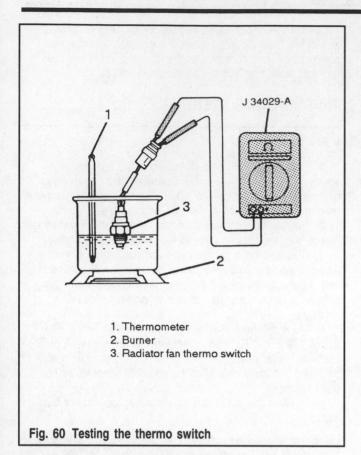

Fig. 60 Testing the thermo switch

1. Thermometer
2. Burner
3. Radiator fan thermo switch

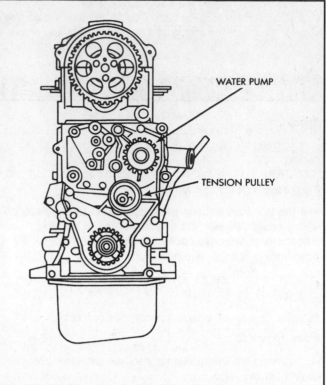

Fig. 61 Water pump and timing belt tension pulley — SOHC engines

6. To install, reverse the removal procedures. Tighten the water pump bolts to 17 ft. lbs. (23 Nm) and the tension pulley to 30 ft. lbs. (40 Nm).

7. Connect the negative battery cable and fill the cooling system, then start the engine and check for leaks.

Twincam Engines

▶ See Figure 63

1.6L DOHC ENGINE

1. Disconnect the negative battery cable and drain the cooling system.

2. Support the engine using a suitable floor jack and remove the right front engine mount.

3. Remove the engine mount bridge and the upper timing belt cover.

4. Remove the power steering belt and the lower timing belt cover.

5. Loosen the timing belt tension pulley and remove the timing belt.

6. Remove the power steering pump and bracket.

7. Remove the water pump attaching bolts, then the water pump from the vehicle. Thoroughly clean all remaining gasket material from the mating surfaces.

8. Reverse procedure to install and tighten the water pump bolts to 17 ft. lbs. (24 Nm). Connect the negative battery cable and refill the cooling system. Start the engine and check for leaks.

1.8L ENGINE

1. Disconnect the negative battery cable and drain the engine cooling system.

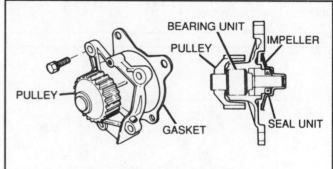

Fig. 62 Cut away view of the water pump assembly — SOHC engines

2. Remove the timing belt covers; refer to the procedure later in this section. Loosen the timing belt tensioner pulley bolt, then remove the belt from the water pump pulley.

3. Remove the 2 bolts from the power steering pump bracket, then position the pump aside with the lines still attached. Be careful not to kink or damage the steering fluid lines.

4. Remove the water pump mounting bolts, then remove the pump from the engine. Thoroughly clean the gasket mating surfaces of all remaining gasket material.

To install:

5. Install the water pump using a new gasket, then tighten the retaining bolts to 18 ft. lbs. (24 Nm).

6. Position the power steering pump assembly, then install the retaining bolts and tighten to 25 ft. lbs. (34 Nm).

7. Install the timing belt to the pump pulley, then tighten the tensioner pulley bolt to 30 ft. lbs. (40 Nm).

8. Install the timing belt covers.

9. Connect the negative battery cable and fill the cooling system, then start the engine and check for leaks.

Cylinder Head

REMOVAL & INSTALLATION

Spectrum

▶ See Figure 64

1. Relieve the fuel system pressure, then disconnect the negative battery cable.

2. Drain the cooling system.

3. Remove the air cleaner. Remove the suction pipe and clips for the air induction system.

4. Disconnect the flex hose and oxygen sensor at the exhaust manifold.

5. Disconnect the exhaust pipe bracket at the block and the exhaust pipe at the manifold.

6. Tag and disconnect the spark plug wires.

7. Remove the thermostat housing, the distributor, the vacuum advance hoses and the ground cable at the cylinder head. Remember to tag all vacuum hoses for assembly purposes.

8. Disconnect the fuel hoses at the fuel pump.

9. From the carburetor, if equipped, remove the necessary hoses and the throttle cable.

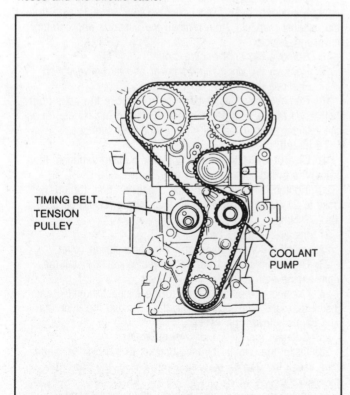

TIMING BELT TENSION PULLEY

COOLANT PUMP

Fig. 63 Water pump and timing belt tension pulley — DOHC engines

10. If applicable, remove the engine harness assembly from fuel injectors.

11. Disconnect the vacuum switching valve electrical connector and the heater hoses.

12. Remove the alternator, power steering and air conditioning adjusting bolts, brackets and drive belts.

13. Support the engine using a vertical hoist. Remove the right hand motor mount and bracket at the front cover.

14. Rotate the engine to align the timing marks, then remove the timing gear cover.

15. Loosen the tension pulley and remove the timing belt from the camshaft timing pulley.

16. Remove the fuel pump.

17. Disconnect the intake manifold coolant hoses.

18. Remove the cylinder head bolts (remove the bolts from both ends at the same time, working toward the middle) and the cylinder head. Clean all of the mounting surfaces.

To install:

19. Use new seals and gaskets, apply oil to the bolt threads and torque the head bolts.

➡**When tightening the cylinder head bolts, work from the middle toward both ends, alternating from one side to the other. Tighten the bolts in at least 2 passes; first, torque the bolts to 29 ft. lbs. (40 Nm). The final torque should be 58 ft. lbs. (79 Nm).**

20. After tightening, adjust the valve clearance and complete the installation procedures, by reversing the removal procedures.

Storm

SOHC ENGINE

▶ See Figure 64

1. Relieve the fuel system pressure, then disconnect the battery negative cable.

2. Drain cooling system.

3. Disconnect the accelerator cable from the throttle body, then the breather hose from the intake air duct.

4. Disconnect the intake air duct from the throttle body, then the MAP sensor hose from the MAP sensor.

5. Disconnect the brake booster hose, then the 2 EVAP canister hoses from the pipes on the intake manifold (common chamber).

6. Disconnect the EGR vacuum hoses, then the oxygen sensor harness electrical connector.

7. Disconnect the ignition coil ground cable from the thermostat housing flange.

8. Unplug both engine coolant temperature sensor connectors from the thermostat housing.

9. Remove the cable harness clip from the coolant outlet pipe bracket.

10. Disconnect the 2 cable harness electrical connectors, located near the left strut tower.

11. Remove the engine heater hoses, then disconnect the upper radiator hose from the radiator.

12. Disconnect the fuel feed and return hoses, then raise and support the vehicle safely.

13. Remove the right undercover, then the front exhaust pipe from the exhaust manifold. Remove the supports and carefully lower the vehicle.

14. Remove the right engine mount, then the alternator drive belt.

15. Remove the power steering belt.

16. Remove the engine mounting bracket from the timing case cover, then remove the timing belt.

17. Remove the valve cover, then remove the cylinder head bolts and the cylinder head.

To install:

18. Clean the cylinder head gasket mounting surfaces, then install the cylinder head with a new gasket.

19. Tighten the bolts in at least 2 passes; first, torque the bolts to 29 ft. lbs. (40 Nm). The final torque should be 58 ft. lbs. (79 Nm).

20. Install the timing belt and the valve cover, then the engine mounting bracket onto the timing case cover.

21. Raise and support the vehicle safely, then install the right engine mount.

22. Install the front exhaust pipe to the exhaust manifold, then right side under cover. Remove the supports and lower the vehicle.

23. Connect the fuel feed line and fuel return hose.

24. Connect the coolant bypass pipe bracket to the cylinder head.

25. Install the upper radiator hose, then the 2 heater hoses onto the engine.

26. Connect the 2 cable harness connectors, located near the left strut tower.

27. Connect the 2 ground cable terminals, located to the right side of the intake manifold (common chamber).

28. Install both engine coolant temperature sensor wiring harness connectors to the thermostat housing.

29. Connect the ignition coil ground cable to the terminal on the thermostat housing flange.

30. Install the oxygen sensor electrical connector.

31. Connect the EVAP canister hoses to the canister pipes on the intake manifold (common chamber).

32. Connect the brake booster vacuum and MAP sensor hoses.

33. Install the intake air duct to the throttle body, then the PCV hose to the intake air duct.

34. Connect the accelerator cable to the throttle body.

35. Connect the battery negative cable and fill cooling system. Start engine and check for leaks.

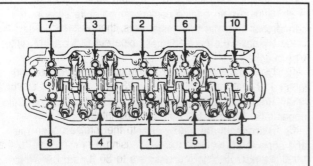

Fig. 64 Cylinder head bolt torque sequence — SOHC engines

1.6L DOHC ENGINE

▶ See Figure 65

1. Relieve the fuel system pressure, then disconnect the battery negative cable.

2. Drain the engine cooling system.

3. Disconnect the accelerator cable from the cable clips (located on the common chamber) and from the throttle body.

4. Remove the PCV hose from the intake air duct, then disconnect the duct from the throttle body.

5. Remove the hose from the MAP sensor, then remove the vacuum hose from the brake booster.

6. Remove the 2 EVAP hoses from the pipes on the common chamber, then remove the MAP sensor and EVAP pipes from the chamber. Remove the EVAP pipe support bracket.

7. Unplug the oxygen sensor electrical connector, then remove the ignition coil ground cable from the thermostat housing flange.

8. Unplug the coolant temperature sensor and thermo unit harness connector from the thermostat housing.

9. Remove the ground cable terminal from the right side of the common chamber, then remove the ground cable from the left front of the chamber.

10. Remove the starter and alternator cable clip.

11. Remove the 2 heater hoses from the engine, then remove the upper radiator hose.

12. Remove the throttle body heating hose from the coolant bypass pipe, then remove the pipe bracket from the cylinder head.

13. Disconnect the fuel feed and return lines.

14. Raise and support the vehicle safely, then remove the right side under cover. Disconnect the front exhaust pipe from the exhaust manifold, then remove the supports and carefully lower the vehicle.

15. Remove the right engine mount.

16. Remove the upper timing cover and the valve cover.

17. Remove the timing belt.

18. Remove the cylinder head bolts (remove the bolts from both ends at the same time, working toward the middle) and the cylinder head. Clean all of the mounting surfaces.

To install:

19. Clean the cylinder head gasket mounting surfaces, then install the cylinder head with a new gasket.

20. Tighten the bolts in at least 2 passes; first, torque the bolts to 29 ft. lbs. (40 Nm). The final torque should be 58 ft. lbs. (79 Nm).

21. Install the timing belt.

22. Install the valve cover and the upper timing cover.

23. Raise and support the vehicle safely, then install the right engine mount.

24. Connect the exhaust pipe to the exhaust manifold and install the right side under cover, then remove the supports and carefully lower the vehicle.

25. Connect the fuel feed and return lines.

26. Install the coolant bypass bracket to the cylinder head, then install the throttle body heating hose to the coolant bypass pipe.

27. Install the upper radiator hose, then connect the 2 heater hoses.

28. Install the starter and alternator harness cable clips to the common chamber.

29. Install the ground cable terminals to the right side and left front of the chamber.

30. Install the coolant temperature sensor and thermo unit harness connector to the thermostat housing.

31. Connect the ignition coil ground cable to the terminal on the thermostat housing flange.

32. Install the wiring harness to the oxygen sensor.

33. Install the EVAP canister pipe support bracket, then install the canister hoses to the pipes on the common chamber.

34. Connect the brake booster vacuum hose, then install the hose to the MAP sensor.

35. Connect the intake air duct to the throttle body, then install the PCV hose to the duct.

36. Connect the accelerator cable to the throttle body, then position the cable into the clips on the common chamber.

37. Connect the negative battery cable and fill the engine cooling system.

38. Start the engine and check for leaks.

1.8L DOHC ENGINE

▶ See Figure 65

1. Relieve the fuel system pressure, then disconnect the battery negative cable.

2. Drain the engine cooling system.

3. Disconnect the accelerator cable from the throttle body and remove the retaining bracket.

4. Tag and disconnect all vacuum hoses from the valve cover.

5. Remove the upper timing belt cover.

6. Remove the valve cover.

7. Unplug the oxygen sensor electrical connector, then remove the heat shield from the exhaust manifold.

8. Raise and support the vehicle safely, then remove the right splash shield.

9. Remove the 3 nuts and the forward exhaust pipe from the exhaust manifold, then remove the supports and carefully lower the vehicle.

10. Remove the power steering pump and support the pump aside. If possible, do not disconnect the steering fluid lines in order to avoid having to fill and bleed the system during installation.

11. Remove the 2 bolts and the EGR pipe from the exhaust manifold, then remove the bolt from the EGR pipe bracket. Loosen the EGR pipe nuts, then disconnect the pipe from the EGR valve.

12. Tag and disconnect the vacuum lines from the EGR valve, then remove the EGR valve from the vehicle.

13. Remove the exhaust manifold from the cylinder head.

14. Remove the air intake duct from the throttle body.

15. Unplug the electrical connectors from the coolant temperature sensor and the thermo unit at the thermostat housing.

16. Tag and disconnect all vacuum hoses from the intake manifold.

17. Remove the throttle body from the common chamber.

18. Disconnect the brake booster vacuum hose.

19. Remove the common chamber from the intake manifold.

20. Unplug the fuel injector electrical connectors, then remove the 2 bolts and the engine wiring harness retainer.

21. Disconnect the fuel return hose from the fuel pressure regulator and the fuel pipe from the injector rail.

22. Unplug the electrical connector from the vacuum switching valve, then remove the valve from the bracket and the bracket from the engine.

23. Remove the coolant hose from the coolant pipe under the intake manifold.

24. Remove the intake manifold from the cylinder head.

25. Support the engine using a floor jack.

26. Remove the right engine mount, by first removing the through bolt, mount bracket bolt/nut and the engine mount. Then remove the center bolt and the serpentine drive belt from the tensioner mounting bracket. Finally, remove the 4 mount bridge retaining bolts and the bridge from the vehicle.

27. Remove the lower timing belt cover, then remove the timing belt from the vehicle.

28. Remove the cylinder head bolts (remove the bolts from both ends at the same time, working toward the middle) and the cylinder head. Clean all of the mounting surfaces.

To install:

29. Clean the cylinder head gasket mounting surfaces, then install the cylinder head with a new gasket.

30. Tighten the bolts in at least 2 passes; first, torque the bolts to 29 ft. lbs. (40 Nm). The final torque should be 58 ft. lbs. (79 Nm).

31. Install the timing belt.

32. Install the upper and lower timing belt covers.

33. Install the right engine mount bridge and tighten the retaining bolts to 30 ft. lbs. (40 Nm).

34. Install the serpentine drive belt tensioner to the mounting bracket and tighten the center bolt to 30 ft. lbs. (40 Nm).

35. Install the right engine mount to the vehicle. Tighten the through bolt to 50 ft. lbs. (68 Nm), then tighten the bracket nut/bolt to 30 ft. lbs. (40 Nm).

36. Remove the floor jack.

37. Install the intake manifold using a new gasket, tighten the retainers to 17 ft. lbs. (23 Nm).

38. Connect the coolant hose to the pipe under the intake manifold.

39. Install the vacuum switching and valve retaining bracket, then install the wiring harness connector to the valve.

40. Connect the fuel feed and return lines.

41. Install the common chamber to the intake manifold and tighten the retainers to 17 ft. lbs. (23 Nm).

42. Install the electrical harness retaining bolts.

43. Install the ground cable bolts to the common chamber and tighten to 71 inch lbs. (8 Nm).

44. Install the brake booster vacuum hose, then install the EGR valve.

45. Install the EGR vacuum hoses, then install the EGR pipe to the EGR valve and tighten the pipe nut to 11 ft. lbs. (15 Nm).

46. Install the throttle body to the common chamber and tighten the retainers to 17 ft. lbs. (23 Nm). Install the electrical connectors to the throttle body.

47. Install the vacuum hoses to the intake manifold.

48. Connect the air intake duct to the throttle body.

49. Install the exhaust manifold, using a new gasket, to the cylinder head. Tighten the retainers to 30 ft. lbs. (39 Nm).

50. Install the EGR pipe to the exhaust manifold, using a new gasket. Tighten the retaining bolts to 11 ft. lbs. (15 Nm).

51. Reposition and install the power steering pump assembly, then raise and support the vehicle safely.

52. Connect the exhaust pipe to the exhaust manifold. Tighten the retainers to 46 ft. lbs. (62 Nm). Install the right splash shield, then lower the vehicle.

53. Connect the heat shield to the manifold and tighten the retainers to 11 ft. lbs. (15 Nm). Install the wiring harness to the oxygen sensor.

54. Install the valve cover.

55. Connect the accelerator cable to the throttle valve.

56. Connect the negative battery cable and refill the engine cooling system, then start the engine and check for leaks.

CLEANING & INSPECTION

▶ See Figure 66

1. Remove carbon deposits from the combustion chambers and valve heads with a drill-mounted wire brush. Be careful not to damage the cylinder head gasket surface. Carbon deposits may be removed with the valves installed in order to protect the valve seats If the head is to the disassembled, proceed to Step 3. If the head is not to be disassembled, proceed to Step 2.

2. Remove all dirt, oil and old gasket material from the cylinder head with solvent. Clean the bolt holes and the oil passage. Be careful not to get solvent on the valve seals as the solvent may damage them. If available, dry the cylinder head with compressed air. Check the head for cracks or other damage, and check the gasket surface for burrs, nicks and flatness. If you are in doubt about the head's serviceability, consult a reputable automotive machine shop.

3. Remove the valves, springs and retainers, then clean the valve guide bores with a valve guide cleaning tool. Remove all dirt, oil and old gasket material from the cylinder head with solvent. Clean the bolt holes and the oil passage.

4. Remove all deposits from the valves with a wire brush or buffing wheel.

5. Check the head for cracks using a dye penetrant in the valve seat area and ports, head surface and top. Check the gasket surface for burrs, nicks and flatness. If you are in doubt about the head's serviceability, consult a reputable automotive machine shop.

➡If the cylinder head was removed due to an overheating condition and a crack is suspected, do not assume that the head is not damaged because a crack is not visually found. A fracture can be so small that it cannot be seen by eye, yet can still pass coolant when the engine is at operating temperature. Consult an automotive machine shop that has pressure testing equipment to make sure the head is not cracked.

RESURFACING

▶ See Figures 67 and 68

Whenever the cylinder head is removed, check the flatness of the cylinder head gasket surface as follows:

1. Make sure all dirt and old gasket material has been cleaned from the cylinder head. Any foreign material left on the head gasket surface can cause a false measurement.

2. Place a precision straight edge diagonally across the gasket surfaces of the cylinder head as shown in Figs. 62 and 63. Using feeler gauges, determine the clearance at the center of the straight edge.

3. If warpage exceeds 0.0080 in. (0.2mm) along any axis, the head must be reground. If the warpage exceeds 0.0158 in. (0.4mm) along any axis, the cylinder head must be replaced.

Valves

REMOVAL & INSTALLATION

▶ See Figures 69 and 70

1. Remove the cylinder head.

Fig. 66 Remove carbon deposits from the cylinder head combustion chambers using a drill-mounted wire brush

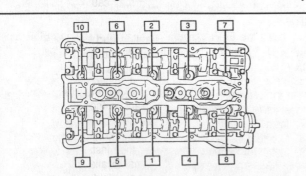

Fig. 65 Cylinder head bolt torque sequence — DOHC engines

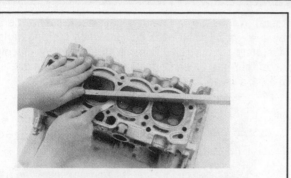

Fig. 67 Checking the cylinder head-to-block mating surface for warpage

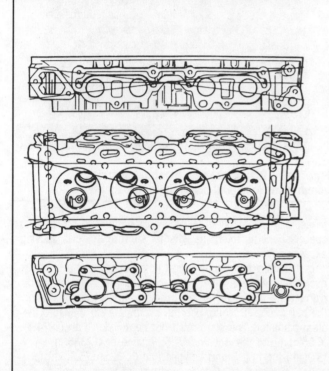

Fig. 68 Check these cylinder head mating surfaces for warpage whenever the head is removed from then engine

2. If not done already, remove the intake and exhaust manifolds.

3. For the SOHC engine, remove the rocker arms/shafts assemblies. Remove the camshaft and oil seal.

➡When disassembling valve trains, parts of which are to be reused, make sure to keep all components labeled or arranged for installation in their original locations. Rocker arms and/or lifters (tappets) must be installed against the same contact surfaces from which they were removed. Store lifters with the camshaft side downward to keep their oil from draining.

4. For the DOHC engine, uniformly remove the camshaft bearing cap fasteners and caps. Begin at the center bearing cap of the exhaust camshaft and work outward, then repeat for the intake camshaft. Remove the camshafts, selective shims and lifters. If necessary a magnet may ease lifter removal.

5. Support the head on suitable blocks with the cylinder side facing downward to facilitate valve removal.

6. Using J-8062, or an equivalent valve spring compressor, and for the DOHC engines, J-37979-A, or an equivalent compressor adapter, remove the valve split collars. With the collars removed, carefully release the spring tension, then remove the upper valve seat, valve spring and valve from the cylinder head.

7. Place the parts from each valve in a separate container, numbered and identified for the valve and cylinder.

8. Remove and discard the valve stem oil seal using an appropriate seal removal tool, a new seal will be used at assembly time.

9. Use an electric drill and rotary wire brush to clean the intake and exhaust valve ports, combustion chamber and valve seats. In some cases, the carbon build-up will have to be chipped away. Use a blunt pointed drift for carbon chipping, being extremely careful around valve seat areas.

10. Use a valve guide cleaning brush and safe solvent to clean the valve guides.

11. Clean the valves with a revolving wire brush. Heavy carbon deposits may be removed with blunt drift.

➡When using a wire brush to remove carbon from the cylinder head or valves, make sure the deposits are actually removed and not just burnished.

12. Wash and clean all valve springs, retainers etc.., in safe solvent. Remember to keep parts from each valve separate.

13. Check the cylinder head for cracks. Cracks usually start around the exhaust valve seat because it is the hottest part of the combustion chamber. If a crack is suspected but cannot be detected visually, have the area checked by pressure testing, with a dye penetrant or other method by an automotive machine shop.

14. Inspect the valves, guides, springs and seats and machine or replace parts, as necessary.

To install:

15. Install new valve seals using the seal removal/installation tool. Do not oil the seal's inner diameter where it contacts the guide.

16. Dip each valve in clean engine oil and install in its original location.

17. Install the valve springs and upper valve seats. Then, using the removal/installation tool to compress the springs, install the valve split collars to the valves. Be careful not to depress the spring cap too far as it may cause seal and stem damage.

➡Once the split collars are installed and the compressor tool is removed, the valve stems should be tapped lightly several times to ensure that the collars are fully seated.

18. For the DOHC engine, lubricate and install the lifters, camshafts and camshaft bearing caps in their proper locations.

19. For the SOHC engine, lubricate and install the camshaft. Oil and install the lifters and shims, then install the rocker arm/shaft assemblies into their original locations.

20. Install the intake and exhaust manifolds to the cylinder head, unless the cylinder head installation procedure includes these components.

21. Install the cylinder head to the vehicle.

INSPECTION

▶ **See Figures 71 and 72**

1. Remove the valves from the cylinder head. Clean the valves, valve guides, valve seats and related components, as explained earlier.

2. Visually check the valves for obvious wear or damage. A burnt valve will have discoloration, severe galling or pitting and even cracks on one area of the valve face. Minor pits, grooves, etc.. can be removed by refacing, but a valve with a cupped head must be replaced. Check the valve stems bends and for obvious wear that is indicated by a step between the part of the stem that travels in the valve guide and the part of the stem near the keeper grooves.

3. Check the valve stem-to-guide clearance in one or more of the following manners, but do not rely on the visual inspection alone:

a. A visual inspection can give you a fairly good idea if the guide, valve stem or both are worn. Insert the valve into the guide until the valve head is slightly away from the valve seat. Wiggle the valve sideways. A small amount of wobble is normal, excessive wobble means a worn guide and/or valve stem.

b. If a dial indicator is on hand, mount the indicator so that gauge stem is 90 degrees to the valve stem as close to the top of the valve guide as possible. Move the valve from the seat, and measure the valve guide-to-stem clearance by rocking the stem back and forth to actuate the dial indicator.

Fig. 70 On DOHC engines, most valve spring compressor tools will also require an adapter

Measure the valve stem using a micrometer and compare to specifications to determine whether stem or guide is causing excessive clearance.

c. If both a ball gauge (small hole gauge) and a micrometer are available. First, measure and note the inside diameter of the valve guide bushing at three locations using the ball gauge. Second, use the micrometer to measure the stem diameter. The stem must not be smaller than 0.274 in. (6.957mm) for the Spectrum 1.5L engine or 0.2335 in. (5.9mm) for 1.6L Storm engines and 0.232 in. (5.9mm) for 1.8L Storm engines. Finally, subtract the valve stem diameter from the corresponding valve guide inside diameter to arrive at the valve clearance.

d. On all engines, if clearance is less than 0.0009 in. (0.023mm) for intake valves or 0.0012 in. (0.030mm) for exhaust valves, the valve guide may be reamed.

e. On the Spectrum, if the clearance is greater than 0.0022 in. (0.056mm) for intake valves or 0.0025 in. (0.063mm) for exhaust valves, the valve and guide must be replaced.

f. On the Storm, if the clearance is greater than 0.0080 in. (0.20mm) for intake or exhaust valves, the valve and guide must be replaced.

4. The valve guide, if worn, must be repaired before the valve seats can be resurfaced. A new valve guide should be installed or, in some cases, knurled. Consult the automotive machine shop.

5. If the valve guide is okay, measure the valve seat concentricity using a run-out gauge. Follow the manufacturers instructions. If run-out is excessive, reface or replace the valve and machine or replace the valve seat.

Fig. 69 Remove the split collars using a suitable valve spring compressor tool to remove spring pressure from the top of the valve stem

6. Valves and seats must always be machined together. Never use a refaced valve on a valve seat that has not been machined; never use a valve that has not been refaced on a machined valve seat.

REFACING

▶ **See Figures 73 and 74**

1. Determine if the valve is usable as explained in the Inspection procedure.

2. The correct valve grinding angle is 45.0 degrees for the Spectrum engine or 45.5 degrees for the Storm engines. Make sure the valve refacer grinding wheels are properly dressed.

3. Reface the valve face only enough to remove the pits and grooves or correct any run-out. If the edge or head margin thickness of the valve head is less than 0.0315 in. (0.8mm) thick after grinding, replace the valve, as the valve will run too hot in the engine.

4. Remove all grooves or score marks from the end of the valve stem, and chamfer it, as necessary. But be careful not to remove too much from the overall length of the valve.

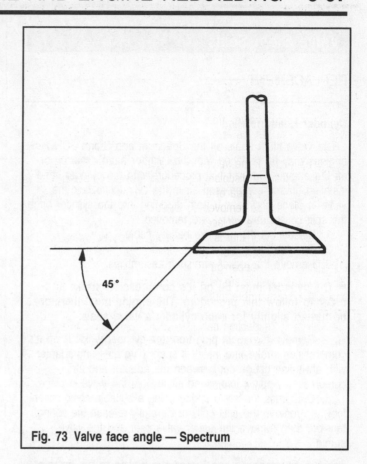

Fig. 73 Valve face angle — Spectrum

Fig. 71 Checking valve stem diameter using a micrometer

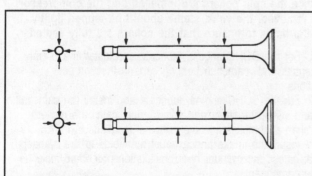

Fig. 72 Check the stem diameter at 3 points along the valve stem

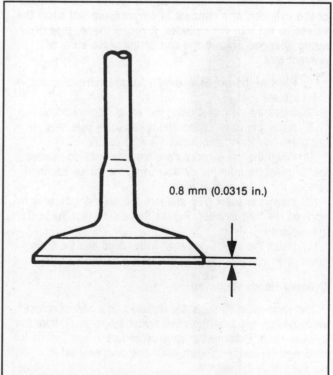

Fig. 74 If the valve margin (head thickness) is less than 0.0315 in. (0.8mm), the valve must be replaced or it will run too hot

Valve Stem Seals

REPLACEMENT

Cylinder Head Installed

The valve stem seals on the Spectrum and Storm SOHC engines may be replaced with the cylinder head either on or off the engine. The removal procedure with the cylinder head installed utilizes compressed air in the cylinder to hold the valve in place and keep it from dropping into the cylinder once the split collars and spring are removed.

1. Disconnect the negative battery cable.
2. Remove the valve cover.
3. Remove the rocker arm/shaft assemblies.

➡The cylinder must be on it's compression stroke in order to follow this procedure. The engine must therefore be turned slightly for each cylinder's valve seals.

4. Remove the spark plug from the cylinder which is on it's compression stroke and install a spark plug air fitting adapter with an in-line gauge set between the adapter and air compressor. Apply compressed air to hold the valve in place.
5. Compress the valve spring using a suitable compressor tool and remove the split collars. Carefully release the spring tension, then remove the upper valve seat and the valve spring.

➡If the air pressure has forced the piston to the bottom of the cylinder, any removal of air pressure will allow the valves to fall into the cylinder. A rubber band, tape or string wrapped around the end of the valve stem will prevent this.

6. Remove the old seal using a suitable removal tool.

To install:

7. Install the new seal using the valve stem seal tool.
8. Install the valve spring and upper valve seat, then compress the spring and install the split collars.
9. When the valve springs are properly installed, release the air pressure from the cylinder using the gauge set, then remove the spark plug adapter.
10. Install the spark plug and turn the engine sufficiently to work on the next cylinder. Repeat Steps 4-11 until the seals are replaced.
11. Install the rocker arm/shaft assemblies and the valve cover, then connect the negative battery cable.

Cylinder Heads Removed

The valve stem oil seals are replaced as a part of normal valve service any time the valve stems are removed from the cylinder head. Refer to the valve procedure in this Section for seal removal and installation when the cylinder head is removed from the vehicle.

Valve Springs

REMOVAL & INSTALLATION

1. Remove the cylinder head.
2. If not done already, remove the intake and exhaust manifolds.
3. For the SOHC engine, remove the rocker arms/shafts assemblies. Remove the camshaft and oil seal.

➡When disassembling valve trains, parts of which are to be reused, make sure to keep all components labeled or arranged for installation in their original locations. Rocker arms and/or lifters (tappets) must be installed against the same contact surfaces from which they were removed. Store lifters with the camshaft side downward to keep their oil from draining.

4. For the DOHC engine, uniformly remove the camshaft bearing cap fasteners and caps. Begin at the center bearing cap of the exhaust camshaft and work outward, then repeat for the intake camshaft. Remove the camshafts, selective shims and lifters. If necessary a magnet may ease lifter removal.
5. Support the head on suitable blocks with the cylinder side facing downward to facilitate valve removal.
6. Using J-8062, or an equivalent valve spring compressor, and for the DOHC engines, J-37979-A, or an equivalent compressor adapter, remove the valve split collars. With the collars removed, carefully release the spring tension, then remove the upper valve seat and the valve spring from the cylinder head.
7. Place the parts from each valve in a separate container, numbered and identified for the valve and cylinder.
8. Inspect the valve springs for damage or wear and replace as necessary. Check the free length and/or spring pressure.

To install:

9. Install the valve springs and upper valve seats. Then, using the removal/installation tool to compress the springs, install the valve split collars to the valves. Be careful not to depress the spring cap too far as it may cause seal and stem damage.

➡Once the split collars are installed and the compressor tool removed, the valve stems should be tapped lightly several times to ensure that the collars are fully seated.

10. For the DOHC engine, lubricate and install the lifters, camshafts and camshaft bearing caps in their proper locations.
11. For the SOHC engine, lubricate and install the camshaft. Oil and install the lifters and shims, then install the rocker arm/shaft assemblies into their original locations.
12. Install the intake and exhaust manifolds to the cylinder head, unless the cylinder head installation procedure includes these components.
13. Install the cylinder head to the vehicle.

INSPECTION

▶ **See Figures 75, 76 and 77**

1. Check the springs for cracks or other damage.

2. Use a ruler to measure the height of each spring at 4 different locations. A bent spring must be replaced. You can also check the spring for squareness using a steel square and a flat surface. Stand the spring and square on end on the flat surface. Slide the spring up to the square, revolve the spring slowly and observe the space between the top coil of the spring and the square. If the space exceeds 0.039 in. (1mm), replace the spring.

3. Measure the free length of the spring using calipers or a suitable service tool:

   a. For the Spectrum, the free length of the valve springs should be approximately 1.9095 in. (48.5mm). The minimum allowable free height is 1.8504 in. (47mm).

   b. For the Storm, SOHC engine, the free length of the valve springs should be approximately 1.73 in. (44.1mm) for intake valves or 1.76 in. (44.7mm) for exhaust valves. The spring must be replaced if the height is less than 1.67 in. (42.6mm) for intake valves or 1.70 in. (43.7mm) for exhaust valves.

4. For the 1.5L Spectrum engine, check the springs for proper pressure at the specified spring lengths using a valve spring tester. First completely compress the spring 3 times, then measure the tension. The pressure should be 47 lbs. (21 Kg) @ 1.57 in. (39.85mm). Replace springs with insufficient tension.

Valve Seats

REMOVAL & INSTALLATION

Due to the high degree of precision and special equipment required, valve seat replacement should be left to an automotive machine shop. Although the seat replacement procedures are virtually the same for all of the Spectrum and Storm engines, the specifications are unique to each cylinder head application. The following procedure can be construed as what is generally acceptable for aluminum cylinder heads; the actual method employed should be the decision of the machinist.

The Chevrolet and Geo engines use replaceable seat inserts. These inserts can be removed by cutting them out to within a few thousandths of their outside diameter and then collapsing the remainder. Another method sometimes used to remove seat inserts is to heat the head to a high temperature and drive the seat out.

Upon installation, the new seat may be installed with the cylinder head heated to a high temperature, then the seat, which is at room temperature or slightly chilled, is pressed into the head. The head is then allowed to cool and as it does, it contracts and grips the seat. In certain applications, the new seat may be driven in with both the head and seat at room temperature. The calculated press-fit interference will then retain the seat in the head.

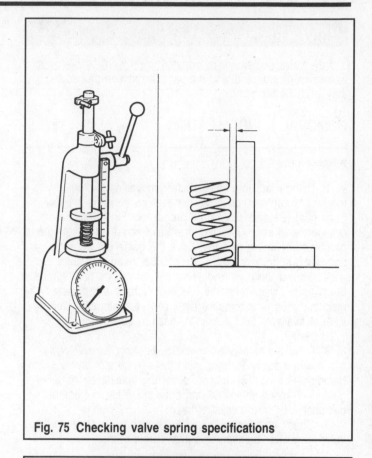
Fig. 75 Checking valve spring specifications

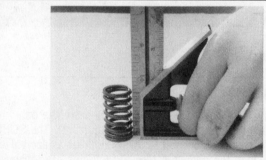
Fig. 76 When checking squareness of valve springs, make sure to hold the square level

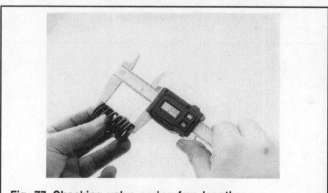
Fig. 77 Checking valve spring free length

Valve Guides

If the valve guides are determined to be worn by discovering excessive clearance during the valve inspection procedure, they must be replaced.

REMOVAL & INSTALLATION

▶ **See Figure 78**

1. Using a suitable valve guide removal/installation service tool and a hammer, drive the old bushing from the cylinder head bore. Be sure to use the proper tool for the applicable cylinder head as an incorrect sized tool could complicate the procedure or cause damage. Drive the guide out from the combustion chamber side of the cylinder head.

2. Inspect the bore to determine if it must be reamed and if an oversized guide must be installed. Consult a reputable machine shop or automotive parts store for information on what is available for the cylinder head in question.

To install:

3. Drive the standard or oversize bushing, as applicable, into the cylinder head bore using the service tool and a hammer. For the 1.5L engine, cover the outside of the valve guide with clean engine oil and drive the guide in from the camshaft side of the cylinder head.

4. Check and assure proper valve clearance. Refer to the valve inspection procedures earlier in this section.

Valve Lifters

REMOVAL & INSTALLATION

▶ **See Figure 79**

➡The Storm 1.6L and 1.8L DOHC engines are the only engines using hydraulic valve lifters (adjusters). The SOHC engines that are being used in these vehicles utilize valve trains in which the camshaft directly actuates the rocker arms. Refer to Section 2 of this manual for lash adjustment.

1. Disconnect the negative battery cable.
2. Remove the camshaft assemblies.

3. Remove the selective shims and valve lifters (adjusters).

➡When removing selective shims and lifters, be sure to arrange them in order of removal to ensure proper installation. Measure the valve lifter (adjuster) outside diameter using a micrometer. If the diameter is less than 1.2l8 in. (31 mm), replace the lifter.

4. Install the selective shims and valve lifters (adjusters).
5. Install the camshaft assemblies. Adjust the valve lash.
6. Connect the negative battery cable.

OVERHAUL

▶ **See Figures 80, 81 and 82**

1. Remove the lifters from the engine and check the outer diameter to determine if they may be reused.

2. Check for air contamination in the lifter oil by attempting to compress the lifter plunger by hand. If the plunger compresses without resistance, the oil must be bled of air; continue with the procedure. If there is resistance, the lifter may be reused.

3. Remove the plunger by gently tapping the lifter against a clean surface such as a small wooden plank.

4. Immerse the lifter in clean, light oil to allow free movement of the inner plunger. Use a wire brush to compress the check ball until the inner plunger stops moving. Refer to Fig. 76.

5. With the lifter immersed in the oil, turn it so the oil hole is facing upward, then install the plunger to the assembly. Refer to the appropriate illustration.

6. Remove the lifter from the oil and attempt to compress the plunger. If no resistance is felt repeat Steps 3-6.

7. Install the lifters to the bores from which they were originally removed.

Oil Pan

REMOVAL & INSTALLATION

Spectrum

▶ **See Figure 83**

1. Disconnect the negative battery cable.

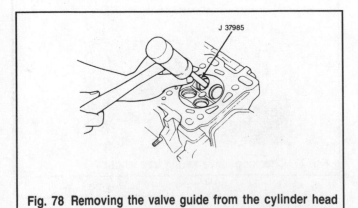

Fig. 78 Removing the valve guide from the cylinder head

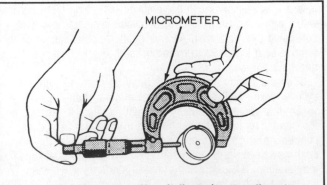

Fig. 79 Checking valve lifter (adjuster) outer diameter

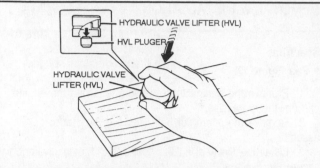

Fig. 80 Remove the plunger from the lifter by gently tapping the assembly on a clean surface

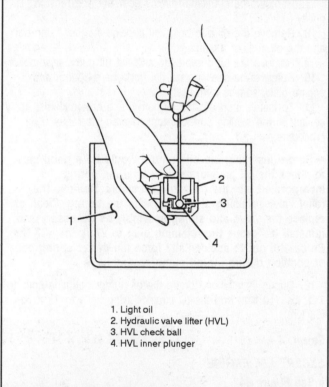

1. Light oil
2. Hydraulic valve lifter (HVL)
3. HVL check ball
4. HVL inner plunger

Fig. 81 While submersed in a clean, light oil, compress the lifter check ball until the plunger stops moving

2. Raise and support the vehicle safely, then drain the crankcase.

3. Disconnect the exhaust pipe bracket from the block and the exhaust pipe at the manifold.

4. Disconnect the right hand tension rod located under the front bumper.

5. Remove the oil pan bolts and oil pan, then clean the sealing surfaces.

6. To install, use a new gasket, apply sealant to the oil pump housing and the rear retainer housing as shown in the illustration, then reverse the removal procedures. Torque the oil pan bolts to 7 ft. lbs. (10 Nm). Torque the exhaust pipe to manifold nuts to 42 ft. lbs. (57 Nm). Torque the exhaust pipe-to-converter bolts and the pipe clamp-to-mounting bracket to 20 ft. lbs. (28 Nm).

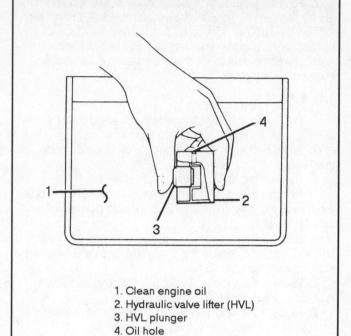

1. Clean engine oil
2. Hydraulic valve lifter (HVL)
3. HVL plunger
4. Oil hole

Fig. 82 With the lifter immersed in the oil and with the oil hole facing upward, install the plunger to the lifter

7. Lower the vehicle, fill the crankcase and connect the negative battery cable.

Storm

EXCEPT 1.8L ENGINE

1. Disconnect the battery negative cable.

2. Raise and support the vehicle safely, then drain engine oil.

3. Remove the right undercover.

4. Remove the front exhaust pipe from the exhaust manifold, then remove the torque rod.

5. Remove the flywheel dust cover. Remove the stiffener from the cylinder head (if so equipped).

6. Remove the oil pan attaching bolts, then remove the oil pan.

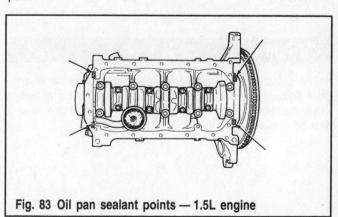

Fig. 83 Oil pan sealant points — 1.5L engine

7. Reverse procedure to install. Apply suitable sealant to the oil pan gasket. Torque oil pan bolts to 89 in. lbs (10 Nm). Tighten the stiffener bolts to 50 ft. lbs. (68 Nm). Connect battery negative cable. Start engine and check for leaks.

8. Lower the vehicle, fill the crankcase and connect the negative battery cable.

1.8L ENGINE

1. Disconnect the negative battery cable and install a suitable engine support fixture and adapter kit.

2. Raise and support the vehicle safely, then drain the crankcase.

3. Remove the left and right splash shields.

4. Remove the forward exhaust pipe bracket, then remove the 3 retaining nuts and the forward exhaust pipe from the exhaust manifold.

5. Remove the torque rod-to-center crossmember through bolt and nut, then remove the 4 retaining bolts and remove the crossmember from the frame.

6. Remove the 2 bolts, 1 nuts and the torque rod along with the bracket from the transaxle.

7. Remove the front and rear cylinder block-to-transaxle braces, then remove the flywheel dust cover.

8. Remove the retaining bolts and nuts, then remove the oil pan from the block. Thoroughly clean the mating surfaces of all remaining gasket material.

To install:

9. Apply a silicone sealant to the oil pan gasket surface, then install the oil pan and tighten the retainers to 89 inch lbs. (10 Nm).

10. Install the flywheel dust cover, then install the front and rear cylinder block-to-transaxle braces.

11. Install the torque rod bracket to the transaxle and secure using the retainers, but do not tighten fully at this time.

12. Install the center crossmember to the frame and tighten the retaining bolts to 45 ft. lbs. (61 Nm).

13. Install the torque rod-to-center crossmember through bolt and nut. Tighten the through-bolt/nut to 51 ft. lbs. (69 Nm), the torque rod bolts to 14 ft. lbs. (19 Nm) and the torque rod nut to 94 ft. lbs. (128 Nm).

14. Install the forward exhaust pipe to the manifold using a new gasket. Tighten the retaining nuts to 46 ft. lbs. (62 Nm).

15. Install the forward exhaust bracket, then install the splash shields and lower the vehicle.

16. Remove the engine support fixture and fill the engine crankcase.

17. Connect the negative battery cable.

Oil Pump

The oil pump is located in a housing mounted to the lower front portion of engine. The pump may be serviced after the cover has been removed. For the Spectrum, the engine must first be removed from the vehicle.

REMOVAL & INSTALLATION

Spectrum

▶ See Figure 84

1. Remove the engine from the vehicle. Drain the engine oil from the crankcase.

2. Remove the alternator belt. Remove the starter assembly.

3. Install the flywheel holding tool J-35271 or equivalent, to secure the flywheel.

4. Remove the crankshaft pulley and boss.

5. Remove the timing cover bolts and the timing cover.

6. Loosen the tension pulley and remove the timing belt.

7. Remove the crankshaft timing gear and the tension pulley.

8. Remove the oil pan bolts, oil pan, oil strainer fixing bolt and the oil strainer assembly.

9. Remove the oil pump bolts and the oil pump assembly.

10. Remove the sealing material from the oil pump and engine block sealing surfaces.

11. To install, lubricate the oil pump, use new gaskets, apply sealant to the sealing surfaces and reverse the removal procedures.

➡Before installing the oil pump it would be a good idea to check the oil pressure relief valve and spring incorporated into the oil pump assembly. Remove the relief valve retaining plug along with the spring. Clean or replace the valve and spring assembly as necessary and reinstall it. Torque the retaining plug to 27 ft. lbs. (37 Nm). Be careful not to accidentally force the garter spring out of position during the oil pump assembly.

12. During installation, torque the oil pump mounting bolts to 7 ft. lbs. (10 Nm) and the oil strainer fixing bolts to 13 ft. lbs. (18 Nm).

Storm

EXCEPT 1.8L ENGINE

▶ See Figure 84

1. Disconnect the battery negative cable.

2. Remove the power steering and alternator belts.

3. Remove the timing belt.

4. Raise and support the vehicle safely.

5. Remove the crankshaft pulley.

6. Remove the oil pump attaching bolts, then the oil pump from the vehicle.

7. Reverse procedure to install. Apply suitable sealant to the oil pump gasket surface. Install bolts and torque to 89 inch lbs. (10 Nm). Connect the battery negative cable. Start engine and check for leaks.

1.8L ENGINE

▶ See Figure 84

1. Disconnect the negative battery cable and drain the engine crankcase.

2. Remove the 6 bolts and the timing belt upper cover.

3. Remove the serpentine drive belt. Support the engine using a floor jack.

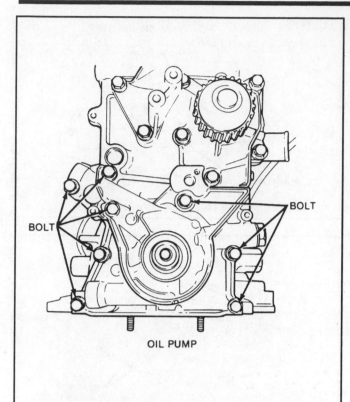

Fig. 84 Remove the oil pump bolts in order to remove the assembly from the engine

4. Remove the bolt and nut from the right engine support bracket, then remove the through bolt and remove the mount from the vehicle.

5. Remove 3 power steering pump bolts and position the pump forward for access to the serpentine drive belt tensioner.

6. Remove the center bolt and the serpentine belt tensioner from the mounting bracket.

7. Remove the 4 bolts and the right engine mount bridge.

8. Remove the 3 bolts and timing belt lower cover.

9. Lower the engine sufficiently for access to the crankshaft pulley, then remove the center bolt and the crankshaft pulley from the engine. Loosen the timing belt tensioner pulley by ½ turn.

10. Remove the timing belt from the crankshaft timing pulley, then using J-28509-A, or an equivalent sprocket removal tool, remove the timing pulley from the crankshaft.

11. Remove the oil pump bolts and the oil pan nuts, then remove the oil pump from the engine block. Thoroughly clean the gasket mating surfaces.

To install:

12. Apply a coat of silicone sealant to the oil pump gasket surface, making sure the no sealant plugs any oil pump ports. Install the pump to the cylinder block, then tighten the bolts and nuts to 89 inch lbs. (10 Nm).

13. Install the timing pulley to the crankshaft, then install the timing belt to the crankshaft pulley. Tighten the tensioner bolt to 31 ft. lbs. (42 Nm). Install the crankshaft pulley to the crankshaft and tighten the pulley center bolt to 108 ft. lbs. (147 Nm).

14. Reposition the engine, then install the timing belt lower cover. Tighten the retaining bolts to 89 inch lbs. (10 Nm).

15. Install the right engine mount bridge and tighten the retaining bolts to 37 ft. lbs. (50 Nm).

16. Install the serpentine drive belt tensioner to the mounting bracket and tighten the center bolt to 30 ft. lbs. (40 Nm).

17. Reposition the power steering pump and tighten the retaining bolts to 15 ft. lbs. (20 Nm).

18. Install the right engine mount to the vehicle, but do not fully tighten the through bolt at this time. Install the bolts and nut to the right engine mount bracket and tighten to 30 ft. lbs. (40 Nm), then tighten the through bolt to 50 ft. lbs. (68 Nm).

19. Remove the floor jack and install the serpentine drive belt.

20. Install the timing belt upper cover and tighten the bolts to 89 inch lbs. (10 Nm).

21. Connect the negative battery cable and fill the engine crankcase.

INSPECTION & OVERHAUL

▶ **See Figures 85, 86, 87, 88 and 89**

1. Remove the oil pump/housing assembly from the vehicle.

2. Inspect the outside of the pump assembly for cracking or other damage. The assembly must be replaced if damage is found.

3. Remove the cover bolts (5 Spectrum or 4 for Storm engines), then remove the cover from the pump housing assembly.

4. Remove the relief valve plug and seal, then remove the spring and valve from the bore in the side of the pump housing.

5. Remove the oil seal from the pump assembly.

6. Using a feeler gauge, measure the clearance between driven gear and the pump body. If clearance exceeds 0.0078 in. (0.20mm) for the Storm or 0.0070 in. (0.18mm) for the Spectrum, replace the oil pump.

7. Using a feeler gauge, measure the clearance between the gear tips. If clearance exceeds 0.012 inch (0.30mm) for the Storm or 0.0138 inch (0.35mm) for the Spectrum, replace the gear set.

8. Using a feeler gauge and a straight edge, check the housing-to-gear set clearance. If clearance exceeds 0.004 inch (0.10mm), replace the oil pump.

Crankshaft Damper/Pulley

REMOVAL & INSTALLATION

Spectrum

Although it may be possible to access the crankshaft damper/pulley while the engine is still in the vehicle, it may be exceedingly difficult. The manufacturer recommends that the engine be removed before attempting to replace components such as the timing belt or the crankshaft damper/gear. To remove these components, refer to the appropriate procedures later in this section.

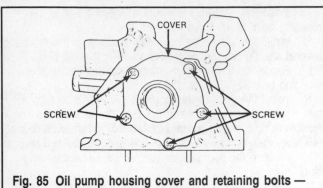

Fig. 85 Oil pump housing cover and retaining bolts — Spectrum (Storm engines similar)

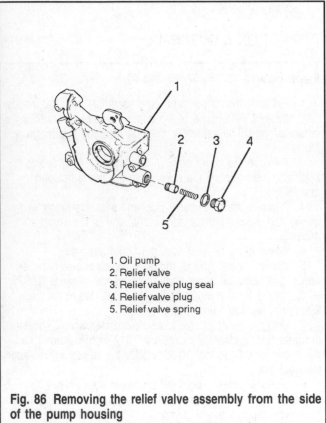

1. Oil pump
2. Relief valve
3. Relief valve plug seal
4. Relief valve plug
5. Relief valve spring

Fig. 86 Removing the relief valve assembly from the side of the pump housing

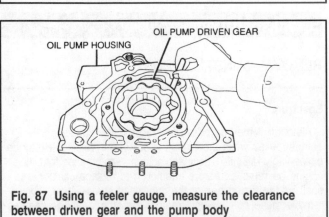

Fig. 87 Using a feeler gauge, measure the clearance between driven gear and the pump body

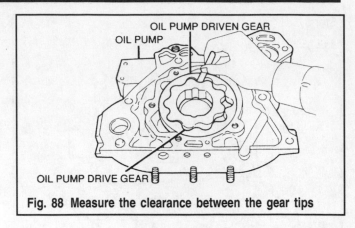

Fig. 88 Measure the clearance between the gear tips

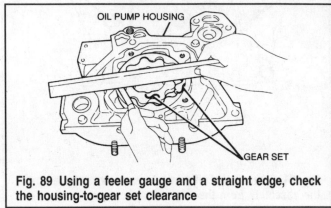

Fig. 89 Using a feeler gauge and a straight edge, check the housing-to-gear set clearance

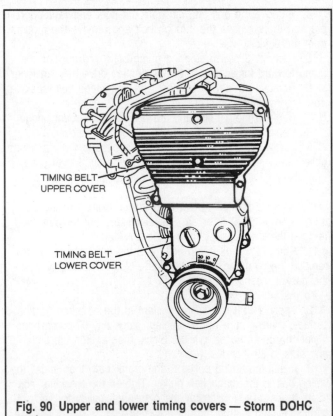

Fig. 90 Upper and lower timing covers — Storm DOHC engines

Storm

1.6L ENGINE

1. Disconnect the negative battery cable.
2. Remove the power steering belt from the crankshaft pulley.
3. Remove the alternator belt.
4. For the DOHC engine, remove the timing belt. Refer to the procedure later in this section.
5. Raise and support the vehicle safely, then remove the right under cover.
6. Remove the crankshaft pulley center bolt. For the DOHC engine, use J-8614-01, or an equivalent pulley holding fixture to prevent the crankshaft from turning.
7. For the SOHC engine, remove the 5 side bolts, then remove the pulley from the engine.
8. For the DOHC engine, use J-1859-03, or an equivalent puller to remove the pulley from the crankshaft.

To install:

9. Align the crankshaft key with the pulley groove, then position the pulley onto the end of the crankshaft.
10. Install the pulley center bolt and tighten to 87 ft. lbs. (118 Nm). For the DOHC engine, use the pulley holding fixture to prevent the crankshaft from turning. For SOHC engines, install the pulley side bolts and tighten to 17 ft. lbs. (23 Nm).
11. Install the right under cover, then remove the supports and carefully lower the vehicle.
12. For the DOHC engine, install the timing belt.
13. Install the alternator belt.
14. Install the power steering belt.
15. Connect the negative battery cable.

1.8L ENGINE

1. Disconnect the negative battery cable.
2. Install an adjustable engine support fixture and adapter kit in order to support the engine weight once the engine mount is removed for access. If an engine hoist is being used as an engine support, raise and support the vehicle sufficiently for both underhood and undervehicle access.
3. Remove the serpentine drive belt from the engine.
4. Remove the bolt and nut from the right engine mount bracket, then remove the through-bolt from the mount. Remove the engine mount from the vehicle.
5. Lower the engine using the support fixture, until the crankshaft pulley may be accessed from underneath the vehicle.
6. If not done already, raise and support the vehicle safely.
7. Remove the right splash shield.
8. Remove the crankshaft pulley center bolt, then remove the pulley from the vehicle.

To install:

9. Align the crankshaft key with the pulley groove, then position the pulley onto the end of the crankshaft.
10. Install the pulley center bolt and tighten to 108 ft. lbs. (147 Nm).
11. Install the right splash shield.
12. If an engine hoist is not being used as the engine support, remove the supports and lower the vehicle.
13. Use the engine support to align the engine with its original position.
14. Install the right engine mount and loosely install the through-bolt. Install and tighten the bracket nut/bolt to 30 ft.

lbs. (40 Nm), then tighten the through-bolt to 50 ft. lbs. (68 Nm).

15. Install the serpentine drive belt.
16. Remove the engine support fixture. If a hoist was use to support the engine, remove the jackstands and carefully lower the vehicle.
17. Connect the negative battery cable.

Timing Belt Cover (Engine Front Cover)

REMOVAL & INSTALLATION

Spectrum

▶ See Figure 37

The Spectrum timing cover may be removed with the engine installed in order to inspect the drive belt, camshaft pulley, timing belt tension pulley and the water pump. If the timing belt or the crankshaft timing pulley must be removed, then engine must first be pulled from the vehicle. Refer to the timing belt procedure later in this section.

1. Disconnect the negative battery cable.
2. Rotate the crankshaft until the No. 4 cylinder is at TDC of the compression stroke and the crankshaft timing mark aligns with the **0** mark on the timing cover toothed gauge. This step must be performed if the timing belt or any of the timing pulleys are to be removed from the engine.
3. Support the engine, then remove the front mount bracket attached to the front cover.
4. Remove the retaining bolts, then remove the timing cover from the engine.

To install:

5. Install the timing cover to the engine and tighten the bolts to 7 ft. lbs. (10 Nm).
6. Install the engine mount bracket and tighten the fasteners to 17 ft. lbs. (23 Nm).
7. Connect the negative battery cable.

Storm

SOHC ENGINE

1. Disconnect the battery negative cable.
2. Remove the alternator belt, then the power steering belt.
3. Support the engine using J-28467-A or an equivalent engine support fixture.
4. Remove the right engine mount.
5. Remove the timing belt cover retaining bolts, then the timing belt cover from the vehicle. It may be necessary to support the vehicle and remove the right under cover in order to access the lower timing cover bolts.
6. Reverse procedure to install. Tighten the cover bolts to 89 inch lbs. (10 Nm). Connect the battery negative cable.

DOHC ENGINE

▶ See Figure 90

Unlike the other Storm engine, the DOHC engines utilize a 2-piece timing cover consisting of an upper and a lower assembly.

1. Disconnect the battery negative cable.

2. Support the engine using J-28467-A or an equivalent engine support fixture.

3. Remove the right engine mount, by first removing the bracket bolt and nut, then removing the mount through-bolt.

4. Remove the alternator and power steering belts (1.6L engine) or the serpentine drive belt (1.8L engine). If necessary, remove the retaining bolt and relocate the wiring harness from the timing belt upper cover.

5. Remove the upper timing belt cover attaching screws, then remove the upper timing belt cover from the vehicle.

6. Raise and support the vehicle safely.

7. Remove the crankshaft pulley. Refer to the procedure earlier in this section.

8. Remove the retaining bolts and the lower timing belt cover.

9. Reverse procedure to install. Tighten the lower and upper cover retaining bolts to 89 inch lbs. (10 Nm). Connect the battery negative cable.

Timing Belt

REMOVAL & INSTALLATION

Although timing belts may last for thousands of miles past the recommended replacement interval, they should be replaced every 60,000 miles to prevent trouble or damage should they snap. Timing belts do not usually give an indication that they are worn or aging without removing the cover(s) and inspecting the belt. A worn or damaged belt could give out at any time. In some cases, should a timing belt snap while the engine is running, damage could be done to the valve trains or pistons requiring a partial or full engine disassembly. Also, should the belt go when the vehicle is far from home, a costly tow or even more costly repair job and considerable inconvenience may be suffered.

➡ Timing belts must always be handled carefully and kept completely free of dirt, grease, fluids and lubricants. This includes any accidental contact from spillage, fingerprints, rags, etc.. These same precautions apply to the pulleys and contact surfaces on which the belt rides. The belt must never be crimped, twisted or bent. Never use tools to pry or wedge the belt into place. Such actions will damage the structure of the belt and possibly cause breakage.

Spectrum

▶ See Figures 91, 92 and 93

The engine must be removed from the vehicle for this procedure to be performed.

1. Remove the engine and mount it to an engine stand.

2. Remove the accessory drive belts.

3. Remove the engine mounting bracket from the timing cover.

4. Rotate the crankshaft until the notch on the crankshaft pulley aligns with the 0 degree mark on the timing cover and the No. 4 cylinder is on TDC of the compression stroke.

5. Remove the starter and install the flywheel holding tool No. J-35271 or equivalent.

6. Remove the crankshaft bolt, boss and pulley.

7. Remove the timing cover bolts and the timing cover.

8. Loosen the tension pulley bolt.

9. Insert an Allen wrench into the tension pulley hexagonal hole and loosen the timing belt by turning the tension pulley clockwise.

10. Remove the timing belt.

11. Remove the head cover.

➡Inspect the timing belt for signs of cracking, abnormal wear and hardening. Never expose the belt to oil, sunlight or heat. Avoid excessive bending, twisting or stretching.

To install:

12. Position the Woodruff key in the crankshaft followed by the crankshaft timing gear. Align the groove on the timing gear with the mark on the oil pump.

13. Align the camshaft timing gear mark with the upper surface of the cylinder head and the dowel pin in its uppermost position.

14. Place the timing belt arrow in the direction of the engine rotation and install the timing belt, first to the crankshaft pulley, next to the camshaft pulley, then to the water pump pulley and finally to the tension pulley. Tighten the tension pulley bolt.

➡Once installed, there must be not slack in the timing belt. The belt teeth must be in perfect alignment with the gears.

15. Turn the crankshaft 2 complete revolutions and realign the crankshaft timing gear groove with the mark on the oil pump.

16. Loosen the tension pulley bolt and apply tension to the belt using an Allen wrench in the hexagonal pulley hole. Torque the pulley bolt to 37 ft. lbs. (50 Nm) while holding the pulley stationary.

17. Check the timing belt tension using a belt tension gauge, it should be 40-48 lbs. (18-22 Kg).

18. Adjust the valve clearances.

19. To complete the installation, reverse the removal procedures. Torque the crankshaft pulley-to-crankshaft bolt to 108 ft. lbs. (147 Nm).

Storm

SOHC ENGINE

▶ See Figures 91, 92 and 93

1. Disconnect the battery negative cable.

2. Remove the timing belt cover. If necessary, raise and support the vehicle, then remove the right under cover to access the lower timing cover bolts.

3. If not done already, rotate the crankshaft so that the No. 4 cylinder is at TDC on its compression stroke by aligning the camshaft pulley timing mark to the 9 o'clock position.

4. Raise and support the vehicle safely.

5. Remove the crankshaft pulley center bolt, the 4 crankshaft pulley side bolts and the crankshaft pulley from the vehicle.

6. Loosen the belt tension pulley bolt, then remove the timing belt from around the tensioner and other pulleys. Remove the timing belt from the vehicle.

To install:

7. Make sure the crankshaft pulley keyway and groove is aligned with the oil pump timing mark and the camshaft pulley

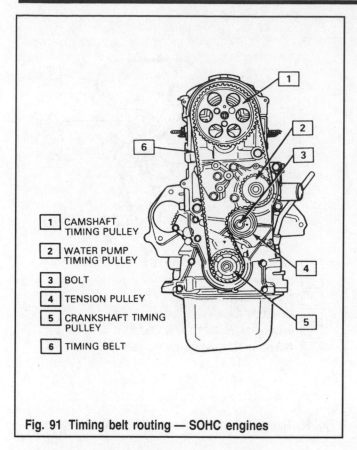

Fig. 91 Timing belt routing — SOHC engines

1 CAMSHAFT TIMING PULLEY
2 WATER PUMP TIMING PULLEY
3 BOLT
4 TENSION PULLEY
5 CRANKSHAFT TIMING PULLEY
6 TIMING BELT

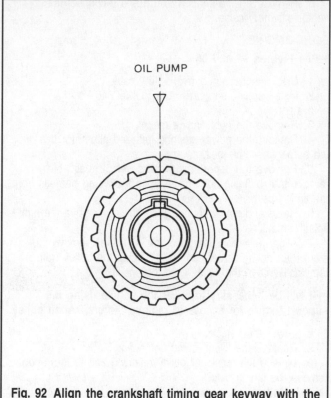

Fig. 92 Align the crankshaft timing gear keyway with the mark in the oil pump — SOHC engines

timing mark is in the 9 o'clock position. Install the timing belt around the crankshaft timing pulley, followed by the tensioner pulley, water pump pulley and the camshaft timing pulley.

8. Tighten the belt tensioner retaining bolt. Make sure that the belt is properly tightened and is aligned evenly around all the pulleys:

a. Turn the crankshaft 2 complete revolutions and realign the crankshaft timing gear groove with the mark on the oil pump.

b. Loosen the tension pulley bolt and apply tension to the belt using an Allen wrench in the hexagonal pulley hole. Torque the pulley bolt to 37 ft. lbs. (50 Nm) while holding the pulley stationary.

c. Check the timing belt tension/deflection using a belt tension gauge. The belt should deflect 0.63-0.79 in. (16-20mm) when 22 lbs. (98 N) of pressure is applied to the center of the longest belt stretch.

9. Check that the camshaft is still aligned to the 9 o'clock position.

10. Install the timing belt cover, secure it with the 2 lower mounting bolts, then torque the bolts to 89 in. lbs. (10 Nm).

11. Install the crankshaft pulley to the crankshaft dampener, secure the center bolt and the 4 side bolts. Torque the center bolt to 87 ft. lbs. (118 Nm) and the 4 side bolts to 17 ft. lbs. (23 Nm).

12. If removed, install the right side under cover.

13. Lower the vehicle. Install the 4 upper timing belt cover retaining bolts and tighten to 89 inch lbs. (10 Nm).

14. Install the right engine mount.

15. Install the power steering pump drive belt and alternator drive belt. Adjust them to the proper belt tension.

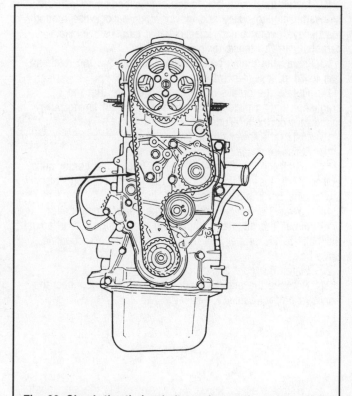

Fig. 93 Check the timing belt tension at the center of the longest point between pulleys — SOHC engines

16. Remove engine support fixture and reconnect the negative battery cable.

DOHC ENGINE

▶ See Figures 94 and 95

1. Disconnect the negative battery cable.
2. Install engine support fixture tool J-28467-A or equivalent.
3. Remove the right engine mount.
4. Remove the power steering belt and alternator belt or the serpentine drive belt, as applicable.
5. Remove the upper timing belt cover. If applicable, remove the retaining bolt and relocate the wiring harness from the timing cover.
6. Raise and safely support the vehicle. Remove the right splash shield.
7. Align the crankshaft pulley to TDC, then remove the crankshaft pulley center bolt while holding the pulley from turning. Remove the pulley from the engine.

➡It will be necessary to lower the engine using the support fixture for access to remove the crankshaft pulley.

8. Lower the vehicle.
9. Remove the lower timing belt cover.
10. Loosen the tensioner pulley retaining bolt ½ turn and remove the timing belt.

To install:

11. Make sure the camshaft pulleys' timing marks are properly aligned.
12. Install the timing belt to the engine beginning with the crankshaft timing pulley and moving counterclockwise around the pulleys (water pump, idler, exhaust camshaft, intake camshaft) to the tensioner pulley.
13. Install the timing belt tensioner and torque the retaining bolt to 31 ft. lbs. (42 Nm).
14. Rotate the crankshaft 2 turns to ensure that the crankshaft timing pulley mark and the camshaft timing pulley marks are correctly aligned.
15. Install the lower timing belt cover.
16. Raise and safely support the vehicle.
17. Install the crankshaft pulley and torque the center pulley bolt to 87 ft. lbs. (118 Nm). Using the engine support, raise the engine back into position.
18. Lower the vehicle and install the upper timing cover.
19. Install the alternator and power steering belt, then adjust the belts to the proper belt tension or install the serpentine drive belt.
20. Install the right engine mount.
21. Remove the engine support fixture tool. Reconnect the negative battery cable.

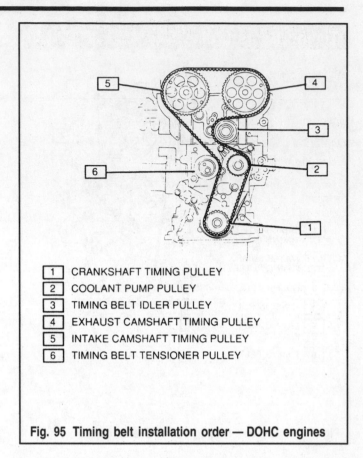

1	CRANKSHAFT TIMING PULLEY
2	COOLANT PUMP PULLEY
3	TIMING BELT IDLER PULLEY
4	EXHAUST CAMSHAFT TIMING PULLEY
5	INTAKE CAMSHAFT TIMING PULLEY
6	TIMING BELT TENSIONER PULLEY

Fig. 95 Timing belt installation order — DOHC engines

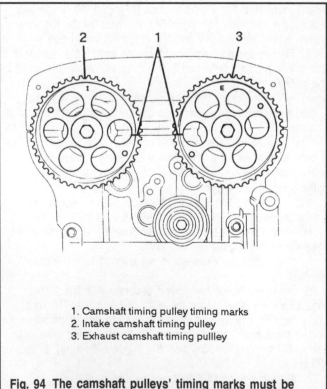

1. Camshaft timing pulley timing marks
2. Intake camshaft timing pulley
3. Exhaust camshaft timing pullley

Fig. 94 The camshaft pulleys' timing marks must be properly aligned before the timing belt is installed — DOHC engines

Timing Gears (Pulleys)

REMOVAL & INSTALLATION

Spectrum

CAMSHAFT/TENSION PULLEYS

▶ See Figures 96 and 97

Unlike the Spectrum crankshaft timing pulley, both the camshaft and tension pulleys may be removed with the engine installed in the vehicle.

1. Disconnect the negative battery cable.
2. Remove the timing belt cover; refer to the procedure earlier in this section.
3. Make sure the timing mark on the camshaft pulley is aligned with the upper surface of the cylinder head and that the camshaft dowel pin is positioned to the top of the gear.
4. Loosen the camshaft pulley retaining bolts.
5. Loosen the timing belt tension pulley and allow the belt to hang.
6. Remove the camshaft timing pulley and/or the tension pulley.

To install:

7. If removed, install the tension pulley assembly and tighten the retaining bolt to 37 ft. lbs. (50 Nm).
8. If removed, install the camshaft pulley and tighten the retaining bolts to 7 ft. lbs. (10 Nm).
9. Make sure the timing marks are aligned, then turn the crankshaft 2 complete revolutions and realign the crankshaft timing gear groove with the mark on the oil pump. The marks camshaft marks should still be properly aligned.
10. Loosen the tension pulley bolt and apply tension to the belt using an Allen wrench in the hexagonal pulley hole. Torque the pulley bolt to 37 ft. lbs. (50 Nm) while holding the pulley stationary.
11. Check the timing belt tension using a belt tension gauge, it should be 40-48 lbs. (18-22 Kg).
12. Install the timing belt cover.
13. Connect the negative battery cable.

CRANKSHAFT PULLEY

1. Disconnect the negative battery cable.
2. Remove the engine assembly from the vehicle. Refer to the procedure earlier in this section.
3. Remove the timing belt. Refer to the procedure earlier in this section.
4. Remove the crankshaft timing pulley from the end of the crankshaft. If necessary use a puller, but be sure that the puller will not damage the crankshaft or the gear.

To install:

5. Position the Woodruff key in the crankshaft followed by the crankshaft timing gear. Align the groove on the timing gear with the mark on the oil pump.
6. Install the timing belt to the engine.
7. Install the engine assembly.
8. Connect the negative battery cable.

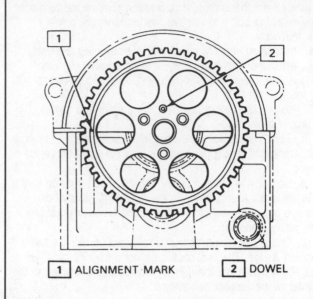

| **1** ALIGNMENT MARK | **2** DOWEL |

Fig. 96 At TDC the timing mark on the camshaft pulley is aligned with the upper surface of the cylinder head and the camshaft dowel pin is positioned to the top of the gear — SOHC engines

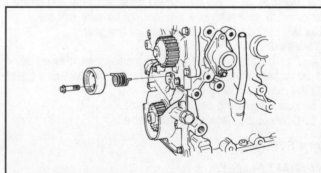

Fig. 97 Exploded view of the timing belt tension pulley assembly — Spectrum

Storm SOHC engine

CAMSHAFT/TENSION PULLEYS

▶ See Figure 96

1. Disconnect the negative battery cable.
2. Remove the timing cover. Refer to the procedure earlier in this section.
3. Remove the crankshaft pulley bolts and remove the pulley from the engine. Refer to the procedure earlier in this section.
4. Turn the engine to the No. 4 cylinder TDC position by aligning the crankshaft timing pulley groove and keyway with the oil pump timing mark.
5. Loosen the tension pulley lock bolt, then loosen the timing belt by turning the tension pulley clockwise.
6. Remove the timing belt from the camshaft pulley.

7. Remove the camshaft pulley retaining bolts and remove the pulley from the engine. If necessary, remove the tensioner pulley retaining bolt and remove the tensioner assembly.

To install:

8. If removed, loosely install the tension pulley assembly.

9. Install the camshaft pulley, making sure to align the timing marks, then install the retaining bolts and tighten to 106 inch lbs. (12 Nm).

10. Position the timing belt over the pulleys and adjust to the proper tension.

   a. Turn the crankshaft 2 complete revolutions and realign the crankshaft timing gear groove with the mark on the oil pump.

   b. Loosen the tension pulley bolt and apply tension to the belt using an Allen wrench in the hexagonal pulley hole. Torque the pulley bolt to 37 ft. lbs. (50 Nm) while holding the pulley stationary.

   c. Check the timing belt tension/deflection using a belt tension gauge. The belt should deflect 0.63-0.79 in. (16-20mm) when 22 lbs. (98 N) of pressure is applied to the center of the longest belt stretch.

11. Install the crankshaft pulley.

12. Install the timing cover.

13. Connect the negative battery cable.

CRANKSHAFT PULLEY

1. Disconnect the negative battery cable.

2. Remove the timing belt. Refer to the procedure earlier in this section.

3. Remove the crankshaft timing pulley from the end of the crankshaft. If necessary use a puller, but be sure that the puller will not damage the crankshaft or the gear.

To install:

4. Position the Woodruff key in the crankshaft followed by the crankshaft timing gear. Align the groove on the timing gear with the mark on the oil pump.

5. Install the timing belt to the engine.

6. Connect the negative battery cable.

Storm DOHC engines

CAMSHAFT PULLEYS

▶ See Figure 94

1. Disconnect the negative battery cable.

2. Remove the camshaft cover from the cylinder head. Refer to the procedure earlier in this section.

3. Rotate the crankshaft until the No. 1 cylinder is at the TDC position which will be achieved when the camshaft pulleys' timing marks are aligned, facing each other. Refer to the illustration shown earlier in this section.

4. Remove the tension adjusting hole cover, then loosen the tension pulley lock bolt and loosen the timing belt by turning the tension pulley clockwise. If the engine is not equipped with a tension adjusting hole cover, the timing cover must be removed for access to the tension pulley bolt.

5. Remove the timing belt from the camshaft pulleys.

6. Remove the camshaft pulley retaining bolts, then remove the pulleys from the ends of the camshafts.

To install:

7. Install the pulleys to the camshafts, while aligning the timing marks. Secure the pulleys with the retaining bolts and tighten to 44 ft. lbs. (59 Nm).

8. Position the timing belt over the camshaft pulleys.

9. Rotate the timing belt tensioner into contact with the timing belt and torque the retaining bolt to 31 ft. lbs. (42 Nm).

10. Rotate the crankshaft 2 turns to ensure that the camshaft timing pulley marks are correctly aligned.

11. Install the tensioner adjusting hole cover or the timing covers, as applicable.

12. Install the camshaft cover to the cylinder head.

13. Connect the negative battery cable.

CRANKSHAFT PULLEY

1. Disconnect the negative battery cable.

2. Remove the timing belt. Refer to the procedure earlier in this section.

3. Remove the crankshaft timing pulley from the end of the crankshaft.

To install:

4. Position the crankshaft timing pulley to the end of the crankshaft.

5. Install the timing belt to the engine.

6. Connect the negative battery cable.

Camshaft and Bearings

REMOVAL & INSTALLATION

Spectrum

▶ See Figure 98

1. Disconnect the negative battery cable.

2. Align the crankshaft pulley notch with the **0** degree mark on the timing cover.

3. Remove the cylinder head cover.

4. Remove the timing cover.

5. Loosen the camshaft timing gear bolts; Be careful not rotate the engine.

6. Loosen the timing belt tensioner and remove the timing belt from the camshaft timing gear.

7. Remove the rocker arm shaft/rocker arm assembly. Remove the timing gear from the camshaft.

8. Remove the distributor bolt and the distributor.

9. Remove the camshaft and the camshaft seal.

10. To install, drive a new camshaft seal on the camshaft using the seal installation tool No. J-35268 or equivalent, reverse the removal procedures, adjust the valves and the timing belt.

Storm

▶ See Figures 99, 100 and 101

1. Disconnect the battery negative cable.

2. Remove the cylinder head cover.

3. Rotate the crankshaft to position No. 1 at TDC on its compression stroke by aligning the camshaft(s) pulley timing mark with the cylinder head cover.

4. Loosen the timing belt tensioner.

5. Remove the timing belt pulley(s) from the camshaft(s).

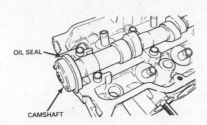

Fig. 98 Remove the camshaft and seal from the cylinder head — Spectrum

6. Remove the distributor.

➡When removing the camshaft bearing caps, be sure to note location and orientation of all the caps to assure they are reinstalled in the same positions. On some engines the caps may be numbered, labelled (E or I for exhaust or Intake) and/or may contain arrows showing proper direction for installation.

7. Remove the camshaft(s) bearing cap bolts, starting at the center and moving outward, then remove the camshaft and seal from the vehicle. Discard seal.

8. Reverse procedure to install. For the DOHC engines, apply sealant to the appropriate points on the bearing caps as shown. Torque the camshaft bearing cap bolts to 89 inch lbs. (10 Nm). Connect the battery negative cable. Start the engine and check for leaks.

INSPECTION

▶ **See Figures 102, 103, 104, 105, 106, 107 and 108**

1. Clean the camshaft in solvent and allow to dry.
2. Inspect the camshaft for obvious signs of wear: scores, nicks or pits on the journals or lobes. Light scuffs or nicks can be removed with an oil stone.
3. Position the camshaft in V-blocks with the front and rear journals riding on the blocks. Check if the camshaft is bent using a dial indicator on the center bearing journal. The run-out limit at the center journal is 0.00394 in. (0.1mm). Replace the camshaft if run-out is excessive.

Fig. 99 Check to see if the camshaft bearing caps are labelled like this one, to assure installation in the proper positions. If necessary, arrange and/or tag the caps to assure proper orientation

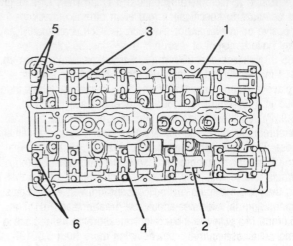

1. Intake camshaft
2. Exhaust camshaft
3. Intake camshaft bearing caps
4. Exhaust camshaft bearing caps
5. Intake camshaft bearing cap bolts
6. Exhaust camshaft bearing cap bolts

Fig. 100 Camshafts and bearing caps — Storm DOHC engines

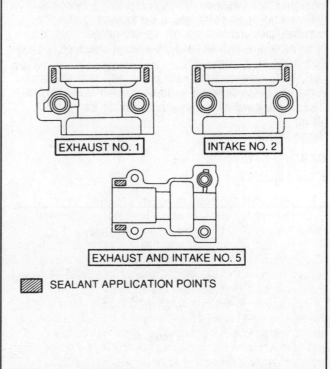

EXHAUST NO. 1   INTAKE NO. 2

EXHAUST AND INTAKE NO. 5

▨ SEALANT APPLICATION POINTS

Fig. 101 For the DOHC camshafts apply sealant to these points on the exhaust No. 1, intake No. 2 and both No. 5 bearing caps

4. Using a micrometer, measure the camshaft lobe heights and compare to specification and each other to check for excessive or uneven wear. Replace a SOHC camshaft if any lobes have a height of less than 1.426 in. (36.22mm) for 1985-92 vehicles or 1.399 in. (35.54mm) on intake lobes and 1.413 in. (35.89mm) on exhaust lobes for 1993 vehicles. Replace a DOHC camshaft if any lobe heights are less than 1.503 in. (38.17mm) for 1.6L DOHC engines or 1.531 in. (38.9mm) for the 1.8L DOHC engine. Compare the measurements of all the camshaft's lobes. Replace a camshaft whose wear deviates more than 0.00197 in. (0.05mm).

5. Using a micrometer, measure the diameter of the journals and replace any camshaft containing a journal that is less than the minimum or that contains uneven wear. For all engines, journal diameter should be greater than 1.0157 in. (25.8mm). As with the lobe height measurements, replace a camshaft whose journal wear deviates more than 0.00197 in. (0.05mm).

6. Measure the bearing oil clearance using a plastic-type gauging material. Temporarily install the camshaft to the cylinder head. Place a strip of the gauge material on the top of each journal, then install the bearing caps and tighten to 89 inch lbs. (10 Nm). DO NOT ROTATE THE CAMSHAFT or the measurement will be ruined and the process must be repeated. Remove the bearing caps and compare the width of the strip to the gauge. If the gauging material reveals an oil clearance of more than 0.0059 in. (0.15mm), the camshaft and/or the cylinder head must be replaced.

7. With the camshaft and bearing cap temporarily installed, mount a dial gauge to 1 end of the camshaft in order to measure thrust clearance. Carefully pry on the other end of the camshaft or on either side of the journals to slide the camshaft back and forth against the dial gauge. Replace camshaft and/or cylinder head if the thrust clearance is greater than 0.008 in. (0.2mm).

8. Finally, measure the width of the distributor slot located in the end of the camshaft (exhaust shaft on DOHC engines). Replace the camshaft if slot width is greater than 0.196 in. (5mm).

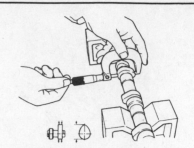

Fig. 103 Measure the camshaft lobe height using an outside micrometer

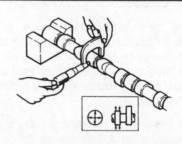

Fig. 104 Measure camshaft journal diameter using an outside micrometer

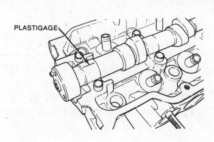

Fig. 105 Apply a strip of plastic-type gauging material to the top of each journal

Pistons and Connecting Rods

REMOVAL

▶ **See Figures 109, 110, 111, 112, 113 and 114**

1. Remove the engine from the vehicle and mount it on a suitable workstand.
2. Remove the cylinder head and the oil pan.
3. Check the connecting rod side clearance vertically along the side of the rod using a feeler gauge while moving the rod back and forth. The maximum allowable clearance is 0.158 in.

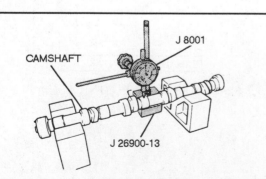

Fig. 102 Measure camshaft run-out at the center bearing journal using a dial gauge

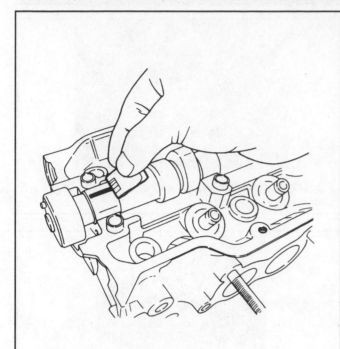

Fig. 106 After tightening, then removing the bearing caps, compare the plastic material width to the gauge in order to determine journal oil clearance

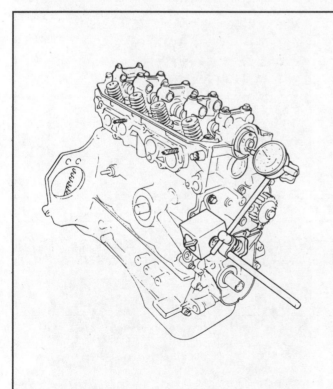

Fig. 107 Mount a dial gauge on the end of the camshaft to measure thrust clearance

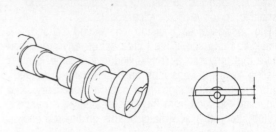

Fig. 108 Measure the distributor slot width in the end of the camshaft

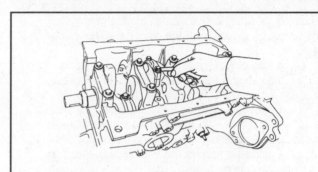

Fig. 109 Check the connecting rod side (thrust) clearance using a feeler gauge

Fig. 110 Apply a strip of plastic-type gauging material to the rod journal

(0.40mm). Replace the connecting rod assembly or the crankshaft to correct extreme clearance(s).

4. The position of each piston, connecting rod and connecting rod cap should be noted before any are removed, to assure that they can be reinstalled in the same location. Connecting rods and caps may be color coded or tagged during to prevent interchanging of parts. If necessary, prior to disconnecting the rods from the crankshaft, use a punch or numbering stamp to place match marks on the rod and cap to ensure correct reassembly.

5. Loosen and remove the connecting rod cap nuts, then tap the connecting rod bolts with a plastic-faced hammer to loosen the bearing cap. Remove the bearing cap from the connecting rod.

6. Clean the rod journal and bearing. Inspect the crank pin and bearing for pitting and scratches to determine if rod journals must be ground, or if the bearings and/or crankshaft must be replaced.

7. Lay a strip of Plastigage® across the rod journal, then install the rod cap and tighten the retainers to specification; refer to the torque chart. Remove the retainers and the rod cap, then determine oil clearance by comparing the widest point of the Plastigage® to the chart as per the manufacturers instructions. The maximum allowable clearance is 0.0047 in. (0.12mm). Completely remove the Plastigage® after the measurement has been taken.

8. Cover the connecting rod bolts with a short piece of ¼ in. (6.34mm) inner diameter rubber hose to protect the crankshaft from scoring or damage. The connecting rod should not be removed until measurements are taken and the cylinder ridge, if present, has been removed.

9. Check the top of the cylinder liner for excessive carbon. If necessary, carefully remove the carbon deposits before attempting to remove the piston.

10. Using a hammer handle or piece of wood or plastic, tap the rod and piston upward in the bore until the piston rings clear the cylinder block. Remove the piston and connecting rod assembly from the top of the cylinder bore.

CLEANING AND INSPECTION

♦ See Figures 115, 116, 117, 118 and 119

1. Remove the piston rings using a piston ring expander. Refer to the Piston Ring Replacement procedure.

Fig. 111 Install the bearing cap and torque to specification

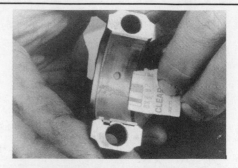

Fig. 112 Remove the bearing cap and compare the plastic strip to the gauge

Fig. 113 Protect the crankshaft and cylinder walls from scoring or damage by installing short lengths of rubber hose over the connecting rod bolts before removing the piston

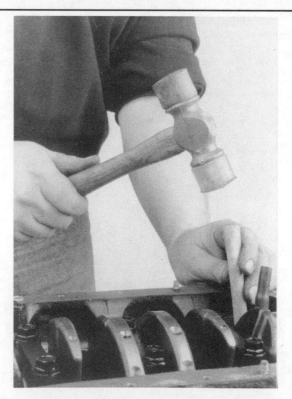

Fig. 114 Using a piece of wood such as a hammer handle, gently tap the piston through the cylinder bore

2. Clean the ring grooves with a ring groove cleaner or a broken piston ring, being careful not to cut into the piston metal. Heavy carbon deposits can be cleaned from the top of the piston with a wire brush, however, do not use a wire wheel on the ring grooves or lands. Clean the oil drain holes in the ring grooves. Clean all remaining dirt, carbon and varnish from the piston with a suitable solvent and a brush; do not use a caustic solution.

3. After cleaning, inspect the piston for scuffing, scoring, cracks, pitting or excessive ring groove wear. Replace any piston that is obviously worn.

4. If the piston appears okay, measure the piston diameter using a micrometer and note the measurement for calculations later. Measure the piston diameter at the grading position, located 1.12 in. (28.5mm) on 1.5L engines or 1.18 in. (30mm) on 1.6L and 1.8L engines, from the top of the piston, perpendicular to the piston pin bore.

5. Measure the cylinder bore diameter using a bore gauge, or using a telescope gauge and micrometer. Make 2 measurements longitudinal and transverse, then average the 2 results and record for calculations.

6. Subtract the piston diameter measurement made in Step 4 from the cylinder bore measurement made in Step 5 to determine the piston-to-bore clearance. Compare the clearance measurements with the specifications. If the clearance is within specification, light finish honing is all that is necessary. If the clearance is excessive, the cylinder must be bored and the piston replaced. Consult an automotive machine shop. If the pistons are replaced, the piston rings must also be replaced.

7. If the piston-to-bore clearance is okay, check the ring groove clearance. Insert the ring that will be used in the ring groove and check the clearance with a feeler gauge, as shown. Compare your measurement with specification. Replace the piston if the ring groove clearance is greater than 0.0059 in. (0.15mm).

8. Next, check the piston ring end gaps. This is done by inserting the ring into the cylinder bore and using the inverted piston to push the ring slightly beyond standard ring travel. The ring must be squared within the bore. Then use a feeler gauge to check the size of the ring gap. If the end gap is greater than 0.059 in. (1.5mm), replace the ring and remeasure. If the gap is still excessive, rebore the cylinder and install oversize pistons and rings.

9. Check the connecting rod for damage or obvious wear. Check for signs of fractures and check the bearing bore for out-of-round and taper.

10. A shiny surface on the pin boss side of the piston usually indicates that the connecting rod is bent or the wrist pin hole is not in proper relation to the piston skirt and ring grooves.

11. Abnormal connecting rod bearing wear can be caused by either a bent connecting rod, an improperly machined journal, or a tapered connecting rod bore.

12. Twisted connecting rods will not create an easily identifiable wear pattern, but badly twisted rods will disturb the action of the entire piston, rings, and connecting rod assembly and may be the cause of excessive oil consumption.

13. Remove and inspect the piston pin from the assembly; refer to the procedure later in this section. If measurements

are good, but a connecting rod problem is still suspected, consult an automotive machine shop to have the rod checked further.

PISTON PIN REPLACEMENT

♦ **See Figures 120, 121 and 122**

1. With the pistons removed from the block, check the fit between the piston and pin. Grasp the piston and try to move it back and forth on the pin. If movement is felt, remove the piston pin and connecting rod in order to check pin to connecting rod clearances.

2. If applicable, remove the snaprings from the piston and pin end.

3. Inspect the piston bore for burrs and remove, if found, using a sharp blade. This will prevent piston pin scoring during removal.

4. Using a wooden block to support the piston, tap or press out the pin from the piston and connecting rod. For the 1.6L engines, a pin service tool kit is available and a press must be used to free the pins.

5. Using an outside micrometer, measure the piston pin diameter. Replace a piston pin whose diameter is less than 0.7075 in. (17.97mm) for all engines except the 1.8L whose piston pins may not be less than 0.7862 in. (19.97mm) in diameter.

6. Using a small hole gauge and outside micrometer, measure the connecting rod small end. Compare the

Fig. 115 The top of the piston may be cleaned using a wire brush

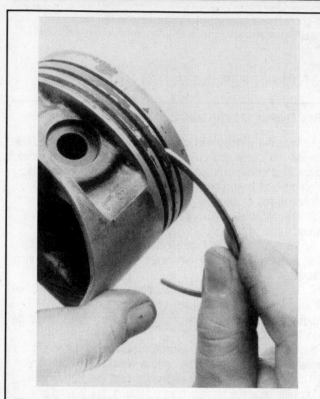

Fig. 116 An old, broken ring may be used to clean the piston ring grooves

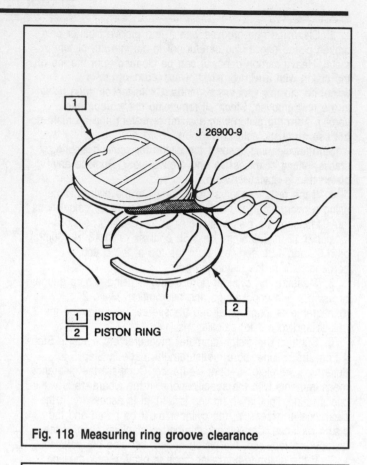

1 PISTON
2 PISTON RING

Fig. 118 Measuring ring groove clearance

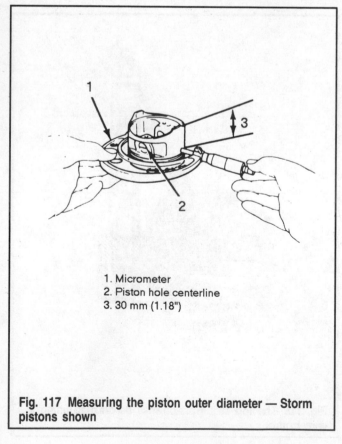

1. Micrometer
2. Piston hole centerline
3. 30 mm (1.18")

Fig. 117 Measuring the piston outer diameter — Storm pistons shown

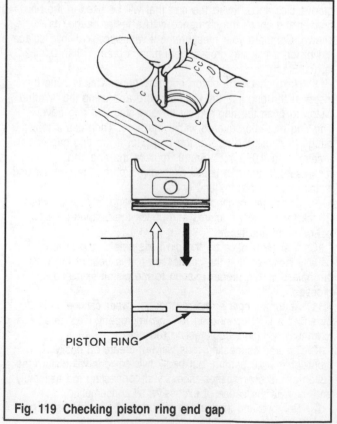

PISTON RING

Fig. 119 Checking piston ring end gap

measurements to the piston pin diameter and replace the rod and piston pin if the clearance exceeds 0.00161 in. (0.041mm).

➡For the 1.5L engine, weigh the piston pin and connecting rods and compare the results. They should not vary more than 0.3527 oz. (10g) or the offending pin and/or rod must be replaced. Before attempting to install the pin, heat the connecting rod in an oven in order to expand the bore and ease installation. Be very careful to use special gloves and precautions when handling the hot connecting rods. Also, be very cautious of overprotective homemakers who have just cleaned their ovens.

7. When ready for assembly, position the piston and connecting rod sideways on a block of wood.

8. Coat the pin with a thin layer of clean engine oil, and if present, align the pin forward marks with the piston forward marks.

9. Tap or press the pin through the piston and connecting rod. Proceed slowly to make sure the pin is properly routed through the bores. For the 1.6L engines, the service tool kit or equivalent must be used along with a base press assembly.

10. If applicable, install the pin retaining snaprings.

11. Make sure the piston and connecting rod move smoothly back and forth on the pin.

PISTON RING REPLACEMENT

1. Remove the rings from the piston using a piston ring expander tool.

2. Clean the piston ring grooves, check the piston-to-cylinder bore clearance and check the ring groove clearance as explained in the piston and connecting rod cleaning and inspection procedure.

3. After the cylinder bores have been finish honed and cleaned, check the piston ring end gap. Compress the piston rings to be used in the cylinder, one at a time, into that cylinder. Using an inverted piston, push the ring down into the cylinder bore area where normal ring wear is not encountered.

4. Measure the ring end gap with a feeler gauge and compare to specification. A gap that is too tight is more harmful than one that is too loose (If ring end gap is excessively loose, the cylinder bore is probably worn beyond specification).

5. If the ring end gap is too tight, carefully remove the ring and file the ends squarely with a fine file or replace the ring to obtain the proper clearance.

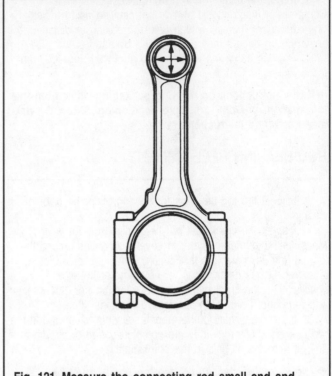

Fig. 121 Measure the connecting rod small end and compare the measurement to the pin diameter in order to check clearance

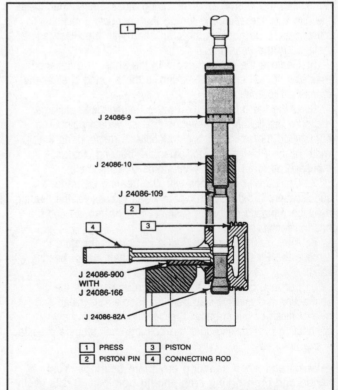

| 1 | PRESS | 3 | PISTON |
| 2 | PISTON PIN | 4 | CONNECTING ROD |

Fig. 122 Example of a piston pin removal/installation service tool set — 1.6L engines

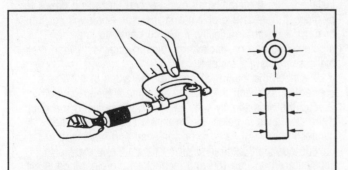

Fig. 120 Check the piston pin outer diameter using an outside micrometer

6. Install the rings on the piston, lowest rings first. Compression rings should always be installed using a piston ring expander. There is a high risk of breaking or distorting the compression rings if they are installed by hand.

7. Position each ring with it's gap about 90 degrees from the next ring.

➡If the instructions on the ring packaging differ from this information regarding ring gap positioning, follow the ring manufacturer's instructions.

ROD BEARING REPLACEMENT

1. Inspect the rod bearings for scoring, chipping or other wear.

2. Inspect the crankshaft rod bearing journal for wear. Measure the journal diameter in several locations around the journal and compare to specification. If the crankshaft journal is scored or has deep ridges, or its diameter is below specification, the crankshaft must be removed from the engine and reground. Consult an automotive machine shop.

3. If the crankshaft journal appears usable, clean it and the rod bearing shells until they are completely free of oil. Blow any oil from the oil hole in the crankshaft.

➡The journal surfaces and bearing shells must be completely free of oil to get an accurate reading with Plastigage®.

4. Place a strip of Plastigage® lengthwise along the crankshaft rod journal as done during disassembly, then install the cap with the shell and torque the connecting rod nuts to specification. Do not turn the crankshaft with the Plastigage® installed in the bearing.

5. Remove the bearing cap with the shell. The flattened Plastigage® will either be sticking to the bearing shell or the crankshaft journal.

6. Using the printed scale on the Plastigage® package, measure the flattened Plastigage® at its widest point. The number on the scale that most closely corresponds to the width of the Plastigage® indicates the bearing clearance in thousandths of an inch or hundredths of a millimeter.

7. Compare your findings with the bearing clearance specification. If the bearing clearance is excessive, the bearing must be replaced or the crankshaft must be ground and the bearing replaced.

8. After clearance measuring is completed, be sure to remove the Plastigage® from the crankshaft and/or bearing shell.

9. For final bearing shell installation, make sure the connecting rod and rod cap bearing saddles are clean and free of nicks or burrs. Install the bearing shells in the connecting rod, making sure the bearing shell tangs are seated in the notches.

➡Be careful when handling any plain bearings. Your hands and the working area should be clean. Dirt is easily embedded in the bearing surface and the bearings are easily scratched or damaged.

INSTALLATION

◆ See Figure 123

1. Make sure the cylinder bore and crankshaft journal are clean.

2. Position the crankshaft journal at its furthest position away from the bottom of the cylinder bore.

3. Coat the cylinder bore and bearing faces with light coat of clean engine oil.

4. Make sure the rod bearing shells are correctly installed. Install the rubber hoses over the connecting rod bolts to protect the crankshaft during installation.

5. Make sure the piston rings are properly installed and the ring end gaps are correctly positioned. Install a piston ring compressor over the piston and rings and compress the piston rings into their grooves. Follow the ring compressor manufacturers instructions.

6. Place the piston and connecting rod assembly into the cylinder bore. Make sure the assembly is the correct one for that bore and that the piston and connecting rod are facing in the proper direction. Most pistons have an arrow or notch on the top of the piston to indicate which side should face the front of the engine.

7. Make sure the ring compressor is seated squarely on the block deck surface. If the compressor is not seated squarely, a ring could pop out from beneath the compressor and hang up on the deck surface, as the piston is tapped into the bore, possibly breaking the ring and/or scoring the cylinder bore as the broken piece is forced into the cylinder.

8. Make sure that the connecting rod is not hung up on the crankshaft counterweights and is in position to come straight on to the crankshaft.

9. Tap the piston slowly into the bore, making sure the compressor remains squarely against the block deck. When the piston is completely in the bore, remove the ring compressor.

10. Coat the crankshaft journal and the bearing shells with engine assembly lube or clean engine oil. Pull the connecting rod onto the crankshaft journal. After the rod is seated, remove the rubber hoses from the rod bolts.

11. Install the rod bearing cap. Match the marked cap to the marked connecting rod. Also, be sure to align the cap and rod tangs on the same side of the connecting rod bore. Lightly oil the connecting rod bolt threads, then install the cap nuts and tighten to specification.

12. After each piston and connecting rod assembly is installed, turn the crankshaft over several times and check for binding. If there is a problem and the crankshaft will not turn, or turns with great difficulty, it will be easier to find the problem (rod cap on backwards, broken ring, etc..) than if all the assemblies are installed.

13. Check the clearance between the sides of the connecting rods and the crankshaft using a feeler gauge. Spread the rods slightly with a screwdriver to insert the gauge. If the clearance is below the minimum specification, the connecting rod will have to be removed and machined to provide adequate clearance. If the clearance is excessive, substitute an unworn rod and recheck. If the clearance is still excessive, the crankshaft must be welded and reground, or replaced.

14. Install the oil pan and cylinder head.
15. Install the engine in the vehicle.

Freeze Plugs

▶ **See Figures 124 and 125**

On most cast iron blocks, round metal plugs are used to seal coolant jackets. These plugs allow for a certain amount of water and block expansion should water (without anti-freeze) ever be left in the coolant system. Although the cooling system should NEVER be filled with plain water only, an emergency and unavailability of coolant could force the situation to occur.

In the event that water only is placed in the cooling system and the engine is subject to sub-freezing temperatures, it is likely that the water will freeze and expand. It is also quite possible that the block will expand and crack. If you are lucky though, the expansion may only cause freeze plugs to become dislodged.

During engine block overhaul, it is often standard procedure to remove and replace all of the freeze plugs.

REMOVAL & INSTALLATION

1. If necessary, remove the engine from the vehicle or remove the interfering components, in order to access the freeze plug(s).
2. Using a hammer and a suitable chisel, cock the plug in the bore.
3. Using the chisel or a small prybar, drive/pry the freeze plug from the bore. Be careful not to score the block or the new freeze plug may not fit well.

To install:

➡**Some auto part stores may offer easy to install freeze plugs consisting of a grommet with metal plates and an adjustment bolt. These plugs are positioned, then the bolt is tightened to expand the grommet sealing the block bore. Although these might be handy to get the vehicle home quickly, they should not be installed for a permanent fix.**

Fig. 123 Tapping the piston into the cylinder bore

4. Freeze plugs are interference fitted to the block. Make sure you have the proper plug size and an equalled sized driver. The proper sized driver will ease the installation process by preventing the plug from cocking in the bore.
5. If possible, shrink the plug(s) by placing them in the freezer for a short period of time.
6. Position the plug to the bore and drive into position. If the plug was cooled to ease installation, allow it to warm to the ambient temperature before filling the engine with coolant.
7. Install the interfering components or the engine, as applicable.

Fig. 124 Using a chisel and hammer, cock the freeze plug in the bore

Fig. 125 Once the plug is cocked, it can be pried from the block

Rear Main Seal

REMOVAL & INSTALLATION

▶ **See Figures 126 and 127**

1. Remove the transaxle. Refer to the procedure in Section 7 of this manual.
2. For the Spectrum, disconnect the exhaust pipe bracket.
3. For the Storm 1.6L engines, remove the right and left undercovers.
4. Remove the pressure plate and clutch on manual transaxle or the torque converter on automatic transaxle, the flywheel bolts and the flywheel from the crankshaft.
5. Drain the crankcase and remove the oil pan from the engine block.
6. Remove the rear oil seal retainer from the engine block, then remove the oil seal from the retainer. Clean the sealing surfaces.

To install:

7. Using J-35264, or an equivalent seal installation tool, drive then new oil seal into the retainer.
8. Apply sealant to the retainer mating surface and clean engine oil to the seal lips, then align the dowel pins of the retainer with the engine block and install the retainer to the rear of the engine.
9. Secure the retainer with the bolts and tighten to 89 inch lbs (10 Nm).
10. Install the oil pan.
11. Install the flywheel and clutch or torque converter assemblies.
12. Install the left and right undercovers or the exhaust pipe bracket, as applicable.
13. Install the transaxle assembly.
14. Lower the vehicle and immediately fill the crankcase with clean engine oil.

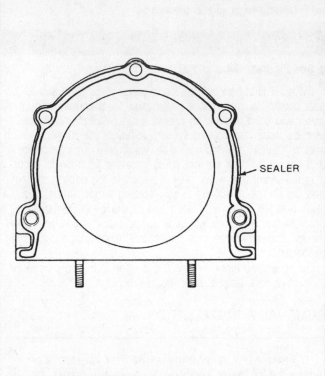

Fig. 127 Apply sealant to the retainer mating surface before installation to the engine block

Crankshaft and Main Bearings

REMOVAL & INSTALLATION

▶ **See Figures 128, 129, 130 and 131**

1. Remove the engine assembly from the vehicle and install on a suitable workstand.
2. Remove the timing belt, oil pan, oil pump, cylinder head and the rear main seal retainer. Refer to the procedures earlier in this section.
3. Remove the piston and connecting rod assemblies. Refer to the procedure in this section.
4. Position a dial indicator at the end of the crankshaft assembly to measure thrust clearance. Carefully pry the crankshaft assembly back and forth with a small prybar and measure the clearance. If the measurement is greater than 0.0118 in. (0.30mm), the thrust washers must be replaced during assembly.
5. Make sure the main bearing caps are numbered so they can be reinstalled in their original positions. Uniformly loosen and remove the bolts in the proper sequence, then remove the bearing caps. If necessary loosen the caps with light blows from a plastic hammer.

➡The bearing caps are loosened from the inside working outward on DOHC engines. The sequence is reversed (from the outward working inside) on SOHC engines.

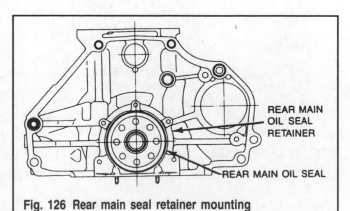

Fig. 126 Rear main seal retainer mounting

6. Position a dial indicator to check crankshaft run-out. Turn the crankshaft and measure run-out; it should not be greater than 0.0039 in. (0.1mm) or the crankshaft must be replaced.

7. Lift the crankshaft from the cylinder block. Inspect the crankshaft and bearings and repair and/or replace as necessary.

To install:

8. After cleaning, inspecting and measuring the crankshaft and checking the main bearing clearance, install the crankshaft. Apply engine assembly lube or clean engine oil to the upper bearing shells prior to installation.

9. Apply engine assembly lube or clean engine oil to the lower bearing shells, then install the main bearing caps in their original positions. Make sure the arrow on the caps is pointing towards the front of the engine. Tighten the bolts in several passes of the proper torque sequence to specification. The torque sequence is the reverse of the removal sequence.

10. After each cap is tightened, check to see and feel that the crankshaft can be rotated by hand. If not, remove the bearing cap and check for the source of the interference.

11. When the caps are all installed, recheck thrust clearance and replace the thrust washers, if clearance is greater than maximum.

12. Install the piston and connecting rod assemblies.

13. Install the rear main seal retainer, cylinder head, oil pump, oil pan and the timing belt.

14. Install the engine assembly to the vehicle.

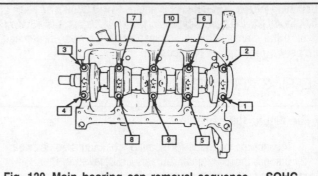

Fig. 130 Main bearing cap removal sequence — SOHC engines

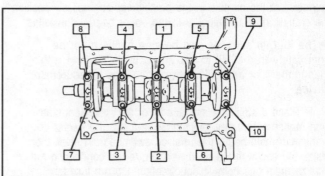

Fig. 131 Main bearing cap removal sequence — DOHC engines

CLEANING AND INSPECTION

▶ See Figure 132

1. Clean the crankshaft with solvent and a brush. Clean the oil passages with a suitable brush, then blow them out with compressed air.

2. Inspect the crankshaft for obvious damage or wear. Check the main and connecting rod journals for cracks, scratches, grooves or scores. Inspect the crankshaft oil seal surface for nicks, sharp edges or burrs that could damage the oil seal or cause premature seal wear.

3. If the crankshaft passes a visual inspection and run-out was not checked prior to removal, check journal run-out. Support the crankshaft in V-blocks and check run-out using a dial indicator. If run-out is greater than 0.0039 in. (0.1mm), the crankshaft must be replaced.

4. Measure the main and connecting rod journals for wear, out-of-roundness or taper, using a micrometer. Measure in at least 4 places around each journal and compare your findings with the journal diameter specifications. The crankshaft must be replaced if the main bearing journal diameter is less than 1.867 in. (47.418mm) for the 1.5L engines or less than 2.0436 in. (51.908mm) for the 1.6L and 1.8L engines. Refer the Piston and Connecting Rods procedure earlier in this section for crankshaft rod journal measurements.

5. Compare the wear measurements of the various journals. The uneven wear limit across similar journals (compare connecting rod-to-connecting rod journal and main bearing-to-main bearing journal measurements) is 0.00196 in.

Fig. 128 Checking crankshaft thrust clearance

Fig. 129 Checking crankshaft run-out

(0.05mm) for the 1.5L and 1.6L engines or 0.0002 in. (0.005mm) for the 1.8L engine.

6. If the crankshaft fails any inspection for wear or damage, it must be reground or replaced.

BEARING REPLACEMENT

▶ **See Figure 133**

1. Inspect the bearings for scoring, chipping or other wear.
2. Inspect the crankshaft journals as detailed in the Cleaning and Inspection procedure.
3. If the crankshaft journals appear usable, clean them and the bearing shells until they are completely free of oil. Blow any oil from the oil hole in the crankshaft. Temporarily position the crankshaft in the block with the upper bearings installed.

➡**The journal surfaces and bearing shells must be completely free of oil to get an accurate reading with Plastigage® or an equivalent plastic-type measurement device.**

4. Place a strip of Plastigage®, or an equivalent plastic-type measurement device, lengthwise along the center of the crankshaft main bearing journal or lower bearing shell, then install the cap with the shell and torque the connecting rod nuts or main cap bolts to specification. Do not turn the crankshaft with the Plastigage® installed in the bearing.
5. Remove the bearing cap with the shell. The flattened Plastigage® will either be sticking to the bearing shell or the crankshaft journal.
6. Using the printed scale on the Plastigage® package, measure the flattened Plastigage® at its widest point. The number on the scale that most closely corresponds to the width of the Plastigage® indicates the bearing clearance in thousandths of an inch or hundredths of a millimeter.
7. Compare your findings with the bearing clearance specification. If the bearing clearance is greater than 0.0047 in. (0.12mm), the bearing must be replaced with an oversized component. If clearance is less than specification, and bearing substitutions do not correct the problem, the crankshaft must be ground or replaced.

➡**Bearing shell sets over standard size are available to correct excessive bearing clearance.**

8. After clearance measuring is completed, be sure to remove the Plastigage® from the crankshaft and/or bearing shell.
9. For final bearing shell installation, make sure the connecting rod and rod cap and/or cylinder block and main cap bearing saddles are clean and free of nicks or burrs. Install the bearing shells in the bearing saddles, making sure the bearing shell tangs are seated in the notches.

➡**Be careful when handling any plain bearings. Your hands and the working area should be clean. Dirt is easily embedded in the bearing surface and the bearings are easily scratched or damaged.**

Flywheel (Flexplate)

REMOVAL & INSTALLATION

▶ **See Figure 134**

1. Disconnect the negative battery cable.
2. Remove the transaxle assembly from the vehicle. Refer to Section 7 of this manual.
3. If equipped with a manual transaxle, remove the clutch assembly. Refer to Section 7 of this manual.
4. Matchmark the position of the flywheel to the engine block.
5. Keep the flywheel from turning, using a holding fixture if necessary, and remove the flywheel retaining bolts.
6. Remove the flywheel from the engine.
7. Clean and inspect the flywheel. On some engines, the ring gear may be replaced if damaged.
   To install:
8. Position the flywheel to the engine, aligning the matchmarks made during removal.
9. Apply a light coat of Loctite® 262, or equivalent thread lock, to the flywheel retaining bolt threads. Be careful not to over-apply the sealant or it could overflow the bolt seat and cause the bolt to work loose during vehicle operation.
10. Tighten the flywheel retaining bolts in a crosswise pattern. For most vehicles, tighten the bolts to 22 ft. lbs. (30 Nm), then tighten each bolt an additional 45-60 degree turn. For 1990 vehicles, tighten the bolts to 47 ft. lbs. (64 Nm) on automatic transaxles or to 58 ft. lbs. (78 Nm) for manual transaxles. For the 1.8L engine, do not tighten the bolts additionally over the 22 ft. lbs. (30 Nm) specification.

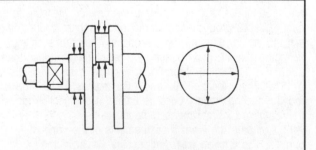

Fig. 132 Measure the crankshaft main bearing and connecting rod journals

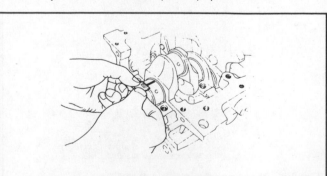

Fig. 133 Use a plastic-type measuring device to check main bearing oil clearance

11. If applicable, install the clutch assembly.
12. Install the transaxle assembly to the vehicle.
13. Connect the negative battery cable.

RING GEAR REPLACEMENT

▶ **See Figures 135 and 136**

1. Remove the flywheel.
2. Tap around the edge of the flywheel at the gear side face using a hammer and brass bar. This will loosen the gear for removal.
3. Remove the gear from the flywheel.

To install:

4. Heat the new gear in an oven to a temperature approaching, but not exceeding, 200°F. If you do not trust your oven, keep the temperature down to 150-175°F.
5. Using special gloves to protect your hands (oven mitts will probably be insufficient and it is painful way to find out), install the expanded ring gear to the flywheel. If necessary, drive the gear into contact with the flywheel.
6. Allow the flywheel and ring gear assembly to cool to the ambient temperature. The ring gear will contract upon cooling, causing a tight interference fit on the flywheel.
7. Measure the ring gear run-out. It must not exceed 0.00394 in. (0.1mm).
8. Install the flywheel to the engine.

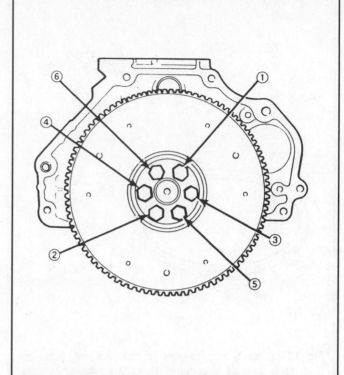

Fig. 134 Flywheel bolt torque sequence — Spectrum (Storm similar)

EXHAUST SYSTEM

Safety Precautions

Exhaust system work can be the most dangerous type of work you can do on your car. Always observe the following precautions:

• Support the car extra securely. Not only will you often be working directly under it, but you'll frequently be using a lot of force, say, heavy hammer blows, to dislodge rusted parts. This can cause a car that's improperly supported to shift and possibly fall.
• Wear goggles. Exhaust system parts are usually rusty. Metal chips can be dislodged, even when you're only turning rusted bolts. Attempting to pry pipes apart with a chisel makes the chips fly even more frequently.
• If you're using a cutting torch, keep it a great distance from either the fuel tank or lines. Stop what you're doing and feel the temperature of the fuel bearing pipes on the vehicle frequently. Even slight heat can expand and/or vaporize fuel, resulting in accumulated vapor, or even a liquid leak, near your torch.
• Watch where your hammer blows fall and make sure you hit squarely. You could easily tap a brake or fuel line when you hit an exhaust system part with a glancing blow. Inspect all lines and hoses in the area where you've been working.

✳✳CAUTION

Be very careful when working on or near the catalytic converter! External temperatures can reach 1,500°F (816°C) and more, causing severe burns. Removal or installation should be performed only on a cold exhaust system.

A number of special exhaust system tools can be rented from auto supply houses or local stores that rent special equipment. A common one is a tail pipe expander, designed to enable you to join pipes of identical diameter. Fortunately, all of the exhaust system components for the Spectrum and Storm are available as bolt on/off replacements, making the need for a pipe expander unnecessary, unless a small portion of pipe must be replaced.

Fig. 135 Removing the ring gear using a hammer and brass bar

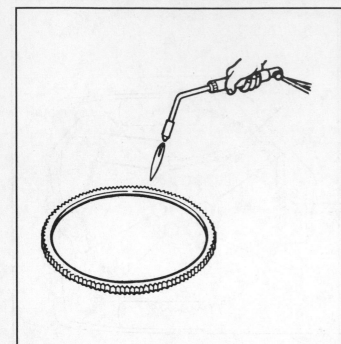

Fig. 136 A torch may be used to heat the ring gear, but it is more difficult to accomplish in this manner because the gear must be heated evenly and to a specific temperature

It may also be quite helpful to use solvents designed to loosen rusted bolts or flanges. Soaking rusted parts the night before you do the job can speed the work of freeing rusted parts considerably. Remember that these solvents are often flammable. Apply only to parts after they are cool!

INSPECTION

▶ **See Figures 137, 138 and 139**

Once or twice a year, check the muffler(s) and pipes for signs of corrosion and damage. Check the hangers for wear, cracks or hardening. Check the heat shields for corrosion or damage. Replace components as necessary.

All vehicles are equipped with a catalytic converter, which is attached to the front exhaust pipe. All the factory exhaust system components are bolted together for ease of replacement or service. Replacement parts are usually the same as or similar to the original system, with the exception of some mufflers. Splash shield removal will be required, in some cases, for removal and installation clearance.

Use only the proper size sockets or wrenches when unbolting system components. Do not tighten completely until all components are attached, aligned, and suspended. Check the system for leaks after the installation is completed.

Front Exhaust Pipe (Converter Inlet Pipe)

REMOVAL & INSTALLATION

1. Raise and support the vehicle safely.
2. Remove the bolts and disconnect the pipe from the front of the catalytic converter.
3. On the Storm, remove the center mounting bracket bolt.
4. On the Spectrum, disconnect the engine-to-pipe bracket.
5. Remove the fasteners and separate the pipe from the exhaust manifold.
6. Release any remaining rubber hangers and remove the pipe from the vehicle.
   To install:
7. Position the pipe to the vehicle and connect any rubber hangers.
8. Connect the pipe to the exhaust manifold, using a new gasket. Loosely install the retainers.
9. Loosely install the center mounting bracket bolt or the engine-to-pipe bracket.
10. Connect the pipe to the catalytic converter and loosely install the bolts.
11. Make sure the exhaust system is properly routed and tighten all the fasteners. Tighten the exhaust manifold fasteners to 42 ft. lbs. (57 Nm) for the Spectrum or to 46 ft. lbs. (62 Nm) for the Storm. Tighten the catalytic converter bolts to 20 ft. lbs. (28 Nm) for the Spectrum or to 32 ft. lbs. (43 Nm) for the Storm.
12. Remove the supports and lower the vehicle.
13. Start the engine and check for leaks.

Catalytic Converter

REMOVAL & INSTALLATION

▶ **See Figures 140 and 141**

1. Raise and support the vehicle safely.
2. Remove the bolts and disconnect the pipe from the front of the catalytic converter.
3. Remove the bolts or nuts and disconnect the pipe from the rear of the catalytic converter.
4. If equipped, remove the retainers or release the rubber hangers.
5. Remove the catalytic converter from the vehicle.
   To install:
6. Position the catalytic converter to the vehicle as shown in Figs. 134 and 135.
7. Loosely install any converter bracket fasteners or rubber hangers.
8. Connect the front and rear pipes to the catalytic converter and loosely install the retaining nuts and/or bolts.
9. Make sure the exhaust system is properly routed and tighten all the fasteners. Tighten the catalytic converter fasteners to 20 ft. lbs. (28 Nm) for the Spectrum or to 32 ft. lbs. (43 Nm) for the Storm.
10. Remove the supports and lower the vehicle.
11. Start the engine and check for leaks.

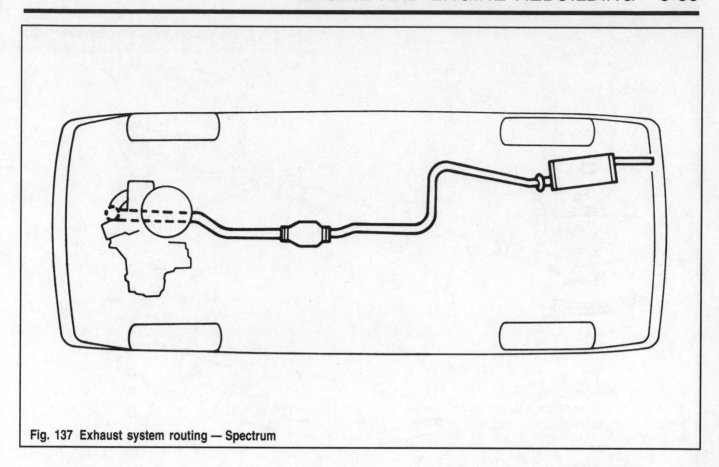

Fig. 137 Exhaust system routing — Spectrum

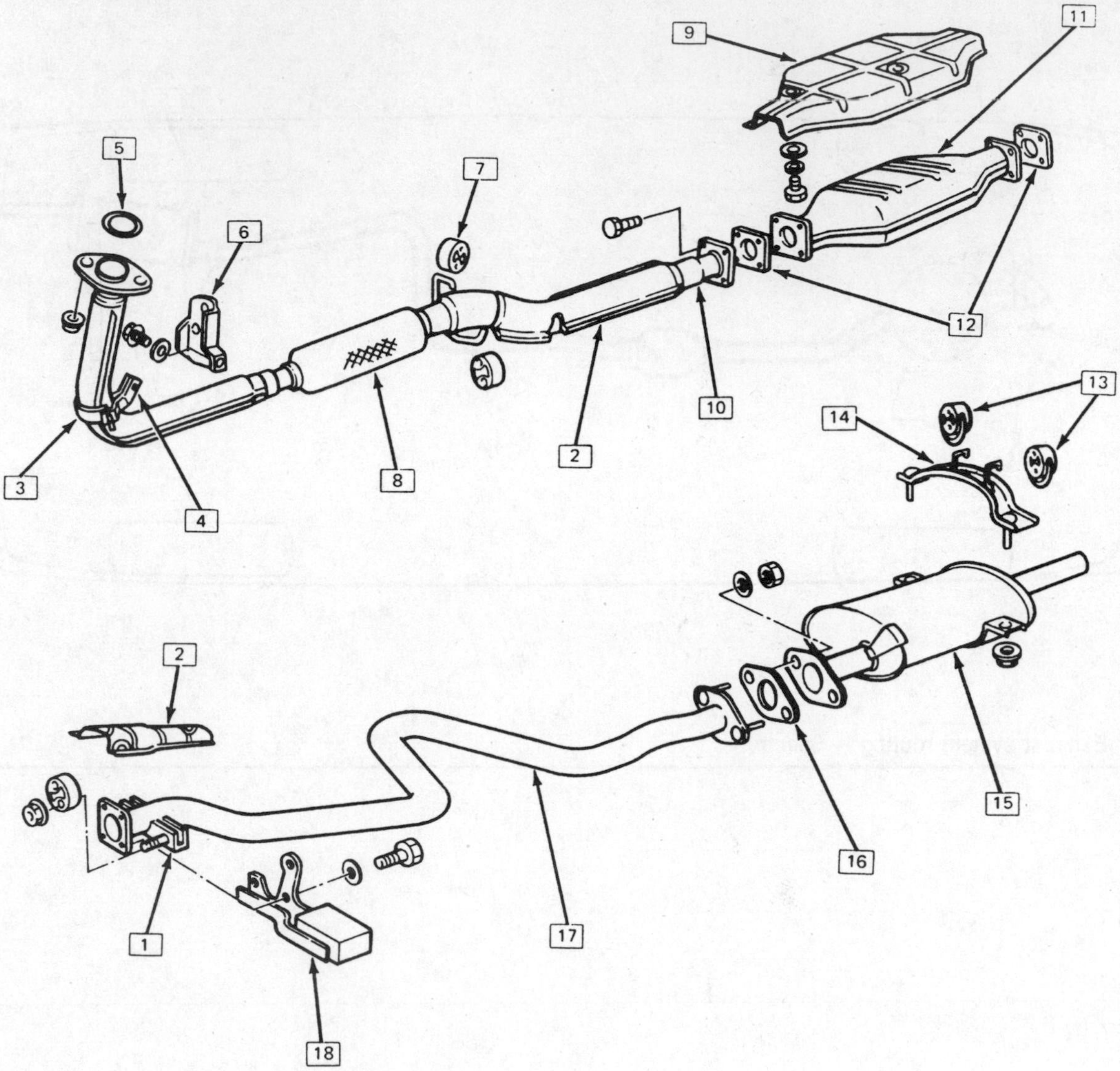

1	HANGER BRACKET	**10**	EXHAUST PIPE FRONT
2	HEAT SHIELD	**11**	CATALYTIC CONVERTER
3	CLAMP, LOWER	**12**	GASKET
4	CLAMP, UPPER	**13**	HANGER RUBBER
5	GASKET	**14**	HANGER BRACKET
6	ENGINE TO PIPE BRACKET	**15**	EXHAUST PIPE REAR
7	HANGER RUBBER	**16**	GASKET
8	FLEXIBLE JOINT	**17**	EXHAUST PIPE CENTER
9	HEAT SHIELD	**18**	MASS DAMPER

Fig. 138 Exhaust system components — Spectrum

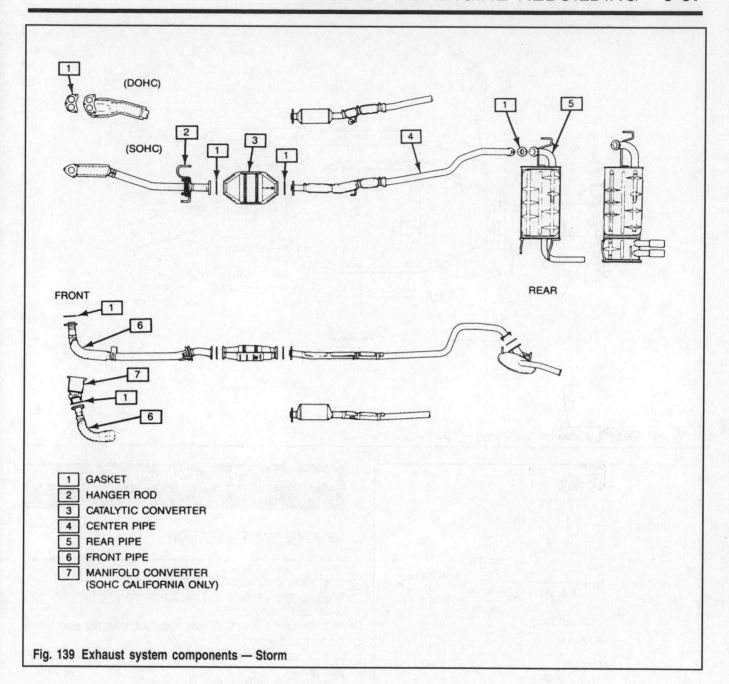

1   GASKET
2   HANGER ROD
3   CATALYTIC CONVERTER
4   CENTER PIPE
5   REAR PIPE
6   FRONT PIPE
7   MANIFOLD CONVERTER
    (SOHC CALIFORNIA ONLY)

Fig. 139 Exhaust system components — Storm

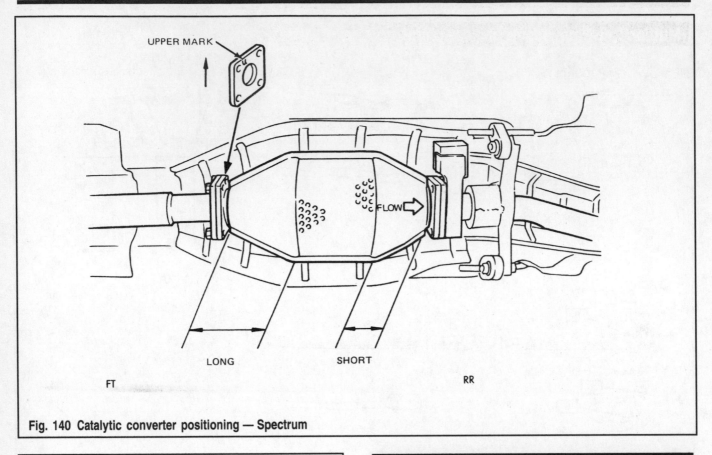

Fig. 140 Catalytic converter positioning — Spectrum

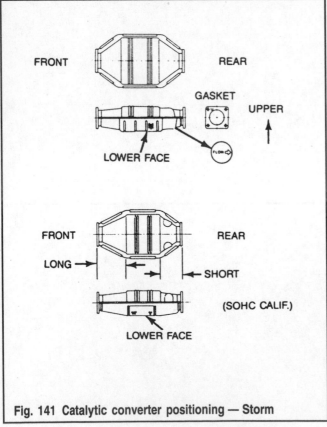

Fig. 141 Catalytic converter positioning — Storm

Intermediate Pipe (Converter-to-Muffler Pipe)

REMOVAL & INSTALLATION

1. Raise and support the vehicle safely.
2. Remove the bolts and disconnect the pipe from the rear of the catalytic converter.
3. Remove the bolts or nuts and disconnect the pipe from the front of the muffler.
4. If applicable, release rubber hangers or disconnect the pipe bracket.
5. Remove the pipe from the vehicle.
   To install:
6. Position the pipe to the vehicle.
7. If applicable install any converter bracket fasteners or rubber hangers.
8. Loosely install the pipe-to-converter and pipe-to-muffler fasteners.
9. Make sure the exhaust system is properly routed and tighten all the fasteners. Tighten the catalytic converter and muffler fasteners to 20 ft. lbs. (28 Nm) for the Spectrum or to 32 ft. lbs. (43 Nm) for the Storm.
10. Remove the supports and lower the vehicle.
11. Start the engine and check for leaks.

Muffler/Tail Pipe Assembly

REMOVAL & INSTALLATION

1. Raise and support the vehicle safely.
2. Remove the bolts or nuts and disconnect the pipe from the front of the muffler.
3. If applicable, release rubber hangers and/or disconnect the muffler bracket.
4. Remove the muffler from the vehicle.

To install:

5. Position the muffler to the vehicle.
6. If applicable install any converter bracket fasteners or rubber hangers.
7. Loosely install the pipe-to-muffler fasteners.
8. Make sure the exhaust system is properly routed and tighten the muffler fasteners to 20 ft. lbs. (28 Nm) for the Spectrum or to 32 ft. lbs. (43 Nm) for the Storm.
9. Remove the supports and lower the vehicle.
10. Start the engine and check for leaks.

ENGINE REBUILDING SPECIFICATIONS CHART

Component	U.S.	Metric
Camshaft:		
Minimum Lobe Height		
SOHC Engines		
1990–92 All	1.426 in.	36.22mm
1993 Intake	1.399 in.	35.54mm
1993 Exhaust	1.413 in.	35.89mm
DOHC Engines		
1.6L All	1.503 in.	38.17mm
1.8L All	1.531 in.	38.90mm
Minimum Journal Diameter	1.0157 in.	25.80mm
Maximum Journal-to-Bearing Clearance	0.0059 in.	0.15mm
Maximum Endplay	0.008 in.	0.02mm
Maximum Camshaft Runout	0.00394 in.	0.1mm
Cylinder Block:		
Maximum Deck Warpage	0.008 in.	0.02mm
Cylinder Bore		
Standard Diameter(s)		
1.5L Engine	3.0315–3.0330 in.	77.000–77.040mm
1.6L Engine	3.1494–3.1512 in.	80.000–80.040mm
1.8L Engine	3.1496–3.1508 in.	80.000–80.030mm
Re-boring Limit		
1.5L Engine	3.0732 in.	78.06mm
1.6L SOHC Engine	3.1990 in.	81.240mm
1.6L DOHC Engine	3.1906 in.	81.040mm
1.8L Engine	3.1968 in.	81.200mm
Wear or Taper Limit	0.005 in.	0.127mm
Cylinder Head:		
Deck Warpage	0.008 in.	0.2mm
Minimum Valve Stem Diameter		
1.5L Engine	0.2740 in.	6.957mm
1.6L Engine	0.2335 in.	5.900mm
1.8L Engine	0.2320 in.	5.900mm
Valve Stem-to-Guide Clearance		
Minimum		
Intake	0.0009 in.	0.023mm
Exhaust	0.0012 in.	0.030mm
Maximum 1.5L Engine		
Intake	0.0022 in.	0.056mm
Exhaust	0.0025 in.	0.063mm
Maximum 1.6L and 1.8L Engines		
Intake	0.0080 in.	0.20mm
Exhaust	0.0080 in.	0.20mm
Valve Face Angle		
1.5L Engine	45°	45°
1.6L and 1.8L Engines	45.5°	45.5°
Valve Seat Angle	45°	45°
Minimum Valve Seat Contact Width		
1.5L Engine	0.0787 in.	2.0mm
1.6L and 1.8L Engine		
Intake	0.0870 in.	2.2mm
Exhaust	0.0790 in.	2.0mm
Minimum Valve Spring Pressure		
1.5L Engine	47.399 lbs. @ 1.57 in.	21.5kg @ 40mm
Minimum Valve Spring Free Length		
1.5L Engine	1.8504 in.	47mm
1.6L SOHC Engine		
Intake	1.67 in.	42.6mm
Exhaust	1.70 in.	43.7mm

ENGINE REBUILDING SPECIFICATIONS CHART

Component	US	Metric
Piston and Connecting Rod:		
Piston Diameter		
1.5L Engine		
A	3.0299–3.0303 in.	76.960–76.970mm
B	3.0304–3.0307 in.	76.971–76.980mm
C	3.0308–3.0311 in.	76.981–76.990mm
D	3.0312–3.0315 in.	76.991–77.000mm
1.6L SOHC Engine		
A	3.1480–3.1484 in.	79.960–79.970mm
B	3.1484–3.1488 in.	79.971–79.980mm
C	3.1488–3.1492 in.	79.981–79.990mm
DOHC Engines		
A	3.1473–3.1477 in.	79.942–79.952mm
B	3.1477–3.1481 in.	79.953–79.962mm
C	3.1481–3.1485 in.	79.963–79.972mm
Piston-to-Bore Clearance		
Standard		
1990–92 SOHC Engines	0.0011–0.0019 in.	0.030–0.050mm
1993 SOHC Engine	0.0012–0.0017 in.	0.030–0.044mm
DOHC Engines	0.0019–0.0027 in.	0.048–0.068mm
Maximum	0.0059 in.	0.15mm
Minimum Piston Pin Diameter		
Except 1.8L Engine	0.7075 in.	17.97mm
1.8L Engine	0.7862 in.	19.97mm
Maximum Piston Pin-to-Piston Clearance	0.00161 in.	0.041mm
Maximum Ring Groove Clearance	0.0059 in.	0.15mm
Maximum Ring End Gap	0.059 in.	1.5mm
Connecting Rod Alignment		
Twist	0.0078 in. per 3.937 in.	0.20mm per 100mm
Bend	0.0059 in. per 3.937 in.	0.15mm per 100mm
Connecting Rod Side Play on Crankshaft		
Standard	0.0079–0.0138 in.	0.20–0.30mm
Maximum	0.0158 in.	0.40mm
Crankshaft:		
Main Journal Diameter		
1.5L Engine	1.8865–1.8873 in.	47.918–47.938mm
1.6L and 1.8L Engines	2.0440–2.0448 in.	51.918–51.938mm
Main Journal Out-of-Round Limit		
1.5L and 1.6L Engines	0.00196 in.	0.05mm
1.8L Engine	0.00020 in.	0.05mm
Main Bearing-to-Crankshaft Oil Clearance		
Standard	0.0008–0.0020 in.	0.020–0.048mm
Maximum	0.0047 in.	0.12mm
Connecting Rod Journal Diameter		
1.5L Engine	1.5720–1.5726 in.	39.930–39.945mm
1.6L SOHC Engine	1.5724–1.5728 in.	39.940–39.950mm
1.6L DOHC Engine	1.5722–1.5728 in.	39.935–39.950mm
1.8L Engine	1.8083–1.8089 in.	45.930–45.945mm
Connecting Rod Journal Out-of-Round Limit		
1.5L and 1.6L Engines	0.00196 in.	0.05mm
1.8L Engine	0.00020 in.	0.05mm
Connecting Rod Bearing-to-Crankshaft Oil Clearance		
Standard		
Except 1.6L SOHC Engine	0.0010–0.0023 in.	0.025–0.058mm
1.6L SOHC Engine	0.0008–0.0019 in.	0.022–0.047mm
Maximum	0.0047 in.	0.12mm
Maximum Crankshaft Runout	0.0039 in.	0.1mm
Maximum Crankshaft Endplay	0.0118 in.	0.3mm

ENGINE REBUILDING SPECIFICATIONS CHART

Component	US	Metric
Oil Pump:		
Maximum Driven Gear-to-Body Clearance		
Spectrum	0.0070 in.	0.18mm
Storm	0.0078 in.	0.20mm
Maximum Gear Tip Clearance		
Spectrum	0.0138 in.	0.35mm
Storm	0.0120 in.	0.30mm
Housing-to-Side of Gear Set Clearance	0.004 in.	0.10mm

TORQUE SPECIFICATIONS

Component	U.S.	Metric
Alternator bracket bolts	24 ft. lbs.	33 Nm
Alternator electrical connection nut	11 ft. lbs.	15 Nm
Battery hold down retainer nut	72 inch lbs.	8 Nm
Battery hold down retainer screw	44 inch lbs.	5 Nm
Belt tension pulley	30 ft. lbs.	40 Nm
Camshaft bearing cap bolts	89 inch lbs.	10 Nm
Camshaft timing pulley bolts		
Spectrum	7 ft. lbs.	10 Nm
Storm DOHC	44 ft. lbs.	59 Nm
Storm SOHC	106 inch lbs.	12 Nm
Catalytic converter bolts		
Spectrum	20 ft. lbs.	28 Nm
Storm	32 ft. lbs.	43 Nm
Crankshaft pulley center bolt		
1.6L engine	87 ft. lbs.	118 Nm
1.8L engine	108 ft. lbs.	147 Nm
Crankshaft pulley side bolts (1.6L SOHC)	17 ft. lbs.	23 Nm
* Cylinder head final torque	58 ft. lbs.	79 Nm
Exhaust manifold		
Spectrum	17 ft. lbs.	23 Nm
Storm	30 ft. lbs.	39 Nm
Exhaust manifold heat shield bolts	11 ft. lbs.	15 Nm
Exhaust pipe		
Spectrum	42 ft. lbs.	56 Nm
Storm	46 ft. lbs.	62 Nm
Flywheel retaining bolts		
Except 1990 initially	22 ft. lbs.	30 Nm
Except 1990 or 1.8L additional	45–60 degree turn	45–60 degree turn
1990 W/ automatic transaxle	47 ft. lbs.	64 Nm
1990 W/ manual transaxle	58 ft. lbs.	78 Nm
Intake manifold common chamber	17 ft. lbs.	23 Nm
Intake manifold fasteners	17 ft. lbs.	23 Nm
Muffler fasteners		
Spectrum	20 ft. lbs.	28 Nm
Storm	32 ft. lbs.	43 Nm
Oil pan bolts	89 inch lbs.	10 Nm
Oil Pressure Sensor	10 ft. lbs.	14 Nm
Oil pump mounting bolts	inch lbs.	10 Nm
Power Steering Pressure Switch	124 inch lbs.	14 Nm
Rear main seal retainer bolts	89 inch lbs.	10 Nm
Rocker arm bracket bolts (Storm)	16 ft. lbs.	22 Nm
Rocker shaft assemblies (Spectrum)	16 ft. lbs.	22 Nm
Solenoid retaining nuts	15 ft. lbs.	20 Nm
Starter frame support (1993 vehicles)	26 ft. lbs.	35 Nm
Starter retainers	29 ft. lbs.	39 Nm
Thermostat cap retaining bolts (1.8L engine)	18 ft. lbs.	24 Nm
Thermostat housing bolts (except 1.8L)	17 ft. lbs.	24 Nm
Throttle body	17 ft. lbs.	23 Nm
Timing cover bolts	89 inch lbs.	10 Nm

TORQUE SPECIFICATIONS

Component	US	Metric
Valve cover retaining bolts		
Spectrum	7 ft. lbs.	10 Nm
Storm 1.6L SOHC and 1.8L	89 inch lbs.	10 Nm
Storm 1.6L DOHC	29 inch lbs.	3 Nm
Water pump bolts		
1.8L engine	18 ft. lbs.	24 Nm
Except 1.8L engine	17 ft. lbs.	23 Nm

* Tighten the bolts in at least 2 passes;
first, torque the bolts to 29 ft. lbs. (40 Nm)

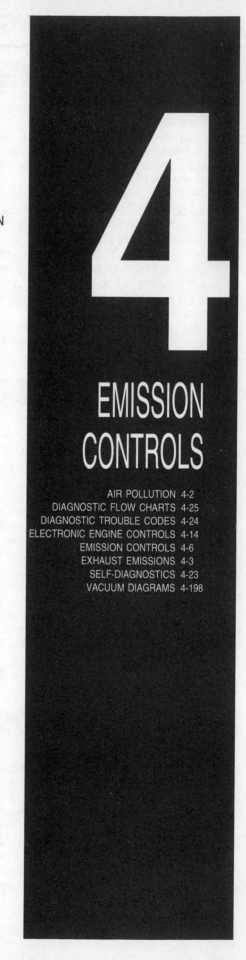

4

EMISSION CONTROLS

AIR POLLUTION

The earth's atmosphere, at or near sea level, consists approximately of 78% nitrogen, 21% oxygen and 1% other gases. If it were possible to remain in this state, 100% clean air would result. However, many varied causes allow other gases and particulates to mix with the clean air, causing the air to become unclean or polluted.

Certain of these pollutants are visible while others are invisible, with each having the capability of causing distress to the eyes, ears, throat, skin and respiratory system. Should these pollutants become concentrated in a specific area and under the right conditions, death could result due to the displacement or chemical change of the oxygen content in the air. These pollutants can also cause great damage to the environment and to the many man made objects that are exposed to the elements.

To better understand the causes of air pollution, the pollutants can be categorized into 3 separate types, natural, industrial and automotive.

Natural Pollutants

Natural pollution has been present on earth since before man appeared and continues to be a factor when discussing air pollution, although it causes only a small percentage of the overall pollution problem existing in our country today. It is the direct result of decaying organic matter, wind born smoke and particulates from such natural events as plain and forest fires (ignited by heat or lightning), volcanic ash, sand and dust which can spread over a large area of the countryside.

Such a phenomenon of natural pollution has been recent volcanic eruptions, with the resulting plume of smoke, steam and volcanic ash blotting out the sun's rays as it spreads and rises higher into the atmosphere, where the upper air currents catch and carry the smoke and ash, while condensing the steam back into water vapor. As the water vapor, smoke and ash traveled on their journey, the smoke dissipates into the atmosphere while the ash and moisture settle back to earth in a trail hundred of miles long. In some cases, lives are lost and millions of dollars of property damage result. Ironically, man can only stand by and watch it happen.

Industrial Pollution

Industrial pollution is caused primarily by industrial processes, the burning of coal, oil and natural gas, which in turn produce smoke and fumes. Because the burning fuels contain large amounts of sulfur, the principal ingredients of smoke and fumes are sulfur dioxide () and particulate matter. This type of pollutant occurs most severely during still, damp and cool weather, such as at night. Even in its less severe form, this pollutant is not confined to just cities. Because of air movements, the pollutants move for miles over the surrounding countryside, leaving in its path a barren and unhealthy environment for all living things.

Working with Federal, State and Local mandated rules, regulations and by carefully monitoring the emissions, industries have greatly reduced the amount of pollutant emitted from their industrial sources, striving to obtain an acceptable level. Because of the mandated industrial emission clean up, many land areas and streams in and around the cities that were formerly barren of vegetation and life, have now begun to move back in the direction of nature's intended balance.

Automotive Pollutants

The third major source of air pollution is automotive emissions. The emissions from the internal combustion engine were not an appreciable problem years ago because of the small number of registered vehicles and the nation's small highway system. However, during the early 1950's, the trend of the American people was to move from the cities to the surrounding suburbs. This caused an immediate problem in transportation because the majority of suburbs were not afforded mass transit conveniences. This lack of transportation created an attractive market for the automobile manufacturers, which resulted in a dramatic increase in the number of vehicles produced and sold, along with a marked increase in highway construction between cities and the suburbs. Multi-vehicle families emerged with a growing emphasis placed on an individual vehicle per family member. As the increase in vehicle ownership and usage occurred, so did pollutant levels in and around the cities, as suburbanites drove daily to their busin esses and employment, returning at the end of the day to their homes in the suburbs.

It was noted that a fog and smoke type haze was being formed and at times, remained in suspension over the cities, taking time to dissipate. At first this 'smog', derived from the words 'smoke' and 'fog', was thought to result from industrial pollution but it was determined that the automobile emissions were also to blame. It was discovered that when normal automobile emissions were exposed to sunlight for a period of time, complex chemical reactions would take place.

It is now known that smog is a photo chemical layer which develops when certain oxides of nitrogen (NOx) and unburned hydrocarbons (HC) from automobile emissions are exposed to sunlight. Pollution was more severe when smog would stagnant over an area in which a warm layer of air settled over the top of the cooler air mass, trapping and holding the cooler mass at ground level. The trapped cooler air would keep the emissions from being dispersed and diluted through normal air flows. This type of air stagnation was given the name 'Temperature Inversion'.

Temperature Inversion

In normal weather situations, the surface air is warmed by heat radiating from the earth's surface and the sun's rays and will rise upward, into the atmosphere. Upon rising it will cool through a convection type heat exchange with the cooler upper air. As warm air rises, the surface pollutants are carried upward and dissipated into the atmosphere.

When a temperature inversion occurs, we find the higher air is no longer cooler but warmer than the surface air, causing the cooler surface air to become trapped. This warm air blanket can extend from above ground level to a few hundred or even a few thousand feet into the air. As the surface air is trapped, so are the pollutants, causing a severe smog condition. Should this stagnant air mass extend to a few thousand feet high, enough air movement with the inversion takes place to allow the smog layer to rise above ground level but the pollutants still cannot dissipate. This inversion can remain for days over an area, with the smog level only rising or lowering from ground level to a few hundred feet high. Meanwhile, the pollutant levels increase, causing eye irritation, respiratory problems, reduced visibility, plant damage and in some cases, disease.

This inversion phenomenon was first noted in the Los Angeles, California area. The city lies terrain resembling a basin and with certain weather conditions, a cold air mass is held in the basin while a warmer air mass covers it like a lid.

Because this type of condition was first documented as prevalent in the Los Angeles area, this type of trapped pollution was named Los Angeles Smog, although it occurs in other areas where a large concentration of automobiles are used and the air remains stagnant for any length of time.

Internal Combustion Engine Pollutants

Consider the internal combustion engine as a machine in which raw materials must be placed so a finished product comes out. As in any machine operation, a certain amount of wasted material is formed. When we relate this to the internal combustion engine, we find that through the input of air and fuel, we obtain power during the combustion process to drive the vehicle. The by-product or waste of this power is, in part, heat and exhaust gases with which we must dispose.

EXHAUST EMISSIONS

Composition Of The Exhaust Gases

The exhaust gases emitted into the atmosphere are a combination of burned and unburned fuel. To understand the exhaust emission and its composition, we must review some basic chemistry.

When the air/fuel mixture is introduced into the engine, we are mixing air, composed of nitrogen (78%), oxygen (21%) and other gases (1%) with the fuel, which is 100% hydrocarbons (HC), in a semi-controlled ratio. As the combustion process is accomplished, power is produced to move the vehicle while the heat of combustion is transferred to the cooling system. The exhaust gases are then composed of nitrogen, a diatomic gas (N_2), the same as was introduced in the engine, carbon dioxide (CO_2), the same gas that is used in beverage carbonation and water vapor (H_2O). The nitrogen (N_2), for the most part passes through the engine unchanged, while the oxygen (O_2) reacts (burns) with the hydrocarbons (HC) and produces the carbon dioxide (CO_2) and the water vapors (H_2O). If this chemical process would be the only process to take place, the exhaust emissions would be harmless. However, during the combustion process, other compounds are formed which are considered dangerous. These pollutants are c arbon monoxide (CO), hydrocarbons (HC), oxides of nitrogen (NOx) oxides of sulfur (SOx) and engine particulates.

Heat Transfer

The heat from the combustion process can rise to over 4000°F (2204°C). The dissipation of this heat is controlled by a ram air effect, the use of cooling fans to cause air flow and having a liquid coolant solution surrounding the combustion area to transfer the heat of combustion through the cylinder walls and into the coolant. The coolant is then directed to a thin-finned, multi-tubed radiator, from which the excess heat is transferred to the atmosphere by 1 of the 3 heat transfer methods, conduction, convection or radiation.

The cooling of the combustion area is an important part in the control of exhaust emissions. To understand the behavior of the combustion and transfer of its heat, consider the air/fuel charge. It is ignited and the flame front burns progressively across the combustion chamber until the burning charge reaches the cylinder walls. Some of the fuel in contact with the walls is not hot enough to burn, thereby snuffing out or quenching the combustion process. This leaves unburned fuel in the combustion chamber. This unburned fuel is then forced out of the cylinder and into the exhaust system, along with the exhaust gases.

Many attempts have been made to minimize the amount of unburned fuel in the combustion chambers due to the snuffing out or quenching, by increasing the coolant temperature and lessening the contact area of the coolant around the combustion area. Design limitations within the combustion chambers prevent the complete burning of the air/fuel charge, so a certain amount of the unburned fuel is still expelled into the exhaust system, regardless of modifications to the engine.

HYDROCARBONS

Hydrocarbons (HC) are essentially fuel which was not burned during the combustion process or which has escaped into the atmosphere through fuel evaporation. The main sources of incomplete combustion are rich air/fuel mixtures, low engine temperatures and improper spark timing. The main sources of hydrocarbon emission through fuel evaporation used to be the vehicle's fuel tank and carburetor bowl.

To reduce combustion hydrocarbon emission, engine modifications were made to minimize dead space and surface area in the combustion chamber. In addition the air/fuel mixture was made more lean through the improved control which fuel injection offers and by the addition of external controls to aid in further combustion of the hydrocarbons outside the engine. Two such methods were the addition of an air injection system, to inject fresh air into the exhaust manifolds and the installation of a catalytic converter, a unit that is able to burn traces of hydrocarbons without affecting the internal combustion process or fuel economy. The Storm utilizes only the second of these methods, the catalytic converter.

To control hydrocarbon emissions through fuel evaporation, modifications were made to the fuel tank to allow storage of the fuel vapors during periods of engine shut-down. Modifications were also made to the air intake system so that at specific times during engine operation, these vapors may be purged and burned by blending them with the air/fuel mixture.

CARBON MONOXIDE

Carbon monoxide is formed when not enough oxygen is present during the combustion process to convert carbon (C) to carbon dioxide (CO_2). An increase in the carbon monoxide (CO) emission is normally accompanied by an increase in the hydrocarbon (HC) emission because of the lack of oxygen to completely burn all of the fuel mixture.

Carbon monoxide (CO) also increases the rate at which the photo chemical smog is formed by speeding up the conversion of nitric oxide (NO) to nitrogen dioxide (NO_2). To accomplish this, carbon monoxide (CO) combines with oxygen (O_2) and nitrogen dioxide (NO_2) to produce carbon dioxide (CO_2) and nitrogen dioxide (NO_2). ($CO + O_2 + NO = CO_2 + NO_2$).

The dangers of carbon monoxide, which is an odorless, colorless toxic gas are many. When carbon monoxide is inhaled into the lungs and passed into the blood stream, oxygen is replaced by the carbon monoxide in the red blood cells, causing a reduction in the amount of oxygen being supplied to the many parts of the body. This lack of oxygen causes headaches, lack of coordination, reduced mental alertness and should the carbon monoxide concentration be high enough, death could result.

NITROGEN

Normally, nitrogen is an inert gas. When heated to approximately 2500°F (1371°C) through the combustion process, this gas becomes active and causes an increase in the nitric oxide (NOx) emission.

Oxides of nitrogen (NOx) are composed of approximately 97-98% nitric oxide (NO2). Nitric oxide is a colorless gas but when it is passed into the atmosphere, it combines with oxygen and forms nitrogen dioxide (NO2). The nitrogen dioxide then combines with chemically active hydrocarbons (HC) and when in the presence of sunlight, causes the formation of photo chemical smog.

OZONE

To further complicate matters, some of the nitrogen dioxide (NO2) is broken apart by the sunlight to form nitric oxide and oxygen. (NO2 + sunlight = NO + O). This single atom of oxygen then combines with diatomic (meaning 2 atoms) oxygen (O2) to form ozone (O3). Ozone is 1 of the smells associated with smog. It has a pungent and offensive odor, irritates the eyes and lung tissues, affects the growth of plant life and causes rapid deterioration of rubber products. Ozone can be formed by sunlight as well as electrical discharge into the air.

The most common discharge area on the automobile engine is the secondary ignition electrical system, especially when inferior quality spark plug cables are used. As the surge of high voltage is routed through the secondary cable, the circuit builds up an electrical field around the wire, acting upon the

oxygen in the surrounding air to form the ozone. The faint glow along the cable with the engine running that may be visible on a dark night, is called the 'corona discharge.' It is the result of the electrical field passing from a high along the cable, to a low in the surrounding air, which forms the ozone gas. The combination of corona and ozone has been a major cause of cable deterioration. Recently, different and better quality insulating materials have lengthened the life of the electrical cables.

Although ozone at ground level can be harmful, ozone is beneficial to the earth's inhabitants. By having a concentrated ozone layer called the 'ozonosphere', between 10 and 20 miles (16-32km) up in the atmosphere much of the ultra violet radiation from the sun's rays are absorbed and screened. If this ozone layer were not present, much of the earth's surface would be burned, dried and unfit for human life.

There is much discussion concerning the ozone layer and its density. A feeling exists that this protective layer of ozone is slowly diminishing and corrective action must be directed to this problem. Much experimentation is presently being conducted to determine if a problem exists and if so, the short and long term effects of the problem and how it can be remedied.

OXIDES OF SULFUR

Oxides of sulfur (SOx) were initially ignored in the exhaust system emissions, since the sulfur content of gasoline as a fuel is less than 1/10 of 1%. Because of this small amount, it was felt that it contributed very little to the overall pollution problem. However, because of the difficulty in solving the sulfur emissions in industrial pollutions and the introduction of catalytic converter to the automobile exhaust systems, a change was mandated. The automobile exhaust system, when equipped with a catalytic converter, changes the sulfur dioxide (SO2) into the sulfur trioxide (SO3).

When this combines with water vapors (H2O), a sulfuric acid mist (H2SO4) is formed and is a very difficult pollutant to handle since it is extremely corrosive. This sulfuric acid mist that is formed, is the same mist that rises from the vents of an automobile storage battery when an active chemical reaction takes place within the battery cells.

When a large concentration of vehicles equipped with catalytic converters are operating in an area, this acid mist will rise and be distributed over a large ground area causing land, plant, crop, paints and building damage.

PARTICULATE MATTER

A certain amount of particulate matter is present in the burning of any fuel, with carbon constituting the largest percentage of the particulates. In gasoline, the remaining particulates are the burned remains of the various other compounds used in its manufacture. When a gasoline engine is in good internal condition, the particulate emissions are low but as the engine wears internally, the particulate emissions increase. By visually inspecting the tail pipe emissions, a determination can be made as to where an engine defect may exist. An engine with light gray smoke emitting from the tail pipe normally indicates an increase in the oil consumption through burning due to internal engine wear. Black smoke would indicate a defective fuel delivery system, causing the engine to operate in a rich mode. Regardless of the color of the smoke, the internal part of the engine or the fuel delivery system should be repaired to a 'like new' condition to prevent excess particulate emissions.

Diesel and turbine engines emit a darkened plume of smoke from the exhaust system because of the type of fuel used. Emission control regulations are mandated for this type of emission and more stringent measures are being used to prevent excess emission of the particulate matter. Electronic components are being introduced to control the injection of the fuel at precisely the proper time of piston travel, to achieve the optimum in fuel ignition and fuel usage. Other particulate after-burning components are being tested to achieve a cleaner emission.

Good grades of engine lubricating oils should be used, which meet the manufacturers specification. 'Cut-rate' oils can contribute to the particulate emission problem because of their low 'flash' or ignition temperature point. Such oils burn prematurely during the combustion process causing emissions of particulate matter.

The cooling system is an important factor in the reduction of particulate matter. With the cooling system operating at a temperature specified by the manufacturer, the optimum of combustion will occur. The cooling system must be maintained in the same manner as the engine oiling system, as each system is required to perform properly in order for the engine to operate efficiently for a long time.

Other Automobile Emission Sources

Before emission controls were mandated on the internal combustion engines, other sources of engine pollutants were discovered, along with the exhaust emission. It was determined the engine combustion exhaust produced 60% of the total emission pollutants, fuel evaporation from the fuel tank and carburetor vents produced 20%, with the another 20% being produced through the crankcase as a by-product of the combustion process.

CRANKCASE EMISSIONS

Crankcase emissions are made up of water, acids, unburned fuel, oil fumes and particulates. The emissions are classified as hydrocarbons (HC) and are formed by the small amount of unburned, compressed air/fuel mixture entering the crankcase from the combustion area during the compression and power strokes, between the cylinder walls and piston rings. The head of the compression and combustion help to form the remaining crankcase emissions.

Since the first engines, crankcase emissions were allowed into the atmosphere through a road draft tube, mounted on the lower side of the engine block. Fresh air came in through an open oil filler cap or breather. The air passed through the crankcase mixing with blow-by gases. The motion of the vehicle and the air blowing past the open end of the road draft tube caused a low pressure area at the end of the tube.

Crankcase emissions were simply drawn out of the road draft tube into the air.

To control the crankcase emission, the road draft tube was deleted. A hose and/or tubing was routed from the crankcase to the intake manifold so the blow-by emission could be burned with the air/fuel mixture. However, it was found that intake manifold vacuum, used to draw the crankcase emissions into the manifold, would vary in strength at the wrong time and not allow the proper emission flow. A regulating type valve was needed to control the flow of air through the crankcase.

Testing, showed the removal of the blow-by gases from the crankcase as quickly as possible, was most important to the longevity of the engine. Should large accumulations of blow-by gases remain and condense, dilution of the engine oil would occur to form water, soots, resins, acids and lead salts, resulting in the formation of sludge and varnishes. This condensation of the blow-by gases occur more frequently on vehicles used in numerous starting and stopping conditions, excessive idling and when the engine is not allowed to attain normal operating temperature through short runs.

FUEL EVAPORATIVE EMISSIONS

Gasoline fuel is a major source of pollution, before and after it is burned in the automobile engine. From the time the fuel is refined, stored, pumped and transported, again stored until it is pumped into the fuel tank of the vehicle, the gasoline gives off unburned hydrocarbons (HC) into the atmosphere. Through redesigning of the storage areas and venting systems, the pollution factor was diminished, but not eliminated, from the refinery standpoint. However, the automobile still remained the primary source of vaporized, unburned hydrocarbon (HC) emissions.

Fuel pumped from an underground storage tank is cool but when exposed to a warmer ambient temperature, will expand. Before controls were mandated, an owner would fill the fuel tank with fuel from an underground storage tank and park the vehicle for some time in warm area, such as a parking lot. As the fuel would warm, it would expand and should no provisions or area be provided for the expansion, the fuel would spill out the filler neck and onto the ground, causing hydrocarbon (HC) pollution and creating a severe fire hazard. To correct this condition, the vehicle manufacturers added overflow plumbing and/or gasoline tanks with built in expansion areas or domes.

However, this did not control the fuel vapor emission from the fuel tank. It was determined that most of the fuel evaporation occurred when the vehicle was stationary and the engine not operating. Most vehicles carry 5-25 gallons (19-95 liters) of gasoline. Should a large concentration of vehicles be parked in one area, such as a large parking lot, excessive fuel vapor emissions would take place, increasing as the temperature increases.

To prevent the vapor emission from escaping into the atmosphere, the fuel system is designed to trap the fuel vapors while the vehicle is stationary, by sealing the fuel system from the atmosphere. A storage system is used to collect and hold the fuel vapors from the carburetor and the fuel tank when the engine is not operating. When the engine is started, the storage system is then purged of the fuel vapors, which are drawn into the engine and burned with the air/fuel mixture.

EMISSION CONTROLS

The emission control system begins at the air intake and ends at the tailpipe. The emission control system includes various sub-systems such as the positive crankcase ventilation system, evaporative emission control system, the exhaust gas recirculation system and exhaust catalyst, as well as the electronic controls that govern the fuel and ignition system. These components are combined to control engine operation for maximum engine efficiency and minimal exhaust emissions.

Positive Crankcase Ventilation System

OPERATION

▶ **See Figures 1 and 2**

The system consists of a tube from the air filter housing to the rocker/camshaft cover and a second tube from the rocker/camshaft cover to the intake manifold. Under normal operating conditions, clean air flows from the air filter into the rocker/camshaft cover where it mixes with crankcase oil vapors. These vapors are drawn through the PCV valve and into the intake manifold to be burned with the air/fuel mixture. The flow to the intake manifold is metered by the PCV valve (either a regulating orifice or vacuum diaphragm type). When manifold vacuum is high, the valve restricts flow to maintain a smooth idle. If crankcase pressure is very high, vapors can flow directly into the air filter housing.

A plugged PCV system may cause a rough idle, stalling, oil leaks and/or a build up of sludge in the engine. An air filter coated with engine oil, indicates excessive crankcase pressure. A leaking valve or hose might cause; a rough or high idle and/or engine stalling.

SERVICE

1. Visually inspect the PCV valve hose and the fresh air supply hose and their attaching nipples or grommets for splits, cuts, damage, clogging, or restrictions. Repair or replace, as necessary.
2. If the hoses pass inspection, start the engine and allow it to warm until normal operating temperature is reached.
3. Remove the PCV valve from the rocker arm cover, but leave it connected to the hose. With the engine at idle, feel the end of the valve for manifold vacuum. If there is no vacuum, check for a plugged or leaking hose, PCV valve or manifold port. Replace a plugged or damaged hose.
4. Stop the engine and remove the PCV valve. Inspect the orifice for plugs or restriction. If restricted, clean the orifice to allow proper flow.

REMOVAL & INSTALLATION

▶ **See Figures 3 and 4**

1. For carbureted vehicles, it may be necessary to the remove the air cleaner assembly for access to the PCV valve.

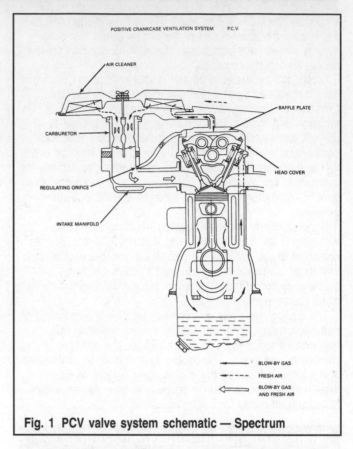

Fig. 1 PCV valve system schematic — Spectrum

2. Remove the PCV valve from the mounting grommet in the rocker/camshaft cover.
3. Disconnect the valve from the PCV hose and remove the valve from the vehicle.
4. Installation is the reverse of the removal procedure.

Fuel Evaporative Emission Control System

OPERATION

▶ **See Figures 5, 6, 7, 8, 9 and 10**

The Evaporative Emission Control System (EECS or EVAP) limits the amount of fuel vapors that are allowed to escape into the air. When the engine is not running, fuel vapors from the sealed fuel tank flow through the single vapor line to the charcoal canister which is normally mounted in the engine compartment. The charcoal absorbs the fuel vapors and retains them until they are purged with fresh air.

Once the engine is started and the appropriate operating conditions are reached, the Engine Control Module (ECM) will operate a solenoid valve in order to provide vacuum to the canister purge valve. The vacuum will open the normally closed purge valve against diaphragm spring pressure. With the purge valve open, intake manifold vacuum is applied to the canister drawing in fresh air and purging the vapors. The

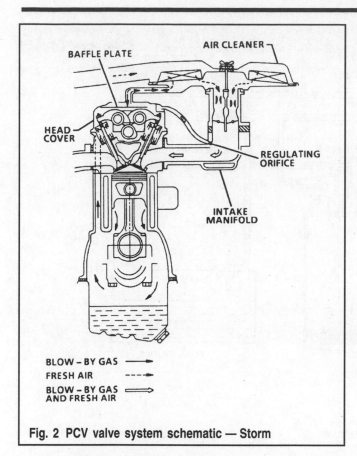

Fig. 2 PCV valve system schematic — Storm

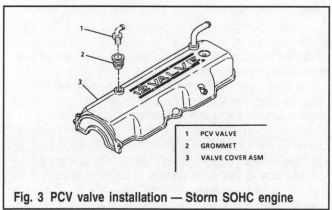

1	PCV VALVE
2	GROMMET
3	VALVE COVER ASM

Fig. 3 PCV valve installation — Storm SOHC engine

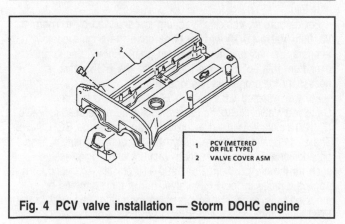

| 1 | PCV (METERED OR FILE TYPE) |
| 2 | VALVE COVER ASM |

Fig. 4 PCV valve installation — Storm DOHC engine

purged vapors are then drawn into the engine and burned efficiently during the normal combustion process.

On carbureted vehicles, a Thermal Vacuum Valve (TVV) is connected in series to the purge signal line. The TVV prevents vapor purge during engine warm up under cold driving conditions in order to assure the proper air/fuel ratio.

For fuel injected vehicles, the ECM uses feedback from the engine coolant temperature and other sensors to determine purge valve activation. The ECM will prevent vapor purge when the engine is cold and while under idle conditions. For these engines, the ECM will wait until a specified coolant temperature is reached and for the engine to run continually for a predetermined amount of time before activating the purge valve.

SERVICE

▶ See Figures 11 and 12

Carefully check for cracks or leaks in the vacuum lines or in the canister itself. The lines and fittings can usually be reached without removing the canister. Cracks or leaks in the system may cause poor idle, stalling, poor driveability, fuel loss or a fuel vapor odor.

Vapor odor and fuel loss may also be caused by; fuel leaking from the lines, tank or injectors, loose, disconnected or kinked lines or an improperly seated air cleaner and gasket.

If the system passes the visual inspection and a problem is still suspected:

1. For Carbureted vehicles:

   a. Locate the tank pressure control valve (inline between the fuel tank and canister) and disconnect the rubber hoses.

   b. Use a hand vacuum pump to apply 7.5-8.5 kPa of vacuum to hose A (valve vacuum fitting). If the valve is operating properly, it should open.

   c. Apply 7.5-8.5 kPa of vacuum to hose B while capping hose C with your finger or a rubber plug. Air should not pass through the valve.

   d. If the tank pressure valve is good, check the purge valve located on top of the canister. Apply 50 kPa of pressure to port marked 'V.C.' and check for air leakage. Air should not leak from the diaphragm.

   e. Apply 380mm Hg (14.96 in. Hg) of vacuum to the port marked 'PURGE' and maintain vacuum. Using a second pump, gradually apply vacuum to the port marked 'V.C.' while watching the first vacuum gauge. If the reading on the 'PURGE' vacuum port decreases as the 2nd gauge approaches 40-80mm Hg (1.6-3.2 in. Hg), then the purge valve is operating normally.

   f. Replace any component which fails to operate sufficiently.

2. For the Storm 1.6L engines:

   a. Connect a length of reasonably clean hose (at least at your end) to the lower tube of the purge valve and attempt to blow through it. Little or no air should pass through the canister. Some vehicles utilize a canister with a constant purge orifice which will allow a minimal amount of air to pass even with the purge diaphragm closed.

   b. Use a hand vacuum pump to apply 51 kPa (15 in. Hg) to the control valve (canister upper tube). If the diaphragm hold the vacuum, attempt to blow through the hose (still

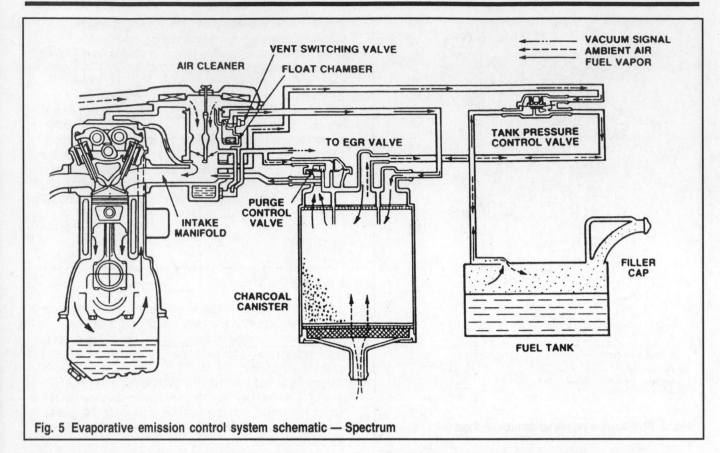

Fig. 5 Evaporative emission control system schematic — Spectrum

connected to the lower tube) again. With the vacuum applied, an increased flow of air should be blown through the tube.

    c. If the valve does not operate properly, then canister/valve assembly must be replaced as a unit.

    3. For the Storm 1.8L engine, refer to the diagnostic charts at the end of this section.

REMOVAL & INSTALLATION

Charcoal Canister

    1. Disconnect the negative battery cable if any tools might come in contact with electrical connections, wires or switches.

    2. Tag and disconnect the vacuum hoses from the canister.

    3. Remove the canister or canister bracket fastener, then remove the charcoal canister assembly from the vehicle.

    4. Installation is the reverse of the removal procedure. Be sure to fully seat, but not overtighten the canister and/or bracket retainers. The vacuum hoses MUST be properly installed for the system to operate correctly.

Exhaust Gas Recirculation System

OPERATION

▶ **See Figures 13 and 14**

    The Exhaust Gas Recirculation (EGR) valve is used to allow a controlled amount of exhaust gas to be recirculated into the

intake system. This limits peak flame temperature in the combustion chamber so the engine produces less NOx (oxides of nitrogen). On all vehicles, the amount of gas recirculated is controlled by a combination of exhaust gas backpressure and the vacuum applied to the EGR valve.

    The same basic EGR valve is used on all systems, with minor housing modifications made for mounting on the various engines and for the various control systems. The valve contains a diaphragm which is normally held closed by spring pressure. When vacuum is applied to the valve port, the diaphragm will be raised and held against the spring pressure, allowing exhaust gas to recirculate. The greater amount of vacuum applied, the more the diaphragm will open allowing a greater amount of exhaust gas to be recirculated to the intake manifold.

    For carbureted vehicles, vacuum is controlled by a Thermal Vacuum Valve (TVV) which opens once the engine coolant temperature has reached a certain point. Engine vacuum takes over from this point to open and close the EGR valve, as necessary for proper engine operation.

    For fuel injected vehicles, an ECM controlled Vacuum Switching Valve (VSV) or Electronic Vacuum Regulating Valve (EVRV) solenoid is used to provide vacuum to the EGR valve. The ECM controlled valve allows for vacuum regulation based on additional factors other than vacuum and backpressure, such as throttle position. For 1990-91 vehicles, the vacuum is applied directly to the EGR valve, but is then throttled or modified by a exhaust backpressure modulator attached to the EGR valve through a second vacuum port. For 1992-93 vehicles, the backpressure modulator (or transducer) is located inline between the solenoid valve and the EGR valve. On this second group of vehicles, the backpressure modulator still

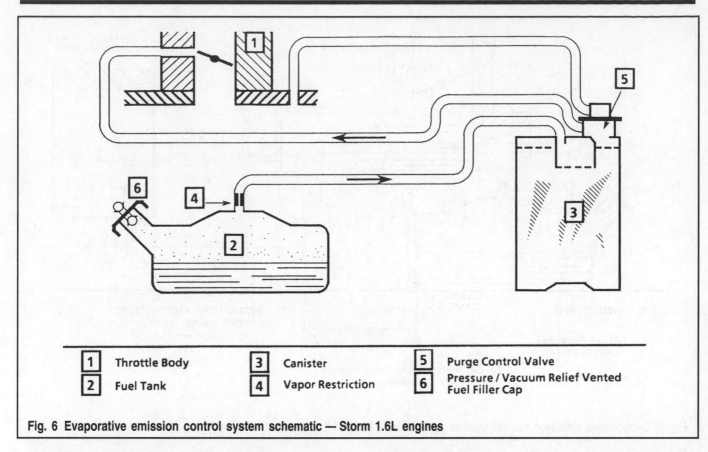

| 1 | Throttle Body | 3 | Canister | 5 | Purge Control Valve |
| 2 | Fuel Tank | 4 | Vapor Restriction | 6 | Pressure / Vacuum Relief Vented Fuel Filler Cap |

Fig. 6 Evaporative emission control system schematic — Storm 1.6L engines

works on the same principles to modify the amount of vacuum applied to the EGR valve, but it does so before vacuum is ever allowed to reach the EGR valve.

The modulator or transducer controls vacuum (thereby controlling the amount of exhaust gas which is recirculated) based on exhaust backpressure. Exhaust backpressure pushes against the valve and keeps the diaphragm pushed against a bleed hole. When the rpm is high but the throttle is closed, exhaust backpressure becomes negative and the diaphragm is pulled down just enough to uncover the bleed hole. The vacuum on top of the diaphragm leaks off and the EGR valve slowly closes.

For ECM controlled EGR systems (fuel injected, not carbureted) the solenoid valve will close, preventing vacuum and thereby preventing exhaust gas recirculation, under any one of the following conditions:

1. Engine coolant temperature below a specified point (during engine warm up)
2. When the throttle valve is at the idle position.
3. When the engine is running under a low load.
4. When intake manifold pressure is low.

SERVICE

Carbureted Vehicles

CHECKING THE EGR SYSTEM

▶ See Figures 15 and 16

1. Locate and disconnect the 3-way vacuum hose connector to the charcoal canister, between the EGR valve

and the TVV. Install a vacuum gauge between the EGR valve and the TVV.

➡ **Before disconnecting ANY vacuum hose, always note and/or tag the position of each hose to be removed. Proper hoses routing is essential to proper system and engine operation. Although it may seem obvious where each hose is connected, before removal, vacuum hoses begin to look strangely similar come installation time.**

2. With the engine cold, turn the ignition **ON** and start the engine. Make sure the vacuum gauge indicates 0 kPa at any speed, while the engine is still cold.

3. When the engine reaches normal operating temperature, check that the vacuum gauge indicates 0 kPa at idle and 6.7 kPa or more at 3500 rpm.

4. With the engine running at 3500 rpm, disconnect and plug the vacuum hose to the EGR valve. Engine speed should increase slightly.

5. Stop the engine, then push the EGR diaphragm by hand and release it. Make sure the diaphragm plate returns smoothly to the original position.

6. If a problem is found, begin by inspecting the EGR valve. Connect a hand vacuum pump to the valve hose and apply 24 kPa of vacuum. The diaphragm should move fully upward and hold without leaking down.

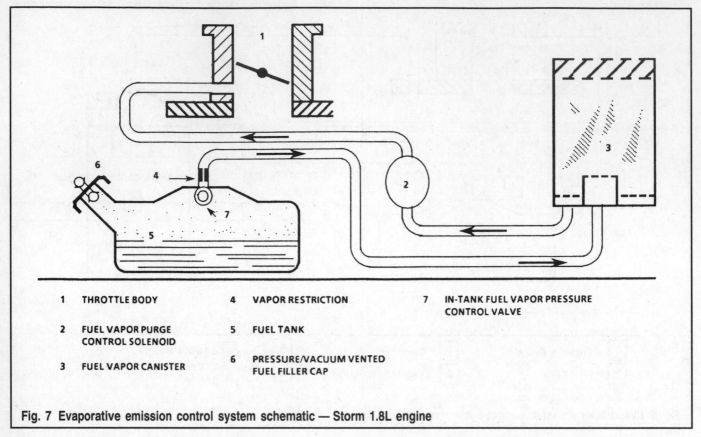

1	THROTTLE BODY	**4**	VAPOR RESTRICTION	**7**	IN-TANK FUEL VAPOR PRESSURE CONTROL VALVE	
2	FUEL VAPOR PURGE CONTROL SOLENOID	**5**	FUEL TANK			
3	FUEL VAPOR CANISTER	**6**	PRESSURE/VACUUM VENTED FUEL FILLER CAP			

Fig. 7 Evaporative emission control system schematic — Storm 1.8L engine

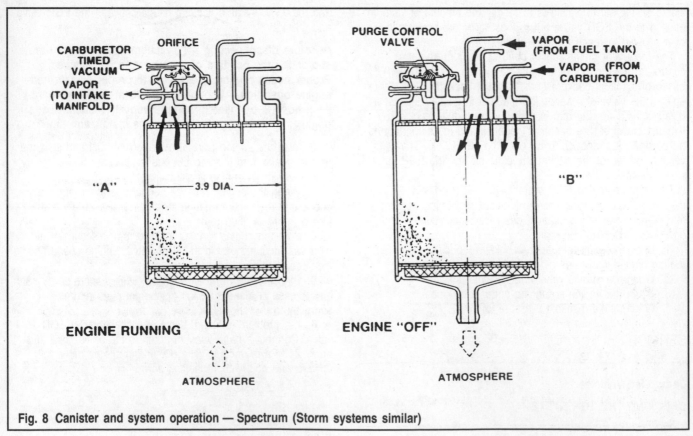

Fig. 8 Canister and system operation — Spectrum (Storm systems similar)

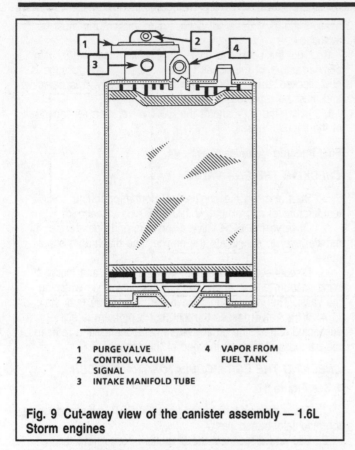

1 PURGE VALVE
2 CONTROL VACUUM
   SIGNAL
3 INTAKE MANIFOLD TUBE
4 VAPOR FROM
   FUEL TANK

Fig. 9 Cut-away view of the canister assembly — 1.6L Storm engines

1 VAPOR FROM FUEL TANK
2 CANISTER PURGE VACUUM
3 CANISTER BODY
4 CARBON
5 FILTER
6 GRID
7 AIR FLOW
   DURING PURGE

Fig. 10 Cut-away view of the canister assembly — 1.8L Storm engine

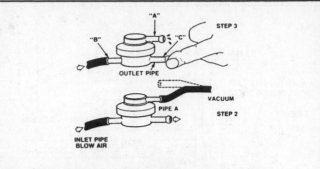

Fig. 11 Testing the tank pressure control valve — Spectrum

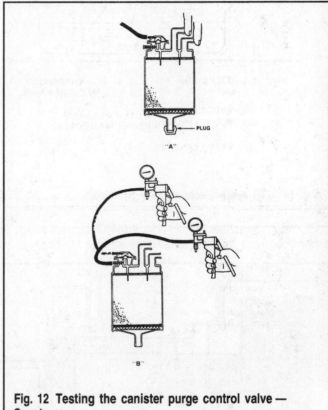

Fig. 12 Testing the canister purge control valve — Spectrum

7. If necessary, remove the EGR valve and check for excessive build-up of deposits which might prevent it from opening or operating properly. Clean any deposits.

➡**The EGR valve must be replaced if cracks in the diaphragm prevent it from holding vacuum or if deformation of the valve seat cause the valve to stick open.**

8. If the EGR valve is good, and a problem is still suspected, check the TVV valve. Remove the valve from the engine, install 2 short lengths of vacuum hose (through which to blow air and check for passage) and heat the sensing portion using hot water. Be very careful when working around the hot water, most oven mits will NOT protect you if they become soaked with boiling water.

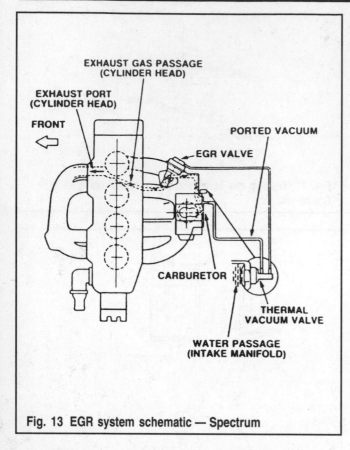

Fig. 13 EGR system schematic — Spectrum

9. When the sensor reaches 130°F (54°C) blow air into 1 of the hoses and check for air passage through the other

hose. If the TVV does not open, it is defective and must be replaced.

10. Cool the sensor to 95°F (35°C) using cool water, then blow air into 1 of the hoses to make sure that air passage is now blocked. If the TVV does not close properly, it is defective and must be replaced.

11. Install the TVV and/or the EGR valve, then reconnect all of the vacuum hoses.

Fuel Injected Vehicles

CHECKING THE EGR VALVE

1. Start and run the engine until normal operating temperature of approximately 120°F (60°C) is reached.

2. Observe the EGR valve diaphragm and operate the throttle lever to accelerate the engine. The diaphragm should move.

3. Disconnect the hose from the EGR valve and install a hand vacuum pump. Apply 10 in. of vacuum while watching the valve. The valve should move and the engine may stall.

4. If the valve passes the test, but a problem is still suspected. Check the other system components and refer to the diagnostic charts at the end of the section.

CHECKING THE EGR MODULATOR/TRANSDUCER

▶ **See Figure 17**

1. Trace the vacuum hoses from the EGR valve and locate the modulator/transducer.

2. Tag and disconnect the 3 vacuum hoses from the modulator/transducer.

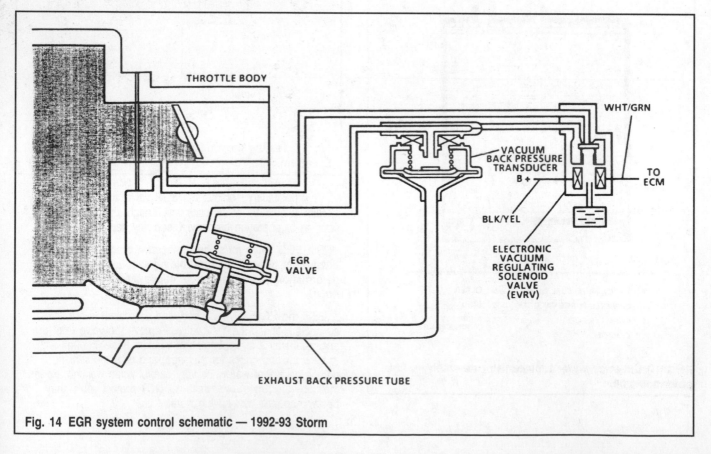

Fig. 14 EGR system control schematic — 1992-93 Storm

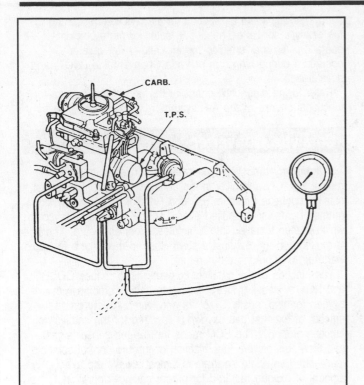

Fig. 15 Install a vacuum gauge between the TVV and EGR valves in order to check system operation — Carbureted vehicles

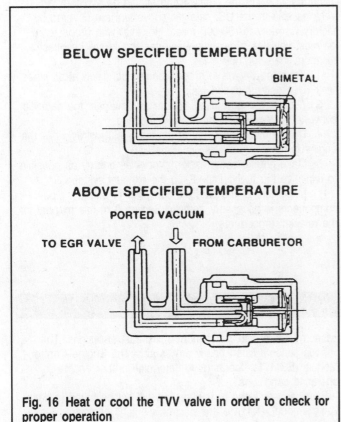

Fig. 16 Heat or cool the TVV valve in order to check for proper operation

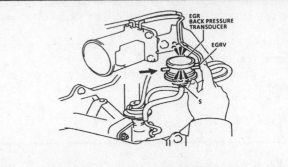

Fig. 17 Checking the EGR modulator/transducer — Fuel injected vehicles

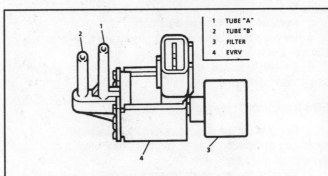

Fig. 18 Checking the VSV/EVRV solenoid — Fuel injected vehicles

3. For 1990-91 vehicles:

a. Place a finger over the tubes marked 'P' and 'R' and blow air into the tube marked 'Q'. Air should pass through the filter portion of the modulator.

b. Connect a vacuum pump to the tube marked 'S' and plug the tubes marked 'P' and 'R' using your finger.

c. You should NOT be able to obtain vacuum on the pump.

4. For 1992-93 vehicles:

a. Place a finger over the tube marked 'VSV' and blow air into the tube marked 'EGRV'. Air should pass through the filter portion of the transducer.

b. Connect a vacuum pump to the tube marked 'VSV' and plug the tube marked 'EGRV' using your finger.

c. You SHOULD be able to obtain vacuum on the pump.

5. If the modulator/transducer does not perform as specified, it is defective and must be replaced.

CHECKING THE EGR VSV/EVRV SOLENOID

▶ See Figure 18

1. Tag and disconnect the 2 vacuum hoses from the solenoid

2. Make sure the ignition is **OFF**, then unplug the electrical connector from the solenoid.

3. Use an ohmmeter, check resistance across the 2 terminals. Resistance must be between 33-39 ohms, or the solenoid must be replaced.

4. Blow air into tube A (closest to the electrical terminal); air should exit only through the filter and NOT through tube B.

5. Install the electrical connector.

6. Turn the ignition **ON** and ground the diagnostic terminal of the check connector. Refer to Self-Diagnostics, later in this section.

7. Blow air into tube A (closest to the electrical terminal); air should now exit through tube B.

8. The solenoid must be replaced if it fails to perform as specified.

REMOVAL & INSTALLATION

EGR Valve

1. Remove the air cleaner assembly for access.
2. Tag and disconnect the vacuum hoses from the EGR valve.
3. Remove the valve retaining bolts.
4. Remove the EGR valve and gasket from the mounting surface. Discard the old gasket.
5. To install, reverse the removal procedure and always use a new gasket.

EGR Modulator/Transducer

1. Remove the air cleaner assembly for access.
2. Tag and disconnect the vacuum hoses from the modulator/transducer.
3. Remove the modulator/transducer from the vehicle.
4. Installation is the reverse of removal.

EGR VSV/EVRV

1. Disconnect the negative battery cable.
2. Unplug the electrical connector from the solenoid.
3. Tag and disconnect the solenoid vacuum hoses.
4. Remove the 2 fasteners securing the solenoid to the intake manifold.
5. Remove the solenoid from the engine.
6. Installation is the reverse of removal.

Air Injection Reaction (AIR) System

The Carbureted vehicles covered by this manual utilize an additional emission control known as the AIR system. The purpose of the system is to reduce emissions in the exhaust while quickly heating the catalytic converter during cold engine starts. The faster the converter reaches operating temperature, the quicker it can begin to reduce engine emissions.

The system operates by allowing air flow through an ECM controlled valve to the exhaust ports during a cold engine start. This additional air speeds up the reactions occurring in the catalytic converter, heating it faster for more efficient operation. Air is diverted to the air cleaner (for quieter operation) during high rpm or Wide Open Throttle (WOT) and deceleration.

Refer to the diagnostic charts at the end of this section for functional checks of the AIR system.

Catalytic Converter

A three-way reduction type catalytic converter is used to reduce HC, CO and NOx in the engine's exhaust. The actual catalyst contains Platinum (Pt) and Rhodium (Rh). A few grams of catalyst is applied evenly onto a ceramic honeycomb, which is then installed into a stainless-steel enclosure. The unit is mounted in the exhaust system close to the engine for rapid warm-up to operating temperature.

The function of the catalytic converter is to reduce CO, HC, and NOx by causing these gasses to easily combine with oxygen forming mostly CO_2, N_2 and water. A very precise amount of exhaust gas oxygen is required for the catalyst to function properly. The ECM reads the oxygen sensor signal and then controls the fuel injection or mixture control solenoid (carbureted vehicles) so there is almost always the exact amount of oxygen required for proper catalyst operation.

A catalytic converter operates at temperatures up to 1500°F (815°C). It can be damaged by prolonged idling, a rich air/fuel ratio or by a constant misfire. Excess fuel will cause the unit to overheat and melt the ceramic substrate. Use of leaded fuel will quickly poison the catalyst and should be avoided. On vehicles sold in the US, catalytic converters are covered by factory warranty for 50,000 miles. However with proper care, on most vehicles a catalytic converter should still be effective for more than 100,000 miles.

1. Keep the engine in proper running condition at all times.
2. Use only unleaded fuel.
3. Avoid prolonged idling. Proper air flow past the catalytic converter is required to prevent overheating.
4. Do not disconnect any of the spark plug wires while the engine is running.
5. Make engine compression checks as quickly as possible to minimize the fuel pumped into the exhaust system.

If replacement of the catalytic converter or exhaust pipe components is necessary, refer to Section 3 of this manual for the relevant procedures.

ELECTRONIC ENGINE CONTROLS

Operation

▶ **See Figures 19, 20, 21, 22, 23 and 24**

The fuel injection or carburetor system, described in detail in Section No. 5 of this manual, is operated along with the ignition system to obtain optimum performance and fuel economy along with a minimum of exhaust emissions. The various sensors listed below are used by the Engine Control Module (ECM) for feedback to determine proper engine operating conditions.

Every sensor listed in this section will not be found in each vehicle/model. Refer to the electronic engine control component diagrams to determine if your vehicle uses a sensor in question, and if so, for the sensor's location.

➡**Although many of the tests listed in the diagnostic section of this manual may be conducted using a Digital Volt/Ohm Meter (DVOM), certain steps or procedures may require use of the Tech1® scan tool (a specialized GM tester) or an equivalent scan/testing tool. If these testers are not available, the vehicle should be taken to a reputable service station which has the appropriate equipment.**

Engine Control Module

REMOVAL & INSTALLATION

✳✳CAUTION

To prevent the possibility of permanent ECM damage, the ignition switch must always be OFF when disconnecting power from or reconnecting power to the ECM. This includes unplugging the ECM connector, disconnecting the negative battery cable, removing the ECM fuse or even attempting to jump your dead battery using jumper cables.

Spectrum

▶ **See Figures 25 and 26**

The ECM is located in the passenger compartment, above the passenger kick pad. The ECM used in the Spectrum contains a Programmable Read Only Memory (PROM) chip which contains data relevant to the specific vehicle model. If the ECM is replaced, the PROM must be switched to the new ECM.

1. Make sure the ignition is **OFF**, then disconnect the negative battery cable.
2. Unplug the wiring harness connectors from the ECM.
3. Remove the ECM mounting hardware, then remove the ECM from the passenger compartment.
4. If the ECM is being replaced, remove the PROM access cover, then use a PROM extraction tool to carefully remove the PROM chip from the old ECM:

   a. Starting at the opposite end from the reference mark, gently work the extraction tool tan under the PROM using a slight rocking motion.

   b. Go to the reference end of the PROM and push the tang under the PROM with your thumb pressing on the tool as close to the tang end as possible.

   c. Make sure the tang end is completely under the PROM, but above the mating socket, then grasp the PROM firmly between your thumb and forefinger while pulling upward and remove the PROM from the mating socket.

   d. Position the PROM on a clean flat surface with the leads pointing downward, then carefully press the PROM inserting tool firmly over the PROM. Make sure the reference end can be seen at the tool cut out end.

e. Compare the service number on the new ECM to the old ECM to double check it is the correct model, then remove the PROM access cover.

✳✳WARNING

Any time the PROM is installed backwards and the ignition switch is turned ON, the PROM is destroyed.

   f. Using the insertion tool, mate the PROM to the circuit board. Make sure the reference ends of both the RPOM and socket are aligned in the same direction. The PROM chip will not be fully seated at this point.

   g. Turn the insertion tool over and using the blunt end, press the PROM down until fully seated. Check that the PROM pins are properly seated in the socket and that the PROM and socket ends are properly aligned.

   h. Install the access cover.
5. To install, reverse Steps 1-3.
6. Turn the ignition **ON** and activate the self-diagnostics to check for proper ECM operation. Refer to the procedure later in this section.

Storm

▶ **See Figure 27**

The ECM is located under the instrument panel, left of the steering column. Unlike the model used in the Spectrum, the Geo Storm's ECM does not have any serviceable components. Data relevant to the vehicle model (which is necessary for proper ECM operation) is programmed into the ECM's Electronically Erasable Programmable Read Only Memory (EEPROM). If the ECM is replaced, the TECH1® or an equivalent scan tool must be used to program the EEPROM in the new ECM. If a proper tool is not available, the vehicle should be taken to a reputable repair shop that has the proper equipment.

1. Disconnect the negative battery cable.
2. Remove the lower trim panel or sound insulator, as necessary for access.
3. Remove the two 10mm nuts securing the ECM.
4. Unplug the wiring harness connectors from the ECM.

✳✳WARNING

To prevent the possibility of electrostatic discharge damage to the ECM, DO NOT touch the connector pins or soldered components on the circuit board.

5. Reverse the removal procedure to install.
6. If installing a new ECM, use the TECH1® or an equivalent scan tool to program the EEPROM. Be sure to follow all of the tool manufacturer's instructions.

Engine Coolant Temperature Sensor

REMOVAL & INSTALLATION

1. Make sure the engine is cold, then relieve the cooling system pressure.
2. Disconnect the negative battery cable.

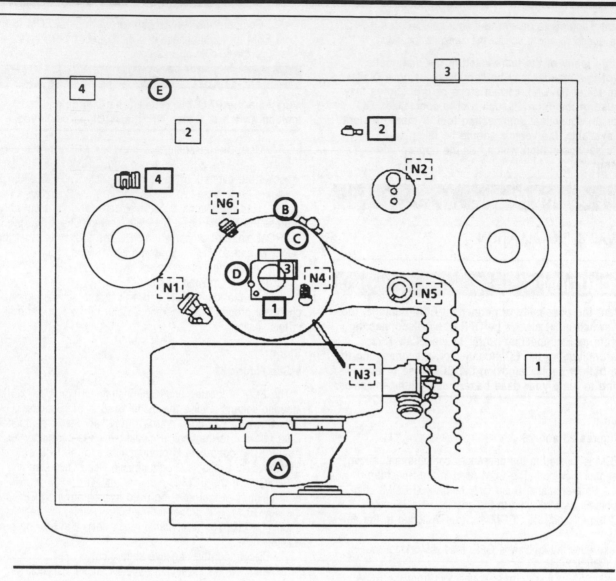

Fig. 19 Electronic engine control components — Carbureted Spectrum

☐ **COMPUTER HARNESS**

1 TACH TEST LEAD
2 DWELL TEST LEAD
3 "CHECK ENGINE" LIGHT
4 ECM

○ **INFORMATION SENSORS**

A O₂ SENSOR
B MAT SENSOR
C COOLANT SENSOR
D TPS AND IDLE SENSORS
E ALTITUDE SWITCH

☐ **CONTROLLED DEVICES**

1 EFE
2 AIR VSV
3 M/C SOLENOID
4 HI ALTITUDE SOLENOID VALVE

⬚ **NOT ECM CONNECTED**

N1 EGR
N2 CHARCOAL CANISTER
N3 PCV
N4 ITC VALVE
N5 THERMAC
N6 MC VALVE

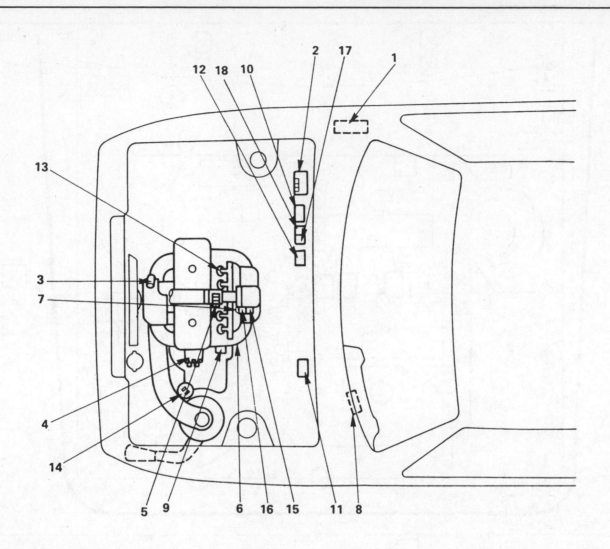

1. Control unit -ECM
    (Under the glove box)
2. MAP sensor
3. Oxygen sensor
4. Distributor
5. Detonation sensor
    (On the cyl. body)
6. Coolant temp. sensor
7. Throttle valve position sensor
8. Vehicle speed sensor
    (Built in the speedometer)

9. Vacuum switching valve : wastegate
10. Vacuum switching valve: EGR
11. Vacuum switching valve: TPCV
12. Vacuum switching valve: AIR
13. Fuel injector
14. Ignition coil
15. Idle air control valve
16. MAT sensor
17. Relay; Fuel pump
18. Vacuum switching valve: vapor canister

Fig. 20 Electronic engine control components — Turbo Spectrum

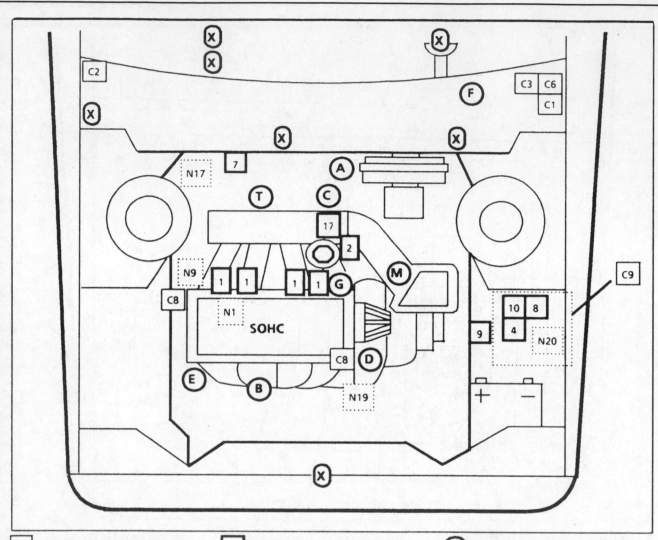

COMPUTER HARNESS
- C1 Electronic Control Module (ECM)
- C2 ALDL Connector
- C3 "Check Engine" Light
- C6 Fuse Panel
- C8 ECM Grounds
- C9 Underhood Relay/Fuse Center

NOT ECM CONNECTED
- N1 Crankcase Vent Valve (PCV) Diaphram Type
- N9 Fuel Pressure Regulator Valve
- N17 Fuel Vapor Canister
- N19 Fan Switch
- N20 A/C Compressor Relay

CONTROLLED DEVICES
- 1 Fuel Injectors
- 2 IAC Valve
- 4 EFI Main Relay
- 7 EGR Vacuum Switching Valve (VSV)
- 8 Cooling Fan Relay
- 9 Ignition Coil
- 10 Fuel Pump Relay
- 17 Throttle Body

Exhaust Gas Recirculation (EGR) Valve

INFORMATION SENSORS
- A Manifold Absolute Pressure (MAP) Sensor
- B Oxygen (O_2) Sensor
- C Throttle Position Sensor (TPS)
- D Coolant Temperature Sensor (CTS)
- E Power Steering Pressure Switch *
- F Vehicle Speed Sensor (VSS)
- G EGR Gas Temperature Sensor
- M Park/Neutral (P/N) Switch
- T Intake Air Temperature (IAT) Sensor

X SIR System Components Refer to Section 9J of the Service Manual, for "Cautions" and Information on SIR System Components.

NOTE: *Power Steering Pressure Switch is part of the Power Steering Pump.

Fig. 21 Electronic engine control components — 1990-91 1.6L SOHC Storm

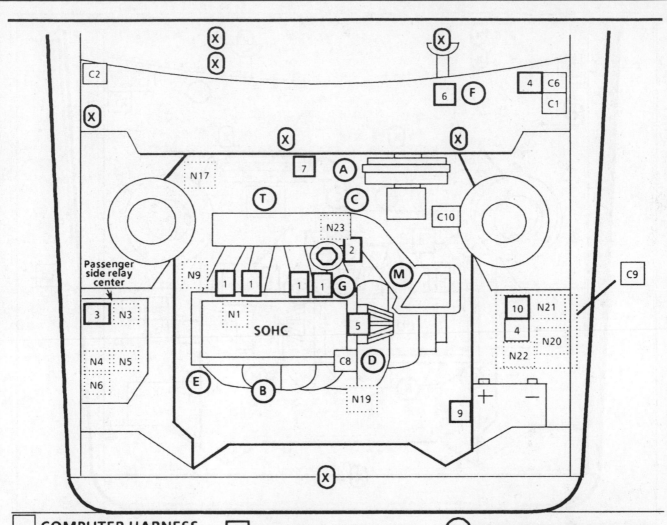

COMPUTER HARNESS
- **C1** Engine Control Module (ECM)
- **C2** DLC Connector
- **C4** ECM Main Relay
- **C6** Fuse Panel
- **C8** ECM Grounds (4 wires) (mounted on thremostat housing)
- **C9** Underhood Relay/Fuse Center
- **C10** Engine Harness Connectors (2)

NOT ECM CONNECTED
- **N1** Crankcase Vent Valve (PCV)
- **N3** A/C Thermo Relay
- **N4** A/C Diode
- **N5** Horn Relay
- **N6** Fog Lamp Relay (if equipped)
- **N9** Fuel Pressure Regulator Valve
- **N17** Fuel Vapor Canister
- **N19** Fan Switch
- **N20** A/C Condensor Relay
- **N21** Cooling Fan Relay
- **N22** Neutral Start Relay
- **N23** Throttle Body

CONTROLLED DEVICES
- **1** Fuel Injectors
- **2** IAC Valve
- **3** A/C compressor clutch relay
- **4** MIL
- **5** Distributor Ignition Control Module
- **6** Shift Light (M/T Only)
- **7** EGR EVRV
- **9** Ignition Coil
- **10** Fuel Pump Relay

Exhaust Gas Recirculation (EGR) Valve

★ California Only.

NOTE: *Power Steering Pressure Switch is part of the Power Steering Pump.

INFORMATION SENSORS
- **A** Manifold Absolute Pressure (MAP) Sensor
- **B** Oxygen Sensor (O2S)
- **C** Throttle Position (TP) Sensor
- **D** Engine Coolant Temperature (ECT) Sensor
- **E** Power Steering Pressure Switch *
- **F** Vehicle Speed Sensor (VSS)
- **G** EGR Gas Temperature Sensor ★
- **M** Park/Neutral Position (PNP) Switch
- **T** Intake Air Temperature (IAT) Sensor

X SIR System Components Refer to Section 9J of the Service Manual, for "Cautions" and Information on SIR System Components.

Fig. 22 Electronic engine control components — 1992-93 1.6L SOHC Storm

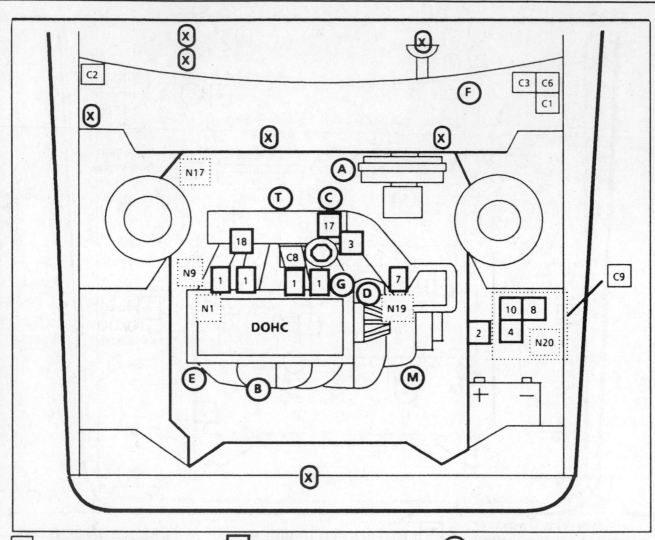

☐ COMPUTER HARNESS

C1 Electronic Control Module (ECM)
C2 ALDL Connector
C3 "Check Engine" Light
C6 Fuse Panel
C8 ECM Grounds
C9 Underhood Relay/Fuse Center

⋯ NOT ECM CONNECTED

N1   Crankcase Vent Valve (PCV)
N9   Fuel Pressure Regulator Valve
N17 Fuel Vapor Canister
N19 Fan Switch
N20 A/C Compressor Relay

☐ CONTROLLED DEVICES

1   Fuel Injectors
2   Ignition Coil
3   IAC Valve
4   Main Relay
7   EGR Vacuum Switching Valve (VSV)
8   Cooling Fan Relay
10 Fuel Pump Relay
17 Throttle Body
18 Secondary Air Vacuum Switching
    Valve (VSV) (Located Under Intake
    Plenum)

⬡ Exhaust Gas Recirculation (EGR) Valve

◯ INFORMATION SENSORS

A Manifold Absolute Pressure (MAP)
   Sensor
B Oxygen (O_2) Sensor
C Throttle Position Sensor
D Coolant Temperature Sensor (CTS)
E Power Steering Pressure Switch *
F Vehicle Speed Sensor (VSS)
G EGR Gas Temperature Sensor
M Park/Neutral (P/N) Switch
T Intake Air Temperature (IAT) Sensor

☒ SIR System Components Refer To
   Section 9J of the Service Manual for
   "Caution's" and Information on SIR
   System Components.

NOTE: *Power Steering Pressure Switch is
       part of the Power Steering Pump.

Fig. 23 Electronic engine control components — 1.6L DOHC Storm

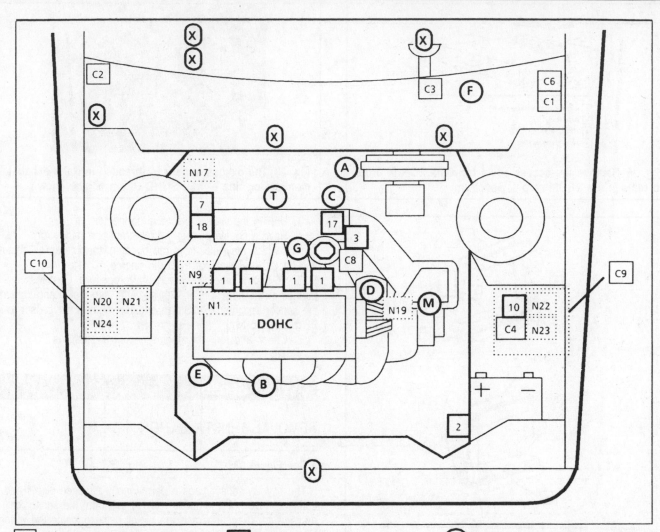

COMPUTER HARNESS

- C1 Electronic Control Module (ECM)
- C2 DLC
- C3 MIL
- C4 ECM Main Relay
- C6 Fuse Panel
- C8 ECM Grounds
- C9 Underhood Relay/Fuse Center
- C10 A/C Relay Center

NOT ECM CONNECTED

- N1 Crankcase Vent Valve (PCV)
- N9 Fuel Pressure Regulator Valve
- N17 Fuel Vapor Canister
- N19 Fan Switch
- N20 A/C Compressor Relay
- N21 A/C Thermo Relay
- N22 Cooling Fan Relay
- N23 Condenser Fan Relay
- N24 A/C Diode

CONTROLLED DEVICES

- 1 Fuel Injectors
- 2 Ignition Coil
- 3 IAC Valve
- 7 EGR EVRV
- 10 Fuel Pump Relay
- 17 Throttle Body
- 18 Canister Purge EVRV

Exhaust Gas Recirculation (EGR) Valve

★ California only.

NOTE: *Power Steering Pressure Switch is part of the Power Steering Pump.

INFORMATION SENSORS

- A Manifold Absolute Pressure (MAP) Sensor
- B Heated Oxygen Sensor (HO2S)
- C Throttle Position (TP) Sensor
- D Engine Coolant Temperature (ECT) Sensor
- E Power Steering Pressure Switch *
- F Vehicle Speed Sensor (VSS)
- G EGR Gas Temperature Sensor ★
- M Park/Neutral Position (PNP) Switch
- T Intake Air Temperature (IAT) Sensor

X SIR System Components Refer To Section 9J of the Service Manual for "Cautions" and Information on SIR System Components.

Fig. 24 Electronic engine control components — 1.8L DOHC Storm

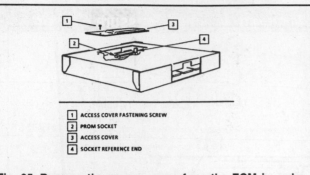

1. ACCESS COVER FASTENING SCREW
2. PROM SOCKET
3. ACCESS COVER
4. SOCKET REFERENCE END

Fig. 25 Remove the access cover from the ECM in order to remove the PROM chip — Spectrum

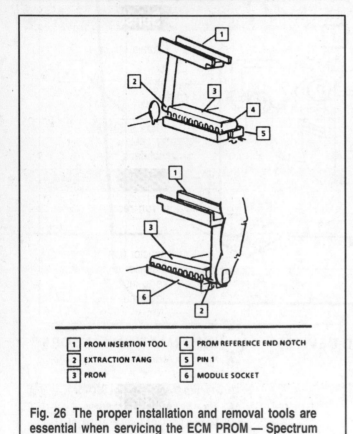

1. PROM INSERTION TOOL
2. EXTRACTION TANG
3. PROM
4. PROM REFERENCE END NOTCH
5. PIN 1
6. MODULE SOCKET

Fig. 26 The proper installation and removal tools are essential when servicing the ECM PROM — Spectrum

1. ECM
2. Instrument main panel
3. Steering wheel

Fig. 27 ECM location — Storm

Fig. 28 The oxygen sensor is threaded into the exhaust manifold or pipe — 1.6L SOHC Storm engine shown

3. Unplug the sensor electrical connector.

4. Have a couple of rags and a drain pan handy for coolant which may leak from the opening, then carefully loosen and back the sensor out from the engine.

5. To install, reverse the removal procedure. Coat the threads of the new sensor with sealant, then install and tighten the sensor securely. For Storm engines, tighten the sensor to 22 ft. lbs. (30 Nm).

6. Check and refill the engine cooling system, as necessary.

Oxygen Sensor

REMOVAL & INSTALLATION

▶ **See Figure 28**

The oxygen sensor uses a permanently attached pigtail and connector. Do not attempt to remove this from the sensor or damage could occur. Trace the pigtail back to locate the wiring harness connector.

1. The sensor may be difficult to remove when the engine temperature is below 120°F (60°C). If necessary, start and warm the engine before removing the sensor, BUT BE VERY CAREFUL. The oxygen sensor is threaded into the exhaust system and will be extremely hot if the engine was run recently. Always use proper protective gloves to prevent burns.

2. Disconnect the negative battery cable.

3. Unplug the wiring harness from the sensor pigtail connector.

4. Carefully loosen the sensor, making sure not to force and damage the threads, exhaust manifold or pipe.

➡ **The inline electrical connector and louvered end of the sensor must be kept free of dirt, grease or other contaminants. Also, avoid using cleaning solvents of any type. The sensor must not be dropped or handled roughly in any way.**

5. To install, reverse the removal procedure. New sensors will have an anti-seize compound already applied to the threads. If reinstalling a sensor, be sure to apply anti-seize ONLY to the threaded portion of the sensor.

6. Tighten the sensor to 30 ft. lbs. (41 Nm).

Throttle Position Sensor

REMOVAL & INSTALLATION

1. Disconnect the negative battery cable.
2. Unplug the sensor electrical connector.
3. Remove the sensor attaching screws and lock washers or retainers.
4. Remove the sensor from the carburetor or throttle body.
To install:
5. With the throttle valve in the normal closed idle position, install the sensor to the carburetor or throttle body.
6. Install the screws and retainers or lock washers and tighten to 18 inch lbs (2 Nm).
7. Install the wiring harness connector to the sensor, then connect the negative battery cable.
8. Check and adjust the sensor as necessary, using a voltmeter (carbureted vehicles) or a scan tool (fuel injected vehicles). Refer to the adjustment procedures in Section 5 of this manual or to the diagnostic charts later in this section.

Intake Air Temperature Sensor

The fuel injected vehicles covered in this manual utilize an Intake Air Temperature (IAT) sensor mounted in the air intake manifold.

REMOVAL & INSTALLATION

1. Disconnect the negative battery cable.
2. Unplug the sensor electrical connector.
3. Carefully back out the sensor from the manifold.
4. Reverse the removal procedure to install. Coat the sensor threads using sealant, then install and tighten the IAT sensor to 22 ft. lbs. (30 Nm).

Manifold Absolute Pressure Sensor

REMOVAL & INSTALLATION

1. Disconnect the negative battery cable.
2. Disconnect the vacuum hose from the sensor.
3. Unplug the sensor electrical connector.
4. Remove the attaching screws, then remove the sensor from the engine.
5. Reverse the removal procedure to install. Be sure to fully seat, but not overtigten the retaining screws.

EGR Gas Temperature Sensor

Some fuel injected vehicles in California utilize an EGR gas temperature sensor.

REMOVAL & INSTALLATION

1. Disconnect the negative battery cable.
2. Remove the air cleaner assembly and related duct work.

✲✲WARNING

Be very careful if the engine was run recently; the sensor may still be HOT.

3. Unplug the wiring harness connector from the sensor.
4. Loosen and carefully back the sensor out of the engine.
5. Reverse the removal procedure to install. Coat the sensor threads with an anti-seize compound, then install and tighten the sensor to 22 ft. lbs. (30 Nm).

SELF-DIAGNOSTICS

General Information

The Engine Control Module (ECM) performs a continual self-diagnosis on many circuits of the engine control system. If a problem or irregularity is detected, the ECM will set a Diagnostic Trouble Code or DTC in the ECM memory. A DTC indicates a suspected failure that currently exists or that has recently existed in an engine system. A currently present code will usually illuminate the CHECK ENGINE light, also known as the the Malfunction Indicator Lamp (MIL).

Diagnostic codes are stored in ECM memory until they are manually erased by a scan tool or until power is disconnected from the ECM for a certain length of time. If an ECM detected problem is intermittent and disappears, the MIL will normally extinguish after 10 seconds, but the DTC will remain in diagnostic memory. Intermittent problems are often caused by corroded, dirty or loose electrical connections. A thorough inspection of the affected system should always be the first step in trouble shooting a DTC.

➡The CHECK ENGINE MIL will illuminate whenever the ignition is turned ON with the engine not running. This occurs for a bulb circuit check. As long as the light extinguishes after the engine is started, there are no currently detected trouble codes. Do not confuse the bulb check with an ECM detected DTC.

Assembly Line Diagnostic Link (ALDL)/Diagnostic Link Connector (DLC)

▶ See Figures 29 and 30

There are many test procedures that require the connecting a scan tool or connecting a jumper wire to terminals 1 and 3 of the 3-terminal ALDL (the main diagnostic tool connector). The ALDL is used during vehicle assembly to test the engine before it leaves the assembly plant and after the factory to communicate with the ECM. The ALDL is located in the passenger compartment. For most vehicles, it is under the right side of the dashboard, to the right of the glove compartment. Terminal 1 is the diagnostic test terminal and is located on the far left of the connector. Terminal 3, located to the far right of the connector, is the engine ground. When these terminals are jumpered together and the ignition switch turned **ON**, the CHECK ENGINE MIL will flash Code 12. This indicates that the internal diagnostic system is operating and that specific output device signals are being generated.

Entering Self-Diagnosis

To enter the diagnostics, either connect a scan tool to the ALDL or use a jumper wire to connect terminals 1 and 3. Turn

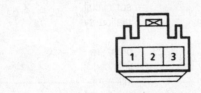

1. **DIAGNOSTIC TEST TERMINAL**
2. **SERIAL DATA**
3. **ENGINE GROUND**

Fig. 29 ALDL connector and terminals — Spectrum

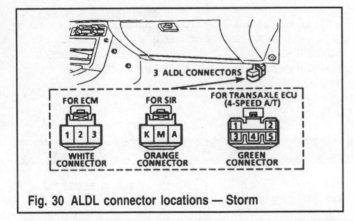

Fig. 30 ALDL connector locations — Storm

the ignition switch **ON**, then the ECM will enter the diagnostic program and report trouble Codes on the scan tool or by flashing the CHECK ENGINE light.

All Codes are 2 digits between 12 and 51. Codes are displayed on the CHECK ENGINE light by flashing the MIL with short and long pauses to distinguish digits of 1 code from digits of another. The short pause is used between digits of the same code, long pauses are between codes. For Code 12, the sequence will be: flash, pause, flash-flash, long pause.

1. When the diagnostic mode is entered, Code 12 is displayed 3 or 4 times, depending on the vehicle. This indicates that the internal diagnostic system is operating. If Code 12 is not displayed, the self-diagnostic program is not functioning properly. If only Code 12 is displayed, no system malfunctions have been stored.

2. After code 12 flashes to indicate diagnostic display, any existing system fault Codes are displayed in order from lowest to highest code number. Each Code is displayed 3 times, followed by the next Code, if any.

3. When all engine and transaxle Codes have been displayed, Code 12 will flash again.

Clearing Codes

On most vehicles, the TECH1®, or an equivalent scan tool may be used to clear codes from the ECM memory. If a scan tool is unavailable or your tool does not have this capability, power must be removed from the ECM for a minimum of 30 seconds. The lower the ambient temperature, the longer period of time the power must be removed.

Remember, to prevent ECM damage, the ignition must always be **OFF** when removing power. Power may be removed through various methods. The preferable method is to remove the 30A main ECM fuse from the underhood relay/fuse box. The ECM pigtail may also be unplugged. If necessary, the negative battery cable may be disconnected, but other onboard data such as radio presets will be lost and the ECM may have to undergo a brief relearning period before normal performance returns.

DIAGNOSTIC TROUBLE CODES

Spectrum

CARBURETED VEHICLES

Code 12 — Diagnostic system check/No distributor reference pulse

Code 13 — Oxygen sensor circuit (open)

Code 14 — Coolant temperature sensor circuit (high temperature indicated)

Code 15 — Coolant temperature sensor circuit (low temperature indicated)

Code 21 — Throttle position sensor and idle switch circuit

Code 22 — Fuel cut-off relay circuit (open or grounded)

Code 23 — Mixture control solenoid circuit (open or grounded)

Code 25 — AIR system VSV solenoid circuit (open or grounded)

Code 42 — Fuel cut-off relay circuit (voltage high)

Code 44 — Oxygen sensor circuit (lean exhaust indicated)

Code 45 — Oxygen sensor circuit (rich exhaust indicated)
Code 51 — PROM error (faulty or incorrect PROM)
Code 53 — AIR system VSV solenoid circuit (voltage high)
Code 54 — Mixture control solenoid circuit (signal voltage high)
Code 55 — ECM error

Turbo Vehicles

Code 12 — Diagnostic system check/No distributor reference pulse
Code 13 — Oxygen sensor circuit
Code 14 — Coolant temperature sensor (signal voltage low)
Code 15 — Coolant temperature sensor (signal voltage high)
Code 21 — Throttle position sensor (signal voltage high)
Code 22 — Throttle position sensor (signal voltage low)
Code 23 — Manifold air temperature sensor (signal voltage high)
Code 24 — Vehicle speed sensor
Code 25 — Manifold air temperature sensor (signal voltage low)
Code 31 — Turbocharger wastegate control
Code 33 — MAP sensor (signal voltage high)
Code 34 — MAP sensor (signal voltage low)

Code 42 — Electronic spark timing
Code 43 — Detonation sensor
Code 44 — Lean exhaust indicated
Code 45 — Rich exhaust indicated
Code 51 — PROM failure

Storm

Code 12 — Diagnostic system check
Code 13 — Oxygen sensor circuit (open)
Code 14 — Engine coolant temperature sensor circuit (high/low temperature indicated)
Code 21 — Throttle positions sensor circuit (high/low signal voltage)
Code 23 — Intake air temperature sensor circuit (high/low temperature indicated)
Code 24 — Vehicle speed sensor circuit
Code 32 — Exhaust gas recirculation system error (California only)
Code 33 — Manifold absolute pressure sensor circuit (signal voltage high/low or vacuum high/low)
Code 42 — Ignition control circuit error
Code 44 — Oxygen sensor circuit (lean exhaust indicated)
Code 45 — Oxygen sensor circuit (rich exhaust indicated)
Code Code 51 — ECM or EEPROM failure

DIAGNOSTIC FLOW CHARTS

The following flow charts may be used to diagnose the causes of various trouble codes which may be recorded by the ECM or to verify proper operation of systems.

→Although many of the following tests may be conducted using a Digital Volt/Ohm Meter (DVOM), certain steps or procedures may require use of the Tech1® scan tool (a specialized GM tester) or an equivalent scan/testing tool. If these testers are not available, the vehicle should be taken to a reputable service station which has the appropriate equipment.

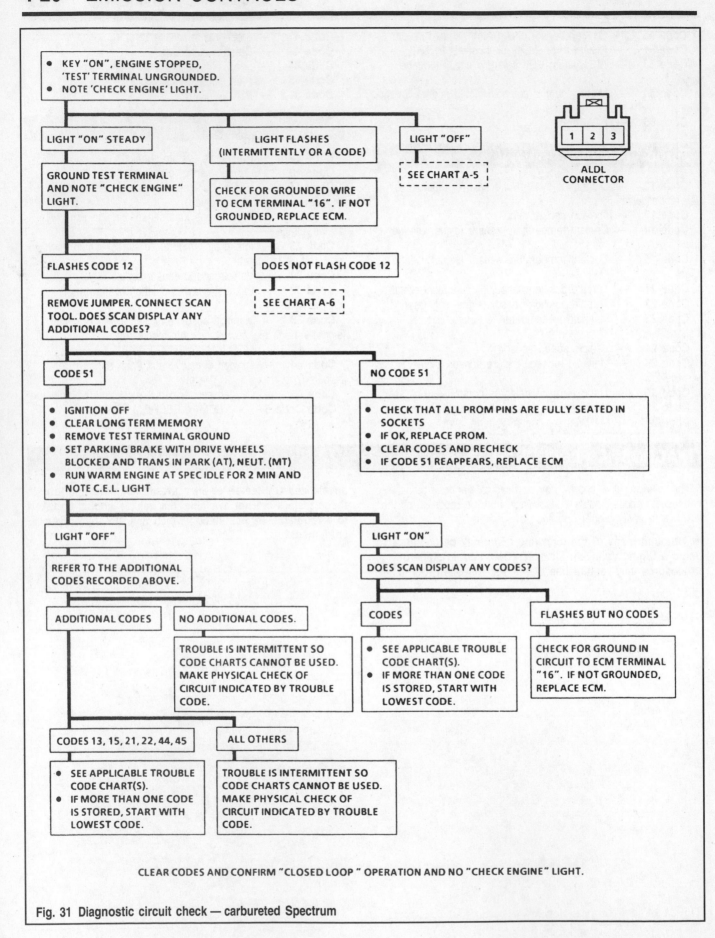

Fig. 31 Diagnostic circuit check — carbureted Spectrum

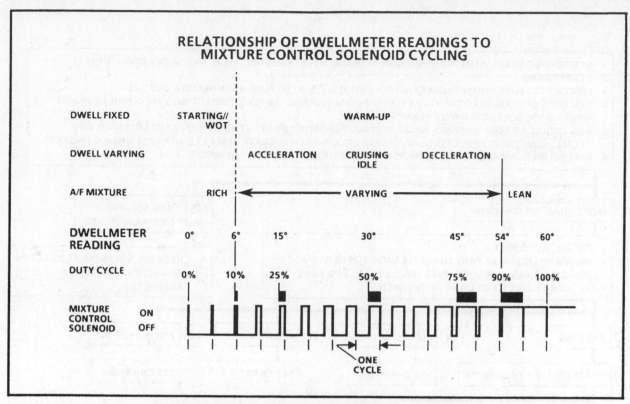

RELATIONSHIP OF DWELLMETER READINGS TO MIXTURE CONTROL SOLENOID CYCLING

SYSTEM PERFORMANCE CHECK
1.5L (VIN 7) "R" CARLINE (CARB)

Test Description: Numbers below refer to circled numbers on the diagnostic chart.

1. Checks for the ability of the carburetor main metering system to change the Air/Fuel mixture. Disconnecting the M/C solenoid makes the carburetor operate full-rich (0% Duty Cycle) and reconnecting it with the dwell lead grounded makes it operate full-lean (100% Duty Cycle). Normal response is for rpm to drop, as M/C solenoid is reconnected. Normal drop should be within a 300 to 1000 rpm range.

1A. If plugging the PCV, Purge, or Bowl Vent vacuum hose causes rpm to drop over 300 rpm, that hose leads to the source of the problem. If rpm increases as M/C solenoid is connected, it indicates the system is running extremely rich. This can sometimes be caused by incorrect valve timing.

2. Checks for proper control of idle circuit.

2A. Normal reading - operates in "Closed Loop" - dwell is between 10°-50°, but varying. Run engine for 1 minute at fast idle to make sure the oxygen sensor is warm.

2B. There is an "Open Loop" condition. It can be caused by:
1. An open oxygen sensor circuit or bad sensor.
2. An open in coolant sensor circuit.
3. An open CKT 413 from ECM terminal "20" to ground.

2C. This is a full-rich command to the carburetor and can be caused by:
1. Lean engine condition.
2. Grounded oxygen sensor CKT 412 to ECM terminal "3", or bad sensor.
3. Open CKT 413, from ECM terminal "14" to ground.
4. Open CKT 452 to ECM terminal "22".
5. Open in coolant sensor CKTs 410 or 452.

2D. This is a full lean command which can be caused by:
1. Rich engine condition caused by:
    a. M/C Solenoid wire connections reversed.
    b. Leaking Bowl Vent valve, excessive fuel in vapor canister, fuel in crankcase, faulty carburetor calibration or carburetor, or silicon contaminated oxygen sensor.

3. Checks for proper control of main metering system. Rpm must be at least 3000 to get into the main metering system operation.

Fig. 32 System performance test — carbureted Spectrum

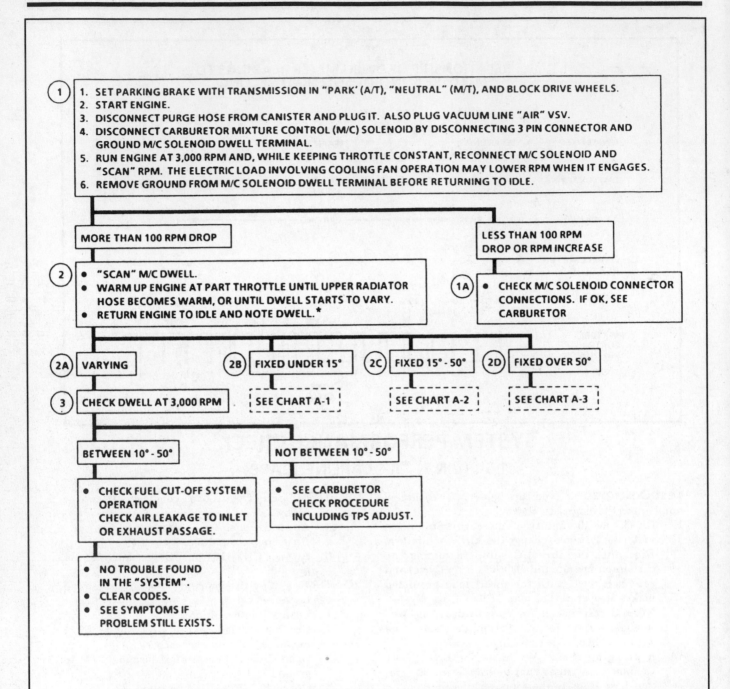

① 1. SET PARKING BRAKE WITH TRANSMISSION IN "PARK' (A/T), "NEUTRAL" (M/T), AND BLOCK DRIVE WHEELS.
2. START ENGINE.
3. DISCONNECT PURGE HOSE FROM CANISTER AND PLUG IT. ALSO PLUG VACUUM LINE "AIR" VSV.
4. DISCONNECT CARBURETOR MIXTURE CONTROL (M/C) SOLENOID BY DISCONNECTING 3 PIN CONNECTOR AND GROUND M/C SOLENOID DWELL TERMINAL.
5. RUN ENGINE AT 3,000 RPM AND, WHILE KEEPING THROTTLE CONSTANT, RECONNECT M/C SOLENOID AND "SCAN" RPM. THE ELECTRIC LOAD INVOLVING COOLING FAN OPERATION MAY LOWER RPM WHEN IT ENGAGES.
6. REMOVE GROUND FROM M/C SOLENOID DWELL TERMINAL BEFORE RETURNING TO IDLE.

MORE THAN 100 RPM DROP

LESS THAN 100 RPM DROP OR RPM INCREASE

② • "SCAN" M/C DWELL.
• WARM UP ENGINE AT PART THROTTLE UNTIL UPPER RADIATOR HOSE BECOMES WARM, OR UNTIL DWELL STARTS TO VARY.
• RETURN ENGINE TO IDLE AND NOTE DWELL.*

①A • CHECK M/C SOLENOID CONNECTOR CONNECTIONS. IF OK, SEE CARBURETOR

②A VARYING   ②B FIXED UNDER 15°   ②C FIXED 15° - 50°   ②D FIXED OVER 50°

③ CHECK DWELL AT 3,000 RPM   SEE CHART A-1   SEE CHART A-2   SEE CHART A-3

BETWEEN 10° - 50°   NOT BETWEEN 10° - 50°

• CHECK FUEL CUT-OFF SYSTEM OPERATION
CHECK AIR LEAKAGE TO INLET OR EXHAUST PASSAGE.

• SEE CARBURETOR CHECK PROCEDURE INCLUDING TPS ADJUST.

• NO TROUBLE FOUND IN THE "SYSTEM".
• CLEAR CODES.
• SEE SYMPTOMS IF PROBLEM STILL EXISTS.

* OXYGEN SENSORS MAY COOL OFF AT IDLE AND THE DWELL MAY CHANGE FROM VARYING TO FIXED. IF THIS HAPPENS, RUNNING THE ENGINE AT FAST IDLE WILL WARM IT UP AGAIN.

CLEAR CODES AND CONFIRM "CLOSED LOOP " OPERATION AND NO "CHECK ENGINE" LIGHT.

Fig. 33 System performance test — carbureted Spectrum

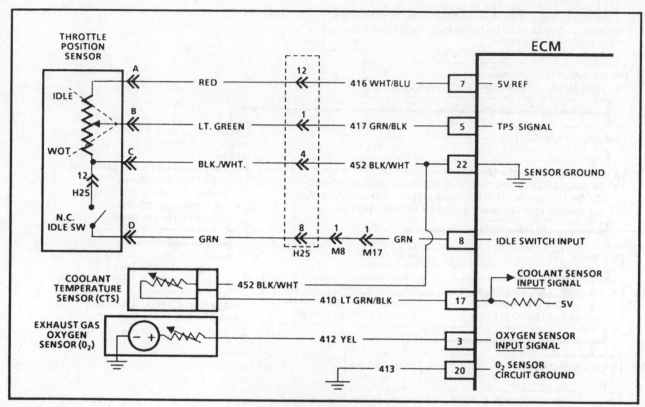

CHART A-1

DWELL FIXED UNDER 15°
(LEAN EXHAUST INDICATED)

Test Description: Numbers below refer to circled numbers on the diagnostic chart.

1. Determines if the problem is CCC related or engine related. Dwell should start increasing as soon as engine is choked and go higher as it is choked more, until it goes over 50°. With severe choking, the dwell could move up the scale momentarily even if it is not engine related, but it will move right back to a low dwell. If dwell responds the problem is a lean engine.

2. Checks for ECM response to input of O_2 sensor circuit. The voltmeter is used to put a voltage on the oxygen sensor circuit to simulate a rich condition. Dwell should increase (a lean command) if ECM and harness are good.

3. Checks for normal coolant sensor circuit condition. Voltage on a normalized, hot engine should be under 2.5V.

4. This step checks for an open CKT 413 to ECM terminal "22" and grounded O_2 sensor CKT 412. Terminal "5" voltage should be under 1.0 volt, at idle. A high voltage could be caused by an open CKT 452 to terminal "22".

5. Checks for cause of lean condition that resulted in full rich command.

Fig. 34 Chart A-1: dwell fixed under 15 degrees — carbureted Spectrum

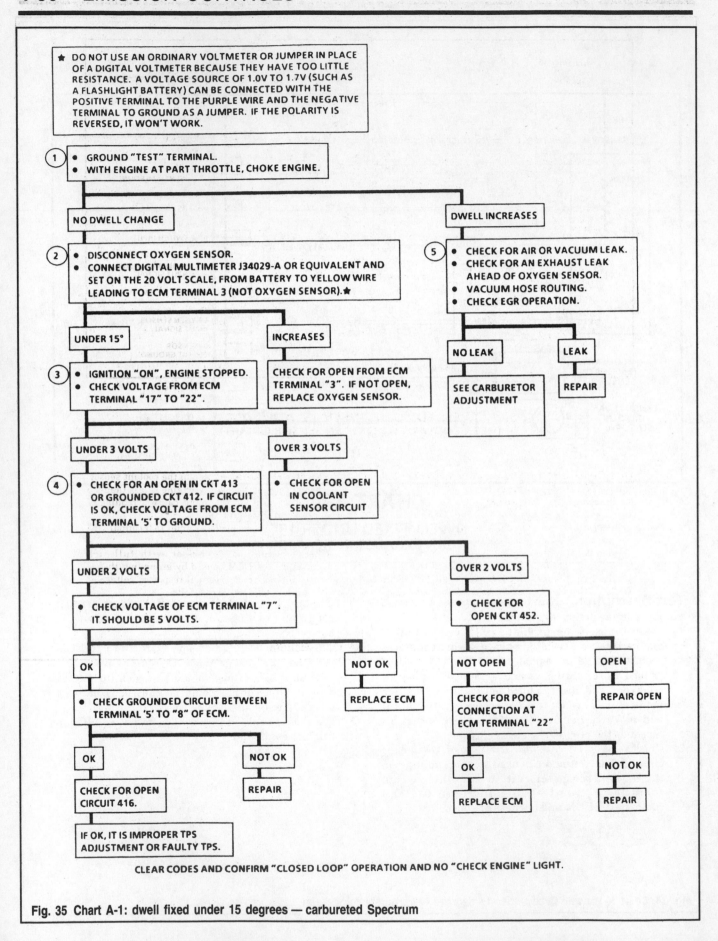

★ DO NOT USE AN ORDINARY VOLTMETER OR JUMPER IN PLACE OF A DIGITAL VOLTMETER BECAUSE THEY HAVE TOO LITTLE RESISTANCE. A VOLTAGE SOURCE OF 1.0V TO 1.7V (SUCH AS A FLASHLIGHT BATTERY) CAN BE CONNECTED WITH THE POSITIVE TERMINAL TO THE PURPLE WIRE AND THE NEGATIVE TERMINAL TO GROUND AS A JUMPER. IF THE POLARITY IS REVERSED, IT WON'T WORK.

1
- GROUND "TEST" TERMINAL.
- WITH ENGINE AT PART THROTTLE, CHOKE ENGINE.

NO DWELL CHANGE

DWELL INCREASES

2
- DISCONNECT OXYGEN SENSOR.
- CONNECT DIGITAL MULTIMETER J34029-A OR EQUIVALENT AND SET ON THE 20 VOLT SCALE, FROM BATTERY TO YELLOW WIRE LEADING TO ECM TERMINAL 3 (NOT OXYGEN SENSOR).★

5
- CHECK FOR AIR OR VACUUM LEAK.
- CHECK FOR AN EXHAUST LEAK AHEAD OF OXYGEN SENSOR.
- VACUUM HOSE ROUTING.
- CHECK EGR OPERATION.

UNDER 15°

INCREASES

NO LEAK

LEAK

3
- IGNITION "ON", ENGINE STOPPED.
- CHECK VOLTAGE FROM ECM TERMINAL "17" TO "22".

CHECK FOR OPEN FROM ECM TERMINAL "3". IF NOT OPEN, REPLACE OXYGEN SENSOR.

SEE CARBURETOR ADJUSTMENT

REPAIR

UNDER 3 VOLTS

OVER 3 VOLTS

4
- CHECK FOR AN OPEN IN CKT 413 OR GROUNDED CKT 412. IF CIRCUIT IS OK, CHECK VOLTAGE FROM ECM TERMINAL '5' TO GROUND.

- CHECK FOR OPEN IN COOLANT SENSOR CIRCUIT

UNDER 2 VOLTS

OVER 2 VOLTS

- CHECK VOLTAGE OF ECM TERMINAL "7". IT SHOULD BE 5 VOLTS.

- CHECK FOR OPEN CKT 452.

OK

NOT OK

NOT OPEN

OPEN

REPLACE ECM

- CHECK GROUNDED CIRCUIT BETWEEN TERMINAL '5' TO "8" OF ECM.

CHECK FOR POOR CONNECTION AT ECM TERMINAL "22"

REPAIR OPEN

OK

NOT OK

OK

NOT OK

CHECK FOR OPEN CIRCUIT 416.

REPAIR

REPLACE ECM

REPAIR

IF OK, IT IS IMPROPER TPS ADJUSTMENT OR FAULTY TPS.

CLEAR CODES AND CONFIRM "CLOSED LOOP" OPERATION AND NO "CHECK ENGINE" LIGHT.

Fig. 35 Chart A-1: dwell fixed under 15 degrees — carbureted Spectrum

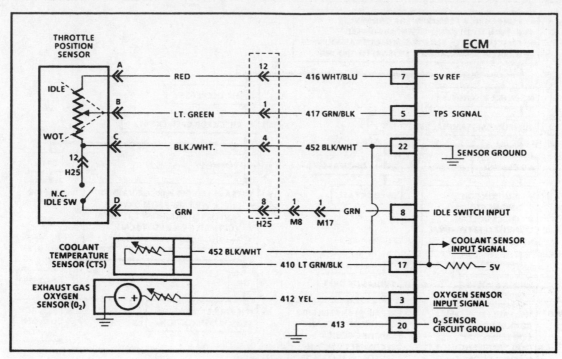

CHART A-2

DWELL FIXED BETWEEN 15° AND 50°
(OPEN COOLANT OR OXYGEN SENSOR CIRCUIT)

Test Description: Numbers below refer to circled numbers on the diagnostic chart.

1. Running engine at part throttle, for one minute, warms up the oxygen sensor. Grounding O_2 sensor input checks ECM response to a "lean" signal. Normal response; dwell decreases to full rich command.

2. This step grounds O_2 sensor circuit at the ECM to check for an open in the wiring to ECM Terminal "3". Normal response is to "lean" the signal. Dwell decreases (rich command).

3. This step checks for voltage to the coolant sensor. Normal reading on a warm engine is less than 2.5 volts. An open circuit would cause a reading of approximately 5 volts.

4. On some ECMs, an open in circuit to terminal "20" can cause "Open Loop".

5. Checks output of O_2 sensor with full rich command from ECM caused by grounding the O_2 sensor input circuit. Normal response; voltage at O_2 sensor should be over .8 volts.

Fig. 36 Chart A-2: dwell fixed between 15-50 degrees — carbureted Spectrum

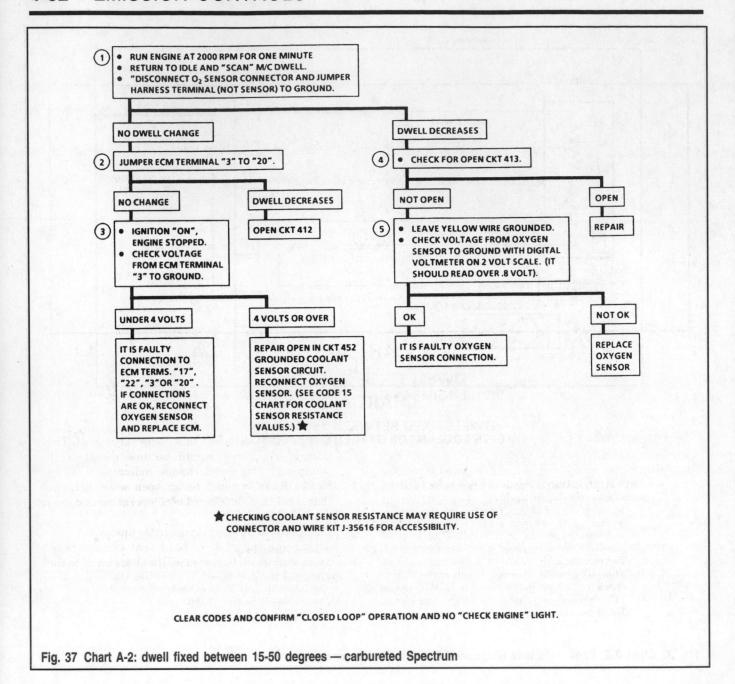

① • RUN ENGINE AT 2000 RPM FOR ONE MINUTE
  • RETURN TO IDLE AND "SCAN" M/C DWELL.
  • "DISCONNECT O₂ SENSOR CONNECTOR AND JUMPER HARNESS TERMINAL (NOT SENSOR) TO GROUND.

NO DWELL CHANGE

② JUMPER ECM TERMINAL "3" TO "20".

DWELL DECREASES

④ • CHECK FOR OPEN CKT 413.

NO CHANGE

③ • IGNITION "ON", ENGINE STOPPED.
  • CHECK VOLTAGE FROM ECM TERMINAL "3" TO GROUND.

DWELL DECREASES

OPEN CKT 412

NOT OPEN

⑤ • LEAVE YELLOW WIRE GROUNDED.
  • CHECK VOLTAGE FROM OXYGEN SENSOR TO GROUND WITH DIGITAL VOLTMETER ON 2 VOLT SCALE. (IT SHOULD READ OVER .8 VOLT).

OPEN

REPAIR

UNDER 4 VOLTS

IT IS FAULTY CONNECTION TO ECM TERMS. "17", "22", "3" OR "20". IF CONNECTIONS ARE OK, RECONNECT OXYGEN SENSOR AND REPLACE ECM.

4 VOLTS OR OVER

REPAIR OPEN IN CKT 452 GROUNDED COOLANT SENSOR CIRCUIT. RECONNECT OXYGEN SENSOR. (SEE CODE 15 CHART FOR COOLANT SENSOR RESISTANCE VALUES.) ★

OK

IT IS FAULTY OXYGEN SENSOR CONNECTION.

NOT OK

REPLACE OXYGEN SENSOR

★ CHECKING COOLANT SENSOR RESISTANCE MAY REQUIRE USE OF CONNECTOR AND WIRE KIT J-35616 FOR ACCESSIBILITY.

CLEAR CODES AND CONFIRM "CLOSED LOOP" OPERATION AND NO "CHECK ENGINE" LIGHT.

Fig. 37 Chart A-2: dwell fixed between 15-50 degrees — carbureted Spectrum

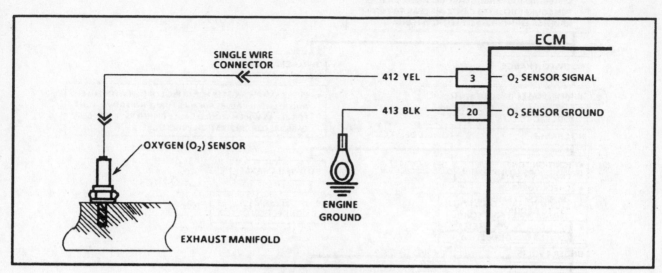

CHART A-3

DWELL FIXED OVER 50°
(RICH ENGINE CONDITION INDICATION)

Test Description: Numbers below refer to circled numbers on the diagnostic chart.

1. Determines whether problem is related to engine or electronics. The normal response would be dwell decreases (rich command), indicating that electronics (O_2 sensor, harness, and ECM) are OK, and fault is a rich engine condition. This may require a large air leak, if engine is very rich. When the mixture is lean enough, the engine will start to run rough.

2. Checks ECM response to a "lean" O_2 signal. The normal response would be low dwell (rich command). No dwell change indicates a faulty ECM. Fault couldn't be an open wire, because that would cause "Open Loop" operation and may set Code 13.

3. Checks for excessive voltage in O_2 line.

4. If plugging the PCV, or bowl vent vacuum hose, causes the dwell to decrease, that hose leads to the source of the problem.

Fig. 38 Chart A-3: dwell fixed over 50 degrees — carbureted Spectrum

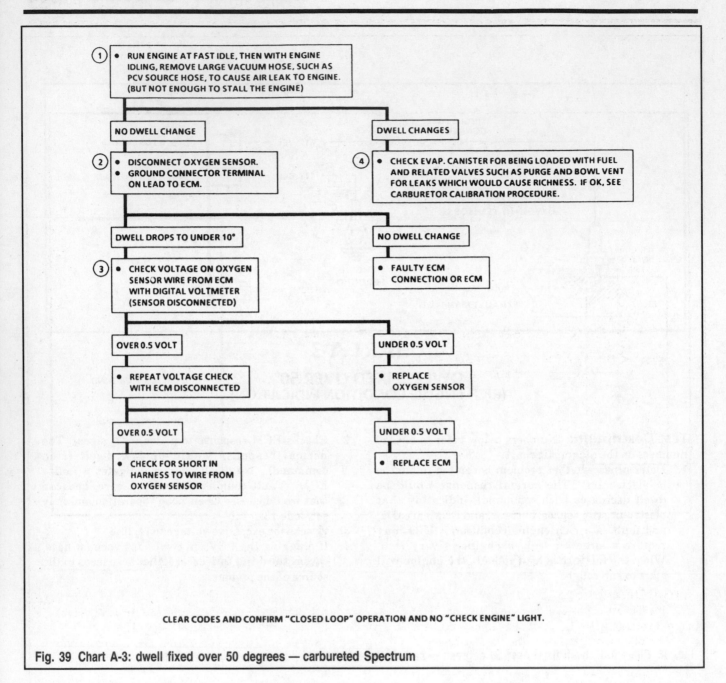

1. • RUN ENGINE AT FAST IDLE, THEN WITH ENGINE IDLING, REMOVE LARGE VACUUM HOSE, SUCH AS PCV SOURCE HOSE, TO CAUSE AIR LEAK TO ENGINE. (BUT NOT ENOUGH TO STALL THE ENGINE)

NO DWELL CHANGE

2. • DISCONNECT OXYGEN SENSOR.
   • GROUND CONNECTOR TERMINAL ON LEAD TO ECM.

DWELL DROPS TO UNDER 10°

3. • CHECK VOLTAGE ON OXYGEN SENSOR WIRE FROM ECM WITH DIGITAL VOLTMETER (SENSOR DISCONNECTED)

OVER 0.5 VOLT

• REPEAT VOLTAGE CHECK WITH ECM DISCONNECTED

OVER 0.5 VOLT

• CHECK FOR SHORT IN HARNESS TO WIRE FROM OXYGEN SENSOR

DWELL CHANGES

4. • CHECK EVAP. CANISTER FOR BEING LOADED WITH FUEL AND RELATED VALVES SUCH AS PURGE AND BOWL VENT FOR LEAKS WHICH WOULD CAUSE RICHNESS. IF OK, SEE CARBURETOR CALIBRATION PROCEDURE.

NO DWELL CHANGE

• FAULTY ECM CONNECTION OR ECM

UNDER 0.5 VOLT

• REPLACE OXYGEN SENSOR

UNDER 0.5 VOLT

• REPLACE ECM

CLEAR CODES AND CONFIRM "CLOSED LOOP" OPERATION AND NO "CHECK ENGINE" LIGHT.

Fig. 39 Chart A-3: dwell fixed over 50 degrees — carbureted Spectrum

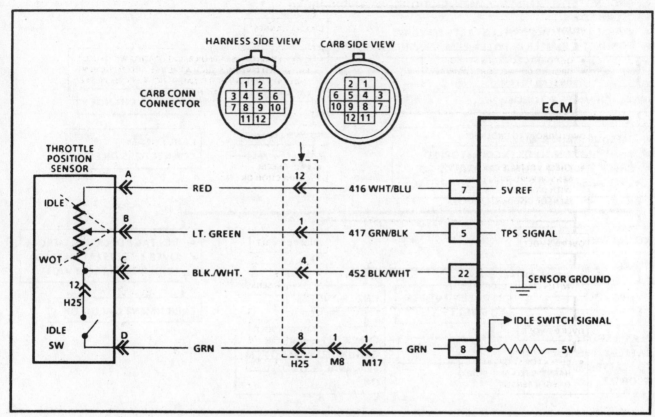

CHART A-4

TPS WIDE-OPEN-THROTTLE ENRICHMENT CIRCUIT CHECK

Circuit Description:

The Throttle Position Sensor (TPS) provides a voltage signal that changes relative to the throttle valve. Signal voltage will vary from less than .80 volts at idle to about 4.5 volts at wide open throttle (WOT).

The idle switch provides the ECM with information used to decide closed loop operation and indicates the off-idle condition to the ECM. This switch is normally closed at idle and opens above 1800 RPM, which is then the off-idle condition.

The TPS signal is one of the most important inputs used by the ECM for fuel control and for many of the ECM controlled outputs.

Diagnostic Aids:

A "Scan" tool displays throttle position in volts. Closed throttle voltage should be less than .80 volts. TPS voltage should increase at a steady rate as throttle is moved to WOT.

Fig. 40 Chart A-4: tps wide-open throttle enrichment circuit check — carbureted Spectrum

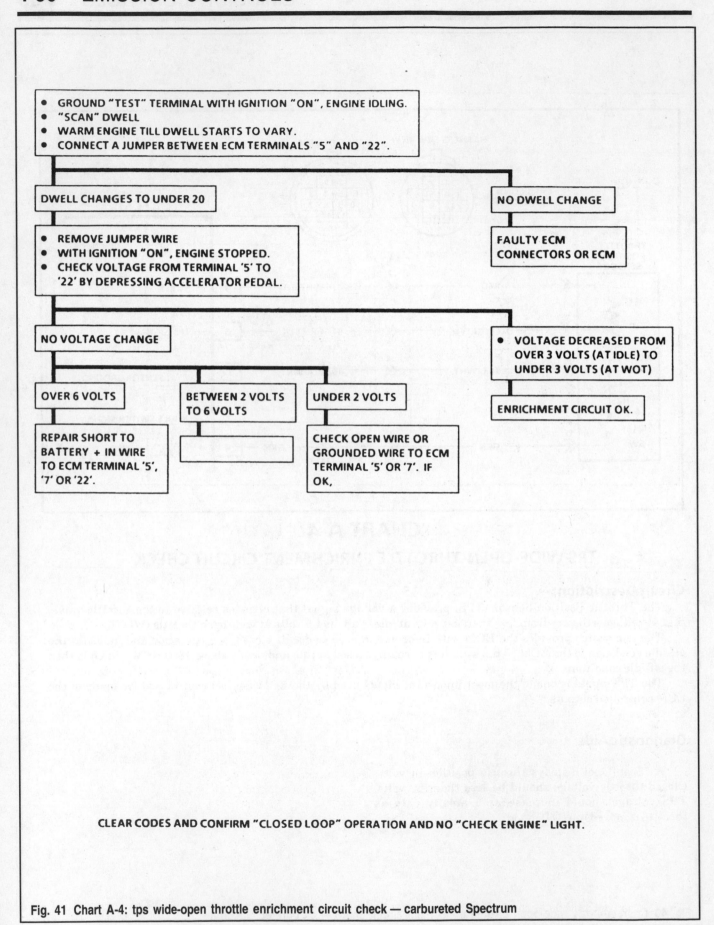

- GROUND "TEST" TERMINAL WITH IGNITION "ON", ENGINE IDLING.
- "SCAN" DWELL
- WARM ENGINE TILL DWELL STARTS TO VARY.
- CONNECT A JUMPER BETWEEN ECM TERMINALS "5" AND "22".

DWELL CHANGES TO UNDER 20

NO DWELL CHANGE

- REMOVE JUMPER WIRE
- WITH IGNITION "ON", ENGINE STOPPED.
- CHECK VOLTAGE FROM TERMINAL '5' TO '22' BY DEPRESSING ACCELERATOR PEDAL.

FAULTY ECM CONNECTORS OR ECM

NO VOLTAGE CHANGE

- VOLTAGE DECREASED FROM OVER 3 VOLTS (AT IDLE) TO UNDER 3 VOLTS (AT WOT)

OVER 6 VOLTS

BETWEEN 2 VOLTS TO 6 VOLTS

UNDER 2 VOLTS

ENRICHMENT CIRCUIT OK.

REPAIR SHORT TO BATTERY + IN WIRE TO ECM TERMINAL '5', '7' OR '22'.

CHECK OPEN WIRE OR GROUNDED WIRE TO ECM TERMINAL '5' OR '7'. IF OK,

CLEAR CODES AND CONFIRM "CLOSED LOOP" OPERATION AND NO "CHECK ENGINE" LIGHT.

Fig. 41 Chart A-4: tps wide-open throttle enrichment circuit check — carbureted Spectrum

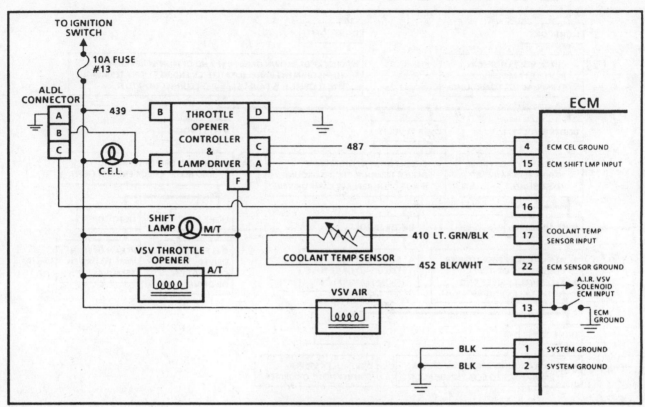

CHART A-5
"CHECK ENGINE" LIGHT INOPERATIVE

Circuit Description:

When the engine is started, the ECM grounds terminal "G" to turn out the "Check Engine" light. It alternately grounds and opens it to flash a code.

Test Description: Numbers below refer to circled numbers on the diagnostic chart.

1. This checks for open gage fuse, or open in "Check Engine" light circuit, including IP connector, printed circuit, and "Check Engine" lamp. Normal response is lamp "ON".
2. This checks for grounded CKT 487 from terminal "C" of lamp driver, to ECM terminal "4", an open CKT 439 to terminal "B" of lamp driver, a bad ground or faulty lamp driver. A normal reading is about 9 to 11 volts, because of the drop through the upper resistor in the lamp driver. Over 11 volts indicates there is no drop in the lamp driver. This indicates a bad ground, or faulty lamp driver.

3. This step checks for an open in the wire to terminal "B". Normal voltage is approximately battery voltage.
3A. This checks for an open CKT 439 to terminal "E" from the "Check Engine" lamp. With terminal "E" grounded, the lamp should normally light. Lamp "OFF" indicates an open, and lamp "ON" indicates faulty lamp driver connection or lamp driver.
4. This checks for a grounded CKT 487 from driver terminal "C" to ECM terminal "4". Normal response is light "ON".

Fig. 42 Chart A-5: check engine light inoperative — carbureted Spectrum

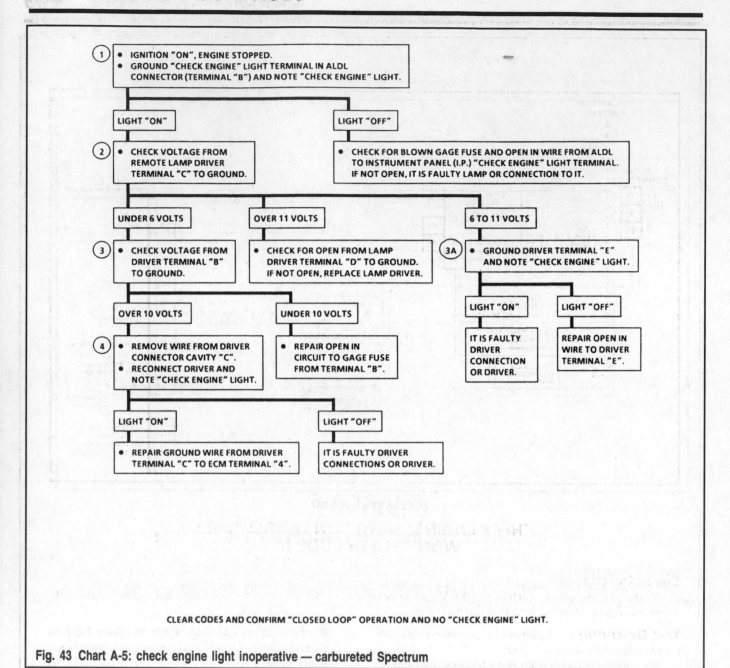

① • IGNITION "ON", ENGINE STOPPED.
• GROUND "CHECK ENGINE" LIGHT TERMINAL IN ALDL CONNECTOR (TERMINAL "B") AND NOTE "CHECK ENGINE" LIGHT.

LIGHT "ON" — LIGHT "OFF"

② • CHECK VOLTAGE FROM REMOTE LAMP DRIVER TERMINAL "C" TO GROUND.

• CHECK FOR BLOWN GAGE FUSE AND OPEN IN WIRE FROM ALDL TO INSTRUMENT PANEL (I.P.) "CHECK ENGINE" LIGHT TERMINAL. IF NOT OPEN, IT IS FAULTY LAMP OR CONNECTION TO IT.

UNDER 6 VOLTS — OVER 11 VOLTS — 6 TO 11 VOLTS

③ • CHECK VOLTAGE FROM DRIVER TERMINAL "B" TO GROUND.

• CHECK FOR OPEN FROM LAMP DRIVER TERMINAL "D" TO GROUND. IF NOT OPEN, REPLACE LAMP DRIVER.

③A • GROUND DRIVER TERMINAL "E" AND NOTE "CHECK ENGINE" LIGHT.

OVER 10 VOLTS — UNDER 10 VOLTS

LIGHT "ON" — LIGHT "OFF"

IT IS FAULTY DRIVER CONNECTION OR DRIVER.

REPAIR OPEN IN WIRE TO DRIVER TERMINAL "E".

④ • REMOVE WIRE FROM DRIVER CONNECTOR CAVITY "C".
• RECONNECT DRIVER AND NOTE "CHECK ENGINE" LIGHT.

• REPAIR OPEN IN CIRCUIT TO GAGE FUSE FROM TERMINAL "B".

LIGHT "ON" — LIGHT "OFF"

• REPAIR GROUND WIRE FROM DRIVER TERMINAL "C" TO ECM TERMINAL "4".

IT IS FAULTY DRIVER CONNECTIONS OR DRIVER.

CLEAR CODES AND CONFIRM "CLOSED LOOP" OPERATION AND NO "CHECK ENGINE" LIGHT.

Fig. 43 Chart A-5: check engine light inoperative — carbureted Spectrum

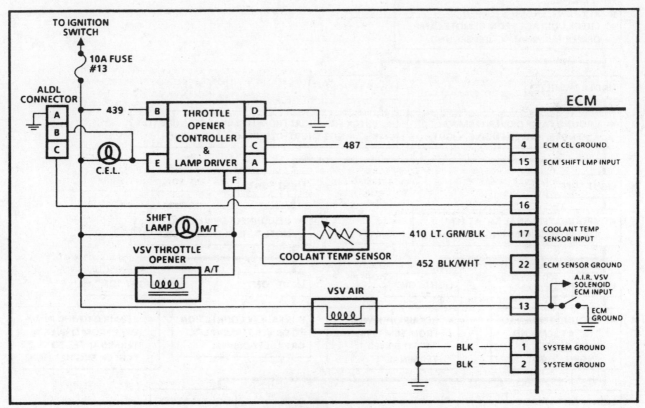

CHART A-6

"CHECK ENGINE" LIGHT "ON" AT ALL TIMES
WON'T FLASH CODE 12

Circuit Description:

When the engine is started, the ECM grounds terminal "G" to turn out the "Check Engine" light. It alternately grounds and opens it to flash a code.

Test Description: Numbers below refer to circled numbers on the diagnostic chart.

1. This step checks for short to battery voltage in wire to terminal "C" or faulty lamp driver. Normal voltage reading is 9-11 volts.
2. This step checks to see if problem is related to the ECM or the lamp driver. Normally, grounding terminal "C" should turn lamp "OFF". If it does, the problem is related to the ECM and its wiring. If not, it is related to the lamp driver and its wiring.
3. Grounding terminal "4" at ECM and finding light "ON" indicates an open in CKT 487 to terminal "C" of lamp driver. Normally, grounding Terminal "4" should turn lamp "OFF".

4. This step checks for open CKT 451 from ECM to test terminal in ALDL connector. The lamp should flash Code 12, when terminal "16" is grounded.
5. Checks for proper voltage supply to ECM. Both should read over 9 volts.
6. Checks for a bad ground to ECM - terminals "1" and "2" are connected together in the ECM.
7. This step distinguishes between a faulty ECM and PROM. Normal response is for Code 51 to flash, even though the PROM is not installed in the ECM. If it doesn't, it means that the ECM is faulty.

Fig. 44 Chart A-6: check engine light on at all times — carbureted Spectrum

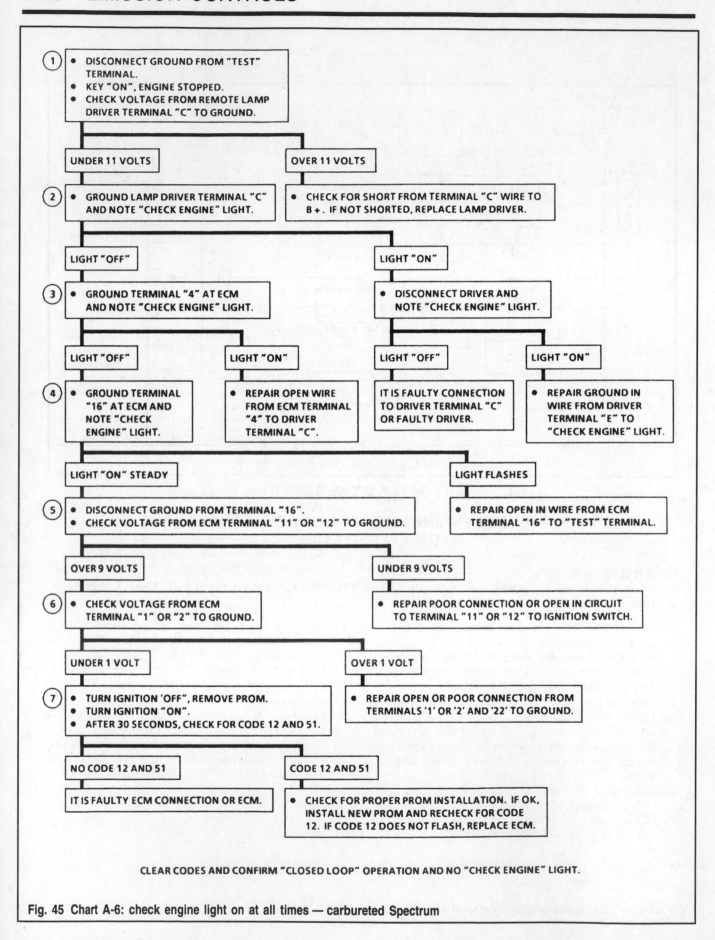

Fig. 45 Chart A-6: check engine light on at all times — carbureted Spectrum

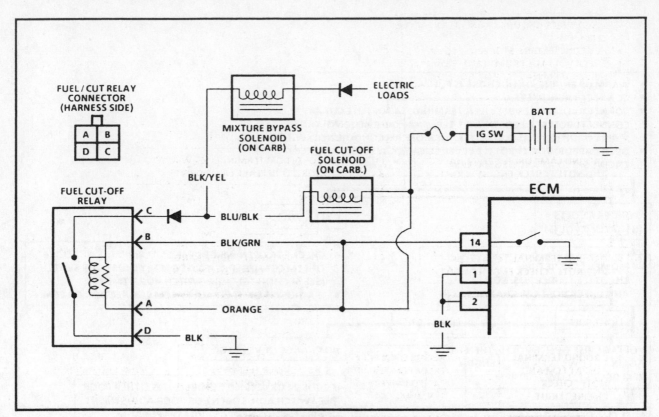

CHART A-7

FUEL CUT-OFF SYSTEM OPERATIONAL CHECK
(INCLUDING IDLE-SWITCH)

Circuit Description:

The fuel cut relay is supplied B+ by fuse 13, and grounded by the ECM driver when in a deceleration mode. The ECM senses a deceleration condition from the TPS and an engine RPM signal above 2300 RPM. With the relay open fuel flow is decreased. Code 42 sets when the voltage on the driver circuit remains high when commanded "low".

Fig. 46 Chart A-7: fuel cut-off system operational check — carbureted Spectrum

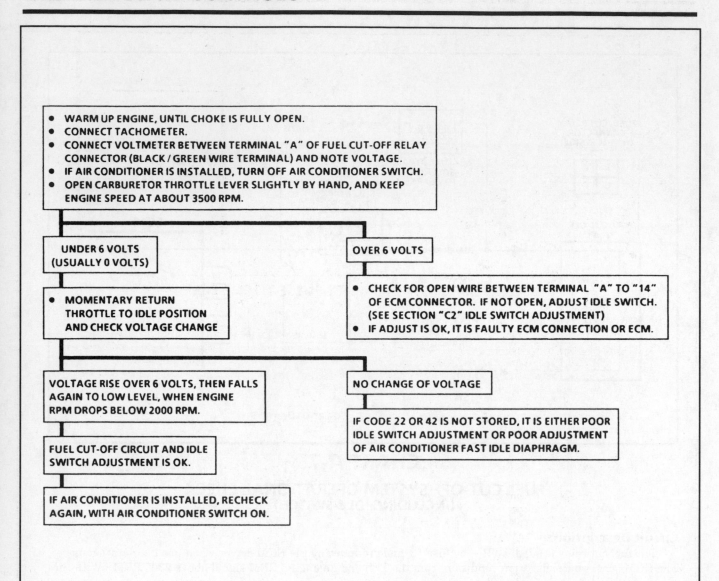

- WARM UP ENGINE, UNTIL CHOKE IS FULLY OPEN.
- CONNECT TACHOMETER.
- CONNECT VOLTMETER BETWEEN TERMINAL "A" OF FUEL CUT-OFF RELAY CONNECTOR (BLACK / GREEN WIRE TERMINAL) AND NOTE VOLTAGE.
- IF AIR CONDITIONER IS INSTALLED, TURN OFF AIR CONDITIONER SWITCH.
- OPEN CARBURETOR THROTTLE LEVER SLIGHTLY BY HAND, AND KEEP ENGINE SPEED AT ABOUT 3500 RPM.

UNDER 6 VOLTS (USUALLY 0 VOLTS)

OVER 6 VOLTS

- MOMENTARY RETURN THROTTLE TO IDLE POSITION AND CHECK VOLTAGE CHANGE

- CHECK FOR OPEN WIRE BETWEEN TERMINAL "A" TO "14" OF ECM CONNECTOR. IF NOT OPEN, ADJUST IDLE SWITCH. (SEE SECTION "C2" IDLE SWITCH ADJUSTMENT)
- IF ADJUST IS OK, IT IS FAULTY ECM CONNECTION OR ECM.

VOLTAGE RISE OVER 6 VOLTS, THEN FALLS AGAIN TO LOW LEVEL, WHEN ENGINE RPM DROPS BELOW 2000 RPM.

NO CHANGE OF VOLTAGE

FUEL CUT-OFF CIRCUIT AND IDLE SWITCH ADJUSTMENT IS OK.

IF CODE 22 OR 42 IS NOT STORED, IT IS EITHER POOR IDLE SWITCH ADJUSTMENT OR POOR ADJUSTMENT OF AIR CONDITIONER FAST IDLE DIAPHRAGM.

IF AIR CONDITIONER IS INSTALLED, RECHECK AGAIN, WITH AIR CONDITIONER SWITCH ON.

CLEAR CODES AND CONFIRM "CLOSED LOOP" OPERATION AND NO "CHECK ENGINE" LIGHT.

Fig. 47 Chart A-7: fuel cut-off system operational check — carbureted Spectrum

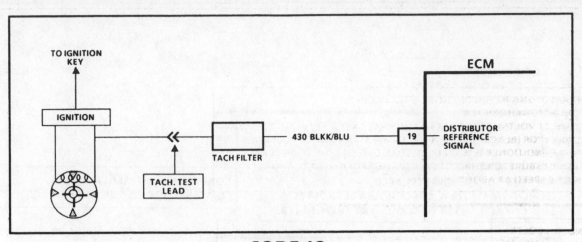

CODE 12
NO DISTRIBUTOR REFERENCE PULSE TO THE ECM

Circuit Description:

The ECM recieves a signal from the ignition system in the form of a pulse delivered from the tach. filter. This pulse is present when the engine is not running and in the absence of any other codes indicates a normal condition. This code will not store in memory and will only flash when when the fault is actually happening.

The actual fault that could cause Code 12 to flash would be an open or ground in the circuit between the ECM and the ignition coil.

Test Description: Numbers below refer to circled numbers on the diagnostic chart.
1. Code 12 will flash if:
   - Ignition is on.
   - ALDL is grounded.
   - Sysystem is functioning normally.
   Under these conditions a Code 12 is normal and a fault should be suspected if it does not flash. A scan tool should display RPM if the tach. signal is being supplied to the ECM.
2. This determines if signal voltage is present at ECM.
3. The rest of the voltage checks determine if there is a short or open in the circuits between the ignition and the tach. filter.

Diagnostic Aids:

Before replacing ECM be sure to check for bent pins or loose connections at the ECM connector.

If Code 12 or the Symptoms are Intermittent refer to Section "B".

Fig. 48 Code 12: circuit check/no distributor reference pulse — carbureted Spectrum

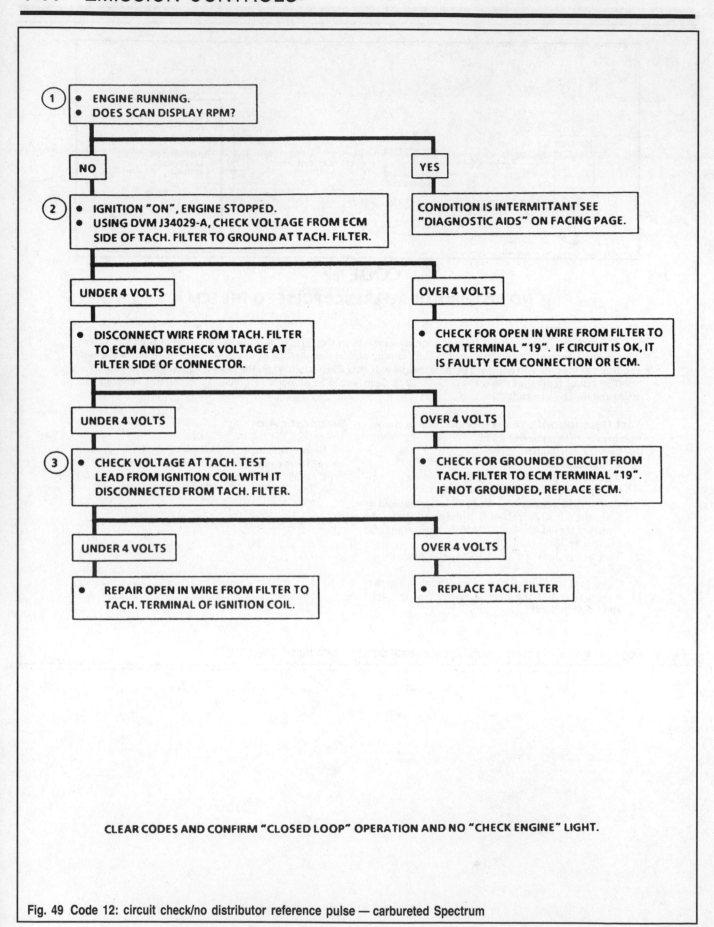

① • ENGINE RUNNING.
   • DOES SCAN DISPLAY RPM?

NO

YES

② • IGNITION "ON", ENGINE STOPPED.
   • USING DVM J34029-A, CHECK VOLTAGE FROM ECM SIDE OF TACH. FILTER TO GROUND AT TACH. FILTER.

CONDITION IS INTERMITTANT SEE "DIAGNOSTIC AIDS" ON FACING PAGE.

UNDER 4 VOLTS

OVER 4 VOLTS

• DISCONNECT WIRE FROM TACH. FILTER TO ECM AND RECHECK VOLTAGE AT FILTER SIDE OF CONNECTOR.

• CHECK FOR OPEN IN WIRE FROM FILTER TO ECM TERMINAL "19". IF CIRCUIT IS OK, IT IS FAULTY ECM CONNECTION OR ECM.

UNDER 4 VOLTS

OVER 4 VOLTS

③ • CHECK VOLTAGE AT TACH. TEST LEAD FROM IGNITION COIL WITH IT DISCONNECTED FROM TACH. FILTER.

• CHECK FOR GROUNDED CIRCUIT FROM TACH. FILTER TO ECM TERMINAL "19". IF NOT GROUNDED, REPLACE ECM.

UNDER 4 VOLTS

OVER 4 VOLTS

• REPAIR OPEN IN WIRE FROM FILTER TO TACH. TERMINAL OF IGNITION COIL.

• REPLACE TACH. FILTER

CLEAR CODES AND CONFIRM "CLOSED LOOP" OPERATION AND NO "CHECK ENGINE" LIGHT.

Fig. 49 Code 12: circuit check/no distributor reference pulse — carbureted Spectrum

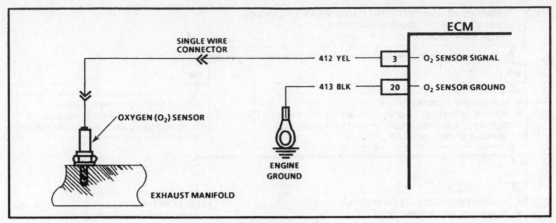

CODE 13
OXYGEN SENSOR CIRCUIT
(OPEN CIRCUIT)

Circuit Description:

The ECM supplies a voltage of about of .45 volt between terminals "3" and "20". (If measured with 10 megohm digital voltmeter, this may read as low as .32 volts).

The O_2 sensor varies the voltage within a range of about 1 volt, if the exhaust is rich, down through about .10 volt, if exhaust is lean.

The sensor is like an open circuit and produces no voltage, when it is below 360° C (600°F). An open sensor circuit, or cold sensor, causes "Open Loop" operation.

Test Description: Numbers below refer to circled numbers on the diagnostic chart.

Code 13 WILL SET:

- Engine at normal operating temperature.
- At least 5 minutes engine run time after start at part throttle.
- O_2 signal voltage steady between .35 and .55 volts.
- Throttle angle is at off-idle condition.
- All conditions must be met for about 60 seconds.

If the conditions for a Code 13 exist, the system will not go "Closed Loop".

1. This test determines if the O_2 sensor is the problem, or, if the ECM and wiring are at fault.

Diagnostic Aids:

Normal "Scan" voltage varies between 100 mv to 999 mv (.1 and 1.0 volt).

Verify a clean, tight ground connection for CKT 413. Open CKT(s), 412 or 413 will result in a Code 13.

If Code 13 is intermittent, refer to Section "B".

Fig. 50 Code 13: oxygen sensor circuit — carbureted Spectrum

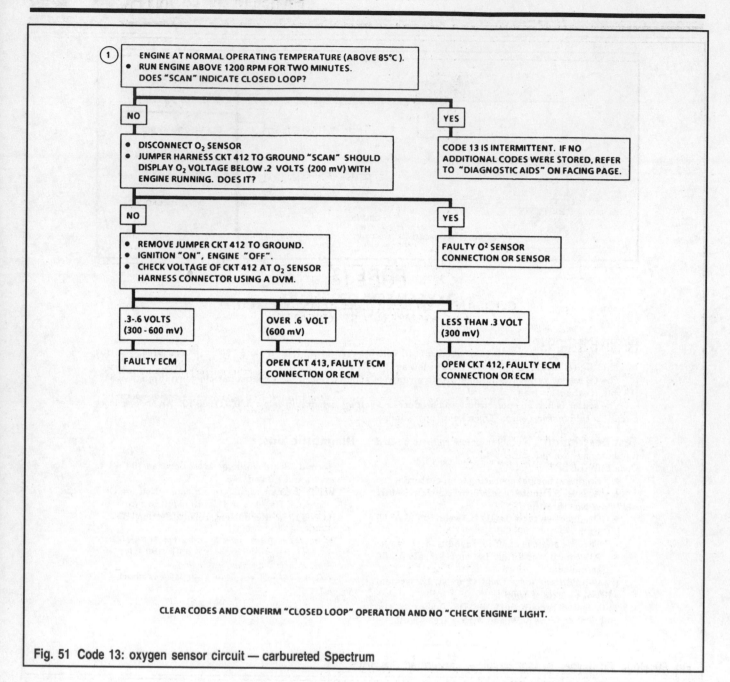

Fig. 51 Code 13: oxygen sensor circuit — carbureted Spectrum

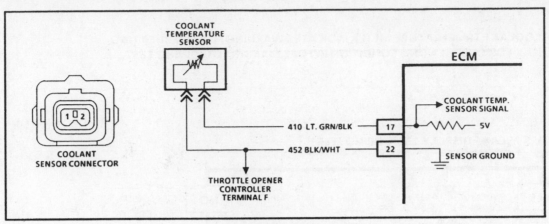

CODE 14

COOLANT TEMPERATURE SENSOR CIRCUIT
(HIGH TEMPERATURE INDICATED)

Circuit Description:

The Coolant Temperature Sensor uses a thermistor to control the signal voltage at the ECM. The ECM applies a voltage on CKT 410 to the sensor. When the engine is cold, the sensor (thermistor) resistance is high, therefore, the ECM will see high signal voltage.

As the engine warms, the sensor resistance becomes less, and the voltage drops. At normal engine operating temperature, the voltage will measure about 2.5 to 3.0 volts at the ECM terminal "17".

Coolant temperature is one of the inputs used by the ECM to control:

- Open Loop timing
- Fuel delivery (M/C solenoid operation)
- EFE (Early Fuel Evaporation)

Test Description: Numbers below refer to circled numbers on the diagnostic chart.

1. Checks to see if code was set as result of hard failure or intermittent condition.
   Code 14 will set if:
   - Signal Voltage indicates a coolant temperature above 185°C (365°F) for 2 minutes.
2. This test simulates conditions for a Code 15. If the ECM recognizes the open circuit (high voltage), and displays a low temperature, the ECM and wiring are OK.

Diagnostic Aids:

A "Scan" tool reads engine temperature in degrees centigrade and Farenheit.

After the engine is started, the temperature should rise steadily to about 194°F (90°C), then stabilize, when the thermostat opens.

A Code 14 will result if CKT 410 is shorted to ground.

Fig. 52 Code 14: coolant temperature sensor circuit — carbureted Spectrum

IF COOLANT TEMPERATURE METER INDICATES WARNING FOR OVERHEATING,
CHECK FOR OVERHEATING CONDITION BEFORE MAKING FOLLOWING TEST.

(1) | DOES "SCAN" DISPLAY 130°C OR HOTTER?

YES

NO

(2) • DISCONNECT SENSOR. "SCAN" SHOULD DISPLAY TEMP. BELOW -30°C. DOES IT?

CODE 14 IS INTERMITTENT. IF NO ADDITIONAL CODES WERE STORED, REFER TO "DIAGNOSTIC AIDS" ON FACING PAGE.

YES

NO

FAULTY SENSOR

CKT 410 SHORTED TO GROUND, SHORTED TO SENSOR GROUND CKT, OR FAULTY ECM.

CLEAR CODES AND CONFIRM "CLOSED LOOP" OPERATION AND NO "CHECK ENGINE" LIGHT.

Fig. 53 Code 14: coolant temperature sensor circuit — carbureted Spectrum

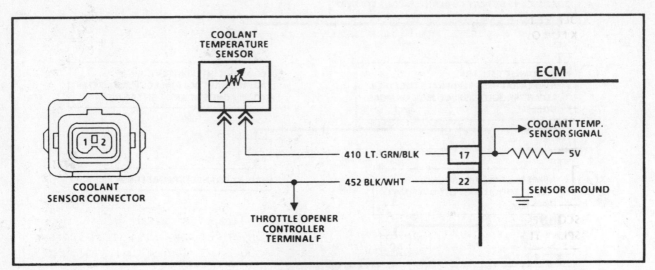

CODE 15
COOLANT TEMPERATURE SENSOR CIRCUIT
(LOW TEMPERATURE INDICATED)

Circuit Description:

The Coolant Temperature Sensor uses a thermistor to control the signal voltage at the ECM. The ECM applies a voltage on CKT 410 to the sensor. When the engine is cold, the sensor (thermistor) resistance is high, therefore, the ECM will see high signal voltage.

As the engine warms, the sensor resistance becomes less, and the voltage drops. At normal engine operating temperature, the voltage will measure about 2.5 to 3.0 volts at the ECM terminal "17".

Coolant temperature is one of the inputs used to control:
- Open Loop timing
- Fuel delivery (M/C solenoid operation)
- EFE (Early Fuel Evaporation)

Test Description: Numbers below refer to circled numbers on the diagnostic chart.

1. Checks to see if code was set as result of hard failure or intermittent condition.
   Code 15 will set if:
   - The engine has been running for 5 minutes.
   - Signal voltage indicates a coolant temperature below 0°C (32°F).
   - Conditions are present for mre than 5 minutes.
2. This test simulates conditions for a Code 14. If the ECM recognizes the grounded circuit (low voltage), and displays a high temperature, the ECM and wiring are OK.
3. This test will determine if there is a wiring problem or a faulty ECM. If CKT 452 is open, there may also be a Code 33 stored. Be sure to carefully check terminals at the engine harness connectors.

Diagnostic Aids:

A "Scan" tool reads engine temperature in degrees centigrade. After the engine is started, the temperature should rise steadily to about 194°F (90°C), then stabilize, when the thermostat opens.

A Code 15 will result if CKT's 410 or 452 is open.

With the coolant sensor circuit open the ECM senses a cold engine and will increase the idle to above 2000 RPM, by increasing the duty cycle of the M/C solenoid.

Fig. 54 Code 15: coolant temperature sensor circuit — carbureted Spectrum

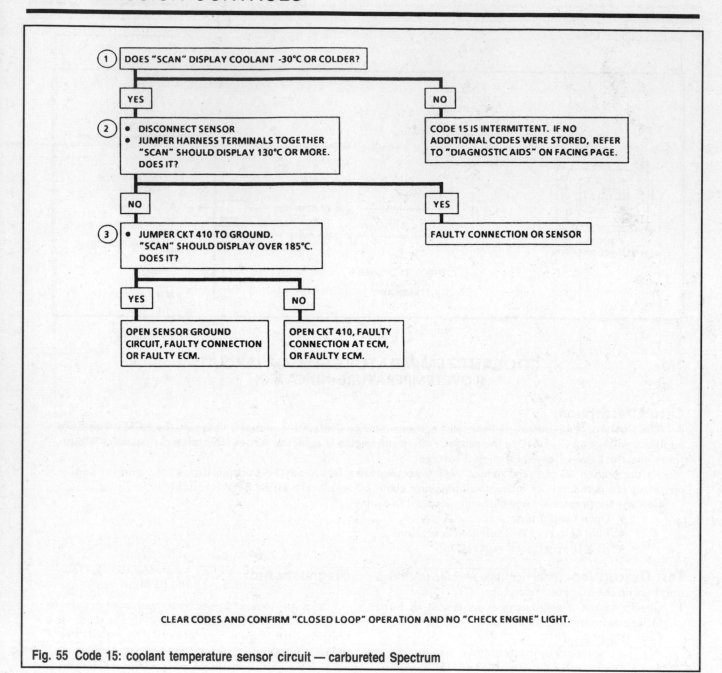

Fig. 55 Code 15: coolant temperature sensor circuit — carbureted Spectrum

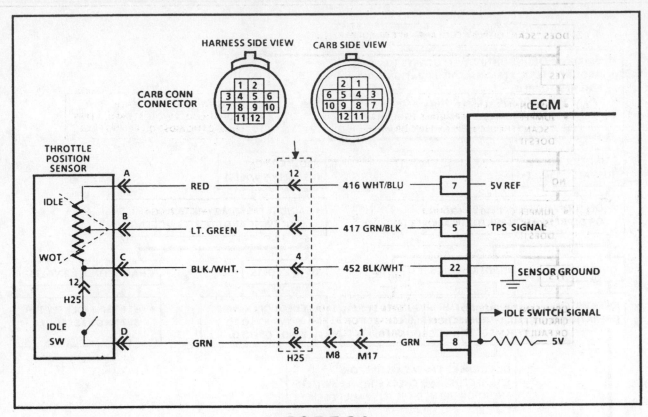

CODE 21

THROTTLE POSITION SENSOR (TPS) AND IDLE SWITCH CIRCUIT

Circuit Description:

The Throttle Position Sensor (TPS) provides a voltage signal that changes relative to the throttle valve. Signal voltage will vary from less than .80 volts at idle to about 4.5 volts at wide open throttle (WOT).

The idle switch provides the ECM with information used to decide closed loop operation and indicates the off-idle condition to the ECM. This switch is normally closed at idle and opens above 1800 RPM, which is then the off-idle condition.

The TPS signal is one of the most important inputs used by the ECM for fuel control and for many of the ECM controlled outputs.

Test Description: Numbers below refer to circled numbers on the diagnostic chart.

1. These tests will determine if the idle switch portion of the circuit is at fault when a code 21 is set.
2. This step checks to see if Code 21 is the result of a hard failure or an intermittent condition.
   A Code 21 will set if:
   - Both WOT and idle are detected for more than one second.

     OR
   - TPS is in OFF-IDLE or WOT position.
   - All of the above conditions present for 32 seconds.
   - Engine speed is between 500 and 600 rpm.

3. If the ECM recognizes the change of state, the ECM and CKTs 416 and 417 are OK.
4. This step isolates a faulty sensor, ECM, or an open CKT 452.

Diagnostic Aids:

A "Scan" tool displays throttle position in volts. Closed throttle voltage should be less than .80 volts. TPS voltage should increase at a steady rate as throttle is moved to WOT.

A Code 21 will result if CKT 452 is open or CKT 417 is shorted to voltage.

Fig. 56 Code 21: throttle position sensor and idle switch circuit — carbureted Spectrum

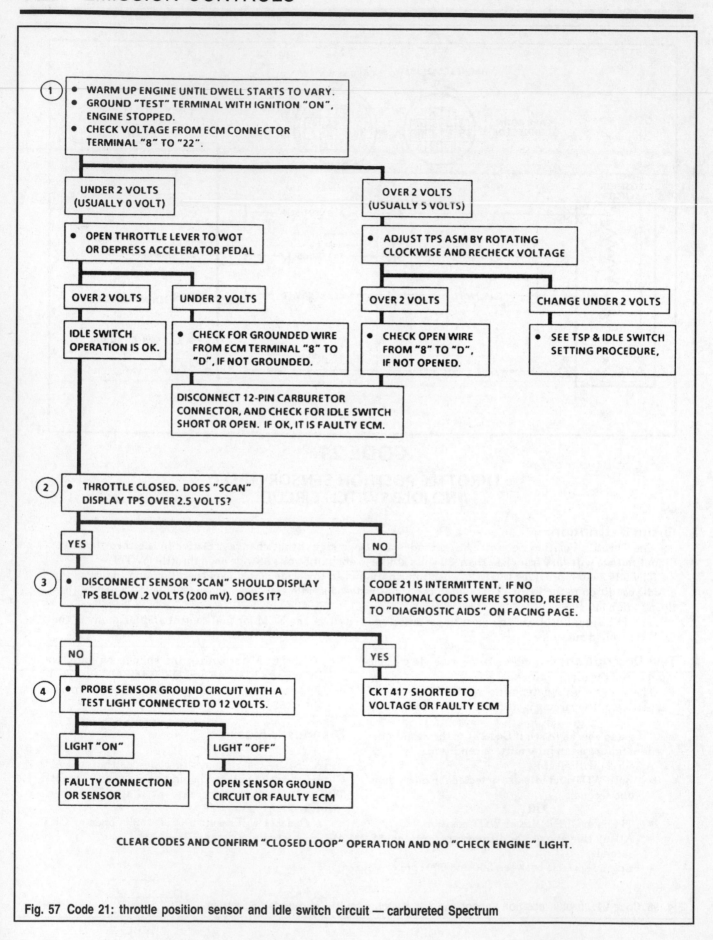

Fig. 57 Code 21: throttle position sensor and idle switch circuit — carbureted Spectrum

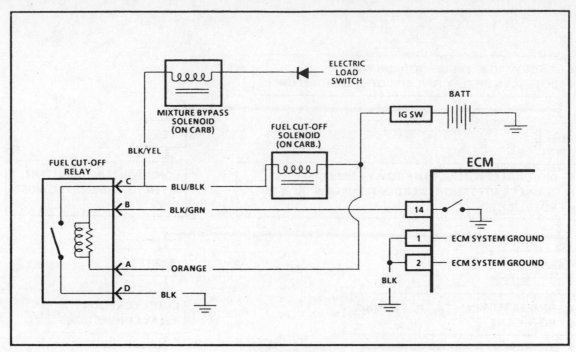

CODE 22
FUEL CUT-OFF (F/C) RELAY CIRCUIT
(OPEN OR GROUNDED)

Circuit Description:
 The Fuel Cut-off solenoid is energized by the Fuel Cut-off Relay with the the ignition switch "ON". When the ignition switch is turned "OFF" the Fuel Cut-off solenoid is de-energized and fuel is immediatly cut-off to prevent dieseling.
 Using the signal from the idle switch the ECM also shuts down fuel when it senses the coasting condition after off-idle condition.

Test Description: Numbers below refer to circled numbers on the diagnostic chart.
1. Checks to see if code 22 is intermittant.
2. Determines if relay or ECM circuits are at fault.

Diagnostic Aids:

 Check Fuel Cut Off relay connector, located behind I.P. Check for loose connections or backed out terminals.

Fig. 58 Code 22: fuel cut-off relay circuit — carbureted Spectrum

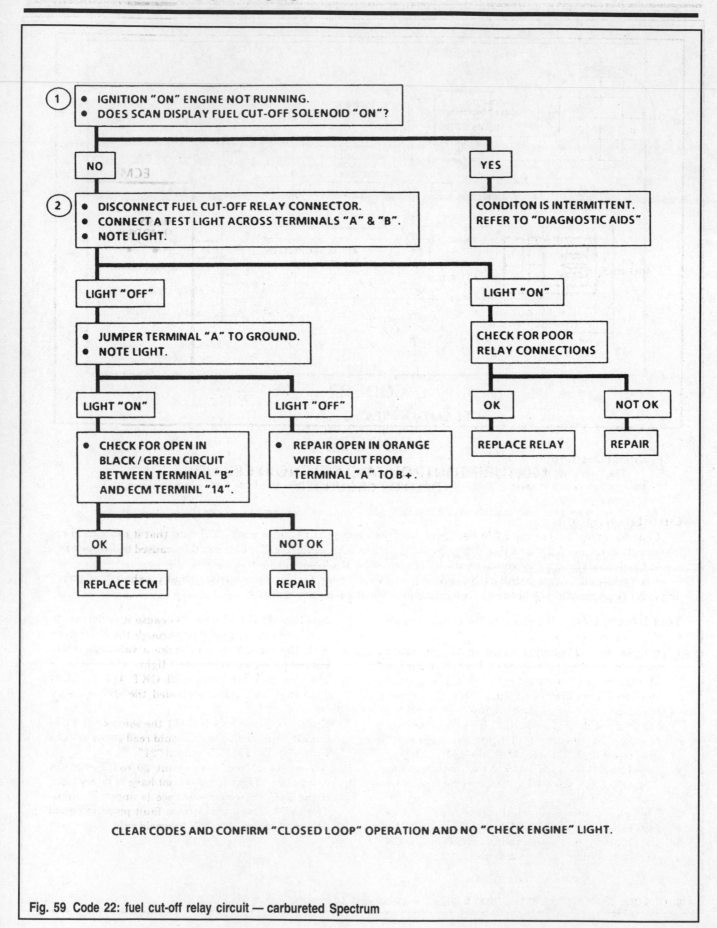

Fig. 59 Code 22: fuel cut-off relay circuit — carbureted Spectrum

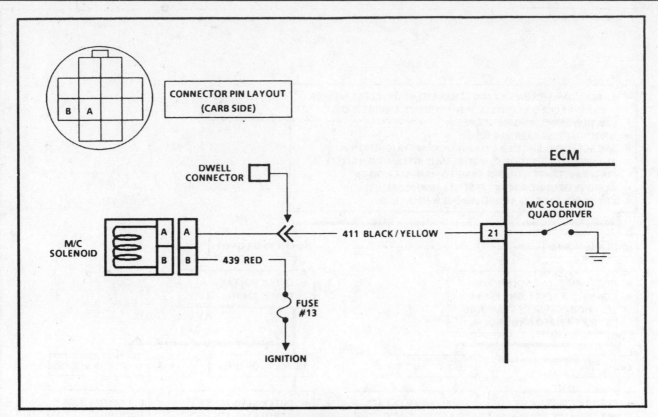

CODE 23

MIXTURE CONTROL (M/C) SOLENOID CIRCUIT
(OPEN OR GROUNDED)

Circuit Description:

Code 23 indicates that the ECM has monitored the voltage at ECM terminal "21" and that it remains low, instead of rising and falling as the M/C solenoid is turned "ON" and "OFF". This could be caused by an open in the M/C solenoid circuit or a ground on the ECM side of the M/C solenoid.

An open would cause a full rich condition and cause poor fuel economy, odor, smoky exhaust or poor driveability. A ground would cause a full lean condition and poor driveability.

Test Description: Numbers below refer to circled numbers on the diagnostic chart.

1. Checks for a complete circuit from the battery through the M/C solenoid dwell lead. Voltage here should be battery voltage. Battery voltage indicates there may be an open CKT 411 between the dwell connector and ground. A 0 voltage reading could be caused either by an open between the dwell connector and ignition source or a ground on the ECM side of the M/C solenoid.

2. Checks for B+ on CKT 439 to the ignition source. The test light should light between the ignition source and ground.

3. This step determines whether the fault is in the M/C solenoid, a grounded CKT 411 to the ECM, or the ECM. A light would indicate a grounded CKT 411 to terminal "21", or a faulty ECM.

A voltmeter can't be used because it is normal to have enough current flow through the ECM even with the circuit open to make a voltmeter read, but not enough to light a test light.

4. This checks for grounded CKT 411 to ECM Terminal "21". If it is grounded, the light will stay "ON".

5. Checks for an open CKT 411 the solenoid to ECM circuit. A normal circuit would read about battery voltage at the ECM Terminal "21".

6. A normal solenoid has about 20 to 32 ohms of resistance. The ECM does not have to be replaced if the M/C solenoid resistance is under 10 ohms. The ECM is equipped with a fault protected quad driver so replace the M/C solenoid only.

Fig. 60 Code 23: mixture control solenoid circuit — carbureted Spectrum

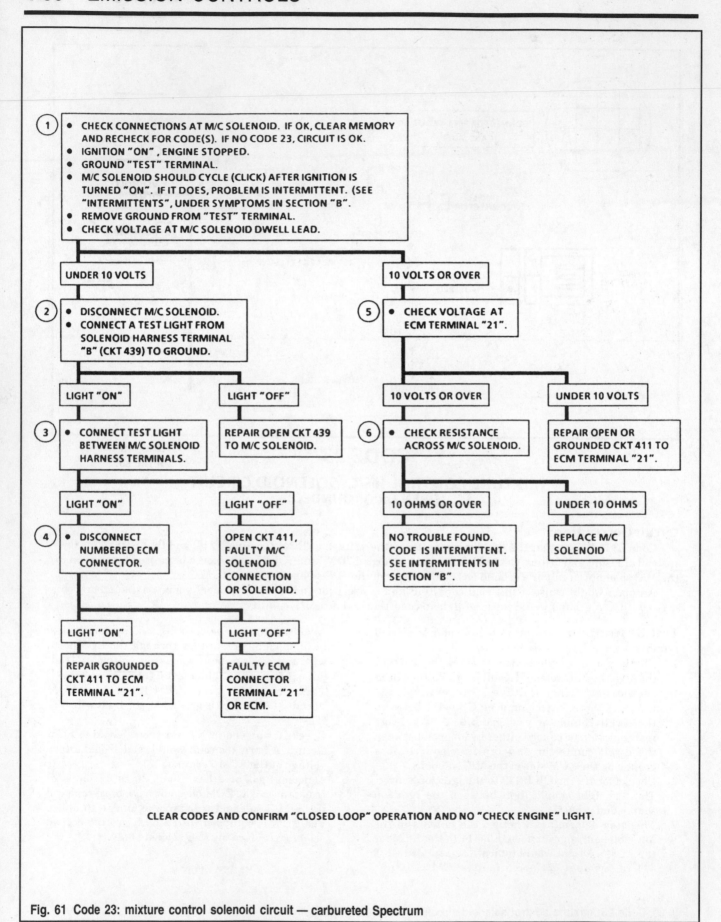

1. • CHECK CONNECTIONS AT M/C SOLENOID. IF OK, CLEAR MEMORY AND RECHECK FOR CODE(S). IF NO CODE 23, CIRCUIT IS OK.
   • IGNITION "ON", ENGINE STOPPED.
   • GROUND "TEST" TERMINAL.
   • M/C SOLENOID SHOULD CYCLE (CLICK) AFTER IGNITION IS TURNED "ON". IF IT DOES, PROBLEM IS INTERMITTENT. (SEE "INTERMITTENTS", UNDER SYMPTOMS IN SECTION "B".
   • REMOVE GROUND FROM "TEST" TERMINAL.
   • CHECK VOLTAGE AT M/C SOLENOID DWELL LEAD.

UNDER 10 VOLTS

10 VOLTS OR OVER

2. • DISCONNECT M/C SOLENOID.
   • CONNECT A TEST LIGHT FROM SOLENOID HARNESS TERMINAL "B" (CKT 439) TO GROUND.

5. • CHECK VOLTAGE AT ECM TERMINAL "21".

LIGHT "ON"

LIGHT "OFF"

10 VOLTS OR OVER

UNDER 10 VOLTS

3. • CONNECT TEST LIGHT BETWEEN M/C SOLENOID HARNESS TERMINALS.

REPAIR OPEN CKT 439 TO M/C SOLENOID.

6. • CHECK RESISTANCE ACROSS M/C SOLENOID.

REPAIR OPEN OR GROUNDED CKT 411 TO ECM TERMINAL "21".

LIGHT "ON"

LIGHT "OFF"

10 OHMS OR OVER

UNDER 10 OHMS

4. • DISCONNECT NUMBERED ECM CONNECTOR.

OPEN CKT 411, FAULTY M/C SOLENOID CONNECTION OR SOLENOID.

NO TROUBLE FOUND. CODE IS INTERMITTENT. SEE INTERMITTENTS IN SECTION "B".

REPLACE M/C SOLENOID

LIGHT "ON"

LIGHT "OFF"

REPAIR GROUNDED CKT 411 TO ECM TERMINAL "21".

FAULTY ECM CONNECTOR TERMINAL "21" OR ECM.

CLEAR CODES AND CONFIRM "CLOSED LOOP" OPERATION AND NO "CHECK ENGINE" LIGHT.

Fig. 61 Code 23: mixture control solenoid circuit — carbureted Spectrum

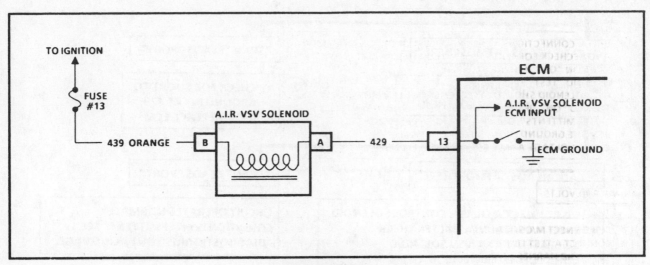

CODE 25

A.I.R. VSV SOLENOID CIRCUIT
(OPEN OR GROUNDED)

Circuit Description:
During cold operation the ECM grounds the circuit, energizing the solenoid and permitting air to go to the exhaust and catalytic converter. During off idle, the air is diverted to the atmosphere when the solenoid is de-energized by the ECM.

Test Description: Numbers below refer to circled numbers on the diagnostic chart.
1. Checks for proper operation of solenoid.
2. Checks for grounded circuit 429 or ECM.
3. Checks to see if voltage is available to circuit.

Diagnostic Aids:
Verify clean tight connections at ECM Terminal "13" and at A.I.R. VSV Solenoid.

Fig. 62 Code 25: air system VSV solenoid circuit — carbureted Spectrum

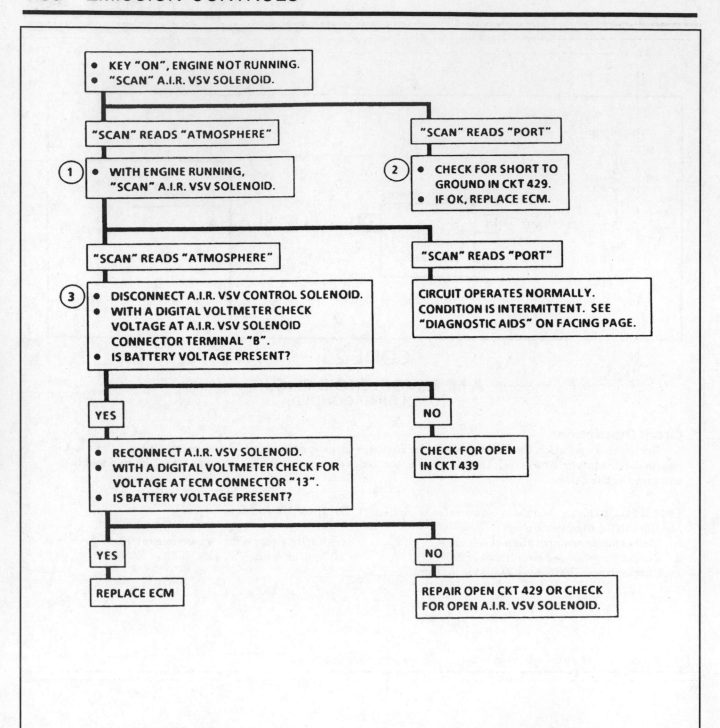

CLEAR CODES AND CONFIRM "CLOSED LOOP" OPERATION AND NO "CHECK ENGINE" LIGHT.

Fig. 63 Code 25: air system VSV solenoid circuit — carbureted Spectrum

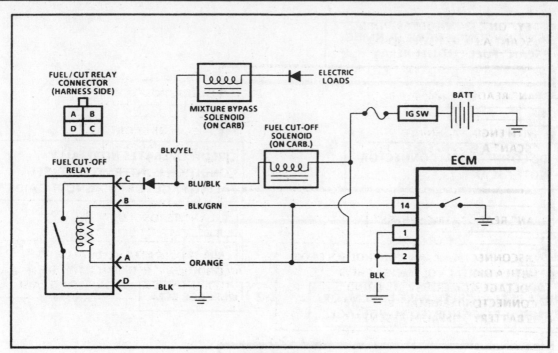

CODE 42
FUEL CUT-OFF (F/C) RELAY CIRCUIT
(VOLTAGE HIGH)

Circuit Description:

The fuel cut relay is supplied B+ by fuse 13, and grounded by the ECM driver when in a deceleration mode. The ECM senses a deceleration condition from the TPS and an engine RPM signal above 2300 RPM. With the relay open fuel flow is decreased. Code 42 sets when the voltage on the driver circuit remains high when commanded "low".

Test Description: Numbers below refer to circled numbers on the diagnostic chart.

1. Checks for short to voltage and for faulty ECM.
2. Code 42 means the ECM has seen an open or short to voltage in the Fuel Cut Relay circuits. This test checks for a shorted F/C relay.
3. Shorts to voltage may have caused damage to the ECM preventing code 42 from being cleared.

Diagnostic Aids:

Check for normal operation of TPS and idle switch. If ECM is receiving wrong signal from throttle switches a false deceleration could be sensed. See Section "C2".

Fig. 64 Code 42: fuel cut-off relay circuit — carbureted Spectrum

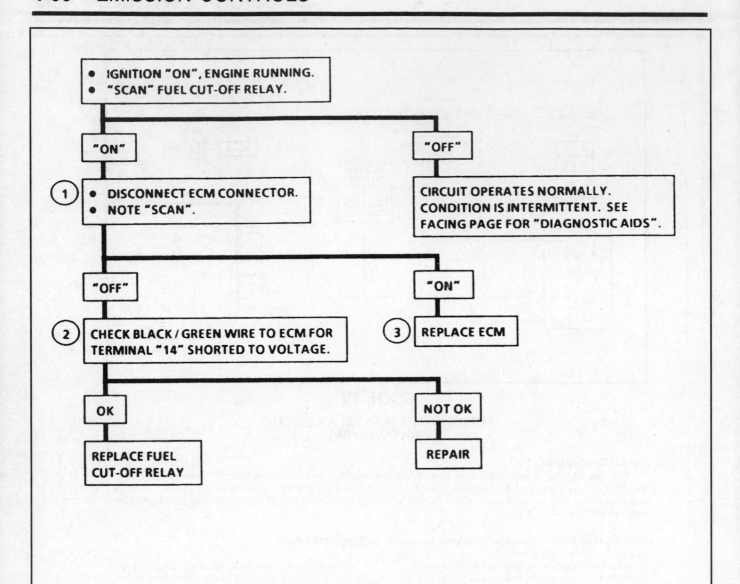

Fig. 65 Code 42: fuel cut-off relay circuit — carbureted Spectrum

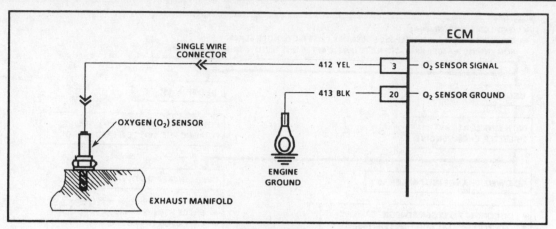

CODE 44

OXYGEN SENSOR CIRCUIT
(LEAN EXHAUST INDICATED)

Circuit Description:

The ECM supplies a voltage of about .45 volt between Terminals "3" and "20". (If measured with a 10 megohm digital voltmeter, this may read as low as .32 volts.) The O_2 sensor varies the voltage within a range of about 1 volt, if the exhaust is rich, down through about .10 volt, if exhaust is lean.

The sensor is like an open circuit and produces no voltage, when it is below about 360°C (600°F). An open sensor circuit, or cold sensor, causes "Open Loop" operation.

Test Description: Numbers below refer to circled numbers on the diagnostic chart.

1. Code 44 is set, when the O_2 sensor signal voltage on CKT 412:
   - Remains below .3 volt for 2 minutes or more;
   - And the system is operating in "Closed Loop".
   - O_2 sensor must reach a temperature of 70°C (158°F).
   - Throttle is off-idle. Inlet air temperature switch is "OFF".
   - Vehicle is at low altitude.

Diagnostic Aids:

- O_2 Sensor Wire - Sensor pigtail may be mispositioned and contacting the exhaust manifold.
- Check for ground in wire between connector and sensor.
- Exhaust Leaks - If there is an exhaust leak, the engine can cause outside air to be pulled into the exhaust and past the sensor. Vacuum or crankcase leaks can cause a lean condition.
- If M/C Solenoid does not "click" with ignition "ON" and test terminal grounded and there is no Code 23, check for sticking solenoid.
- Inlet air temperature switch may be open. Should be closed below 32°F.

Fig. 66 Code 44: oxygen sensor circuit — carbureted Spectrum

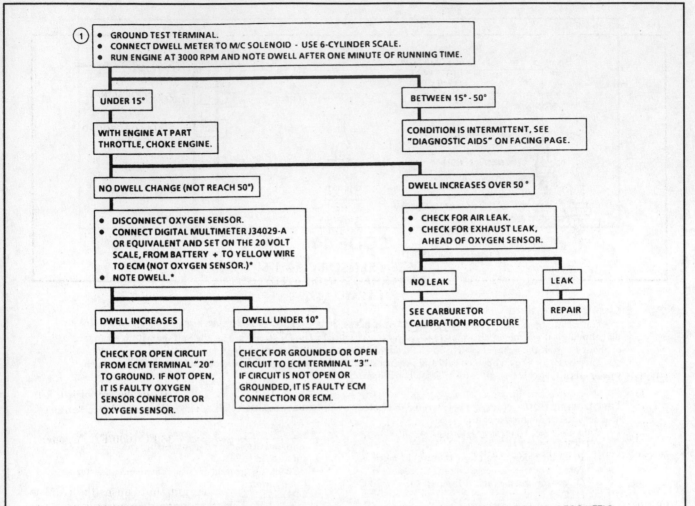

① • GROUND TEST TERMINAL.
• CONNECT DWELL METER TO M/C SOLENOID - USE 6-CYLINDER SCALE.
• RUN ENGINE AT 3000 RPM AND NOTE DWELL AFTER ONE MINUTE OF RUNNING TIME.

UNDER 15°

WITH ENGINE AT PART THROTTLE, CHOKE ENGINE.

NO DWELL CHANGE (NOT REACH 50°)

• DISCONNECT OXYGEN SENSOR.
• CONNECT DIGITAL MULTIMETER J34029-A OR EQUIVALENT AND SET ON THE 20 VOLT SCALE, FROM BATTERY + TO YELLOW WIRE TO ECM (NOT OXYGEN SENSOR.)*
• NOTE DWELL.*

DWELL INCREASES

CHECK FOR OPEN CIRCUIT FROM ECM TERMINAL "20" TO GROUND. IF NOT OPEN, IT IS FAULTY OXYGEN SENSOR CONNECTOR OR OXYGEN SENSOR.

DWELL UNDER 10°

CHECK FOR GROUNDED OR OPEN CIRCUIT TO ECM TERMINAL "3". IF CIRCUIT IS NOT OPEN OR GROUNDED, IT IS FAULTY ECM CONNECTION OR ECM.

BETWEEN 15° - 50°

CONDITION IS INTERMITTENT, SEE "DIAGNOSTIC AIDS" ON FACING PAGE.

DWELL INCREASES OVER 50°

• CHECK FOR AIR LEAK.
• CHECK FOR EXHAUST LEAK, AHEAD OF OXYGEN SENSOR.

NO LEAK

SEE CARBURETOR CALIBRATION PROCEDURE

LEAK

REPAIR

* DO NOT USE AN ORDINARY VOLTMETER OR JUMPER IN PLACE OF THE DIGITAL VOLTMETER BECAUSE THEY HAVE TOO LITTLE RESISTANCE. A VOLTAGE SOURCE OF 1.0V TO 1.7V (SUCH AS A FLASHLIGHT BATTERY) CAN BE CONNECTED WITH THE POSITIVE TERMINAL TO THE YELLOW WIRE AND THE NEGATIVE TERMINAL TO GROUND AS A JUMPER. IF THE POLARITY IS REVERSED, IT WON'T WORK.

CLEAR CODES AND CONFIRM "CLOSED LOOP" OPERATION AND NO "CHECK ENGINE" LIGHT.

Fig. 67 Code 44: oxygen sensor circuit — carbureted Spectrum

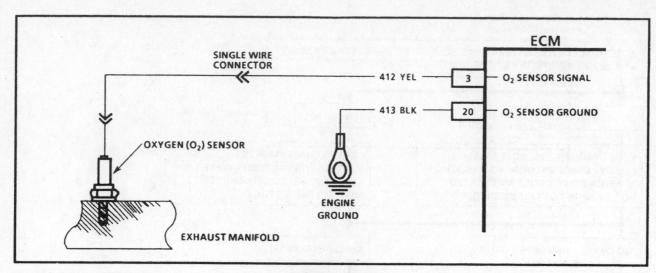

CODE 45

OXYGEN SENSOR CIRCUIT
(RICH EXHAUST INDICATED)

Circuit Description:

The ECM supplies a voltage of about .45 volt between terminals "3" and "20". (If measured with a 10 megohm digital voltmeter, this may read as low as .32 volts.) The O_2 sensor varies the voltage within a range of about 1 volt, if the exhaust is rich, down through about .10 volt, if exhaust is lean.

The sensor is like an open circuit and produces no voltage, when it is below about 360°C (600°F). An open sensor circuit, or cold sensor, causes "Open Loop" operation.

Test Description:
Numbers below refer to circled numbers on the diagnostic chart.

1. Code 45 is set, when the O_2 sensor signal voltage on CKT 412:
   - Remains above .6V for 2 minutes or more.
   - System operating in "Closed Loop".
   - O_2 sensor must reach a temperature of 70°C (158°F).
   - Engine running 5 minutes or more, at part throttle.

Diagnostic Aids:

The Code 45, or rich exhaust, is most likely caused by one of the flowing:

- If M/C solenoid does not click with ignition "ON" and "ALDL" terminal grounded, and there is no code 23, check for sticking solenoid.
- EEC - Check for fuel saturation. If full of fuel, check canister control and hoses.

- MAP Sensor - An output that causes the ECM to sense a higher than normal manifold pressure (low vacuum) can cause the system to go rich. Disconnecting the MAP sensor will allow the ECM to set a fixed value for the MAP sensor. Substitute a different MAP sensor, if the rich condition is gone, while the sensor is disconnected.
- TPS - An intermittent TPS output will cause the system to go rich, due to a false indication of the engine accelerating.
- O_2 Sensor Contamination - Inspect Oxygen Sensor for silicone contamination from fuel, or use of improper RTV sealant. The sensor may have a white, powdery coating and result in a high, but false signal voltage (rich exhaust indication). The ECM will then reduce the amount of fuel delivered to the engine, causing a severe surge driveability problem.

- If the EGR valve is stuck open it may result in a rich exhaust indication and could possibly set a Code 45, especially at idle. Refer to CHART C-7 to check EGR system.
- Faulty Reed Valve in Air System.

Fig. 68 Code 45: oxygen sensor circuit — carbureted Spectrum

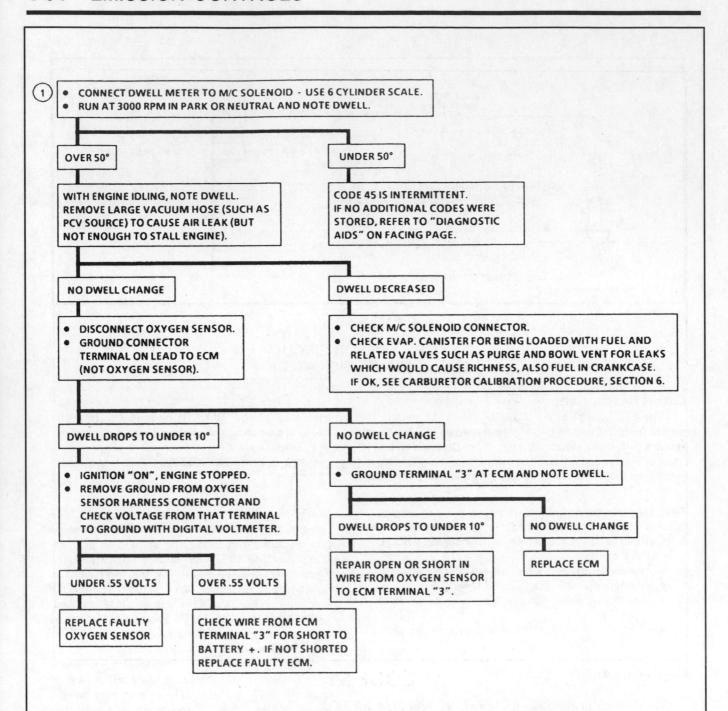

* DO NOT USE AN ORDINARY VOLTMETER OR JUMPER IN PLACE OF THE DIGITAL VOLTMETER BECAUSE THEY HAVE TOO LITTLE RESISTANCE. A VOLTAGE SOURCE OF 1.0V TO 1.7V (SUCH AS A FLASHLIGHT BATTERY) CAN BE CONNECTED WITH THE POSITIVE TERMINAL TO THE YELLOW WIRE AND THE NEGATIVE TERMINAL TO GROUND AS A JUMPER. IF THE POLARITY IS REVERSED, IT WON'T WORK.

CLEAR CODES AND CONFIRM "CLOSED LOOP" OPERATION AND NO "CHECK ENGINE" LIGHT.

Fig. 69 Code 45: oxygen sensor circuit — carbureted Spectrum

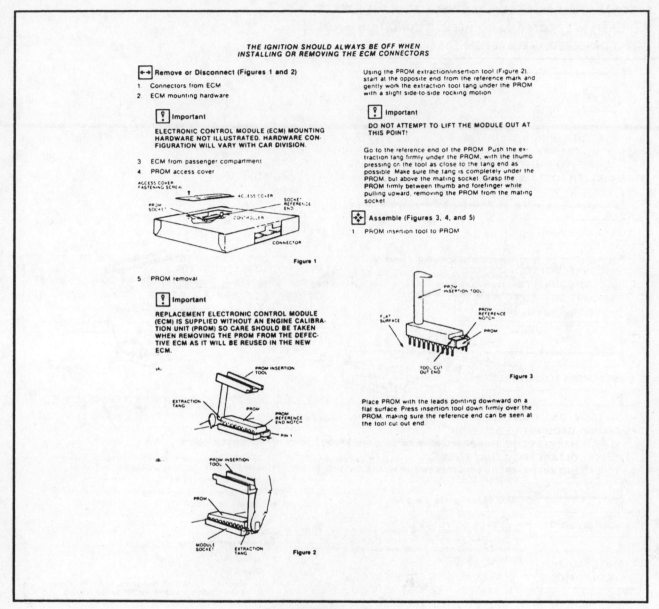

THE IGNITION SHOULD ALWAYS BE OFF WHEN
INSTALLING OR REMOVING THE ECM CONNECTORS

← → Remove or Disconnect (Figures 1 and 2)

1. Connectors from ECM
2. ECM mounting hardware

⚠ Important

ELECTRONIC CONTROL MODULE (ECM) MOUNTING HARDWARE NOT ILLUSTRATED. HARDWARE CONFIGURATION WILL VARY WITH CAR DIVISION.

3. ECM from passenger compartment
4. PROM access cover

Figure 1

5. PROM removal

⚠ Important

REPLACEMENT ELECTRONIC CONTROL MODULE (ECM) IS SUPPLIED WITHOUT AN ENGINE CALIBRATION UNIT (PROM) SO CARE SHOULD BE TAKEN WHEN REMOVING THE PROM FROM THE DEFECTIVE ECM AS IT WILL BE REUSED IN THE NEW ECM.

Figure 2

Using the PROM extraction/insertion tool (Figure 2), start at the opposite end from the reference mark and gently work the extraction tool tang under the PROM with a slight side-to-side rocking motion

⚠ Important

DO NOT ATTEMPT TO LIFT THE MODULE OUT AT THIS POINT!

Go to the reference end of the PROM. Push the extraction tang firmly under the PROM, with the thumb pressing on the tool as close to the tang end as possible. Make sure the tang is completely under the PROM, but above the mating socket. Grasp the PROM firmly between thumb and forefinger while pulling upward, removing the PROM from the mating socket

✦ Assemble (Figures 3, 4, and 5)

1. PROM insertion tool to PROM

Figure 3

Place PROM with the leads pointing downward on a flat surface. Press insertion tool down firmly over the PROM, making sure the reference end can be seen at the tool cut out end.

CODE 51

PROM ERROR
(FAULTY OR INCORRECT PROM)

Circuit Description:

Code 51 sets if any one of the following occur:

- Faulty PROM unit.
- PROM unit improperly installed (may not set a code if installed backwards).
- Some PROM pins not making contact (i.e., bent).

Always check to see that the PROM pins are not bent and are inserted properly into the ECM.

Make certain the PROM is installed in the proper direction as shown in the chart.

Fig. 70 Code 51: prom error — carbureted Spectrum

CHECK THAT ALL PINS ARE FULLY INSERTED IN THE SOCKET.
IF OK, REPLACE PROM AND RECHECK. IF CONDITION IS NOT
CORRECTED, REPLACE ECM.

◄—► **Remove or Disconnect (Figure 4)**

1. New electronic control module out of its packaging
    and check the service number to make sure it is the
    same as the defective ECM.
2. Access cover

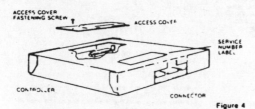

Figure 4

! **Important (Before installing new PROM)**

ANY TIME THE PROM IS INSTALLED BACKWARDS
AND THE IGNITION SWITCH TURNED ON, THE
PROM IS DESTROYED.

✦ **Assemble (Figures 5 and 6)**

1. PROM in PROM socket

Mate the PROM held by the insertion tool to the
PROM socket on the circuit board. Make sure
reference ends of both PROM and socket are aligned
in the same direction.

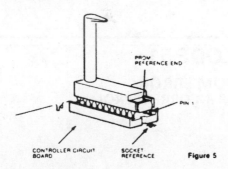

Figure 5

! **Important**

THE MODULE WILL NOT BE FULLY SEATED AT THIS
POINT.

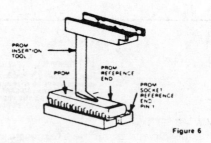

Figure 6

Turn the insertion tool over and using the blunt end
press the PROM down until fully seated.

👁 **Inspect (Figure 6)**

For bent pins, properly seated in socket or installed
with PROM and socket ends aligned

2. Access cover on ECM
3. ECM in passenger compartment
4. Connectors to ECM

🔧 **Measure or Check**

1. Ignition on
2. Diagnostics

    A   Code 12 should flash four times (No other codes
        present.) This indicates the PROM is installed
        properly

    B   If trouble code 51 occurs or if the check engine
        light is on constantly with no codes, the PROM is
        not fully seated, installed backwards, has bent
        pins, or is defective.

    •   If not fully seated, press firmly on PROM
    •   If it is necessary to remove the PROM, follow
        instructions
    •   If installed backwards, REPLACE THE PROM
    •   If pins bend, remove PROM, straighten pins, and
        reinstall. If bent pins break or crack during
        straightening, discard PROM and replace it

! **Important (Before installing new PROM)**

ANY TIME THE PROM IS INSTALLED BACKWARDS
AND THE IGNITION SWITCH TURNED ON, THE
PROM IS DESTROYED.

Fig. 71 Code 51: prom error — carbureted Spectrum

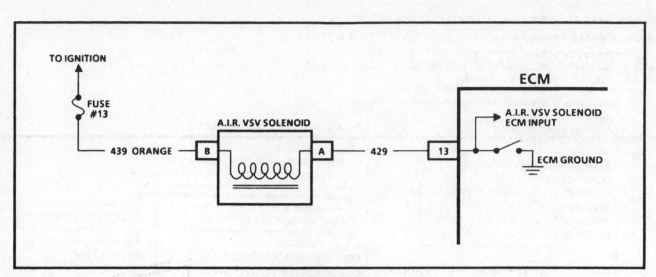

CODE 53

A.I.R. VSV SOLENOID CIRCUIT
(VOLTAGE HIGH)

Circuit Description:

During cold operation the ECM grounds the circuit, energizing the solenoid and permitting air to go to the exhaust and catalytic converter. During off idle, the air is diverted to the atmosphere when the solenoid is de-energized by the ECM.

Test Description: Numbers below refer to circled numbers on the diagnostic chart.

1. Checks for proper operation of solenoid.
2. Checks for short to B+.
3. Checks for open solenoid or open connector terminals.
4. Checks for presence of B+.

Diagnostic Aids:

Verify clean tight connections at ECM Terminal "13" and at A.I.R. VSV Solenoid.

Fig. 72 Code 53: air system VSV solenoid circuit — carbureted Spectrum

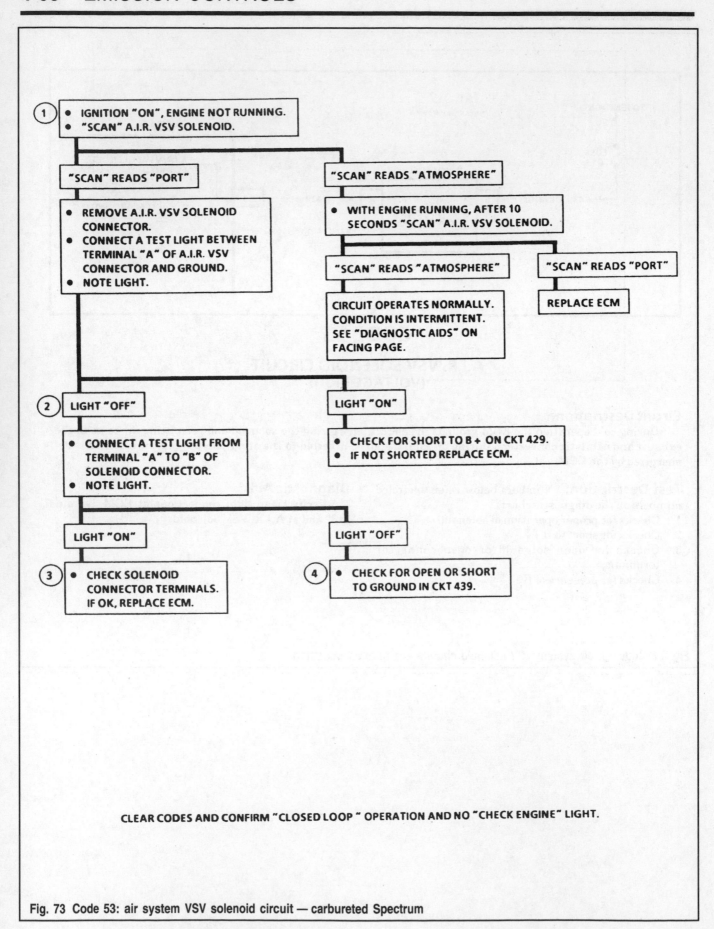

1
- IGNITION "ON", ENGINE NOT RUNNING.
- "SCAN" A.I.R. VSV SOLENOID.

"SCAN" READS "PORT"

"SCAN" READS "ATMOSPHERE"

- REMOVE A.I.R. VSV SOLENOID CONNECTOR.
- CONNECT A TEST LIGHT BETWEEN TERMINAL "A" OF A.I.R. VSV CONNECTOR AND GROUND.
- NOTE LIGHT.

- WITH ENGINE RUNNING, AFTER 10 SECONDS "SCAN" A.I.R. VSV SOLENOID.

"SCAN" READS "ATMOSPHERE"

"SCAN" READS "PORT"

CIRCUIT OPERATES NORMALLY. CONDITION IS INTERMITTENT. SEE "DIAGNOSTIC AIDS" ON FACING PAGE.

REPLACE ECM

2 LIGHT "OFF"

LIGHT "ON"

- CONNECT A TEST LIGHT FROM TERMINAL "A" TO "B" OF SOLENOID CONNECTOR.
- NOTE LIGHT.

- CHECK FOR SHORT TO B + ON CKT 429.
- IF NOT SHORTED REPLACE ECM.

LIGHT "ON"

LIGHT "OFF"

3
- CHECK SOLENOID CONNECTOR TERMINALS. IF OK, REPLACE ECM.

4
- CHECK FOR OPEN OR SHORT TO GROUND IN CKT 439.

CLEAR CODES AND CONFIRM "CLOSED LOOP" OPERATION AND NO "CHECK ENGINE" LIGHT.

Fig. 73 Code 53: air system VSV solenoid circuit — carbureted Spectrum

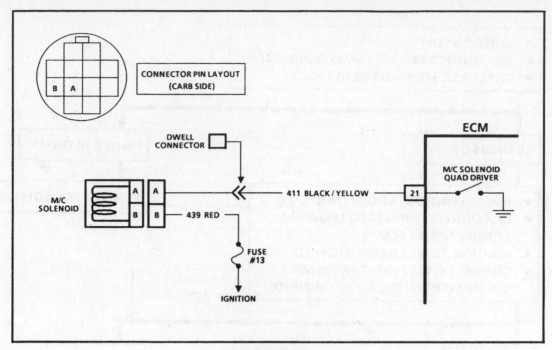

CODE 54

MIXTURE CONTROL (M/C) SOLENOID CIRCUIT
(SIGNAL VOLTAGE HIGH)

Circuit Description:

Code 54 will be set if there is constant high voltage at ECM terminal "21".

A shorted solenoid or shorted CKT 411 to 12V would cause the solenoid to remain in the full rich position, resulting in potential ECM damage, excessive fuel consumption, and excessive exhaust odor.

Test Description: Numbers below refer to circled numbers on the diagnostic chart.

1. Checks the M/C solenoid resistance to determine if the fault is in the solenoid, ECM harness, or ECM. A normal solenoid has about 20 to 32 ohms of resistance. The ECM is equipped with a fault protected quad driver. If the M/C solenoid is under 10 ohms, only the solenoid has to be replaced, not the ECM.

2. Checks to see if reason for high voltage to terminal "21" is a faulty ECM or a short to 12V in CKT 411. If the test light illuminates with both ends of harness disconnected, there is a short to 12V in CKT 411.

Fig. 74 Code 54: mixture control solenoid circuit — carbureted Spectrum

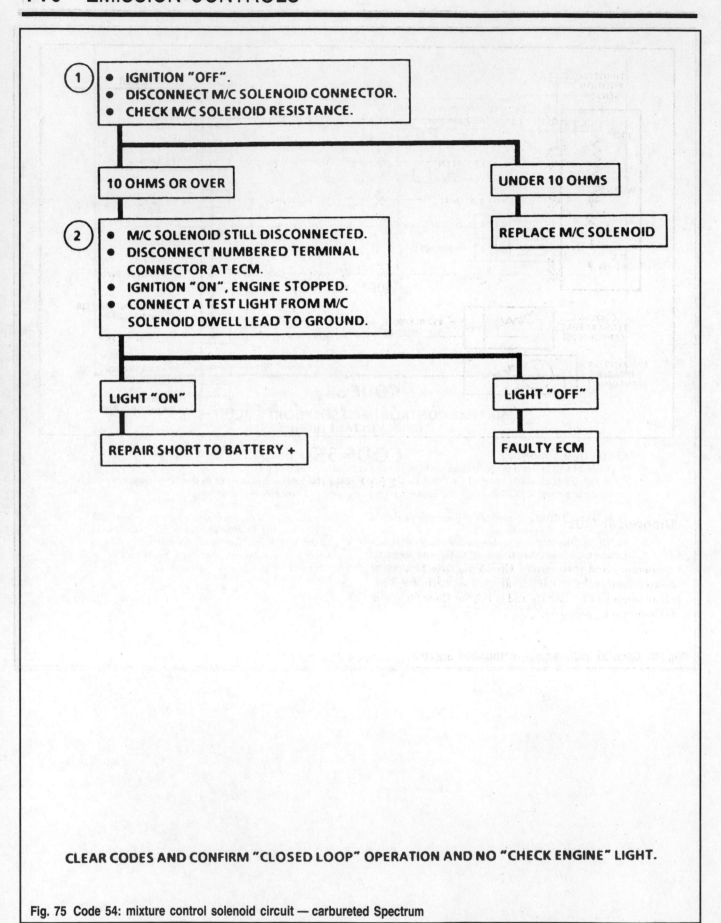

① • IGNITION "OFF".
  • DISCONNECT M/C SOLENOID CONNECTOR.
  • CHECK M/C SOLENOID RESISTANCE.

10 OHMS OR OVER

UNDER 10 OHMS

REPLACE M/C SOLENOID

② • M/C SOLENOID STILL DISCONNECTED.
  • DISCONNECT NUMBERED TERMINAL CONNECTOR AT ECM.
  • IGNITION "ON", ENGINE STOPPED.
  • CONNECT A TEST LIGHT FROM M/C SOLENOID DWELL LEAD TO GROUND.

LIGHT "ON"

LIGHT "OFF"

REPAIR SHORT TO BATTERY +

FAULTY ECM

CLEAR CODES AND CONFIRM "CLOSED LOOP" OPERATION AND NO "CHECK ENGINE" LIGHT.

Fig. 75 Code 54: mixture control solenoid circuit — carbureted Spectrum

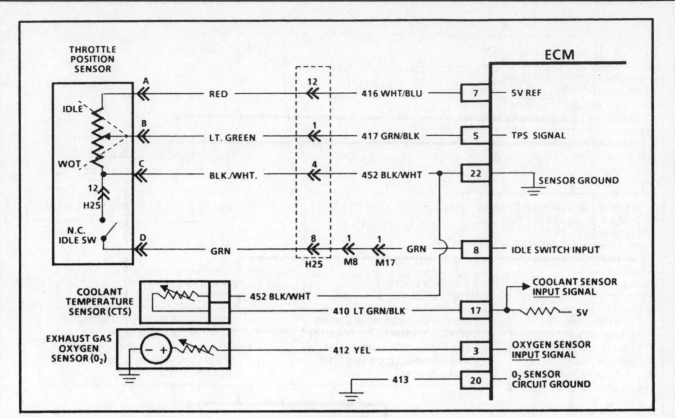

CODE 55
ECM ERROR

Diagnostic Aids:

Check for corrosion at ECM edgeboard connectors and terminals. Check for windshield or heater core leaks. If leaks are present, repair leak, clear connector terminals and check for Code 55 again. If Code resets, replace ECM.

Fig. 76 Code 55: ECM error — carbureted Spectrum

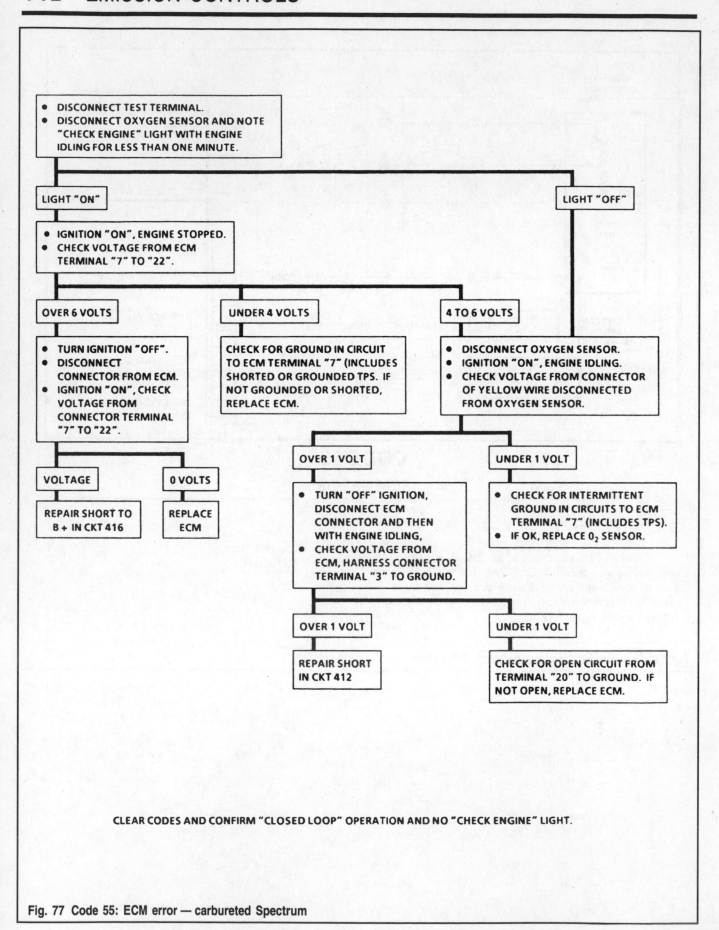

Fig. 77 Code 55: ECM error — carbureted Spectrum

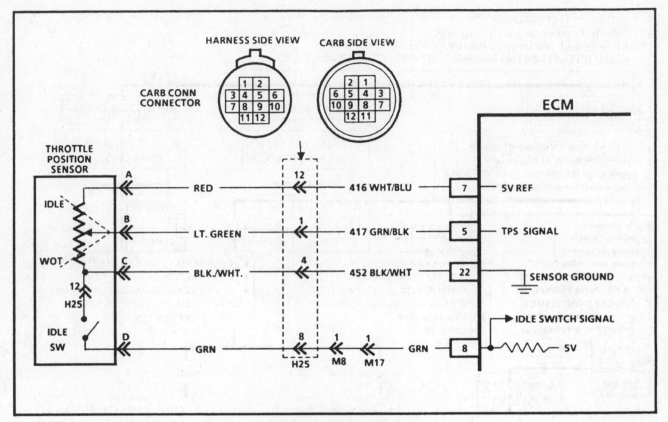

CHART C-1A

THROTTLE POSITION SENSOR (TPS)
(ASSEMBLY FUNCTIONAL CHECK)

Circuit Description:

The Throttle Position Sensor (TPS) provides a voltage signal that changes relative to the throttle valve. Signal voltage will vary from less than .80 volts at idle to about 4.5 volts at wide open throttle (WOT).

The idle switch provides the ECM with information used to decide closed loop operation and indicates the off-idle condition to the ECM. This switch is normally closed at idle and opens above 1800 RPM, which is then the off-idle condition.

The TPS signal is one of the most important inputs used by the ECM for fuel control and for many of the ECM controlled outputs.

Diagnostic Aids:

A "Scan" tool displays throttle position in volts.
Closed throttle voltage should be less than .80 volts.
TPS voltage should increase at a steady rate as throttle is moved to WOT.

Fig. 78 Chart C-1a: throttle position sensor functional check — carbureted Spectrum

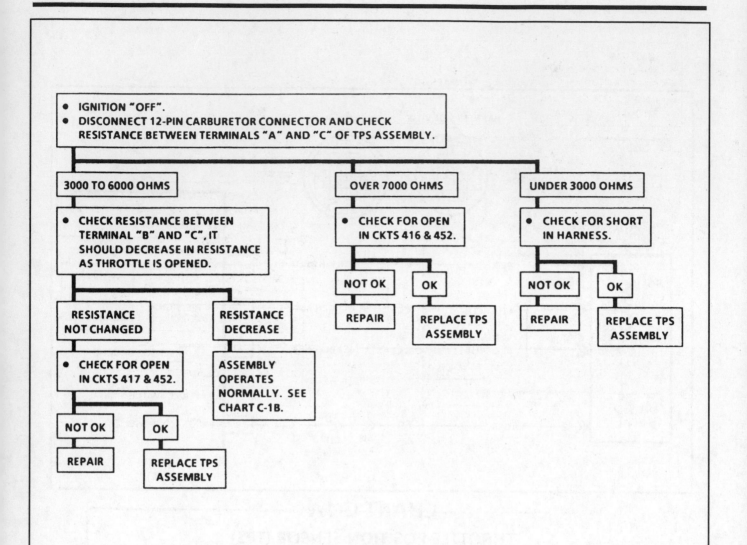

- IGNITION "OFF".
- DISCONNECT 12-PIN CARBURETOR CONNECTOR AND CHECK RESISTANCE BETWEEN TERMINALS "A" AND "C" OF TPS ASSEMBLY.

3000 TO 6000 OHMS

- CHECK RESISTANCE BETWEEN TERMINAL "B" AND "C", IT SHOULD DECREASE IN RESISTANCE AS THROTTLE IS OPENED.

RESISTANCE NOT CHANGED

- CHECK FOR OPEN IN CKTS 417 & 452.

NOT OK → REPAIR

OK → REPLACE TPS ASSEMBLY

RESISTANCE DECREASE

ASSEMBLY OPERATES NORMALLY. SEE CHART C-1B.

OVER 7000 OHMS

- CHECK FOR OPEN IN CKTS 416 & 452.

NOT OK → REPAIR

OK → REPLACE TPS ASSEMBLY

UNDER 3000 OHMS

- CHECK FOR SHORT IN HARNESS.

NOT OK → REPAIR

OK → REPLACE TPS ASSEMBLY

CLEAR CODES AND CONFIRM "CLOSED LOOP" OPERATION AND NO "CHECK ENGINE" LIGHT.

Fig. 79 Chart C-1a: throttle position sensor functional check — carbureted Spectrum

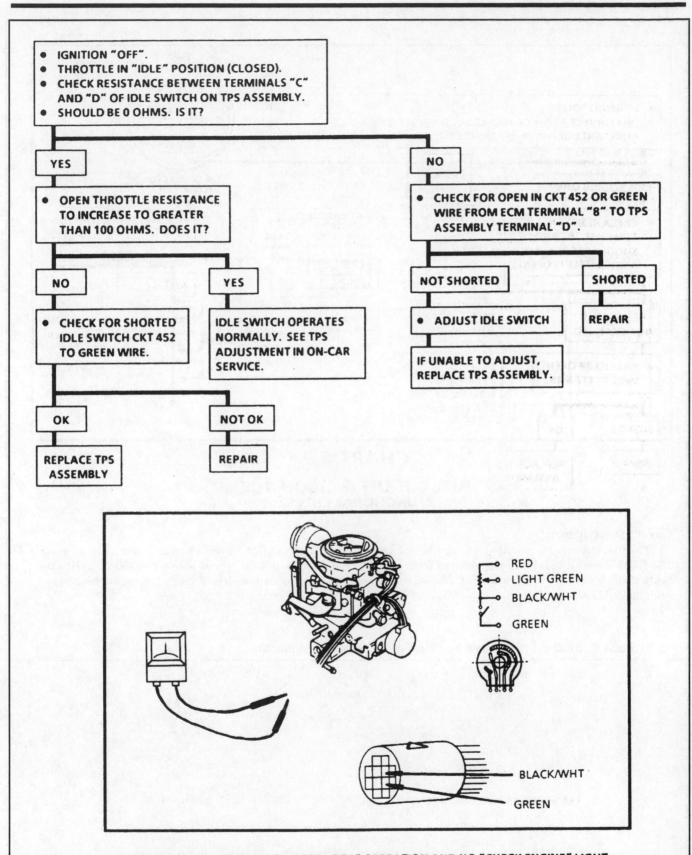

- IGNITION "OFF".
- THROTTLE IN "IDLE" POSITION (CLOSED).
- CHECK RESISTANCE BETWEEN TERMINALS "C" AND "D" OF IDLE SWITCH ON TPS ASSEMBLY.
- SHOULD BE 0 OHMS. IS IT?

YES

- OPEN THROTTLE RESISTANCE TO INCREASE TO GREATER THAN 100 OHMS. DOES IT?

NO

- CHECK FOR SHORTED IDLE SWITCH CKT 452 TO GREEN WIRE.

YES

IDLE SWITCH OPERATES NORMALLY. SEE TPS ADJUSTMENT IN ON-CAR SERVICE.

OK

REPLACE TPS ASSEMBLY

NOT OK

REPAIR

NO

- CHECK FOR OPEN IN CKT 452 OR GREEN WIRE FROM ECM TERMINAL "8" TO TPS ASSEMBLY TERMINAL "D".

NOT SHORTED

- ADJUST IDLE SWITCH

IF UNABLE TO ADJUST, REPLACE TPS ASSEMBLY.

SHORTED

REPAIR

RED
LIGHT GREEN
BLACK/WHT
GREEN

BLACK/WHT
GREEN

CLEAR CODES AND CONFIRM "CLOSED LOOP" OPERATION AND NO "CHECK ENGINE" LIGHT.

Fig. 80 Chart C-1b: idle switch functional check — carbureted Spectrum

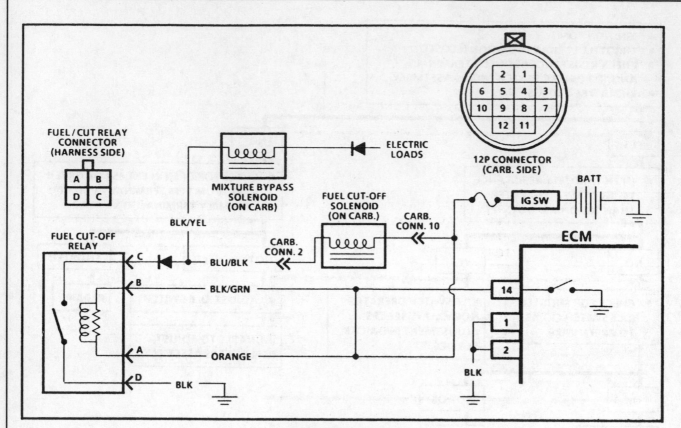

CHART C-2

FUEL CUT-OFF (F/C) SOLENOID
(FUNCTIONAL CHECK)

Circuit Description:

The fuel cut relay is supplied B+ by fuse 13, and grounded by the ECM driver when in a deceleration mode. The ECM senses a deceleration condition from the TPS and an engine RPM signal above 2300 RPM. With the relay open fuel flow is decreased. Code 42 sets when the voltage on the driver circuit remains high when commanded "low".

Fig. 81 Chart C-2: fuel cut-off solenoid functional check — carbureted Spectrum

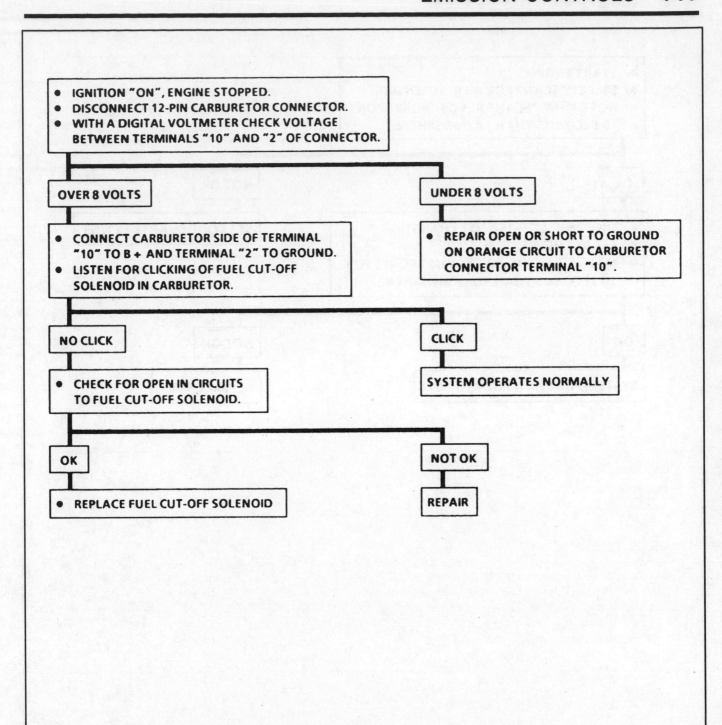

- IGNITION "ON", ENGINE STOPPED.
- DISCONNECT 12-PIN CARBURETOR CONNECTOR.
- WITH A DIGITAL VOLTMETER CHECK VOLTAGE BETWEEN TERMINALS "10" AND "2" OF CONNECTOR.

OVER 8 VOLTS

UNDER 8 VOLTS

- CONNECT CARBURETOR SIDE OF TERMINAL "10" TO B + AND TERMINAL "2" TO GROUND.
- LISTEN FOR CLICKING OF FUEL CUT-OFF SOLENOID IN CARBURETOR.

- REPAIR OPEN OR SHORT TO GROUND ON ORANGE CIRCUIT TO CARBURETOR CONNECTOR TERMINAL "10".

NO CLICK

CLICK

- CHECK FOR OPEN IN CIRCUITS TO FUEL CUT-OFF SOLENOID.

SYSTEM OPERATES NORMALLY

OK

NOT OK

- REPLACE FUEL CUT-OFF SOLENOID

REPAIR

CLEAR CODES AND CONFIRM "CLOSED LOOP" OPERATION AND NO "CHECK ENGINE" LIGHT.

Fig. 82 Chart C-2: fuel cut-off solenoid functional check — carbureted Spectrum

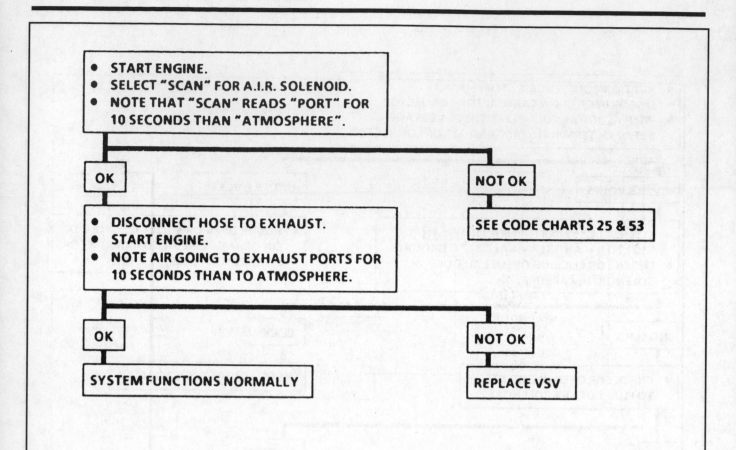

- START ENGINE.
- SELECT "SCAN" FOR A.I.R. SOLENOID.
- NOTE THAT "SCAN" READS "PORT" FOR 10 SECONDS THAN "ATMOSPHERE".

OK

NOT OK

- DISCONNECT HOSE TO EXHAUST.
- START ENGINE.
- NOTE AIR GOING TO EXHAUST PORTS FOR 10 SECONDS THAN TO ATMOSPHERE.

SEE CODE CHARTS 25 & 53

OK

NOT OK

SYSTEM FUNCTIONS NORMALLY

REPLACE VSV

CLEAR CODES AND CONFIRM "CLOSED LOOP" OPERATION AND NO "CHECK ENGINE" LIGHT.

Fig. 83 Chart C-6: air system vsv solenoid functional check — carbureted Spectrum

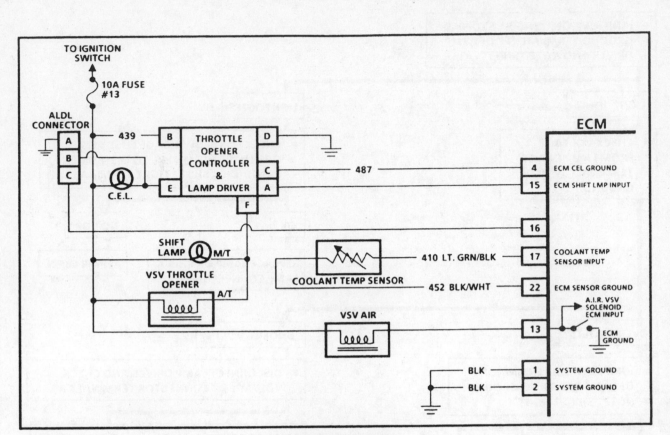

CHART C-8A

SHIFT LIGHT INOPERATIVE

Circuit Description:

When the engine is started, the ECM grounds terminal "G" to turn out the "Check Engine" light. It alternately grounds and opens it to flash a code.

Fig. 84 Chart C-8a: shift light inoperative — carbureted Spectrum

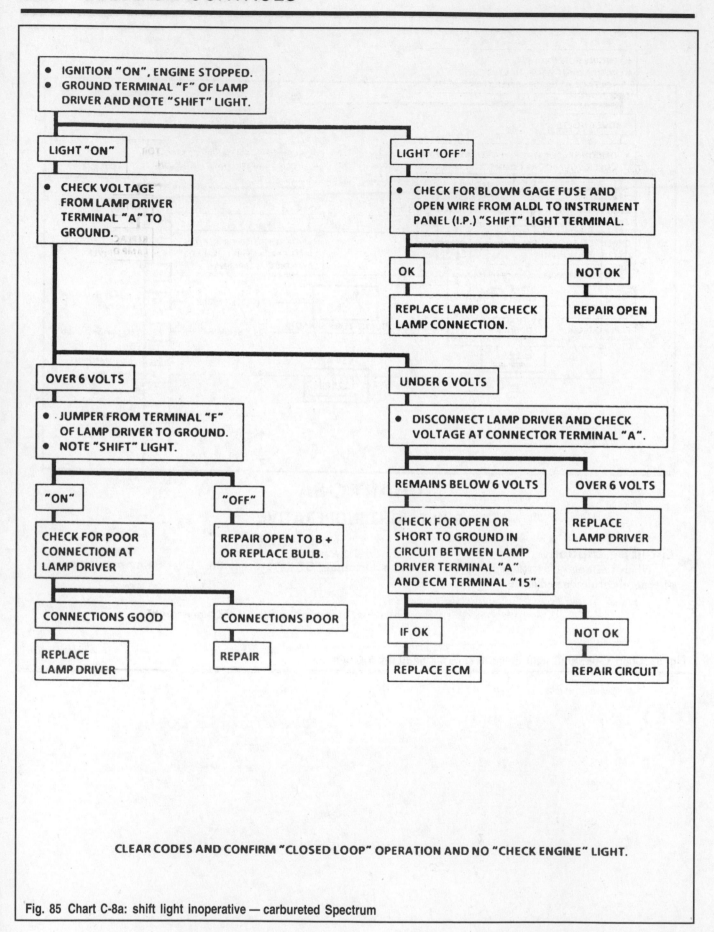

- IGNITION "ON", ENGINE STOPPED.
- GROUND TERMINAL "F" OF LAMP DRIVER AND NOTE "SHIFT" LIGHT.

LIGHT "ON"

- CHECK VOLTAGE FROM LAMP DRIVER TERMINAL "A" TO GROUND.

LIGHT "OFF"

- CHECK FOR BLOWN GAGE FUSE AND OPEN WIRE FROM ALDL TO INSTRUMENT PANEL (I.P.) "SHIFT" LIGHT TERMINAL.

OK

REPLACE LAMP OR CHECK LAMP CONNECTION.

NOT OK

REPAIR OPEN

OVER 6 VOLTS

- JUMPER FROM TERMINAL "F" OF LAMP DRIVER TO GROUND.
- NOTE "SHIFT" LIGHT.

UNDER 6 VOLTS

- DISCONNECT LAMP DRIVER AND CHECK VOLTAGE AT CONNECTOR TERMINAL "A".

"ON"

CHECK FOR POOR CONNECTION AT LAMP DRIVER

"OFF"

REPAIR OPEN TO B + OR REPLACE BULB.

REMAINS BELOW 6 VOLTS

CHECK FOR OPEN OR SHORT TO GROUND IN CIRCUIT BETWEEN LAMP DRIVER TERMINAL "A" AND ECM TERMINAL "15".

OVER 6 VOLTS

REPLACE LAMP DRIVER

CONNECTIONS GOOD

REPLACE LAMP DRIVER

CONNECTIONS POOR

REPAIR

IF OK

REPLACE ECM

NOT OK

REPAIR CIRCUIT

CLEAR CODES AND CONFIRM "CLOSED LOOP" OPERATION AND NO "CHECK ENGINE" LIGHT.

Fig. 85 Chart C-8a: shift light inoperative — carbureted Spectrum

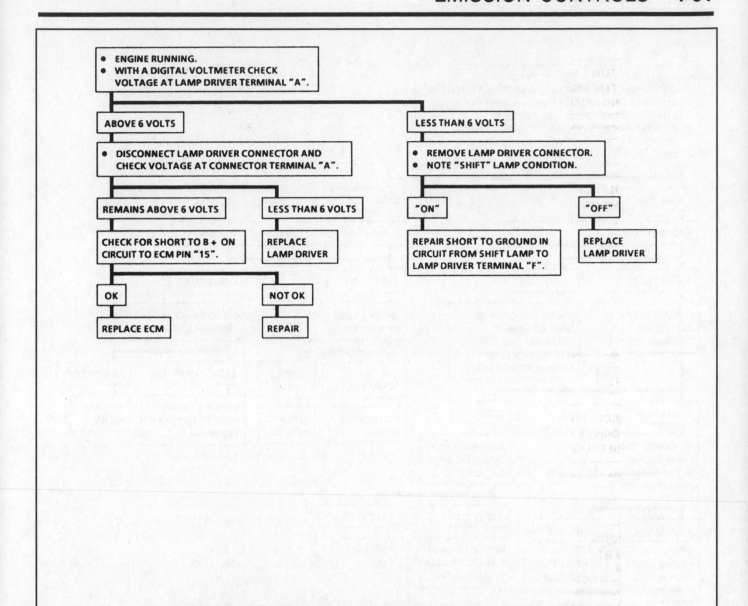

Fig. 86 Chart C-8b: shift light on at all times — carbureted Spectrum

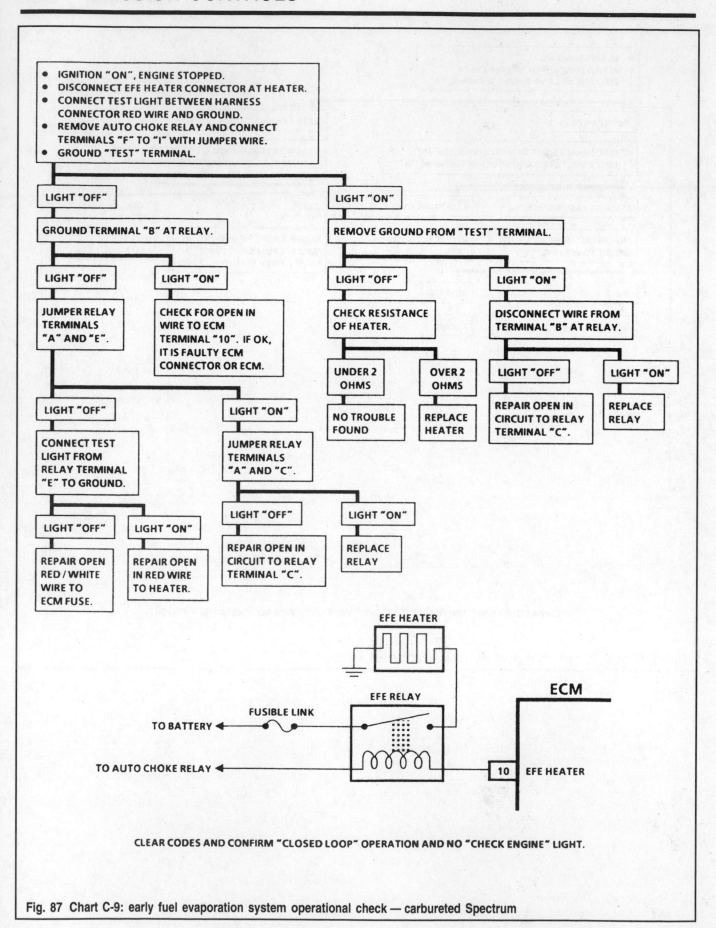

Fig. 87 Chart C-9: early fuel evaporation system operational check — carbureted Spectrum

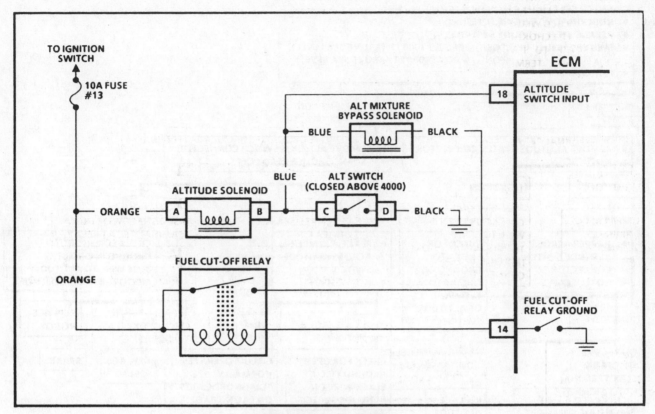

CHART C-16A

HIGH ALTITUDE EMISSION CONTROL SYSTEM
(ALTITUDE SWITCH CIRCUIT CHECK)

Circuit Description:

At high altitudes (above 4000 ft.) the Altitude Sensing Switch will close the circuits between the battery and the Altitude Mixture Bypass Solenoid and the Altitude Solenoid.

The Altitude Solenoid Valve will open the passage between the air cleaner and the carburetor. At this time the Mixture Bypass Solenoid Valve will be activated and will open the port for additional air/fuel mixture to stabilize RPM.

The Altitude Switch is:
- Closed at high altitude and,
- Open at low altitude.

Test Description: Numbers below refer to circled numbers on the diagnostic chart.

1. Determines whether Altitude Switch is functioning normally.
2. Looks for faulty Altitude Solenoid.
3. Determines if ECM is faulty.

Diagnostic Aids:

If High Altitude circuit malfunctions at **very high altitude**, Code 45 may be stored.
- If engine operation is badly affected, carburetor passages may be plugged.

Fig. 88 Chart C-16a: high altitude emission control system functional check — carbureted Spectrum

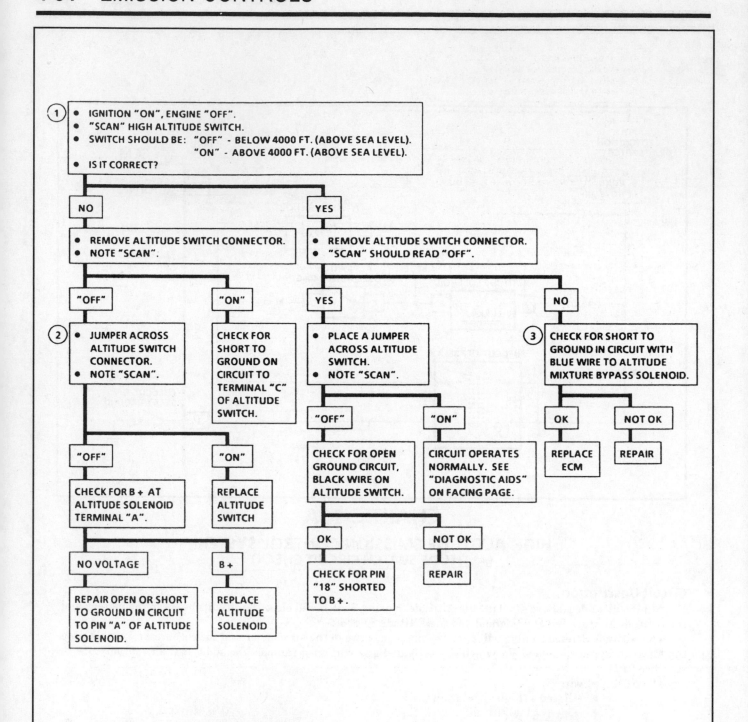

①
- IGNITION "ON", ENGINE "OFF".
- "SCAN" HIGH ALTITUDE SWITCH.
- SWITCH SHOULD BE: "OFF" - BELOW 4000 FT. (ABOVE SEA LEVEL).
  "ON" - ABOVE 4000 FT. (ABOVE SEA LEVEL).
- IS IT CORRECT?

NO
- REMOVE ALTITUDE SWITCH CONNECTOR.
- NOTE "SCAN".

YES
- REMOVE ALTITUDE SWITCH CONNECTOR.
- "SCAN" SHOULD READ "OFF".

"OFF"

②
- JUMPER ACROSS ALTITUDE SWITCH CONNECTOR.
- NOTE "SCAN".

"ON"
CHECK FOR SHORT TO GROUND ON CIRCUIT TO TERMINAL "C" OF ALTITUDE SWITCH.

YES
- PLACE A JUMPER ACROSS ALTITUDE SWITCH.
- NOTE "SCAN".

NO

③
CHECK FOR SHORT TO GROUND IN CIRCUIT WITH BLUE WIRE TO ALTITUDE MIXTURE BYPASS SOLENOID.

"OFF"
CHECK FOR B + AT ALTITUDE SOLENOID TERMINAL "A".

"ON"
REPLACE ALTITUDE SWITCH

"OFF"
CHECK FOR OPEN GROUND CIRCUIT, BLACK WIRE ON ALTITUDE SWITCH.

"ON"
CIRCUIT OPERATES NORMALLY. SEE "DIAGNOSTIC AIDS" ON FACING PAGE.

OK
REPLACE ECM

NOT OK
REPAIR

NO VOLTAGE
REPAIR OPEN OR SHORT TO GROUND IN CIRCUIT TO PIN "A" OF ALTITUDE SOLENOID.

B +
REPLACE ALTITUDE SOLENOID

OK
CHECK FOR PIN "18" SHORTED TO B +.

NOT OK
REPAIR

CLEAR CODES AND CONFIRM "CLOSED LOOP" OPERATION AND NO "CHECK ENGINE" LIGHT.

Fig. 89 Chart C-16a: high altitude emission control system functional check — carbureted Spectrum

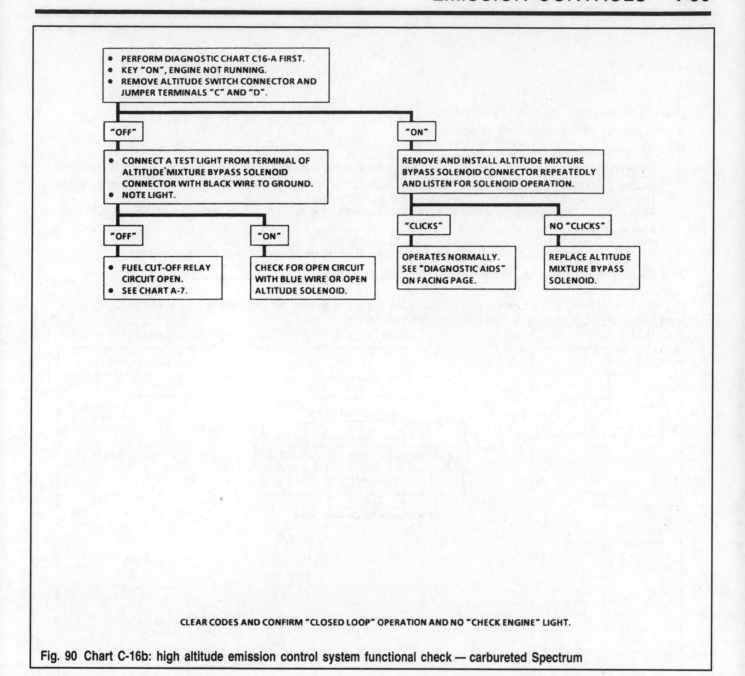

- PERFORM DIAGNOSTIC CHART C16-A FIRST.
- KEY "ON", ENGINE NOT RUNNING.
- REMOVE ALTITUDE SWITCH CONNECTOR AND JUMPER TERMINALS "C" AND "D".

"OFF"

- CONNECT A TEST LIGHT FROM TERMINAL OF ALTITUDE MIXTURE BYPASS SOLENOID CONNECTOR WITH BLACK WIRE TO GROUND.
- NOTE LIGHT.

"OFF"

- FUEL CUT-OFF RELAY CIRCUIT OPEN.
- SEE CHART A-7.

"ON"

CHECK FOR OPEN CIRCUIT WITH BLUE WIRE OR OPEN ALTITUDE SOLENOID.

"ON"

REMOVE AND INSTALL ALTITUDE MIXTURE BYPASS SOLENOID CONNECTOR REPEATEDLY AND LISTEN FOR SOLENOID OPERATION.

"CLICKS"

OPERATES NORMALLY. SEE "DIAGNOSTIC AIDS" ON FACING PAGE.

NO "CLICKS"

REPLACE ALTITUDE MIXTURE BYPASS SOLENOID.

CLEAR CODES AND CONFIRM "CLOSED LOOP" OPERATION AND NO "CHECK ENGINE" LIGHT.

Fig. 90 Chart C-16b: high altitude emission control system functional check — carbureted Spectrum

Code 13 will set under the following conditions:

- Engine at normal operating temperature
- At least 2 minutes after engine start.
- O_2 signal voltage at terminal M2-23 of ECM steadily reading between 0.35 and 0.55 volts for more than one minute. The ECM supplies a voltage of about 0.5 volts between terminals M2-23 and M2-22. (If measured with a 10 megohm digital voltmeter, this may read as low as 0.32 volts).
The O_2 sensor varies voltage within a range of about 1 volt if the exhaust is rich, down through about 0.10 volts if exhaust is lean.

- Throttle position sensor signal above 7 % (about 0.35 volts above closed throttle voltage.)
- All conditions must be met for about 60 seconds.

The sensor acts like an open circuit and produces no voltage when the temperature is below 360°C (600°F). An open sensor circuit or cold sensor causes open loop operation.

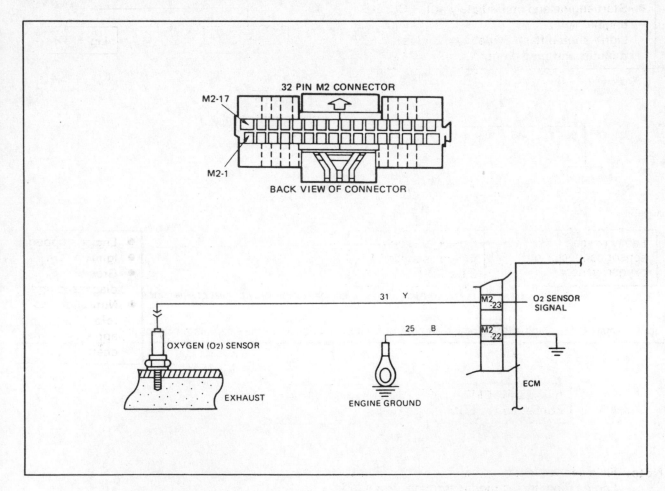

Fig. 91 Code 13: oxygen sensor circuit open — turbo Spectrum

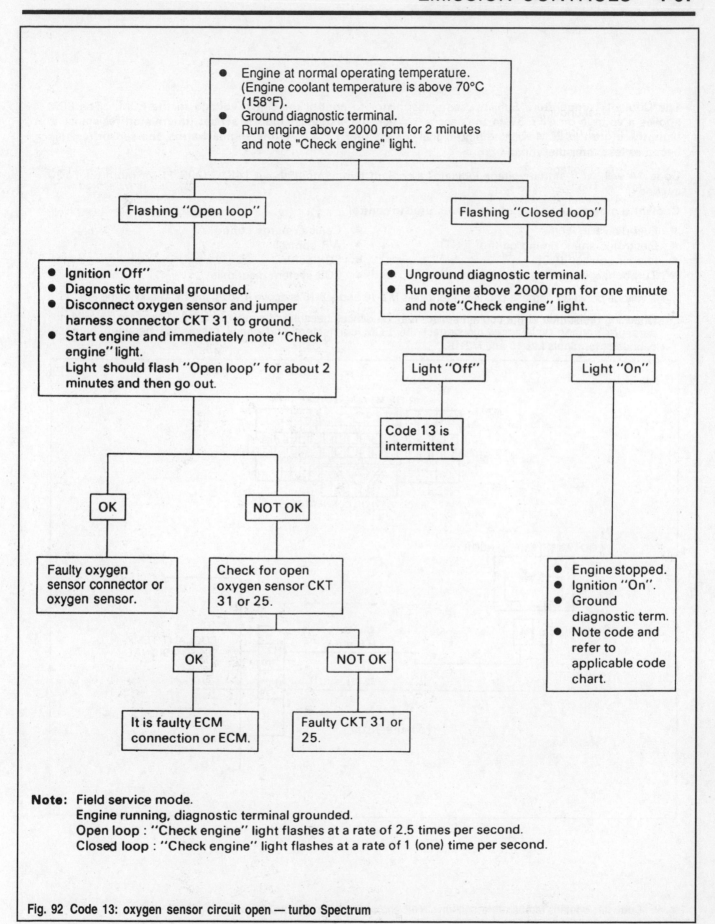

Fig. 92 Code 13: oxygen sensor circuit open — turbo Spectrum

The Coolant Temperature Sensor uses a thermistor to control the signal voltage to the ECM. The ECM applies a voltage on CKT 37 to the sensor. When the engine is cold the sensor (thermistor) resistance is high, therefore the ECM will see high signal voltage on CKT 37. As the engine warms, the sensor resistance becomes less, and the voltage drops.

Code 14 will set if signal voltage indicates a coolant temperature above 145°C (293°F) for more than 120 seconds.

Coolant temperature is one of the inputs used to control:

- Fuel delivery
- Electronic spark timing control (EST)
- Idle air control (IAC)
- Turbocharger wastegate control

- Canister purge control
- AIR control
- EGR control
- EGR system diagnosis

1. If voltage between harness connector terminals M2-10 and M2-18 is above 4 volts, the ECM and wiring are OK.

2. Checking resistance at the coolant sensor may be difficult because of sensor location. Therefore, in order to measure sensor resistance, disconnect the ECM connectors and check resistance between harness connector terminals M2-10 and M2-18.

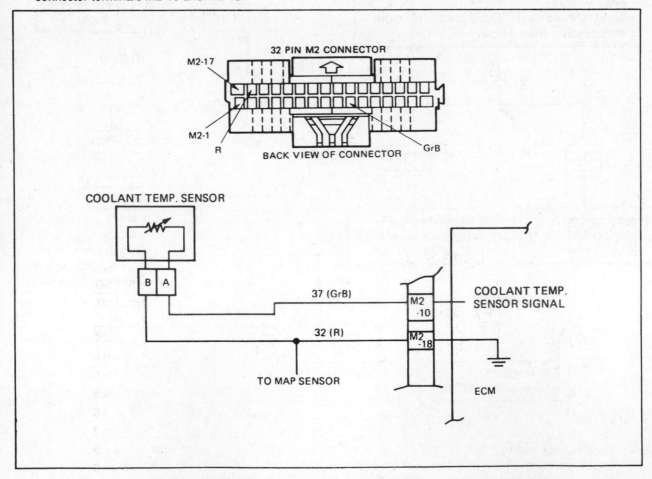

Fig. 93 Code 14: coolant temperature sensor circuit shorted — turbo Spectrum

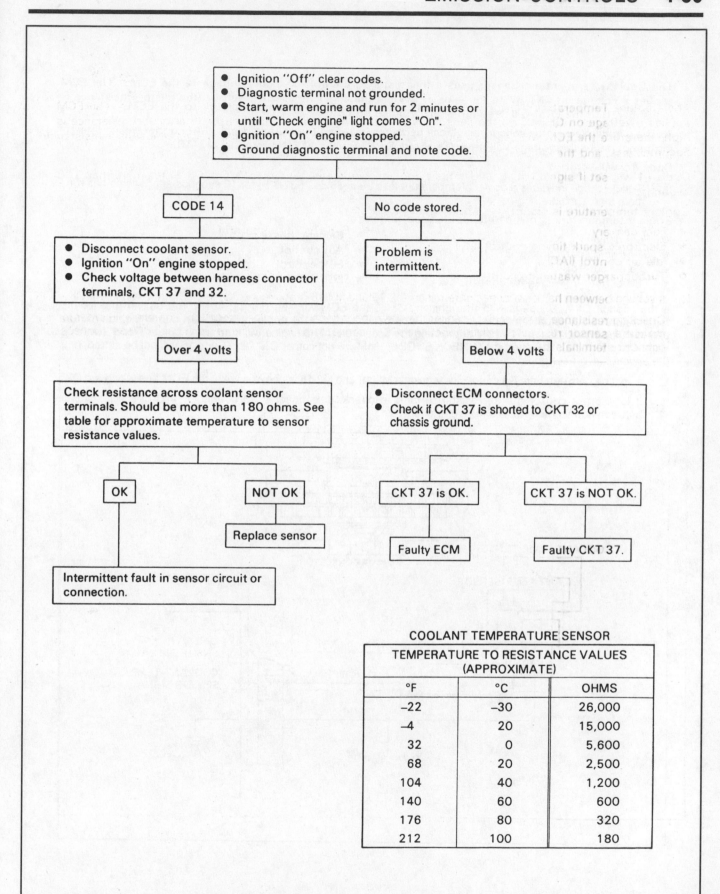

- Ignition "Off" clear codes.
- Diagnostic terminal not grounded.
- Start, warm engine and run for 2 minutes or until "Check engine" light comes "On".
- Ignition "On" engine stopped.
- Ground diagnostic terminal and note code.

CODE 14

No code stored.

- Disconnect coolant sensor.
- Ignition "On" engine stopped.
- Check voltage between harness connector terminals, CKT 37 and 32.

Problem is intermittent.

Over 4 volts

Below 4 volts

Check resistance across coolant sensor terminals. Should be more than 180 ohms. See table for approximate temperature to sensor resistance values.

- Disconnect ECM connectors.
- Check if CKT 37 is shorted to CKT 32 or chassis ground.

OK

NOT OK

CKT 37 is OK.

CKT 37 is NOT OK.

Replace sensor

Faulty ECM

Faulty CKT 37.

Intermittent fault in sensor circuit or connection.

COOLANT TEMPERATURE SENSOR

TEMPERATURE TO RESISTANCE VALUES (APPROXIMATE)		
°F	°C	OHMS
–22	–30	26,000
–4	20	15,000
32	0	5,600
68	20	2,500
104	40	1,200
140	60	600
176	80	320
212	100	180

Fig. 94 Code 14: coolant temperature sensor circuit shorted — turbo Spectrum

The Coolant Temperature Sensor uses a thermistor to control the signal voltage to the ECM. The ECM applies a voltage on CKT 37 to the sensor. When the engine is cold the sensor (thermistor) resistance is high, therefore the ECM will see high signal voltage on CKT 37.

As the engine warms, the sensor resistance becomes less, and the voltage drops. At normal engine operating temperature the voltage will measure about 1 to 1.5 volts at ECM terminal M2-10.

Code 15 will set if:

● Signal voltage indicates a coolant temperature less than -38.5°C (-37.3°F) for 10 seconds after engine has run more than 1 minute.

Coolant temperature is one of the inputs used to control:

● Fuel delivery
● Electronic spark timing (EST)
● Idle air control (IAC)
● Turbocharger wastegate control

● Canister purge control
● AIR control
● EGR control
● EGR system diagnostic

If the coolant CKT 37 opens with the ignition "OFF", the ECM will see -40°C (-40°F) and deliver fuel for this temperature. If the actual temperature is above approx. -7°C (20°F) the engine will not start due to the rich mixture unless "Clear Flood" is used by fully depressing the accelerator. The engine will start using "Clear Flood" (which is Wide Open Throttle). However, the "CHECK ENGINE" light will not come "ON", and Code 15 will not be stored, until the engine has run for one minute.

1. If voltage between harness connector terminals M2-10 and M2-18 is above 4 volts, the ECM and wiring are OK.

2. If location of sensor makes resistance hard to check, disconnect ECM connector and check resistance between connector terminals M2-10 and M2-18.

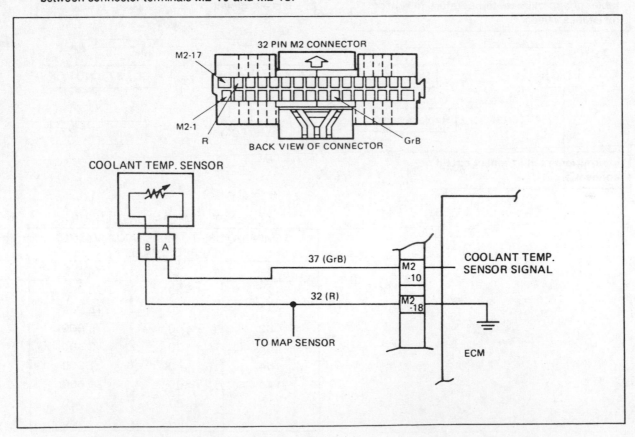

Fig. 95 Code 15: coolant temperature sensor circuit open — turbo Spectrum

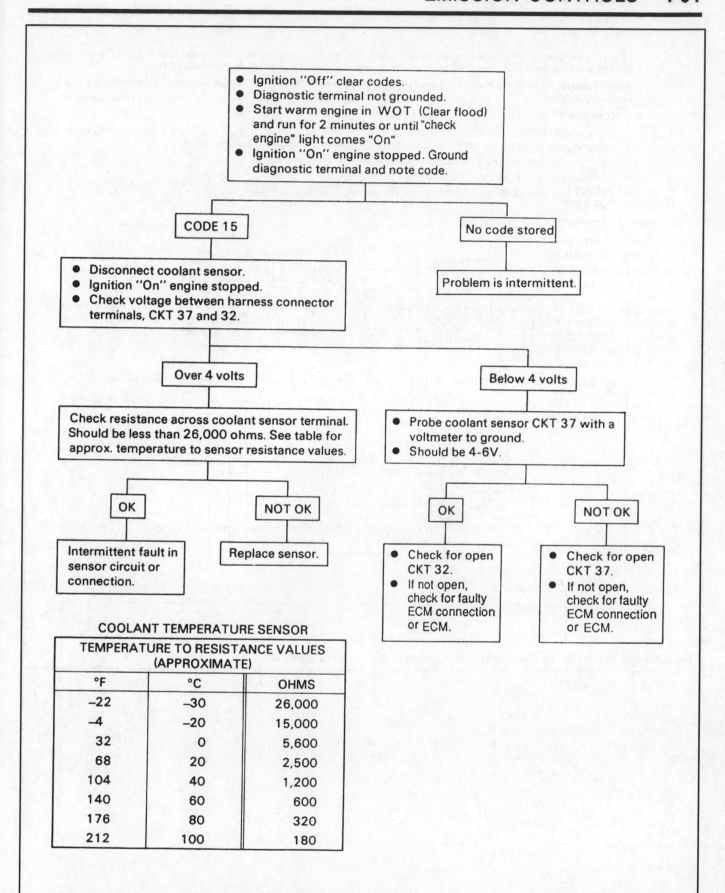

- Ignition "Off" clear codes.
- Diagnostic terminal not grounded.
- Start warm engine in WOT (Clear flood) and run for 2 minutes or until "check engine" light comes "On"
- Ignition "On" engine stopped. Ground diagnostic terminal and note code.

CODE 15

- Disconnect coolant sensor.
- Ignition "On" engine stopped.
- Check voltage between harness connector terminals, CKT 37 and 32.

No code stored

Problem is intermittent.

Over 4 volts

Check resistance across coolant sensor terminal. Should be less than 26,000 ohms. See table for approx. temperature to sensor resistance values.

Below 4 volts

- Probe coolant sensor CKT 37 with a voltmeter to ground.
- Should be 4-6V.

OK

Intermittent fault in sensor circuit or connection.

NOT OK

Replace sensor.

OK

- Check for open CKT 32.
- If not open, check for faulty ECM connection or ECM.

NOT OK

- Check for open CKT 37.
- If not open, check for faulty ECM connection or ECM.

COOLANT TEMPERATURE SENSOR

TEMPERATURE TO RESISTANCE VALUES (APPROXIMATE)		
°F	°C	OHMS
–22	–30	26,000
–4	–20	15,000
32	0	5,600
68	20	2,500
104	40	1,200
140	60	600
176	80	320
212	100	180

Fig. 96 Code 15: coolant temperature sensor circuit open — turbo Spectrum

The Throttle Sensor (TPS) provides a voltage signal that changes relative to the throttle valve. Signal voltage will vary from less than 0.45 volts at idle to about 4.0 volts at wide open throttle (WOT).

The TPS signal is one of the most important inputs used by the ECM for fuel control and for many of the ECM controlled outputs.

Code 21 will set if:

- TPS signal voltage is greater than 4.7 volts for 5 seconds.
- Engine speed is less than 1200 rpm. This is the purpose for placing shift lever in "Drive."
- MAP is less than 50 kPa (7.5 psi) or equal to a no load condition.

1. Confirms Code 21, and that fault is present.
2. Simulates Code 22: If the ECM recognizes the low signal voltage and sets Code 22 the ECM and wiring are OK.

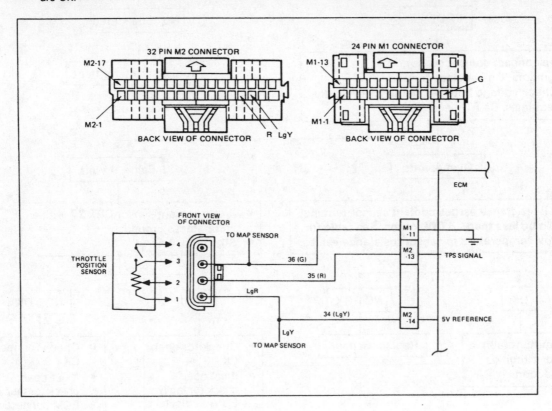

Fig. 97 Code 21: throttle position sensor signal voltage high — turbo Spectrum

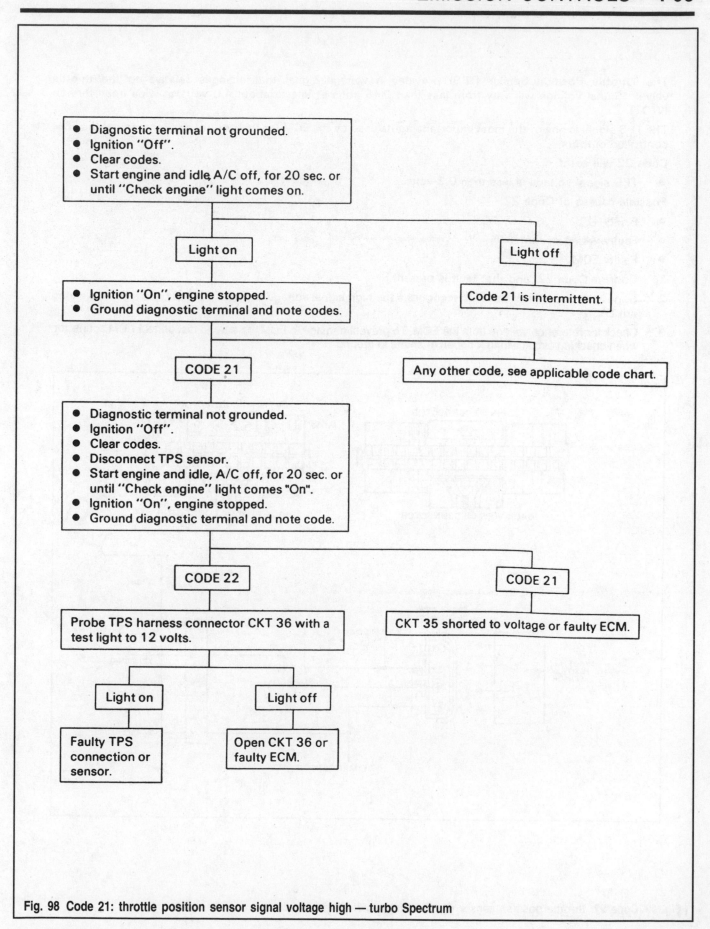

Fig. 98 Code 21: throttle position sensor signal voltage high — turbo Spectrum

The Throttle Position Sensor (TPS) provides a voltage signal that changes relative to the throttle valve. Signal voltage will vary from less than 0.45 volts at idle to about 4.0 volts at wide open throttle (WOT).

The TPS signal is one of the most important inputs used by the ECM for fuel control and for many of the ECM controlled outputs.

Code 22 will set if:

- TPS signal voltage is less than 0.2 volts.

Possible causes of Code 22:

- Faulty TPS
- Faulty wiring or terminals
- Faulty ECM

1. Confirm Code 22, and that fault is present.

2. Simulates Code 21: If the ECM recognizes the high signal voltage and sets Code 21 the ECM and wiring are OK.

3. Check for reference voltage from the ECM. To prevent damage to ECM, be sure to disconnect ECM connector when checking circuit wiring for open or shorts to ground.

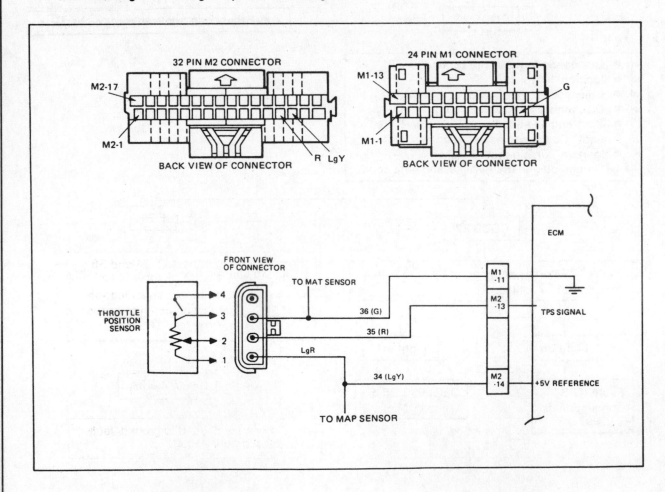

Fig. 99 Code 22: throttle position sensor signal voltage low — turbo Spectrum

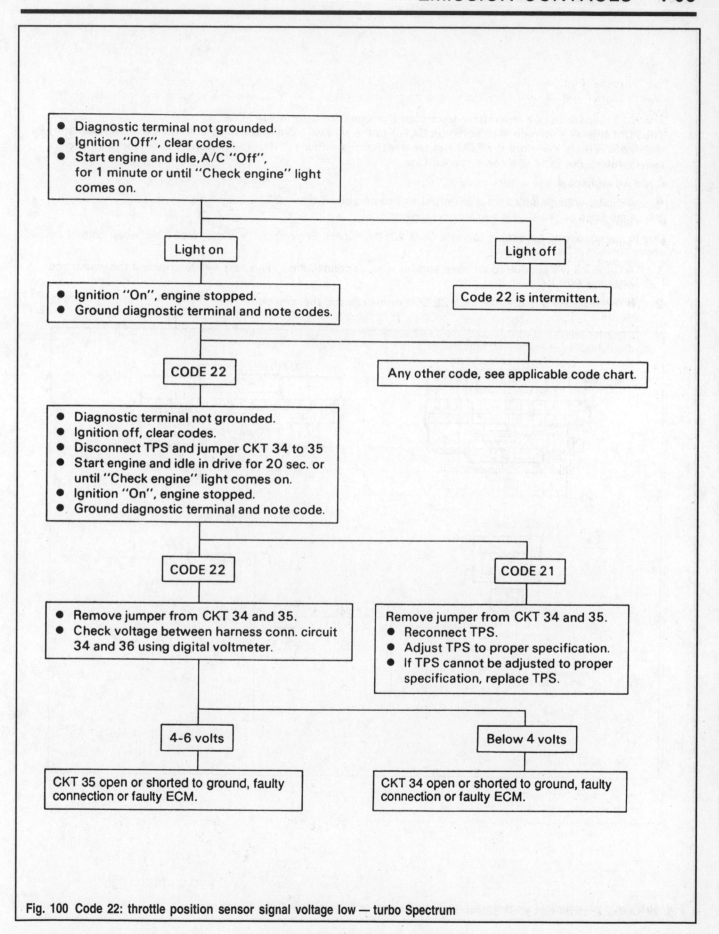

Fig. 100 Code 22: throttle position sensor signal voltage low — turbo Spectrum

The MAT Sensor uses a thermistor to control the signal voltage to the ECM.

The ECM applies a voltage (4-6 volts) on CKT 9 to the sensor. When the air is cold the sensor (thermistor) resistance is high, therefore the ECM will see a high signal voltage. If the air is warm the sensor resistance is low therefore the ECM will see a low voltage.

Code 23 will set if:

● A signal voltage indicates a manifold air temperature below –38°C (–36.4°F).
● Time since engine start is 1 minute or longer.

Due to the conditions necessary to set a Code 23, the "Check Engine" light will only stay "ON" when both of the above conditions have been met.

1. A Code 23 will set due to an open sensor, wire, or connection. This test will determine if the wiring and ECM are OK.

2. If the resistance is greater than 25,000 ohms replace the sensor.

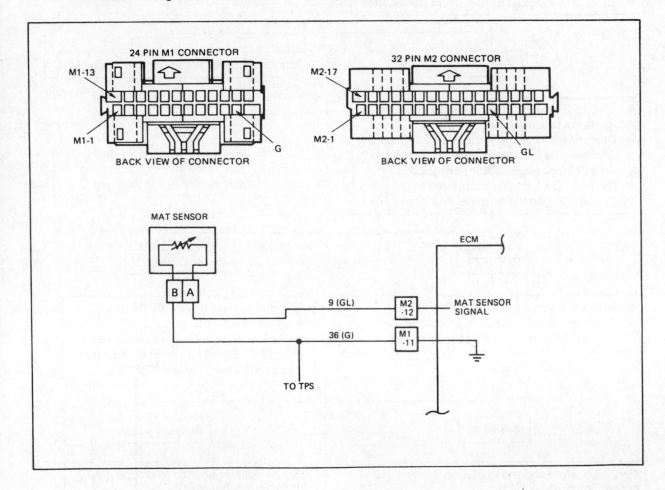

Fig. 101 Code 23: manifold air temperature sensor signal voltage high — turbo Spectrum

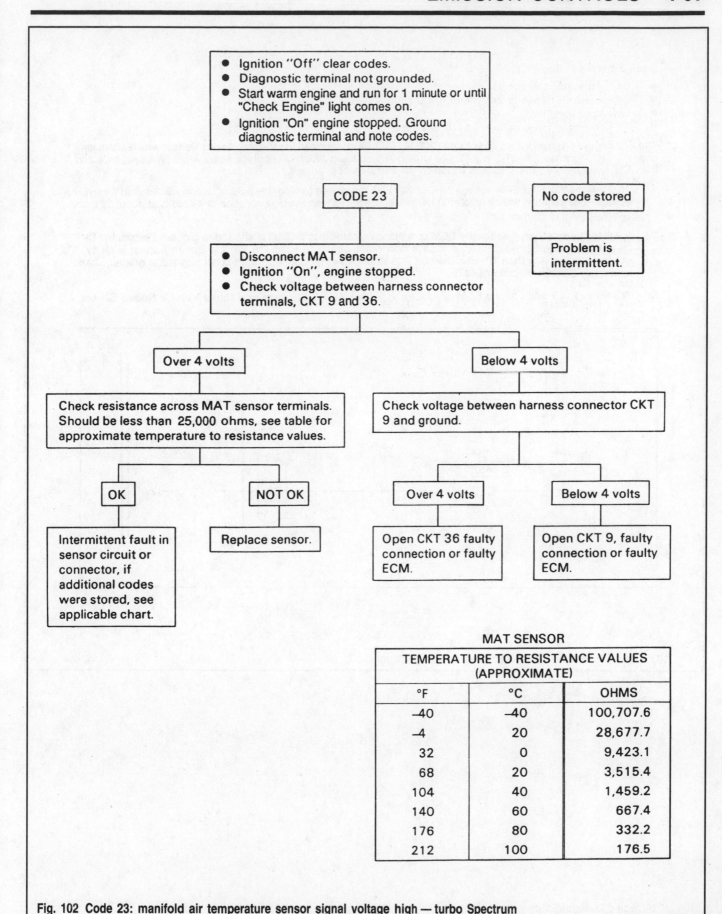

Fig. 102 Code 23: manifold air temperature sensor signal voltage high — turbo Spectrum

Code 24 will set if:

- CKT 38 voltage is constant.
- Engine speed between 2400 and 4400 rpm.
- Low load condition.
- All conditions must be met for 10 seconds.

The ECM applies and monitors 12 volts on CKT 38. CKT 38 connects to the Vehicle Speed Sensor which alternately grounds CKT 38 when the drive wheels are turning. This pulsing action takes place about 4096 times per mile and the ECM will calculate vehicle speeds based on the time between "pulses".

1. This test monitors the ECM voltage on CKT 38. With the wheels turning, the pulsing action will result in a varying voltage. The variation will be greater at low wheel speeds with an average variation of 4-6 volts at about 20 mph. (32 km/h).

2. A voltage of less than 1 volt at the ECM connector indicates that CKT 38 is shorted to ground. Disconnect CKT 38 at the Vehicle Speed Sensor. If voltage now reads above 10 volts, the Vehicle Speed Sensor is faulty. If voltage remains less than 10 volts, then CKT 38 is shorted to ground. If CKT 38 is not shorted to ground, check for a faulty ECM connector or ECM.

3. A steady 8-12 volts at the ECM connector indicates CKT 38 is open or a faulty Vehicle Speed Sensor.

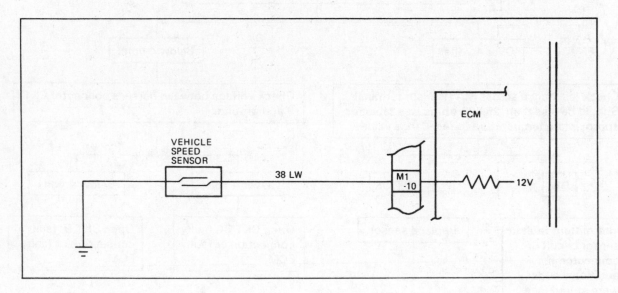

Fig. 103 Code 24: vehicle speed sensor — turbo Spectrum

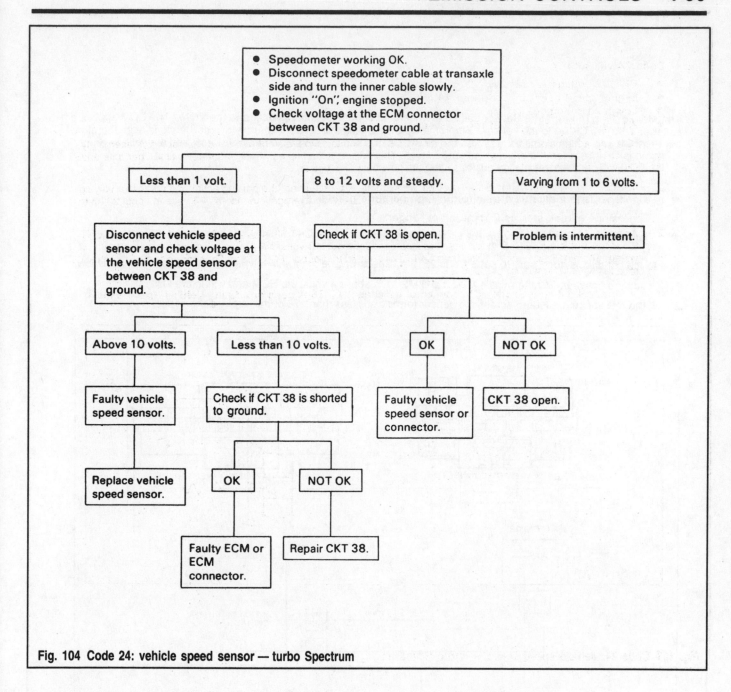

Fig. 104 Code 24: vehicle speed sensor — turbo Spectrum

The Manifold Air Temperature Sensor uses a thermistor to control the signal-voltage to the ECM. The ECM applies a voltage (4-6V) on CKT 9 to the sensor. When manifold air is cold the sensor (Thermistor) resistance is high, therefore the ECM will see a high signal voltage. As the air warms, the sensor resistance becomes less, and the voltage drops.

Code 25 will set if:

- Signal voltage indicates a manifold air temperature greater than 145°C (293°F).
- Time since engine start is 2 minutes or longer.
- Turbocharger wastegate control is not operated.

Due to the conditions necessary to set a Code 25, the "Check Engine" light will only remain on while the signal is low.

1. If voltage between ECM terminals M2-12 and M2-11 is above 4 volts, the ECM and wiring are OK.
2. If the resistance measured across the sensor terminals is less than 176 ohms, replace the sensor.

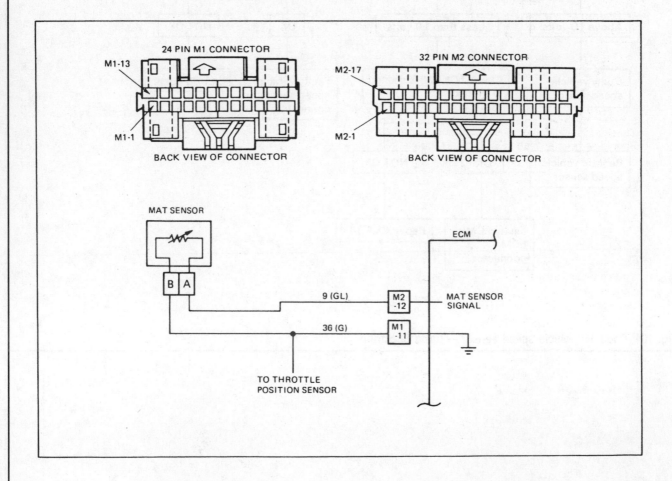

Fig. 105 Code 25: manifold -->air temperature sensor signal voltage low — turbo Spectrum

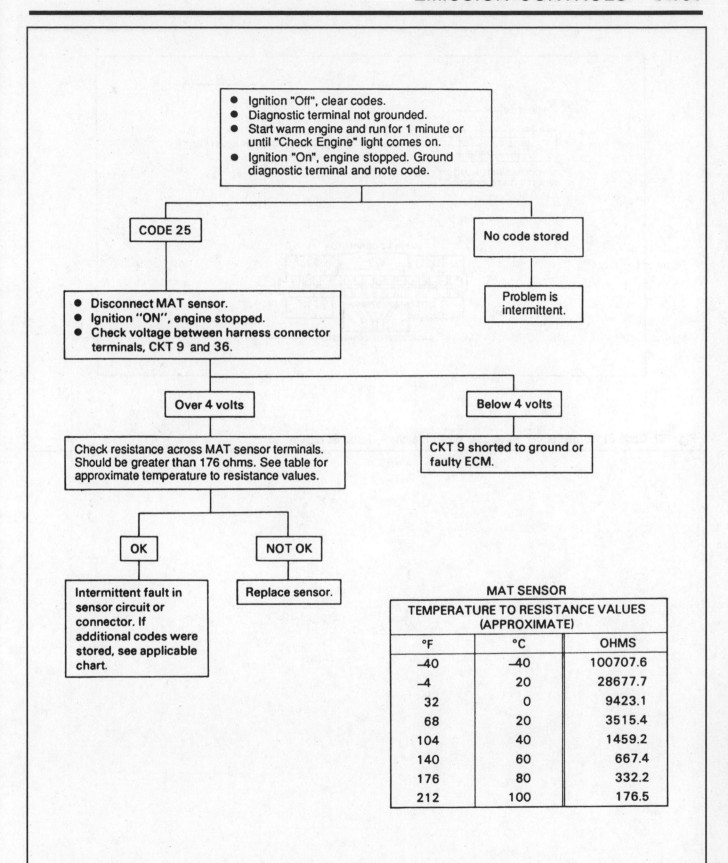

- Ignition "Off", clear codes.
- Diagnostic terminal not grounded.
- Start warm engine and run for 1 minute or until "Check Engine" light comes on.
- Ignition "On", engine stopped. Ground diagnostic terminal and note code.

CODE 25

No code stored

- Disconnect MAT sensor.
- Ignition "ON", engine stopped.
- Check voltage between harness connector terminals, CKT 9 and 36.

Problem is intermittent.

Over 4 volts

Below 4 volts

Check resistance across MAT sensor terminals. Should be greater than 176 ohms. See table for approximate temperature to resistance values.

CKT 9 shorted to ground or faulty ECM.

OK

NOT OK

Intermittent fault in sensor circuit or connector. If additional codes were stored, see applicable chart.

Replace sensor.

MAT SENSOR

TEMPERATURE TO RESISTANCE VALUES (APPROXIMATE)		
°F	°C	OHMS
−40	−40	100707.6
−4	20	28677.7
32	0	9423.1
68	20	3515.4
104	40	1459.2
140	60	667.4
176	80	332.2
212	100	176.5

Fig. 106 Code 25: manifold air temperature sensor signal voltage low — turbo Spectrum

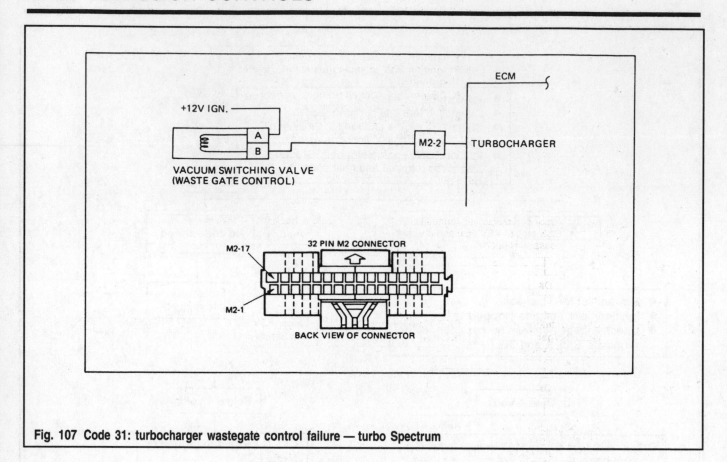

Fig. 107 Code 31: turbocharger wastegate control failure — turbo Spectrum

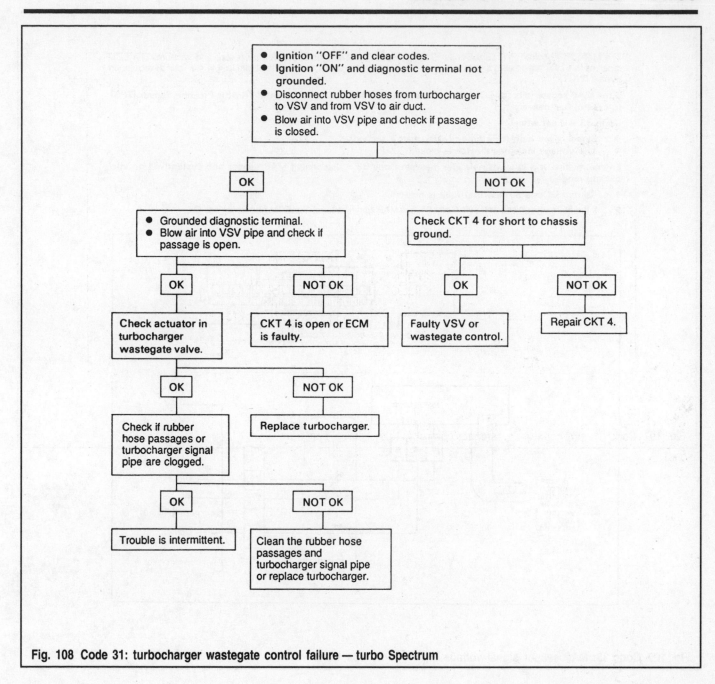

Fig. 108 Code 31: turbocharger wastegate control failure — turbo Spectrum

The Manifold Absolute Pressure Sensor (MAP) responds to changes in manifold pressure and vacuum. The ECM receives this information as a signal voltage that will vary from about 1 to 1.5 volts at idle to 4 to 4.5 volts at wide open throttle (WOT).

If the MAP sensor fails, the ECM will substitute a fixed MAP value and use the Throttle Position Sensor (TPS) to control fuel delivery.

Code 33 will set when:

- Signal is too high for a time greater than 5 seconds.
- TPS voltage indicates throttle is closed.

Engine misfire or a low unstable idle may set Code 33. Disconnect MAP sensor and system will go into backup mode.

1. Confirms Code 33 and that fault is present.

2. If the ECM recognizes and sets Code 34, low MAP signal voltage, the ECM and wiring are OK.

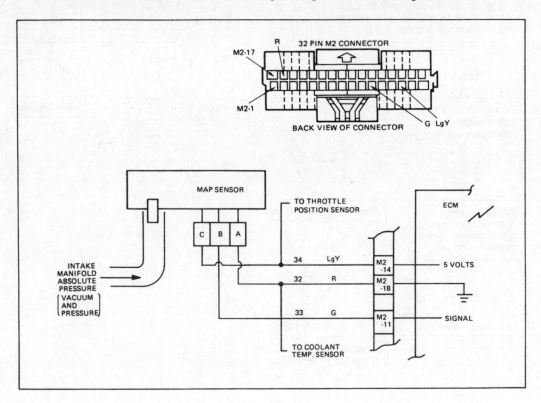

Fig. 109 Code 33: MAP sensor signal voltage high — turbo Spectrum

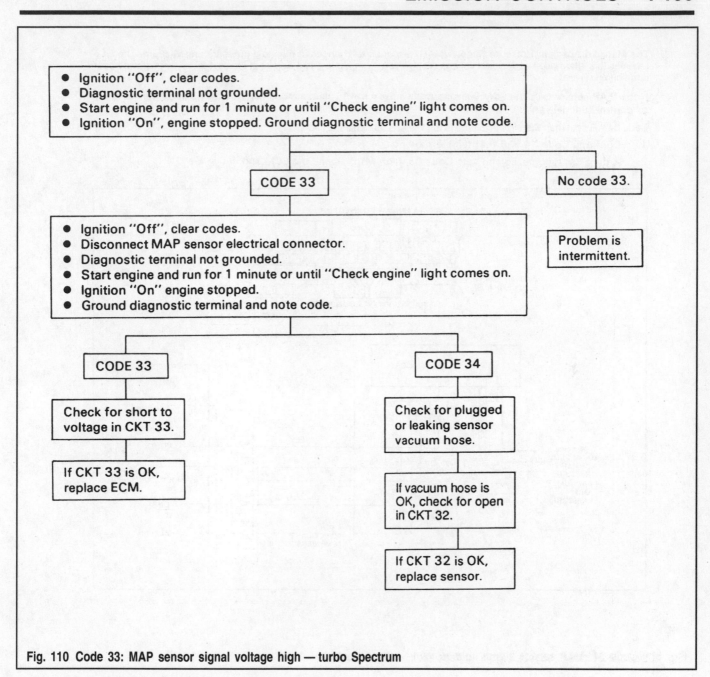

Fig. 110 Code 33: MAP sensor signal voltage high — turbo Spectrum

The Manifold Absolute Pressure Sensor (MAP) responds to changes in manifold pressure and vacuum. The ECM receives this information as a signal voltage that will vary from about 1 to 1.5 volts at idle to 4 to 4.5 volts at wide open throttle (WOT).

If the MAP sensor fails the ECM will substitute a fixed MAP value and use the Throttle Position Sensor (TPS) to control fuel delivery.

Code 34 will set when the signal voltage is too low and the ignition is "ON".

1. Confirms Code 34 and that fault is present.
2. If the ECM recognizes and sets Code 33, high MAP signal, the ECM and wiring are OK.

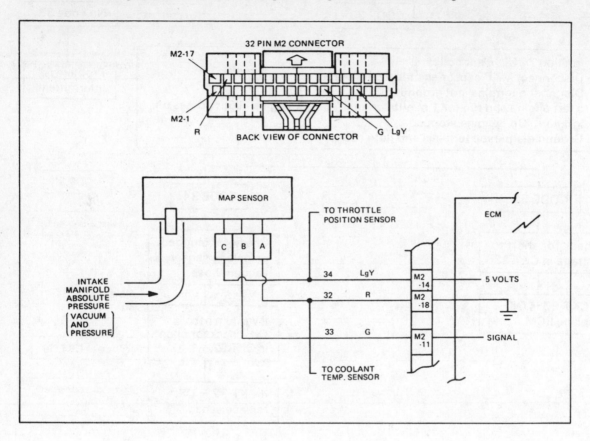

Fig. 111 Code 34: MAP sensor signal voltage low — turbo Spectrum

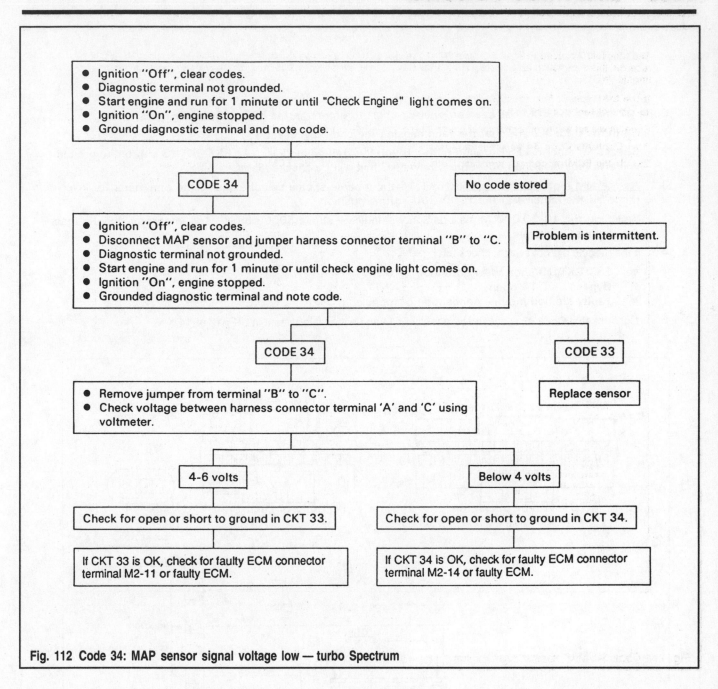

- Ignition "Off", clear codes.
- Diagnostic terminal not grounded.
- Start engine and run for 1 minute or until "Check Engine" light comes on.
- Ignition "On", engine stopped.
- Ground diagnostic terminal and note code.

CODE 34   No code stored

- Ignition "Off", clear codes.
- Disconnect MAP sensor and jumper harness connector terminal "B" to "C.
- Diagnostic terminal not grounded.
- Start engine and run for 1 minute or until check engine light comes on.
- Ignition "On", engine stopped.
- Grounded diagnostic terminal and note code.

Problem is intermittent.

CODE 34   CODE 33

- Remove jumper from terminal "B" to "C".
- Check voltage between harness connector terminal 'A' and 'C' using voltmeter.

Replace sensor

4-6 volts   Below 4 volts

Check for open or short to ground in CKT 33.   Check for open or short to ground in CKT 34.

If CKT 33 is OK, check for faulty ECM connector terminal M2-11 or faulty ECM.   If CKT 34 is OK, check for faulty ECM connector terminal M2-14 or faulty ECM.

Fig. 112 Code 34: MAP sensor signal voltage low — turbo Spectrum

Code 42 means the ECM has seen an open or short to ground in the EST or bypass circuits.

1. Confirms Code 42 and that the fault causing the code is present.

2. Checks for a normal EST ground path through the ignition module.   An EST CKT 13 shorted to ground will also read less than 500 ohms; however, this will be checked later.

3. As the test high voltage touches CKT 14 the module should switch causing the ohmmeter to "over-range" if the meter is in the 1000-2000 ohms position.

   Selecting the 10-20,000 ohms position will indicate above 5000 ohms.   The important thing is that the module "switched".

4. If the module did not switch, check for:

   • EST CKT 13 shorted to ground.
   • Bypass CKT 14 open.
   • Faulty ignition module connection or module.

5. Confirms that Code 42 is caused by a faulty ECM and not an intermittent in CKT 13 or 14.

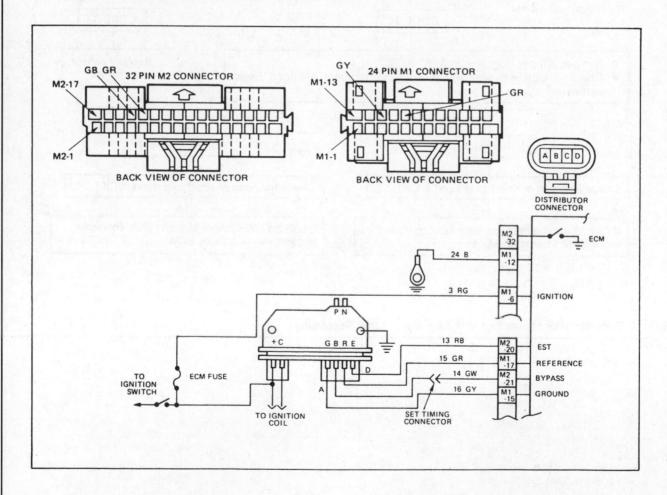

Fig. 113 Code 42: electronic spark timing — turbo Spectrum

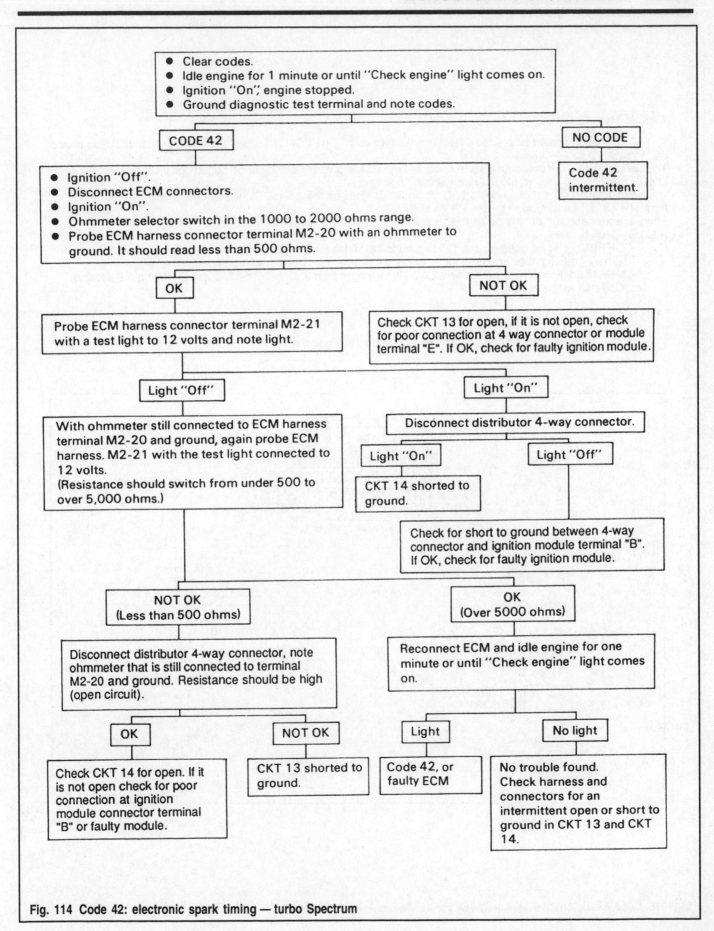

Fig. 114 Code 42: electronic spark timing — turbo Spectrum

Circuit Description;

The detonation sensor is used to detect engine detonation. The ECM will retard the electronic spark timing based on the signal being received.

The circuity, within the detonation sensor, causes the ECM's 5 volt reference to be pulled down so that under a no knock condition, CKT 26 would measure about 2.5 volts.

The detonation sensor produces an AC signal, which rides on the 2.5 volt DC signal. The amplitude and signal frequency is dependent upon the knock level.

There are two tests run on this circuit by the ECM to determine if it is operating correctly.

A Code 43 will be set if:

- CKT 26 becomes open, or shorted to ground the voltage will either go above 3.5 volts or below 1.5 volts. If either of these conditions are met for about 0.6 seconds, a code 43 will be stored.
- The detonation sensor produces an AC signal longer then 3.67 seconds in duration, during 3.9 second. Code 43 will be stored.

The tests are performed when;

Coolant temp. is over 50°C (122°F).

High engine load based on MAP and rpm between 1000 and 5800.

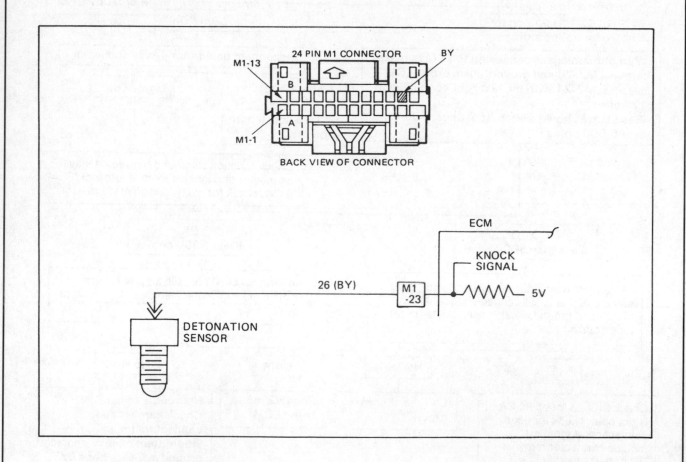

Fig. 115 Code 43: detonation sensor/knock control failure — turbo Spectrum

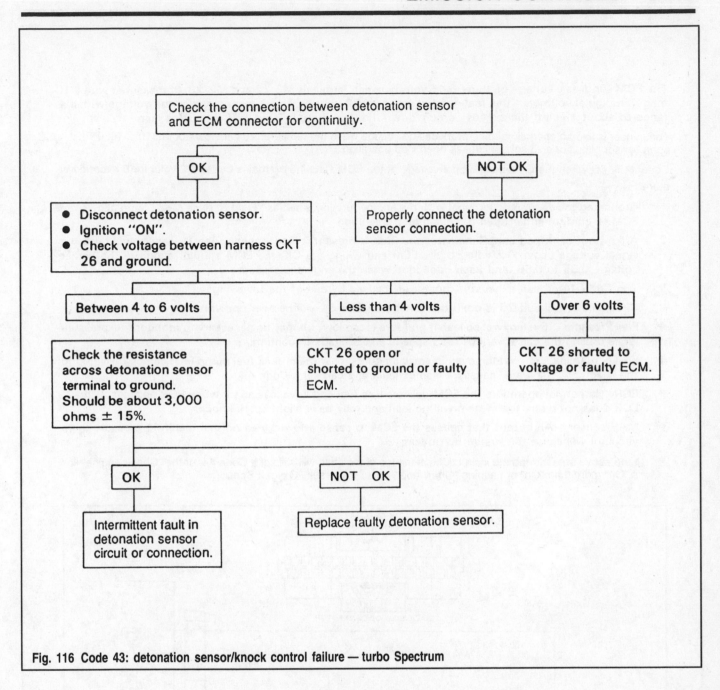

Fig. 116 Code 43: detonation sensor/knock control failure — turbo Spectrum

The ECM supplies a voltage of about 0.45 volts between terminals M2-22 and M2-23. (If measured with a 10 megohm digitial voltmeter, this may read as low as 0.32 volts.) The O_2 sensor varies the voltage within a range of about 1 volt if the exhaust is rich, down through about 0.10 volts if exhaust is lean.

The sensor is like an open circuit and produces no voltage when the temperature is below about 310°C (600°F). An open sensor circuit or cold sensor causes open loop operation.

Code 44 is set when the O_2 sensor signal voltage at the ECM Circuit 31 remains below 0.2 volts for 8 seconds or more.

1. Grounding the diagnostic terminal with the engine running, enables "Field Service Mode" and allows the ECM to confirm either open or closed loop operation.

2. A light out or "Open Loop" indicates the fault is present. Disconnecting the O_2 sensor will raise the signal voltage above 0.2 volts. If the ECM and wiring are OK, the ECM should recognize the higher voltage, 0.35 to 0.55, and flash open loop when the engine is started.

3. The Code 44 or lean exhaust is most likely caused by one of the following:

- Circuit 25. If circuit 25 is open, the voltage on CKT 31 will be over one volt.

- Fuel Pressure. System will be lean if pressure is too low. It may be necessary to monitor fuel pressure while driving the car at various road speeds and/or loads to confirm.

- Fuel contamination. Water, even in small amounts, near the in-tank fuel pump inlet can be delivered to the injector. The water causes a lean exhaust and can set a Code 44.

- EGR. In normal operation, the ECM delivers less fuel and advances spark when EGR engages. If the EGR does not open, the system will go lean and may have slight spark knock.

- MAP sensor. An output that causes the ECM to sense a lower than normal manifold pressure (high vacuum) will cause the system to go lean.

- If the above are OK, and the instructions at the top of the chart will still set a Code 44, or the "Check engine" light is "Off" more than "On" or flashing "Open loop", check for a faulty Oxygen Sensor.

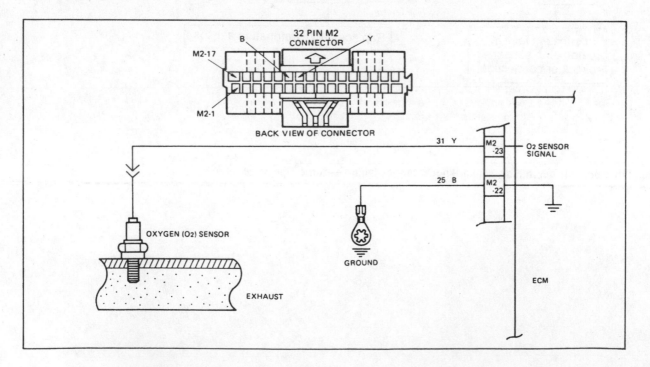

Fig. 117 Code 44: lean exhaust indication — turbo Spectrum

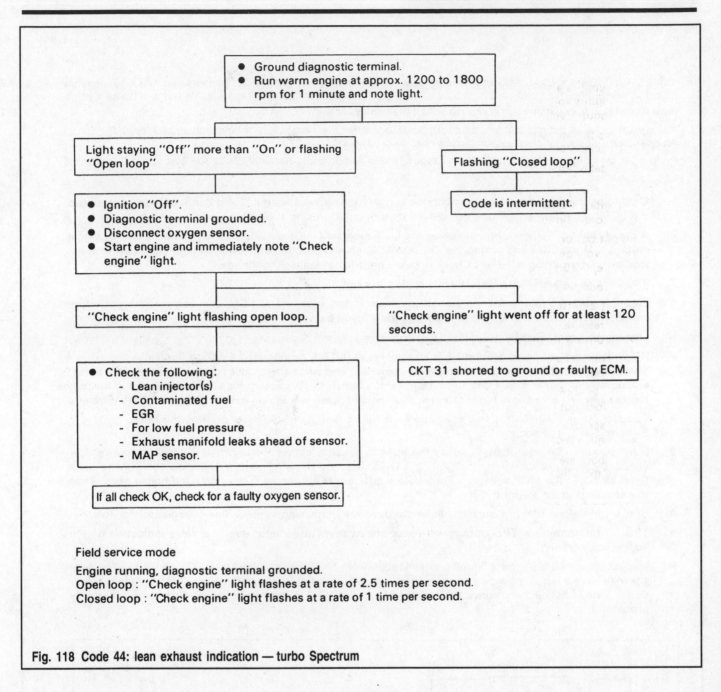

Fig. 118 Code 44: lean exhaust indication — turbo Spectrum

The ECM supplies a voltage of about 0.45 volts between terminals M2-23 and M2-22. (If measured with a 10 megohm digital voltmeter, this may read as low as 0.32 volts.) The O_2 sensor varies the voltage within a range of about 1 volt if the exhaust is rich, down through about .10 volts if the exhaust is lean.

The sensor is like an open circuit and produces no voltage when the temperature is below about 360° (600°F). An open sensor circuit or cold sensor causes open loop operation.

Code 45 is set when the O_2 sensor signal voltage at the ECM connector terminal M2-22 remains above 0.6 volts for 120 seconds.

1. Grounding the diagnostic terminal with the engine running, enables the "Field Service Mode" and allows the ECM to confirm either open or closed loop operation using the "Check engine" light.

2. A steady light or "Open loop" indicates the fault is present. Grounding CKT 31 causes a low O_2 signal voltage. If the ECM and wiring are OK, the ECM should recognize the low voltage and confirm the lean signal by turning off the "Check engine" light for at least 30 seconds.

3. The Code 44 is most likely caused by one of the following:

●   Fuel Pressure. System will go rich if pressure is too high. The ECM can compensate for some increase. However, if it gets too high, a Code 45 will be set.

●   Leaking injector. See Fuel System Diagnosis chart.

●   HEI Shielding. An open ground CKT 16 may result in EMI, or indicated electrical "noise". The ECM looks at this "noise" as distributor pulses. The additional pulses result in a higher than actual engine speed signal. The ECM then delivers too much fuel, causing the system to go rich. The engine tachometer will also show higher than actual engine speed, which can help in diagnosing this problem.

●   Canister purge. Check for fuel saturation. If full of fuel, check canister control and hoses. See canister purge section.

●   MAP sensor. An output that causes the ECM to sense a higher than normal manifold pressure (low vacuum) can cause the system to go rich. Disconnecting the MAP sensor will allow the ECM to set a fixed value for the MAP sensor. Substitute a different MAP sensor if the rich condition is gone while the sensor is disconnected.

●   Check for leaking fuel pressure regulator diaphragm by checking vacuum line to regulator for fuel.

●   TPS. An intermittent TPS output will cause the system to go rich, due to a false indication of the engine accelerating.

●   Inspect Oxygen Sensor for silicone contamination from fuel, or use of improper RTV sealant. The sensor may have a white, powdery coating and result in a high but false signal voltage (rich exhaust indication). The ECM will then reduce the amount of fuel delivered to the engine, causing a severe driveability problem.

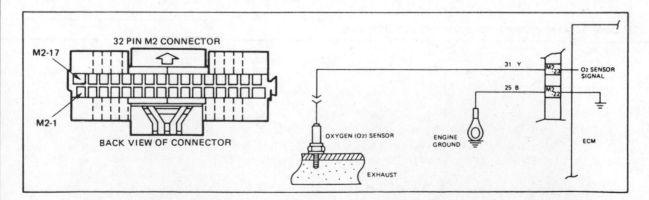

Fig. 119 Code 45: rich exhaust indication — turbo Spectrum

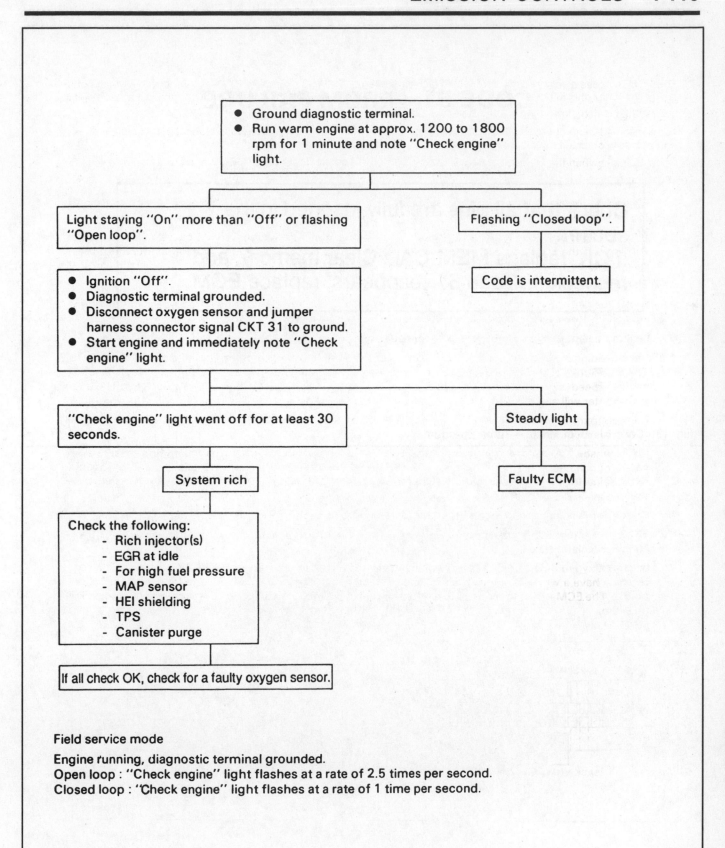

- Ground diagnostic terminal.
- Run warm engine at approx. 1200 to 1800 rpm for 1 minute and note "Check engine" light.

Light staying "On" more than "Off" or flashing "Open loop".

Flashing "Closed loop".

Code is intermittent.

- Ignition "Off".
- Diagnostic terminal grounded.
- Disconnect oxygen sensor and jumper harness connector signal CKT 31 to ground.
- Start engine and immediately note "Check engine" light.

"Check engine" light went off for at least 30 seconds.

Steady light

System rich

Faulty ECM

Check the following:
- Rich injector(s)
- EGR at idle
- For high fuel pressure
- MAP sensor
- HEI shielding
- TPS
- Canister purge

If all check OK, check for a faulty oxygen sensor.

Field service mode

Engine running, diagnostic terminal grounded.
Open loop : "Check engine" light flashes at a rate of 2.5 times per second.
Closed loop : "Check engine" light flashes at a rate of 1 time per second.

Fig. 120 Code 45: rich exhaust indication — turbo Spectrum

CODE 51   PROM FAILURE

Check that all pins are fully inserted in the socket.
If OK, replace MEM-CAL. Clear memory, and recheck. If Code 51 reappears, replace ECM.

Fig. 121 Code 51: prom failure — turbo Spectrum

The ECM will control the engine idle speed by moving the IAC valve to control air flow around the throttle plate. It does this by sending voltage pulses to the proper motor winding for each IAC motor. This will cause the motor shaft and valve to move "IN" or "OUT" of the motor a given distance for each pulse received. ECM pulses are referred to as "counts".

- To increase idle speed - ECM will send enough counts to retract the IAC valve and allow more air to flow through the idle air passage and bypass the throttle plate until idle speed reaches the proper RPM.   This will increase the ECM counts.

- To decrease idle speed - ECM will send enough counts to extend the IAC valve and reduce air flow through the idle passage around the throttle plate. This will reduce the number of ECM counts.

Each time the engine is started and then the ignition is turned "OFF", the ECM will reset the IAC valve. This is done by sending enough counts to seat the valve. The fully seated valve is the ECM zero reference. A given number of counts are then issued to open the valve, and normal ECM control of IAC will begin from this point. The number of counts needed to move the valve are then added or subtracted. This is how the ECM knows what the motor position is for a given idle speed.

The ECM uses the following information to control idle speed:

- Battery voltage
- Coolant temperature
- Throttle position sensor
- Engine speed
- A/C clutch signal
- Power steering pressure switch
- Vehicle speed sensor

Don't apply battery voltage across the IAC motor terminals.   It will permanently damage the IAC motor windings.

1. Be sure to disconnect the IAC valve prior to this test.   The test light will confirm the ECM signals by a steady or flashing light, for all circuits.

2. Before replacing an ECM, be sure to check the resistance at the IAC motor windings. Failure to do so may result in a repeat ECM failure.

3. Diagnostic aids
Engine idle speed can be adversely affected by the following:

- Leaking injector(s) will cause fuel imbalance and poor idle quality due to excess fuel.

- Vacuum leaks can cause higher than normal idle.

- When the throttle shaft or throttle position sensor is binding or sticking in an open throttle position, the ECM does not know if the vehicle has stopped and does not control idle.

- Faulty battery cables can result in voltage variations.   The ECM will try to compensate, which results in erratic idle speeds.

- The ECM will compensate for A/C compressor clutch loads. Loss of this signal would be most apparent in neutral.

- Power steering pressure switch - If the ECM thinks the pressure switch is closed the idle may be too high.

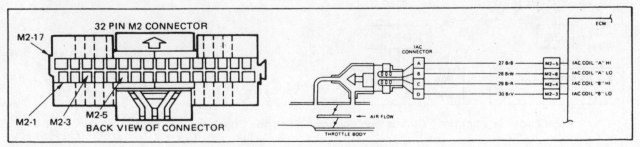

Fig. 122 Code 51: prom failure — turbo Spectrum

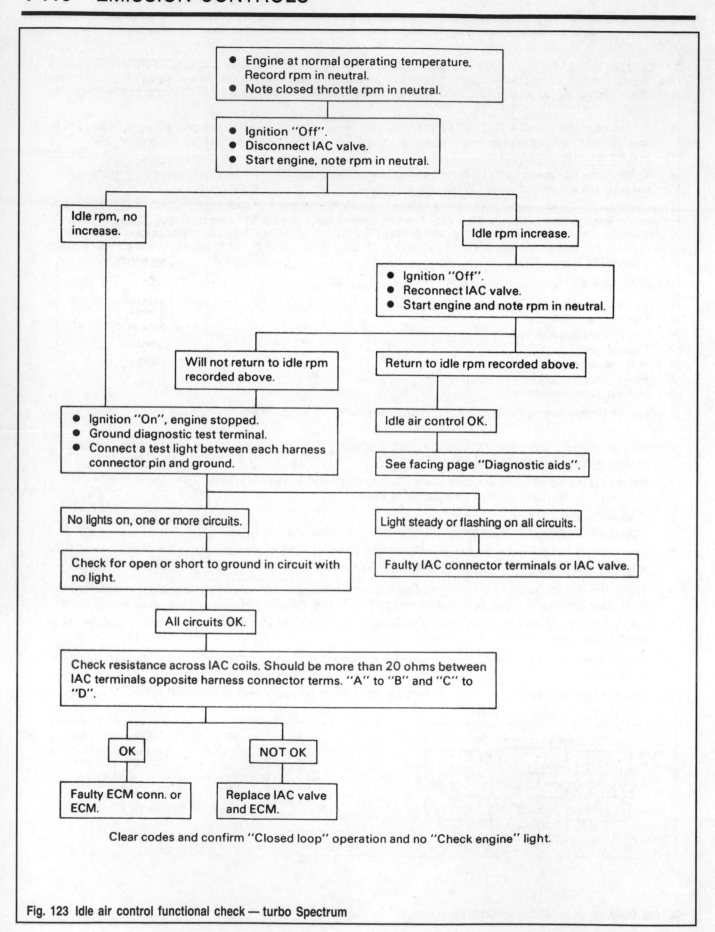

Fig. 123 Idle air control functional check — turbo Spectrum

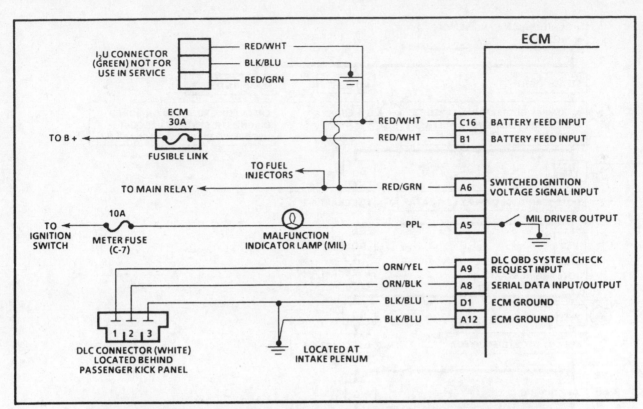

ON-BOARD DIAGNOSTIC (OBD) SYSTEM CHECK

Circuit Description:

The OBD system check is an organized approach to identifying a problem created by a malfunction in the engine control system. It must be the starting point for any driveability complaint diagnosis, because it directs the service technician to the next logical step in diagnosing the complaint. Understanding the chart and using it correctly will reduce diagnostic time and prevent the unnecessary replacement of good parts.

Test Description: Number(s) below refer to circled number(s) on the diagnostic chart.

1. This step is a check for the proper operation of the malfunction indication lamp. The MIL should be "ON" steady.
2. No MIL at this point indicates that there is a problem with the MIL circuit or the ECM control of that circuit.
3. This test checks the ability of the ECM to control the MIL. With the DLC grounded, the MIL should flash a DTC 12 three times, followed by any DTC stored in memory. Depending upon the type of ECM, an ECM error may result in the inability to flash DTC 12.
4. Most of the 6E procedures use a scan tool to aid diagnosis, therefore, serial data must be available. If an ECM or EEPROM error is present, the ECM may have been able to flash DTC 12/51, but not enable serial data.
5. Although the ECM is powered up, a "Cranks But Will Not Run" symptom could exist because of an ECM or system problem.
6. This step will isolate if the customer complaint is a MIL or a driveability problem with no MIL. Refer to diagnostic trouble code in this section for a list of valid DTC(s). An invalid DTC may be the result of a faulty scan tool or ECM.
7. Comparison of actual control system data with the typical values is a quick check to determine if any parameter is not within limits. Keep in mind that a base engine problem (i.e. advanced cam timing) may substantially alter sensor values.
8. Installation of a scan tool will provide a good ground path for the ECM and may hide a driveability complaint due to poor ECM grounds.

Fig. 124 On-board diagnostic system check — Storm

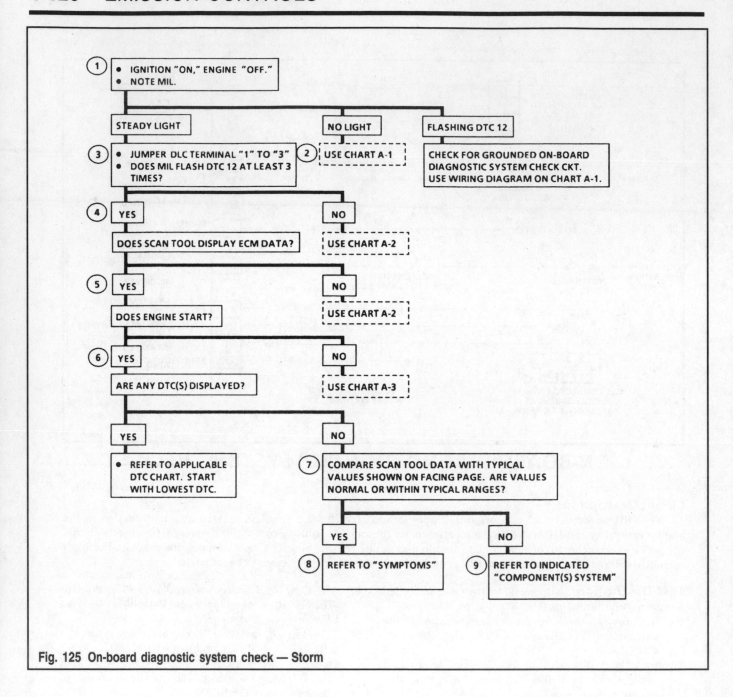

Fig. 125 On-board diagnostic system check — Storm

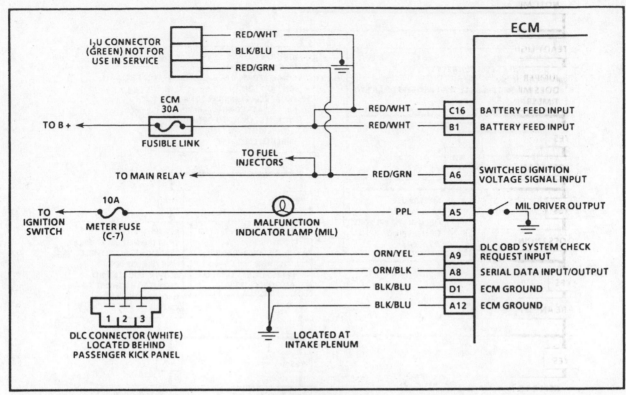

CHART A-1

WON'T FLASH DTC 12
NO MALFUNCTION INDICATOR LAMP (MIL)

Circuit Description:

There should always be a steady Malfunction Indicator Lamp (MIL), when the ignition is "ON" and engine stopped. Battery voltage is supplied directly to the light bulb. The Engine Control Module (ECM) will control the MIL and turn it "ON" by providing a ground path through the MIL circuit from the ECM to the bulb.

Test Description: Number(s) below refer to circled number(s) on the diagnostic chart.

1. Battery feed terminals "C16" and "B1" are protected by a fusible link in relay/fuse center under the hood near the battery.
2. If terminals "C16" and "B1" have voltage, the ECM grounds or the ECM are faulty.
3. Using a test light connected to 12 volts, probe each of the system ground circuits to be sure a good ground is present. Refer to the ECM terminal end view in front of this section for ECM pin locations of ground circuits.

Diagnostic Aids:

Engine runs OK, check:
- Faulty light bulb.
- PPL wire open.
- Meter fuse blown. This will result in no oil or generator lights, seat belt reminder, etc.

Engine cranks, but will not run.
- Continuous battery - fuse or fusible link open.
- ECM ignition fuse open.
- Battery RED/WHT wire to ECM open.
- Ignition RED/GRN wire to ECM open.
- Poor connection to ECM.

Fig. 126 Chart A-1: no code 12/mil won't flash — Storm

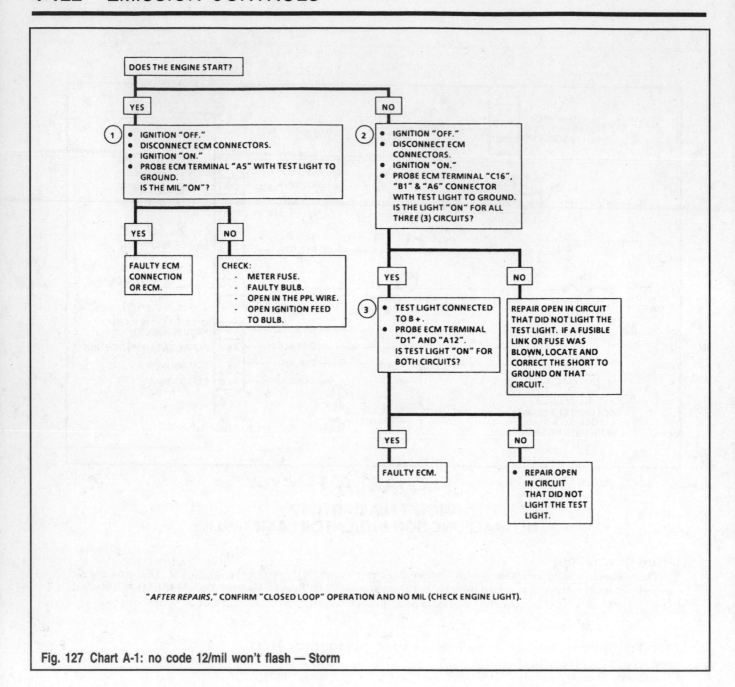

Fig. 127 Chart A-1: no code 12/mil won't flash — Storm

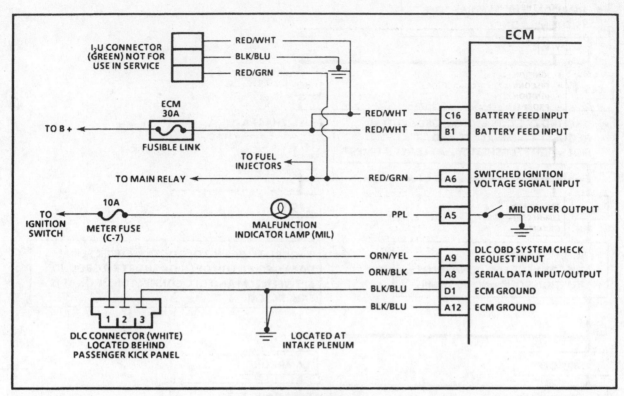

CHART A-2

NO DLC DATA OR WON'T FLASH DTC 12
MALFUNCTION INDICATOR LAMP (MIL) "ON" STEADY

Circuit Description:

There should always be a steady Malfunction Indicator Lamp (MIL) when the ignition is "ON" and engine stopped. Battery mounted is supplied directly to the light bulb. The Engine Control Module (ECM) will turn the light "ON" by grounding MIL circuit at the ECM.

With the on-board diagnostic terminal grounded, the light should flash a DTC 12, followed by any trouble DTC(S) stored in memory.

A steady light suggests a short to ground in the MIL circuit, or an open in OBD system check request circuit.

Test Description: Number(s) below refer to circled number(s) on the diagnostic chart.

1. If there is a problem with the ECM that causes a scan tool to not read Serial data, then the ECM should not flash a DTC 12. If DTC 12 does flash, be sure that the scan tool is working properly on another vehicle. If the scan tool is functioning properly and OBD system request circuit is OK, the ECM may be at fault for the NO DLC symptom.
2. If the light goes "OFF" when the ECM connector is disconnected, then the MIL circuit is not shorted to ground.

3. This step will check for an open OBD system check request circuit.
4. At this point, the MIL wiring is OK. The problem is a faulty ECM. If DTC 12 does not flash, the ECM should be replaced.

Diagnostic Aid:

If the Malfunction Indicator Lamp (MIL) starts to flash DTC 12 but does not flash DTC at least 3 times, the cause of this condition could be a short in one of the QDM circuits. Check the following circuits for a possible short:
- A/C clutch circuit.
- Canister purge circuit.
- EGR valve EVRV circuit.
- Shift light circuit.

If no problem is found the ECM is the cause of the problem.

Fig. 128 Chart A-2: no code 12/mil on steady — Storm

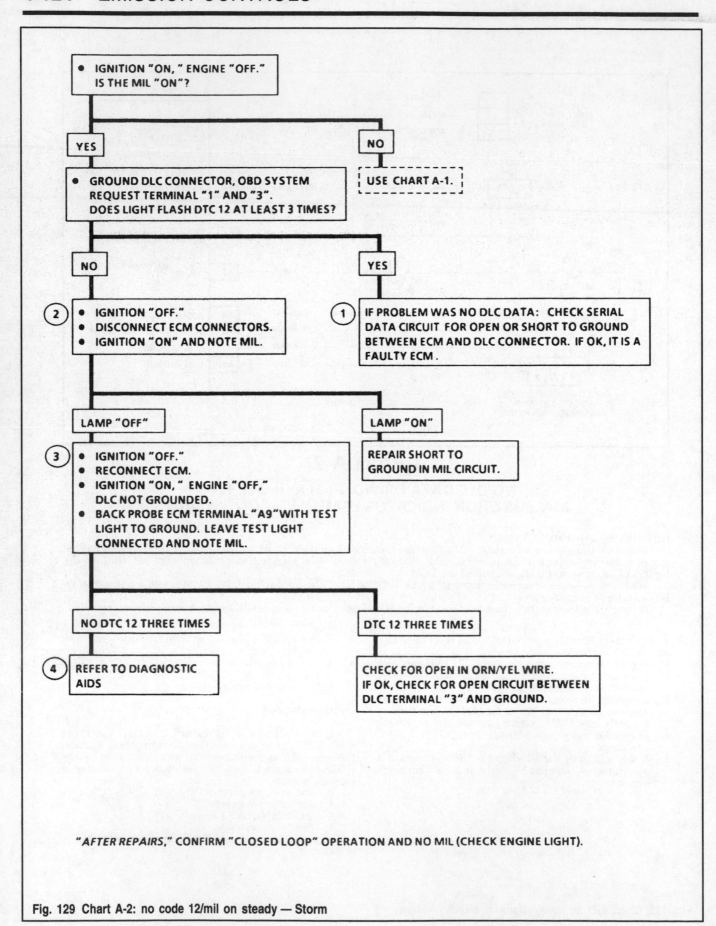

Fig. 129 Chart A-2: no code 12/mil on steady — Storm

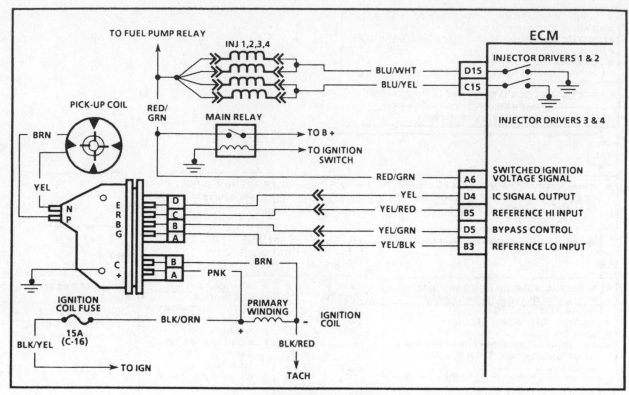

CHART A-3

(Page 1 of 2)
ENGINE CRANKS BUT WON'T RUN

Circuit Description:

Before using this chart, battery condition, engine cranking speed, and fuel quantity should be checked and verified as being OK.

Test Description: Number(s) below refer to circled number(s) on the diagnostic chart.

1. An MIL "ON" is a basic test to determine if there is battery voltage and ignition voltage supplied to the ECM. No DLC data may be due to an ECM problem. CHART A-2 will diagnose the ECM. If TP sensor voltage is over 2.5 volts, the engine may be in the "clear flood" mode, which will cause starting problems. The engine will not start without reference pulses and, therefore, the scan tool should indicate engine speed during cranking.

2. If engine speed was indicated during crank, the DI control module is receiving a crank signal, but "no spark" at this test indicates the DI control module is not triggering the coil or there is a secondary ignition problem.

3. The test light should flash, indicating the ECM is controlling the injectors. The brightness of the light is not important.

4. This test will determine if the DI control module is not generating the reference pulse, or if the wiring or ECM are at fault. By touching and removing a test light to battery voltage on YEL/RED wire, a reference pulse should be generated. If engine speed is indicated, the ECM and wiring are OK.

Diagnostic Aids:

- Water or foreign material can cause a no start condition during freezing weather. The engine may start after 5 or 6 minutes in a heated shop. The problem may recur after an overnight park in freezing temperatures.
- An EGR sticking open can cause a low air/fuel ratio during cranking. Unless the system enters "clear flood" at the first indication of a flooding condition it can result in a no start.
- Fuel pressure: Low fuel pressure can result in a very lean air/fuel ratio. See CHART A-7.

Fig. 130 Chart A-3: engine cranks but won't run (SOHC engine) — Storm

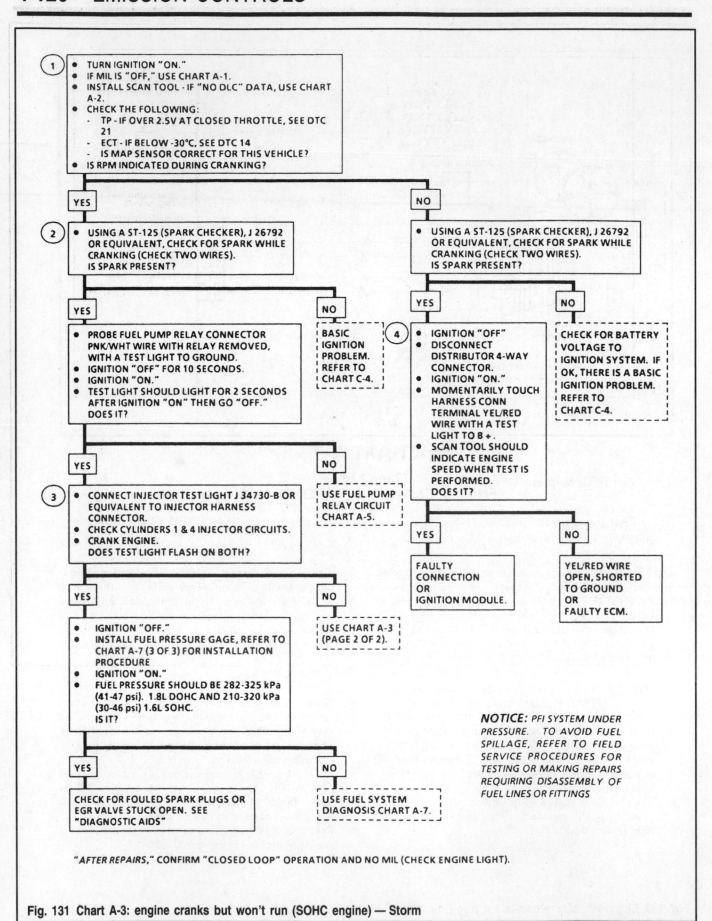

1
- TURN IGNITION "ON."
- IF MIL IS "OFF," USE CHART A-1.
- INSTALL SCAN TOOL - IF "NO DLC" DATA, USE CHART A-2.
- CHECK THE FOLLOWING:
  - TP - IF OVER 2.5V AT CLOSED THROTTLE, SEE DTC 21
  - ECT - IF BELOW -30°C, SEE DTC 14
  - IS MAP SENSOR CORRECT FOR THIS VEHICLE?
- IS RPM INDICATED DURING CRANKING?

YES / **NO**

2
- USING A ST-125 (SPARK CHECKER), J 26792 OR EQUIVALENT, CHECK FOR SPARK WHILE CRANKING (CHECK TWO WIRES).
  IS SPARK PRESENT?

- USING A ST-125 (SPARK CHECKER), J 26792 OR EQUIVALENT, CHECK FOR SPARK WHILE CRANKING (CHECK TWO WIRES).
  IS SPARK PRESENT?

YES / **NO** / **YES** / **NO**

3
- PROBE FUEL PUMP RELAY CONNECTOR PNK/WHT WIRE WITH RELAY REMOVED, WITH A TEST LIGHT TO GROUND.
- IGNITION "OFF" FOR 10 SECONDS.
- IGNITION "ON."
- TEST LIGHT SHOULD LIGHT FOR 2 SECONDS AFTER IGNITION "ON" THEN GO "OFF." DOES IT?

BASIC IGNITION PROBLEM. REFER TO CHART C-4.

4
- IGNITION "OFF"
- DISCONNECT DISTRIBUTOR 4-WAY CONNECTOR.
- IGNITION "ON."
- MOMENTARILY TOUCH HARNESS CONN TERMINAL YEL/RED WIRE WITH A TEST LIGHT TO B+.
- SCAN TOOL SHOULD INDICATE ENGINE SPEED WHEN TEST IS PERFORMED. DOES IT?

CHECK FOR BATTERY VOLTAGE TO IGNITION SYSTEM. IF OK, THERE IS A BASIC IGNITION PROBLEM. REFER TO CHART C-4.

YES / **NO**

- CONNECT INJECTOR TEST LIGHT J 34730-B OR EQUIVALENT TO INJECTOR HARNESS CONNECTOR.
- CHECK CYLINDERS 1 & 4 INJECTOR CIRCUITS.
- CRANK ENGINE.
  DOES TEST LIGHT FLASH ON BOTH?

USE FUEL PUMP RELAY CIRCUIT CHART A-5.

YES / **NO**

FAULTY CONNECTION OR IGNITION MODULE.

YEL/RED WIRE OPEN, SHORTED TO GROUND OR FAULTY ECM.

YES / **NO**

- IGNITION "OFF."
- INSTALL FUEL PRESSURE GAGE, REFER TO CHART A-7 (3 OF 3) FOR INSTALLATION PROCEDURE
- IGNITION "ON."
- FUEL PRESSURE SHOULD BE 282-325 kPa (41-47 psi). 1.8L DOHC AND 210-320 kPa (30-46 psi) 1.6L SOHC.
  IS IT?

USE CHART A-3 (PAGE 2 OF 2).

NOTICE: *PFI SYSTEM UNDER PRESSURE. TO AVOID FUEL SPILLAGE, REFER TO FIELD SERVICE PROCEDURES FOR TESTING OR MAKING REPAIRS REQUIRING DISASSEMBLY OF FUEL LINES OR FITTINGS*

YES / **NO**

CHECK FOR FOULED SPARK PLUGS OR EGR VALVE STUCK OPEN. SEE "DIAGNOSTIC AIDS"

USE FUEL SYSTEM DIAGNOSIS CHART A-7.

"AFTER REPAIRS," CONFIRM "CLOSED LOOP" OPERATION AND NO MIL (CHECK ENGINE LIGHT).

Fig. 131 Chart A-3: engine cranks but won't run (SOHC engine) — Storm

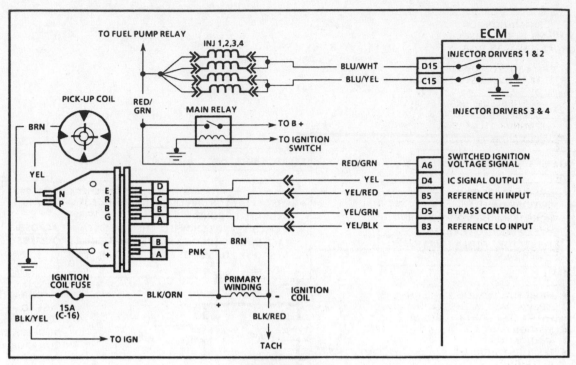

CHART A-3

(Page 2 of 2)
ENGINE CRANKS BUT WON'T RUN

Circuit Description:

Before using this chart, battery condition, engine cranking, speed and fuel quantity should be checked and verified as being OK.

Test Description: Number(s) below refer to circled number(s) on the diagnostic chart.

1. This step checks for ignition voltage at the injector harness connector. Disconnect harness connector before probing terminal "B". Reconnect connector after test.

2. Checks for open in BLU/WHT wire or BLU/YEL wire from connector to ECM. Be sure injector harness is connected.

Fig. 132 Chart A-3: engine cranks but won't run (SOHC continued) — Storm

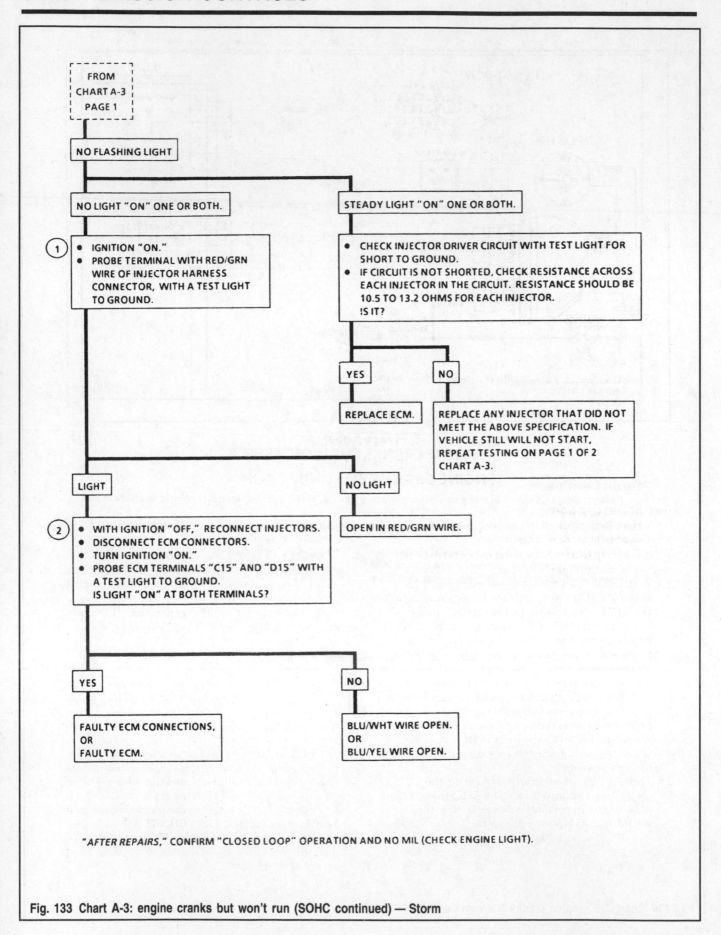

FROM
CHART A-3
PAGE 1

NO FLASHING LIGHT

NO LIGHT "ON" ONE OR BOTH.

STEADY LIGHT "ON" ONE OR BOTH.

①
- IGNITION "ON."
- PROBE TERMINAL WITH RED/GRN WIRE OF INJECTOR HARNESS CONNECTOR, WITH A TEST LIGHT TO GROUND.

- CHECK INJECTOR DRIVER CIRCUIT WITH TEST LIGHT FOR SHORT TO GROUND.
- IF CIRCUIT IS NOT SHORTED, CHECK RESISTANCE ACROSS EACH INJECTOR IN THE CIRCUIT. RESISTANCE SHOULD BE 10.5 TO 13.2 OHMS FOR EACH INJECTOR. IS IT?

YES

NO

REPLACE ECM.

REPLACE ANY INJECTOR THAT DID NOT MEET THE ABOVE SPECIFICATION. IF VEHICLE STILL WILL NOT START, REPEAT TESTING ON PAGE 1 OF 2 CHART A-3.

LIGHT

NO LIGHT

②
- WITH IGNITION "OFF," RECONNECT INJECTORS.
- DISCONNECT ECM CONNECTORS.
- TURN IGNITION "ON."
- PROBE ECM TERMINALS "C15" AND "D15" WITH A TEST LIGHT TO GROUND. IS LIGHT "ON" AT BOTH TERMINALS?

OPEN IN RED/GRN WIRE.

YES

NO

FAULTY ECM CONNECTIONS, OR FAULTY ECM.

BLU/WHT WIRE OPEN. OR BLU/YEL WIRE OPEN.

"AFTER REPAIRS," CONFIRM "CLOSED LOOP" OPERATION AND NO MIL (CHECK ENGINE LIGHT).

Fig. 133 Chart A-3: engine cranks but won't run (SOHC continued) — Storm

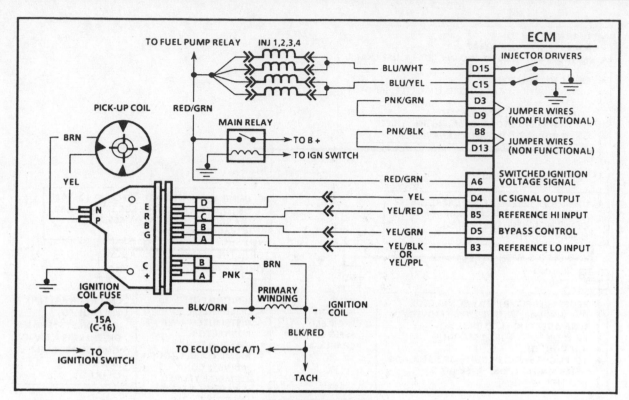

CHART A-3

(Page 1 of 2)
ENGINE CRANKS BUT WON'T RUN

Circuit Description:

Before using this chart, battery condition, engine cranking speed, and fuel quantity should be checked and verified as being OK.

Test Description: Number(s) below refer to circled number(s) on the diagnostic chart.

1. A MIL "ON" is a basic test to determine if there is battery voltage and ignition voltage supplied to the ECM. No DLC data may be due to an ECM problem. CHART A-2 will diagnose the ECM. If TP sensor voltage is over 2.5 volts, the engine may be in the "clear flood" mode, which will cause starting problems. The engine will not start without reference pulses and, therefore, the scan tool should indicate engine speed during cranking.

2. If engine speed was indicated during crank, the DI control module is receiving a crank signal, but "no spark" at this test indicates the DI control module is not triggering the coil or there is a secondary ignition problem.

3. The test light should flash, indicating the ECM is controlling the injectors. The brightness of the light is not important. However, the test light should be a J 34730 or equivalent.

4. This test will determine if the DI control module is not generating the reference pulse, or if the wiring or ECM are at fault. By touching and removing a test light to battery voltage on YEL/RED wire, a reference pulse should be generated. If engine speed is indicated, the ECM and wiring are OK.

Diagnostic Aids:

- Water or foreign material can cause a no start condition during freezing weather. The engine may start after 5 or 6 minutes in a heated shop. The problem may recur after an overnight park in freezing temperatures.

- An EGR sticking open can cause a low air/fuel ratio during cranking. Unless the system enters "clear flood" at the first indication of a flooding condition it can result in a no start.

- Fuel pressure: Low fuel pressure can result in a very lean air/fuel ratio. See CHART A-7.

- The peak and hold wires have no useable purpose and will not affect the injector circuits if open and/or shorted.

Fig. 134 Chart A-3: engine cranks but won't run (DOHC engine) — Storm

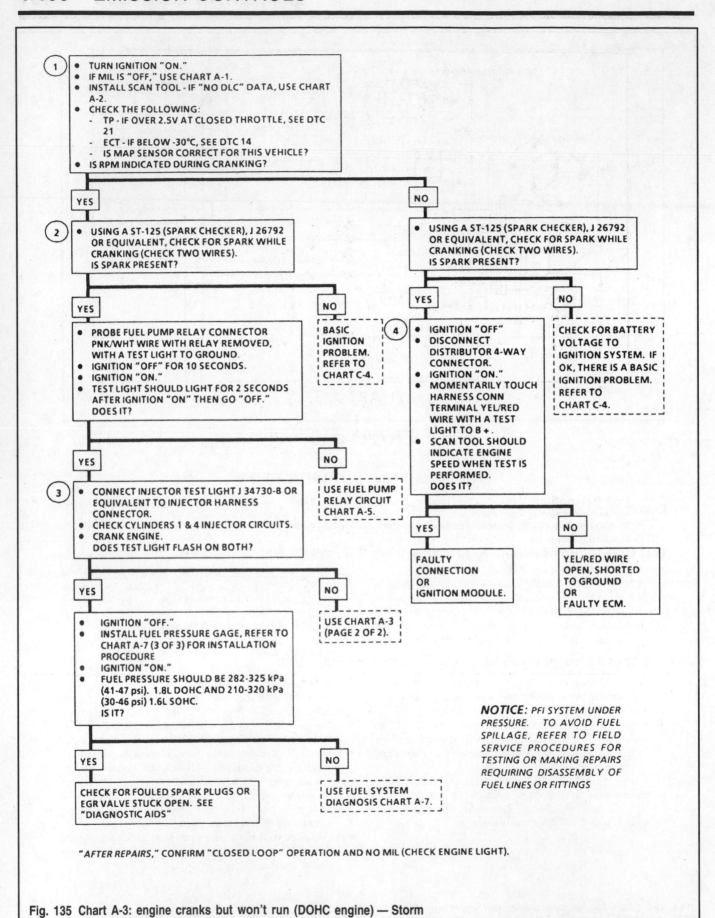

Fig. 135 Chart A-3: engine cranks but won't run (DOHC engine) — Storm

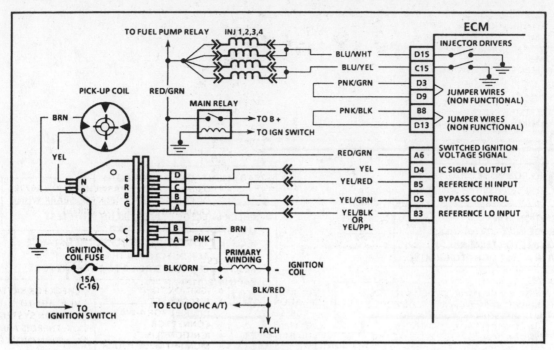

CHART A-3

(Page 2 of 2)
ENGINE CRANKS BUT WON'T RUN

Test Description: Number(s) below refer to circled number(s) on the diagnostic chart.

1. This step checks for ignition voltage at the injector harness connector. Disconnect harness connector before probing terminal "B". Reconnect connector after test.

2. Checks for open in BLU/WHT wire or BLU/YEL wire from connector to ECM. Be sure injector harness is connected.

Diagnostic Aids:

- The peak and hold wires have no useable purpose and do not affect injector circuits if open and/or shorted.

Fig. 136 Chart A-3: engine cranks but won't run (DOHC continued) — Storm

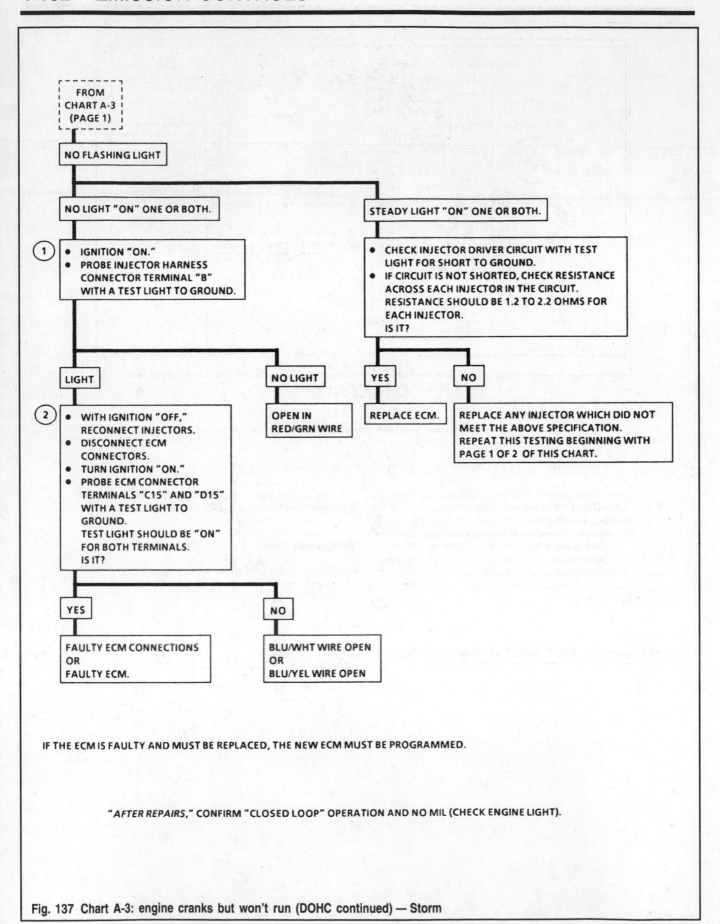

Fig. 137 Chart A-3: engine cranks but won't run (DOHC continued) — Storm

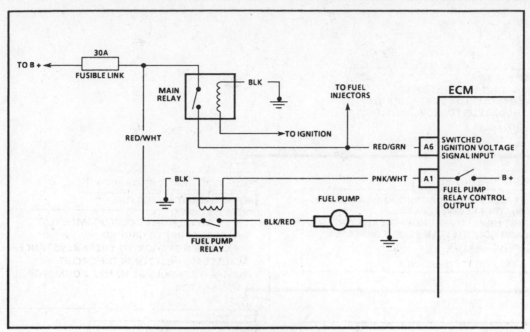

CHART A-5
FUEL PUMP RELAY CIRCUIT

Circuit Description:

When the ignition switch is turned "ON," the Engine Control Module (ECM) will activate the fuel pump relay and operate the in-tank fuel pump. The fuel pump will operate as long as the engine is cranking or running and the ECM is receiving ignition reference pulses.

If there are no reference pulses, the ECM will shut "OFF" the fuel pump within 2 seconds after key "ON."

Test Description: Number(s) below refer to circled number(s) on the diagnostic chart.

1. Checks for the presence of B+ at switching portion of fuel pump relay.
2. Checks circuit between fuel pump relay and ground (including the fuel pump).
3. This test will confirm if voltage is available to the relay coil.

Diagnostic Aids:

A visual inspection of wiring and connectors should be made if an intermittent problem exists.

Fig. 138 Chart A-5: fuel pump delay circuit — Storm

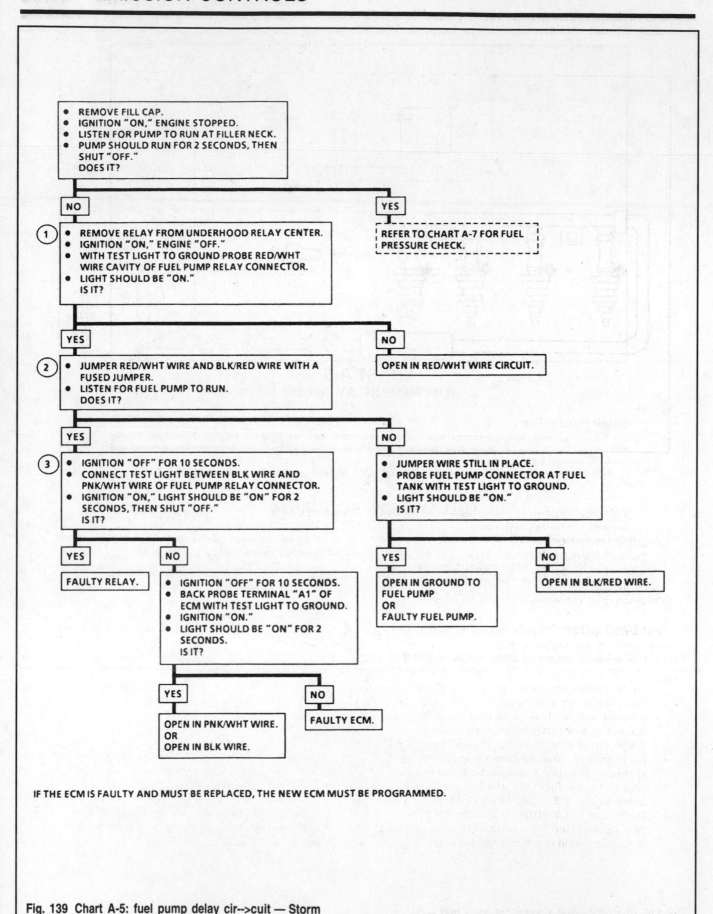

- REMOVE FILL CAP.
- IGNITION "ON," ENGINE STOPPED.
- LISTEN FOR PUMP TO RUN AT FILLER NECK.
- PUMP SHOULD RUN FOR 2 SECONDS, THEN SHUT "OFF."
  DOES IT?

NO

①
- REMOVE RELAY FROM UNDERHOOD RELAY CENTER.
- IGNITION "ON," ENGINE "OFF."
- WITH TEST LIGHT TO GROUND PROBE RED/WHT WIRE CAVITY OF FUEL PUMP RELAY CONNECTOR.
- LIGHT SHOULD BE "ON."
  IS IT?

YES

REFER TO CHART A-7 FOR FUEL PRESSURE CHECK.

YES

②
- JUMPER RED/WHT WIRE AND BLK/RED WIRE WITH A FUSED JUMPER.
- LISTEN FOR FUEL PUMP TO RUN.
  DOES IT?

NO

OPEN IN RED/WHT WIRE CIRCUIT.

YES

③
- IGNITION "OFF" FOR 10 SECONDS.
- CONNECT TEST LIGHT BETWEEN BLK WIRE AND PNK/WHT WIRE OF FUEL PUMP RELAY CONNECTOR.
- IGNITION "ON," LIGHT SHOULD BE "ON" FOR 2 SECONDS, THEN SHUT "OFF."
  IS IT?

NO

- JUMPER WIRE STILL IN PLACE.
- PROBE FUEL PUMP CONNECTOR AT FUEL TANK WITH TEST LIGHT TO GROUND.
- LIGHT SHOULD BE "ON."
  IS IT?

YES

FAULTY RELAY.

NO

- IGNITION "OFF" FOR 10 SECONDS.
- BACK PROBE TERMINAL "A1" OF ECM WITH TEST LIGHT TO GROUND.
- IGNITION "ON."
- LIGHT SHOULD BE "ON" FOR 2 SECONDS.
  IS IT?

YES

OPEN IN GROUND TO FUEL PUMP
OR
FAULTY FUEL PUMP.

NO

OPEN IN BLK/RED WIRE.

YES

OPEN IN PNK/WHT WIRE.
OR
OPEN IN BLK WIRE.

NO

FAULTY ECM.

IF THE ECM IS FAULTY AND MUST BE REPLACED, THE NEW ECM MUST BE PROGRAMMED.

Fig. 139 Chart A-5: fuel pump delay cir-->cuit — Storm

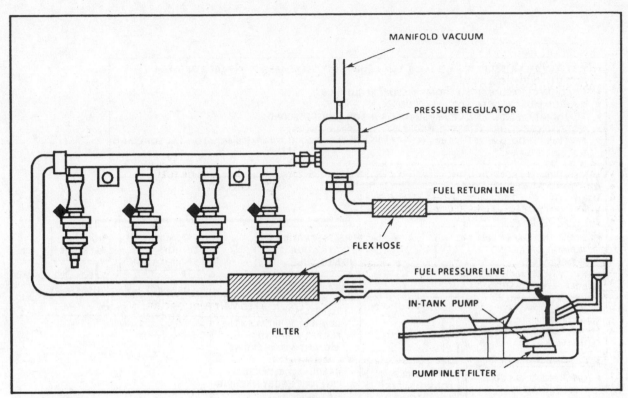

CHART A-7

(Page 1 of 3)
FUEL SYSTEM PRESSURE TEST

Circuit Description:

The fuel pump delivers fuel to the fuel rail and injectors, where the system pressure is controlled from 282 to 325 kPa (41 to 47 psi) on 1.8L DOHC and 1.6L SOHC 210-320 kPa (30-46 psi) by the fuel pressure regulator. Excess fuel is returned to the fuel tank. When the engine is stopped, the pump can be energized by jumpering the fuel pump relay connector with a fused jumper.

Test Description: Number(s) below refer to circled number(s) on the diagnostic chart.

1. Use pressure gage J 34730-1 and adapter J 35957-10. Wrap a shop towel around the fuel pressure tap to absorb any small amount of fuel leakage that may occur when installing the gage. (The pressure will not leak down after the fuel pump is stopped on a correctly functioning system.)
2. While the engine is idling, manifold pressure is low (vacuum). When vacuum is applied to the fuel pressure regulator diaphragm more fuel is returned to the fuel tank, the fuel pressure will be lower at about 282-303 kPa (41-44 psi) on 1.8L DOHC and 1.6L SOHC 210-260 kPa (30-37 psi).
3. The application of vacuum to the pressure regulator should result in a fuel pressure drop.

4. Pressure leak-down may be caused by one of the following:
   - In-tank fuel pump check valve not holding.
   - Pump coupling hose leaking.
   - Fuel pressure regulator valve leaking.
   - Injector sticking open/leaking.

Diagnostic Aids:

Improper fuel system pressure may contribute to one or all of the following symptoms:
   - Cranks but won't run.
   - DTC 44 or 45.
   - Cutting out (May feel like ignition problem).
   - Hesitation, loss of power or poor fuel economy.
   Refer to "Symptoms "

Fig. 140 Chart A-7: fuel system pressure test — Storm

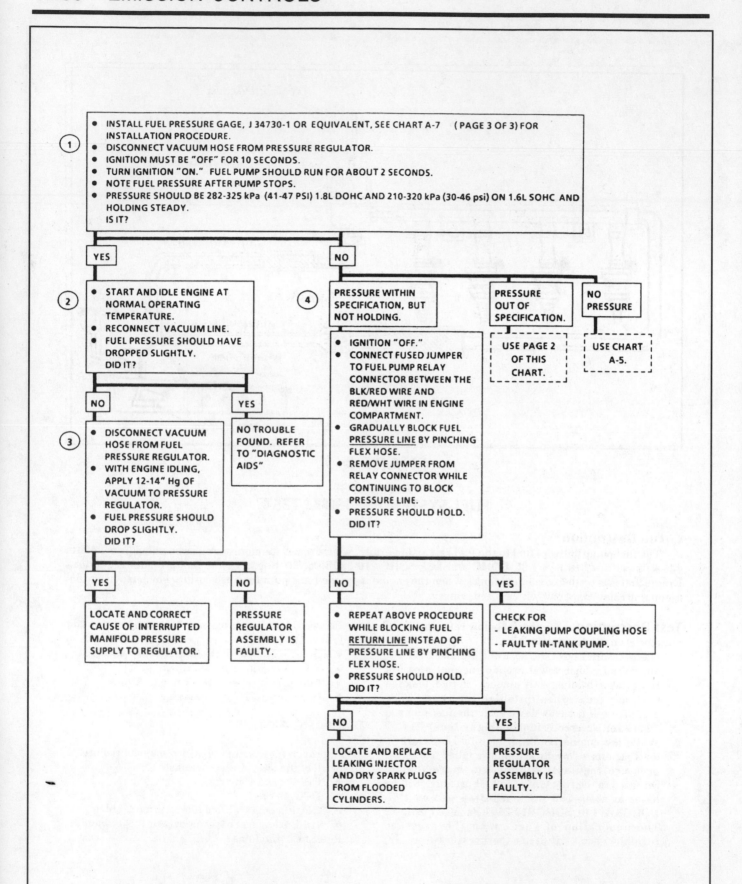

① • INSTALL FUEL PRESSURE GAGE, J 34730-1 OR EQUIVALENT, SEE CHART A-7   (PAGE 3 OF 3) FOR
    INSTALLATION PROCEDURE.
  • DISCONNECT VACUUM HOSE FROM PRESSURE REGULATOR.
  • IGNITION MUST BE "OFF" FOR 10 SECONDS.
  • TURN IGNITION "ON." FUEL PUMP SHOULD RUN FOR ABOUT 2 SECONDS.
  • NOTE FUEL PRESSURE AFTER PUMP STOPS.
  • PRESSURE SHOULD BE 282-325 kPa (41-47 PSI) 1.8L DOHC AND 210-320 kPa (30-46 psi) ON 1.6L SOHC AND
    HOLDING STEADY.
    IS IT?

YES

NO

② • START AND IDLE ENGINE AT
    NORMAL OPERATING
    TEMPERATURE.
  • RECONNECT VACUUM LINE.
  • FUEL PRESSURE SHOULD HAVE
    DROPPED SLIGHTLY.
    DID IT?

④ PRESSURE WITHIN
  SPECIFICATION, BUT
  NOT HOLDING.

PRESSURE
OUT OF
SPECIFICATION.

NO
PRESSURE

USE PAGE 2
OF THIS
CHART.

USE CHART
A-5.

NO

YES

③ • DISCONNECT VACUUM
    HOSE FROM FUEL
    PRESSURE REGULATOR.
  • WITH ENGINE IDLING,
    APPLY 12-14" Hg OF
    VACUUM TO PRESSURE
    REGULATOR.
  • FUEL PRESSURE SHOULD
    DROP SLIGHTLY.
    DID IT?

NO TROUBLE
FOUND. REFER
TO "DIAGNOSTIC
AIDS"

• IGNITION "OFF."
• CONNECT FUSED JUMPER
  TO FUEL PUMP RELAY
  CONNECTOR BETWEEN THE
  BLK/RED WIRE AND
  RED/WHT WIRE IN ENGINE
  COMPARTMENT.
• GRADUALLY BLOCK FUEL
  PRESSURE LINE BY PINCHING
  FLEX HOSE.
• REMOVE JUMPER FROM
  RELAY CONNECTOR WHILE
  CONTINUING TO BLOCK
  PRESSURE LINE.
• PRESSURE SHOULD HOLD.
  DID IT?

YES

NO

LOCATE AND CORRECT
CAUSE OF INTERRUPTED
MANIFOLD PRESSURE
SUPPLY TO REGULATOR.

PRESSURE
REGULATOR
ASSEMBLY IS
FAULTY.

NO

YES

• REPEAT ABOVE PROCEDURE
  WHILE BLOCKING FUEL
  RETURN LINE INSTEAD OF
  PRESSURE LINE BY PINCHING
  FLEX HOSE.
• PRESSURE SHOULD HOLD.
  DID IT?

CHECK FOR
- LEAKING PUMP COUPLING HOSE
- FAULTY IN-TANK PUMP.

NO

YES

LOCATE AND REPLACE
LEAKING INJECTOR
AND DRY SPARK PLUGS
FROM FLOODED
CYLINDERS.

PRESSURE
REGULATOR
ASSEMBLY IS
FAULTY.

Fig. 141 Chart A-7: fuel system pressure test — Storm

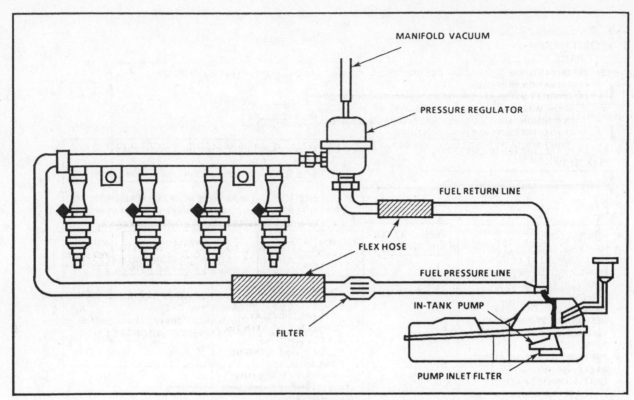

MANIFOLD VACUUM

PRESSURE REGULATOR

FUEL RETURN LINE

FLEX HOSE

FUEL PRESSURE LINE

IN-TANK PUMP

FILTER

PUMP INLET FILTER

CHART A-7

(Page 2 of 3)
FUEL SYSTEM PRESSURE TEST

Circuit Description:

The fuel pump delivers fuel to the fuel rail and injectors, where the system pressure is controlled from 282 to 325 kPa (41 to 47 psi) 1.8L DOHC and 210-320 kPa (30-46 psi) 1.6L SOHC by the fuel pressure regulator. Excess fuel is returned to the fuel tank. When the engine is stopped, the pump can be energized by jumpering the fuel pump relay connector with a fused jumper.

Test Description: Number(s) below refer to circled number(s) on the diagnostic chart.

5. Pressure less than 282 kPa (41 psi) 1.8L DOHC and 210 kPa (30 psi) 1.6L SOHC may be caused by one of two problems.
   - The regulated fuel pressure is too low. The system will be running lean and may set DTC 44. Also, hard cold starting and overall poor performance is possible.
   - Restricted flow is causing a pressure drop. Normally, a vehicle with a fuel pressure loss at idle will not be driveable. However, if the pressure drop occurs only while driving, the engine will surge and then stop as pressure begins to drop rapidly.

6. Restricting the fuel return line allows the fuel pump to build above regulated pressure. When battery voltage is applied to the pump test terminal, pressure should be above 413 kPa (60 psi).

7. This test determines if the high fuel pressure is due to a restricted fuel return line or a pressure regulator problem.

Fig. 142 Chart A-7: fuel system pressure test (continued) — Storm

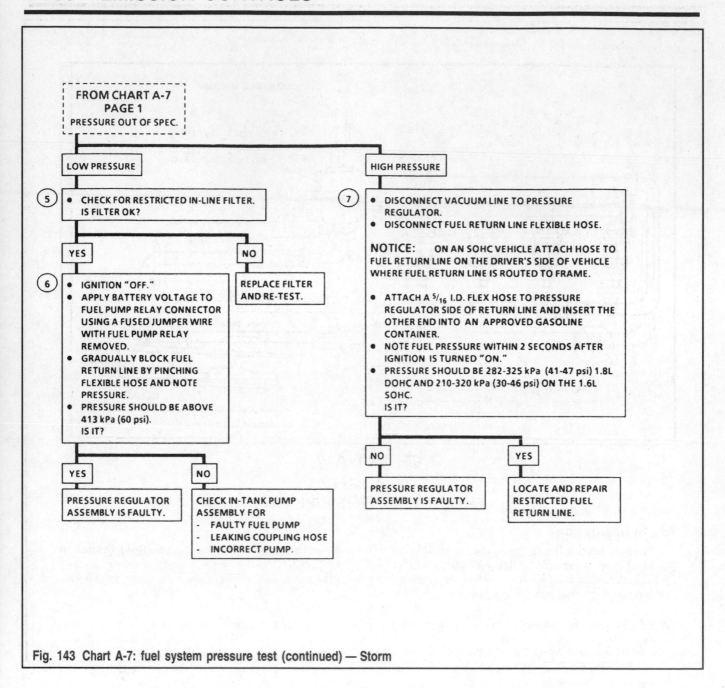

FROM CHART A-7
PAGE 1
PRESSURE OUT OF SPEC.

LOW PRESSURE

HIGH PRESSURE

(5)
- CHECK FOR RESTRICTED IN-LINE FILTER.
  IS FILTER OK?

YES

NO

(6)
- IGNITION "OFF."
- APPLY BATTERY VOLTAGE TO FUEL PUMP RELAY CONNECTOR USING A FUSED JUMPER WIRE WITH FUEL PUMP RELAY REMOVED.
- GRADUALLY BLOCK FUEL RETURN LINE BY PINCHING FLEXIBLE HOSE AND NOTE PRESSURE.
- PRESSURE SHOULD BE ABOVE 413 kPa (60 psi).
  IS IT?

REPLACE FILTER AND RE-TEST.

(7)
- DISCONNECT VACUUM LINE TO PRESSURE REGULATOR.
- DISCONNECT FUEL RETURN LINE FLEXIBLE HOSE.

NOTICE: ON AN SOHC VEHICLE ATTACH HOSE TO FUEL RETURN LINE ON THE DRIVER'S SIDE OF VEHICLE WHERE FUEL RETURN LINE IS ROUTED TO FRAME.

- ATTACH A $5/16$ I.D. FLEX HOSE TO PRESSURE REGULATOR SIDE OF RETURN LINE AND INSERT THE OTHER END INTO AN APPROVED GASOLINE CONTAINER.
- NOTE FUEL PRESSURE WITHIN 2 SECONDS AFTER IGNITION IS TURNED "ON."
- PRESSURE SHOULD BE 282-325 kPa (41-47 psi) 1.8L DOHC AND 210-320 kPa (30-46 psi) ON THE 1.6L SOHC.
  IS IT?

YES

NO

NO

YES

PRESSURE REGULATOR ASSEMBLY IS FAULTY.

CHECK IN-TANK PUMP ASSEMBLY FOR
- FAULTY FUEL PUMP
- LEAKING COUPLING HOSE
- INCORRECT PUMP.

PRESSURE REGULATOR ASSEMBLY IS FAULTY.

LOCATE AND REPAIR RESTRICTED FUEL RETURN LINE.

Fig. 143 Chart A-7: fuel system pressure test (continued) — Storm

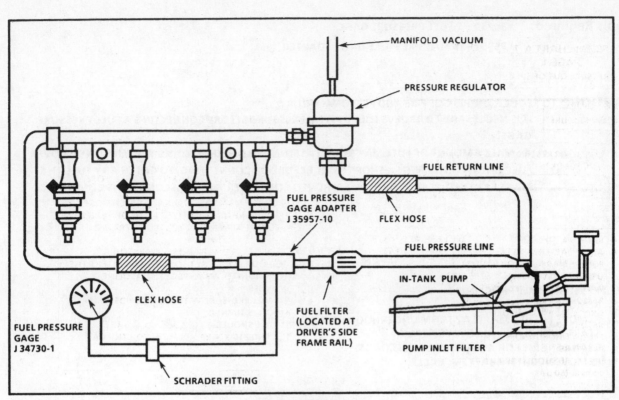

CHART A-7

(Page 3 of 3)
FUEL SYSTEM PRESSURE TEST

Circuit Description:

The fuel rail is not equipped with a fuel system test fitting. In order to install fuel pressure gage J 34730-1, gage adapter J 23597-10 must be installed as shown.

Fig. 144 Chart A-7: fuel system pressure test (continued) — Storm

Tools Required: J 34730 - 1 FUEL PRESSURE GAGE

J 35957 - 10 FUEL PRESSURE GAGE ADAPTER

CAUTION: TO REDUCE THE RISK OF FIRE AND PERSONAL INJURY:
- IT IS NECESSARY TO RELIEVE FUEL SYSTEM PRESSURE BEFORE CONNECTING A FUEL PRESSURE GAGE.
- A SMALL AMOUNT OF FUEL MAY BE RELEASED WHEN DISCONNECTING THE FUEL LINES. COVER FUEL LINE FITTINGS WITH A SHOP TOWEL BEFORE DISCONNECTING, TO CATCH ANY FUEL THAT MAY LEAK OUT. PLACE TOWEL IN APPROVED CONTAINER WHEN DISCONNECT IS COMPLETED.

FUEL PRESSURE RELIEF PROCEDURE
1. REMOVE FUEL CAP.
2. REMOVE FUEL PUMP RELAY FROM UNDERHOOD RELAY CENTER.
3. START ENGINE AND ALLOW TO STALL.
4. CRANK ENGINE FOR ADDITIONAL 30 SECONDS.
5. REMOVE NEGATIVE BATTERY CABLE.

FUEL GAGE ADAPTER INSTALLATION
1. DISCONNECT FUEL PRESSURE LINE AT THE FUEL FILTER.
   USE A SHOP TOWEL TO CATCH ANY ADDITIONAL FUEL
   THAT WAS LEFT IN THE LINE.
2. INSTALL FUEL GAGE ADAPTER J 35957 - 10 BETWEEN FUEL PRESSURE LINE
   AND FUEL FILTER AT FRAME RAIL.
3. INSTALL FUEL GAGE J 34730 - 1 TO ADAPTER.
4. REINSTALL FUEL PUMP RELAY.
5. CONNECT NEGATIVE BATTERY CABLE.
6. INSTALL FUEL CAP.
7. START ENGINE AND CHECK FOR LEAKS.

NOTE: REVERSE THE PROCEDURE ABOVE TO REMOVE FUEL GAGE ADAPTER.

Fig. 145 Chart A-7: fuel system pressure test (continued) — Storm

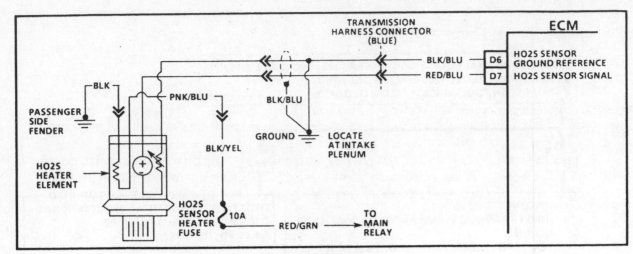

DTC 13
HEATED OXYGEN SENSOR (HO2S) CIRCUIT
(OPEN CIRCUIT)

Circuit Description:

The ECM supplies a voltage of about .45 volt between terminals "D7" and "D6". (If measured with a 10 megohm digital voltmeter, this may read as low as .32 volt.)

The heater circuit of the HO2S is turned "ON" when the engine is running. The HO2S as it heats up will begin to send a varying voltage signal to the ECM. This voltage will vary from about .1 volt (lean exhaust) to about 1.0 volts (rich exhaust) depending on the condition of the exhaust gases in the exhaust manifold.

The sensor is like an open circuit and produces no voltage when it is below 315°C (600°F). An open sensor circuit causes "Open Loop" operation.

Test Description: Number(s) below refer to circled number(s) on the diagnostic chart.

1. DTC 13 will set under if:
   - Engine operating temperature above 69.5°C (183°F).
   - At least 2 minutes have elapsed since engine start-up.
   - HO2S signal voltage is steady between .347 volt and .547 volt.
   - Vehicle speed > 3 mph.
   - Throttle angle is above 5%.
   - All above conditions are met for about 40 seconds.

   If the conditions for a DTC 13 exist, the system will not go "Closed Loop."

2. This test determines if the HO2S is the problem or if the ECM and wiring are at fault.

3. Use only a 10 megohm digital when performing this test. This test checks the continuity of "D7" and "D6". If "D6" is open, the ECM voltage on "D7" will be over .6 volt (600 mV).

Diagnostic Aids:

Normal scan tool HO2S voltage varies between 100 mV to 999 mV (.1 and 1.0 volt) while in "Closed Loop." DTC 13 sets in one minute if sensor signal voltage remains between .347 volt and .547 volt, but the system will go to "Open Loop" in about 15 seconds after DTC 13 has set.

Verify a clean, tight ground connection for "D6". Open "D7" or "D6" will result in a DTC 13. If DTC 13 is intermittent, refer to "Symptoms."

- Check the oxygen sensor wire for induced voltage (EMI). Disconnect the oxygen sensor signal wire at the sensor and the ECM. Using DVM measure the wire with the engine running for any voltage. If 300 mV or more are indicated, check the signal wire shield and/or reroute the signal wire away from any high voltage sources. Such source could be ignition wires, battery cables, Alternator "B" circuit, ect.

Fig. 146 Code 13: oxygen sensor circuit open (DOHC engine) — Storm

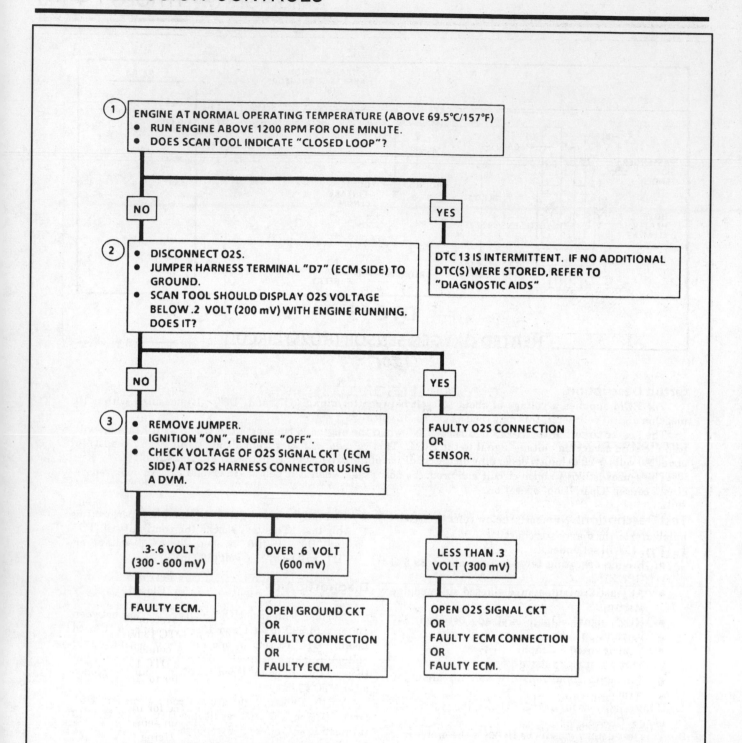

1. ENGINE AT NORMAL OPERATING TEMPERATURE (ABOVE 69.5°C/157°F)
   - RUN ENGINE ABOVE 1200 RPM FOR ONE MINUTE.
   - DOES SCAN TOOL INDICATE "CLOSED LOOP"?

NO

YES

2. - DISCONNECT O2S.
   - JUMPER HARNESS TERMINAL "D7" (ECM SIDE) TO GROUND.
   - SCAN TOOL SHOULD DISPLAY O2S VOLTAGE BELOW .2 VOLT (200 mV) WITH ENGINE RUNNING. DOES IT?

DTC 13 IS INTERMITTENT. IF NO ADDITIONAL DTC(S) WERE STORED, REFER TO "DIAGNOSTIC AIDS"

NO

YES

3. - REMOVE JUMPER.
   - IGNITION "ON", ENGINE "OFF".
   - CHECK VOLTAGE OF O2S SIGNAL CKT (ECM SIDE) AT O2S HARNESS CONNECTOR USING A DVM.

FAULTY O2S CONNECTION
OR
SENSOR.

.3-.6 VOLT
(300 - 600 mV)

OVER .6 VOLT
(600 mV)

LESS THAN .3
VOLT (300 mV)

FAULTY ECM.

OPEN GROUND CKT
OR
FAULTY CONNECTION
OR
FAULTY ECM.

OPEN O2S SIGNAL CKT
OR
FAULTY ECM CONNECTION
OR
FAULTY ECM.

IF THE ECM IS FAULTY AND MUST BE REPLACED, THE NEW ECM MUST BE PROGRAMMED.

"AFTER REPAIRS," CONFIRM "CLOSED LOOP" OPERATION AND NO MIL (CHECK ENGINE LIGHT).

Fig. 147 Code 13: oxygen sensor circuit open (DOHC engine) — Storm

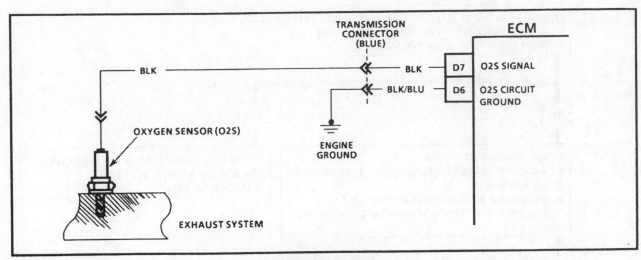

DTC 13

OXYGEN SENSOR (O2S) CIRCUIT
(OPEN CIRCUIT)

Circuit Description:

The ECM supplies a voltage of about of .45 volt between terminals "D7" and "D6". (If measured with 10 megohm digital voltmeter, this may read as low as .32 volt).

The oxygen sensor varies the voltage within a range of about 1.0 volts, if the exhaust is rich, down to about .1 volt, if exhaust is lean.

The sensor is like an open circuit and produces no voltage, when it is below 315°C (600°F). An open sensor circuit causes "Open Loop" operation.

Test Description: Number(s) below refer to circled number(s) on the diagnostic chart.

1. DTC 13 will set if:
   - Engine operating temperature above 69.5°C (183°F).
   - At least 50 seconds engine run time after start.
   - O2S signal voltage steady between .347 volt and .547 volt.
   - Throttle angle above 5%.
   - Vehicle speed > 3 mph.
   - All conditions must be met for about 60 seconds.

   If the conditions for a DTC 13 exist, the system will not go "Closed Loop."
2. This test determines if the oxygen sensor is the problem, or if the ECM/wiring are at fault.
3. Use only a high impedance digital volt ohmmeter when preforming this test. This test checks the continuity of "D7" and "D6". If "D6" is open, the ECM voltage on "D7" will be over .6 volt (600 mV).

Diagnostic Aids:

Normal scan voltage varies between 100 mV to 999 mV (.1 and 1.0 volt), while in "Closed Loop." DTC 13 sets within one minute, if voltage remains between .347 volt and .547 volt, but the system will go "Open Loop" in about 15 seconds after DTC 13 has set.

Verify a clean, tight ground connection for "D6". Open "D7" or "D6" will result in a DTC 13.

If DTC 13 is intermittent, refer to "Intermittents," in "Symptoms."

- Check the oxygen sensor wire for induced voltage (EMI). Disconnect the oxygen sensor signal wire at the sensor and the ECM. Using DVM measure the wire with the engine running for any voltage. If 300 mV or more are indicated, check the signal wire shield and/or reroute the signal wire away from any high voltage sources. Such source could be ignition wires, battery cables, Alternator "B" circuit, ect.

Fig. 148 Code 13: oxygen sensor circuit open (SOHC engine) — Storm

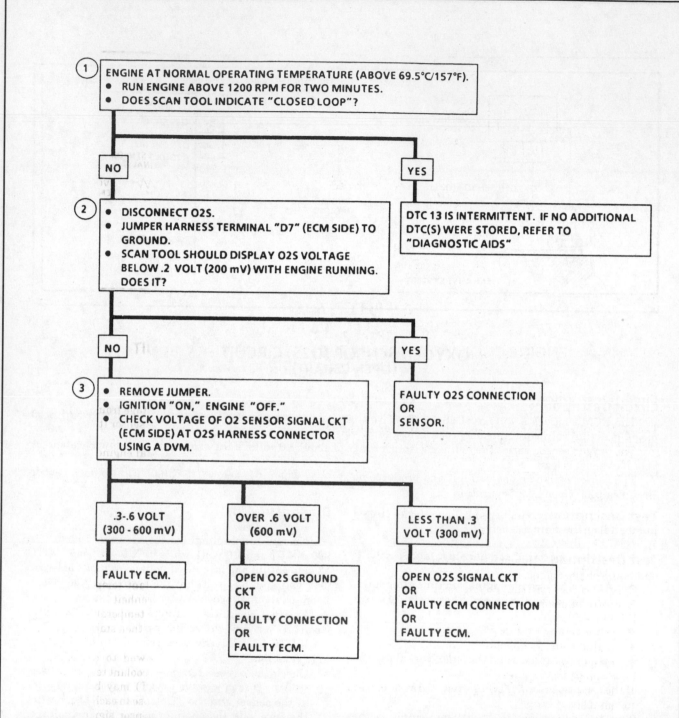

① ENGINE AT NORMAL OPERATING TEMPERATURE (ABOVE 69.5°C/157°F).
- RUN ENGINE ABOVE 1200 RPM FOR TWO MINUTES.
- DOES SCAN TOOL INDICATE "CLOSED LOOP"?

NO

YES

② - DISCONNECT O2S.
- JUMPER HARNESS TERMINAL "D7" (ECM SIDE) TO GROUND.
- SCAN TOOL SHOULD DISPLAY O2S VOLTAGE BELOW .2 VOLT (200 mV) WITH ENGINE RUNNING. DOES IT?

DTC 13 IS INTERMITTENT. IF NO ADDITIONAL DTC(S) WERE STORED, REFER TO "DIAGNOSTIC AIDS"

NO

YES

③ - REMOVE JUMPER.
- IGNITION "ON," ENGINE "OFF."
- CHECK VOLTAGE OF O2 SENSOR SIGNAL CKT (ECM SIDE) AT O2S HARNESS CONNECTOR USING A DVM.

FAULTY O2S CONNECTION OR SENSOR.

.3-.6 VOLT (300 - 600 mV)

OVER .6 VOLT (600 mV)

LESS THAN .3 VOLT (300 mV)

FAULTY ECM.

OPEN O2S GROUND CKT OR FAULTY CONNECTION OR FAULTY ECM.

OPEN O2S SIGNAL CKT OR FAULTY ECM CONNECTION OR FAULTY ECM.

IF THE ECM IS FAULTY AND MUST BE REPLACED, THE NEW ECM MUST BE PROGRAMMED.

"AFTER REPAIRS," CONFIRM "CLOSED LOOP" OPERATION AND NO MIL (CHECK ENGINE LIGHT).

Fig. 149 Code 13: oxygen sensor circuit open (SOHC engine) — Storm

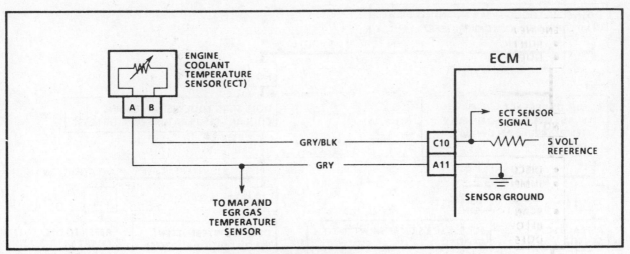

DTC 14
(Page 1 of 2)
ENGINE COOLANT TEMPERATURE (ECT) SENSOR CIRCUIT
(HIGH/LOW TEMPERATURE INDICATED)

Circuit Description:

The Engine Coolant Temperature (ECT) sensor uses a thermistor to control the signal voltage from the ECM. The ECM applies a reference voltage on GRY wire to the sensor. When the engine is cold, the sensor (thermistor) resistance is high. The ECM will then sense a high signal voltage.

As the engine warms up, the sensor resistance decreases and the voltage drops. At normal engine operating temperature, the voltage will measure about 1.5 to 2.0 volts at ECM terminal.

Engine coolant temperature is one of the inputs used to control the following:
- Fuel Delivery.
- Ignition Control (IC).
- Idle Air Control (IAC).

Test Description: Number(s) below refer to circled number(s) on the diagnostic chart.
1. Checks to see if a DTC was set as result of hard failure or intermittent condition.
   DTC 14 will set if:
   High Temperature Criteria:
   - Signal voltage indicates an engine coolant temperature above 213°C (412°F) for 3 seconds.
   Low Temperature Criteria:
   - Engine has been running for at least two (2) minutes.
   - Coolant temperature is indicated below -37°C (-35°F).
2. This test simulates conditions for a DTC 14 (Low Temperature Indicated). If the ECM recognizes the open circuit (high voltage) and displays a low temperature, the ECM and wiring are OK.

Diagnostic Aids:

A scan tool reads engine coolant temperature in degrees celsius and degrees of fahrenheit..

After the engine is started, the temperature should rise steadily to about 90°C (220°F), then stabilize when the thermostat opens.

If the engine has been allowed to cool to an ambient temperature (overnight), coolant temperature and Intake Air Temperature (IAT) may be checked with a scan tool and should read close to each other.

A DTC 14 will result if the sensor signal wire is shorted to ground.

If DTC 14 is intermittent, refer to "Intermittents" in "Symptoms."

Fig. 150 Code 14: engine coolant temperature sensor circuit — Storm

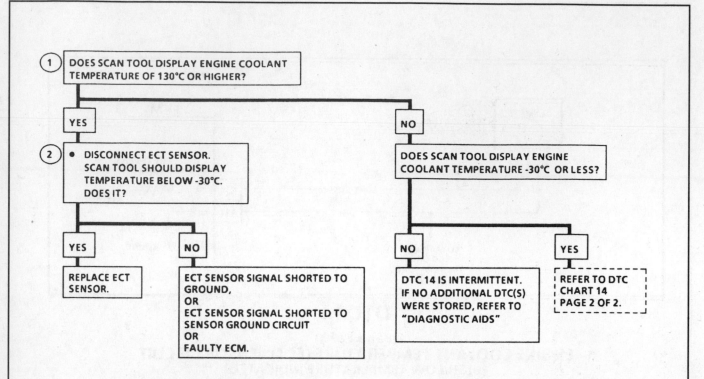

DIAGNOSTIC AID

ENGINE COOLANT TEMPERATURE SENSOR		
TEMPERATURE VS. RESISTANCE VALUES (APPROXIMATE)		
°C	°F	OHMS
100	212	177
90	194	241
80	176	332
70	158	467
60	140	667
50	122	973
45	113	1188
40	104	1459
35	95	1802
30	86	2238
25	77	2796
20	68	3520
15	59	4450
10	50	5670
5	41	7280
0	32	9420
-5	23	12300
-10	14	16180
-15	5	21450
-20	-4	28680
-30	-22	52700
-40	-40	100700

"AFTER REPAIRS," CONFIRM "CLOSED LOOP" OPERATION AND NO MIL (CHECK ENGINE LIGHT).

Fig. 151 Code 14: engine coolant temperature sensor circuit — Storm

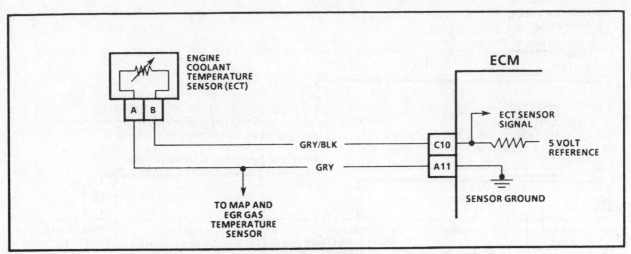

DTC 14

(Page 2 of 2)
ENGINE COOLANT TEMPERATURE (ECT) SENSOR CIRCUIT
(HIGH/LOW TEMPERATURE INDICATED)

Circuit Description:

The Engine Coolant Temperature (ECT) sensor uses a thermistor to control the signal voltage to the ECM. The ECM applies a voltage on the sensor signal wire to the sensor. When the engine is cold, the sensor (thermistor) resistance is high, therefore, the ECM will see high signal voltage.

As the engine warms, the sensor resistance becomes less and the voltage drops. At normal engine operating temperature, the voltage will measure about 1.5 to 2.0 volts at the ECM terminal.

Engine coolant temperature is one of the inputs used to control:
- Fuel Delivery.
- Ignition Control (IC).
- Engine Idle Speed (IAC).

Test Description: Number(s) below refer to circled number(s) on the diagnostic chart.

1. Checks to see if code was set as a result of hard failure or intermittent condition.
2. This test simulates conditions for a DTC 14 (High Temperature Indicated). If the ECM recognizes the grounded circuit (low voltage), and displays a high temperature, the ECM and wiring are OK.
3. This test will determine if there is a wiring problem or a faulty ECM.

Diagnostic Aids:

A scan tool reads engine temperature in degrees centigrade and degrees in fahrenheit. After the engine is started, the temperature should rise steadily to about 90°C (220°F), then stabilize when the thermostat opens.

If the engine has been allowed to cool to an ambient temperature (overnight), coolant and IAT temperatures may be checked with a scan tool and should read close to each other.

A DTC 14 will result if the sensor ground wire or the sensor signal wire are open.

If DTC 14 is intermittent, refer to "Intermittents" in "Symptoms."

Fig. 152 Code 14: engine coolant temperature sensor circuit (continued) — Storm

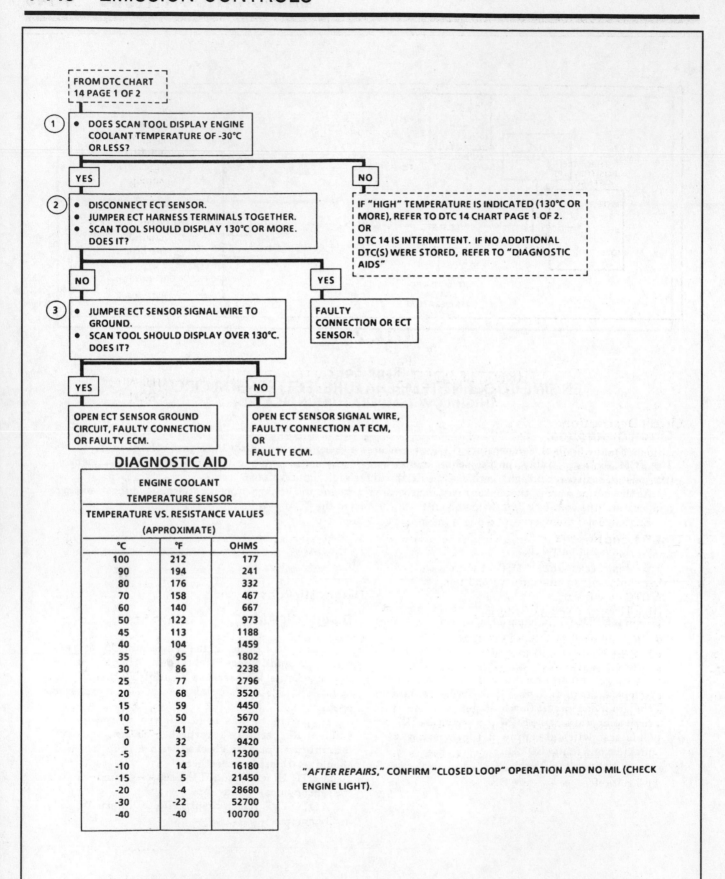

FROM DTC CHART 14 PAGE 1 OF 2

1
- DOES SCAN TOOL DISPLAY ENGINE COOLANT TEMPERATURE OF -30°C OR LESS?

YES

NO

2
- DISCONNECT ECT SENSOR.
- JUMPER ECT HARNESS TERMINALS TOGETHER.
- SCAN TOOL SHOULD DISPLAY 130°C OR MORE. DOES IT?

IF "HIGH" TEMPERATURE IS INDICATED (130°C OR MORE), REFER TO DTC 14 CHART PAGE 1 OF 2.
OR
DTC 14 IS INTERMITTENT. IF NO ADDITIONAL DTC(S) WERE STORED, REFER TO "DIAGNOSTIC AIDS"

NO

YES

3
- JUMPER ECT SENSOR SIGNAL WIRE TO GROUND.
- SCAN TOOL SHOULD DISPLAY OVER 130°C. DOES IT?

FAULTY CONNECTION OR ECT SENSOR.

YES

NO

OPEN ECT SENSOR GROUND CIRCUIT, FAULTY CONNECTION OR FAULTY ECM.

OPEN ECT SENSOR SIGNAL WIRE, FAULTY CONNECTION AT ECM, OR FAULTY ECM.

DIAGNOSTIC AID

ENGINE COOLANT TEMPERATURE SENSOR		
TEMPERATURE VS. RESISTANCE VALUES (APPROXIMATE)		
°C	°F	OHMS
100	212	177
90	194	241
80	176	332
70	158	467
60	140	667
50	122	973
45	113	1188
40	104	1459
35	95	1802
30	86	2238
25	77	2796
20	68	3520
15	59	4450
10	50	5670
5	41	7280
0	32	9420
-5	23	12300
-10	14	16180
-15	5	21450
-20	-4	28680
-30	-22	52700
-40	-40	100700

"AFTER REPAIRS," CONFIRM "CLOSED LOOP" OPERATION AND NO MIL (CHECK ENGINE LIGHT).

Fig. 153 Code 14: engine coolant temperature sensor circuit (continued) — Storm

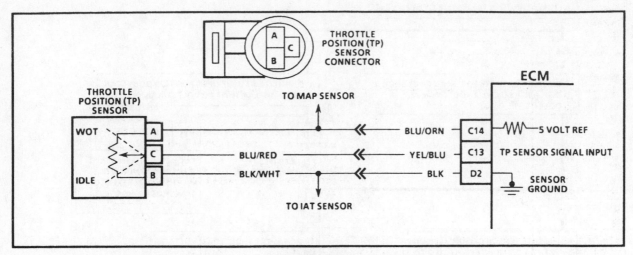

DTC 21

(Page 1 of 2)
THROTTLE POSITION (TP) SENSOR CIRCUIT
(SIGNAL VOLTAGE HIGH/LOW INDICATED)

Circuit Description:

The Throttle Position (TP) sensor provides a voltage signal that changes relative to the throttle valve position. Signal voltage will vary from less than 1.25 volts at idle to about 5 volts at Wide Open Throttle (WOT).

The TP sensor signal is one of the most important inputs used by the ECM for fuel control and for many of the ECM controlled outputs.

Test Description: Number(s) below refer to circled number(s) on the diagnostic chart.

1. This step checks to see if DTC 21 is the result of a hard failure or an intermittent condition.
   A DTC 21 will set if:
   High TP Sensor Voltage Criteria:
   - TP sensor reading above 2.5 volts.
   - Engine speed less than 1800 RPM.
   - MAP reading below 60 kPa.
   - All of the above conditions present for 2 seconds.
   Low TP Sensor Voltage Criteria:
   - Engine running.
   - TP sensor voltage below .2 volt (200 mV).
2. This step simulates conditions for a DTC 21 (Signal Voltage Low). If the ECM recognizes the change, the ECM, and the signal circuit wire and the 5 volt reference wire are OK.

3. This step isolates a faulty sensor ECM or an open BLK/WHT wire. If the BLK/WHT wire is open, there may also be a DTC 23.

Diagnostic Aids:

A scan tool displays throttle position in volts. Closed throttle voltage should be less than 1.25 volts. TP sensor voltage should increase at a steady rate as throttle is moved to WOT.

A DTC 21 will result if the sensor ground wire is open or the signal circuit wire is shorted to voltage. If DTC 21 is intermittent, refer to "Intermittents" in "Symptoms."

NOTICE: On the 1.8L DOHC vehicles with A/T transaxles, the "ECONO" light will also be flashing when DTC 21 is logged in the ECM's memory or the circuit fault is still present. An incorrectly programmed EEPROM may also cause the "ECONO" light to be flashing.

Fig. 154 Code 21: throttle position sensor circuit — Storm

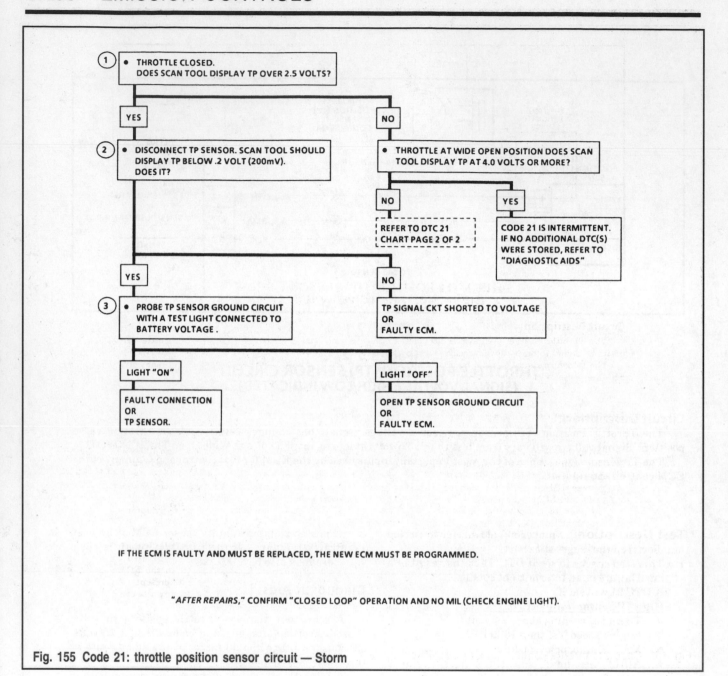

Fig. 155 Code 21: throttle position sensor circuit — Storm

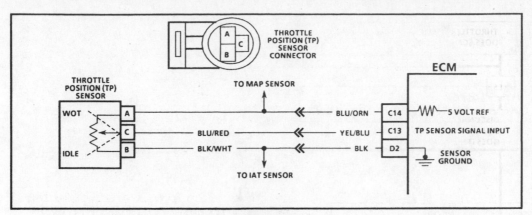

DTC 21

(Page 2 of 2)
THROTTLE POSITION (TP) SENSOR CIRCUIT
(SIGNAL VOLTAGE HIGH/LOW INDICATED)

Circuit Description:

The Throttle Position (TP) sensor provides a voltage signal that changes, relative to the throttle valve position. Signal voltage will vary from less than 1.25 volts at idle to about 5 volts at Wide Open Throttle (WOT).

The TP sensor signal is one of the most important inputs used by the ECM for fuel control and for many of the ECM controlled outputs.

Test Description: Number(s) below refer to circled number(s) on the diagnostic chart.
1. This step checks to see if DTC 21 is the result of a hard failure or an intermittent condition.
2. This step simulates conditions for a DTC 21 (Signal Voltage High). If a DTC 21 (Signal Voltage High) is set, or the scan tool displays over 4 volts, the ECM and wiring are OK.
3. The scan tool may not display 12 volts. The important thing is that the ECM recognizes the voltage as over 4 volts, indicating that the signal circuit wire and the ECM are OK.
4. If the 5 volt reference wire is open or shorted to ground, there may also be a stored DTC 33.

Diagnostic Aids:

A scan tool displays throttle position in volts. Closed throttle voltage should be less than 1.25 volts. TP sensor voltage should increase at a steady rate as throttle is moved to WOT.

An open or grounded 5 volt reference wire or signal circuit wire will result in a DTC 21.

If DTC 21 is intermittent, refer to "Symptoms."

NOTICE: On the 1.8L DOHC vehicles with A/T transaxles, the "ECONO" light will also be flashing when DTC 21 is logged in the ECM's memory or the circuit fault is still present. An incorrectly programmed EEPROM may also cause the "ECONO" light to be flashing.

Fig. 156 Code 21: throttle position sensor circuit (continued) — Storm

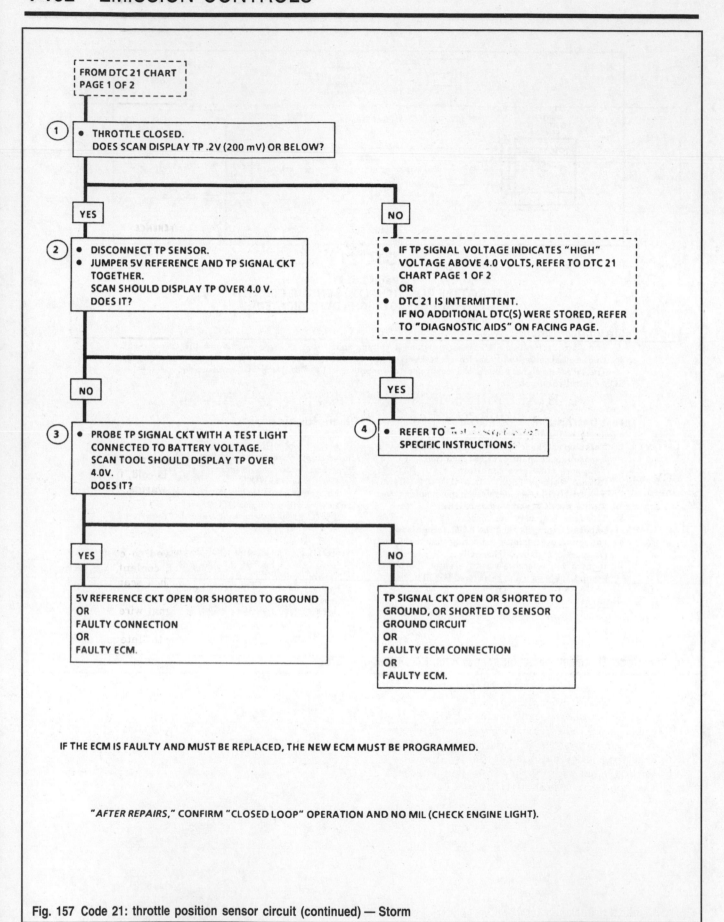

FROM DTC 21 CHART
PAGE 1 OF 2

1
- THROTTLE CLOSED.
  DOES SCAN DISPLAY TP .2V (200 mV) OR BELOW?

YES

NO

2
- DISCONNECT TP SENSOR.
- JUMPER 5V REFERENCE AND TP SIGNAL CKT TOGETHER.
  SCAN SHOULD DISPLAY TP OVER 4.0 V.
  DOES IT?

- IF TP SIGNAL VOLTAGE INDICATES "HIGH" VOLTAGE ABOVE 4.0 VOLTS, REFER TO DTC 21 CHART PAGE 1 OF 2
  OR
- DTC 21 IS INTERMITTENT.
  IF NO ADDITIONAL DTC(S) WERE STORED, REFER TO "DIAGNOSTIC AIDS" ON FACING PAGE.

NO

YES

3
- PROBE TP SIGNAL CKT WITH A TEST LIGHT CONNECTED TO BATTERY VOLTAGE.
  SCAN TOOL SHOULD DISPLAY TP OVER 4.0V.
  DOES IT?

4
- REFER TO Test Description for SPECIFIC INSTRUCTIONS.

YES

NO

5V REFERENCE CKT OPEN OR SHORTED TO GROUND
OR
FAULTY CONNECTION
OR
FAULTY ECM.

TP SIGNAL CKT OPEN OR SHORTED TO GROUND, OR SHORTED TO SENSOR GROUND CIRCUIT
OR
FAULTY ECM CONNECTION
OR
FAULTY ECM.

IF THE ECM IS FAULTY AND MUST BE REPLACED, THE NEW ECM MUST BE PROGRAMMED.

"AFTER REPAIRS," CONFIRM "CLOSED LOOP" OPERATION AND NO MIL (CHECK ENGINE LIGHT).

Fig. 157 Code 21: throttle position sensor circuit (continued) — Storm

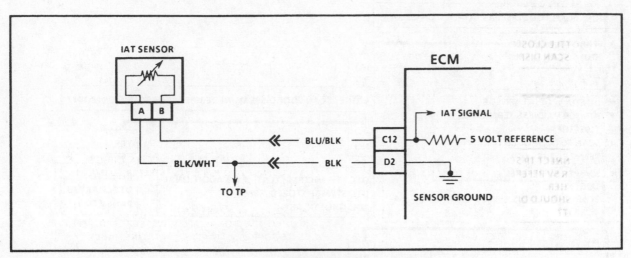

DTC 23

(Page 1 of 2)
INTAKE AIR TEMPERATURE (IAT) SENSOR CIRCUIT
(HIGH/LOW TEMPERATURE INDICATED)

Circuit Description:

The Intake Air Temperature (IAT) sensor uses a thermistor to control the signal voltage from the ECM. The ECM applies a voltage on the sensor signal wire to the sensor. When intake manifold air is cold, the sensor (thermistor) resistance is high, therefore, the ECM will see a high signal voltage. As the air warms, the sensor resistance becomes less and the voltage drops.

Test Description: Number(s) below refer to circled number(s) on the diagnostic chart.

1. This step checks to see if DTC 23 is the result of a hard failure or an intermittent condition.
   A DTC 23 will set if:
   Low Temperature Criteria:
   - Engine has been running for longer than 2 minutes.
   - Signal voltage indicates an IAT temperature less than -38°C (-36°F).
   High Temperature Criteria:
   - IAT temperature above 199°C (390°F).
   - Detected for at least 2 minutes.
2. This test simulates conditions for a DTC 23 (High Temperature Indicated). If the scan tool displays a high temperature, the ECM and wiring are OK.
3. This step checks continuity of the signal wire and sensor ground wire. If the sensor ground wire is open, there may also be a DTC 21.

Diagnostic Aids:

If the engine has been allowed to cool to an ambient temperature (overnight), coolant and IAT temperatures may be checked with a scan tool and should read close to each other.

A DTC 23 will result if the signal wire or sensor ground wire become open.

If DTC 23 is intermittent, refer to "Intermittents" in "Symptoms."

Fig. 158 Code 23: intake air temperature sensor circuit — Storm

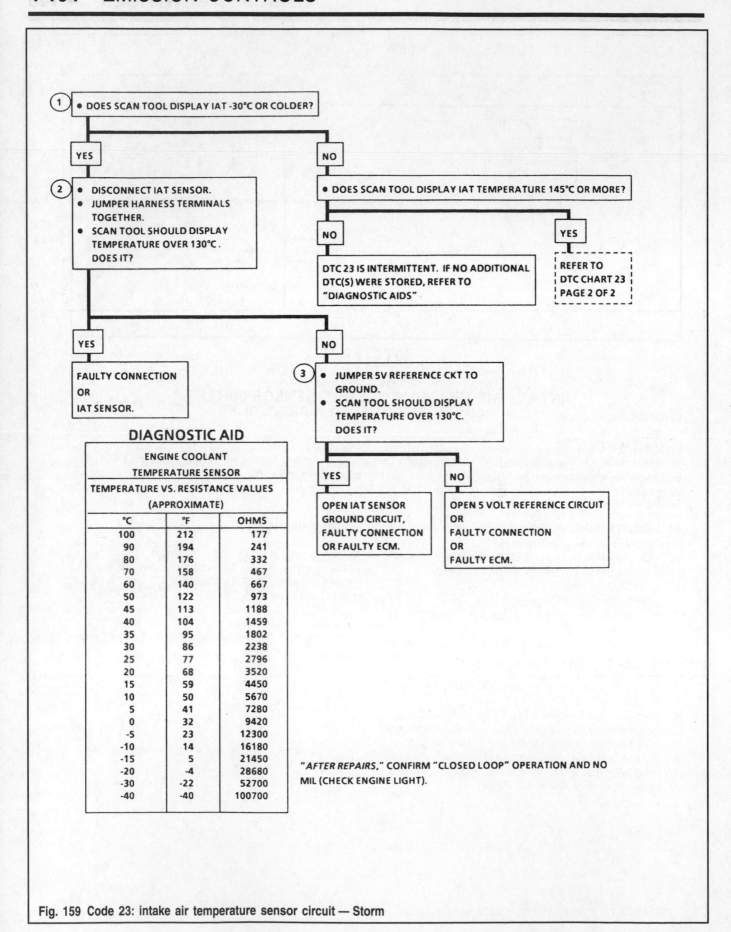

1 ● DOES SCAN TOOL DISPLAY IAT -30°C OR COLDER?

YES

NO

2 ● DISCONNECT IAT SENSOR.
● JUMPER HARNESS TERMINALS TOGETHER.
● SCAN TOOL SHOULD DISPLAY TEMPERATURE OVER 130°C. DOES IT?

● DOES SCAN TOOL DISPLAY IAT TEMPERATURE 145°C OR MORE?

NO

YES

DTC 23 IS INTERMITTENT. IF NO ADDITIONAL DTC(S) WERE STORED, REFER TO "DIAGNOSTIC AIDS"

REFER TO DTC CHART 23 PAGE 2 OF 2

YES

NO

FAULTY CONNECTION
OR
IAT SENSOR.

3 ● JUMPER 5V REFERENCE CKT TO GROUND.
● SCAN TOOL SHOULD DISPLAY TEMPERATURE OVER 130°C. DOES IT?

YES

NO

OPEN IAT SENSOR GROUND CIRCUIT, FAULTY CONNECTION OR FAULTY ECM.

OPEN 5 VOLT REFERENCE CIRCUIT OR FAULTY CONNECTION OR FAULTY ECM.

DIAGNOSTIC AID

ENGINE COOLANT TEMPERATURE SENSOR		
TEMPERATURE VS. RESISTANCE VALUES (APPROXIMATE)		
°C	°F	OHMS
100	212	177
90	194	241
80	176	332
70	158	467
60	140	667
50	122	973
45	113	1188
40	104	1459
35	95	1802
30	86	2238
25	77	2796
20	68	3520
15	59	4450
10	50	5670
5	41	7280
0	32	9420
-5	23	12300
-10	14	16180
-15	5	21450
-20	-4	28680
-30	-22	52700
-40	-40	100700

"AFTER REPAIRS," CONFIRM "CLOSED LOOP" OPERATION AND NO MIL (CHECK ENGINE LIGHT).

Fig. 159 Code 23: intake air temperature sensor circuit — Storm

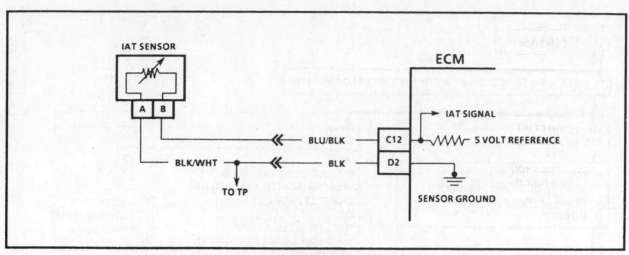

DTC 23

(Page 2 of 2)
INTAKE AIR TEMPERATURE (IAT) SENSOR CIRCUIT
(HIGH/LOW TEMPERATURE INDICATED)

Circuit Description:

The Intake Air Temperature (IAT) sensor uses a thermistor to control the signal voltage from the ECM. The ECM applies a voltage on the sensor signal wire to the sensor. When intake manifold air is cold, the sensor (thermistor) resistance is high, therefore, the ECM will see a high signal voltage. As the air warms the sensor resistance becomes less and the voltage drops.

Test Description: Number(s) below refer to circled number(s) on the diagnostic chart.

1. This check determines if the DTC 23 is the result of a hard failure or an intermittent condition.

Diagnostic Aids:

If the engine has been allowed to cool to an ambient temperature (overnight), coolant and IAT temperatures may be checked with a scan tool and should read close to each other.

A DTC 23 will result if the signal wire is shorted to ground.

Fig. 160 Code 23: intake air temperature sensor circuit (continued) — Storm

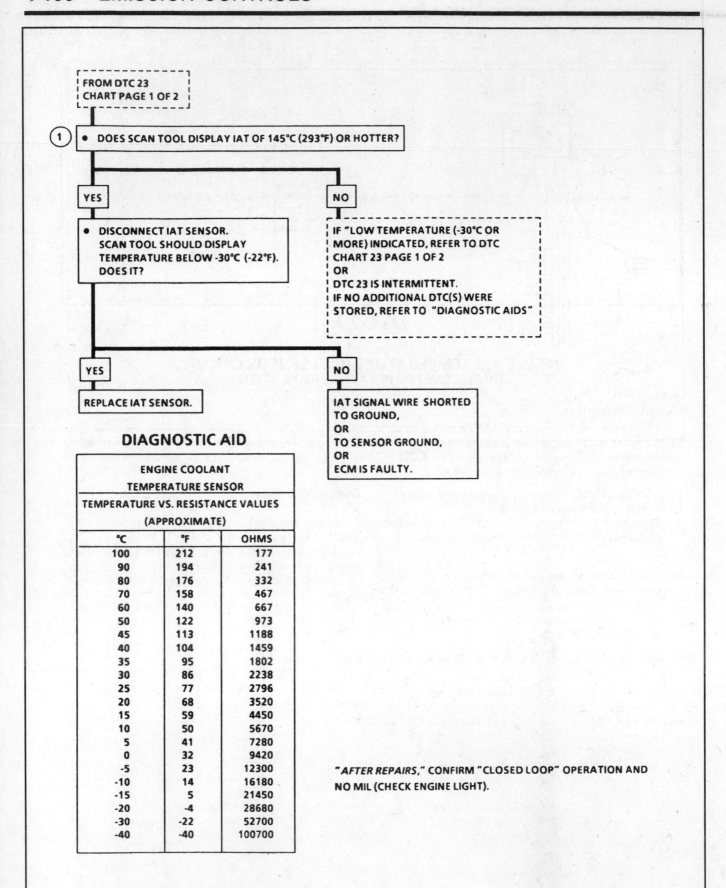

FROM DTC 23
CHART PAGE 1 OF 2

1 ● DOES SCAN TOOL DISPLAY IAT OF 145°C (293°F) OR HOTTER?

YES

● DISCONNECT IAT SENSOR.
SCAN TOOL SHOULD DISPLAY
TEMPERATURE BELOW -30°C (-22°F).
DOES IT?

NO

IF "LOW TEMPERATURE (-30°C OR
MORE) INDICATED, REFER TO DTC
CHART 23 PAGE 1 OF 2
OR
DTC 23 IS INTERMITTENT.
IF NO ADDITIONAL DTC(S) WERE
STORED, REFER TO "DIAGNOSTIC AIDS"

YES

REPLACE IAT SENSOR.

NO

IAT SIGNAL WIRE SHORTED
TO GROUND,
OR
TO SENSOR GROUND,
OR
ECM IS FAULTY.

DIAGNOSTIC AID

ENGINE COOLANT TEMPERATURE SENSOR		
TEMPERATURE VS. RESISTANCE VALUES (APPROXIMATE)		
°C	°F	OHMS
100	212	177
90	194	241
80	176	332
70	158	467
60	140	667
50	122	973
45	113	1188
40	104	1459
35	95	1802
30	86	2238
25	77	2796
20	68	3520
15	59	4450
10	50	5670
5	41	7280
0	32	9420
-5	23	12300
-10	14	16180
-15	5	21450
-20	-4	28680
-30	-22	52700
-40	-40	100700

"*AFTER REPAIRS*," CONFIRM "CLOSED LOOP" OPERATION AND
NO MIL (CHECK ENGINE LIGHT).

Fig. 161 Code 23: intake air temperature sensor circuit (continued) — Storm

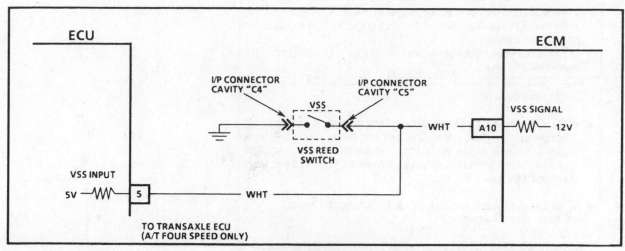

DTC 24
VEHICLE SPEED SENSOR (VSS) CIRCUIT

Circuit Description:

The Vehicle Speed Sensor (VSS), which is located in the instrument panel is a magnetic reed switch type. The ECM provides battery voltage to the switch, which will toggle the voltage high and low as a magnet that is part of the speedometer, pass by the reed switch. This pulsed signal to the ECM is used by the ECM to determine mph/km/h.

Test Description: Number(s) below refer to circled number(s) on the diagnostic chart.

1. DTC 24 will set if vehicle speed equals 0 mph when:
   - Engine speed is between 1500 and 4400 RPM.
   - Vehicle speed is indicated less than 5 km/h (3 mph).
   - No DTC 33 set.
   - MAP sensor is less than 43 kPa.
   - Not in park or neutral (A/T).
   - All conditions met for 5 seconds.

These conditions are met during a road load deceleration. Disregard DTC 24 that sets when drive wheels are not turning.

Diagnostic Aids:

- An open in the ECM circuit will result in 4-5 volts at terminal "C5" of the instrument panel connector. This voltage is sourced from the transaxle ECU for 4 speed transaxle only.

  Scan should indicate a vehicle speed whenever the drive wheels are turning greater than 3 mph (5 km/h).

  Check the VSS signal wire for proper connections to be sure they are clean and tight and the harness is routed correctly. Refer to "Intermittents" in "Symptoms."

  (A/T) - A faulty or misadjusted Park/Neutral switch can result in a false DTC 24. Use a scan tool and check for proper signal while in drive. Refer to CHART C-1A for PNP switch check.
- A faulty reed switch in the I/P can be the cause of an intermittent DTC 24. Inspect reed switch for poor connections and/or a crack in the glass vapor tube.

Fig. 162 Code 24: vehicle speed sensor circuit — Storm

DISREGARD DTC 24 IF SET WHILE DRIVE WHEELS ARE NOT TURNING.

- VERIFY SPEEDOMETER IS WORKING, IF NOT REFER TO APPROPRIATE SECTION OF THE SERVICE MANUAL FOR NECESSARY REPAIR PROCEDURES.
- CLEAR DTC FROM ECM AND RETEST. IF DTC RESETS PROCEED WITH DTC 24 CHART.

(1)

- RAISE DRIVE WHEELS.
- **NOTICE:** DO NOT PERFORM THIS TEST WITHOUT SUPPORTING THE LOWER CONTROL ARMS SO THAT THE DRIVE AXLES ARE IN A NORMAL HORIZONTAL POSITION. RUNNING THE VEHICLE IN GEAR WITH THE WHEELS HANGING DOWN AT FULL TRAVEL MAY DAMAGE THE DRIVE AXLES.
- WITH ENGINE IDLING IN GEAR, SCAN TOOL SHOULD DISPLAY VEHICLE SPEED ABOVE 0. DOES IT?

NO

- IGNITION "ON" ENGINE "OFF."
- USING A DVM BACKPROBE ECM TERMINAL "A10" WITH DRIVE WHEELS ROTATING.
- VOLTAGE SHOULD BE VARYING BETWEEN 0-12 VOLTS. IS IT?

YES

DTC 24 IS INTERMITTENT. IF NO ADDITIONAL DTC(S) WERE STORED, REFER TO "DIAGNOSTIC AIDS"

NO

USING A DVM BACKPROBE THE I/P CONNECTOR CAVITIES "C4" AND "C5". SHOULD HAVE 12 VOLTS OR MORE. DOES IT?

YES

POOR CONNECTION AT ECM OR FAULTY ECM.

YES

FAULTY CONNECTION AT I/P OR FAULTY REED SWITCH.

NO

REPEAT TEST WITH DVM AT TERMINAL "C5" AND GROUND. SHOULD HAVE 12 VOLTS OR MORE. DOES IT?

YES

FAULTY I/P GROUND.

NO

OPEN CIRCUIT OR FAULTY ECM.

"AFTER REPAIRS," CONFIRM "CLOSED LOOP" OPERATION AND NO MIL (CHECK ENGINE LIGHT).

Fig. 163 Code 24: vehicle speed sensor circuit — Storm

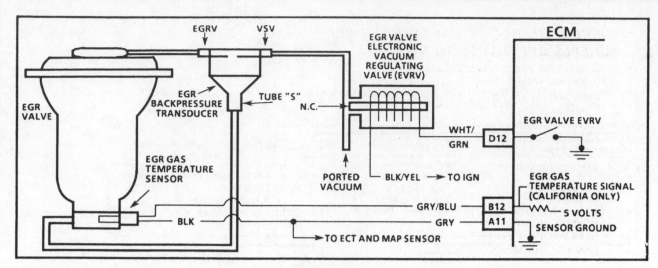

DTC 32
EXHAUST GAS RECIRCULATION (EGR) SYSTEM ERROR
(CALIFORNIA ONLY)

Circuit Description:

EGR valve operation is ECM controlled. A driver inside the ECM provides a ground source to the EGR Electronic Vacuum Regulating Valve (EVRV). By turning the EVRV "ON" and "OFF," the ECM controls the vacuum source to the EGR back-pressure transducer. The EGR back-pressure transducer then regulates vacuum to the EGR valve using back pressure provided by the exhaust system. For more information, refer to "Exhaust Gas Recirculation (EGR) System."   The ECM uses an EGR gas temperature sensor mounted in the base of the EGR valve for diagnosing if the EGR system is functioning properly. This temperature sensor contains a thermistor. The ECM provides a 5 volt reference and a ground for the sensor. The ECM monitors a change in the exhaust gas temperature to determine if the EGR valve is working when the EGR is commanded "ON." If the EGR valve fails to open, the gas temperature sensor signal will indicate "Low" Temperature to the ECM. If the EGR valve is stuck open, the gas temperature sensor signal will indicate "High" Temperature to the ECM. As a result, DTC 32 will be logged in the ECM's memory, and the "Check Engine" light will come "ON." A failure in the EGR gas temperature circuit will also set a DTC 32.

DTC 32 will set if any of the following conditions exist:
- "High" Temperature indicated at idle.
- "Low" Temperature indicated when EGR is commanded "ON."
- Open or short in the EGR gas temperature sensor circuit.
- One of the above conditions exist for 120 seconds.

EGR is not enabled if coolant temperature is below 69°C (182°F).

Test Description: Number(s) below refer to circled number(s) on the diagnostic chart.

1. Checks for the gas temperature sensors 5 volts reference.
2. Looking for a poor or open ground wire.
3. Checks for short to voltage or ground in sensor 5 volts reference circuit.
4. Checking the EGR gas temperatures sensors resistance.
5. A non-functioning EGR valve can cause DTC 32 to set.

Diagnostic Aids:

A poor connection or "shifted" EGR gas temperature sensor could cause a DTC 32 to set. To check for a "shifted" sensor, monitor the sensor resistance at ambient temperature with a DVM connected to GRY/BLU wire and BLK wire. Start and run the engine noting the resistance change in the sensor as engine temperature increases. Refer to Temperature to Resistance chart on diagnostic chart. If the sensor fails the check, replace the sensor.

Fig. 164 Code 32: exhaust gas recirculation system error — Storm

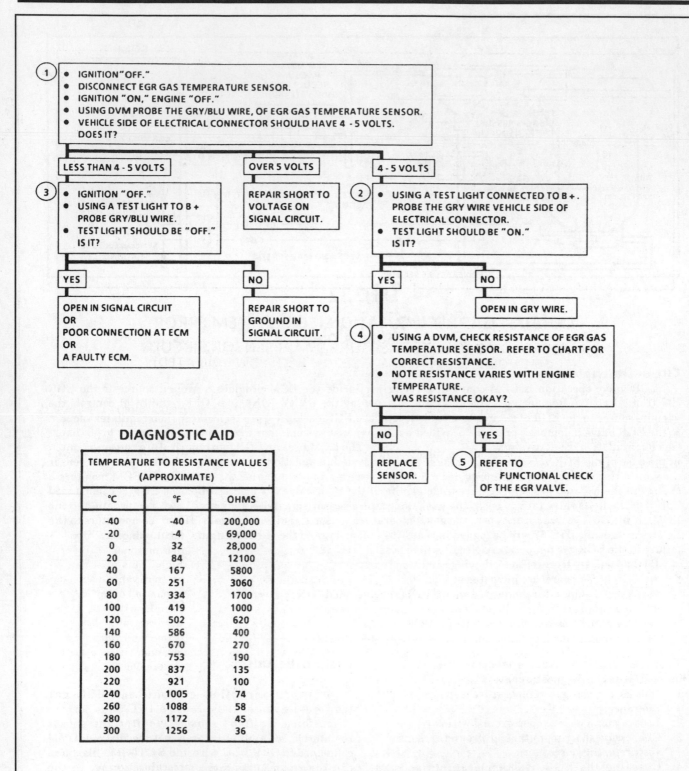

① • IGNITION "OFF."
   • DISCONNECT EGR GAS TEMPERATURE SENSOR.
   • IGNITION "ON," ENGINE "OFF."
   • USING DVM PROBE THE GRY/BLU WIRE, OF EGR GAS TEMPERATURE SENSOR.
   • VEHICLE SIDE OF ELECTRICAL CONNECTOR SHOULD HAVE 4 - 5 VOLTS.
     DOES IT?

LESS THAN 4 - 5 VOLTS

OVER 5 VOLTS

4 - 5 VOLTS

③ • IGNITION "OFF."
   • USING A TEST LIGHT TO B + PROBE GRY/BLU WIRE.
   • TEST LIGHT SHOULD BE "OFF." IS IT?

REPAIR SHORT TO VOLTAGE ON SIGNAL CIRCUIT.

② • USING A TEST LIGHT CONNECTED TO B +. PROBE THE GRY WIRE VEHICLE SIDE OF ELECTRICAL CONNECTOR.
   • TEST LIGHT SHOULD BE "ON." IS IT?

YES

OPEN IN SIGNAL CIRCUIT
OR
POOR CONNECTION AT ECM
OR
A FAULTY ECM.

NO

REPAIR SHORT TO GROUND IN SIGNAL CIRCUIT.

YES

NO

OPEN IN GRY WIRE.

④ • USING A DVM, CHECK RESISTANCE OF EGR GAS TEMPERATURE SENSOR. REFER TO CHART FOR CORRECT RESISTANCE.
   • NOTE RESISTANCE VARIES WITH ENGINE TEMPERATURE.
     WAS RESISTANCE OKAY?

NO

REPLACE SENSOR.

YES

⑤ REFER TO FUNCTIONAL CHECK OF THE EGR VALVE.

DIAGNOSTIC AID

TEMPERATURE TO RESISTANCE VALUES (APPROXIMATE)		
°C	°F	OHMS
-40	-40	200,000
-20	-4	69,000
0	32	28,000
20	84	12100
40	167	5800
60	251	3060
80	334	1700
100	419	1000
120	502	620
140	586	400
160	670	270
180	753	190
200	837	135
220	921	100
240	1005	74
260	1088	58
280	1172	45
300	1256	36

"AFTER REPAIRS," CONFIRM "CLOSED LOOP" OPERATION AND NO MIL (CHECK ENGINE LIGHT).

Fig. 165 Code 32: exhaust gas recirculation system error — Storm

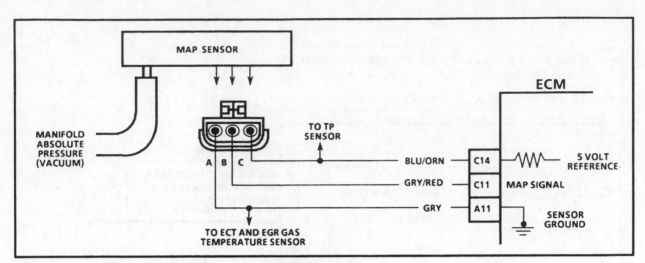

DTC 33

(Page 1 of 2)
MANIFOLD ABSOLUTE PRESSURE (MAP) SENSOR CIRCUIT
(SIGNAL VOLTAGE HIGH/LOW-VACUUM HIGH/LOW INDICATED)

Circuit Description:

The Manifold Absolute Pressure (MAP) sensor responds to changes in manifold pressure (vacuum). The ECM receives this information as a signal voltage that will vary from about 1 to 1.5 volts, at closed throttle idle, to 4 - 4.5 volts at Wide Open Throttle (low vacuum).

If the MAP sensor fails, the ECM will substitute a fixed MAP value and use the Throttle Position (TP) sensor to control fuel delivery.

Test Description: Number(s) below refer to circled number(s) on the diagnostic chart.

1. This step will determine if DTC 33 is the result of a hard failure or an intermittent condition.
   A DTC 33 will set if:
   High Voltage-Low Vacuum Criteria:
   - MAP signal indicates greater than 84 kPa (low vacuum).
   - No DTC 21 is set.
   - TP sensor less than 5%.
   - These conditions are present longer than 5 seconds.
   Low Voltage-High Vacuum Criteria:
   - Engine RPM > 1200 RPM.
   - No DTC 21 is set.
   - TP sensor is > 15%.
   - MAP voltage indicated too low.

2. This step simulates conditions for a DTC 33 (Signal Voltage Low-High Vacuum). If the ECM recognizes the change, the ECM and sensor ground wire and signal circuit wire are OK. If the 5 volt reference wire is open, there may also be a stored DTC 23.

Diagnostic Aids:

With the ignition "ON" and the engine stopped, the manifold pressure is equal to atmospheric pressure and the signal voltage will be high. This information is used by the ECM as an indication of vehicle altitude and is referred to as BARO. Comparison of this BARO reading with a known good vehicle with the same sensor is a good way to check accuracy of a "suspect" sensor. Readings should be the same ± .4 volt.

A DTC 33 will result if the ground wire is open, or if the signal wire is shorted to voltage or to the 5 volt reference wire.

If DTC 33 is intermittent, refer to "Intermittents" in "Symptoms."

NOTICE: If MAP sensor is mounted below intake manifold, you may set a false DTC 33. Be sure sensor is mounted in the correct location.

Fig. 166 Code 33: manifold absolute pressure sensor circuit — Storm

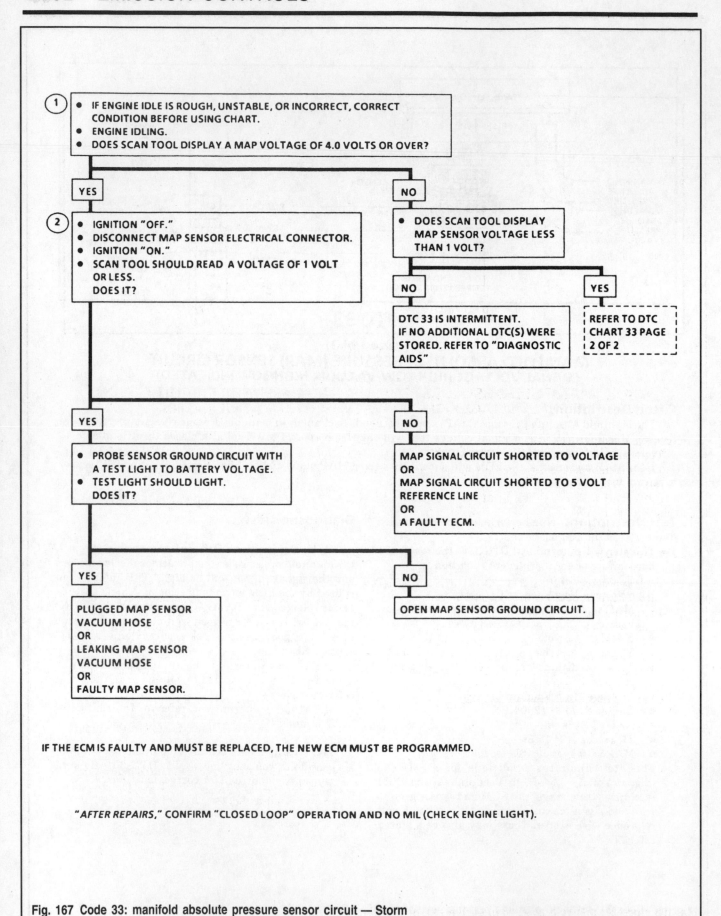

1
- IF ENGINE IDLE IS ROUGH, UNSTABLE, OR INCORRECT, CORRECT CONDITION BEFORE USING CHART.
- ENGINE IDLING.
- DOES SCAN TOOL DISPLAY A MAP VOLTAGE OF 4.0 VOLTS OR OVER?

YES

NO

2
- IGNITION "OFF."
- DISCONNECT MAP SENSOR ELECTRICAL CONNECTOR.
- IGNITION "ON."
- SCAN TOOL SHOULD READ A VOLTAGE OF 1 VOLT OR LESS. DOES IT?

- DOES SCAN TOOL DISPLAY MAP SENSOR VOLTAGE LESS THAN 1 VOLT?

NO

YES

DTC 33 IS INTERMITTENT. IF NO ADDITIONAL DTC(S) WERE STORED. REFER TO "DIAGNOSTIC AIDS"

REFER TO DTC CHART 33 PAGE 2 OF 2

YES

NO

- PROBE SENSOR GROUND CIRCUIT WITH A TEST LIGHT TO BATTERY VOLTAGE.
- TEST LIGHT SHOULD LIGHT. DOES IT?

MAP SIGNAL CIRCUIT SHORTED TO VOLTAGE OR MAP SIGNAL CIRCUIT SHORTED TO 5 VOLT REFERENCE LINE OR A FAULTY ECM.

YES

NO

PLUGGED MAP SENSOR VACUUM HOSE OR LEAKING MAP SENSOR VACUUM HOSE OR FAULTY MAP SENSOR.

OPEN MAP SENSOR GROUND CIRCUIT.

IF THE ECM IS FAULTY AND MUST BE REPLACED, THE NEW ECM MUST BE PROGRAMMED.

"AFTER REPAIRS," CONFIRM "CLOSED LOOP" OPERATION AND NO MIL (CHECK ENGINE LIGHT).

Fig. 167 Code 33: manifold absolute pressure sensor circuit — Storm

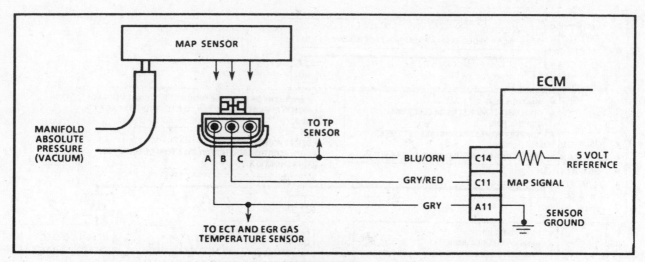

DTC 33

(Page 2 of 2)
MANIFOLD ABSOLUTE PRESSURE (MAP) SENSOR CIRCUIT
(SIGNAL VOLTAGE HIGH/LOW-VACUUM HIGH/LOW INDICATED)

Circuit Description:

The Manifold Absolute Pressure (MAP) sensor responds to changes in manifold pressure (vacuum). The ECM receives this information as a signal voltage that will vary from about 1 to 1.5 volts at closed throttle idle, to 4 - 4.5 volts at Wide Open Throttle (WOT).

If the MAP sensor fails, the ECM will substitute a fixed MAP value and use the Throttle Position (TP) sensor to control fuel delivery.

Test Description: Number(s) below refer to circled number(s) on the diagnostic chart.

1. This step determines if DTC 33 is the result of a hard failure or an intermittent condition.
2. Jumpering harness terminals "B" to "C", 5 volts to signal will determine if the sensor is at fault or if there is a problem with the ECM or wiring.
3. The scan tool may not display 12 volts. The important thing is that the ECM recognizes the voltage as more than 4 volts, indicating that the ECM and the signal circuit wire are OK.

Diagnostic Aids:

With the ignition "ON" and the engine stopped, the manifold pressure is equal to atmospheric pressure and the signal voltage will be high. This information is used by the ECM as an indication of vehicle altitude and is referred to as BARO. Comparison of this BARO reading with a known good vehicle with the same sensor is a good way to check accuracy of a "suspect" sensor. Readings should be the same ± .4 volt.

A DTC 33 will result if the 5 volt reference wire or the signal wire are open or shorted to ground.

If DTC 33 is intermittent, refer to "Intermittents" in "Symptoms."

NOTICE: If MAP sensor is mounted below intake manifold, you may set a false DTC 33. Be sure sensor is mounted in the correct location.

Fig. 168 Code 33: manifold absolute pressure sensor circuit (continued) — Storm

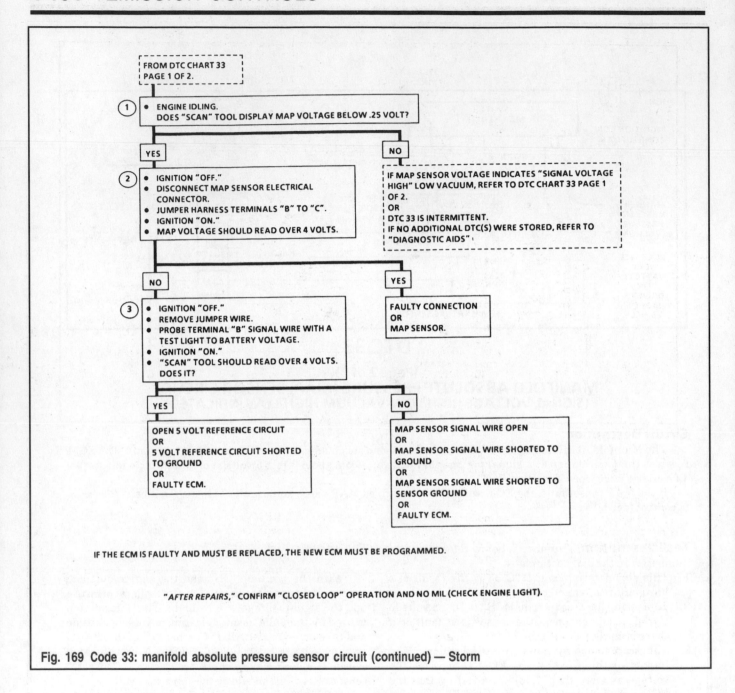

FROM DTC CHART 33
PAGE 1 OF 2.

1. • ENGINE IDLING.
     DOES "SCAN" TOOL DISPLAY MAP VOLTAGE BELOW .25 VOLT?

YES

NO

2. • IGNITION "OFF."
   • DISCONNECT MAP SENSOR ELECTRICAL CONNECTOR.
   • JUMPER HARNESS TERMINALS "B" TO "C".
   • IGNITION "ON."
   • MAP VOLTAGE SHOULD READ OVER 4 VOLTS.

IF MAP SENSOR VOLTAGE INDICATES "SIGNAL VOLTAGE HIGH" LOW VACUUM, REFER TO DTC CHART 33 PAGE 1 OF 2.
OR
DTC 33 IS INTERMITTENT.
IF NO ADDITIONAL DTC(S) WERE STORED, REFER TO "DIAGNOSTIC AIDS"

NO

YES

3. • IGNITION "OFF."
   • REMOVE JUMPER WIRE.
   • PROBE TERMINAL "B" SIGNAL WIRE WITH A TEST LIGHT TO BATTERY VOLTAGE.
   • IGNITION "ON."
   • "SCAN" TOOL SHOULD READ OVER 4 VOLTS. DOES IT?

FAULTY CONNECTION
OR
MAP SENSOR.

YES

NO

OPEN 5 VOLT REFERENCE CIRCUIT
OR
5 VOLT REFERENCE CIRCUIT SHORTED TO GROUND
OR
FAULTY ECM.

MAP SENSOR SIGNAL WIRE OPEN
OR
MAP SENSOR SIGNAL WIRE SHORTED TO GROUND
OR
MAP SENSOR SIGNAL WIRE SHORTED TO SENSOR GROUND
OR
FAULTY ECM.

IF THE ECM IS FAULTY AND MUST BE REPLACED, THE NEW ECM MUST BE PROGRAMMED.

"AFTER REPAIRS," CONFIRM "CLOSED LOOP" OPERATION AND NO MIL (CHECK ENGINE LIGHT).

Fig. 169 Code 33: manifold absolute pressure sensor circuit (continued) — Storm

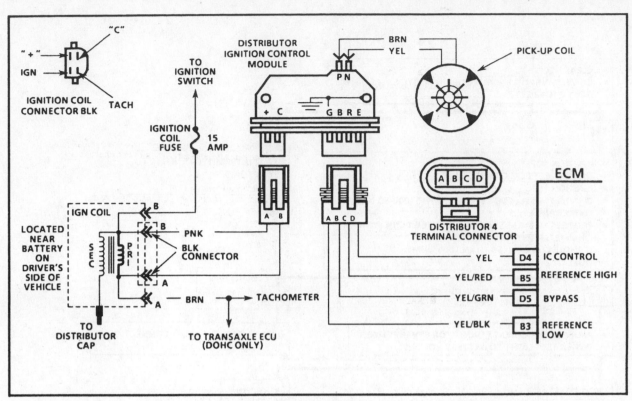

DTC 42

IGNITION CONTROL (IC) CIRCUIT ERROR

Circuit Description:

The Distributor Ignition (DI) module sends a reference signal (YEL/RED wire) to the ECM, when the engine is cranking. While the engine speed is under 400 RPM, the DI module will control ignition timing. When the engine speed exceeds 400 RPM, the ECM applies 5 volts to the bypass line to switch the timing to ECM control.

When the system is running on the DI module, that is, no voltage on the bypass line, the DI module grounds the IC circuit. The ECM expects to sense or detect no voltage on the IC line during this condition. If it senses or detects a voltage, it sets DTC 42 and will not go into the IC mode.

When the RPM for IC is reached (about 400 RPM), voltage will be applied to the bypass line. The IC should no longer be grounded in the DI module, so the IC voltage should be varying.

If the bypass line is open or grounded, the DI module will not switch to IC mode, so the IC voltage will be low and DTC 42 will be set.

If the IC line is grounded, the DI module will switch to IC but, because the line is grounded, there will be no IC signal. A DTC 42 will be set.

Test Description: Number(s) below refer to circled number(s) on the diagnostic chart.

1. DTC 42 means the ECM has detected an open or short to ground in the IC or bypass circuits. This test confirms DTC 42 and that the fault causing the DTC is present.
2. Checks for a normal IC ground path through the ignition module. An IC circuit wire shorted to ground, will also read less than 500 ohms; however, this will be checked later.
3. As the test light voltage touches bypass circuit wire, the DI module should switch, causing the ohmmeter to

"overrange" if the meter is in the 1000-2000 ohms position. Selecting the 10-20,000 ohms position will indicate above 5000 ohms. The important thing is that the DI module "switched."

4. The DI module did not switch and this step checks for:
   - IC circuit wire shorted to ground.
   - Bypass circuit wire open.
   - Faulty distributor ignition module connection or faulty DI module.
5. Confirms that DTC 42 is a faulty ECM and not an intermittent in circuit wire or bypass circuit wire.

Fig. 170 Code 42: ignition control circuit error — Storm

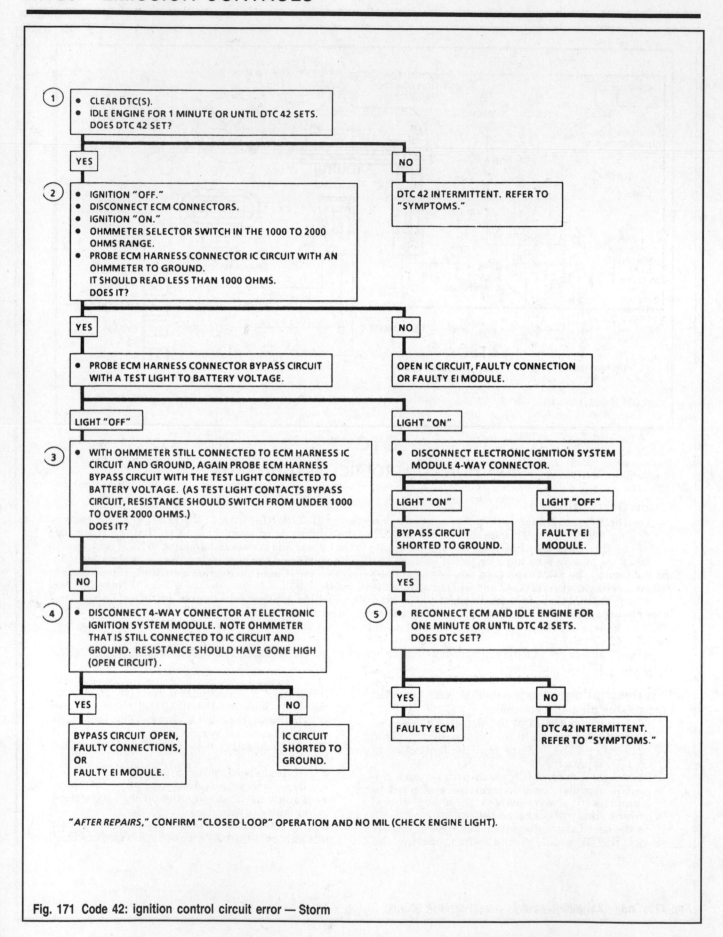

① • CLEAR DTC(S).
• IDLE ENGINE FOR 1 MINUTE OR UNTIL DTC 42 SETS.
  DOES DTC 42 SET?

YES

NO

② • IGNITION "OFF."
• DISCONNECT ECM CONNECTORS.
• IGNITION "ON."
• OHMMETER SELECTOR SWITCH IN THE 1000 TO 2000 OHMS RANGE.
• PROBE ECM HARNESS CONNECTOR IC CIRCUIT WITH AN OHMMETER TO GROUND.
  IT SHOULD READ LESS THAN 1000 OHMS.
  DOES IT?

DTC 42 INTERMITTENT. REFER TO "SYMPTOMS."

YES

NO

• PROBE ECM HARNESS CONNECTOR BYPASS CIRCUIT WITH A TEST LIGHT TO BATTERY VOLTAGE.

OPEN IC CIRCUIT, FAULTY CONNECTION OR FAULTY EI MODULE.

LIGHT "OFF"

LIGHT "ON"

③ • WITH OHMMETER STILL CONNECTED TO ECM HARNESS IC CIRCUIT AND GROUND, AGAIN PROBE ECM HARNESS BYPASS CIRCUIT WITH THE TEST LIGHT CONNECTED TO BATTERY VOLTAGE. (AS TEST LIGHT CONTACTS BYPASS CIRCUIT, RESISTANCE SHOULD SWITCH FROM UNDER 1000 TO OVER 2000 OHMS.)
  DOES IT?

• DISCONNECT ELECTRONIC IGNITION SYSTEM MODULE 4-WAY CONNECTOR.

LIGHT "ON"

LIGHT "OFF"

BYPASS CIRCUIT SHORTED TO GROUND.

FAULTY EI MODULE.

NO

YES

④ • DISCONNECT 4-WAY CONNECTOR AT ELECTRONIC IGNITION SYSTEM MODULE. NOTE OHMMETER THAT IS STILL CONNECTED TO IC CIRCUIT AND GROUND. RESISTANCE SHOULD HAVE GONE HIGH (OPEN CIRCUIT).

⑤ • RECONNECT ECM AND IDLE ENGINE FOR ONE MINUTE OR UNTIL DTC 42 SETS.
  DOES DTC SET?

YES

NO

YES

NO

BYPASS CIRCUIT OPEN, FAULTY CONNECTIONS, OR FAULTY EI MODULE.

IC CIRCUIT SHORTED TO GROUND.

FAULTY ECM

DTC 42 INTERMITTENT. REFER TO "SYMPTOMS."

"AFTER REPAIRS," CONFIRM "CLOSED LOOP" OPERATION AND NO MIL (CHECK ENGINE LIGHT).

Fig. 171 Code 42: ignition control circuit error — Storm

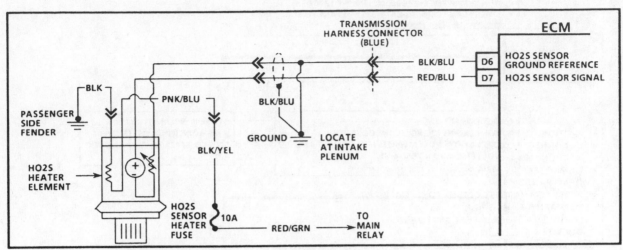

DTC 44

HEATED OXYGEN SENSOR (HO2S) CIRCUIT
(LEAN EXHAUST INDICATED)

Circuit Description:

The ECM supplies a voltage of about .45 volt between terminals "D7" and "D6". (If measured with a 10 megohm digital voltmeter, this may read as low as .32 volt.)

The heater circuit of the oxygen sensor is turned "ON" when the engine is running. The oxygen sensor as it heats up will begin to send a varying voltage signal to the ECM. This voltage will vary from about .1 volt (lean exhaust) to about 1.0 volts (rich exhaust) depending on the condition of the exhaust gases in the exhaust manifold.

The sensor is like an open circuit and produces no voltage when it is below 315°C (600°F). An open sensor circuit causes "Open Loop" operation.

Test Description: Number(s) below refer to circled number(s) on the diagnostic chart.
1. DTC 44 is set when the O2 sensor signal voltage is fixed above 280 mV) and the following:
   - TP sensor greater than 3%.
   - No DTC 21 or 33.
   - System is operating in "Closed Loop."
   - Engine Coolant Temperature (ECT) above 69.5°C (183°F).
   - Short term fuel trim not at 128.
   - VSS > 3 mph.

Diagnostic Aids:

Using the scan tool, observe the long term fuel trim value at different RPMs. The scan tool also displays the long term fuel trim cells, so the long term fuel trim values can be checked in each of the cells, to determine when the DTC 44 may have been set. If the conditions for DTC 44 exist, the long term fuel trim values will be around 150.
- HO2 Sensor Wire - Sensor pigtail may be mispositioned and contacting the exhaust manifold.
- Check for ground in wire between connector and sensor.

- Fuel Contamination - Water, even in small amounts, near the in-tank fuel pump inlet can be delivered to the injector. The water causes a lean exhaust and can set a DTC 44.
- Fuel Pressure - System will be lean if pressure is too low. It may be necessary to monitor fuel pressure, while driving the vehicle at various road speeds and/or loads to confirm. See "Fuel System Diagnosis," CHART A-7.
- Exhaust Leaks - If there is an exhaust leak, the engine can cause outside air to be pulled into the exhaust and past the sensor. Vacuum or crankcase leaks can cause a lean condition.
- If DTC 44 intermittent, refer to "Symptoms,"

- If the heater part of the O2 sensor fails, this may cause a DTC 44 or DTC 45 to set.

- Check the oxygen sensor wire for induced voltage (EMI). Disconnect the oxygen sensor signal wire at the sensor and the ECM. Using DVM measure the wire with the engine running for any voltage. If 300 mV or more are indicated, check the signal wire shield and/or reroute the signal wire away from any high voltage sources. Such source could be ignition wires, battery cables, Alternator "B" circuit, etc.

Fig. 172 Code 44: oxygen sensor circuit (DOHC engine) — Storm

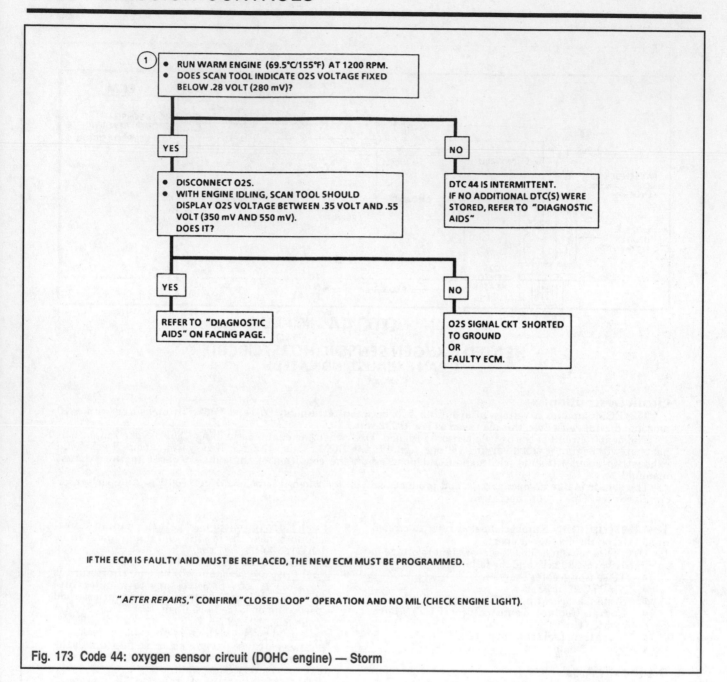

Fig. 173 Code 44: oxygen sensor circuit (DOHC engine) — Storm

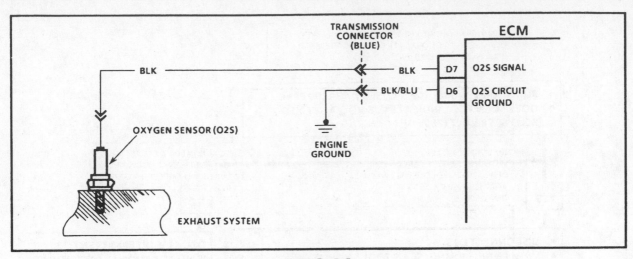

DTC 44
OXYGEN SENSOR (O2S) CIRCUIT
(LEAN EXHAUST INDICATED)

Circuit Description:

The ECM supplies a voltage of about .43 volt between terminals "D7" and "D6". (If measured with a 10 megohm digital voltmeter, this may read as low as .32 volt.) The oxygen sensor varies the voltage within a range of about 1.0 volt, if the exhaust is rich, down to about .10 volt, if exhaust is lean.

The sensor is like an open circuit and produces no voltage, when it is below about 315°C (600°F). An open sensor circuit causes "Open Loop" operation.

Test Description: Number(s) below refer to circled number(s) on the diagnostic chart.

1. DTC 44 will set when the following occurs:
    - No DTC 21 or DTC 33.
    - Engine running for 50 seconds or more.
    - O2S voltage below 278 mV for 99 seconds.
    - System is in "Closed Loop."
    - Engine coolant temperature above 69.5°C (183°F).
    - TP sensor is above 3%.
    - Short term fuel trim not at 128.
    - VSS > 3 mph.

Diagnostic Aids:

Using the scan tool, observe the long term fuel trim value at different RPMs. The scan tool also displays the long term fuel trim cells, so the long term fuel trim values can be checked in each of the cells, to determine when the DTC 44 may have been set. If the conditions for DTC 44 exist, the long term fuel trim values will be around 150.
- Oxygen Sensor Wire - Sensor pigtail may be mispositioned and contacting the exhaust manifold.
- Check for ground in wire between connector and sensor.

- Fuel Contamination - Water, even in small amounts, near the in-tank fuel pump inlet can be delivered to the injector. The water causes a lean exhaust and can set a DTC 44.
- Fuel Pressure - System will be lean if pressure is too low. It may be necessary to monitor fuel pressure, while driving the vehicle at various road speeds and/or loads to confirm. See "Fuel System Diagnosis," CHART A-7.
- Exhaust Leaks - If there is an exhaust leak, the engine can cause outside air to be pulled into the exhaust and past the sensor. Vacuum or crankcase leaks can cause a lean condition.
- If DTC 44 intermittent, refer to "Symptoms."

- Fuel Injectors - The wrong fuel injector(s) could be the cause of a lean exhaust condition. Verify that the correct fuel injector(s) are installed in the vehicle. Refer to the service parts manual for correct part and part number.
- Check the oxygen sensor wire for induced voltage (EMI). Disconnect the oxygen sensor signal wire at the sensor and the ECM. Using DVM, measure the wire with the engine running for any voltage. If 300 mV or more are indicated, check the signal wire shield and/or reroute the signal wire away from any high voltage sources. Such source could be ignition wires, battery cables, Alternator "B" circuit, etc.

Fig. 174 Code 44: oxygen sensor circuit (SOHC engine) — Storm

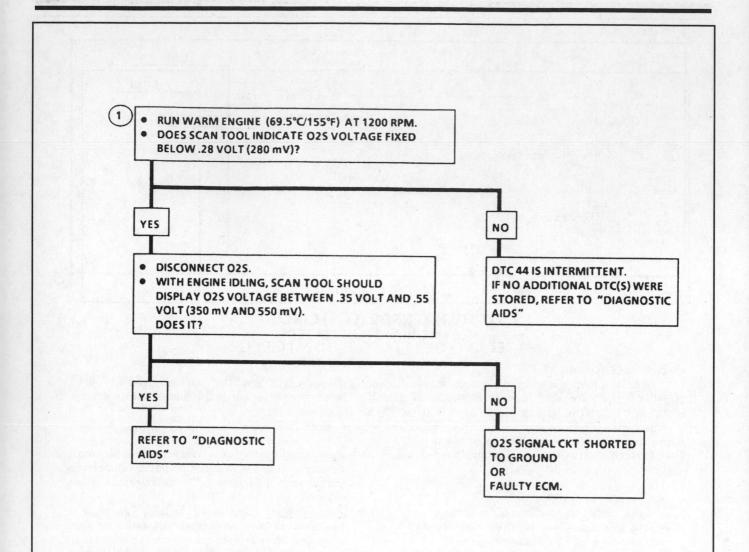

① • RUN WARM ENGINE (69.5°C/155°F) AT 1200 RPM.
• DOES SCAN TOOL INDICATE O2S VOLTAGE FIXED BELOW .28 VOLT (280 mV)?

YES

NO

• DISCONNECT O2S.
• WITH ENGINE IDLING, SCAN TOOL SHOULD DISPLAY O2S VOLTAGE BETWEEN .35 VOLT AND .55 VOLT (350 mV AND 550 mV). DOES IT?

DTC 44 IS INTERMITTENT.
IF NO ADDITIONAL DTC(S) WERE STORED, REFER TO "DIAGNOSTIC AIDS"

YES

NO

REFER TO "DIAGNOSTIC AIDS"

O2S SIGNAL CKT SHORTED TO GROUND
OR
FAULTY ECM.

IF THE ECM IS FAULTY AND MUST BE REPLACED, THE NEW ECM MUST BE PROGRAMMED.

"AFTER REPAIRS," CONFIRM "CLOSED LOOP" OPERATION AND NO MIL (CHECK ENGINE LIGHT).

Fig. 175 Code 44: oxygen sensor circuit (SOHC engine) — Storm

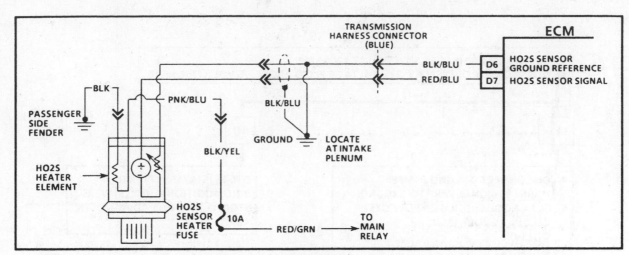

DTC 45

HEATED OXYGEN SENSOR (HO2S) CIRCUIT
(RICH EXHAUST INDICATED)

Circuit Description:

The ECM supplies a voltage of about .45 volt between terminals "D7" and "D6". (If measured with a 10 megohm digital voltmeter, this may read as low as .32 volt.)

The heater circuit of the oxygen sensor is turned "ON" when the engine is running. The oxygen sensor as it heats up will begin to send a varying voltage signal to the ECM. This voltage will vary from about .1 volt (lean exhaust) to about 1.0 volts (rich exhaust) depending on the condition of the exhaust gases in the exhaust manifold.

The sensor is like an open circuit and produces no voltage when it is below 315°C (600°F). An open sensor circuit or cold sensor causes "Open Loop" operation.

Test Description: Number(s) below refer to circled number(s) on the diagnostic chart.
1. DTC 45 is set, when the O2 sensor signal voltage is fixed above .75 (750 mV) and the following:
   - TP sensor greater than 3%.
   - No DTC 21 or 33.
   - System is operating in "Closed Loop."
   - Engine Coolant Temperature (ECT) above 69.5°C (183°F).
   - Short term fuel trim not at 128.
   - VSS > 3 mph.

Diagnostic Aids:

The DTC 45, or rich exhaust, is most likely caused by one of the following:
- Fuel Pressure - System will go rich if pressure is too high. The ECM can compensate for some increase. However, if it gets too high, a DTC 45 will be set. See "Fuel System Diagnosis" CHART A-7.
- HEI Shielding - An open ground YEL/BLK wire may result in EMI, or induced electrical "noise." The ECM looks at this "noise" as reference pulses. The additional pulses result in a higher than actual engine speed signal. The ECM then delivers too much fuel, causing system to go rich. Engine tachometer will also show higher than actual engine speed, which can help in diagnosing this problem.
- Canister Purge - Check for fuel saturation. If full of fuel, check canister control and hoses. See "Evaporative Emission (EVAP) Control System,"
- MAP Sensor - An output that causes the ECM to sense a higher than normal manifold pressure (low vacuum) can cause the system to go rich. Disconnecting the MAP sensor will allow the ECM to set a fixed value for the MAP sensor. Substitute a different MAP sensor if the rich condition is gone, while the sensor is disconnected.
- TP Sensor - An intermittent TP sensor output will cause the system to go rich, due to a false indication of the engine accelerating.
- Oxygen Sensor Contamination - Inspect oxygen sensor for silicone contamination from fuel, or use of improper RTV sealant. The sensor may have a white, powdery coating and result in a high, but false signal voltage (rich exhaust indication). The ECM will then reduce the amount of fuel delivered to the engine, causing a severe surge driveability problem.
- EGR - Valve sticking open at idle, usually accompanied by a rough idle, stall complaint. If DTC 45 is intermittent, refer to "Symptoms."

Fig. 176 Code 45: oxygen sensor circuit (DOHC engine) — Storm

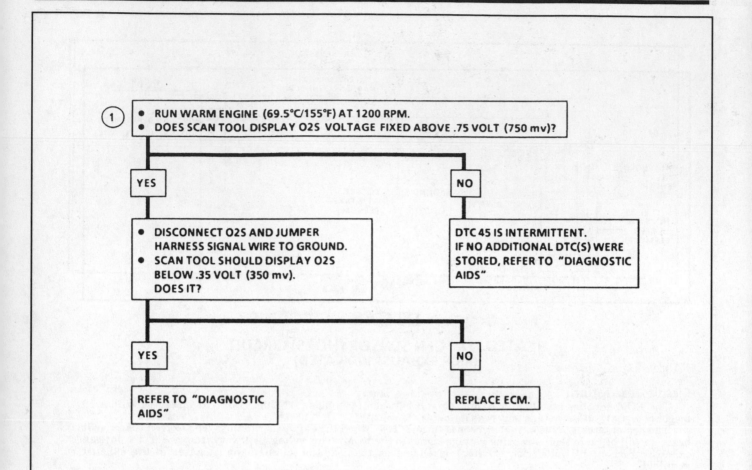

1.
   - RUN WARM ENGINE (69.5°C/155°F) AT 1200 RPM.
   - DOES SCAN TOOL DISPLAY O2S VOLTAGE FIXED ABOVE .75 VOLT (750 mv)?

YES

- DISCONNECT O2S AND JUMPER HARNESS SIGNAL WIRE TO GROUND.
- SCAN TOOL SHOULD DISPLAY O2S BELOW .35 VOLT (350 mv). DOES IT?

NO

DTC 45 IS INTERMITTENT. IF NO ADDITIONAL DTC(S) WERE STORED, REFER TO "DIAGNOSTIC AIDS"

YES

REFER TO "DIAGNOSTIC AIDS"

NO

REPLACE ECM.

IF THE ECM IS FAULTY AND MUST BE REPLACED, THE NEW ECM MUST BE PROGRAMMED.

"AFTER REPAIRS," CONFIRM "CLOSED LOOP" OPERATION AND NO MIL (CHECK ENGINE LIGHT).

Fig. 177 Code 45: oxygen sensor circuit (DOHC engine) — Storm

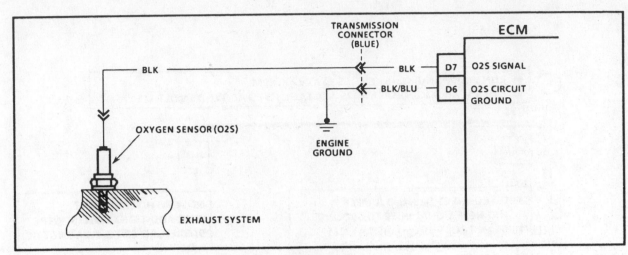

DTC 45
OXYGEN SENSOR (O2S) CIRCUIT
(RICH EXHAUST INDICATED)

Circuit Description:

The ECM supplies a voltage of about .43 volt between terminals "D7" and "D6". (If measured with a 10 megohm digital voltmeter, this may read as low as .32 volt.) The oxygen sensor varies the voltage within a range of about 1.0 volt, if the exhaust is rich, down to about .10 volt, if exhaust is lean.

The sensor is like an open circuit and produces no voltage, when it is below about 315°C (600°F). An open sensor circuit causes "Open Loop" operation.

Test Description: Number(s) below refer to circled number(s) on the diagnostic chart.
1. DTC 45 is set, when the O2 sensor signal voltage is fixed above .75 (750 mV) and the following:
   - TP sensor greater than 3%.
   - No DTC 21 or 33.
   - System is operating in "Closed Loop."
   - Engine Coolant Temperature (ECT) above 69.5°C (183°F).
   - Short term fuel trim not at 128.
   - VSS > 3 mph.

Diagnostic Aids:

The DTC 45, or rich exhaust, is most likely caused by one of the following:
- Fuel Pressure - System will go rich if pressure is too high. The ECM can compensate for some increase. However, if it gets too high, a DTC 45 will be set. See "Fuel System Diagnosis" CHART A-7.
- HEI Shielding - An open ignition ref low wire may result in EMI, or induced electrical "noise." The ECM looks at this "noise" as reference pulses. The additional pulses result in a higher than actual engine speed signal. Refer to

  ECM wiring schematics for ignition system wiring. The ECM then delivers too much fuel, causing system to go rich. Engine tachometer will also show higher than actual engine speed, which can help in diagnosing this problem.

- Canister Purge - Check for fuel saturation. If full of fuel, check canister control and hoses. See "Evaporative Emission (EVAP) Control System."
- MAP Sensor - An output that causes the ECM to sense a higher than normal manifold pressure (low vacuum) can cause the system to go rich. Disconnecting the MAP sensor will allow the ECM to set a fixed value for the MAP sensor. Substitute a different MAP sensor if the rich condition is gone, while the sensor is disconnected.
- TP Sensor - An intermittent TP sensor output will cause the system to go rich, due to a false indication of the engine accelerating.
- Oxygen Sensor Contamination - Inspect oxygen sensor for silicone contamination from fuel, or use of improper RTV sealant.
- Fuel Injectors - The wrong fuel injector(s) could be the cause of a rich exhaust condition. Verify the correct injector(s) are installed in the vehicle. Refer to the service parts manual for the correct part and part number.
- EGR - Valve sticking open at idle, usually accompanied by a rough idle, stall complaint.

If DTC 45 is intermittent, refer to "Intermittents" in "Symptoms,"

Fig. 178 Code 45: oxygen sensor circuit (SOHC engine) — Storm

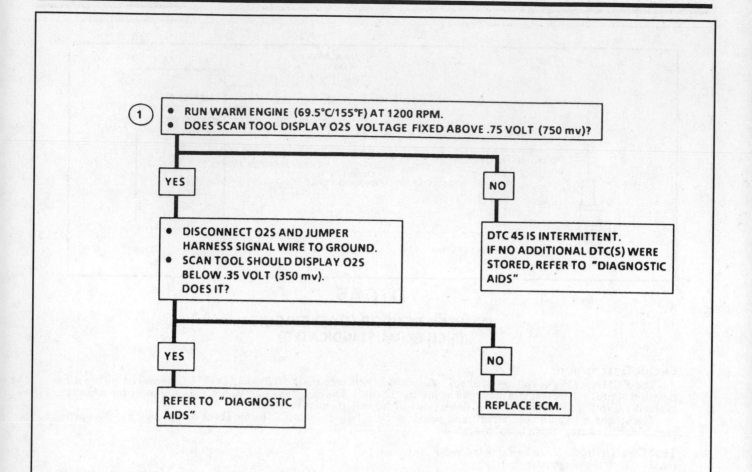

① • RUN WARM ENGINE (69.5°C/155°F) AT 1200 RPM.
• DOES SCAN TOOL DISPLAY O2S VOLTAGE FIXED ABOVE .75 VOLT (750 mv)?

YES

• DISCONNECT O2S AND JUMPER HARNESS SIGNAL WIRE TO GROUND.
• SCAN TOOL SHOULD DISPLAY O2S BELOW .35 VOLT (350 mv). DOES IT?

NO

DTC 45 IS INTERMITTENT.
IF NO ADDITIONAL DTC(S) WERE STORED, REFER TO "DIAGNOSTIC AIDS"

YES

REFER TO "DIAGNOSTIC AIDS"

NO

REPLACE ECM.

IF THE ECM IS FAULTY AND MUST BE REPLACED, THE NEW ECM MUST BE PROGRAMMED.

"AFTER REPAIRS," CONFIRM "CLOSED LOOP" OPERATION AND NO MIL (CHECK ENGINE LIGHT).

Fig. 179 Code 45: oxygen sensor circuit (SOHC engine) — Storm

DTC 51
ECM FAILURE
(ECM FAILED OR EEPROM FAILURE)

CHECK THAT ALL ECM CONNECTIONS ARE GOOD.
IF OK, CLEAR MEMORY AND RECHECK ECM.
IF DTC 51 REAPPEARS, REPLACE ECM AND REPROGRAM.

IF THE ECM IS FAULTY AND MUST BE REPLACED, THE NEW ECM MUST BE PROGRAMMED.

"AFTER REPAIRS," CONFIRM "CLOSED LOOP" OPERATION AND NO MIL (CHECK ENGINE LIGHT).

Fig. 180 Code 51: ecm or eeprom failure — Storm

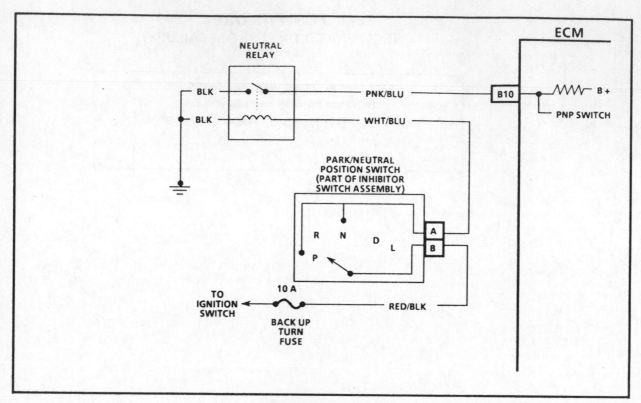

CHART C-1A

PARK/NEUTRAL POSITION (PNP) SWITCH DIAGNOSIS
(AUTO TRANSAXLE ONLY)

Circuit Description:

The Park/Neutral Position (PNP) switch contacts are a part of the inhibitor switch assembly. When the PNP is in park or neutral the neutral relay is "Closed" indicating to the ECM the vehicle is in park/neutral (low voltage at ECM terminal "B10"). When the gear selector is moved to reverse or drive the neutral relay is "Open" (high voltage at ECM terminal "B10") the ECM will raise the engine RPM for the additional load the transaxle put on the engine.

The ECM uses the PNP signal as one of the inputs to control idle air, VSS diagnostics, and EGR.

If signal wire indicates PNP (grounded), while in drive range, the EGR would be inoperative, resulting in possible detonation.

If PNP signal wire indicates drive (closed), a dip in the idle may exist when the gear selector is moved into drive range a harsh bump may be felt. If the ECM thinks the vehicle is in drive range all of the time, a "High" idle condition may exist.

Test Description: Number(s) below refer to circled number(s) on the diagnostic chart.

1. Checks for a closed switch to ground in park position. Different makes of scan tools will read PNP differently. Refer to tool operator's manual for type of display used for a specific tool.

2. Checks for an open switch in drive range.
3. Be sure scan indicates drive, even while wiggling shifter, to test for an intermittent or misadjusted switch in drive or overdrive range.
4. Checking for an open in the power feed circuit.

Fig. 181 Chart C-1a: park/neutral position switch diagnosis — Storm

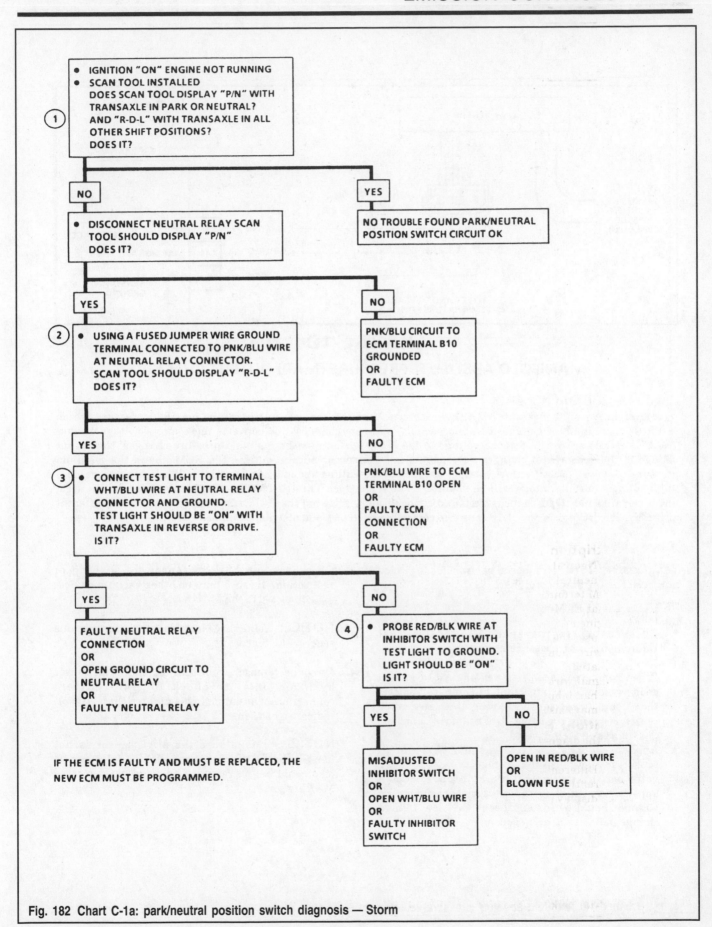

Fig. 182 Chart C-1a: park/neutral position switch diagnosis — Storm

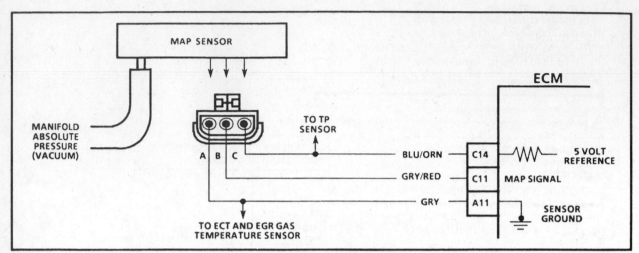

CHART C-1D
MANIFOLD ABSOLUTE PRESSURE (MAP) OUTPUT CHECK

Circuit Description:

Manifold Absolute Pressure (MAP) sensor measures the changes in the intake manifold pressure which result from engine load (intake manifold vacuum) and rpm changes; and converts these into a voltage output. The ECM sends a 5-volt reference voltage to the MAP sensor. As the manifold pressure changes, the output voltage of the sensor also changes. By monitoring the sensor output voltage, the ECM knows the manifold pressure. A lower pressure (low voltage) output voltage will be about 1-2 volts at idle. While higher pressure (high voltage) output voltage will be about 4-4.8 at Wide Open Throttle (WOT). The MAP sensor is also used, under certain conditions, to measure barometric pressure, allowing the ECM to make adjustments for different altitudes. The ECM uses the MAP sensor to control fuel delivery and distributor ignition timing.

Test Description: Number(s) below refer to circled number(s) on the diagnostic chart.

> ⚠ **Important**

- Be sure to use the same Diagnostic Test Equipment for all measurements.

1. When comparing scan tool readings to a known good vehicle, it is important to compare vehicles that use a MAP sensor having the same color insert or having the same "Hot Stamped" number. See figures on facing page.
2. Applying 34 kPa (10" Hg) vacuum to the MAP sensor should cause the voltage to be 1.5 to 2.1 volts less than the voltage at Step 1. Upon applying vacuum to the sensor, the change in voltage should be instantaneous. A slow voltage change indicates a faulty sensor.

3. Check vacuum hose to sensor for leaking or restriction. Be sure than no other vacuum devices are connected to the MAP hose.

NOTICE: Make sure electrical connector remains securely fastened.

4. Disconnect sensor from bracket and twist sensor by hand (only) to check for intermittent connection. Output changes greater than .10 volt indicate a bad sensor.

NOTICE: Make sure the MAP sensor is not hanging below the intake manifold, a false engine load could be the result of an improperly located MAP sensor.

Fig. 183 Chart C-1d: manifold absolute pressure sensor output check — Storm

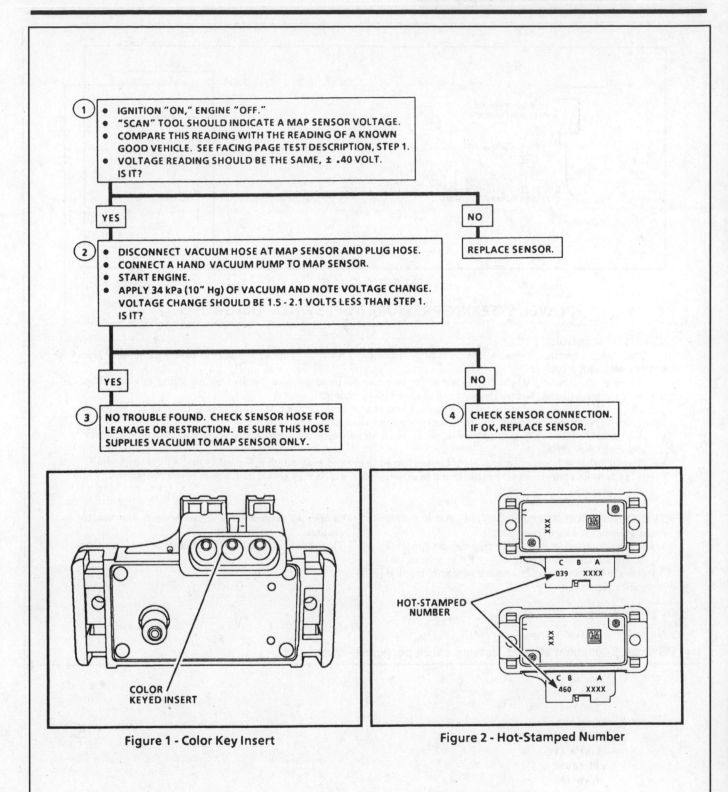

1
- IGNITION "ON," ENGINE "OFF."
- "SCAN" TOOL SHOULD INDICATE A MAP SENSOR VOLTAGE.
- COMPARE THIS READING WITH THE READING OF A KNOWN GOOD VEHICLE. SEE FACING PAGE TEST DESCRIPTION, STEP 1.
- VOLTAGE READING SHOULD BE THE SAME, ± .40 VOLT. IS IT?

YES

NO → REPLACE SENSOR.

2
- DISCONNECT VACUUM HOSE AT MAP SENSOR AND PLUG HOSE.
- CONNECT A HAND VACUUM PUMP TO MAP SENSOR.
- START ENGINE.
- APPLY 34 kPa (10" Hg) OF VACUUM AND NOTE VOLTAGE CHANGE. VOLTAGE CHANGE SHOULD BE 1.5 - 2.1 VOLTS LESS THAN STEP 1. IS IT?

YES

NO

3 NO TROUBLE FOUND. CHECK SENSOR HOSE FOR LEAKAGE OR RESTRICTION. BE SURE THIS HOSE SUPPLIES VACUUM TO MAP SENSOR ONLY.

4 CHECK SENSOR CONNECTION. IF OK, REPLACE SENSOR.

COLOR KEYED INSERT

Figure 1 - Color Key Insert

HOT-STAMPED NUMBER

C B A
039 XXXX

C B A
460 XXXX

Figure 2 - Hot-Stamped Number

"AFTER REPAIRS," CONFIRM "CLOSED LOOP" OPERATION AND NO MIL (CHECK ENGINE LIGHT).

Fig. 184 Chart C-1d: manifold absolute pressure sensor output check — Storm

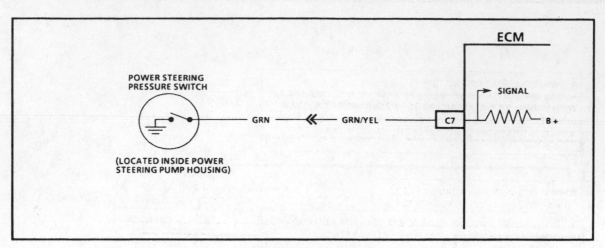

CHART C-1E
POWER STEERING PRESSURE (PSP) SWITCH DIAGNOSIS

Circuit Description:
The Power Steering Pressure Switch (PSPS) is normally open to ground, and signal wire will be near the battery voltage.

Turning the steering wheel increases power steering oil pressure and its load on an idling engine. The pressure switch will close before the load can cause an idle problem.

Closing the switch causes signal wire to read less than 1 volt. The ECM will increase the idle air rate and disengage the A/C relay, and distributor ignition timing will also become fixed.

- A pressure switch that will not close, or an open signal wire may cause the engine to stop when power steering loads are high.
- A switch that will not open or a signal wire shorted to ground may affect idle quality and will cause the A/C relay to be de-energized and spark timing to become fixed, which may result in a lack of power complaint.

Test Description: Number(s) below refer to circled number(s) on the diagnostic chart.
1. Different makes of scan tools may display the state of this switch in different ways. Refer to scan tool operator's manual to determine how this input is indicated.

2. Checks to determine if signal wire is shorted to ground.
3. This should simulate a closed switch.

Fig. 185 Chart C-1e: power steering pressure switch diagnosis — Storm

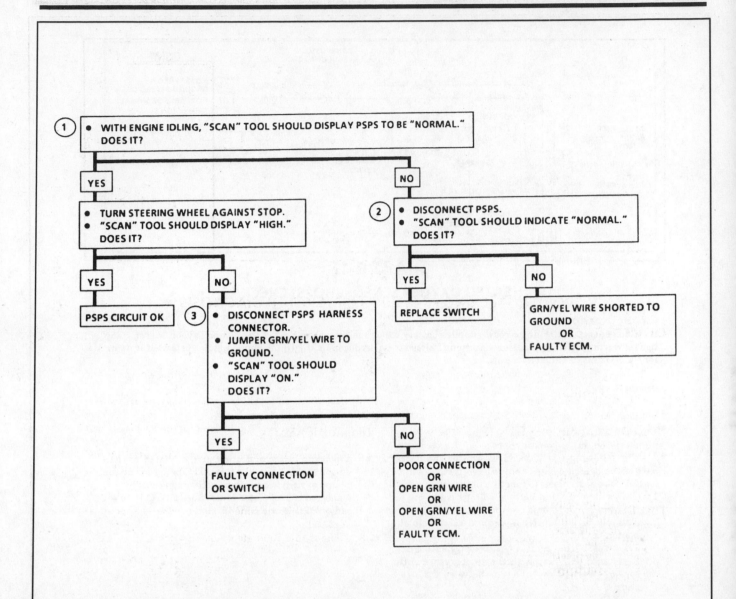

① • WITH ENGINE IDLING, "SCAN" TOOL SHOULD DISPLAY PSPS TO BE "NORMAL." DOES IT?

YES

• TURN STEERING WHEEL AGAINST STOP.
• "SCAN" TOOL SHOULD DISPLAY "HIGH." DOES IT?

YES

PSPS CIRCUIT OK

NO

③ • DISCONNECT PSPS HARNESS CONNECTOR.
• JUMPER GRN/YEL WIRE TO GROUND.
• "SCAN" TOOL SHOULD DISPLAY "ON." DOES IT?

YES

FAULTY CONNECTION OR SWITCH

NO

POOR CONNECTION
OR
OPEN GRN WIRE
OR
OPEN GRN/YEL WIRE
OR
FAULTY ECM.

NO

② • DISCONNECT PSPS.
• "SCAN" TOOL SHOULD INDICATE "NORMAL." DOES IT?

YES

REPLACE SWITCH

NO

GRN/YEL WIRE SHORTED TO GROUND
OR
FAULTY ECM.

IF THE ECM IS FAULTY AND MUST BE REPLACED, THE NEW ECM MUST BE PROGRAMMED.

"AFTER REPAIRS," CONFIRM "CLOSED LOOP" OPERATION AND NO MIL (CHECK ENGINE LIGHT).

Fig. 186 Chart C-1e: power steering pressure switch diagnosis — Storm

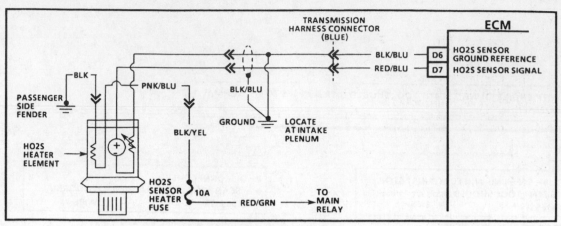

CHART C-1F
HEATED OXYGEN SENSOR (HO2S) CHECK

Circuit Description:

The generator charging circuit supplies battery voltage to the heater part of the heated oxygen sensor. The heater warms the HO2S to allow a varying voltage to be produced by the HO2S more rapidly instead of waiting for the HO2S to heat-up on its own.

Test Description: Number(s) below refer to circled number(s) on the diagnostic chart.

The following test procedures are for the heater part of the heated oxygen sensor. No DTC(s) will be logged if the heater fails to function properly.

1. This will verify that battery voltage is present for the heater.
2. This check will test the ground circuit to the heater.
3. This tests the heater element resistance. Resistance will vary with the temperature of the sensor. Normal resistance is between 3.5 - 14.2 ohms.

Diagnostic Aids:

- A poor or loose connection at the heated oxygen sensor could result in a false DTC being set or the heated oxygen heater not functioning properly.
- A shorted HO2S heater could cause a DTC 13 to set and/or DTC 44 and DTC 45.

Fig. 187 Chart C-1f: heated oxygen sensor check (DOHC engine) — Storm

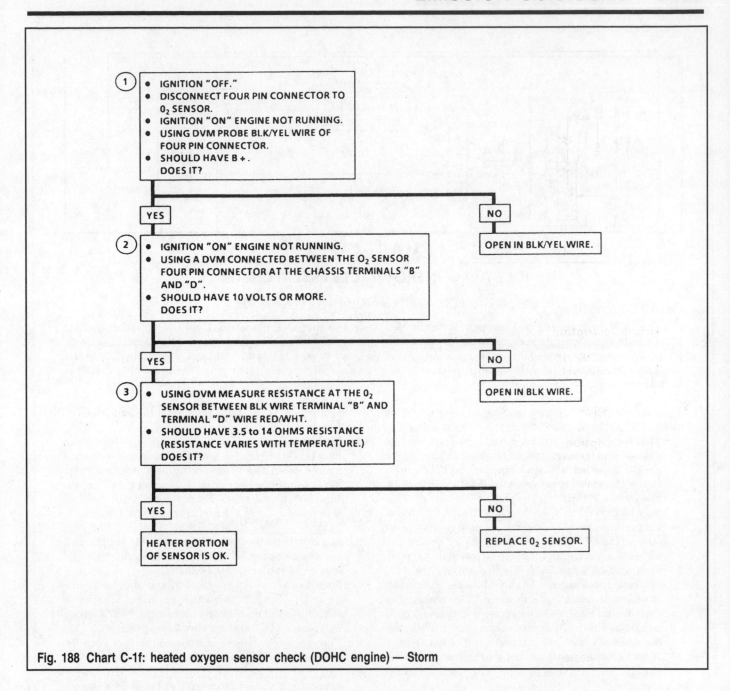

Fig. 188 Chart C-1f: heated oxygen sensor check (DOHC engine) — Storm

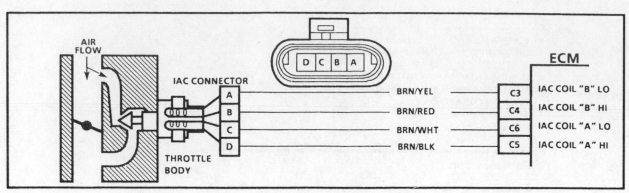

CHART C-2C

IDLE AIR CONTROL (IAC) SYSTEM CHECK

Circuit Description:

The ECM controls engine idle speed with the IAC valve. To increase idle speed, the ECM retracts the IAC valve pintle away from its seat, allowing more air to bypass the throttle bore. To decrease idle speed, it extends the IAC valve pintle towards its seat, reducing bypass air flow. A scan tool will read the ECM commands to the IAC valve in counts. Higher the counts indicate more air bypass (higher idle). The lower the counts indicate less air allowed to bypass (lower idle).

Test Description: Number(s) below refer to circled number(s) on the diagnostic chart.

1. The Tech 1 RPM output control mode is used to extend and retract the IAC valve. The valve should move smoothly within the specified range. If the idle speed is commanded (IAC extended) too low (below 700 RPM), the engine may stall. This may be normal and would not indicate a problem. Retracting the IAC beyond its controlled range (above 1500 RPM) will cause a delay before the RPM's start dropping. This too is normal.

2. This test uses the Tech 1 to command the IAC controlled idle speed. The ECM issues commands to obtain commanded idle speed. The node lights each should flash red and green to indicate a good circuit as the ECM issues commands. While the sequence of color is not important if either light is "OFF" or does not flash red and green, check the circuits for faults, beginning with poor terminal contacts.

Diagnostic Aids:

A slow, unstable, or fast idle may be caused by a non-IAC system problem that cannot be overcome by the IAC valve. Out of control range IAC scan tool counts will be above 60 if idle is too low, and zero counts if idle is too high. The following checks should be made to repair a non-IAC system problem:

- Vacuum Leak (High Idle) - If idle is too high, stop the engine. Fully extend (low) IAC with tester. Start engine. If Idle speed is above 800 RPM, locate and correct vacuum leak including PCV

system. Also check for binding of throttle blade or linkage.

- System too lean (High Air/Fuel Ratio) - Idle speed may be too high or too low. Engine speed may vary up and down and disconnecting IAC does not help. DTC 44 may be set. Scan O2S voltage will be less than 300 mV (.3 volt). Check for low regulated fuel pressure, water in the fuel or a restricted injector.

- System too rich (Low Air/Fuel Ratio) - The idle speed will be too low. Scan tool IAC counts will usually be above 80. System is obviously rich and may exhibit black smoke exhaust.
  Scan tool O2S voltage will be fixed above 800 mV (.8 volt). Check for high fuel pressure, leaking or sticking injector. Silicone contaminated O2 sensor will scan an O2S voltage slow to respond.

- Throttle Body - Remove IAC and inspect bore for foreign material.

- IAC Valve Electrical Connections - IAC valve connections should be carefully checked for proper contact.

- Crankcase Ventilation Valve - An incorrect or faulty PCV valve may result in an incorrect idle speed.

- Refer to "Rough, Unstable, Incorrect Idle or Stalling" in "Symptoms."

- If intermittent, poor driveability or idle symptoms are resolved by disconnecting the IAC, carefully recheck connections, valve terminal resistance, or replace IAC.

Fig. 189 Chart C-2c: idle air control system check — Storm

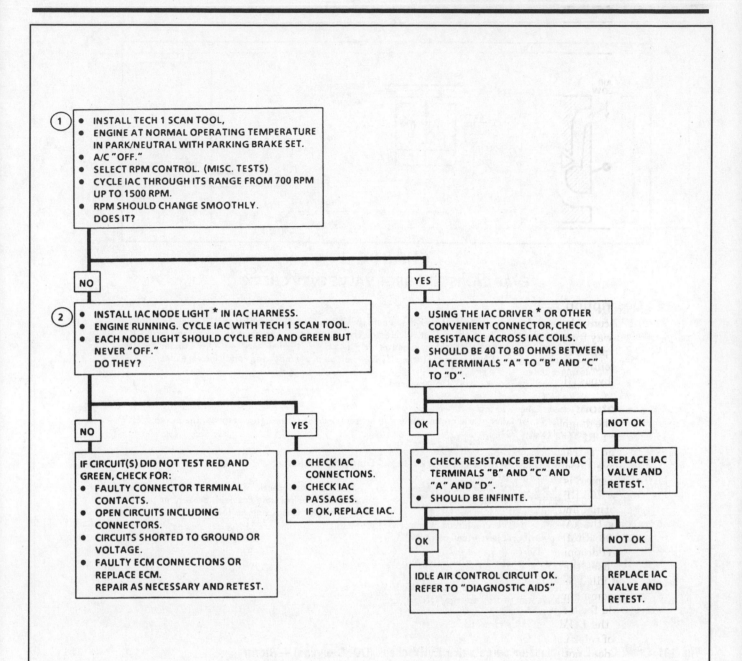

① • INSTALL TECH 1 SCAN TOOL,
   • ENGINE AT NORMAL OPERATING TEMPERATURE
     IN PARK/NEUTRAL WITH PARKING BRAKE SET.
   • A/C "OFF."
   • SELECT RPM CONTROL. (MISC. TESTS)
   • CYCLE IAC THROUGH ITS RANGE FROM 700 RPM
     UP TO 1500 RPM.
   • RPM SHOULD CHANGE SMOOTHLY.
     DOES IT?

NO

YES

② • INSTALL IAC NODE LIGHT * IN IAC HARNESS.
   • ENGINE RUNNING. CYCLE IAC WITH TECH 1 SCAN TOOL.
   • EACH NODE LIGHT SHOULD CYCLE RED AND GREEN BUT
     NEVER "OFF."
     DO THEY?

• USING THE IAC DRIVER * OR OTHER
  CONVENIENT CONNECTOR, CHECK
  RESISTANCE ACROSS IAC COILS.
• SHOULD BE 40 TO 80 OHMS BETWEEN
  IAC TERMINALS "A" TO "B" AND "C"
  TO "D".

NO

YES

OK

NOT OK

IF CIRCUIT(S) DID NOT TEST RED AND
GREEN, CHECK FOR:
• FAULTY CONNECTOR TERMINAL
  CONTACTS.
• OPEN CIRCUITS INCLUDING
  CONNECTORS.
• CIRCUITS SHORTED TO GROUND OR
  VOLTAGE.
• FAULTY ECM CONNECTIONS OR
  REPLACE ECM.
  REPAIR AS NECESSARY AND RETEST.

• CHECK IAC
  CONNECTIONS.
• CHECK IAC
  PASSAGES.
• IF OK, REPLACE IAC.

• CHECK RESISTANCE BETWEEN IAC
  TERMINALS "B" AND "C" AND
  "A" AND "D".
• SHOULD BE INFINITE.

REPLACE IAC
VALVE AND
RETEST.

OK

NOT OK

IDLE AIR CONTROL CIRCUIT OK.
REFER TO "DIAGNOSTIC AIDS"

REPLACE IAC
VALVE AND
RETEST.

IF THE ECM IS FAULTY AND MUST BE REPLACED, THE NEW ECM MUST BE PROGRAMMED.

* IAC DRIVER AND NODE LIGHT REQUIRED KIT
  222-L FROM: CONCEPT TECHNOLOGY, INC.
  J 37027 FROM: KENT-MOORE, INC.

Fig. 190 Chart C-2c: idle air control system check — Storm

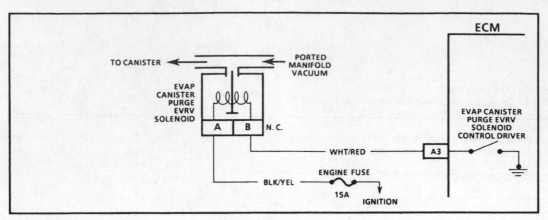

CHART C-3
EVAP CANISTER PURGE VALVE EVRV CHECK

Circuit Description:

EVAP canister purge is controlled by an EVRV solenoid that allows manifold and/or ported vacuum to purge the canister when energized. The Engine Control Module (ECM) supplies a ground to energize the EVRV solenoid (purge "ON"). The purge EVRV solenoid control by the ECM is turned "ON" or "OFF" under specific engine conditions. The purge EVRV solenoid is turned "ON" when all of the following conditions are met.

- DLC is ungrounded.
- Engine run time after start more than 20 seconds.
- ECT above 60°C.
- Vehicle speed is above 15 mph.

Also, if the DLC on-board diagnostic request terminal is grounded with the engine stopped, the purge EVRV solenoid is energized (purge "ON").

Test Description: Number(s) below refer to circled number(s) on the diagnostic chart.

1. Checks to see if the EVRV solenoid is opened or closed. The EVRV solenoid is normally de-energized in this step, so it should be closed.
2. Checks to determine if EVRV solenoid was open due to electrical circuit problem or defective EVRV solenoid.
3. Completes functional check by grounding OBD request terminal. This should normally energize the EVRV solenoid opening the valve which should allow the vacuum to drop (purge "ON").

Diagnostic Aids:

Make a visual check of vacuum hose(s). Check throttle body for possible cracked, broken, or plugged vacuum block. Check engine for possible mechanical problem.

Fig. 191 Chart C-3: EVAP canister purge valve EVRV check (DOHC engine) — Storm

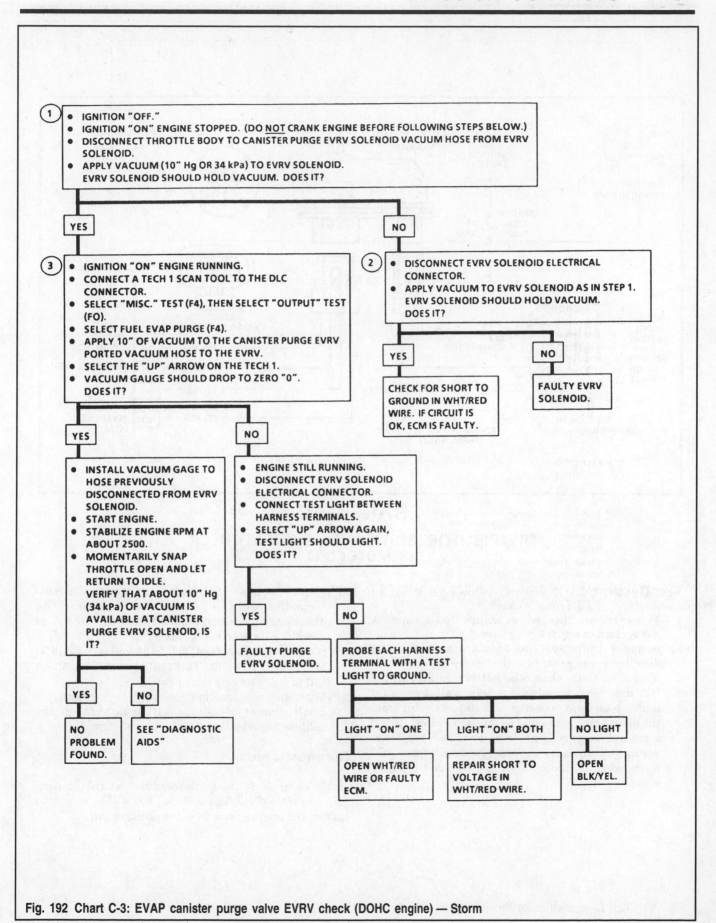

1
- IGNITION "OFF."
- IGNITION "ON" ENGINE STOPPED. (DO NOT CRANK ENGINE BEFORE FOLLOWING STEPS BELOW.)
- DISCONNECT THROTTLE BODY TO CANISTER PURGE EVRV SOLENOID VACUUM HOSE FROM EVRV SOLENOID.
- APPLY VACUUM (10" Hg OR 34 kPa) TO EVRV SOLENOID. EVRV SOLENOID SHOULD HOLD VACUUM. DOES IT?

YES / **NO**

3
- IGNITION "ON" ENGINE RUNNING.
- CONNECT A TECH 1 SCAN TOOL TO THE DLC CONNECTOR.
- SELECT "MISC." TEST (F4), THEN SELECT "OUTPUT" TEST (FO).
- SELECT FUEL EVAP PURGE (F4).
- APPLY 10" OF VACUUM TO THE CANISTER PURGE EVRV PORTED VACUUM HOSE TO THE EVRV.
- SELECT THE "UP" ARROW ON THE TECH 1.
- VACUUM GAUGE SHOULD DROP TO ZERO "0". DOES IT?

2
- DISCONNECT EVRV SOLENOID ELECTRICAL CONNECTOR.
- APPLY VACUUM TO EVRV SOLENOID AS IN STEP 1. EVRV SOLENOID SHOULD HOLD VACUUM. DOES IT?

YES

CHECK FOR SHORT TO GROUND IN WHT/RED WIRE. IF CIRCUIT IS OK, ECM IS FAULTY.

NO

FAULTY EVRV SOLENOID.

YES / **NO**

- INSTALL VACUUM GAGE TO HOSE PREVIOUSLY DISCONNECTED FROM EVRV SOLENOID.
- START ENGINE.
- STABILIZE ENGINE RPM AT ABOUT 2500.
- MOMENTARILY SNAP THROTTLE OPEN AND LET RETURN TO IDLE. VERIFY THAT ABOUT 10" Hg (34 kPa) OF VACUUM IS AVAILABLE AT CANISTER PURGE EVRV SOLENOID, IS IT?

- ENGINE STILL RUNNING.
- DISCONNECT EVRV SOLENOID ELECTRICAL CONNECTOR.
- CONNECT TEST LIGHT BETWEEN HARNESS TERMINALS.
- SELECT "UP" ARROW AGAIN, TEST LIGHT SHOULD LIGHT. DOES IT?

YES / **NO**

YES

NO PROBLEM FOUND.

NO

SEE "DIAGNOSTIC AIDS"

FAULTY PURGE EVRV SOLENOID.

PROBE EACH HARNESS TERMINAL WITH A TEST LIGHT TO GROUND.

LIGHT "ON" ONE

OPEN WHT/RED WIRE OR FAULTY ECM.

LIGHT "ON" BOTH

REPAIR SHORT TO VOLTAGE IN WHT/RED WIRE.

NO LIGHT

OPEN BLK/YEL.

Fig. 192 Chart C-3: EVAP canister purge valve EVRV check (DOHC engine) — Storm

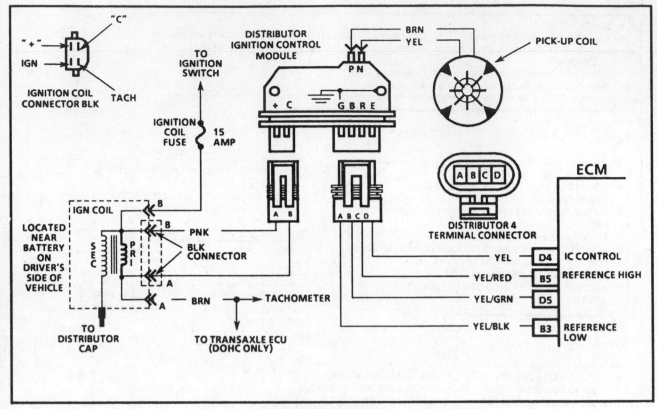

CHART C-4C

DISTRIBUTOR IGNITION (DI) SYSTEM CHECK
(REMOTE COIL)

Test Description: Number(s) below refer to circled number(s) on the diagnostic chart.

1. Two wires are checked, to ensure that an open is not present in a spark plug wire.
2. A spark indicates the problem must be the distributor cap, rotor or coil output wire.
3. Normally, there should be battery voltage at the "C" and "+" terminals. Low voltage would indicate an open or a high resistance circuit from the distributor to the coil or ignition switch. If "C" terminal voltage was low, but "+" terminal voltage is 10 volts or more, circuit from "C" terminal to ignition coil or ignition coil primary winding is open.

4. Checks for a shorted module or grounded circuit from the ignition coil to the module. The distributor module should be turned "OFF," so normal voltage should be about 12 volts.
If the module is turned "ON," the voltage would be low, but above 1 volt. This could cause the ignition coil to fail from excessive heat.
With an open ignition coil primary winding, a small amount of voltage will leak through the module from the "batt" to the "tach" terminal.

Diagnostic Aids:

In order to do the test procedures at the ignition coil, use of the Kent-Moore J 35616-A will be needed to jumper the engine harness at the ignition coil.

Fig. 193 Chart C-4c: distributor ignition system check — Storm

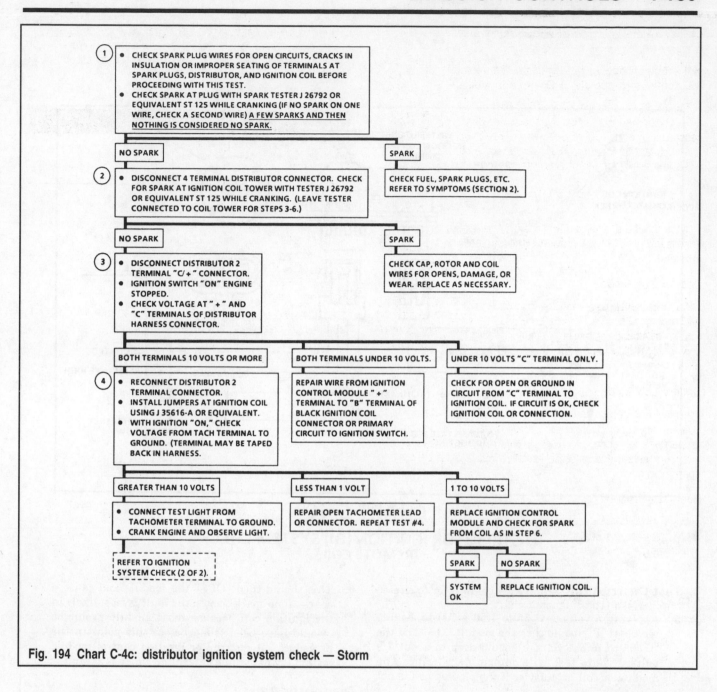

Fig. 194 Chart C-4c: distributor ignition system check — Storm

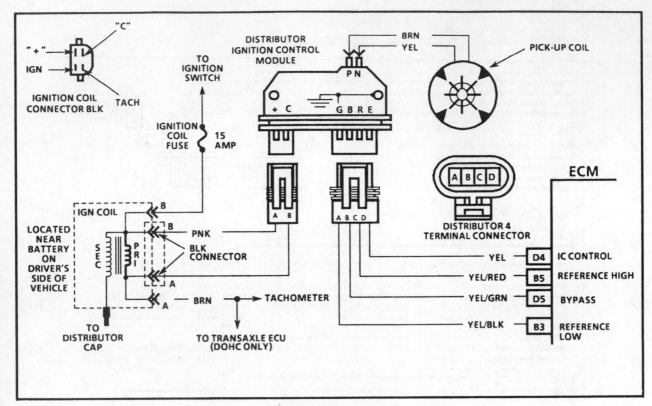

CHART C-4C

DISTRIBUTOR IGNITION (DI) SYSTEM CHECK
(REMOTE COIL)

Test Description: Number(s) below refer to circled number(s) on the diagnostic chart.

5. Applying a voltage (1.35 to 1.50 volts) to module terminal "P" should turn the module "ON" and the "tach" terminal voltage should drop to about 7-9 volts. This test will determine whether the module or coil is faulty or if the pick-up coil is not

generating the proper signal to turn the module "ON." This test can be performed by using a DC test battery with a rating of 1.5 volts. (Such as AA, C, or D cell.) The battery must be a known good battery with a voltage of over 1.35 volts.

6. This should turn "OFF" the module and cause a spark. If no spark occurs, the fault is most likely in the ignition coil because most module problems would have been found before this point in the procedure. A distributor ignition control module tester (J 24642) could determine which is at fault.

Diagnostic Aids:

In order to do the test procedures at the ignition coil, use of the Kent-Moore J 35616-A will be needed to jumper the engine harness at the ignition coil.

Fig. 195 Chart C-4c: distributor ignition system check (continued) — Storm

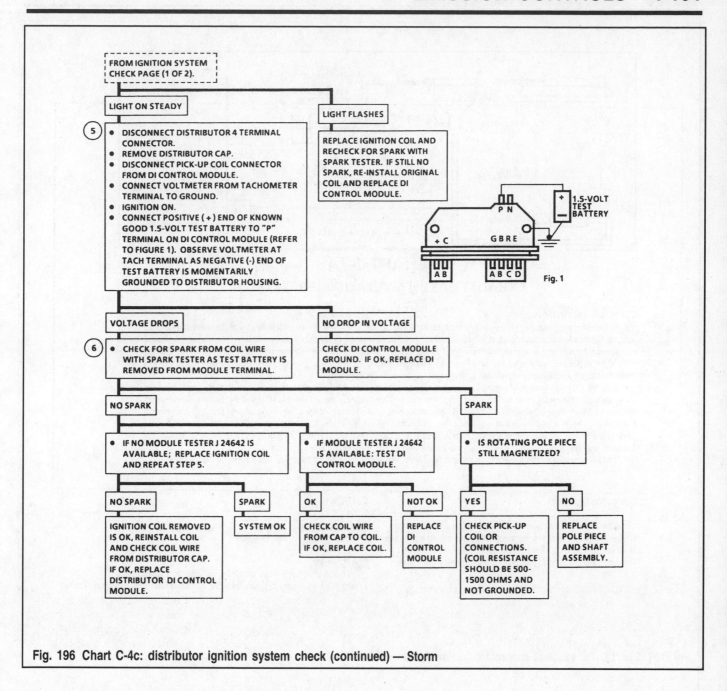

FROM IGNITION SYSTEM CHECK PAGE (1 OF 2).

LIGHT ON STEADY

5
- DISCONNECT DISTRIBUTOR 4 TERMINAL CONNECTOR.
- REMOVE DISTRIBUTOR CAP.
- DISCONNECT PICK-UP COIL CONNECTOR FROM DI CONTROL MODULE.
- CONNECT VOLTMETER FROM TACHOMETER TERMINAL TO GROUND.
- IGNITION ON.
- CONNECT POSITIVE (+) END OF KNOWN GOOD 1.5-VOLT TEST BATTERY TO "P" TERMINAL ON DI CONTROL MODULE (REFER TO FIGURE 1). OBSERVE VOLTMETER AT TACH TERMINAL AS NEGATIVE (-) END OF TEST BATTERY IS MOMENTARILY GROUNDED TO DISTRIBUTOR HOUSING.

LIGHT FLASHES

REPLACE IGNITION COIL AND RECHECK FOR SPARK WITH SPARK TESTER. IF STILL NO SPARK, RE-INSTALL ORIGINAL COIL AND REPLACE DI CONTROL MODULE.

1.5-VOLT TEST BATTERY

P N
+ C   G B R E
A B   A B C D   Fig. 1

VOLTAGE DROPS

6
- CHECK FOR SPARK FROM COIL WIRE WITH SPARK TESTER AS TEST BATTERY IS REMOVED FROM MODULE TERMINAL.

NO DROP IN VOLTAGE

CHECK DI CONTROL MODULE GROUND. IF OK, REPLACE DI MODULE.

NO SPARK

- IF NO MODULE TESTER J 24642 IS AVAILABLE; REPLACE IGNITION COIL AND REPEAT STEP 5.

SPARK

- IF MODULE TESTER J 24642 IS AVAILABLE: TEST DI CONTROL MODULE.

- IS ROTATING POLE PIECE STILL MAGNETIZED?

NO SPARK

IGNITION COIL REMOVED IS OK, REINSTALL COIL AND CHECK COIL WIRE FROM DISTRIBUTOR CAP. IF OK, REPLACE DISTRIBUTOR DI CONTROL MODULE.

SPARK

SYSTEM OK

OK

CHECK COIL WIRE FROM CAP TO COIL. IF OK, REPLACE COIL.

NOT OK

REPLACE DI CONTROL MODULE

YES

CHECK PICK-UP COIL OR CONNECTIONS. (COIL RESISTANCE SHOULD BE 500-1500 OHMS AND NOT GROUNDED.

NO

REPLACE POLE PIECE AND SHAFT ASSEMBLY.

Fig. 196 Chart C-4c: distributor ignition system check (continued) — Storm

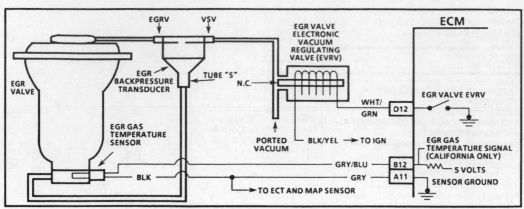

CHART C-7A
EXHAUST GAS RECIRCULATION (EGR) SYSTEM

Circuit Description:

A properly operating EGR system will directly affect the air/fuel requirements of the engine. Since the exhaust gas introduced into the air/fuel mixture is an inert gas (contains very little or no oxygen), less fuel is required to maintain a correct air/fuel ratio. If the EGR system were to become inoperative, the inert exhaust gas would be replaced with air and the air/fuel mixture would be leaner. The ECM would compensate for the lean condition by adding fuel, resulting in higher long term fuel trim values.

The engine control system operates within two long term fuel trim cells, a closed throttle cell and an open throttle cell. Since EGR is not used at idle, the closed throttle cell would not be affected by EGR system operation. The open throttle cell is affected by EGR operation and when the EGR system is operating properly, the long term fuel trim values in both cells should be close to being the same. If the EGR system was inoperative, the long term fuel trim value in the open throttle cell would change (become higher) to compensate for the resulting lean system, but the long term fuel trim value in the closed throttle cell would not change.

This change or difference in long term fuel trim values is used to monitor EGR system performance.

Diagnostic Aids:

The EGR valve chart is a check of the EGR system. If the EGR system works properly, check other items that could result in high long term fuel trim values in the open throttle cell, but not in the closed throttle cell.

CHECK:

<u>EGR Passages</u>
Restricted or blocked.

<u>MAP Sensor</u>
A MAP sensor may shift in calibration enough to affect fuel delivery. Use CHART C-1D, MAP output check.

Fig. 197 Chart C-7a: exhaust gas recirculation system — Storm

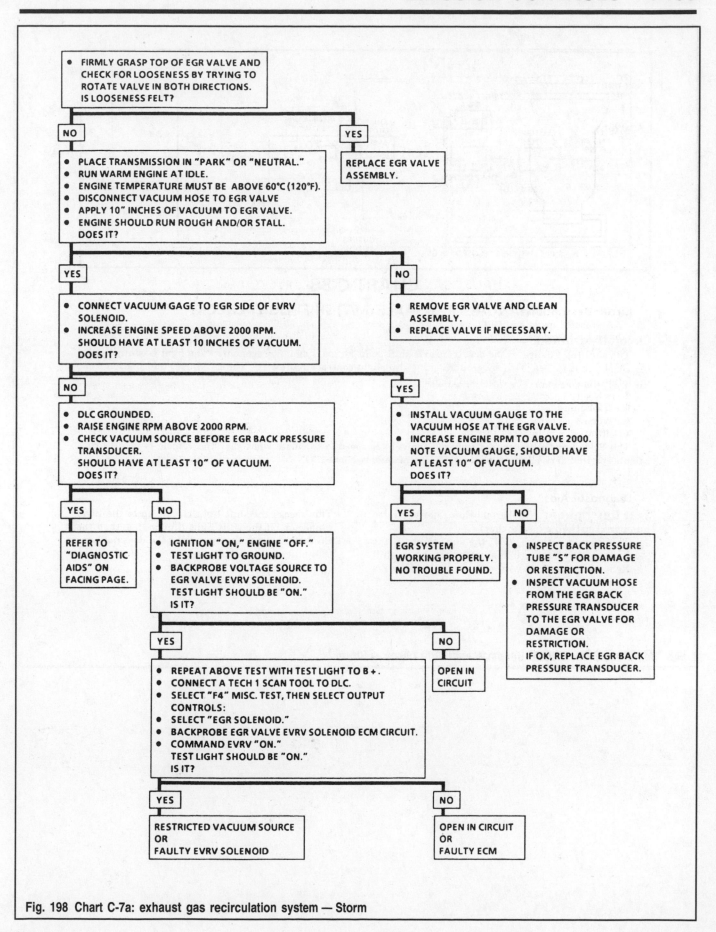

Fig. 198 Chart C-7a: exhaust gas recirculation system — Storm

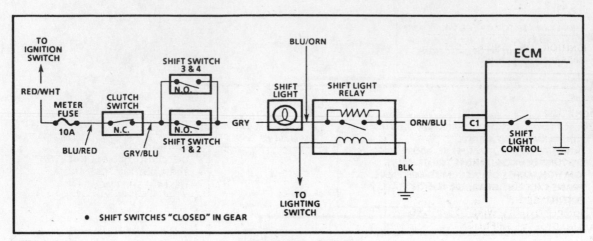

CHART C-8B
MANUAL TRANSAXLE (M/T) SHIFT LIGHT CHECK

Circuit Description:
The shift light indicates the best transaxle shift point for maximum fuel economy. The light is controlled by the ECM and is turned "ON" by grounding the shift light control circuit wire. The ECM uses information from the following inputs to control the shift light:
- ECT
- TP Sensor
- VSS
- RPM

The ECM uses the measured rpm and the vehicle speed to calculate what gear the vehicle is in. It's this calculation that determines when the shift light should be turned "ON."

Test Description: Number(s) below refer to circled number(s) on the diagnostic chart.
1. This should not turn "ON" the shift light. If the light is "ON," there is a short to ground in shift light control circuit wire or a faulty relay, or a fault in the ECM.

2. This checks the shift light circuit up to the ECM connector. If the shift light illuminates, then the ECM connector is faulty or the ECM does not have the ability to ground the circuit.

Fig. 199 Chart C-8b: manual transaxle shift light check — Storm

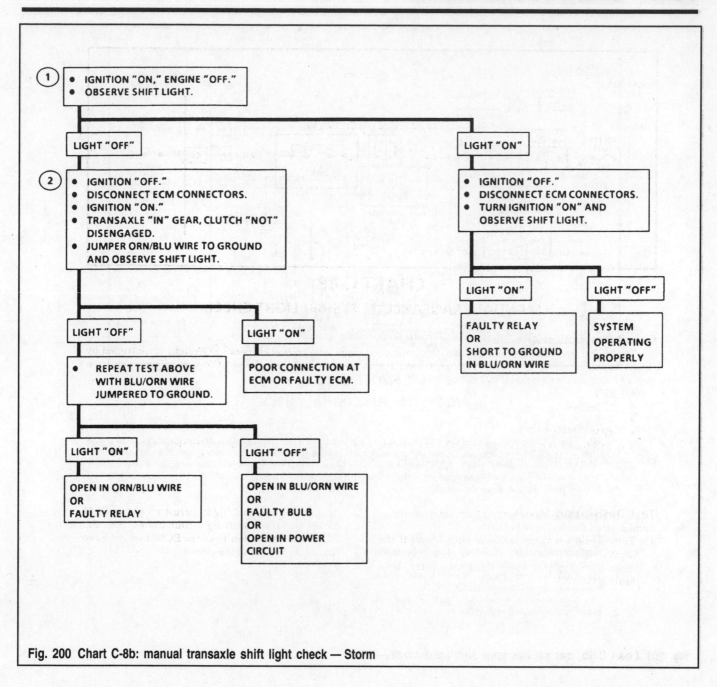

Fig. 200 Chart C-8b: manual transaxle shift light check — Storm

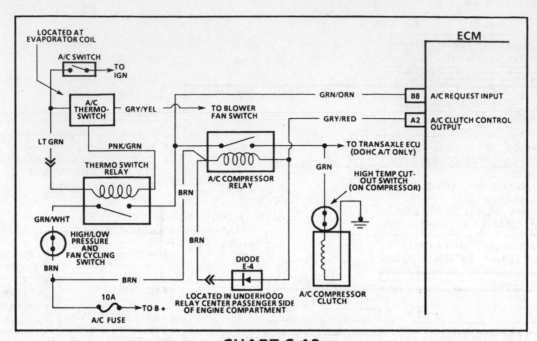

CHART C-10
A/C SYSTEM FUNCTIONAL CHECK

Circuit Description:

When the A/C mode is selected the ECM will supply a ground to the A/C clutch relay. Battery voltage is then supplied to the A/C clutch through the completing of circuit through the thermo switch relay, which is part of the A/C "ON/OFF" switch circuit. If the A/C system exhibits high/low pressure or an overheating condition exist, the A/C system will be disabled by the opening of the A/C high/low pressure switch or the A/C thermo switch, or A/C compressor HIGH temperature cutout switch.

Diagnostic Aids:

- The A/C high/low pressure switch is located in the high pressure side A/C hose. This switch also controls the A/C condenser fan.
- The HIGH temperature cutout switch is located in the back of the A/C compressor.
- The thermo cut-out switch is part of the A/C evaporator mounted under the dash.

Fig. 201 Chart C-10: A/C system functional check — Storm

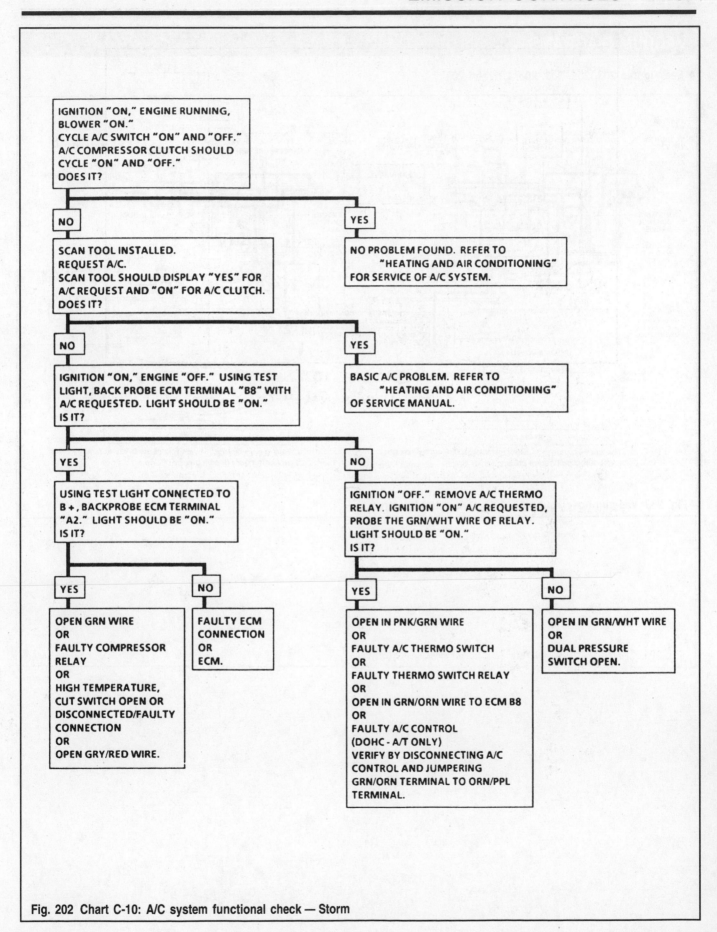

Fig. 202 Chart C-10: A/C system functional check — Storm

VACUUM DIAGRAMS

▶ **See Figures 203, 204, 205, 206, 207 and 208**

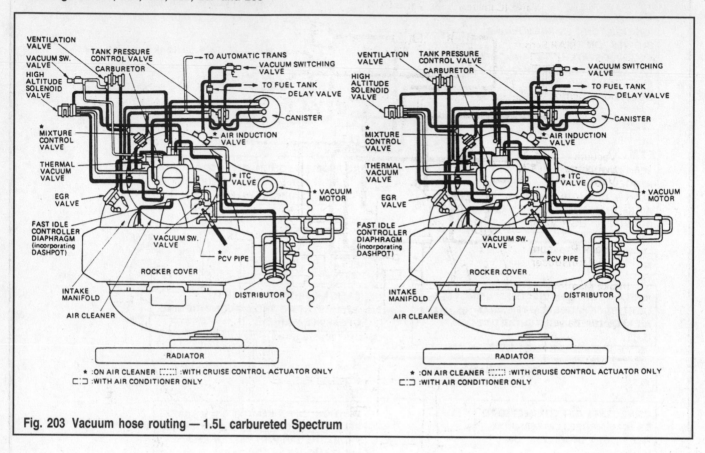

Fig. 203 Vacuum hose routing — 1.5L carbureted Spectrum

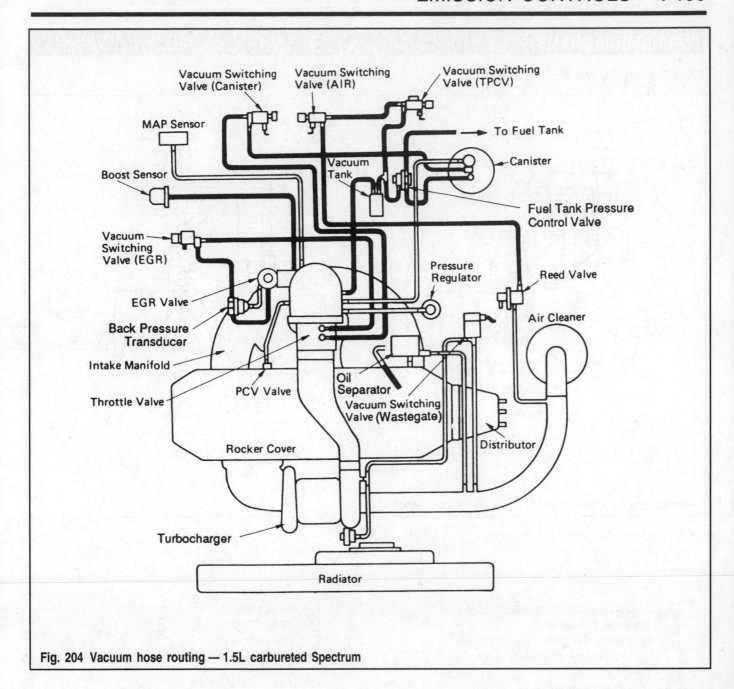

Fig. 204 Vacuum hose routing — 1.5L carbureted Spectrum

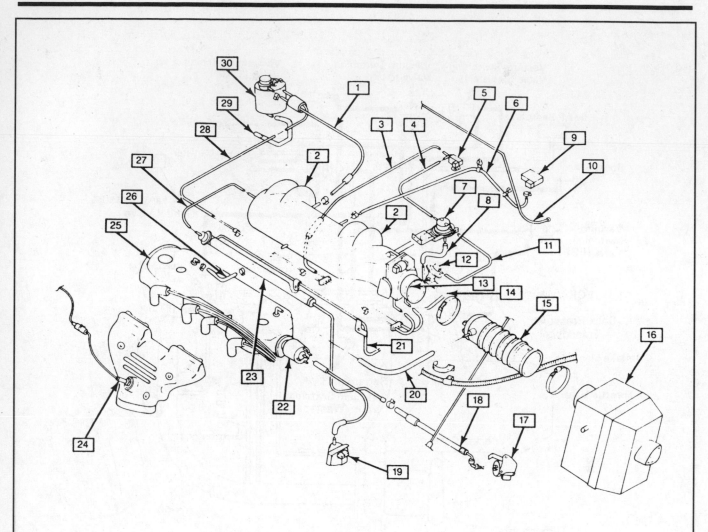

1	CANISTER HOSE TO COMMON CHAMBER
2	COMMON CHAMBER
3	EGR HOSE: THROTTLE VALVE TO VSV
4	EGR HOSE: VSV TO TRANSDUCER
5	EGR VSV
6	MAP SENSOR HOSE
7	EGR TRANSDUCER
8	EGR HOSE: EGR VALVE TO TRANSDUCER
9	MAP SENSOR
10	ACCELERATOR CABLE
11	EGR HOSE: TRANSDUCER TO EGR VALVE
12	EGR VALVE
13	THROTTLE VALVE
14	EGR PIPE
15	AIR DUCT
16	AIR CLEANER

17	FUEL FILTER
18	FUEL FEED HOSE
19	IGNITION COIL
20	PCV HOSE: CYLINDER HEAD COVER TO AIR DUCT
21	FUEL RETURN PIPE
22	DISTRIBUTOR
23	FUEL RAIL
24	OXYGEN SENSOR
25	CYLINDER HEAD COVER
26	PCV HOSE: CYLINDER HEAD COVER TO COMMON CHAMBER
27	VACCUM HOSE: PRESSURE REGULATOR TO COMMON CHAMBER
28	CANISTER HOSE: TO THROTTLE VALVE
29	CANISTER HOSE
30	CANISTER

Fig. 205 Vacuum hose routing — 1990-91 SOHC Storm

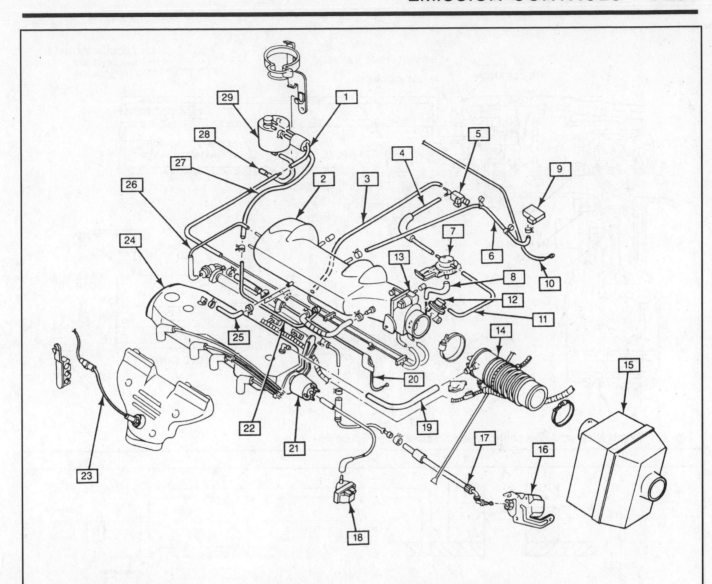

1. EVAP CANISTER HOSE-TO-COMMON CHAMBER
2. COMMON CHAMBER
3. EGR HOSE: TB-TO-EGR SV VALVE
4. EGR HOSE: EGR SV VALVE-TO-EGR TRANSDUCER
5. EGR SOLENOID VACUUM (SV) VALVE
6. MAP SENSOR HOSE
7. EGR TRANSDUCER
8. EGR HOSE: EGR VALVE-TO-EGR TRANSDUCER
9. MANIFOLD ABSOLUTE PRESSURE (MAP) SENSOR
10. ACCELERATOR CABLE
11. EGR HOSE: EGR TRANSDUCER-TO-EGR VALVE
12. EXHAUST GAS RECIRCULATION (EGR) VALVE
13. THROTTLE BODY (TB)
14. AIR DUCT
15. AIR CLEANER (ACL)
16. FUEL FILTER
17. FUEL FEED HOSE
18. IGNITION COIL
19. POSITIVE CRANKCASE VENTILATION (PCV) HOSE: CYLINDER HEAD COVER-TO-AIR DUCT
20. FUEL RETURN PIPE
21. DISTRIBUTOR
22. FUEL RAIL
23. OXYGEN SENSOR (O2S)
24. CYLINDER HEAD COVER
25. PCV HOSE: CYLINDER HEAD COVER-TO-COMMON CHAMBER
26. VACUUM HOSE: PRESSURE REGULATOR-TO-COMMON CHAMBER
27. EVAP CANISTER HOSE TO TB
28. EVAP CANISTER HOSE
29. EVAPORATIVE EMISSIONS (EVAP) CANISTER

Fig. 206 Vacuum hose routing — 1992-93 SOHC Storm

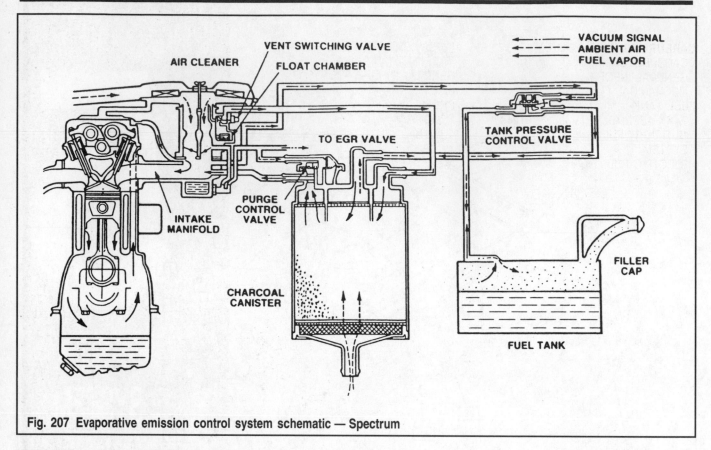

Fig. 207 Evaporative emission control system schematic — Spectrum

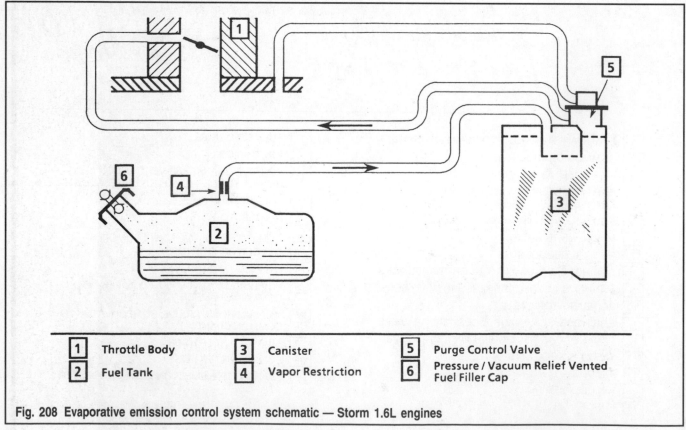

1	Throttle Body	**3**	Canister	**5**	Purge Control Valve
2	Fuel Tank	**4**	Vapor Restriction	**6**	Pressure / Vacuum Relief Vented Fuel Filler Cap

Fig. 208 Evaporative emission control system schematic — Storm 1.6L engines

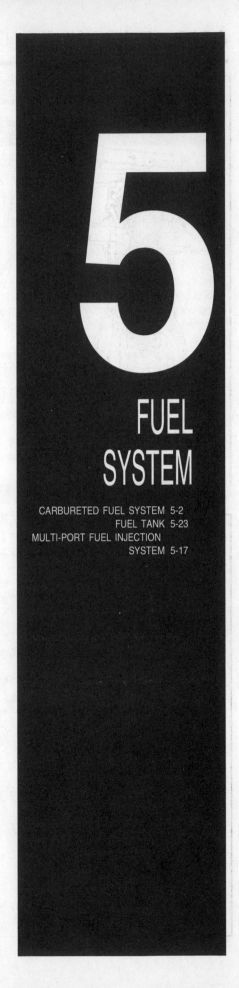

5

FUEL
SYSTEM

CARBURETED FUEL SYSTEM

General Information

The non-turbo Spectrum is the only vehicle covered by this manual which uses a carburetor to deliver fuel to the engine. The remaining vehicles use a fuel injection system, covered later in this section.

The Spectrum carburetor is a downdraft fuel and air metering device with 2 stages of operation. The primary side uses a relatively small bore, double venturi and a bridge nozzle. Primary fuel metering is accomplished using a duty (mixture control) solenoid.

The secondary side of the Spectrum carburetor has one large bore and a secondary main metering system. The metering system supplies fuel to the engine during heavy load conditions.

The Engine Control Module (ECM), which monitors the engine emission system, uses information gathered from various sensors to control the air/fuel ratio. Based on feedback from the oxygen sensor (and other related sensors), the ECM will vary signals to the mixture control solenoid located in the carburetor to control primary side fuel delivery.

The remaining fuel system components are the fuel tank, lines/hoses, inline fuel filter and the mechanical fuel pump.

Mechanical Fuel Pump

REMOVAL & INSTALLATION

▶ **See Figures 1 and 2**

The mechanical fuel pump for Carbureted Spectrum vehicles is located on the engine at the side of the cylinder head intake manifold. It is driven by a camshaft lobe which contacts and 'pumps' the fuel pump rocker arm/lever.

1. Tag and disconnect the fuel hoses from the pump assembly.
2. Remove the retaining bolts from the fuel pump and heat insulator assembly.
3. Remove the fuel pump from the engine.
4. Cover the fuel pump mounting face on the cylinder head to prevent the discharge of oil and to prevent the entry of dirt or contaminants.

To install:
5. Clean the cylinder head and fuel pump mating surfaces.
6. Attach the fuel pump, along with the new heat insulator assembly, to the cylinder head. Depending on camshaft position, it may be difficult to install the pump. Make sure the pump rocker arm is properly in contact with the camshaft or camshaft driver.
7. Hold the pump in position, then install and tighten the retaining bolts.
8. Connect the fuel hoses to the pump assembly.
9. Start the engine and carefully check for leakage or proper operation.

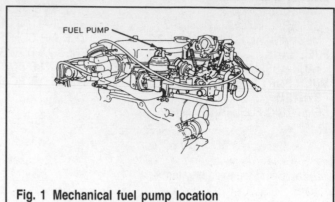

Fig. 1 Mechanical fuel pump location

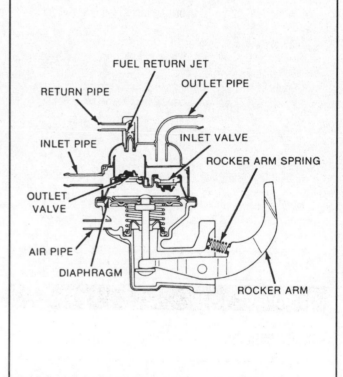

Fig. 2 Cut-away view of the mechanical fuel pump assembly

TESTING

▶ **See Figures 3, 4, 5 and 6**

If a fuel pump problem is suspected, the fuel pump must be removed from the engine for testing.

1. Make a visual inspection of the pump casing for cracks and other damage. If cracks or other visible damage are present, the pump assembly must be replaced.
2. Check for excessive wear between the rocker arm and the camshaft contact faces. The pump must be replaced, if excessive wear is found.

3. Before proceeding with pump testing, the pump valve seals must be moistened by pouring a small amount of fuel into the pump.

4. Remove the rocker arm spring, then measure the force and play of the rocker arm by moving the arm.

5. Check the inlet valve:

a. Move the rocker arm to the pump side and hold it in this position.

b. Shut both the return and outlet pipes.

c. Allow the rocker arm to return to it's original position.

d. When the rocker arm is returned, there should be a noticeable increase in the amount of play.

e. If play doe not increase, replace the pump.

6. Check the outlet valve:

a. Cover the inlet pipe and attempt to move the rocker arm.

b. The rocker arm must not move when the inlet pipe is closed, but DO NOT apply excessive force to the rocker arm.

c. The fuel pump must be replaced, if there is excessive play.

7. Check the diaphragm:

a. Cover the inlet, outlet and return pipes, then attempt to move the rocker arm.

b. The rocker arm must not move when the pipes are closed, but DO NOT apply excessive force to the rocker arm.

c. The fuel pump must be replaced, if the rocker arm moves.

8. Check the oil seal:

a. Cover the air pipe, then attempt to move the rocker arm.

b. The rocker arm must not move when the air pipe is closed, but DO NOT apply excessive force to the rocker arm.

c. The fuel pump must be replaced, if the rocker arm moves.

Carburetor

ADJUSTMENTS

The following adjustments may be performed with the carburetor in service. Additional adjustments are part of the overhaul procedure.

Before performing any adjustments, the following steps must be followed:

1. Set the parking brake, then block both the front and rear wheels.

2. Place the transaxle in **Neutral** (manual vehicles) or in **P** (automatic vehicles).

3. Switch ALL accessories OFF.

4. If equipped with power steering, make sure the front wheels are pointing forward. This must be done to make sure the power steering pump is not placing an additional load on the engine.

5. Check and, if necessary, adjust the ignition timing.

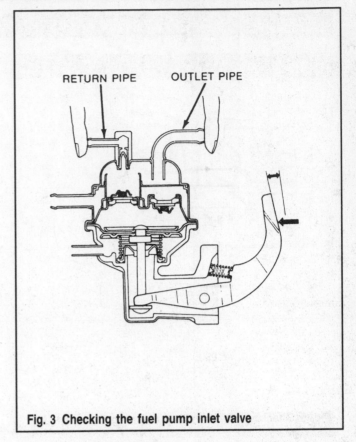

Fig. 3 Checking the fuel pump inlet valve

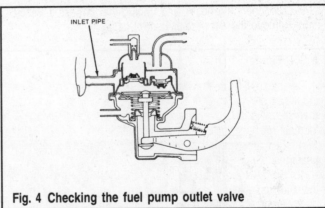

Fig. 4 Checking the fuel pump outlet valve

Idle Speed and Mixture Adjustment

Refer to Section 2 of this manual for idle speed and mixture adjustments. For additional carburetor adjustments, refer to carburetor assembly in the overhaul procedures, later in this section.

REMOVAL & INSTALLATION

▶ **See Figure 7**

1. Disconnect the negative battery cable.
2. Properly drain the engine cooling system.
3. Remove the air cleaner assembly.

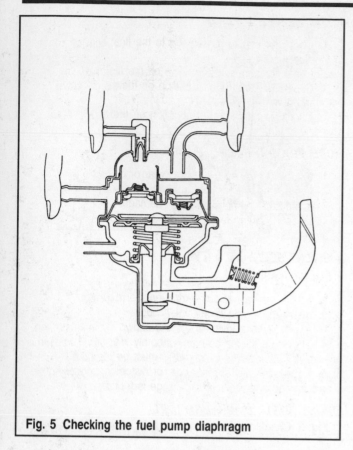

Fig. 5 Checking the fuel pump diaphragm

4. Disconnect the hoses and unplug the harness connector.
5. Remove the accelerator control cable.

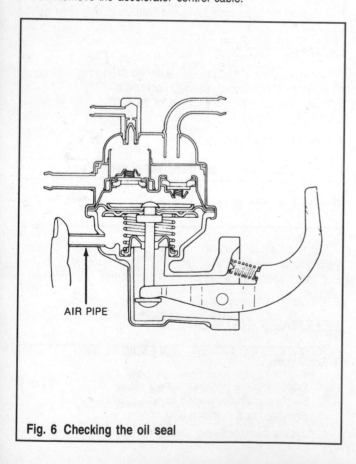

AIR PIPE

Fig. 6 Checking the oil seal

6. Remove the carburetor mounting bolts located on the bottom side of the intake manifold.
7. Remove the carburetor from the engine.
8. Be sure to cover the intake manifold to prevent debris from entering and damaging the engine.
   To install:
9. Replace the insulator holding the Early Fuel Evaporation (EFE) heater with new packings.
10. Install the carburetor and tighten the retaining bolts to 7.2 ft. lbs. (9.8 Nm).
11. Connect the accelerator, then check and adjust as necessary.
12. Connect the removed hoses and connectors.
13. Install the air cleaner assembly.
14. Connect the negative battery cable and fill the engine cooling system, then start the engine and check for leaks.

OVERHAUL

▶ **See Figures 8 and 9**

Once the carburetor has been removed from the engine, and before disassembly, check for traces of abrasion, fuel leakage or other damage on each component. This may help lead to the identification of components which must be replaced.

Be sure to remove the wire pins, necessary for disassembly of each component, from the connectors. Refer to the appropriate illustration for pin locations and wire colors for each connector.

Disassembly

AIR HORN

▶ **See Figures 10, 11, 12, 13, 14, 15, 16 and 17**

1. Remove the pump lever spring, then remove the pump arm assembly.
2. Remove the E-clip and the connecting link from the cam lever of the automatic choke.
3. Remove the 7 air horn attaching screws, then lift the air horn straight up and off the body.
4. Pull out the pin and remove the float assembly.
5. Remove and discard the old gasket.
6. Remove the needle valve assembly, seat and packing.
7. Remove the pump and piston assembly.
8. Remove the 2 screws. then remove the mixture control duty solenoid valve from the air horn. Take care not to tilt of bind the valve during removal.
9. Remove the choke break diaphragm unit by first removing the E-clip, then removing the coupling from the connecting link. Loosen the 2 screws, then remove the choke break diaphragm as a unit.

BODY

▶ **See Figures 18, 19, 20, 21, 22, 23, 24, 25, 26, 27 and 28**

1. Remove the throttle return and 2nd lock spring.
2. Remove the E-clip and remove the diaphragm chamber rod from the secondary valve shaft.
3. Remove the accelerator control cable bracket bolt and the 2 screws on the bottom side of the body.
4. Remove the diaphragm chamber and gasket.
5. Remove the slow cut solenoid valve.

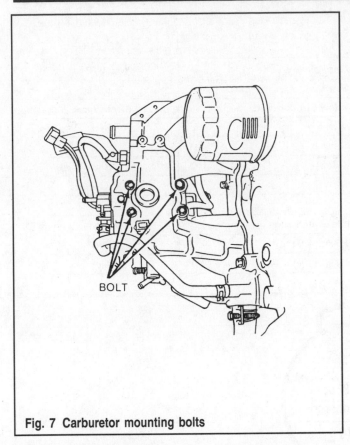

Fig. 7 Carburetor mounting bolts

6. Remove the snapring in the pump well, then take out the filter and the inlet check valve. Be VERY careful not to score the pump bore when removing the snapring.

7. Remove the main jet plug retainer and remove the plug.

8. Remove the primary and secondary main jets with packings.

9. Remove the primary small venturi and secondary small venturi assembly.

10. Remove the main air bleed jets.

11. Remove the plug and take out the P-slow jet.

12. Remove the plug and take out the pump injector.

13. Remove the plug and take out the S-slow jet and S-slow air bleed (2nd).

14. Remove the idle-up (mixture by-pass) jet.

FLANGE

▶ See Figure 29

1. Remove the idle-up (mixture by-pass) solenoid valve(s)

2. Loosen the 2 retaining screws, then remove the Throttle Position Sensor (TPS).

Cleaning & Inspection

1. Clean all removed parts, except O-rings, packing, gaskets and electric parts, using a carburetor cleaner. Take care not to score or damage parts.

2. After cleaning, remove any dirt or foreign material by blowing out each passage of the carburetor using dry compressed air.

FLOAT NEEDLE & VALVE

1. Check for cracks or damage to the float and for abrasion of the float pin hole.

2. Check for abrasion and flaws on the float pin.

3. Check for damage or abrasion on the needle valve, body and spring.

4. Check for damage and abrasion on the needle valve seat and strainer.

ACCELERATING PUMP

1. Inspect the pump piston for wear or damage.

2. Inspect the springs and strainer for damage.

3. Inspect the pump injector for damage.

4. Inspect the acceleration pump piston bore for wear or scratches.

AIR VENT SOLENOID VALVE

▶ See Figure 30

1. Check the valve body and spring for damage.

2. Install the spring to the valve body.

3. Apply 12 volts to the valve, as shown in the illustration.

4. The valve should operate smoothly with power applied. If not, valve and/or air horn assembly must be replaced.

5. Inspect the air horn surface for distortion, scratching or other damage and replace, if damage is found.

CHOKE BREAK DIAPHRAGM UNIT

1. Using a hand-held pump, apply vacuum to the choke break unit.

2. The diaphragm should hold the vacuum for a reasonable amount of time.

3. If the unit diaphragm does not hold vacuum, it must be replaced.

CHOKE HEATER

1. Measure the resistance between the thermostatic spring lead wire and the housing using an ohmmeter.

2. With an ambient temperature of 78°F (25°C), resistance should be 1-11 ohms.

SLOW CUT SOLENOID VALVE

▶ See Figure 31

1. Check for damage to the slow cut solenoid valve body and spring spool.

2. Install the valve assembly to the body.

3. Apply 12 volts to the valve terminals; refer to the illustration.

4. With power applied, make sure the valve operates smoothly. If not, the valve must be replaced.DIAPHRAGM CHAMBER

5. Push in diaphragm chamber rod using your fingers.

6. Block the chamber hole and make sure the rod does not move.

IDLE-UP (MIXTURE BY-PASS) SOLENOID VALVE(S)

1. Check for damage to the valve body, spring and spool.

2. Install the valve assembly to the flange.

3. Apply 12 volts to the solenoid terminals and check that the solenoid operates smoothly.

4. Replace the solenoid if it does not operate smoothly.

PIN NUMBER	CIRCUIT	COLOR
1	Auto Choke Heater—Air Vent Solenoid +	Yellow/Red
2	Duty Solenoid—Slow Cut Solenoid +	Red/Red
3	Mixture by pass Solenoid—Slow Cut Solenoid −	Black/Black
4	Mixture by-pass solenoid valve +	Red
5	Duty solenoid valve −	Black
6	Throttle position sensor (V-Ref.) +	Red
7	Throttle position sensor +	Lt. Green
8	Throttle position sensor −	Black
9	Throttle position sensor—Idle Switch +	Green
10	Mixture by-pass solenoid (Hi-altitude) +	Red
11	Mixture by-pass solenoid (Hi-altitude) −	Black
12	Plug	

12P CONNECTOR

PIN NUMBER	CIRCUIT	COLOR
1	Auto Choke heater	Yellow/Blue
2	Mixture by-pass solenoid valve	Black
3	Duty solenoid valve	Red

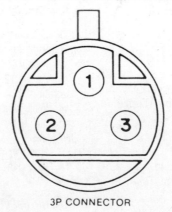

3P CONNECTOR

Fig. 8 Carburetor connector pin locations

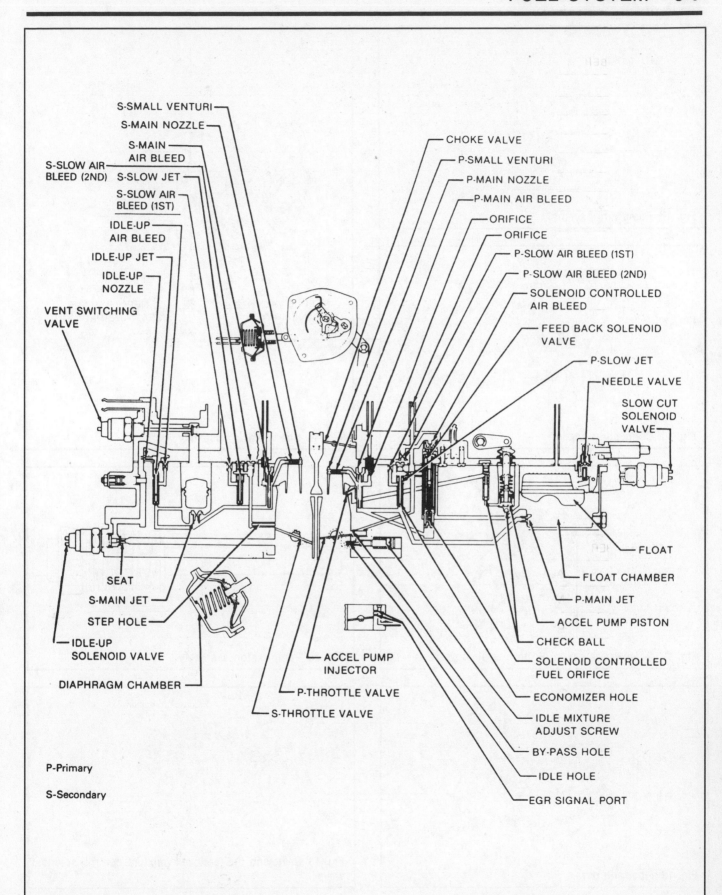

Fig. 9 Carburetor component location

S-SMALL VENTURI

S-MAIN NOZZLE

S-MAIN AIR BLEED

S-SLOW AIR BLEED (2ND)

S-SLOW JET

S-SLOW AIR BLEED (1ST)

IDLE-UP AIR BLEED

IDLE-UP JET

IDLE-UP NOZZLE

VENT SWITCHING VALVE

CHOKE VALVE

P-SMALL VENTURI

P-MAIN NOZZLE

P-MAIN AIR BLEED

ORIFICE

ORIFICE

P-SLOW AIR BLEED (1ST)

P-SLOW AIR BLEED (2ND)

SOLENOID CONTROLLED AIR BLEED

FEED BACK SOLENOID VALVE

P-SLOW JET

NEEDLE VALVE

SLOW CUT SOLENOID VALVE

FLOAT

FLOAT CHAMBER

P-MAIN JET

ACCEL PUMP PISTON

CHECK BALL

SOLENOID CONTROLLED FUEL ORIFICE

ECONOMIZER HOLE

IDLE MIXTURE ADJUST SCREW

BY-PASS HOLE

IDLE HOLE

EGR SIGNAL PORT

SEAT

S-MAIN JET

STEP HOLE

IDLE-UP SOLENOID VALVE

DIAPHRAGM CHAMBER

ACCEL PUMP INJECTOR

P-THROTTLE VALVE

S-THROTTLE VALVE

P-Primary

S-Secondary

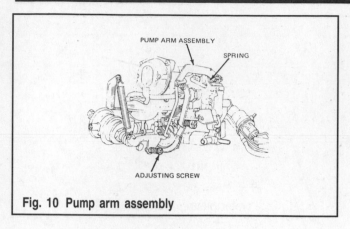

Fig. 10 Pump arm assembly

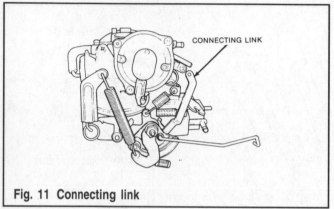

Fig. 11 Connecting link

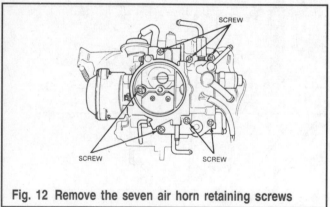

Fig. 12 Remove the seven air horn retaining screws

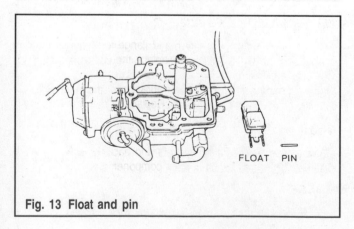

Fig. 13 Float and pin

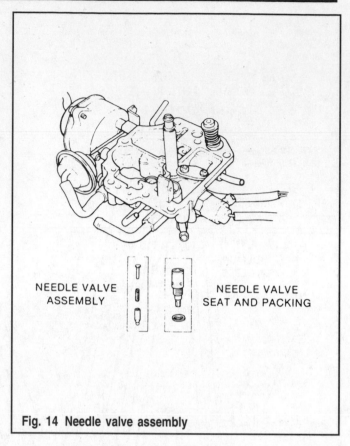

NEEDLE VALVE ASSEMBLY

NEEDLE VALVE SEAT AND PACKING

Fig. 14 Needle valve assembly

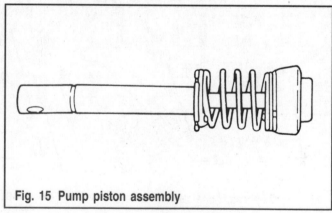

Fig. 15 Pump piston assembly

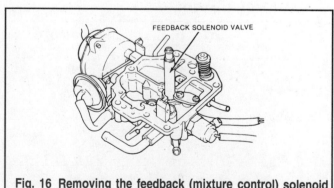

Fig. 16 Removing the feedback (mixture control) solenoid valve

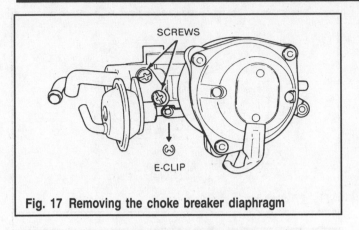

Fig. 17 Removing the choke breaker diaphragm

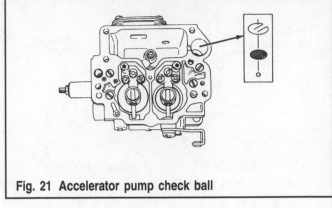

Fig. 21 Accelerator pump check ball

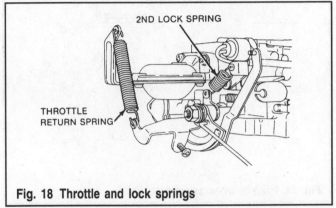

Fig. 18 Throttle and lock springs

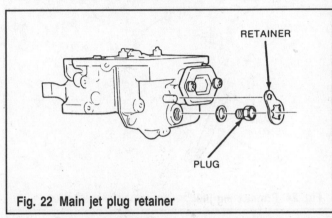

Fig. 22 Main jet plug retainer

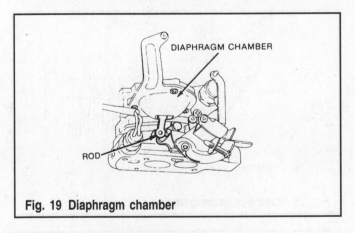

Fig. 19 Diaphragm chamber

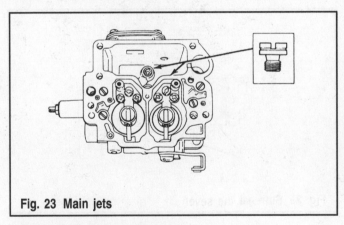

Fig. 23 Main jets

AIR HORN, BODY & FLANGE

1. Inspect the air horn, body and flange for damage, cracks or flaws on the fitting surfaces. Replace the component(s), if problems are found.

2. Inspect for deformation and abrasion of the shaft, link, bushing and related components. Replace, if damage is found.

Assembly

Always use new O-rings, gaskets and packings when assembling the various carburetor components.

FLANGE

1. If the idle mixture adjusting screw was removed, temporarily install it.

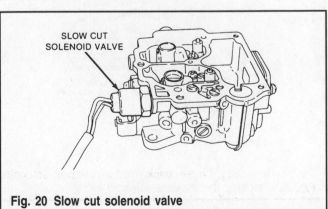

Fig. 20 Slow cut solenoid valve

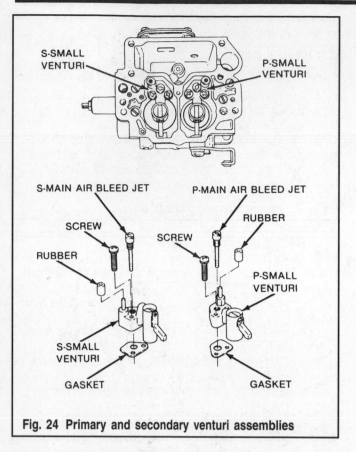

S-SMALL VENTURI

P-SMALL VENTURI

S-MAIN AIR BLEED JET

P-MAIN AIR BLEED JET

SCREW

RUBBER

SCREW

RUBBER

P-SMALL VENTURI

S-SMALL VENTURI

GASKET

GASKET

Fig. 24 Primary and secondary venturi assemblies

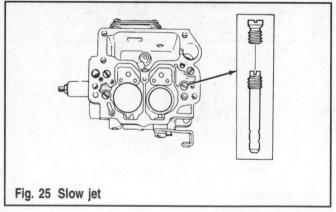

Fig. 25 Slow jet

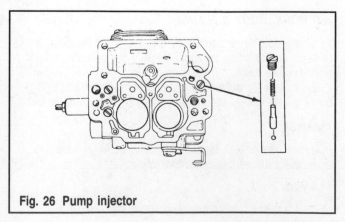

Fig. 26 Pump injector

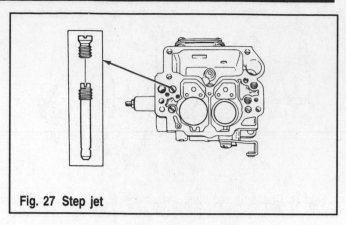

Fig. 27 Step jet

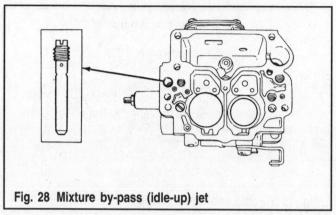

Fig. 28 Mixture by-pass (idle-up) jet

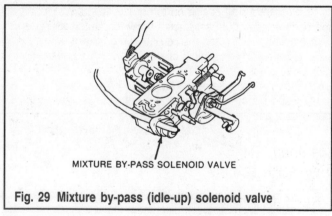

MIXTURE BY-PASS SOLENOID VALVE

Fig. 29 Mixture by-pass (idle-up) solenoid valve

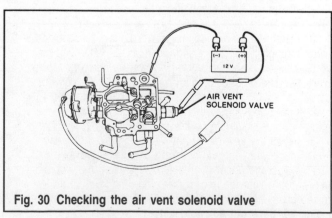

12 V

AIR VENT SOLENOID VALVE

Fig. 30 Checking the air vent solenoid valve

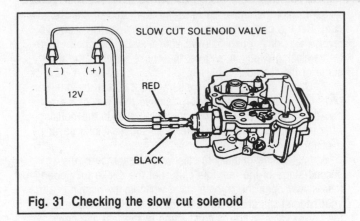

Fig. 31 Checking the slow cut solenoid

2. Install the TPS to the bracket.
3. Install the idle-up (mixture by-pass) solenoid valve using a new gasket.
4. Check that each part moves smoothly.

BODY

1. Assemble each jet in the proper position.
2. Install the accelerating pump filter by first inserting the check ball, then insert the filter followed by the snapring. Be VERY CAREFUL that no damage is done to the bore while inserting the snapring.
3. Install the slow cut solenoid valve using a new gasket.
4. Install the diaphragm chamber using a new gasket.

BODY & FLANGE

1. Position a new gasket on top of the flange, then position the body on top of the assembly. Install the flange screws and wire bracket, then tighten the bolt.
2. Connect the diaphragm chamber rod and the secondary shift valve shaft with the E-clip.
3. Install the throttle return and 2nd lock springs.
4. Insert the accelerating pump return springs into the pump bore and install the piston from the top.
5. Make sure each part of the assembly moves smoothly.

AIR HORN
▶ See Figure 32

1. Install the air vent solenoid valve using a new gasket.
2. Install the choke break diaphragm unit and hose. Connect the rod to the diaphragm then secure using the E-clip.
3. Install the mixture control duty solenoid by passing the wires through the air horn and inserting the valve vertically, holding the valve body. DO not attempt to insert the valve while bending or holding at an angle. Tighten the retainer screw.
4. Install and tighten the needle valve seat with the packing, then install the needle valve onto the valve seat.
5. Install the new gasket on the air horn.
6. Install the float and secure it using the float pin.
7. Adjust the upper float level by checking the clearance between the float top and gasket when the float is in the raised position. Clearance should be 0.59 in. (15mm), if necessary bend tab **A** to adjust. Refer to the figure.
8. Adjust the lower float level by checking the clearance between the float bottom and gasket when the float is in the

lowered position. Clearance should be 1.7 in. (44.3mm), if necessary bend tab **B** to adjust. Refer to the figure.

AIR HORN & BODY
▶ See Figure 33

1. Being careful not to bump the float against the body, assembly the air horn to the body. Check to make sure no wires are pinched between the components.
2. Carefully insert the grooves of the accelerating pump piston rod and boot.
3. Install the screws retaining the air horn to the body. Note that the screws are of varying lengths. Refer to the illustration for proper positioning.
4. Connect the link to the choke cam lever, then install the E-clip.
5. Install the pump arm assembly.
6. Arrange each wire properly:
   a. Position the slow cut solenoid valve wire on the inner side.
   b. Position the automatic choke heater wires on the outer side.
   c. Make sure the wires DO NOT interfere with the throttle valve return spring.
7. Install the wires to their positions in the wiring harness connectors.
8. Make sure that each carburetor part moves smoothly.

Initial Carburetor Adjustment (Prior to Installation)
▶ See Figures 34, 35, 36, 37, 38, 39, 40 and 41

1. If removed, install the idle mixture screw and seat it lightly in the bore, then carefully back the screw out 3 turns

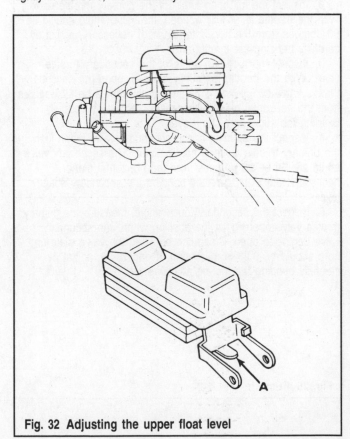

Fig. 32 Adjusting the upper float level

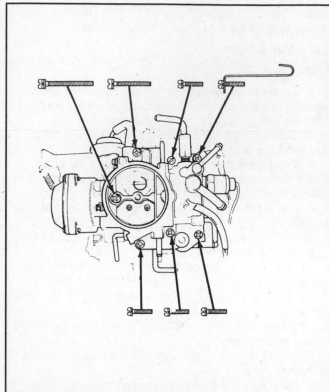

Fig. 33 The seven air horn-to-body screws are of varying lengths. The screws must be positioned properly.

from fully closed for manual transaxles or 2 turns from fully closed for automatic transaxles.

2. Inspect the full open angle of the primary throttle valve. With the throttle lever fully opened, the valve angle should be 90 degrees from the horizontal plane. If necessary, adjust by carefully bending the throttle arm.

3. Inspect the full open angle of the secondary throttle valve. With the throttle lever fully opened, open the secondary throttle valve completely; the valve angle should be 87 degrees from the horizontal plane. If necessary, adjust by carefully bending the secondary shaft lever.

4. Inspect the opening of the secondary valve when just the primary throttle valve is fully opened. The secondary valve angle should be 23 degrees from the horizontal plane. If necessary, adjust by carefully bending the secondary shaft lever.

5. Inspect the secondary touch angle. Measure the primary throttle valve opening, at the position where the secondary valve begins to open. Clearance between the valve plate and bore should be 0.23 in. (5.87mm). If necessary, adjust by carefully bending the throttle adjusting arm.

6. Inspect the choke valve in the third step of the fast idle cam. Set the choke fully open, then slowly open the throttle lever while lightly pushing (with your fingers) the choke valve in the closing direction and set the choke valve to the third stage of the fast idle cam.

7. Check the choke valve clearance; it should be 0.086 in. (2.19mm). If not to specification, remove the rivet of the auto choke and adjust by bending the choke lever in the housing. After adjustment always be sure to install the choke cover by riveting.

8. Inspect the primary throttle valve clearance in the second stage of the fast idle cam. Set the choke fully open, then slowly open the throttle valve while lightly pushing (with your fingers) the choke valve in the closing direction and set the choke valve to the second stage of the fast idle cam.

9. Check the primary throttle clearance; it should be 0.0323 in. (0.82mm) for automatic transaxle vehicles or 0.0256 in. (0.65mm) for manual transaxle vehicles. If necessary, adjust the fast idle screw to achieve the proper clearance.

10. Check the unloader by fully opening the primary throttle valve, then measuring the choke valve clearance; it should be 0.071 in. (1.8mm). If not to specification, remove the auto choke rivet and adjust by bending the choke lever in the housing. After adjustment, always be sure to install the choke cover by riveting.

11. Check the choke break using a hand held vacuum pump. Apply 400mm Hg to the choke break vacuum unit and measure the valve clearance while lightly pushing the valve towards the closing side. Clearance should be 0.057 in. (1.44mm). If necessary, adjust by bending the choke lever.

12. Check and, if necessary, adjust the TPS. Checking and adjustment of the sensor should be completed as quickly as possible:

   a. Make sure the TPS bracket screws are tight.

   b. Make sure there is not play in the TPS arm and primary throttle arm.

   c. Connect an ohmmeter across the green and black leads of the TPS terminal.

   d. Open the primary throttle lever about 1/3, the ohmmeter should indicate NO CONTINUITY. Gradually close the lever and check that there is continuity when the primary throttle valve reaches the prescribed clearance. Specified clearance is 0.015 in. (automatic transaxle vehicles) or 0.011 in. (manual transaxle vehicles).

   e. If not to specification, loosen the retaining screws and adjust the switch to achieve the proper angle. After tightening the screws, check clearance adjustment again using the ohmmeter.

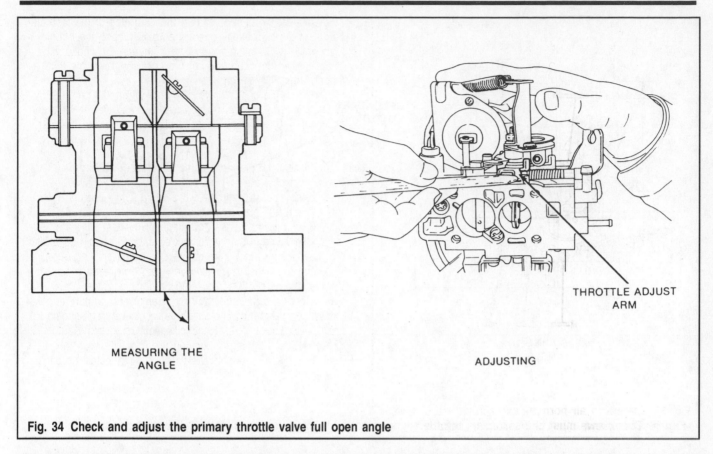

MEASURING THE
ANGLE

THROTTLE ADJUST
ARM

ADJUSTING

Fig. 34 Check and adjust the primary throttle valve full open angle

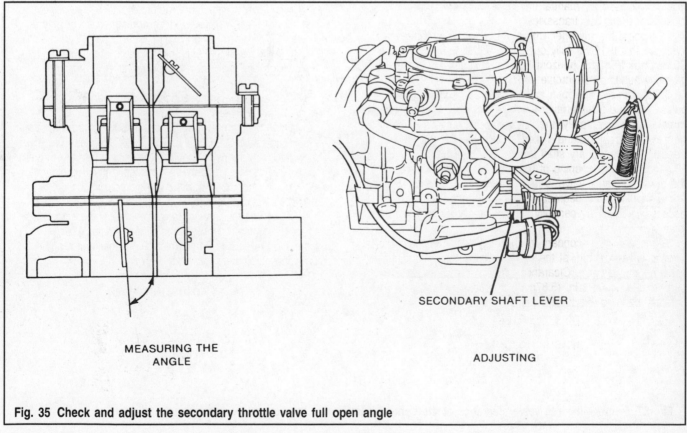

MEASURING THE
ANGLE

SECONDARY SHAFT LEVER

ADJUSTING

Fig. 35 Check and adjust the secondary throttle valve full open angle

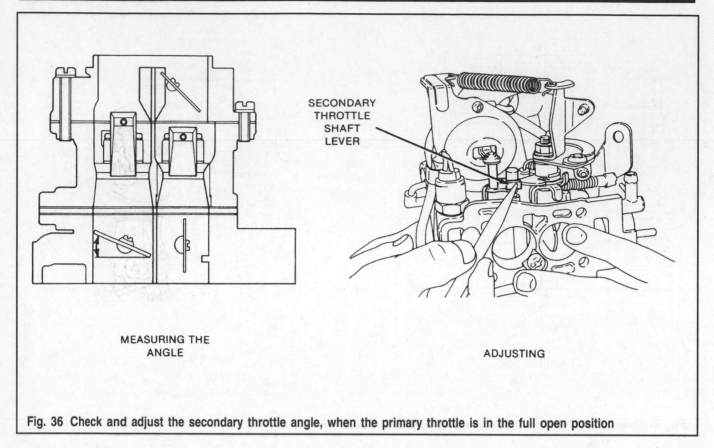

MEASURING THE
ANGLE

SECONDARY
THROTTLE
SHAFT
LEVER

ADJUSTING

Fig. 36 Check and adjust the secondary throttle angle, when the primary throttle is in the full open position

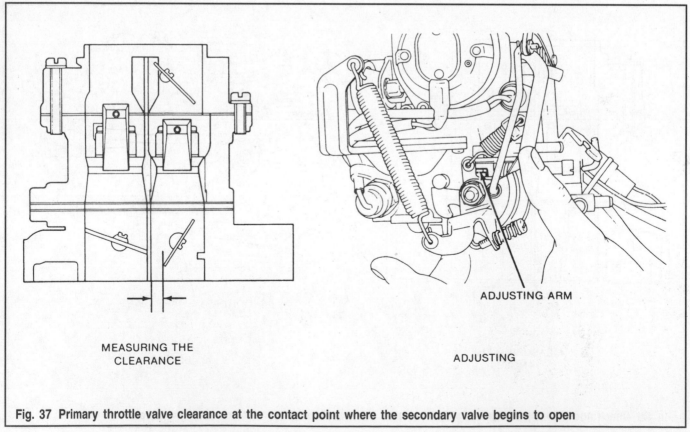

MEASURING THE
CLEARANCE

ADJUSTING ARM

ADJUSTING

Fig. 37 Primary throttle valve clearance at the contact point where the secondary valve begins to open

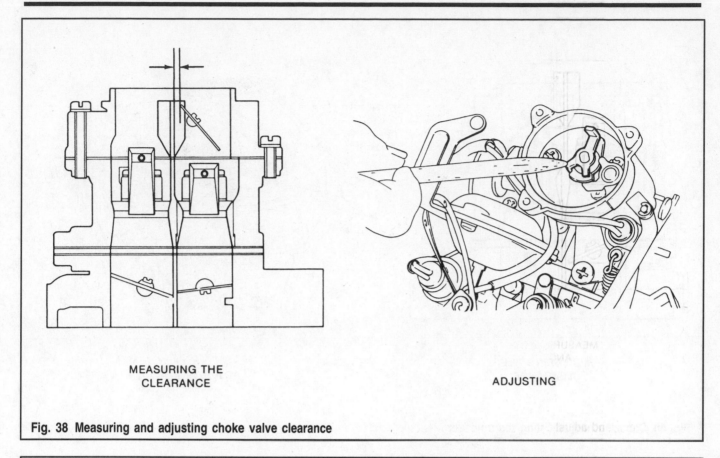

MEASURING THE CLEARANCE

ADJUSTING

Fig. 38 Measuring and adjusting choke valve clearance

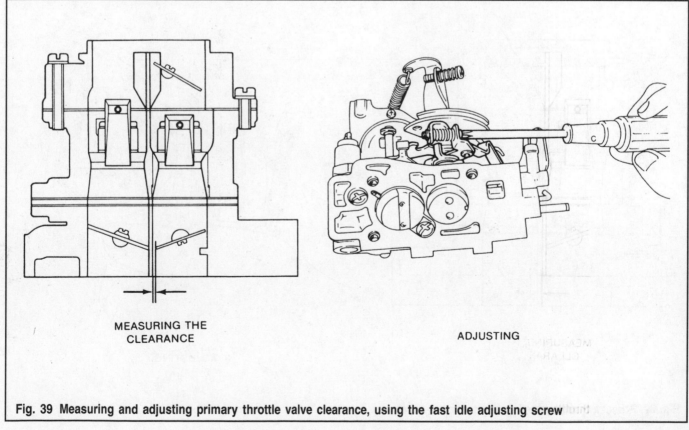

MEASURING THE CLEARANCE

ADJUSTING

Fig. 39 Measuring and adjusting primary throttle valve clearance, using the fast idle adjusting screw

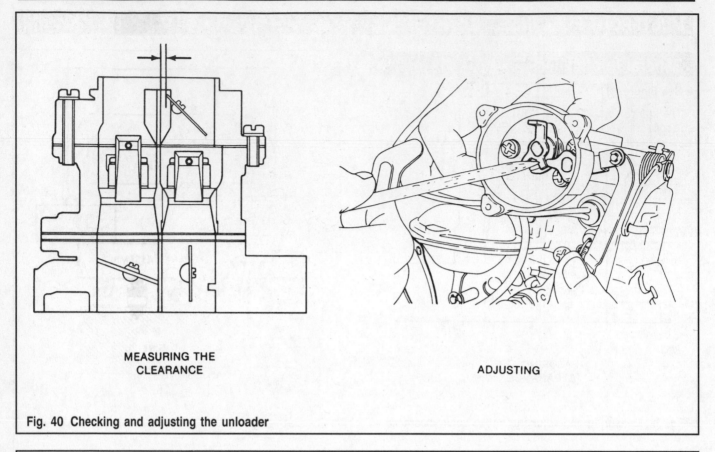

MEASURING THE
CLEARANCE

ADJUSTING

Fig. 40 Checking and adjusting the unloader

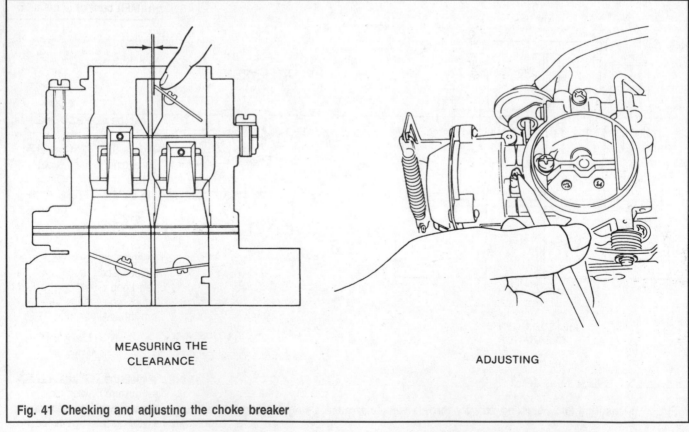

MEASURING THE
CLEARANCE

ADJUSTING

Fig. 41 Checking and adjusting the choke breaker

MULTI-PORT FUEL INJECTION SYSTEM

General Information

▶ See Figure 42

The non-carbureted engines covered in this manual are equipped Multi-port Fuel Injection (MFI) that uses 1 injector for each cylinder. All fuel injection functions are controlled by the Engine Control Module (ECM). It accepts inputs from various sensors and switches, calculates the optimum air/fuel mixture and operates the various output devices to provide peak performance within specific emissions limits. The ECM will attempt to maintain the air/fuel mixture of 14.7:1 in order to optimize catalytic converter operation. If a system failure occurs that is not serious enough to stop the engine, the ECM will illuminate the CHECK ENGINE light and operate the engine in a backup or fail-safe mode.

Fuel is supplied to the engine from a pump mounted in the fuel tank. A separate fuel gauge sending unit is also mounted in the tank. Either component can be replaced separately.

Other related system components include a pressure regulator, an Idle Air Control (IAC) valve, a Throttle Position Sensor (TPS), Intake Air Temperature (IAT) sensor, Engine Coolant Temperature (ECT) sensor, Manifold Absolute Pressure (MAP) sensor, a power steering pressure switch (in some cases) and an oxygen sensor. The fuel injectors are solenoid valves that the ECM pulses on and off many times per second in order to promote good fuel atomization. The pulse width determines how long the injector is ON each cycle and this regulates the amount of fuel supplied to the engine.

The system pressure regulator is mounted on the end of the fuel rail that feeds the injectors. Intake manifold pressure is supplied to the regulator diaphragm, making system pressure partly dependent on engine load. The pressure regulator compensates for engine load by increasing fuel pressure as vacuum drops.

The idle air control valve is a stepper motor that controls the amount of air allowed to bypass the throttle plate. With this valve the ECM can closely control idle speed even when the engine is cold or when there is a high engine load at idle.

The throttle position sensor is mounted on the side of the throttle body and monitors rotation of the throttle shaft. The sensor is a potentiometer (variable resistor) that creates a voltage drop in the reference signal to correspond with throttle position. The sensor is an auto zeroing type that cannot be adjusted.

OPERATING MODES

▶ See Figure 43

Starting Mode

When the ignition switch is first turned ON, the fuel pump relay is energized by the ECM for 2 seconds to build system pressure. When the ECM determines that the engine is turning over or cranking, the pump will run continuously. In the start mode, the ECM checks the MAP sensor, TPS and ECT sensor

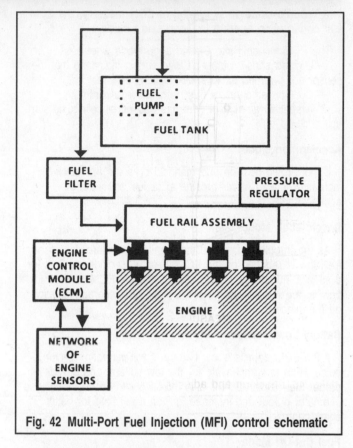

Fig. 42 Multi-Port Fuel Injection (MFI) control schematic

to determine the best air/fuel ratio for starting. Ratios could range from 1.5:1 at -33°F (-36°C), to 14.7:1 at 201°F (94°C) of engine coolant temperature.

Clear Flood Mode

If the engine becomes flooded, it can be cleared by opening the accelerator to the full throttle position. When the throttle is open all the way and engine rpm is less than 400, the ECM will close the fuel injectors while the engine is turning over in order to clear the engine of excess fuel. If throttle position is reduced below about 80 percent, the ECM will return to the start mode.

Open Loop Mode

When the engine first starts and engine speed rises above 400 rpm, the ECM operates in the Open Loop mode until specific parameters are met. In Open Loop operation the ECM ignores oxygen sensor signals and fuel requirements are calculated based on information from the MAP sensor, TPS and ECT sensor.

Closed Loop Mode

When the correct parameters are met, the ECM will use O_2 sensor output and adjust the air/fuel mixture in order to maintain a narrow band of exhaust gas oxygen concentration. When the ECM is correcting and adjusting fuel mixture based on the oxygen sensor signal along with the other sensors, this is known as feedback air/fuel ratio control.

➡**If Trouble Code 13 is logged in ECM memory, the ECM will continue to operate in Open Loop mode.**

The ECM will shift into Closed Loop mode when:
— Oxygen sensor output voltage varies, indicating that the sensor has warmed up to operating temperature.
— Coolant temperature has risen above a minimum.
— A specific amount of time has passed since engine start-up.

Acceleration Mode

If the throttle position and manifold pressure are quickly increased, the ECM will provide extra fuel for smooth acceleration.

Deceleration Mode

As the throttle closes and the manifold pressure decreases, fuel flow is reduced by the ECM. If both conditions remain for a specific number of engine revolutions, the ECM decides fuel flow is not needed and stops the flow by temporarily shutting off the injectors.

Battery Low Mode

If the ECM detects a low battery, it will increase injector pulse width to compensate for the low voltage and provide proper fuel delivery. It will also increase idle speed to increase alternator output and increase ignition dwell time for better spark control.

Fuel Cut-Off Mode

When the ECM is receiving an engine rpm signal above 6800, the injectors are shut off to prevent engine overspeed. When rpm drops below 6800, the injectors will again be pulsed in normal mode.

RELIEVING FUEL SYSTEM PRESSURE

1. Remove the fuel cap to relieve tank pressure.
2. Remove the fuel pump relay from the underhood relay center.
3. Start the engine and run until fuel in the lines is consumed and the engine stalls.

4. Crank the engine for an additional 30 seconds to assure all pressure is released from the lines. It is easier on the starter if the 30 seconds is broken into shorter 10 second bursts, with a pause between each.
5. Disconnect the negative battery cable.

Electric Fuel Pump

REMOVAL & INSTALLATION

▶ **See Figure 44**

Fuel pump replacement or service requires the removal of the fuel tank.

1. Remove the fuel tank from the vehicle. Refer to the procedure later in this section.
2. Remove the 8 fuel pump mounting screws.
3. Remove the fuel pump bracket from the tank.
4. Loosen the screw-type fitting, then disconnect the fuel pump supply hose extension from the bracket.
5. Remove the gasket from the pump bracket or tank.
6. Remove the filter from the pump pick-up tube.
7. Unplug the electrical wires from the pump.
8. Remove the fuel pump bracket.
9. Disconnect the outlet hose from the pump.
To install:
10. Connect the outlet hose to the pump.
11. Install the pump on the bracket.
12. Install the electrical wiring connectors to the pump.
13. Install the filter to the pump pick-up tube.
14. Position the gasket on the pump bracket.
15. Install the fuel pump supply hose extension on the bracket and tighten the screw-type fitting to 25 ft. lbs. (34 Nm).
16. Install the fuel pump bracket to the tank.
17. Install the mounting screws and tighten to 30 inch lbs. (3 Nm).
18. Install the fuel tank assembly to the vehicle.

TESTING

Refer to the appropriate chart in Section 4 of this manual for fuel pump/system pressure checks.

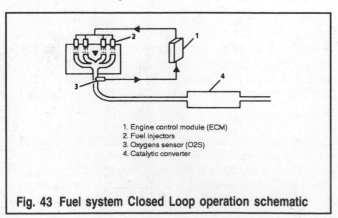

1. Engine control module (ECM)
2. Fuel injectors
3. Oxygens sensor (O2S)
4. Catalytic converter

Fig. 43 Fuel system Closed Loop operation schematic

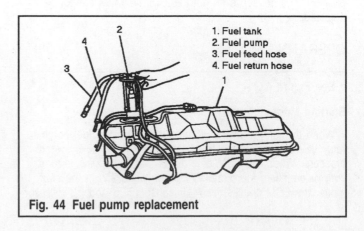

1. Fuel tank
2. Fuel pump
3. Fuel feed hose
4. Fuel return hose

Fig. 44 Fuel pump replacement

Throttle Body

REMOVAL & INSTALLATION

▶ See Figure 45

1. Disconnect the negative battery cable.
2. Partially drain the engine cooling system to a level below the throttle body coolant hoses.
3. Tag and disconnect the vacuum connections from the throttle body.
4. Unplug the IAC valve and TPS wiring from the terminals.
5. Disconnect the air cleaner-to-throttle body duct from the throttle body. If necessary, remove the duct completely for better access.
6. Disconnect the coolant hoses from the fittings on the bottom of the throttle body.
7. Disconnect the throttle and, if applicable, cruise control linkage.
8. Remove the throttle body attaching bolts, then remove the throttle body and flange gasket from the intake. Discard the old flange gasket.

To install:

9. Thoroughly clean the gasket mating surfaces, but be careful not to score the machined aluminum surfaces.
10. Install the throttle body assembly using a new gasket. Secure using the mounting bolts and tighten to 16 ft. lbs. (22 Nm).
11. If removed, install the power steering brace and tighten.
12. Install the throttle linkage, and if equipped, the cruise control cable. Make sure the cable(s) do not hold the throttle open when the accelerator pedal is released.
13. Connect the coolant hoses to the throttle body fittings.
14. Install the air cleaner-to-throttle body duct.
15. Install the wiring harness connectors to the IAC valve and TP sensor terminals.
16. Install the vacuum connections.
17. Refill the engine cooling system.
18. Connect the negative battery cable, then start the engine and check for leaks.

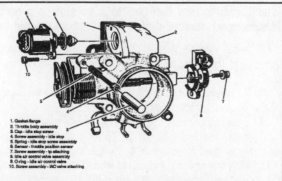

1. Gasket-flange
2. Throttle body assembly
3. Cap - idle stop screw
4. Screw assembly - idle stop
5. Spring - idle stop screw assembly
6. Sensor - throttle position sensor
7. Screw assembly - tp attaching
8. Idle air control valve assembly
9. O-ring - idle air control valve
10. Screw assembly - IAC valve attaching

Fig. 45 Exploded view of the throttle body assembly

ADJUSTMENTS

Idle Speed Check

➡The minimum idle speed is preset at the factory and requires no periodic adjustment. The factory adjustment should not be tampered with.

1. If there is problem with high idle speed, the most likely cause is a vacuum leak. Check all vacuum hoses and connections. Make sure the throttle body is properly mounted and the gasket is intact.
2. If no vacuum leaks are found, perform the IAC valve functional check. Refer to the diagnostic charts in Section 4 of this manual. Also, make sure IAC valve pintle position is not 'lost' which could occur if the battery cable was disconnected. Refer to the IAC valve Idle Learn procedure, later in this section.
3. If the minimum throttle position is still suspect, continue with the procedure. Block the drive wheels and apply the parking brake, then place the transaxle in **N**.
4. Connect a suitable scan tool to the ALDL/DLC. Refer to Section 4 of this manual for information regarding the ECM and self-diagnostics.
5. Start the engine and allow it to idle until normal operating temperature is reached (about 90°C) and the engine enters Closed Loop operation.
6. If equipped with an automatic transaxle, shift to **D**, then back to **N**.
7. Select the power steering pressure switch input on the scan tool. Make sure the A/C and ALL accessories are turned off. The power steering pressure switch reading should be OFF or NORMAL indicating that engine load is at minimum. If reading is incorrect, diagnose and repair and possible faulty pressure switch circuit.
8. Select IAC valve display on the scan tool and monitor IAC valve counts. If between 5-45 counts, the minimum throttle position is acceptable. It is important that the idle speed be stabilized before attempting to read counts.
9. If IAC counts are too low, check for a vacuum leak missed earlier at the hoses, throttle body, and intake manifold. Check for a damaged throttle lever and correct, as necessary. If no causes can be found for the excessive air flow into the intake, the throttle body must be replaced.
10. If IAC counts are too high, check for a damaged throttle lever or air flow restriction by the throttle valve. If no problem is evident, disconnect the inlet duct from the throttle body and use a carburetor cleaner (which does not contain Methyl Ethyl Ketone) along with a shop towel to clean residue from the throttle body bore. Recheck the IAC counts and, if still too high, replace the throttle body.

Fuel Injectors/Fuel Rail Assembly

REMOVAL & INSTALLATION

Except 1993 1.6L Engine
▶ See Figures 46 and 47

1. Relieve the fuel system pressure.

2. Disconnect the negative battery cable.

3. Remove the air duct assembly.

4. Disconnect the throttle cable at the throttle body, the throttle cable from the bracket and the TPS electrical connector.

5. Unplug the idle air control valve and the intake air temperature sensor electrical connectors.

6. Label and disconnect the 2 vacuum hoses, then disconnect the 2 coolant hoses at the throttle body.

7. Remove the 4 throttle body retaining bolts.

8. Remove the throttle body. Then remove and discard the gasket from the mating surface.

9. Tag and disconnect the 4 vacuum hoses at the plenum.

10. Disconnect the PCV valve at the plenum. Disconnect the ECM ground wires.

11. Remove the engine lift hook brackets, then remove the plenum support brackets.

12. Remove the 9 plenum retaining nuts and bolts, then remove the plenum assembly.

13. Unplug the 4 injector electrical connectors.

14. If the fuel rail is to be completely removed from the engine, disconnect the fuel lines. Using a backup wrench to prevent fuel rail/pressure regulator damage, disconnect the fuel pressure line from the rail and return line from the regulator.

15. Remove the fuel rail retaining bolts, then remove the rail/injector assembly from the engine.

16. If fuel injector removal from the fuel rail is necessary, slide the injector retaining clip along the fuel rail ledge away from the injector to disengage, then spread the clip open while pulling downward. Discard the clip after it has been removed. Remove the injector assemblies.

17. Remove the O-ring from the top and bottom of the injectors and discard them. If the injectors are not being removed from the rail, only the bottom O-rings must be replaced.

To install:

➡**Different injectors are calibrated for different flow rates. When ordering new fuel injectors, be sure to order the identical part number that is inscribed on the old injector.**

18. Install new O-rings to the bottom (and if applicable to the top) of the injectors, then lubricate them with clean engine oil.

19. If removed, install the fuel injectors into the fuel rail. Install the new injector retaining clip. Be sure that the clip is parallel to the injector electrical connector.

➡**Be sure to install the injector assembly into the fuel rail injector socket, with the electrical connector and retaining clip facing outward. Line up the injector with the injector socket, push upward slowly to engage the retaining clip on the fuel rail ledge then push the injector all the way in to firmly seat it in the socket.**

20. Install the fuel rail/injector assembly to the engine and secure using the retaining bolts. Tighten the bolts to 19 ft. lbs. (26 Nm).

21. If disconnected, replace the O-rings seals, then connect the fuel lines and tighten using a backup wrench to prevent component damage.

22. Install the 4 wiring harness connectors to the injector terminals.

23. Install the plenum assembly. Install the 9 plenum retaining nuts and bolts. Install the plenum support brackets.

24. Install the engine lift hook brackets.

25. Reconnect the PCV valve at the plenum and the ECM ground wires.

26. Install the 4 vacuum hoses to the plenum.

27. Install the throttle body using a new gasket.

28. Install the 4 retaining bolts at the throttle body assembly. Torque the bolts 16 ft. lbs. (22 Nm).

29. Reconnect the 2 vacuum hose and the 2 coolant hoses to the throttle body.

30. Install the wiring harness connectors to the idle air control valve and the intake air temperature sensor and TPS terminals.

31. Reconnect the throttle cable at the throttle body and the throttle cable to the bracket.

32. Install the air duct assembly.

33. Reconnect the negative battery cable.

34. Cycle the ignition to build system pressure, then check for leaks.

1993 1.6L Engine

▶ **See Figures 48 and 49**

1. Relieve the fuel system pressure, then disconnect the negative battery cable.

2. Disconnect the PCV valve and hose from the plenum.

3. Disconnect the fuel supply line from the retainer bracket.

4. Disconnect the fuel return line from the pressure regulator.

5. Tag and remove the canister purge vacuum hoses from the plenum and fuel rail.

6. Disconnect the pressure regulator vacuum hose.

7. Unplug the wiring harness connectors from the fuel injectors.

8. Unplug the Intake Air Temperature (IAT) sensor connector, then reposition the harness away from the fuel rail.

9. Remove the plenum support bracket and fasteners from the passenger side of the plenum.

10. Using a ¼ in. drive with an 11 in. extension and 12mm universal socket, remove the 2 fasteners with spacers for the fuel rail.

11. Remove the fuel injectors from the fuel rail and intake, then remove and discard the fuel injector O-rings.

12. If necessary, remove the fuel rail by sliding out towards the passenger side of the engine compartment.

To install:

➡**Different injectors are calibrated for different flow rates. When ordering new fuel injectors, be sure to order the identical part number that is inscribed on the old injector.**

13. Install new O-rings to the bottom (and if applicable to the top) of the injectors, then lubricate them with clean engine oil.

14. If removed, slide the fuel rail in from the passenger side of the engine compartment.

15. Connect the fuel line to the pressure regulator.

16. Install the fuel injector assemblies to the fuel rail, then seat the rail and injectors to the intake.

17. With the socket, extension and drive used earlier, install the 2 fuel rail fasteners (with spacers) and tighten to 19 ft. lbs. (26 Nm).

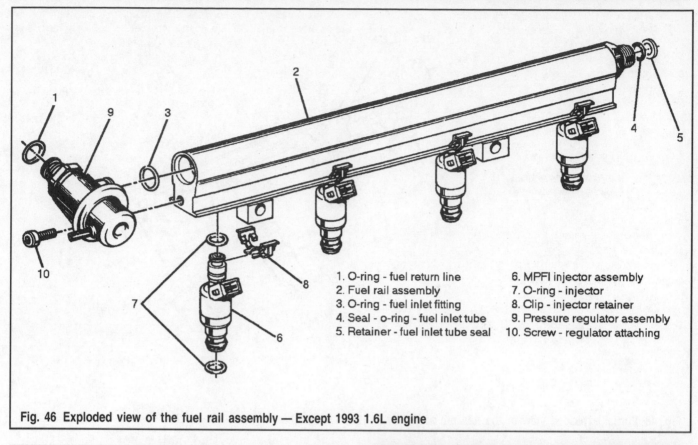

Fig. 46 Exploded view of the fuel rail assembly — Except 1993 1.6L engine

1. O-ring - fuel return line
2. Fuel rail assembly
3. O-ring - fuel inlet fitting
4. Seal - o-ring - fuel inlet tube
5. Retainer - fuel inlet tube seal
6. MPFI injector assembly
7. O-ring - injector
8. Clip - injector retainer
9. Pressure regulator assembly
10. Screw - regulator attaching

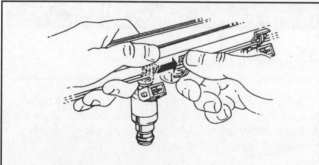

Fig. 47 Removing the fuel injector retaining clip — Except 1993 1.6L engine

18. Connect the vacuum hose to the fuel pressure regulator.
19. Install the canister purge vacuum hoses.
20. Connect the fuel pressure line.
21. Install the wiring harness connectors to the IAT sensor and the fuel injectors.
22. Install the PCV valve and vacuum hose.
23. Install the plenum support bracket to the passenger side of the plenum and tighten the fasteners.
24. Install air cleaner duct.
25. Connect the negative battery cable, then cycle the ignition to build system pressure and check for leaks.

Pressure Regulator

REMOVAL & INSTALLATION

Except 1993 1.6L Engine

1. Relieve fuel system pressure, then disconnect the negative battery cable.
2. Remove the fuel rail/injector assembly from the engine.
3. Remove the pressure regulator retaining screw.
4. Separate the regulator from the fuel rail by twisting back and forth while pulling it apart.
5. Remove and discard the regulator-to-rail and regulator-to-fuel line O-rings seals.

To install:

6. Lubricate new O-rings seals with clean engine oil, then install them to the regulator.
7. Install the regulator assembly to the fuel rail.
8. Install the regulator retaining screw and tighten to 102 inch lbs. (11.5 Nm).
9. Install the fuel rail/injector assembly.
10. Connect the negative battery cable, then cycle the ignition to build system pressure and check for leaks.

1993 1.6L Engine

1. Relieve the fuel system pressure, then disconnect the negative battery cable.
2. Disconnect the vacuum hose from the pressure regulator.
3. Remove the fuel return line from the regulator.

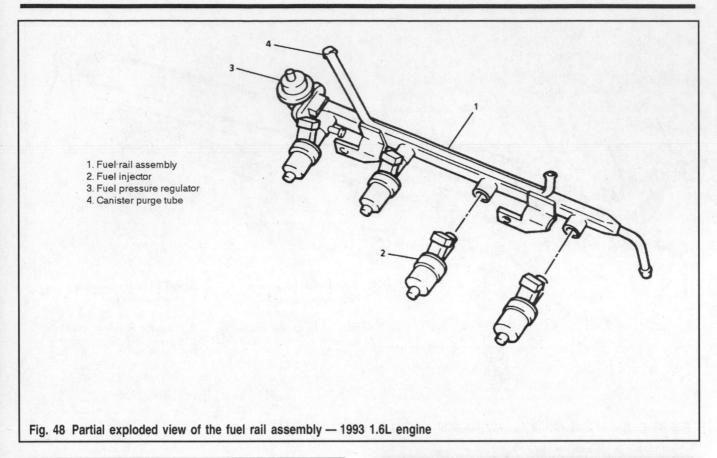

1. Fuel rail assembly
2. Fuel injector
3. Fuel pressure regulator
4. Canister purge tube

Fig. 48 Partial exploded view of the fuel rail assembly — 1993 1.6L engine

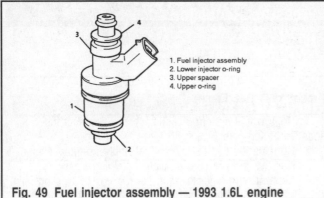

1. Fuel injector assembly
2. Lower injector o-ring
3. Upper spacer
4. Upper o-ring

Fig. 49 Fuel injector assembly — 1993 1.6L engine

4. Remove the 2 fasteners holding the regulator to the fuel rail assembly.
5. Remove the regulator from the fuel rail, then remove and discard the O-ring seals.
To install:
6. Lubricate new O-rings seals with clean engine oil, then install them to the regulator.
7. Connect the fuel return line to the pressure regulator assembly.
8. Install the pressure regulator to the fuel rail, then secure using the 2 fasteners.
9. Connect the vacuum hose to the pressure regulator.
10. Connect the negative battery cable, then cycle the ignition to build system pressure and check for leaks.

Throttle Position Sensor

ADJUSTMENT

The Throttle Position Sensor (TPS) is an automatic zeroing component. No adjustment is necessary or possible. If an idle problem is suspected, refer to the minimum idle check under Throttle Body, earlier in this section.

REMOVAL & INSTALLATION

Refer to Section 4 of this manual for TPS removal and installation procedures.

Idle Air Control Valve

REMOVAL & INSTALLATION

▶ **See Figure 50**

1. Disconnect the negative battery cable.
2. Remove the IAC valve attaching screws.
3. Remove the valve from the throttle body.
To install:

➡**Once an IAC valve has been in service, DO NOT push or pull on the pintle. The force required to move the pintle may damage threads on the worn drive.**

4. Carefully clean the IAC valve mounting surface to assure proper O-ring seal. The IAC valve is an electrical part, do not soak or immerse it in solvent.

➡When replacing the IAC valve, make sure only to use an identical part. The pintle shape and diameter are essential to proper valve operation and may vary from application to application.

5. If installing a new IAC valve, measure the distance from the tip of the pintle to the flange mating surface. If the distance is greater than 28mm, retract the pintle using finger pressure. This will not harm a NEW IAC valve.

6. Inspect the valve O-ring for damage, and replace, if necessary. Lubricate the O-ring with clean engine oil.

7. Install the IAC valve to the throttle body.

8. Install the IAC valve retaining screws and tighten to 27 inch lbs. (3 Nm).

9. Connect the negative battery cable, then follow the Idle Learn Procedure.

IDLE LEARN PROCEDURE

The ECM controls idle speed using the IAC valve by extending or retracting the valve pintle to control air flow. But to do this, the ECM must know at all times exactly where the pintle is located. If the battery cable is removed and power is lost, the pintle position will also be lost.

The ECM will normally reset the pintle position 1 time each ignition cycle, during moderate acceleration, once the vehicle

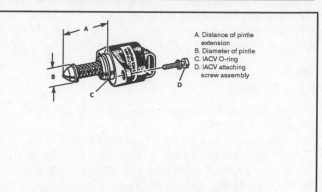

A. Distance of pintle extension
B. Diameter of pintle
C. IACV O-ring
D. IACV attaching screw assembly

Fig. 50 Idle Air Control (IAC) Valve service

speed passes 30-40 mph (depending on the model). The ECM accomplishes this by commanding the pintle to retract completely, then move inward to the fully seated position. This establishes a zero count, from which the ECM can back out the valve to its desired position.

If a problem occurs with the resetting, the ECM will repeat it until a proper count is established.

Any time power has been cut and the pintle position is lost, a drop in performance may be noticeable until the ECM has a chance to relearn proper positioning. To 'teach' the ECM proper pintle position, the vehicle should be driven with the engine in normal closed loop operation (fully warmed) using moderate acceleration and speeds of at least 40 mph for 2-3 miles until normal performance returns.

FUEL TANK

Tank Assembly

REMOVAL & INSTALLATION

➡Before removing fuel system parts, clean them with a spray-type engine cleaner. Follow the instructions on the cleaner. Do not soak fuel system parts in liquid cleaning solvent.

✳✳CAUTION

The fuel injection system is under pressure. Release pressure slowly and contain spillage. Observe no smoking/no open flame precautions. Have a Class B-C (dry powder) fire extinguisher within arm's reach at all times.

Spectrum
▶ See Figure 51

1. Relieve the fuel system pressure and disconnect the negative battery cable.

2. Remove the fuel filler cap from the fuel tank.

3. Have a Class B fire extinguisher near the work area. Use a hand operated pump device to drain as much fuel through the fuel filler neck as possible.

4. Use a siphon to remove the remainder of the fuel in the tank by connecting the siphon to the fuel pump outlet fitting.

✳✳CAUTION

Never drain or store fuel in an open container because there is the possibility of a fire or an explosion.

5. Reinstall the fuel filler cap.

6. Disconnect the sending unit wire from the fuel tank terminal.

7. Unfasten the clips and disconnect the 3 rubber hoses on the rear side of the fuel tank.

8. Unfasten the clips and disconnect the fuel delivery and fuel return hose from the side of the fuel tank.

9. Remove the fuel filler pipe bracket bolts.

10. Using a suitable transaxle jack, support the fuel tank.

11. Remove the fuel tank retaining bolts and carefully lower the tank.

To install:

12. Place the fuel tank in its proper space using the transaxle jack, Install the fuel tank retaining bolts.

13. Install the fuel filler pipe bracket bolts.

14. Install the clips and reconnect the fuel delivery and fuel return hose to the side of the fuel tank.

15. Install the clips and reconnect the 3 rubber hoses on the rear side of the fuel tank.

16. Install the sending unit wire.

17. Fill the fuel tank and check for leaks.

18. Connect the negative battery cable, then start and run the engine. Makes sure the fuel gauge sending unit is working.

Storm

▶ **See Figure 52**

1. Relieve the fuel system pressure and disconnect the negative battery cable.

2. Remove the fuel filler cap from the fuel tank.

3. Have a Class B fire extinguisher near the work area. Use a hand operated pump device to drain as much fuel through the fuel filler neck as possible.

4. Use a siphon to remove the remainder of the fuel in the tank by connecting the siphon to the fuel pump outlet fitting.

✳✳CAUTION

Never drain or store fuel in an open container because there is the possibility of a fire or an explosion.

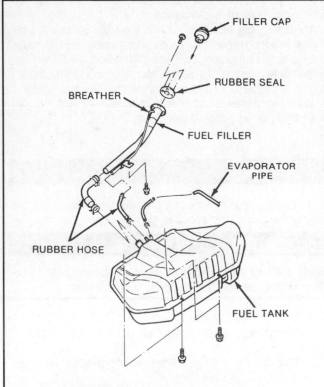

Fig. 51 Exploded view of the fuel tank assembly — Carbureted Spectrum

5. Reinstall the fuel pump outlet hose to its fitting, install the fuel filler cap.

6. Raise and support the vehicle safely.

7. Remove the center exhaust pipe from the catalytic converter. If necessary, completely remove the center exhaust pipe from the vehicle.

8. Loosen the clamp, then remove the fuel filler neck hose from the fuel tank.

9. Loosen the clamp, then remove the fuel overflow pipe hose from the fuel tank.

10. Unplug the fuel gauge sending unit and fuel pump electrical connectors.

11. Disconnect the fuel feed, return and vapor hoses from their respective pipes. For each hose, either spread the retaining clamp or loosen the screw-type retaining nut.

12. For 1993 vehicles, remove the 2 retaining bolts, then disconnect the parking brake cables from the tank.

13. Using a suitable transaxle jack, support the fuel tank.

14. For 1993 vehicles, remove the 4 retaining bolts, then lower the tank and heat shield from the vehicle.

15. Except for 1993 vehicles, remove the 6 fuel tank retaining bolts and lower the tank.

To install:

16. Place the fuel tank in its proper space using the transaxle jack, Install the tank retaining bolts and torque them to 14 ft. lbs. (19 Nm). Remove the transaxle jack.

17. For 1993 vehicles, position the parking brake cables and tighten the bolts to 21 ft. lbs. (28 Nm).

18. Install the fuel supply, return and vapor hoses. If equipped with screw-type retaining nuts tighten to 25 ft. lbs. (34 Nm).

19. Install the wiring harness connectors for the fuel pump and the gauge sending unit. Install the fuel overflow pipe hose and the fuel filler neck.

20. Install the center exhaust pipe and/or connect the pipe to the catalytic converter.

21. Lower the vehicle, then refill the fuel tank and install the fuel filler cap.

22. Connect the negative battery cable, then cycle the ignition to build system pressure and check for leaks.

23. Start the engine and check for proper fuel system and gauge sending unit operation.

FUEL GAUGE SENDING UNIT REPLACEMENT

Storm

▶ **See Figure 53**

1. Relieve the fuel system pressure, then disconnect the negative battery cable.

2. Remove the fuel tank assembly from the vehicle. Refer to the procedure earlier in this section.

3. Remove the 5 or 6 retaining screws from the sending unit, then carefully remove the sending unit from the tank.

4. Remove and discard the old gasket from the unit or from the tank.

To install:

5. Install a new gasket on the sending unit, then carefully insert the unit into the tank.

6. Install the retaining screws and tighten to 30 inch lbs. (3 Nm).

7. Install the fuel tank assembly to the vehicle.

8. Connect the negative battery cable, then start the engine. Check for fuel leaks and for proper sending unit operation.

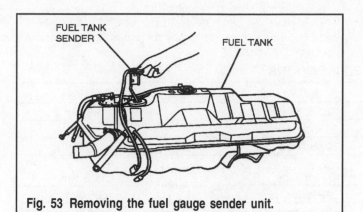

Fig. 53 Removing the fuel gauge sender unit.

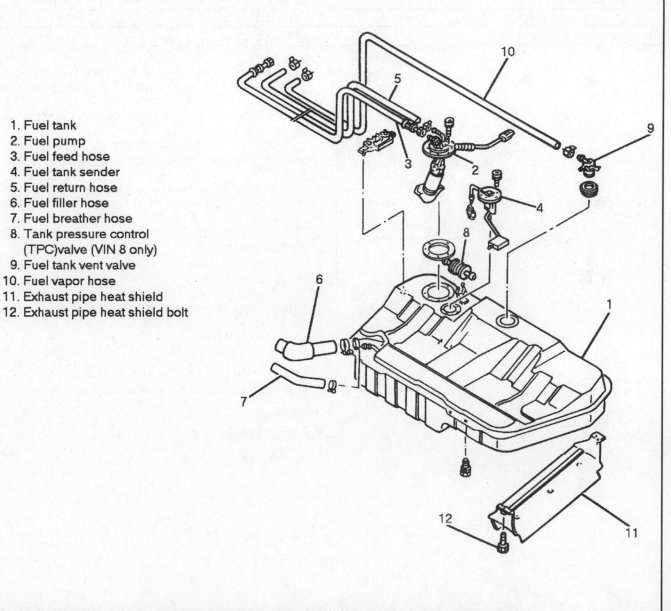

1. Fuel tank
2. Fuel pump
3. Fuel feed hose
4. Fuel tank sender
5. Fuel return hose
6. Fuel filler hose
7. Fuel breather hose
8. Tank pressure control (TPC)valve (VIN 8 only)
9. Fuel tank vent valve
10. Fuel vapor hose
11. Exhaust pipe heat shield
12. Exhaust pipe heat shield bolt

Fig. 52 Exploded view of the fuel tank assembly — 1993 Storm (other fuel injected vehicles similar)

TORQUE SPECIFICATIONS

Component	U.S.	Metric
Carburetor retaining bolts	7.2 ft. lbs.	9.8 Nm
Eletric fuel pump mounting screws	30 inch lbs.	3 Nm
Fuel gauge sending unit screws (Storm)	30 inch lbs.	3 Nm
Fuel pressure regulator: Except 1993 1.6L engine	102 inch lbs.	11.5 Nm
Fuel rail retaining bolts	19 ft. lbs.	26 Nm
Fuel tank hose (screw-type fitting)	25 ft. lbs.	34 Nm
Fuel tank retaining bolts	14 ft. lbs.	19 Nm
IAC valve retaining screws	27 inch lbs.	3 Nm
Parking brake cable brackets (Storm)	21 ft. lbs.	28 Nm
Throttle body mounting bolts	16 ft. lbs.	22 Nm

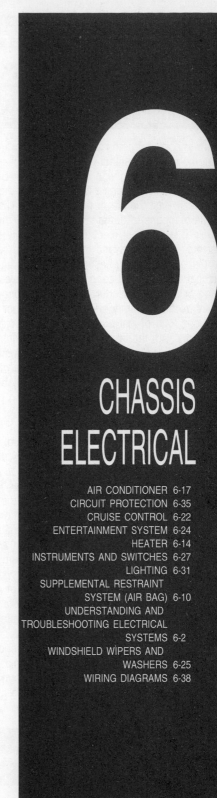

6

CHASSIS ELECTRICAL

UNDERSTANDING AND TROUBLESHOOTING ELECTRICAL SYSTEMS

General Information

Both import and domestic manufacturers are incorporating electronic control systems into their production lines. Most vehicles are equipped with one or more on-board computers. These electronic components (with no moving parts) should theoretically last the life of the vehicle, provided nothing external happens to damage the circuits or memory chips.

While it is true that electronic components should never wear out, in the real world malfunctions do occur. It is also true that any computer-based system is extremely sensitive to electrical voltages and cannot tolerate careless or haphazard testing or service procedures. An inexperienced individual can literally do major damage looking for a minor problem by using the wrong kind of test equipment or connecting test leads or connectors with the ignition switch ON. When selecting test equipment, make sure the manufacturers instructions state that the tester is compatible with whatever type of electronic control system is being serviced. Read all instructions carefully and double check all test points before installing probes or making any test connections.

The following section outlines basic diagnosis techniques for dealing with computerized automotive control systems. Along with a general explanation of the various types of test equipment available to aid in servicing modern electronic automotive systems, basic repair techniques for wiring harnesses and connectors is given. Read the basic information before attempting any repairs or testing on any computerized system, to provide the background of information necessary to avoid the most common and obvious mistakes that can cost both time and money. Although the replacement and testing procedures are simple in themselves, the systems are not, and unless one has a thorough understanding of all components and their function within a particular computerized control system, the logical test sequence these systems demand cannot be followed. Minor malfunctions can make a big difference, so it is important to know how each component affects the operation of the overall electronic system to find the ultimate e cause of a problem without replacing good components unnecessarily. It is not enough to use the correct test equipment; the test equipment must be used correctly.

Safety Precautions

✳✳CAUTION

Whenever working on or around any computer based microprocessor control system, always observe these general precautions to prevent the possibility of personal injury or damage to electronic components.

• Never install or remove battery cables with the key ON or the engine running. Jumper cables should be connected with the key OFF to avoid power surges that can damage electronic control units. Engines equipped with computer controlled systems should avoid both giving and getting jump starts due to the possibility of serious damage to components

from arcing in the engine compartment when connections are made with the ignition ON.

• Always remove the battery cables before charging the battery. Never use a high output charger on an installed battery or attempt to use any type of "hot shot" (24 volt) starting aid.

• Exercise care when inserting test probes into connectors to insure good connections without damaging the connector or spreading the pins. Always probe connectors from the rear (wire) side, NOT the pin side, to avoid accidental shorting of terminals during test procedures.

• Never remove or attach wiring harness connectors with the ignition switch ON, especially to an electronic control unit.

• Do not drop any components during service procedures and never apply 12 volts directly to any component (like a solenoid or relay) unless instructed specifically to do so. Some component electrical windings are designed to safely handle only 4 or 5 volts and can be destroyed in seconds if 12 volts are applied directly to the connector.

• Remove the electronic control unit if the vehicle is to be placed in an environment where temperatures exceed approximately 176°F (80°C), such as a paint spray booth or when arc or gas welding near the control unit location in the car.

ORGANIZED TROUBLESHOOTING

When diagnosing a specific problem, organized troubleshooting is a must. The complexity of a modern automobile demands that you approach any problem in a logical, organized manner. There are certain troubleshooting techniques that are standard:

1. Establish when the problem occurs. Does the problem appear only under certain conditions? Were there any noises, odors, or other unusual symptoms?

2. Isolate the problem area. To do this, make some simple tests and observations; then eliminate the systems that are working properly. Check for obvious problems such as broken wires, dirty connections or split or disconnected vacuum hoses. Always check the obvious before assuming something complicated is the cause.

3. Test for problems systematically to determine the cause once the problem area is isolated. Are all the components functioning properly? Is there power going to electrical switches and motors? Is there vacuum at vacuum switches and/or actuators? Is there a mechanical problem such as bent linkage or loose mounting screws? Doing careful, systematic checks will often turn up most causes on the first inspection without wasting time checking components that have little or no relationship to the problem.

4. Test all repairs after the work is done to make sure that the problem is fixed. Some causes can be traced to more than one component, so a careful verification of repair work is important to pick up additional malfunctions that may cause a problem to reappear or a different problem to arise. A blown fuse, for example, is a simple problem that may require more than another fuse to repair. If you don't look for a problem that

caused a fuse to blow, for example, a shorted wire may go undetected.

Experience has shown that most problems tend to be the result of a fairly simple and obvious cause, such as loose or corroded connectors or air leaks in the intake system; making careful inspection of components during testing essential to quick and accurate troubleshooting. Special, hand held computerized testers designed specifically for diagnosing the system are available from a variety of aftermarket sources, as well as from the vehicle manufacturer, but care should be taken that any test equipment being used is designed to diagnose that particular computer controlled system accurately without damaging the control unit (ECU) or components being tested.

➡**Pinpointing the exact cause of trouble in an electrical system can sometimes only be accomplished by the use of special test equipment. The following describes commonly used test equipment and explains how to put it to best use in diagnosis. In addition to the information covered below, the manufacturer's instructions booklet provided with the tester should be read and clearly understood before attempting any test procedures.**

Test Equipment

JUMPER WIRES

Jumper wires are simple, yet extremely valuable, pieces of test equipment. Jumper wires are merely wires that are used to bypass sections of a circuit. The simplest type of jumper wire is merely a length of multi-strand wire with an alligator clip at each end. Jumper wires are usually fabricated from lengths of standard automotive wire and whatever type of connector (alligator clip, spade connector or pin connector) that is required for the particular vehicle being tested. The well equipped tool box will have several different styles of jumper wires in several different lengths. Some jumper wires are made with three or more terminals coming from a common splice for special purpose testing. In cramped, hard-to-reach areas it is advisable to have insulated boots over the jumper wire terminals in order to prevent accidental grounding, sparks, and possible fire, especially when testing fuel system components.

Jumper wires are used primarily to locate open electrical circuits, on either the ground (-) side of the circuit or on the hot (+) side. If an electrical component fails to operate, connect the jumper wire between the component and a good ground. If the component operates only with the jumper installed, the ground circuit is open. If the ground circuit is good, but the component does not operate, the circuit between the power feed and component is open. You can sometimes connect the jumper wire directly from the battery to the hot terminal of the component, but first make sure the component uses 12 volts in operation. Some electrical components, such as fuel injectors, are designed to operate on about 4 volts and running 12 volts directly to the injector terminals can burn out the wiring. By inserting an inline fuse holder between a set of test leads, a fused jumper wire can be used for bypassing

open circuits. Use a 5 amp fuse to provide protection against voltage spikes. When in doubt, use a voltmeter to check the voltage input to the component and measure how much voltage is being applied normally. By moving the jumper wire successively back from the lamp toward the power source, you can isolate the area of the circuit where the open is located. When the component stops functioning, or the power is cut off, the open is in the segment of wire between the jumper and the point previously tested.

❋❋CAUTION

Never use jumpers made from wire that is of lighter gauge than used in the circuit under test. If the jumper wire is of too small gauge, it may overheat and possibly melt. Never use jumpers to bypass high resistance loads (such as motors) in a circuit. Bypassing resistances, in effect, creates a short circuit which may, in turn, cause damage and fire. Never use a jumper for anything other than temporary bypassing of components in a circuit.

12 VOLT TEST LIGHT

The 12 volt test light is used to check circuits and components while electrical current is flowing through them. It is used for voltage and ground tests. Twelve volt test lights come in different styles but all have three main parts; a ground clip, a probe, and a light. The most commonly used 12 volt test lights have pick-type probes. To use a 12 volt test light, connect the ground clip to a good ground and probe wherever necessary with the pick. The pick should be sharp so that it can penetrate wire insulation to make contact with the wire, without making a large hole in the insulation. The wrap-around light is handy in hard to reach areas or where it is difficult to support a wire to push a probe pick into it. To use the wrap around light, hook the wire to probed with the hook and pull the trigger. A small pick will be forced through the wire insulation into the wire core.

❋❋CAUTION

Do not use a test light to probe electronic ignition spark plug or coil wires. Never use a pick-type test light to probe wiring on computer controlled systems unless specifically instructed to do so. Any wire insulation that is pierced by the test light probe should be taped and sealed with silicone after testing.

Like the jumper wire, the 12 volt test light is used to isolate opens in circuits. But, whereas the jumper wire is used to bypass the open to operate the load, the 12 volt test light is used to locate the presence of voltage in a circuit. If the test light glows, you know that there is power up to that point; if the 12 volt test light does not glow when its probe is inserted into the wire or connector, you know that there is an open circuit (no power). Move the test light in successive steps back toward the power source until the light in the handle does glow. When it does glow, the open is between the probe and point previously probed.

➡️ The test light does not detect that 12 volts (or any particular amount of voltage) is present; it only detects that some voltage is present. It is advisable before using the test light to touch its terminals across the battery posts to make sure the light is operating properly.

SELF-POWERED TEST LIGHT

The self-powered test light usually contains a 1.5 volt penlight battery. One type of self-powered test light is similar in design to the 12 volt test light. This type has both the battery and the light in the handle and pick-type probe tip. The second type has the light toward the open tip, so that the light illuminates the contact point. The self-powered test light is dual purpose piece of test equipment. It can be used to test for either open or short circuits when power is isolated from the circuit (continuity test). A powered test light should not be used on any computer controlled system or component unless specifically instructed to do so. Many engine sensors can be destroyed by even this small amount of voltage applied directly to the terminals.

Open Circuit Testing

To use the self-powered test light to check for open circuits, first isolate the circuit from the vehicle's 12 volt power source by disconnecting the battery or wiring harness connector. Connect the test light ground clip to a good ground and probe sections of the circuit sequentially with the test light. (start from either end of the circuit). If the light is out, the open is between the probe and the circuit ground. If the light is on, the open is between the probe and end of the circuit toward the power source.

Short Circuit Testing

By isolating the circuit both from power and from ground, and using a self-powered test light, you can check for shorts to ground in the circuit. Isolate the circuit from power and ground. Connect the test light ground clip to a good ground and probe any easy-to-reach test point in the circuit. If the light comes on, there is a short somewhere in the circuit. To isolate the short, probe a test point at either end of the isolated circuit (the light should be on). Leave the test light probe connected and open connectors, switches, remove parts, etc., sequentially, until the light goes out. When the light goes out, the short is between the last circuit component opened and the previous circuit opened.

➡️ The 1.5 volt battery in the test light does not provide much current. A weak battery may not provide enough power to illuminate the test light even when a complete circuit is made (especially if there are high resistances in the circuit). Always make sure that the test battery is strong. To check the battery, briefly touch the ground clip to the probe; if the light glows brightly the battery is strong enough for testing. Never use a self-powered test light to perform checks for opens or shorts when power is

applied to the electrical system under test. The 12 volt vehicle power will quickly burn out the 1.5 volt light bulb in the test light.

VOLTMETER

A voltmeter is used to measure voltage at any point in a circuit, or to measure the voltage drop across any part of a circuit. It can also be used to check continuity in a wire or circuit by indicating current flow from one end to the other. Voltmeters usually have various scales on the meter dial and a selector switch to allow the selection of different voltages. The voltmeter has a positive and a negative lead. To avoid damage to the meter, always connect the negative lead to the negative (-) side of circuit (to ground or nearest the ground side of the circuit) and connect the positive lead to the positive (+) side of the circuit (to the power source or the nearest power source). Note that the negative voltmeter lead will always be black and that the positive voltmeter will always be some color other than black (usually red). Depending on how the voltmeter is connected into the circuit, it has several uses.

A voltmeter can be connected either in parallel or in series with a circuit and it has a very high resistance to current flow. When connected in parallel, only a small amount of current will flow through the voltmeter current path; the rest will flow through the normal circuit current path and the circuit will work normally. When the voltmeter is connected in series with a circuit, only a small amount of current can flow through the circuit. The circuit will not work properly, but the voltmeter reading will show if the circuit is complete or not.

Available Voltage Measurement

Set the voltmeter selector switch to the 20V position and connect the meter negative lead to the negative post of the battery. Connect the positive meter lead to the positive post of the battery and turn the ignition switch ON to provide a load. Read the voltage on the meter or digital display. A well charged battery should register over 12 volts. If the meter reads below 11.5 volts, the battery power may be insufficient to operate the electrical system properly. This test determines voltage available from the battery and should be the first step in any electrical trouble diagnosis procedure. Many electrical problems, especially on computer controlled systems, can be caused by a low state of charge in the battery. Excessive corrosion at the battery cable terminals can cause a poor contact that will prevent proper charging and full battery current flow.

Normal battery voltage is 12 volts when fully charged. When the battery is supplying current to one or more circuits it is said to be "under load". When everything is off the electrical system is under a 'no-load' condition. A fully charged battery may show about 12.5 volts at no load; will drop to 12 volts under medium load; and will drop even lower under heavy load. If the battery is partially discharged the voltage decrease under heavy load may be excessive, even though the battery shows 12 volts or more at no load. When allowed to discharge further, the battery's available voltage under load will decrease more severely. For this reason, it is important that the battery be fully charged during all testing procedures to avoid errors in diagnosis and incorrect test results.

Voltage Drop

When current flows through a resistance, the voltage beyond the resistance is reduced (the larger the current, the greater the reduction in voltage). When no current is flowing, there is no voltage drop because there is no current flow. All points in the circuit which are connected to the power source are at the same voltage as the power source. The total voltage drop always equals the total source voltage. In a long circuit with many connectors, a series of small, unwanted voltage drops due to corrosion at the connectors can add up to a total loss of voltage which impairs the operation of the normal loads in the circuit.

Indirect Computation of Voltage Drops

1. Set the voltmeter selector switch to the 20 volt position.
2. Connect the meter negative lead to a good ground.
3. Probe all resistances in the circuit with the positive meter lead.
4. Operate the circuit in all modes and observe the voltage readings.

Direct Measurement of Voltage Drops

1. Set the voltmeter switch to the 20 volt position.
2. Connect the voltmeter negative lead to the ground side of the resistance load to be measured.
3. Connect the positive lead to the positive side of the resistance or load to be measured.
4. Read the voltage drop directly on the 20 volt scale.

Too high a voltage indicates too high a resistance. If, for example, a blower motor runs too slowly, you can determine if there is too high a resistance in the resistor pack. By taking voltage drop readings in all parts of the circuit, you can isolate the problem. Too low a voltage drop indicates too low a resistance. If, for example, a blower motor runs too fast in the MED and/or LOW position, the problem can be isolated in the resistor pack by taking voltage drop readings in all parts of the circuit to locate a possibly shorted resistor. The maximum allowable voltage drop under load is critical, especially if there is more than one high resistance problem in a circuit because all voltage drops are cumulative. A small drop is normal due to the resistance of the conductors.

High Resistance Testing

1. Set the voltmeter selector switch to the 4 volt position.
2. Connect the voltmeter positive lead to the positive post of the battery.
3. Turn on the headlights and heater blower to provide a load.
4. Probe various points in the circuit with the negative voltmeter lead.
5. Read the voltage drop on the 4 volt scale. Some average maximum allowable voltage drops are:

> FUSE PANEL — 7 volts
> IGNITION SWITCH — 5 volts
> HEADLIGHT SWITCH — 7 volts
> IGNITION COIL (+) — 5 volts
> ANY OTHER LOAD — 1.3 volts

➡Voltage drops are all measured while a load is operating; without current flow, there will be no voltage drop.

OHMMETER

The ohmmeter is designed to read resistance (ohms) in a circuit or component. Although there are several different styles of ohmmeters, all will usually have a selector switch which permits the measurement of different ranges of resistance (usually the selector switch allows the multiplication of the meter reading by 10, 100, 1000, and 10,000). A calibration knob allows the meter to be set at zero for accurate measurement. Since all ohmmeters are powered by an internal battery (usually 9 volts), the ohmmeter can be used as a self-powered test light. When the ohmmeter is connected, current from the ohmmeter flows through the circuit or component being tested. Since the ohmmeter's internal resistance and voltage are known values, the amount of current flow through the meter depends on the resistance of the circuit or component being tested.

The ohmmeter can be used to perform continuity test for opens or shorts (either by observation of the meter needle or as a self-powered test light), and to read actual resistance in a circuit. It should be noted that the ohmmeter is used to check the resistance of a component or wire while there is no voltage applied to the circuit. Current flow from an outside voltage source (such as the vehicle battery) can damage the ohmmeter, so the circuit or component should be isolated from the vehicle electrical system before any testing is done. Since the ohmmeter uses its own voltage source, either lead can be connected to any test point.

➡When checking diodes or other solid state components, the ohmmeter leads can only be connected one way in order to measure current flow in a single direction. Make sure the positive (+) and negative (-) terminal connections are as described in the test procedures to verify the one-way diode operation.

In using the meter for making continuity checks, do not be concerned with the actual resistance readings. Zero resistance, or any resistance readings, indicate continuity in the circuit. Infinite resistance indicates an open in the circuit. A high resistance reading where there should be none indicates a problem in the circuit. Checks for short circuits are made in the same manner as checks for open circuits except that the circuit must be isolated from both power and normal ground. Infinite resistance indicates no continuity to ground, while zero resistance indicates a dead short to ground.

Resistance Measurement

The batteries in an ohmmeter will weaken with age and temperature, so the ohmmeter must be calibrated or "zeroed" before taking measurements. To zero the meter, place the selector switch in its lowest range and touch the two ohmmeter leads together. Turn the calibration knob until the meter needle is exactly on zero.

➡ All analog (needle) type ohmmeters must be zeroed before use, but some digital ohmmeter models are automatically calibrated when the switch is turned on. Self-calibrating digital ohmmeters do not have an adjusting knob, but its a good idea to check for a zero readout before use by touching the leads together. All computer controlled systems require the use of a digital ohmmeter with at least 10 megohms impedance for testing. Before any test procedures are attempted, make sure the ohmmeter used is compatible with the electrical system or damage to the on-board computer could result.

To measure resistance, first isolate the circuit from the vehicle power source by disconnecting the battery cables or the harness connector. Make sure the key is OFF when disconnecting any components or the battery. Where necessary, also isolate at least one side of the circuit to be checked to avoid reading parallel resistances. Parallel circuit resistances will always give a lower reading than the actual resistance of either of the branches. When measuring the resistance of parallel circuits, the total resistance will always be lower than the smallest resistance in the circuit. Connect the meter leads to both sides of the circuit (wire or component) and read the actual measured ohms on the meter scale. Make sure the selector switch is set to the proper ohm scale for the circuit being tested to avoid misreading the ohmmeter test value.

✳✳CAUTION

Never use an ohmmeter with power applied to the circuit. Like the self-powered test light, the ohmmeter is designed to operate on its own power supply. The normal 12 volt automotive electrical system current could damage the meter.

AMMETERS

An ammeter measures the amount of current flowing through a circuit in units called amperes or amps. Amperes are units of electron flow which indicate how fast the electrons are flowing through the circuit. Since Ohms Law dictates that current flow in a circuit is equal to the circuit voltage divided by the total circuit resistance, increasing voltage also increases the current level (amps). Likewise, any decrease in resistance will increase the amount of amps in a circuit. At normal operating voltage, most circuits have a characteristic amount of amperes, called "current draw" which can be measured using an ammeter. By referring to a specified current draw rating, measuring the amperes, and comparing the two values, one can determine what is happening within the circuit to aid in diagnosis. An open circuit, for example, will not allow any current to flow so the ammeter reading will be zero. More current flows through a heavily loaded circuit or when the charging system is operating.

An ammeter is always connected in series with the circuit being tested. All of the current that normally flows through the circuit must also flow through the ammeter; if there is any

other path for the current to follow, the ammeter reading will not be accurate. The ammeter itself has very little resistance to current flow and therefore will not affect the circuit, but it will measure current draw only when the circuit is closed and electricity is flowing. Excessive current draw can blow fuses and drain the battery, while a reduced current draw can cause motors to run slowly, lights to dim and other components to not operate properly. The ammeter can help diagnose these conditions by locating the cause of the high or low reading.

MULTIMETERS

Different combinations of test meters can be built into a single unit designed for specific tests. Some of the more common combination test devices are known as Volt/Amp testers, Tach/Dwell meters, or Digital Multimeters. The Volt/Amp tester is used for charging system, starting system or battery tests and consists of a voltmeter, an ammeter and a variable resistance carbon pile. The voltmeter will usually have at least two ranges for use with 6, 12 and 24 volt systems. The ammeter also has more than one range for testing various levels of battery loads and starter current draw and the carbon pile can be adjusted to offer different amounts of resistance. The Volt/Amp tester has heavy leads to carry large amounts of current and many later models have an inductive ammeter pickup that clamps around the wire to simplify test connections. On some models, the ammeter also has a zero-center scale to allow testing of charging and starting systems without switching leads or polarity. A digital multimeter i s a voltmeter, ammeter and ohmmeter combined in an instrument which gives a digital readout. These are often used when testing solid state circuits because of their high input impedance (usually 10 megohms or more).

The tach/dwell meter combines a tachometer and a dwell (cam angle) meter and is a specialized kind of voltmeter. The tachometer scale is marked to show engine speed in rpm and the dwell scale is marked to show degrees of distributor shaft rotation. In most electronic ignition systems, dwell is determined by the control unit, but the dwell meter can also be used to check the duty cycle (operation) of some electronic engine control systems. Some tach/dwell meters are powered by an internal battery, while others take their power from the car battery in use. The battery powered testers usually require calibration much like an ohmmeter before testing.

Special Test Equipment

A variety of diagnostic tools are available to help troubleshoot and repair computerized engine control systems. The most sophisticated of these devices are the console type engine analyzers that usually occupy a garage service bay, but there are several types of aftermarket electronic testers available that will allow quick circuit tests of the engine control system by plugging directly into a special connector located in the engine compartment or under the dashboard. Several tool and equipment manufacturers offer simple, hand held testers that measure various circuit voltage levels on command to check all system components for proper operation. Although these testers usually cost about $300-$500, consider that the average computer control unit (or ECM) can cost just as much and the money saved by not replacing perfectly good sensors or components in an attempt to correct a problem could justify the purchase price of a special diagnostic tester the first time it's used.

These computerized testers can allow quick and easy test measurements while the engine is operating or while the car is being driven. In addition, the on-board computer memory can be read to access any stored trouble codes; in effect allowing the computer to tell you where it hurts and aid trouble diagnosis by pinpointing exactly which circuit or component is malfunctioning. In the same manner, repairs can be tested to make sure the problem has been corrected. The biggest advantage these special testers have is their relatively easy hookups that minimize or eliminate the chances of making the wrong connections and getting false voltage readings or damaging the computer accidentally.

➡**It should be remembered that these testers check voltage levels in circuits; they don't detect mechanical problems or failed components if the circuit voltage falls within the preprogrammed limits stored in the tester PROM unit. Also, most of the hand held testers are designed to work only on one or two systems made by a specific manufacturer.**

A variety of aftermarket testers are available to help diagnose different computerized control systems. Owatonna Tool Company (OTC), for example, markets a device called the OTC Monitor which plugs directly into the diagnostic connector. The OTC tester makes diagnosis a simple matter of pressing the correct buttons and, by changing the internal PROM or inserting a different diagnosis cartridge, it will work on any model from full size to subcompact, over a wide range of years. By inserting an updated PROM into the tester, it can be easily updated to diagnose any new modifications of computerized control systems.

Wiring Harnesses

The average automobile contains about ½ mile of wiring, with hundreds of individual connections. To protect the many wires from damage and to keep them from becoming a confusing tangle, they are organized into bundles, enclosed in plastic or taped together and called wire harnesses. Different wiring harnesses serve different parts of the vehicle. Individual wires are color coded to help trace them through a harness where sections are hidden from view.

A loose or corroded connection or a replacement wire that is too small for the circuit will add extra resistance and an additional voltage drop to the circuit. A ten percent voltage drop can result in slow or erratic motor operation, for example, even though the circuit is complete. Automotive wiring or circuit conductors can be in any one of three forms:
1. Single strand wire
2. Multistrand wire
3. Printed circuitry

Single strand wire has a solid metal core and is usually used inside such components as alternators, motors, relays and other devices. Multistrand wire has a core made of many small strands of wire twisted together into a single conductor. Most of the wiring in an automotive electrical system is made up of multi-strand wire, either as a single conductor or grouped together in a harness. All wiring is color coded on the insulator, either as a solid color or as a colored wire with an identification stripe. A printed circuit is a thin film of copper or other conductor that is printed on an insulator backing. Occasionally, a printed circuit is sandwiched between two sheets of plastic for more protection and flexibility. A complete printed circuit, consisting of conductors, insulating material and connectors for lamps or other components is called a printed circuit board. Printed circuitry is used in place of individual wires or harnesses in places where space is limited, such as behind instrument panels.

WIRE GAUGE

Since computer controlled automotive electrical systems are very sensitive to changes in resistance, the selection of properly sized wires is critical when systems are repaired. The wire gauge number is an expression of the cross section area of the conductor. The most common system for expressing wire size is the American Wire Gauge (AWG) system.

Wire cross section area is measured in circular mils. A mil is 1/1000" (0.001"); a circular mil is the area of a circle one mil in diameter. For example, a conductor ¼" in diameter is 0.250 in. or 250 mils. The circular mil cross section area of the wire is 250 squared or 62,500 circular mils. Imported car models usually use metric wire gauge designations, which is simply the cross section area of the conductor in square millimeters (mm).

Gauge numbers are assigned to conductors of various cross section areas. As gauge number increases, area decreases and the conductor becomes smaller. A 5 gauge conductor is smaller than a 1 gauge conductor and a 10 gauge is smaller than a 5 gauge. As the cross section area of a conductor decreases, resistance increases and so does the gauge number. A conductor with a higher gauge number will carry less current than a conductor with a lower gauge number.

➡**Gauge wire size refers to the size of the conductor, not the size of the complete wire. It is possible to have two wires of the same gauge with different diameters because one may have thicker insulation than the other.**

12 volt automotive electrical systems generally use 10, 12, 14, 16 and 18 gauge wire. Main power distribution circuits and larger accessories usually use 10 and 12 gauge wire. Battery cables are usually 4 or 6 gauge, although 1 and 2 gauge wires are occasionally used. Wire length must also be considered when making repairs to a circuit. As conductor length increases, so does resistance. An 18 gauge wire, for example, can carry a 10 amp load for 10 feet without excessive voltage drop; however if a 15 foot wire is required for the same 10 amp load, it must be a 16 gauge wire.

An electrical schematic shows the electrical current paths when a circuit is operating properly. It is essential to understand how a circuit works before trying to figure out why it doesn't. Schematics break the entire electrical system down into individual circuits and show only one particular circuit. In a schematic, no attempt is made to represent wiring and components as they physically appear on the vehicle; switches and other components are shown as simply as possible. Face views of harness connectors show the cavity or terminal locations in all multi-pin connectors to help locate test points.

If you need to probe a connector while it is on the component, the order of the terminals must be mentally reversed. The wire color code can help in this situation, as well as a keyway, lock tab or other reference mark.

WIRING REPAIR

Soldering is a quick, efficient method of joining metals permanently. Everyone who has the occasion to make wiring repairs should know how to solder. Electrical connections that are soldered are far less likely to come apart and will conduct electricity much better than connections that are only "pig-tailed" together. The most popular (and preferred) method of soldering is with an electrical soldering gun. Soldering irons are available in many sizes and wattage ratings. Irons with higher wattage ratings deliver higher temperatures and recover lost heat faster. A small soldering iron rated for no more than 50 watts is recommended, especially on electrical systems where excess heat can damage the components being soldered.

There are three ingredients necessary for successful soldering; proper flux, good solder and sufficient heat. A soldering flux is necessary to clean the metal of tarnish, prepare it for soldering and to enable the solder to spread into tiny crevices. When soldering, always use a resin flux or resin core solder which is non-corrosive and will not attract moisture once the job is finished. Other types of flux (acid core) will leave a residue that will attract moisture and cause the wires to corrode. Tin is a unique metal with a low melting point. In a molten state, it dissolves and alloys easily with many metals. Solder is made by mixing tin with lead. The most common proportions are 40/60, 50/50 and 60/40, with the percentage of tin listed first. Low priced solders usually contain less tin, making them very difficult for a beginner to use because more heat is required to melt the solder. A common solder is 40/60 which is well suited for all-around general use, but 60/40 melts easier, has more tin f or a better joint and is preferred for electrical work.

SOLDERING TECHNIQUES

Successful soldering requires that the metals to be joined be heated to a temperature that will melt the solder — usually 360-460°F (182-238°C). Contrary to popular belief, the purpose of the soldering iron is not to melt the solder itself, but to heat the parts being soldered to a temperature high enough to melt the solder when it is touched to the work. Melting flux-cored solder on the soldering iron will usually destroy the effectiveness of the flux.

➡**Soldering tips are made of copper for good heat conductivity, but must be 'tinned'' regularly for quick transference of heat to the project and to prevent the solder from sticking to the iron. To "tin" the iron, simply heat it and touch the flux-cored solder to the tip; the solder will flow over the hot tip. Wipe the excess off with a clean rag, but be careful as the iron will be hot.**

After some use, the tip may become pitted. If so, simply dress the tip smooth with a smooth file and "tin" the tip again. An old saying holds that "metals well cleaned are half soldered." Flux-cored solder will remove oxides but rust, bits of insulation and oil or grease must be removed with a wire brush or emery cloth. For maximum strength in soldered parts, the joint must start off clean and tight. Weak joints will result in gaps too wide for the solder to bridge.

If a separate soldering flux is used, it should be brushed or swabbed on only those areas that are to be soldered. Most solders contain a core of flux and separate fluxing is unnecessary. Hold the work to be soldered firmly. It is best to solder on a wooden board, because a metal vise will only rob the piece to be soldered of heat and make it difficult to melt the solder. Hold the soldering tip with the broadest face against the work to be soldered. Apply solder under the tip close to the work, using enough solder to give a heavy film between the iron and the piece being soldered, while moving slowly and making sure the solder melts properly. Keep the work level or the solder will run to the lowest part and favor the thicker parts, because these require more heat to melt the solder. If the soldering tip overheats (the solder coating on the face of the tip burns up), it should be retained. Once the soldering is completed, let the soldered joint stand until cool. Tape and seal all soldered wire splices after the repair has cooled.

WIRE HARNESS AND CONNECTORS

The on-board computer (ECM) wire harness electrically connects the control unit to the various solenoids, switches and sensors used by the control system. Most connectors in the engine compartment or otherwise exposed to the elements are protected against moisture and dirt which could create oxidation and deposits on the terminals. This protection is important because of the very low voltage and current levels used by the computer and sensors. All connectors have a lock which secures the male and female terminals together, with a secondary lock holding the seal and terminal into the connector. Both terminal locks must be released when disconnecting ECM connectors.

These special connectors are weather-proof and all repairs require the use of a special terminal and the tool required to service it. This tool is used to remove the pin and sleeve terminals. If removal is attempted with an ordinary pick, there is a good chance that the terminal will be bent or deformed. Unlike standard blade type terminals, these terminals cannot be straightened once they are bent. Make certain that the connectors are properly seated and all of the sealing rings in place when connecting leads. On some models, a hinge-type flap provides a backup or secondary locking feature for the terminals. Most secondary locks are used to improve the connector reliability by retaining the terminals if the small terminal lock tangs are not positioned properly.

Molded-on connectors require complete replacement of the connection. This means splicing a new connector assembly into the harness. All splices in on-board computer systems should be soldered to insure proper contact. Use care when probing the connections or replacing terminals in them as it is possible to short between opposite terminals. If this happens to the wrong terminal pair, it is possible to damage certain components. Always use jumper wires between connectors for circuit checking and never probe through weatherproof seals.

Open circuits are often difficult to locate by sight because corrosion or terminal misalignment are hidden by the connectors. Merely wiggling a connector on a sensor or in the wiring harness may correct the open circuit condition. This should always be considered when an open circuit or a failed sensor is indicated. Intermittent problems may also be caused by oxidized or loose connections. When using a circuit tester for diagnosis, always probe connections from the wire side. Be careful not to damage sealed connectors with test probes.

All wiring harnesses should be replaced with identical parts, using the same gauge wire and connectors. When signal wires are spliced into a harness, use wire with high temperature insulation only. With the low voltage and current levels found in the system, it is important that the best possible connection at all wire splices be made by soldering the splices together. It is seldom necessary to replace a complete harness. If replacement is necessary, pay close attention to insure proper harness routing. Secure the harness with suitable plastic wire clamps to prevent vibrations from causing the harness to wear in spots or contact any hot components.

➡**Weatherproof connectors cannot be replaced with standard connectors. Instructions are provided with replacement connector and terminal packages. Some wire harnesses have mounting indicators (usually pieces of colored tape) to mark where the harness is to be secured.**

In making wiring repairs, it's important that you always replace damaged wires with wires that are the same gauge as the wire being replaced. The heavier the wire, the smaller the gauge number. Wires are color-coded to aid in identification and whenever possible the same color coded wire should be used for replacement. A wire stripping and crimping tool is necessary to install solderless terminal connectors. Test all crimps by pulling on the wires; it should not be possible to pull the wires out of a good crimp.

Wires which are open, exposed or otherwise damaged are repaired by simple splicing. Where possible, if the wiring harness is accessible and the damaged place in the wire can be located, it is best to open the harness and check for all possible damage. In an inaccessible harness, the wire must be bypassed with a new insert, usually taped to the outside of the old harness.

When replacing fusible links, be sure to use fusible link wire, NOT ordinary automotive wire. Make sure the fusible segment is of the same gauge and construction as the one being replaced and double the stripped end when crimping the terminal connector for a good contact. The melted (open) fusible link segment of the wiring harness should be cut off as close to the harness as possible, then a new segment spliced in as described. In the case of a damaged fusible link that feeds two harness wires, the harness connections should be replaced with two fusible link wires so that each circuit will have its own separate protection.

➡**Most of the problems caused in the wiring harness are due to bad ground connections. Always check all vehicle ground connections for corrosion or looseness before performing any power feed checks to eliminate the chance of a bad ground affecting the circuit.**

Repairing Hard Shell Connectors

Unlike molded connectors, the terminal contacts in hard shell connectors can be replaced. Weatherproof hard-shell connectors with the leads molded into the shell have non-replaceable terminal ends. Replacement usually involves the use of a special terminal removal tool that depress the locking tangs (barbs) on the connector terminal and allow the connector to be removed from the rear of the shell. The connector shell should be replaced if it shows any evidence of burning, melting, cracks, or breaks. Replace individual terminals that are burnt, corroded, distorted or loose.

➡**The insulation crimp must be tight to prevent the insulation from sliding back on the wire when the wire is pulled. The insulation must be visibly compressed under the crimp tabs, and the ends of the crimp should be turned in for a firm grip on the insulation.**

The wire crimp must be made with all wire strands inside the crimp. The terminal must be fully compressed on the wire strands with the ends of the crimp tabs turned in to make a firm grip on the wire. Check all connections with an ohmmeter to insure a good contact. There should be no measurable resistance between the wire and the terminal when connected.

Mechanical Test Equipment

VACUUM GAUGE

Most gauges are graduated in inches of mercury (in.Hg), although a device called a manometer reads vacuum in inches of water (in. H_2O). The normal vacuum reading usually varies between 18 and 22 in.Hg at sea level. To test engine vacuum, the vacuum gauge must be connected to a source of manifold vacuum. Many engines have a plug in the intake manifold which can be removed and replaced with an adapter fitting. Connect the vacuum gauge to the fitting with a suitable rubber hose or, if no manifold plug is available, connect the vacuum gauge to any device using manifold vacuum, such as EGR valves, etc. The vacuum gauge can be used to determine if enough vacuum is reaching a component to allow its actuation.

HAND VACUUM PUMP

Small, hand-held vacuum pumps come in a variety of designs. Most have a built-in vacuum gauge and allow the component to be tested without removing it from the vehicle. Operate the pump lever or plunger to apply the correct amount of vacuum required for the test specified in the diagnosis routines. The level of vacuum in inches of Mercury (in.Hg) is indicated on the pump gauge. For some testing, an additional vacuum gauge may be necessary.

Intake manifold vacuum is used to operate various systems and devices on late model vehicles. To correctly diagnose and solve problems in vacuum control systems, a vacuum source is necessary for testing. In some cases, vacuum can be taken from the intake manifold when the engine is running, but vacuum is normally provided by a hand vacuum pump. These hand vacuum pumps have a built-in vacuum gauge that allow testing while the device is still attached to the component. For some tests, an additional vacuum gauge may be necessary.

SUPPLEMENTAL RESTRAINT SYSTEM (AIR BAG)

General Information

The air bag system used on the Storm is referred to as the Supplemental Inflatable Restraint (SIR) system. The SIR system provides additional protection for the driver, if a forward collision of sufficient force is encountered. The SIR assists the normal seatbelt restraining system by deploying an air bag, via the steering column. A knee bolster, located beneath the driver's side instrument panel, also aids in absorbing the collision's impact. The steering column, as in previous design, still continues to be collapsible.

SYSTEM OPERATION

The SIR system contains a deployment loop and a Diagnostic Energy Reserve Module (DERM). The function of the deployment loop is to supply current through the inflator module in the steering wheel, which will cause air bag deployment during a severe accident. The DERM supplies the necessary power, even if the battery has been damaged.

The deployment loop is made up of the arming sensors, coil assembly, inflator module and the discriminating sensors. The inflator module is only supplied sufficient current to deploy the air bag when the arming sensors and at least 1 of the discriminating sensors close simultaneously. The function of the DERM is to supply the deployment loop a 36 Volt Loop Reserve (36VLR) to assure air bag deployment for seconds after ignition voltage is lost during an accident.

The DERM in conjunction with the resistors make it possible to detect circuit and component faults within the deployment loop. If the voltages monitored by the DERM fall outside expected limits, the DERM will indicate a fault code through the storage of a malfunction code and turning ON the INFLATABLE RESTRAINT lamp.

SYSTEM COMPONENTS

♦ See Figure 1

Diagnostic Energy Reserve Module

The Diagnostic Energy Reserve Module (DERM) is designed to perform 5 main functions. It maintains an energy reserve of 36 volts for several seconds and can maintain sufficient voltage to cause a deployment for up to 10 minutes after the ignition switch is turned OFF and the battery disconnected. The DERM performs diagnostic monitoring of the SIR system and records malfunction codes, which can be obtained from a hand scan tool or the INFLATABLE RESTRAINT lamp. It warns the driver of a malfunction by controlling the INFLATABLE RESTRAINT lamp and keeps a record of the SIR system during a vehicle accident.

The DERM is connected to the system with a 24 pin connector. This harness has a shorting bar across certain terminals in the contact areas. The shorting bar connects the INFLATABLE RESTRAINT lamp input to ground when the DERM is disconnected causing the lamp to light when the ignition switch is ON.

The DERM does not need to be replaced after each air bag deployment. After 4 deployments the DERM will register a Code 52. The Code 52 informs that the accident memory is full and the DERM must be replaced.

Inflatable Restraint Indicator

The indicator lamp is used to verify the DERM operation by flashing 7-9 times when the ignition is first turned ON. It is also used to warn the driver of a SIR malfunction. For certain tests it can provide diagnostic information by flashing the fault code when the fault code diagnostic mode is enabled.

Arming Sensor

The arming sensor, mounted at the center of the upper dash panel, is a protective switch in the power feed side of the deployment loop. It is calibrated to close at low level velocity changes. This insures that the inflator module is connected to the 36VLR output of the DERM or ignition 1 voltage.

The sensor consists of a sensing element, a normally open switch, a diagnostic resistor and 2 steering diodes. The resistor is connected in parallel with the switch and allows a small amount of current to flow through the deployment loop during normal non-deployment operation. The DERM monitors this voltage to determine component faults.

When the arming sensor is located in the same housing as the passenger compartment discrimination sensor, the assembly is referred to as the dual sensor.

Discrimination Sensor

There are 2 discriminating sensors wired in parallel on the low side of the deployment loop. The forward sensor is located in front of the radiator and the passenger sensor is located on the floor ahead of the transmission selector lever. These sensors are located on the low side of the deployment loop and are calibrated to close with velocity changes which are severe enough to warrant air bag deployment.

The sensors consist of a sensing element, normally open switch and a diagnostic resistor. The diagnostic resistor is wired in parallel with the switch within each sensor. They provide a ground for current to pass during normal non-deployment operation. The DERM measures this current to determine component faults.

SIR Coil Assembly

The coil assembly, or clockspring, connects the air bag to the DERM. It is attached to the steering column and allows the rotation of the steering wheel, while maintaining continuous electrical continuity to the air bag in case a deployment is needed.

There is a shorting bar on the lower steering column connector, which connects the SIR coil to the SIR harness.

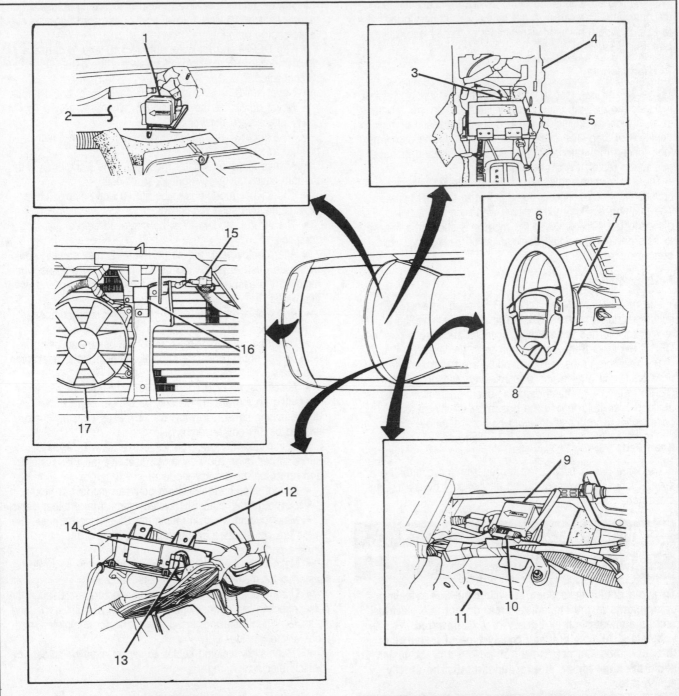

1. Arming sensor
2. Cowl panel
3. Derm connector
4. Console bracket
5. Derm
6. Steering wheel
7. SIR coil assembly
8. Inflator module
9. Passenger compartment discriminating sensor
10. Passenger compartment discriminating sensor connector
11. Floor panel
12. Wiring harness retainer
13. Junction connector
14. Resustor module
15. Forward discriminating sensor connector
16. Forward discriminating sensor
17. Condenser fan

Fig. 1 Air bag component locations — Storm

The shorting bar shorts the circuit when the connector is disconnected. The circuit to the module is shorted in this way to help prevent unwanted deployment of the air bag, while performing service.

Air Bag Module

The SIR air bag module is located in the steering wheel. It includes the air bag, inflator and initiator. When the vehicle is in an accident of sufficient force, current is passed through the deployment loop. The current passing through the deployment loop ignited the material in the inflator module and produces a gas which rapidly inflates the air bag.

There is a shorting bar on the lower steering column connector, which connects the SIR coil to the SIR harness. The shorting bar shorts the circuit when the connector is disconnected. The circuit to the module is shorted in this way to help prevent unwanted deployment of the air bag, while performing service.

Resistor Module

The resistor module is in the SIR harness between the inflator module and the DERM. The resistor allows the DERM to monitor the deployment loop for faults and also allows the DERM to detect if the air bag has been deployed.

The resistors in the resistor module are balanced with the resistors in the arming and discriminating sensors to allow the DERM to monitor voltage drops across the circuits. These resistors also help reduce the possibility of unwanted deployment in the case of wiring harness damage.

Knee Pad

The knee pad is used to absorb energy and control the driver's forward movement during an accident by limiting leg movement.

SERVICE PRECAUTIONS

✳✳CAUTION

To avoid deployment when servicing the SIR system or components in the immediate area, do not use electrical test equipment such as battery or A.C. powered voltmeters, ohmmeters, etc. or any type of tester other than specified. Do not use a non-powered probe tester. To avoid personal injury, all precautions must be strictly adhered to.

• Never disconnect any electrical connection with the ignition switch **ON** unless instructed to do so in a test.
• Before disconnecting the negative battery cable, make a record of the contents memorized by each memory system like the clock, audio, etc. When service or repairs are completed, make certain to reset these memory systems.
• Always wear a grounded wrist static strap when servicing any control module or component labeled with a Electrostatic Discharge (ESD) sensitive device symbol.
• Avoid touching module connector pins.
• Leave new components and modules in the shipping package until ready to install them.

• Always touch a vehicle ground after sliding across a vehicle seat or walking across vinyl or carpeted floors to avoid static charge damage.
• The DERM can maintain sufficient voltage to cause a deployment for up to 10 minutes, even if the battery is disconnected.
• Never strike or jar a sensor, or deployment could happen.
• Never power up the SIR system when any sensor is not rigidly attached to the vehicle.
• Always carry an inflator module with the trim cover pointed away.
• Always place an inflator module on the workbench with the trim cover up, away from loose objects.
• The inflator module is to be stored and shipped under DOT flammable solid regulations.
• The inflator module must be deployed before it is scrapped.
• After deployment, the air bag surface may contain sodium hydroxide dust. Always wear gloves and safety glasses when handling the assembly. Wash hands with mild soap and water afterwards.
• Any visible damage to the sensors requires component replacement.
• Wire and connector repair must be performed using kit J-38125, or equivalent. Use special crimping tools, heat torch and seals.
• Absolutely no wire connector, or terminal repair is to be attempted on the arming sensor, passenger compartment discriminating sensor, forward discriminating sensor, inflator module or SIR coil assembly.
• Never bake dry paint on vehicle or allow to exceed temperatures over 300°F, without disabling the SIR system and removing the inflator module.
• Do not interchange sensors between models or years.
• Do not install used SIR system parts from another vehicle.
• Make certain when installing the SIR wiring harness, the wires are not pinched or interfering with any of the other vehicle parts.
• Make certain all SIR grounds are clean and securely fastened for maximum metal-to-metal contact.
• Orange color double-lock type connectors are used. When disconnecting the connectors, unlock them at both inside and outside. When installing, insert the connector completely and lock at the outside.
• Never allow welding cables to lay on, near or across any vehicle electrical wiring.

DISARMING THE SYSTEM

▶ See Figures 2 and 3

1. Turn the ignition switch to the **OFF** position.
2. Disconnect the battery negative cable.
3. Remove fuses C-22 and C-23 from the fuse box.
4. Disconnect the orange 3-way connector at the base of the steering column.

ENABLING THE SYSTEM

1. Turn the ignition switch to the **OFF** position.

3. Install fuses C-22 and C-23 to the fuse box.
4. Connect the battery negative cable.

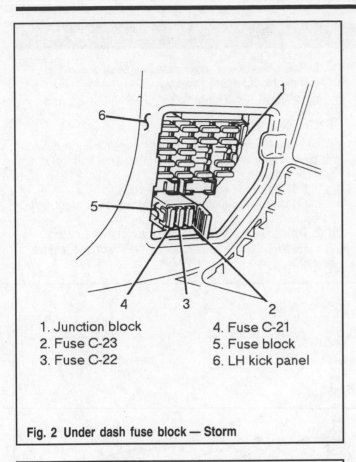

1. Junction block
2. Fuse C-23
3. Fuse C-22
4. Fuse C-21
5. Fuse block
6. LH kick panel

Fig. 2 Under dash fuse block — Storm

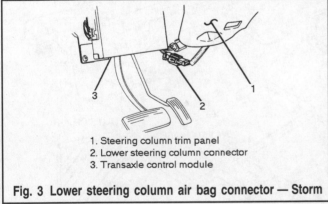

1. Steering column trim panel
2. Lower steering column connector
3. Transaxle control module

Fig. 3 Lower steering column air bag connector — Storm

2. Connect the orange 3-way connector at the base of the steering column.

HEATER

Blower Motor

REMOVAL & INSTALLATION

▶ **See Figures 4 and 5**

Spectrum

1. Disconnect the negative battery cable. Disconnect the blower motor electrical connector at the motor case.

2. If equipped with air conditioning, remove the rubber hose from the blower case.

3. Rotate the blower motor case counterclockwise and remove the blower motor assembly.

4. To install, reverse the removal procedures.

Storm

The blower motor is located under the instrument panel at the far right side of the vehicle. It is accessible from below the instrument panel.

1. Disconnect the negative battery cable.

2. Disconnect the rubber air duct between the motor and the heater assembly.

3. Disconnect the electrical connector from the motor.

4. Remove the 3 screws retaining the motor and remove the motor.

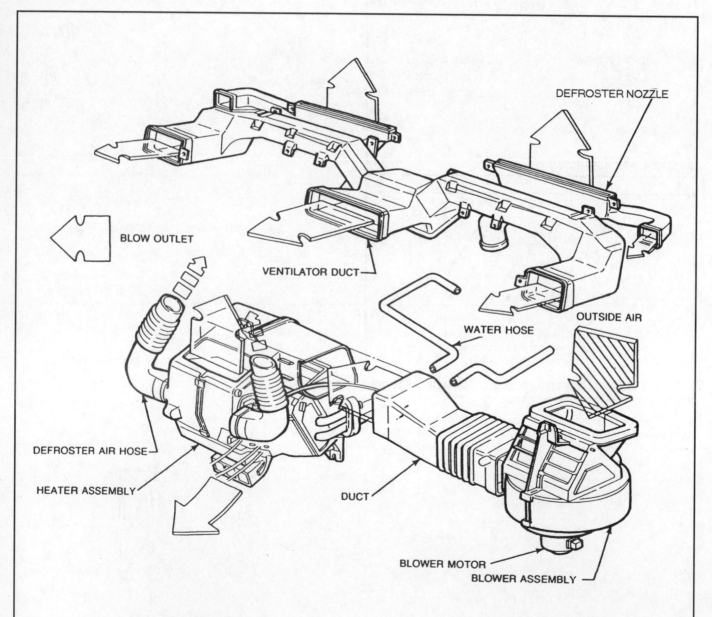

DEFROSTER NOZZLE

BLOW OUTLET

VENTILATOR DUCT

WATER HOSE

OUTSIDE AIR

DEFROSTER AIR HOSE

HEATER ASSEMBLY

DUCT

BLOWER MOTOR

BLOWER ASSEMBLY

Fig. 4 Heater components — Spectrum

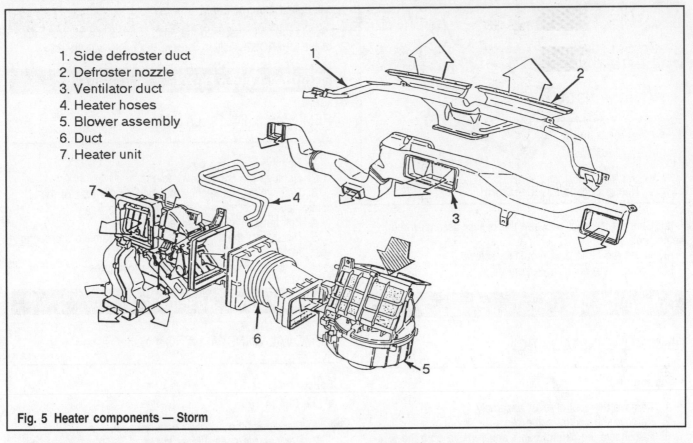

1. Side defroster duct
2. Defroster nozzle
3. Ventilator duct
4. Heater hoses
5. Blower assembly
6. Duct
7. Heater unit

Fig. 5 Heater components — Storm

5. Installation is the reverse of removal.

Heater Core

REMOVAL & INSTALLATION

Spectrum

1. Disconnect the negative battery cable.
2. Disconnect the heater hose at the engine compartment.
3. Remove the six clips holding the lower part of the heater unit case, then remove the lower part of the case.
4. Carefully pry open the lower part of the case.
5. Remove the insulator from the core assembly.
6. Remove the core assembly from the heater case.

To install:

7. Install the core assembly into the heater case.
8. Place the insulator into the core assembly.
9. Snap the heater unit case closed at the bottom.
10. Install the lower part of the heater unit case and the six clips to hold the lower part of the case.
11. Connect the heater hose at the engine compartment.
12. Connect the negative battery cable.

Storm

♦ **See Figures 6 and 7**

1. Disconnect the negative battery cable. Drain the cooling system.
2. Remove the three duct mounting screws.

3. Disconnect the duct between the blower assembly and the heater unit.
4. Remove the five screws attaching the mode control case to the heater core case.
5. Remove the mode control case. Do not remove the link assembly.
6. Remove the five screws to separate the two halves of the heater core case.
7. Remove the core assembly.

To install:

8. Install the core assembly.
9. Install the five screws to join the two halves of the heater core case.
10. Install the control case.
11. Install the five screws attaching the mode control case to the heater core case.

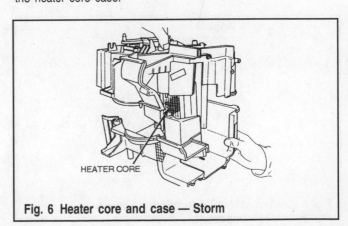

HEATER CORE

Fig. 6 Heater core and case — Storm

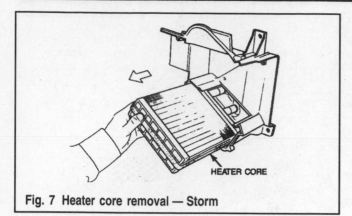

Fig. 7 Heater core removal — Storm

12. Connect the duct between the blower assembly and heater unit.
13. Install the three duct mounting screws.
14. Connect the negative battery cable.

Control Cables

REMOVAL & INSTALLATION

▶ See Figure 8

1. Remove the control lever assembly.
2. Remove the control cable clip.
3. Disconnect the control cable and remove from the vehicle.
4. Installation is the reverse of the removal procedure.

ADJUSTMENT

▶ See Figure 9

Air Source Control Cable

Slide the select lever to the left, then connect the control cable at the **CIRC** position. Secure the cable with the clip.

Temperature Control Cable

Slide the select lever to the left, connect the control cable at the **COLD** position. Secure the cable with the clip.

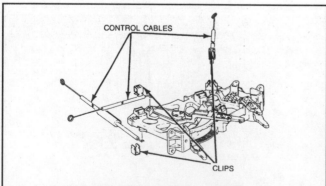

Fig. 8 Control cable clip locations — Storm

Air Select Control Cable

Slide the select lever to the right, connect the control cable at the **DEFROST** position. Secure the cable with the clip.

Control Lever Bezel

REMOVAL & INSTALLATION

1. Remove the glove box.
2. Remove the control lever knobs.
3. Remove the six latches attached on the rear of the control lever bezel.
4. Pull the control lever bezel to remove it.
5. Disconnect the illumination lamp and remove the control lever bezel.
6. To install, reverse the removal procedures.

Control Lever Assembly

REMOVAL & INSTALLATION

Spectrum
▶ See Figure 10

1. Disconnect the negative battery cable.
2. Remove the control lever knobs.
3. Remove the control assembly lens and disconnect the bulb.
4. Disconnect the control cables at the blower assembly and the heater assembly.
5. Remove the control assembly fasteners.
6. Pull the control assembly from the instrument panel and disconnect the electrical connection.
7. Disconnect the control cables from the control lever assembly.
8. Remove the blower switch.
9. Remove the A/C switch, if equipped.
10. Remove the heater switch.
 To install:
11. Install the heater switch, A/C switch, if equipped, and the blower switch.
12. Connect the control cables to the control lever assembly and adjust the cables.
13. Connect the electrical connection to the control assembly and install the assembly to the instrument panel.
14. Install the control assembly fasteners.
15. Connect and adjust the control cables to the blower assembly and the heater assembly.
16. Connect the bulb and install the control assembly lens.
17. Install the control lever knobs.
18. Connect the negative battery cable.

Storm
▶ See Figure 11

1. Disconnect the negative battery cable.
2. Remove the console and the glove box.

AIR SELECTOR CABLE >

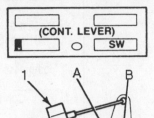

(CONT. LEVER) SW

TEMPERATURE CONTROL CABLE

(CONT. LEVER) SW

AIR SOURCE SELECT CABLE

(CONT. LEVER) SW

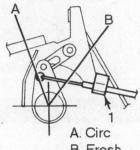

A B C D E

A. Defrost
B. Defrost/floor
C. Floor
D. Bi-level
E. Vent
1. Clip

1 A B

A. Hot
B. Cold
1. Clip

A B

A. Circ
B. Fresh
1. Clip

Fig. 9 Control lever adjustments — Storm

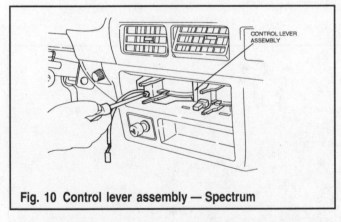

CONTROL LEVER ASSEMBLY

Fig. 10 Control lever assembly — Spectrum

3. Remove the control cables at the blower assembly and the heater assembly.

4. Remove the four screws attaching the control lever assembly.

5. Remove the control lever assembly.

6. Disconnect the A/C, if equipped, and blower switch connectors.

7. Remove the control lever assembly.

To install:

8. Connect the A/C, if equipped, and the blower switch connectors.

9. Install the control lever assembly.

10. Install the four screws attaching the control lever assembly.

11. Connect and adjust the control cables at the blower assembly and the heater unit.

12. Install the glove box and the console.

13. Connect the negative battery cable.

AIR CONDITIONER

➡Refer to Section 1 for discharging and charging of the air conditioning system.

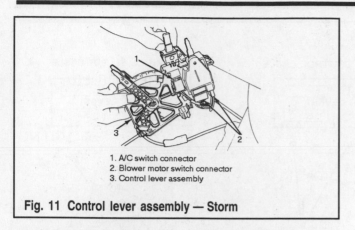

1. A/C switch connector
2. Blower motor switch connector
3. Control lever assembly

Fig. 11 Control lever assembly — Storm

Compressor

REMOVAL & INSTALLATION

Spectrum

▶ See Figure 12

1. Disconnect the negative battery cable and properly discharge the refrigerant system.
2. Disconnect the clutch harness connector.
3. Remove the connector attaching the pipes from the rear head of the compressor. Carefully handle the O-rings when removing the compressor.
4. Loosen the bolts attaching the compressor and remove the drive belt.

5. Remove the compressor attaching bolt, and remove the compressor.

To install:

6. Install the compressor and tighten the attaching bolt.
7. Install the drive belt. Adjust the belt to the correct tension and tighten the compressor mounting bolts.
8. Inspect the O-rings and replace if necessary. Connect the connector attaching the pipes to the rear head of the compressor.
9. Connect the clutch harness connector.
10. Connect the negative battery terminal.

Storm

▶ See Figure 13

1. Disconnect the negative battery cable and properly discharge the refrigerant system.
2. Disconnect the compressor/power steering pump drive belt from the air conditioning compressor clutch pulley on the 1.6L engine.
3. Loosen the power steering pump adjustment and pivot bolts.
4. Move the power steering pump toward the engine and remove the drive belt from pump and air conditioning compressor clutch pulleys.
5. Remove the serpentine drive belt by pulling up on the belt tension idler pulley with a breaker bar and removing the belt from the generator and air conditioning compressor clutch pulleys on the 1.8L engine.
6. Disconnect the air conditioning compressor clutch electrical connector.

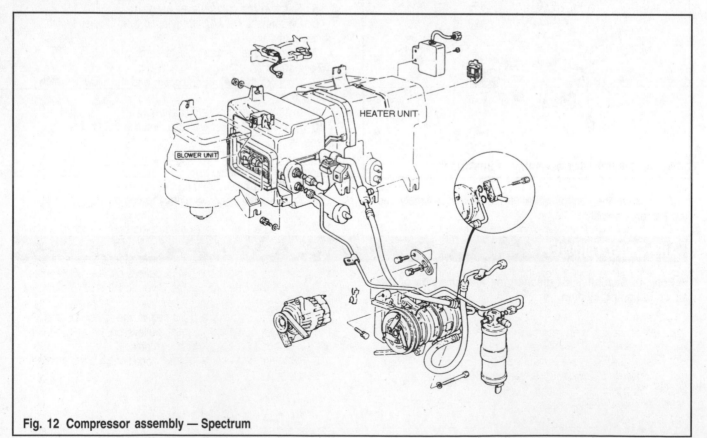

Fig. 12 Compressor assembly — Spectrum

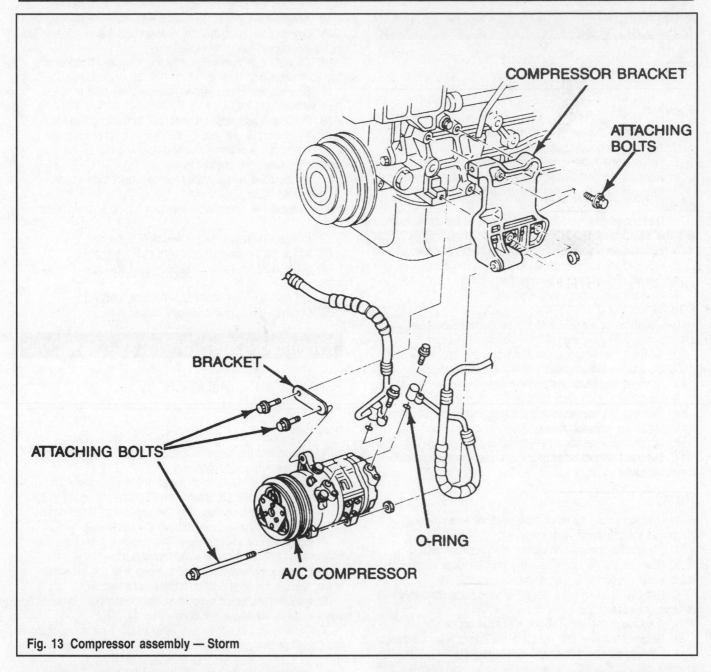

Fig. 13 Compressor assembly — Storm

7. Disconnect the discharge pipe from the compressor fitting by removing the bolt.

8. Disconnect the suction pipe from the compressor fitting by removing the bolt.

9. Raise and support the vehicle safely.

10. Remove the right lower splash shield.

11. Remove the upper and lower compressor mounting bolts and the compressor from the mounting bracket.

To install:

12. Install the compressor to the mounting bracket and secure with the upper and lower mounting bolts.

13. Install the right lower splash shield. Lower the vehicle.

14. Coat new O-rings with refrigerant oil and install the O-rings to the compressor fittings.

15. Connect the discharge pipe to the compressor fitting and tighten the bolt.

16. Connect the suction pipe to the compressor fitting and tighten the bolt.

17. Connect the air conditioning compressor clutch electrical connector.

18. Install the drive belt to the power steering pump and the air conditioning compressor clutch pulleys on the 1.6L engine. Tighten the power steering pump pivot and the adjustment bolt.

19. Install the serpentine drive belt to the generator and the air conditioning compressor clutch pulleys on the 1.8L engine.

20. Connect the negative battery cable.

21. Evacuate and charge the air conditioning system and check for leaks.

Condenser

REMOVAL & INSTALLATION

Spectrum

1. Disconnect the negative battery cable and properly discharge the refrigerant system.
2. Remove the radiator grille and emblem.
3. Remove the compressor discharge line at the condenser.
4. Remove the accumulator/dehydrator outlet line at the dehydrator.
5. Disconnect the electrical connections at the condenser and the drier.
6. Remove the upper end of the hood latch support.
7. Remove the condenser fasteners and the condenser.
8. Transfer all of the necessary parts.
9. Replace the O-rings and lubricate.
   To install:
10. Install the condenser and the condenser fasteners.
11. Install the upper end of the hood latch support.
12. Connect the electrical connectors to the condenser and the drier.
13. Connect the accumulator/dehydrator outlet line to the dehydrator.
14. Connect the compressor discharge line at the condenser.
15. Install the radiator grille and emblem.
16. Connect the negative battery cable.
17. Evacuate and charge the air conditioning system and check for leaks.

Storm

1. Disconnect the negative battery cable and properly discharge the refrigerant system.
2. Disconnect the condenser fan electrical connector.
3. Remove the six bolts from the radiator core support and remove the support.
4. Remove the two bolts from the hood latch assembly and remove the assembly.
5. Disconnect the triple switch electrical connector.
6. Remove the one bolt securing the compressor discharge pipe to the condenser fitting and disconnect the pipe from the fitting.
7. Remove the one bolt securing the receiver/drier-to-evaporator pipe at the receiver/drier fitting and disconnect.
8. Disconnect the chassis harness retaining clip from the front end panel near the receiver/drier.
9. Remove the two condenser retaining bolts.
10. Remove the condenser, condenser fan and receiver/drier from the vehicle as a unit.
11. Disconnect the condenser-to-receiver/drier pipe at the receiver/drier.
12. Remove the one screw securing the receiver/drier to the mounting bracket and remove the receiver/drier.
13. Remove the four bolts securing the fan to the condenser and remove the fan.
14. Remove the bolt from the receiver/drier mounting bracket and remove the condenser.

To install:

15. Connect the receiver/drier bracket and the condenser fan to the condenser and tighten the bolts.
16. Connect the receiver/drier to the mounting bracket and tighten the screw.
17. Connect the condenser-to-receiver/drier pipe at the receiver/drier.
18. Install the condenser, condenser fan, and receiver/drier to the vehicle as a unit and tighten the two retaining bolts.
19. Connect the chassis harness retaining clip to the front end panel, near the receiver/drier.
20. Connect the receiver/drier-to-evaporator pipe at the receiver/drier fitting.
21. Connect the compressor discharge pipe to the condenser fitting.
22. Connect the triple switch electrical connector.
23. Install the hood latch and tighten the two bolts.
24. Install the radiator core support and tightened the six bolts.
25. Connect the condenser fan electrical connector.
26. Connect the negative battery cable.

Evaporator Core

REMOVAL & INSTALLATION

Spectrum

1. Disconnect the negative battery cable and properly discharge the refrigerant system.
2. Remove the insulator at outlet of the evaporator and blower joint. Remove the thermo switch from the upper case.
3. Remove the clips retaining the upper and lower halves of the evaporator case, then remove the upper half.
4. Carefully pull the thermo-switch capillary tube from the evaporator core. Remove the thermo-switch.
5. Remove the evaporator core along with the expansion valve, leaving the inlet and outlet lines attached.
6. Peel the insulation tape from the thermo bulb expansion valve and the equalizer line connection.
7. Disconnect the expansion valve intake pipe connection, the equalizer line and the evaporator outlet line and remove the core. Cap or plug all open connections at once.
   To install:

➡**Lubricate the line fittings with clean refrigeration oil prior to installation.**

8. Install the core. Add 1.7 fluid oz. (50 ml) of new refrigeration oil to a new core. Connect the expansion valve intake pipe connection, the equalizer line and the evaporator outlet line.
9. With fresh insulation tape, tape the thermo bulb expansion valve and the equalizer line connection.
10. Install the evaporator core with the expansion valve.
11. Install the thermo-switch capillary tube to the evaporator core.
12. Install the upper half of the evaporator case and install the clips retaining the upper and lower halves.
13. Connect the thermo-switch to the upper case.

14. Install the insulator at the outlet of the evaporator and blower joint.
15. Connect the negative battery cable.
16. Evacuate, charge and check the operation of the system.

Storm

1. Disconnect the negative battery cable and properly discharge the refrigerant system.
2. Disconnect the lines from the expansion valve.
3. Remove the retaining clip and the expansion valve from the evaporator.
4. Remove the glove box from the instrument panel.
5. Remove the lower instrument panel reinforcement bracket.
6. Disconnect the electrical connectors from the thermostatic switch and the blower motor resistor.
7. Disconnect the air inlet cable from the blend door.
8. Remove the retaining nuts from the evaporator case.
9. Remove the evaporator case from the instrument panel.
10. Remove the retaining clips from the evaporator case.
11. Remove the four case screws.
12. Remove the case halves.
13. Remove the evaporator core from the case.

To install:
14. Install the evaporator core into the case.
15. Install the case halves and tighten the four screws.
16. Install the retaining clips.
17. Install the evaporator case into the instrument panel and tighten the retaining nuts.
18. Connect the air inlet cable to the blend door.
19. Connect the electrical connectors to the thermostatic switch and the blower motor resistor.
20. Install the lower instrument panel reinforcement bracket.
21. Install the glove box into the instrument panel.
22. Install the expansion valve to the evaporator and install the retaining clip.
23. Connect the lines to the expansion valve.
24. Connect the negative battery cable.
25. Evacuate, charge and check the operation of the system.

Control Panel

REMOVAL & INSTALLATION

For removal and installation of the control panel and the control cable adjustment, refer to the procedures under 'HEATER", in this Section.

Expansion Valve

REMOVAL & INSTALLATION

Spectrum

For removal and installation of the expansion valve, refer to the procedures under EVAPORATOR CORE, in this section.

Storm

1. Disconnect the negative battery cable and properly discharge the refrigerant system.
2. Remove the clamp attaching refrigerant pipes.
3. Remove the two nuts attaching refrigerant pipes to the expansion valve.
4. Remove the expansion valve retaining clip.
5. Remove the expansion valve.

To install:
6. Install the expansion valve and retaining clip.
7. Connect the refrigerant pipes to the expansion valve with the two retaining nuts and tighten them to 70 inch lbs. (8 Nm). Make sure to use new O-ring before installation.
8. Install the clamp attaching the refrigerant pipes.
9. Connect the negative battery cable.
10. Evacuate, charge and check the operation of the system.

Receiver/Drier

REMOVAL & INSTALLATION

Spectrum

1. Disconnect the negative battery cable and properly discharge the refrigerant system.
2. Remove the radiator grille.
3. Remove the receiver/drier inlet and outlet lines at the drier.
4. Disconnect the electrical connections at the drier switch.
5. Remove the receiver/drier.
6. Transfer the electrical switch.

To install:
7. Install the receiver/drier.
8. Connect the electrical connections to the drier switch.
9. Install the receiver/drier inlet and outlet lines at the drier. Make sure to use new O-rings prior to installation, if equipped.
10. Install the radiator grille.
11. Connect the negative battery cable.
12. Evacuate, charge and check the operation of the system.

Storm

▶ **See Figure 14**

1. Disconnect the negative battery cable and properly discharge the refrigerant system.
2. Remove the core support bracket.
3. Disconnect the compressor discharge line at the condenser.
4. Remove the two condenser retaining bolts.
5. Disconnect the inlet and outlet lines at the receiver/drier.
6. Disconnect the triple switch connector.
7. Remove the retaining bolts from the receiver/drier mounting bracket.
8. Remove the receiver/drier.

To install:
9. Install the receiver/drier and install the retaining bolts to the receiver/drier mounting bracket.
10. Connect the triple switch connector.
11. Connect the inlet and outlet lines at the receiver/drier. Make sure to use new O-rings prior to installation, if equipped.

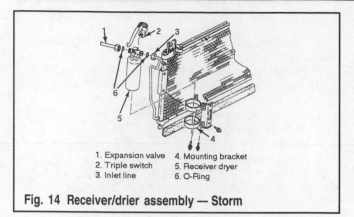

1. Expansion valve
2. Triple switch
3. Inlet line
4. Mounting bracket
5. Receiver dryer
6. O-Ring

Fig. 14 Receiver/drier assembly — Storm

12. Install the two condenser retaining bolts.
13. Connect the compressor discharge line at the condenser.
14. Install the core support bracket.
15. Connect the negative battery cable.
16. Evacuate, charge and check the operation of the system.

Refrigerant Lines

DISCONNECT AND CONNECT

Spectrum

1. Disconnect the negative battery cable and properly discharge the refrigerant system.
2. Remove the radiator grille.
3. Loosen the bolt attaching the connector at the compressor.
4. Loosen the connector attaching the pipe at the condenser, then remove the hoses (high and low pressure).
5. Remove the clips attaching the pipes.
6. Loosen the connectors attaching the pipes at the evaporator assembly.
7. Loosen the connector attaching the pipe at the receiver/drier, loosen the harness that links the shock tower with the intake manifold. Remove the clips and the receiver/drier to the evaporator pipe.
To install:
8. Connect the receiver/drier to the evaporator pipe and attach the clips. Tighten the harness that links the shock tower

CRUISE CONTROL

Control Switches

REMOVAL & INSTALLATION

Spectrum
♦ **See Figures 15 and 16**

For removal and installation of the control switches, refer to the procedures under COMBINATION SWITCH, in Section 8.

with the intake manifold, and tighten the connector attaching the pipe at the receiver/drier.
9. Tighten the connectors attaching the pipes at the evaporator assembly.
10. Install the clips attaching the pipes.
11. Install the high and low pressure hoses and tighten the connector attaching the pipe at the condenser.
12. Tighten the bolt attaching the connector at the compressor.
13. Install the radiator grille.
14. Connect the negative battery cable.
15. Evacuate, charge and check the operation of the system.

Storm

1. Disconnect the negative battery cable and properly discharge the refrigerant system.
2. Replace any faulty or damaged lines and plug open fittings immediately to prevent moisture from entering the lines.
3. Connect the negative battery cable.
4. Evacuate, charge and check the operation of the system.

Control Cables

REMOVAL & INSTALLATION

For removal and installation of the control panel and the control cable adjustment, refer to the procedures under 'HEATER" in this Section.

Cycling Clutch Switch

REMOVAL & INSTALLATION

1. Disconnect the negative battery cable and properly discharge the refrigerant system.
2. Disconnect the electrical connector on the switch.
3. Remove the switch.
To install:
4. Connect the switch and the electrical connector.
5. Connect the negative battery cable.
6. Evacuate, charge and check the operation of the system.

Speed Sensor

REMOVAL & INSTALLATION

Spectrum

1. Disconnect the negative battery cable.
2. Loosen and remove the speed sensor from the top right of the transaxle.
3. To install reverse removal procedure.

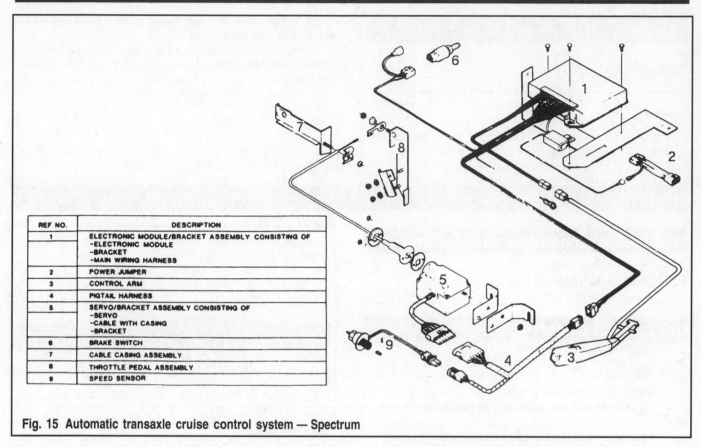

REF NO.	DESCRIPTION
1	ELECTRONIC MODULE/BRACKET ASSEMBLY CONSISTING OF -ELECTRONIC MODULE -BRACKET -MAIN WIRING HARNESS
2	POWER JUMPER
3	CONTROL ARM
4	PIGTAIL HARNESS
5	SERVO/BRACKET ASSEMBLY CONSISTING OF -SERVO -CABLE WITH CASING -BRACKET
6	BRAKE SWITCH
7	CABLE CASING ASSEMBLY
8	THROTTLE PEDAL ASSEMBLY
9	SPEED SENSOR

Fig. 15 Automatic transaxle cruise control system — Spectrum

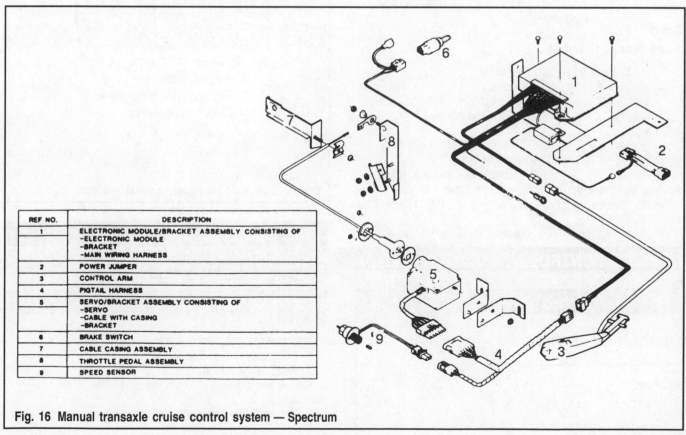

REF NO.	DESCRIPTION
1	ELECTRONIC MODULE/BRACKET ASSEMBLY CONSISTING OF -ELECTRONIC MODULE -BRACKET -MAIN WIRING HARNESS
2	POWER JUMPER
3	CONTROL ARM
4	PIGTAIL HARNESS
5	SERVO/BRACKET ASSEMBLY CONSISTING OF -SERVO -CABLE WITH CASING -BRACKET
6	BRAKE SWITCH
7	CABLE CASING ASSEMBLY
8	THROTTLE PEDAL ASSEMBLY
9	SPEED SENSOR

Fig. 16 Manual transaxle cruise control system — Spectrum

Servo

LINKAGE ADJUSTMENT

Spectrum

1. Position the accelerator pedal so that the engine runs at a normal idling speed. Hold the accelerator pedal in this position.

2. Lightly secure the cable casing to the bracket using the cable clamp and self locking hex nut.
3. Adjust the cable casing so that there is a light tension on the servo cable. Make sure not to pull the throttle off the idle setting.
4. Tighten the clamp securely.

ENTERTAINMENT SYSTEM

Radio Receiver/Amplifier/Tape Player

REMOVAL & INSTALLATION

Spectrum

1. Disconnect battery negative cable.
2. Remove the radio cover attaching screws and the radio cover.
3. Remove the radio and bracket.
4. Disconnect electrical connectors and antenna from the radio.
5. Reverse procedure to install. Connect battery negative cable.

Storm

▶ **See Figures 17 and 18**

1. Disconnect battery negative cable.
2. Remove 4 heater control knobs.
3. Remove 4 radio bezel attaching screws and the bezel.
4. Disconnect the illumination light and harness from the radio bezel.
5. Remove the 3 left hand console side panel attaching screws, then the left hand console side panel.
6. Remove the 3 right hand console side panel attaching screws, then the right hand console side panel.
7. Remove the radio attaching screws and the radio from the instrument panel.
8. Disconnect electrical connectors and antenna. Reverse procedure to install and connect the battery negative cable.

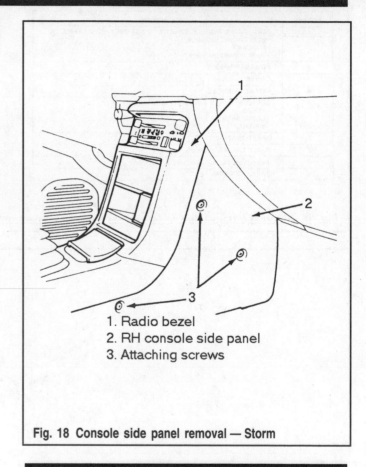

1. Radio bezel
2. RH console side panel
3. Attaching screws

Fig. 18 Console side panel removal — Storm

Front Speakers

REMOVAL & INSTALLATION

Spectrum

1. Disconnect the negative battery cable.
2. Disconnect the speaker connector.
3. Remove the attaching screws.
4. Remove the speaker from the lower side of the instrument panel.
5. To install, reverse the removal procedure.

Storm

1. Disconnect the negative battery cable.

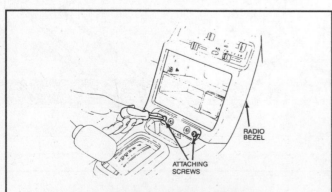

RADIO BEZEL

ATTACHING SCREWS

Fig. 17 Radio bezel removal screws — Storm

2. Pry off the bottom of the speaker grille.

3. Remove the four speaker mounting screws and remove the speaker from the door.

4. Disconnect the electrical connector from the speaker.

5. To install, reverse the removal procedure.

Rear Speakers

REMOVAL & INSTALLATION

1. Disconnect the negative battery cable.

WINDSHIELD WIPERS AND WASHERS

Windshield Wiper Blade and Arm

REMOVAL & INSTALLATION

Spectrum

▶ See Figure 19

1. Remove the lock nuts at the base of the wiper arm.
2. Remove the wiper arm.
3. Depress the blade assembly release lever.
4. Slide the blade assembly downward until it clear the arm.
5. To install, reverse the removal procedure.

Storm

▶ See Figure 20

1. Remove the wiper arm cap.
2. Remove the wiper arm attaching nut.
3. Remove the wiper arm.
4. Depress the blade assembly release lever.
5. Slide the blade assembly downward until it clear the arm.
6. To install, reverse the removal procedure.

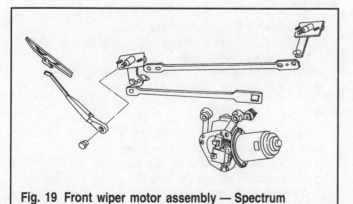

Fig. 19 Front wiper motor assembly — Spectrum

2. Remove the ten plugs securing the rear trim panel and remove the trim panel.

3. Disconnect the electrical connector from the speaker.

4. Remove the two mounting screws securing the speaker to the trim panel and remove the speaker.

5. To install, reverse the removal procedure.

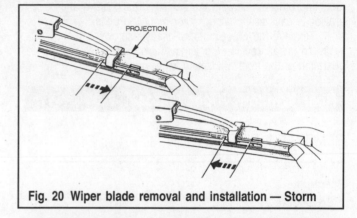

Fig. 20 Wiper blade removal and installation — Storm

Rear Window Wiper Blade and Arm

REMOVAL & INSTALLATION

Spectrum

1. Remove the lock nuts at the base of the wiper arm.
2. Remove the wiper arm.
3. To install, reverse the removal procedure.

Storm

1. Remove the wiper arm cap.
2. Remove the wiper arm attaching nut.
3. Remove the wiper arm.
4. Depress the blade assembly release lever.
5. Slide the blade assembly downward until it clear the arm.
6. To install, reverse the removal procedure.

Front Windshield Wiper Motor

REMOVAL & INSTALLATION

Spectrum

1. Disconnect the negative battery terminal from the battery.

2. Remove the locknuts retaining the wiper arms and the wiper arms.

3. Remove the cowl cover, wiper motor cover and the electrical connector.

4. Disconnect the drive arm from the wiper link.

5. Remove the mounting bolts and the wiper motor.

6. To install, reverse the removal procedures.

Storm

1. Disconnect the negative terminal from the battery.

2. Remove the cowl vent grille. From the engine compartment, disconnect the electrical connector from the windshield wiper motor.

3. Disconnect the wiper motor from the windshield wiper crank arm; be careful not to bend the linkage.

4. Remove the 2 retaining bolts from the charcoal canister mounting bracket, allowing the canister to slip down and provide access to the wiper motor mounting bolts.

5. Remove the wiper motor-to-chassis screws.

6. To install, reverse the removal procedures. Check the operation of the front windshield wiper motor.

Rear Window Wiper Motor

REMOVAL & INSTALLATION

Spectrum

▶ **See Figure 21**

1. Disconnect the negative battery terminal from the battery.

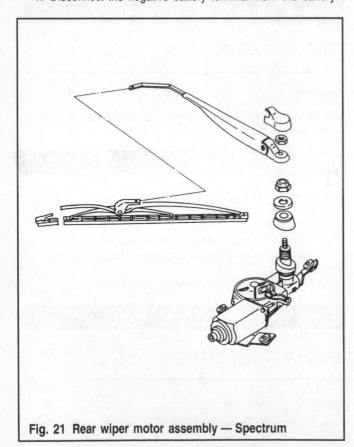

Fig. 21 Rear wiper motor assembly — Spectrum

2. Remove the trim pad and the wiper arm assemblies.

3. Remove the mounting bolts and the motor assembly.

4. Disconnect the electrical connector.

5. To install, reverse the removal procedures.

Storm

1. Disconnect the negative terminal from the battery.

2. Remove the rear wiper arm-to-wiper motor nut and wiper arm.

3. From inside the rear hatch, remove the rear wiper cover (hatch trim panel), then, disconnect the electrical connector from the rear wiper motor.

4. Remove the wiper motor-to-hatch screws and the wiper motor from the hatch.

5. To install, reverse the removal procedures. Check the operation of the rear wiper motor.

Wiper Linkage

REMOVAL & INSTALLATION

1. Disconnect the negative battery terminal from the battery.

2. Remove the locknuts retaining the wiper arms and the wiper arms.

3. Remove the cowl cover, wiper motor cover and the electrical connector.

4. Disconnect the drive arm from the wiper link.

5. Remove the mounting bolts and the wiper motor.

6. Remove the wiper linkage.

To install:

7. Install the wiper linkage.

8. Install the wiper motor and the mounting bolts.

9. Connect the drive arm to the wiper link.

10. Connect the electrical connector.

11. Install the wiper motor cover and the cowl cover.

12. Install the wiper arms and tighten the lock nuts.

13. Connect the negative battery cable.

Windshield Washer Fluid Reservoir

REMOVAL & INSTALLATION

Spectrum

1. Disconnect the negative battery cable.

2. Disconnect the pump wiring at the connector.

3. Disconnect the vinyl tube.

4. Remove the washer fluid reservoir attaching screw.

5. To install, reverse the removal procedure.

Storm

1. Disconnect the negative battery cable.

2. Remove the engine coolant reservoir.

3. Remove the power steering fluid reservoir.

4. Disconnect the electrical connector.

5. Disconnect the washer fluid hose.

6. Remove the attaching bolt.

7. Remove the washer fluid reservoir.

To install:

8. Install the washer fluid reservoir and install the attaching bolt.
9. Connect the washer fluid hose.
10. Connect the electrical connector.
11. Install the power steering fluid reservoir.
12. Install the engine coolant reservoir.
13. Connect the negative battery cable.

Windshield Washer Motor

REMOVAL & INSTALLATION

Spectrum

The windshield washer motor and reservoir are the same assembly. For removal procedure, see Windshield Washer Reservoir, in this section.

Storm

1. Disconnect the negative battery cable.
2. Remove the cowl cover.
3. Disconnect the electrical connector.
4. Disconnect the wiper linkage from the wiper motor arm.
5. Remove the canister attaching clip.
6. Remove the wiper motor attaching bolt.
7. Remove the wiper link attaching nut.
8. Remove the wiper motor.

To install:

9. Install the wiper motor.
10. Install the wiper link attaching nut.
11. Install the wiper motor attaching bolt.
12. Install the canister attaching clip.
13. Connect the wiper linkage to the wiper motor arm.
14. Connect the electrical connector.
15. Install the cowl cover.
16. Connect the negative battery cable.

INSTRUMENTS AND SWITCHES

Instrument Cluster

REMOVAL & INSTALLATION

Spectrum
▶ See Figure 22

1. Disconnect the negative battery terminal from the battery.
2. Remove the instrument cluster bezel retaining screws and bezel.
3. Disconnect the windshield wiper and lighting switch connectors.
4. Remove the instrument cluster retaining screws and pull out the assembly.
5. Remove the trip reset knob and the assembly glass.

Rear Window Washer Reservoir

REMOVAL & INSTALLATION

Spectrum

1. Disconnect the negative battery cable.
2. Remove the rear quarter trim.
3. Disconnect the pump wiring at the connector.
4. Remove the washer tank assembly.
5. To install, reverse the removal procedure.

Storm

1. Disconnect the negative battery cable.
2. Remove the end trim panel.
3. Remove the side trim panel.
4. Remove the washer tank assembly.
5. To install, reverse the removal procedure.

Rear Window Washer Motor

REMOVAL & INSTALLATION

Spectrum

1. Disconnect the negative battery cable.
2. Remove the rear quarter trim.
3. Disconnect the pump wiring at the connector.
4. Remove the washer pump assembly.
5. To install, reverse the removal procedure.

Storm

1. Disconnect the negative battery cable.
2. Remove the end trim panel.
3. Remove the side trim panel.
4. Remove the washer pump motor assembly.
5. To install, reverse the removal procedure.

6. Remove the buzzer, sockets and bulbs.
7. Remove the speedometer assembly, fuel and temperature gauge.
8. Remove the tachometer, if equipped.
9. To install, reverse the removal procedures.

Storm
▶ See Figure 23

1. Disconnect battery negative cable.
2. Remove the cluster switch panel.
3. Remove the 4 screws securing the instrument cluster. Disconnect the electrical connectors and speedometer from the back of the instrument cluster.
4. Remove the cluster assembly.
5. Installation is the reverse order of the removal procedure.

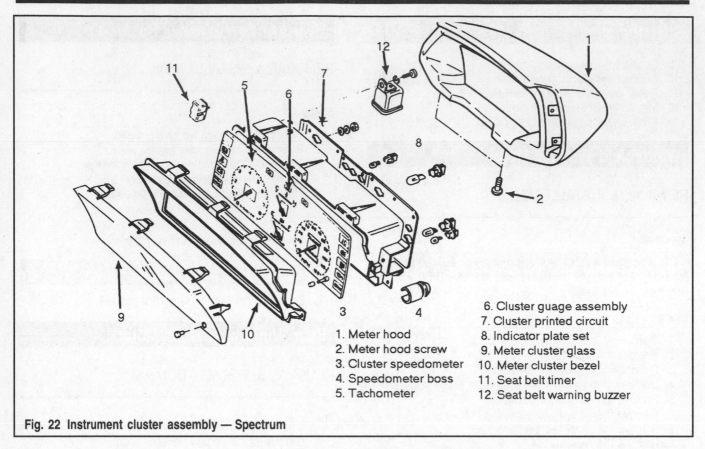

1. Meter hood
2. Meter hood screw
3. Cluster speedometer
4. Speedometer boss
5. Tachometer
6. Cluster guage assembly
7. Cluster printed circuit
8. Indicator plate set
9. Meter cluster glass
10. Meter cluster bezel
11. Seat belt timer
12. Seat belt warning buzzer

Fig. 22 Instrument cluster assembly — Spectrum

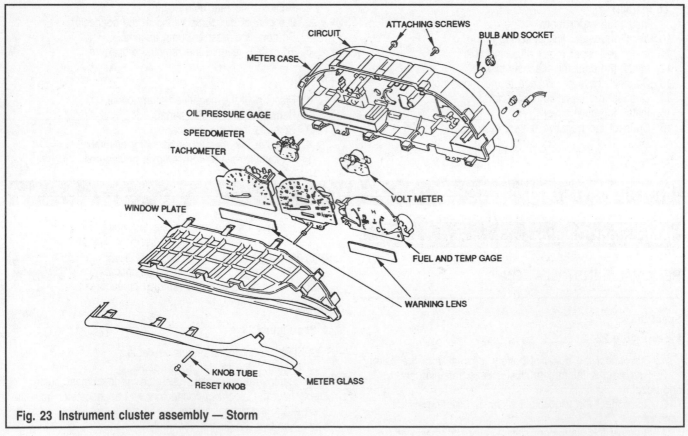

Fig. 23 Instrument cluster assembly — Storm

Speedometer

REMOVAL & INSTALLATION

1. Disconnect the negative battery cable.
2. Remove the instrument cluster from the instrument panel.
3. Remove the cluster lens and retainer from the cluster.
4. Remove the speedometer retaining screws from the rear of the cluster.
5. Remove the speedometer-odometer from the cluster.
6. Installation is the reverse order of the removal procedure. Connect battery negative cable.

Tachometer

REMOVAL & INSTALLATION

Spectrum

1. Disconnect the negative battery cable.
2. Remove the instrument cluster from the instrument panel.
3. Remove the cluster lens and retainer from the cluster.
4. Remove the tachometer retaining screws from the rear of the cluster.
5. Remove the tachometer from the cluster.
6. Installation is the reverse order of the removal procedure. Connect battery negative cable.

Storm

1. Disconnect the negative battery cable.
2. Remove the instrument cluster from the instrument panel.
3. Remove the cluster lens and retainer from the cluster.
4. Remove the five tachometer retaining screws.
5. Remove the tachometer from the cluster.
6. Installation is the reverse order of the removal procedure. Connect battery negative cable.

Speedometer Cable

REMOVAL & INSTALLATION

1. Disconnect negative battery cable.
2. Remove the instrument cluster assembly.
3. Disconnect the speedometer cable at the meter assembly.
4. Disconnect the speedometer cable at the transaxle.
5. Remove the grommet and pull the cable toward the engine compartment.
6. To install, reverse the removal procedure.

Oil Pressure Gauge

REMOVAL & INSTALLATION

Storm

1. Disconnect the negative battery cable.
2. Remove the instrument cluster from the instrument panel.
3. Remove the cluster lens and retainer from the cluster.
4. Remove the two oil pressure gauge retaining screws.
5. Remove the oil pressure gauge from the cluster.
6. Installation is the reverse order of the removal procedure. Connect battery negative cable.

Fuel Gauge

REMOVAL & INSTALLATION

Spectrum

1. Disconnect the negative battery cable.
2. Remove the instrument cluster from the instrument panel.
3. Remove the cluster lens and retainer from the cluster.
4. Remove the fuel gauge retaining screws from the rear of the cluster.
5. Remove the fuel gauge from the cluster.
6. Installation is the reverse order of the removal procedure. Connect battery negative cable.

Storm

1. Disconnect the negative battery cable.
2. Remove the instrument cluster from the instrument panel.
3. Remove the cluster lens and retainer from the cluster.
4. Remove the six engine coolant temperature and fuel gauge retaining screws.
5. Remove the engine coolant temperature and fuel gauge from the cluster.
6. Installation is the reverse order of the removal procedure. Connect battery negative cable.

Engine Coolant Temperature Gauge

REMOVAL & INSTALLATION

Spectrum

1. Disconnect the negative battery cable.
2. Remove the instrument cluster from the instrument panel.
3. Remove the cluster lens and retainer from the cluster.
4. Remove the engine coolant temperature gauge retaining screws from the rear of the cluster.
5. Remove the engine coolant temperature gauge from the cluster.

6. Installation is the reverse order of the removal procedure. Connect battery negative cable.

Storm

For removal and installation of the engine coolant temperature gauge, refer to the procedures under FUEL GAUGE, in this section.

Printed Circuit Board

REMOVAL & INSTALLATION

Spectrum

1. Disconnect the negative battery cable.
2. Remove the instrument cluster from the instrument panel.
3. Remove the cluster lens and retainer from the cluster.
4. Remove the circuit board retaining screws from the rear of the cluster.
5. Remove the circuit board from the cluster.
6. Installation is the reverse order of the removal procedure. Connect battery negative cable.

Storm

1. Disconnect the negative battery cable.
2. Remove the instrument cluster from the instrument panel.
3. Remove the cluster lens and retainer from the cluster.
4. Remove the gauges.
5. Remove the circuit board from the cluster.
6. Installation is the reverse order of the removal procedure. Connect battery negative cable.

Voltmeter

REMOVAL & INSTALLATION

Storm

1. Disconnect the negative battery cable.
2. Remove the instrument cluster from the instrument panel.
3. Remove the cluster lens and retainer from the cluster.
4. Remove the voltmeter retaining screws.
5. Remove the voltmeter from the cluster.
6. Installation is the reverse order of the removal procedure. Connect battery negative cable.

Windshield Wiper Switch

REMOVAL & INSTALLATION

Spectrum

1. Disconnect the negative battery cable.

2. Remove the instrument cluster hood attaching screws and remove the cluster hood.
3. Disconnect the windshield wiper switch connector and the lighting switch connector.
4. Remove the instrument cluster hood inside attaching nuts and bracket and then push the switches out of the cluster hood from the inside.
5. To install, reverse the removal procedures.

Storm

▶ See Figure 24

1. Disconnect the negative battery cable.
2. Remove the cluster switch panel.
3. Remove the 2 screws securing the wiper/washer switch assembly to the cluster switch panel.
4. Remove the wiper/washer switch assembly from the cluster switch panel.
5. Installation is the reverse order of the removal procedure.

Rear Window Wiper Switch

REMOVAL & INSTALLATION

Spectrum

1. Disconnect the negative battery cable. Using a small tool, pry the switch panel from the dash.
2. Pull the switch out and disconnect the electrical connector.
3. To install, reverse the removal procedures.

Headlight Switch

REMOVAL & INSTALLATION

Spectrum

The headlight control switch is a 3 position, push type switch which is located at the left side of the instrument panel.

1. Disconnect the negative battery cable. Remove the instrument cluster bezel retaining screw and the bezel.
2. Disconnect the electrical connectors.
3. Place the bezel on a bench and remove the 2 nuts securing the headlight control switch.
4. Remove the headlight control switch.
5. To install, reverse the removal procedures.

Storm

The headlight control switch is located at the left hand side of the instrument panel on the meter hood.

1. Disconnect the battery negative cable.
2. Remove the meter hood.
3. Remove the instrument cluster from the meter hood.
4. Remove the 2 clips attaching headlight control harness.
5. Remove the 4 screws attaching the headlight switch to the meter hood.

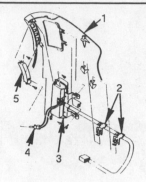

1. Meter hood
2. Clips
3. Windshield wiper switch
4. Illumination bulb
5. Illumination box

Fig. 24 Windshield wiper-washer switch — Storm

6. Disconnect electrical connectors from the switch and remove the switch.

7. Reverse procedure to install. Connect battery negative cable.

Clock

REMOVAL & INSTALLATION

Spectrum

1. Disconnect the negative battery cable.

LIGHTING

Headlights

REMOVAL & INSTALLATION

1985-1986 Spectrum

1. Disconnect the negative battery cable.
2. Remove the radiator grille, and the headlight bezel.
3. Remove the four seal beam unit attaching screws.
4. Remove the headlight.

To install:

5. Fit the bosses on the headlight lens into the grooves so that the TOP mark is up, and install the four attaching screws.
6. Install the headlight bezel.
7. Install the radiator grille.
8. Connect the negative battery cable.

1987-1989 Spectrum

1. Disconnect the negative battery cable.
2. Twist the headlight bulb connector.
3. Disconnect the connector to the bulb.

To install:

4. Do not touch the bulb when installing into the connector.
5. Twist the headlight bulb connector.
6. Connect the negative battery cable.

2. Remove the instrument panel from the vehicle.
3. Remove the clock connectors.
4. Remove the clock attaching screws.
5. Remove the clock assembly.
6. To install, reverse the removal procedure.

Storm

The clock is part of the radio. For removal and installation of the clock, refer to the procedures under RADIO/RECEIVER, in this section.

1990-1991 Storm

▶ **See Figures 25, 26, 27 and 28**

1. Raise the headlight cover.
2. Disconnect the negative battery cable.
3. Remove the upper headlamp garnish retaining screws and the garnish. Remove the lower headlamp garnish retaining screws and the garnish.
4. Remove the four attaching screws and remove the sealed beam unit.
5. To install, reverse the removal procedure.

1992-1993 Storm

1. Disconnect the negative battery cable.

Fig. 25 Headlamp cover adjustment — 1990-1991 Storm

Fig. 26 Headlamp cover adjustment — 1990-1991 Storm

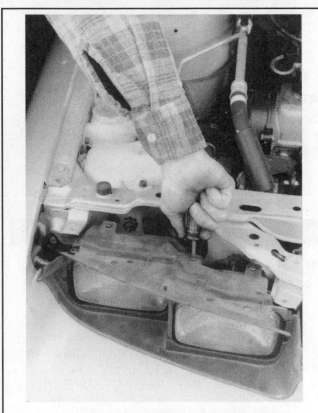

Fig. 27 Headlamp upper garnish — 1990-1991 Storm

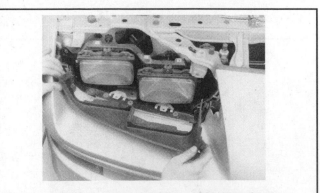

Fig. 28 Headlamp lower garnish — 1990-1991 Storm

2. Remove the two retaining screws and the lower headlamp garnish.

3. Remove the three retaining screws and the upper headlamp garnish.

4. Remove the four retaining screws and the headlamp retaining ring.

5. Disconnect the headlamp electrical connectors.

6. Remove the headlamp bulb from the vehicle.

To install:

7. Install the headlamp bulb and connect the electrical connectors.

8. Install the retaining ring and tighten the four retaining screws.

9. Install the upper headlamp garnish and tighten the three retaining screws.

10. Install the lower headlamp garnish and tighten the two retaining screws.

11. Connect the negative battery cable.

AIMING

1985-1986 Spectrum

1. With the vehicle at empty weight, check and adjust the tire inflation pressures, clean the headlights and park the vehicle on a level surface.

2. Use the screw above the headlight to adjust the vertical aim and the screw on the side of the headlight to adjust the horizontal aim.

1987-1989 Spectrum

▶ **See Figure 29**

1. With the vehicle at empty weight, check and adjust the tire inflation pressures, clean the headlights and park the vehicle on a level surface.

2. Use the screw above the headlight to adjust the vertical aim and the screw in the front engine compartment support, to the rear of the headlight, to adjust the horizontal aim.

1990-1991 Storm

1. With the vehicle at empty weight, check and adjust the tire inflation pressures, clean the headlights and park the vehicle on a level surface.

2. Use the knob above the headlight to adjust the vertical aim and the screw on the side of the headlight to adjust the horizontal aim.

1992-1993 Storm

1. With the vehicle at empty weight, check and adjust the tire inflation pressures, clean the headlights and park the vehicle on a level surface.

2. Use the screw above the headlight to adjust the vertical aim and the screw in the front engine compartment support, to the rear of the headlight, to adjust the horizontal aim.

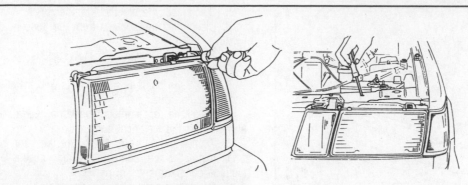

Fig. 29 Headlamp adjusting screws — 1987-1989 Spectrum

Headlamp Cover

REMOVAL & INSTALLATION

Storm

1. Raise the headlamp cover.
2. Disconnect the negative battery cable.
3. Remove the headlamp lower garnish retaining screws and remove the garnish.
4. Remove the nut securing the link joint, on the inside of the cover, and remove the link joint.
5. Remove the four bolts securing the headlamp cover and remove the cover.

To install:

6. Install the headlamp cover and tighten the four bolts to 89 in. lbs. (10 Nm).
7. Install the link joint and tighten the nut.
8. Install the headlamp lower garnish and tighten the retaining screws.

Signal and Marker Lights

REMOVAL & INSTALLATION

Front Turn Signal and Parking Lights

SPECTRUM

1. Disconnect the negative battery cable.
2. Remove the 2 screws attaching the turn signal lens and the housing to the front bumper.
3. Disconnect the wiring at the 3 pole connector and remove the front turn signal as a unit.
4. Remove the light lens to replace the light bulb.
5. To install, reverse the removal procedure.

STORM

1. Disconnect the negative battery cable.
2. Remove the two screws attaching the turn signal lamp lens and housing to the front bumper.
3. Disconnect the 3 pole connector.
4. Remove the turn signal lamp unit.

5. Remove the bulb by turning the bulb socket counterclockwise.
6. To install, reverse the removal procedure.

Side Marker Lights

SPECTRUM

1. Disconnect the negative battery cable.
2. Remove the screws attaching the side marker lens.
3. Disconnect the wiring at the connector and remove the side marker lens.
4. Remove the light lens to replace the light bulb.
5. To install, reverse the removal procedure.

STORM

1. Disconnect the negative battery cable.
2. Remove the two screws attaching the side marker lens and remove the lamp from the fender.
3. Remove the bulb by turning the bulb socket counterclockwise.
4. To install, reverse the removal procedure.

Rear Turn Signal, Brake and Parking Lights

SPECTRUM

1. Disconnect the negative battery cable.
2. Open the trunk lid and open the combination light lid (remove the 3 screws on the sedan).
3. Remove the bulb by turning the attaching knob and pull it out.
4. Remove the screw attaching the rear end trim cover and remove the light lens.
5. To install, reverse the removal procedure.

STORM COUPE

▶ See Figure 30

1. Disconnect the negative battery cable.
2. Lift the luggage compartment floor carpet toward the front of the vehicle and remove the spare tire cover panel.
3. Remove the ten plastic retaining clips from the rear end trim panel.
4. Disconnect the luggage compartment lamp electrical connector.
5. Remove the luggage compartment trim panel and the rear end trim panel.
6. Disconnect the rear combination lamp assembly electrical connector.

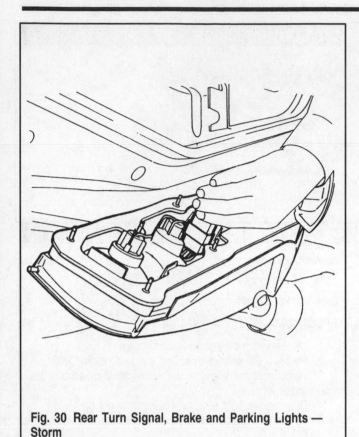

**Fig. 30 Rear Turn Signal, Brake and Parking Lights —
Storm**

7. Remove the seven nuts and the rear combination lamp assembly from the vehicle.

8. Disconnect the rear combination lamp electrical connector.

9. Remove the four bulb sockets from the rear combination lamp assembly and remove the four bulbs from the sockets.

To install:

10. Install the four bulbs to the sockets and install the four bulb sockets to the rear combination lamp assembly.

11. Connect the rear combination lamp electrical connector.

12. Install the rear combination lamp assembly to the vehicle and the seven nuts.

13. Connect the rear combination lamp assembly electrical connector.

14. Install the rear end trim panel and the luggage compartment trim panel.

15. Connect the luggage compartment lamp electrical connector.

16. Install the ten plastic retaining clips to the rear end trim panel.

17. Install the spare tire cover panel and the luggage compartment floor carpet.

18. Connect the negative battery cable.

STORM HATCHBACK

1. Disconnect the negative battery cable.

2. Remove the rear combination lamp access panel from the luggage compartment trim panel.

3. Disconnect the five nuts retaining the lamp housing.

4. Remove the rear combination lamp housing from the vehicle.

5. Disconnect the electrical connector.

6. Disconnect the sockets from the lamp housing by twisting.

7. Remove the bulbs from the sockets.

To install:

8. Install the bulbs in the sockets and install the sockets into the lamp housing.

9. Install the rear combination lamp housing to the vehicle and connect the electrical connector.

10. Tighten the five nuts to secure the lamp housing.

11. Install the rear combination lamp access panel to the luggage compartment trim panel.

12. Connect the negative battery cable.

High-mount Brake Light

STORM

1. Disconnect the negative battery cable.

2. Remove the spare tire cover.

3. Remove the ten clips attaching the rear end trim panel and remove the rear end trim panel.

4. Disconnect the luggage room lamp connector.

5. Remove the rear side trim panel.

6. Disconnect the connector.

7. Remove the seven nuts and the attachment to the rear combination lamp.

8. Disconnect the high mount stop lamp connector.

9. Remove the four inside and the four outside bolts from the rear garnish, and remove the rear garnish.

10. Peel the pad. Remove the two attachment screws to the lens and the housing.

11. Remove the lens and the housing assembly.

To install:

12. Install the lens and housing assembly.

13. Tighten the two attachment screws to the lens and housing. Replace the pad.

14. Install the rear garnish and tighten the four inside and four outside bolts.

15. Connect the high mount stop lamp connector.

16. Tighten the seven nuts and install the attachment to the rear combination lamp.

17. Install the rear side trim panel.

18. Connect the luggage room lamp connector.

19. Install the rear end trim panel and attach the ten clips.

20. Install the spare tire cover.

21. Connect the negative battery cable.

Dome Light

1. Disconnect the negative battery cable.

2. Remove the dome light cover.

3. Remove the screws and the light housing.

4. Disconnect the electrical connectors.

5. To install, reverse the removal procedure.

Cargo Area Lamps

1. Disconnect the negative battery cable.

2. Remove the cargo area light cover.

3. Remove the screws and the light housing.

4. Disconnect the electrical connectors.

5. To install, reverse the removal procedure.

License Plate Lights

1. Disconnect the negative battery cable.
2. Remove the screws and the lens.
3. Remove the license plate lens and the socket.
4. Disconnect the electrical connectors.
5. To install, reverse the removal procedure.

Fog/Driving Lights

REMOVAL & INSTALLATION

Storm

1. Disconnect the negative battery cable.
2. Disconnect the connector to the fog lamp.
3. Remove the two bolt attaching the fog lamp bracket.
4. Remove the fog lamp assembly.
5. To install, reverse the removal procedure.

CIRCUIT PROTECTION

Fuses, Circuit Breakers and Relays

LOCATION

Fusible Links

Fusible links are located in the engine harness at the starter solenoid and the left hand front of the dash at the battery junction block.

Circuit Breakers

The circuit breakers can be found incorporated in the switch it represents or they can be found on the fuse and relay boards, mounted to the boards with blades similar to the fuses. Before removing a breaker, always disconnect the negative battery cable to prevent potentially damaging electrical "spikes" within the system. Simply remove the breaker by pulling straight out from the relay board. Do not twist the relay; damage may occur to the connectors inside the housing.

Reinstall the circuit breaker by pressing it straight into its mount. Make certain the blades line up correctly and that the circuit breaker is fully seated. Reconnect the negative battery cable and check the circuit for function.

Fuse Panel

SPECTRUM

The fuse panel is located at the lower left hand side of the instrument panel, concealed by a cover.

STORM

▶ **See Figures 31, 32 and 33**

The main fuse panel is attached to the junction block behind the left hand kick panel inside the vehicle. There is also a fuse/relay box located on the left hand side of the engine compartment near the battery. There is also a relay box located on the right hand side of the engine compartment near the strut tower.

Relays

Various relays are attached to the brackets under the left-side of the dash. All units are easily replaced with plug-in modules.

Fig. 31 Main fuse panel — Storm

Fig. 32 Fuse/relay panel — Storm

Fig. 33 Relay panel — Storm

Computers

LOCATION

Storm

The Electronic Control Module (ECM) is located under the dash on the left hand side of the steering column.

Spectrum

The Electronic Control Module (ECM) controls the operation of the engine and is located under the dash on the right side of the vehicle.

Flashers

LOCATION

Storm

The turn signal and hazard flasher are located above the fuse box, under the left hand dash panel.

Spectrum

The turn signal flasher is located behind the instrument panel, on the left-hand side of the steering column. Replacement is accomplished by unplugging the old flasher and inserting a new one.

The hazard flasher is located behind the instrument panel, on the left-hand side of the steering column. Replacement is accomplished by unplugging the old flasher and inserting a new one.

Relays, Sensors and Computer Locations

SPECTRUM

- **A/C Cycling Switch** — is located behind the A/C compressor on the front grille support, if so equipped.
- **A/C Dual Pressure Switch** — is mounted on the top of the A/C condenser, in the engine compartment.
- **A/C Relay** — is located under the left side of the instrument panel, near the left kick panel.
- **A/C Resistor** — is located behind the center console.
- **A/C Thermo Switch** — is located on the A/C evaporator housing.
- **Air Inlet Temperature Sensor** — is located on the bottom of the air cleaner assembly.
- **Altitude Sensing Switch** — is located on the front of the carburetor.
- **Assembly Line Diagnostic Link** — is located under the right side of the dash panel near the kick panel.
- **Back-Up Switch (manual transaxle)** — is located on the top of the clutch pedal bracket.
- **Clutch/Start Switch (manual transaxle)** — is located on the top of the clutch pedal bracket.
- **Check Engine Lamp Driver** — is located under the right side of the dash panel near the kick panel, if so equipped.
- **Choke Relay** — is located on the right side of the fire wall, in the engine compartment.
- **Coolant Temperature Sensor** — see Engine Coolant Temperature Sensor.
- **Cooling Fan Relay** — is located on the left front inner fender panel, in front of the battery.
- **Cruise Control Brake Disengage Switch** — is located on top of the brake pedal bracket.
- **Cruise Control Clutch Disengage Switch (manual transaxle)** — is located on top of the clutch pedal bracket.
- **Cruise Control Controller Unit** — is located under the instrument panel, mounted to the steering support bracket.
- **Cruise Control Servo** — is located in the left rear side of the engine compartment.
- **Diode Box** — is located under the right side of the dash panel near the kick panel, if so equipped.
- **Early Fuel Evaporation Relay** — is located on the right side of the firewall, in the engine compartment.
- **Electronic Control Module (ECM)** — is located under the right side of the dash panel, behind the kick panel.
- **Engine Coolant Temperature Sensor** — is located on the intake manifold on the engine.
- **FICD Relay** — is located on the right side of the firewall, in the engine compartment.
- **Front Harness Diodes** — are located under the left hand side of the instrument panel.
- **High Altitude Solenoid Valve** — is located in the right rear of the engine compartment.
- **Key Warning Buzzer** — is located near the center of the dash, to the right of the instrument panel.

- **Kick-Down Solenoid (automatic transaxle)** — is located in the left side of the engine compartment.
- **Ignition Main Relay** — is located behind the left hand side of the instrument panel.
- **Inhibit Switch (automatic transaxle)** — is located on the right rear side of the transaxle.
- **Noise Filter** — is located on the right front shock tower.
- **Oil Pressure Switch** — is located on the lower right rear section of the engine.
- **Oxygen Sensor** — is located in the exhaust manifold.
- **Power Steering Pressure Switch** — is located on the power steering hydraulic pressure line.
- **Rear Window Defogger Relay** — is located behind the left hand side of the instrument panel.
- **Restart Relay** — is located under the left side of the instrument panel, near the left kick panel.
- **Seatbelt Timer** — is located on the back of the instrument panel cluster.
- **Seatbelt Switch** — is located in the driver's seatbelt.
- **Stop Light Relay** — is located in the rear trunk panel, if so equipped.
- **Throttle Positioner Switch** — is located on the side of the carburetor.
- **Transaxle Gear Switches** — are located on the top rear side of the transaxle.
- **Turn Signal/Hazard Flasher Relay** — is located behind the left hand side of the instrument panel.
- **Upshift Relay** — is located under the left side of the instrument panel, near the left kick panel.
- **Vehicle Speed Sensor** — is located on the side of the transaxle, if so equipped.
- **Windshield Wiper Delay Relay** — is located behind the left hand side of the instrument panel.

STORM

- **A/C Cut Control Unit** — is mounted of top of evaporator housing.
- **A/C Switch** — is located in center of instrument panel.
- **A/C Thermo Switch** — is located in the left front of the engine compartment, near the distributor.
- **Air Bag** — see Supplement Inflatable Restraint (SIR).
- **Assembly Line Diagnostic Link (ALDL)** — is located behind the right side kick panel.
- **Audio Alarm Module** — is located behind the left side kick panel, attached to the junction block.
- **Automatic Transaxle Controller** — is located behind the dash, left of the steering column.
- **Automatic Transaxle Kickdown Switch** — is located on top of the accelerator pedal assembly.
- **Back-Up Lamp Switch** — is located on top center of transaxle.
- **Brake Fluid Switch** — is mounted on brake fluid reservoir.
- **Canister Purge Vacuum Switching Valve** — is located in the rear of the engine compartment, near the bulkhead.
- **Clutch Interrupt Switch** — is located above clutch pedal.
- **Clutch Start Switch** — is located above clutch pedal.
- **Combination Switch** — is located on left side of steering column.

- **Coolant Temperature Sensor** — is located on thermostat housing.
- **Diagnostic Connector** — is located in the right lower kick panel.
- **Diagnostic Energy Reserve Module (DERM)** — is located under center console.
- **Door Switch (left)** — is located in left door jam.
- **Door Switch (right)** — is located in right door jam.
- **Economy Switch** — is located in center of console.
- **EGR Temperature Sensor** — is located in rear of engine compartment, near the bulkhead.
- **EGR Vacuum Switching Valve** — is located in rear of engine compartment.
- **Electronic Thermo Switch** — is located on top of the evaporator housing.
- **Engine Control Module (ECM)** — is located behind the left kick panel.
- **Fan Relay** — is located in the relay box.
- **Fan Switch** — is located behind center of instrument panel.
- **Flasher Unit** — is located behind lower left instrument panel.
- **Fog Lamp Switch** — is located on instrument panel, left of steering column.
- **Fuel Pump Relay** — is located in the relay box.
- **Fuse Block** — is located behind left kick panel.
- **Fuse and Relay Box** — is located in left engine compartment.
- **Horn Relay** — is located in the relay box.
- **Idle Air Control Valve** — is located on the rear of the engine, near the bulkhead.
- **Ignition Switch** — is located on the right steering column.
- **Inhibitor Switch** — is located on top center of transaxle.
- **Intake Air Temperature Sensor** — is located rear of engine compartment, near the bulkhead.
- **Intake Air Vacuum Switching Valve** — is located rear of engine compartment.
- **Intermittent Windshield Wiper Relay** — is located behind lower left of instrument panel.
- **Junction Connector** — is located behind center of instrument panel.
- **Junction Block** — is located behind the left side kick panel.
- **Manifold Absolute Pressure (MAP) Sensor** — is located center of bulkhead.
- **Oil Pressure Switch** — is located right rear corner of engine.
- **Oxygen Sensor** — is located in engine compartment, on exhaust manifold.
- **Parking Brake Switch** — is located on parking brake.
- **Park/Neutral Switch** — is located on top center of transaxle.
- **Power Steering Pressure Switch** — is located on power steering pump.
- **Radiator Fan Thermo Switch** — is located on lower left side of radiator.
- **Rear Defogger Relay** — is located behind left side of instrument panel, in junction block.
- **Relay Box** — in right side of engine compartment, near the strut tower.
- **Safety Belt Switch** — is located on base of driver's safety belt buckle.

- **Shift Interlock Control Module** — is located under the center console, near the gear selector.
- **SIR Arming Sensor** — is located behind center of instrument panel
- **SIR Forward Discriminating Sensor** — is located in engine compartment behind grille.
- **SIR Module** — is located behind steering wheel.
- **SIR Passenger Compartment Sensor** — is located under console assembly.
- **Stop Lamp Switch** — is located above the brake pedal.
- **Throttle Position Sensor** — is located on common chamber of engine.

- **Upshift Indicator Relay** — is located behind the right kick panel.
- **Upshift Indicator Switch** — is located on the transaxle, near the battery.
- **Triple Switch** — is located on the right front of the engine, near the radiator.
- **Vehicle Speed Sensor** — is located on rear of transaxle.
- **Windshield Wiper/Washer Switch** — is located on instrument panel, right of cluster.

WIRING DIAGRAMS

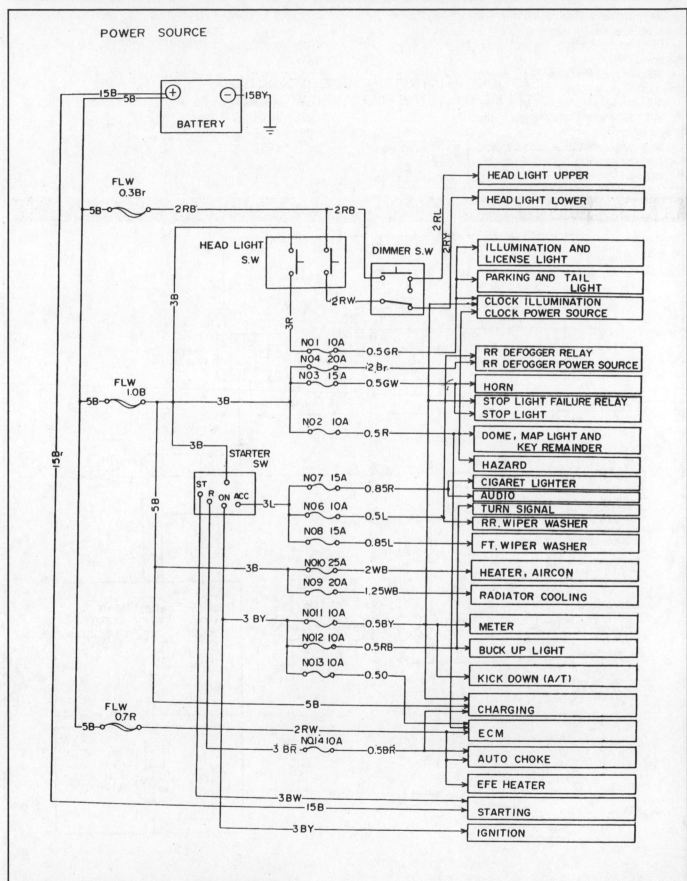

Fig. 34 Fuse block circuitry — 1985-1986 Spectrum

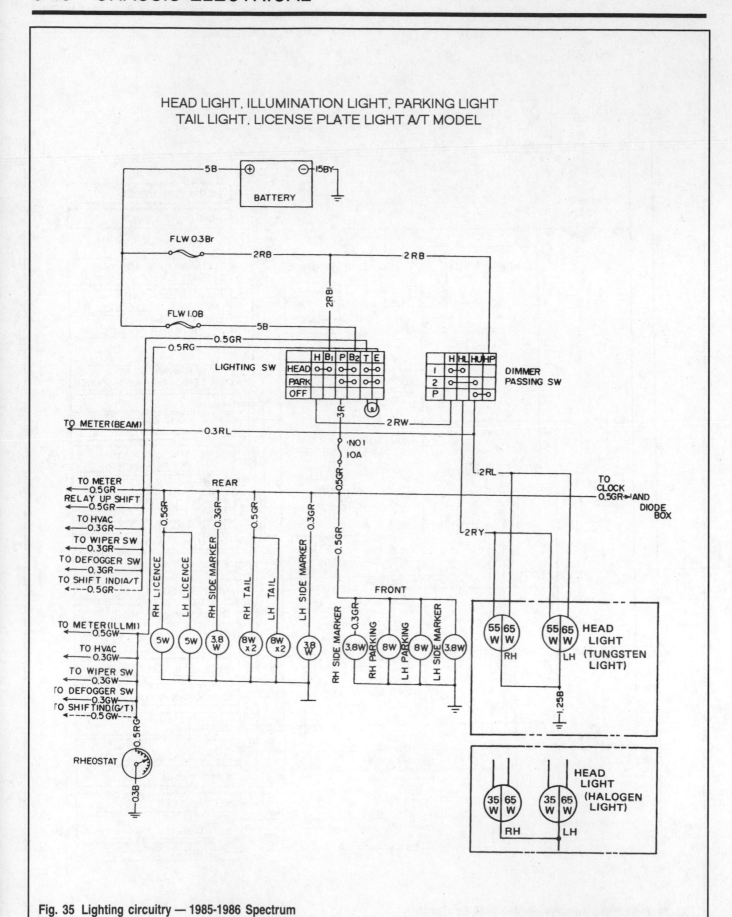

Fig. 35 Lighting circuitry — 1985-1986 Spectrum

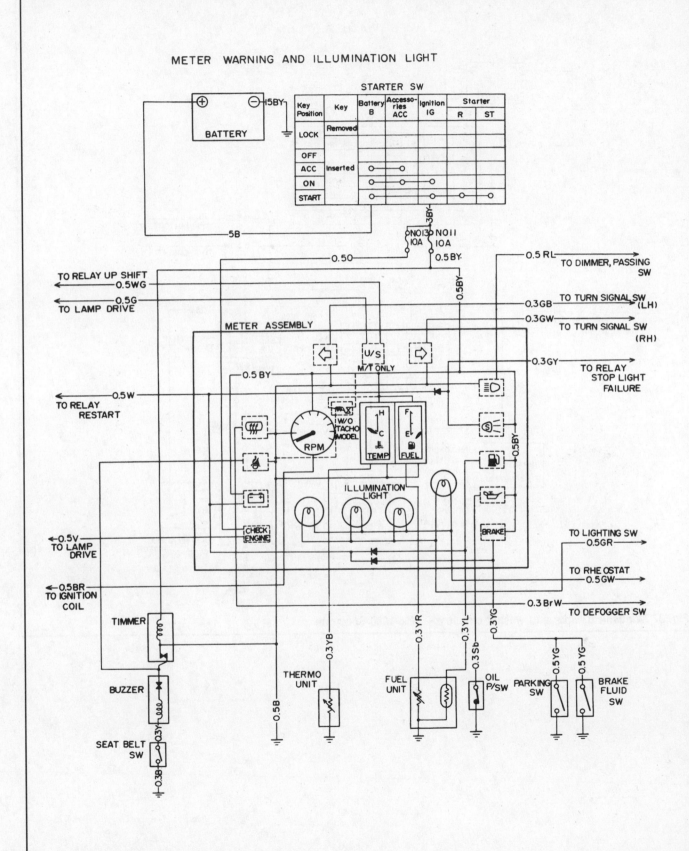

METER WARNING AND ILLUMINATION LIGHT

Key Position	Key	Battery B	Accessories ACC	Ignition IG	Starter	
					R	ST
LOCK	Removed					
OFF						
ACC	Inserted	o——o	o——o			
ON		o——o		o——o		
START		o——o			o——o	o——o

Fig. 36 Meter and warning lamps circuitry — 1985-1986 Spectrum

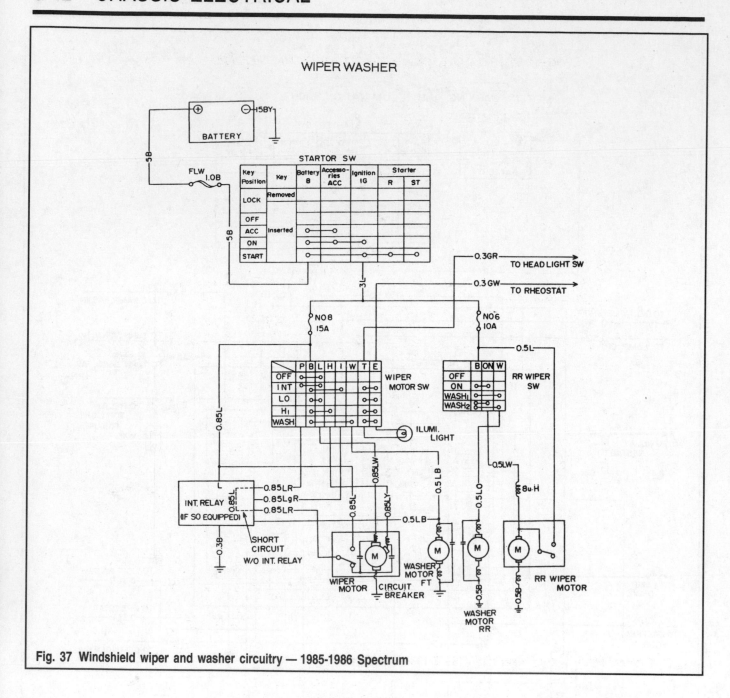

Fig. 37 Windshield wiper and washer circuitry — 1985-1986 Spectrum

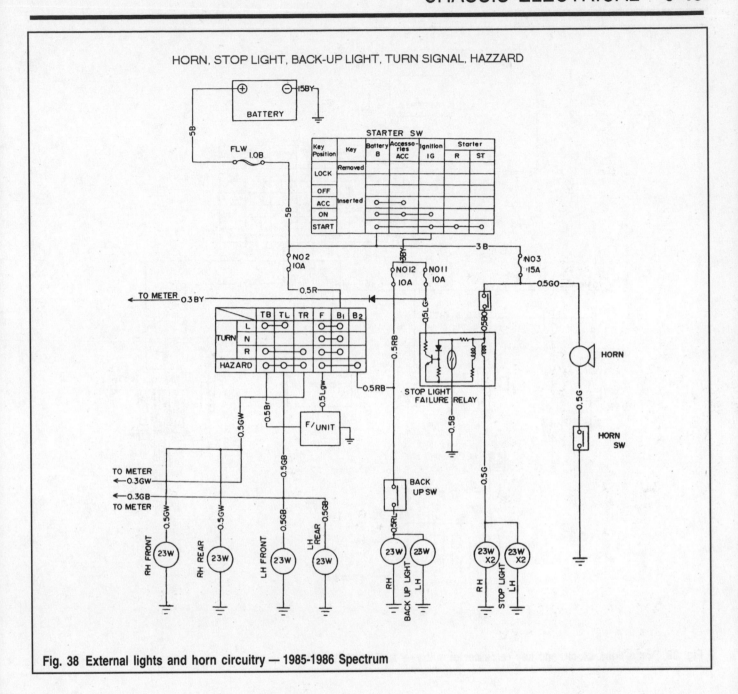

Fig. 38 External lights and horn circuitry — 1985-1986 Spectrum

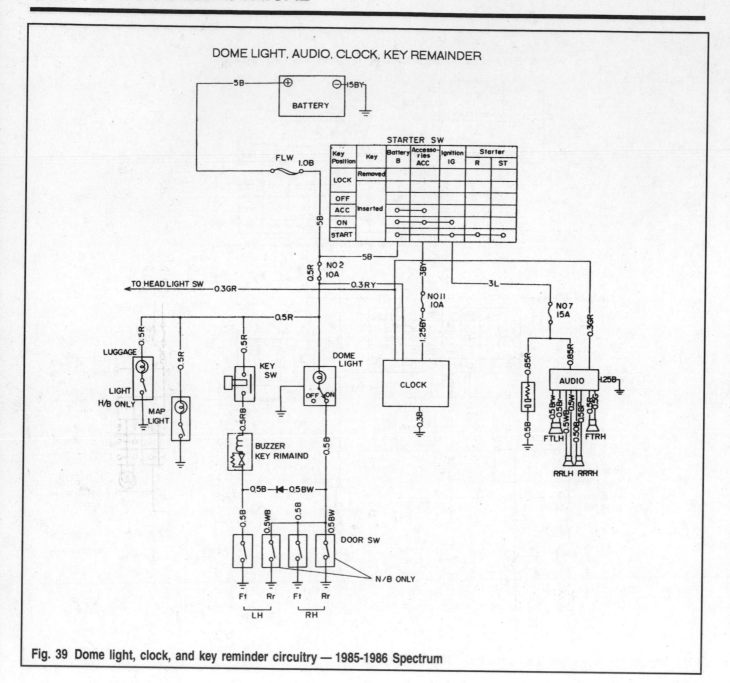

Fig. 39 Dome light, clock, and key reminder circuitry — 1985-1986 Spectrum

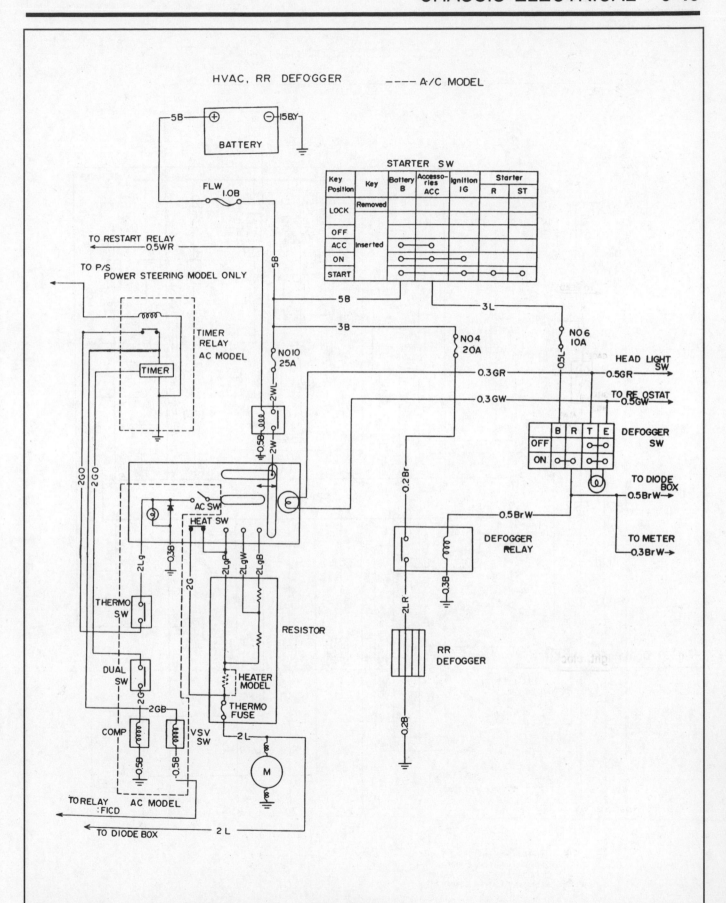

Fig. 40 Heater, A/C and rear deffoger circuitry — 1985-1986 Spectrum

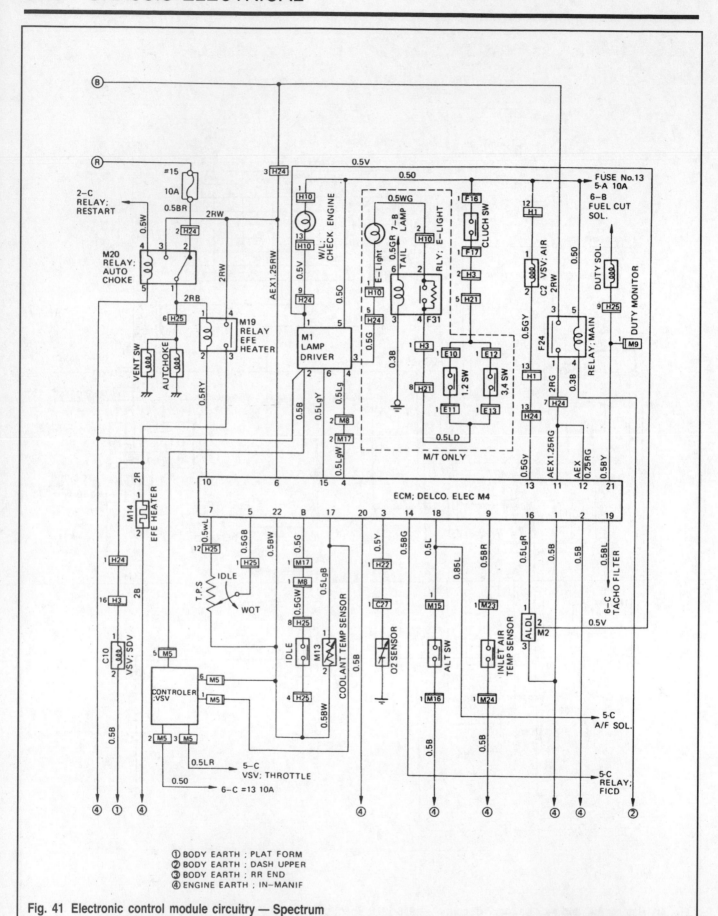

Fig. 41 Electronic control module circuitry — Spectrum

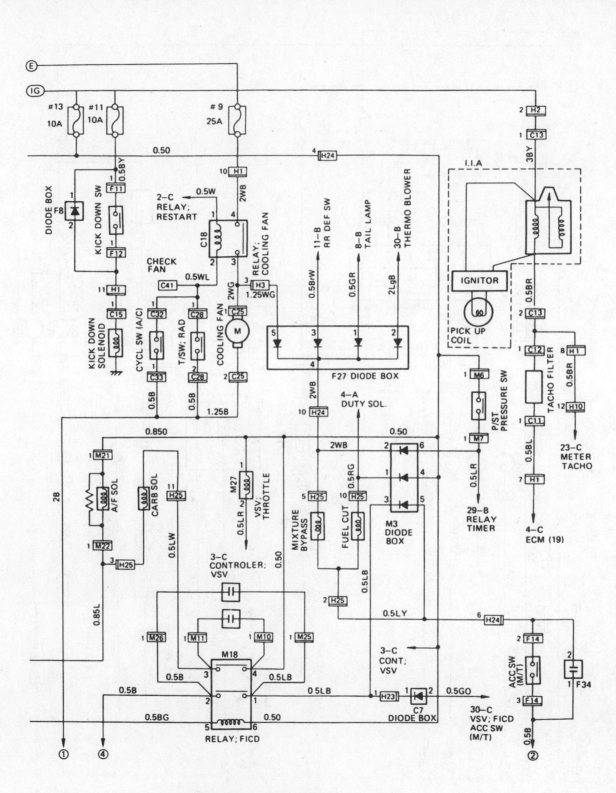

Fig. 42 Cooling fan circuitry — Spectrum

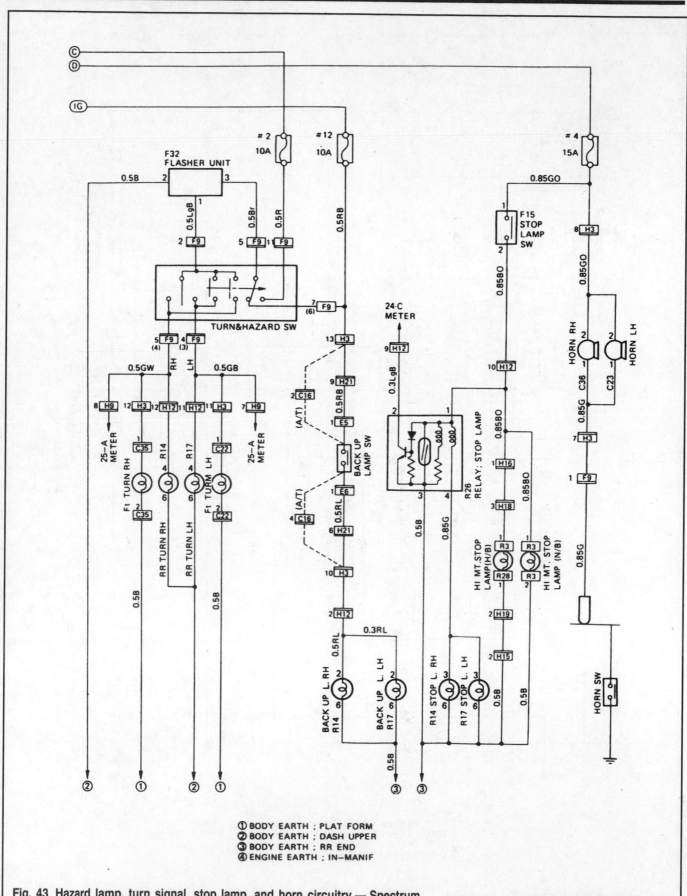

Fig. 43 Hazard lamp, turn signal, stop lamp, and horn circuitry — Spectrum

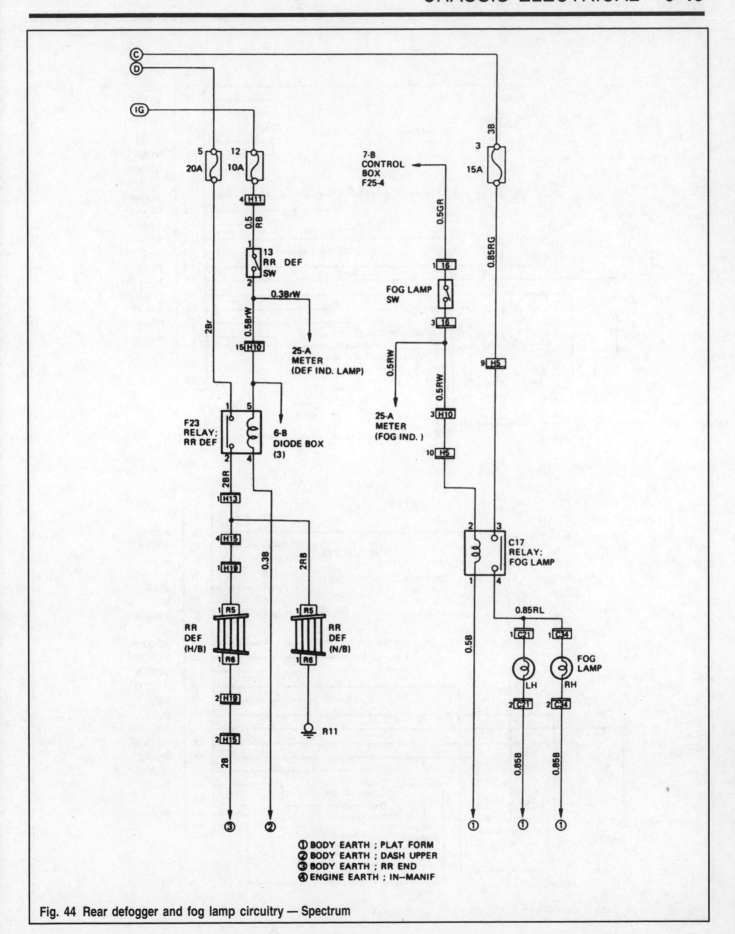

Fig. 44 Rear defogger and fog lamp circuitry — Spectrum

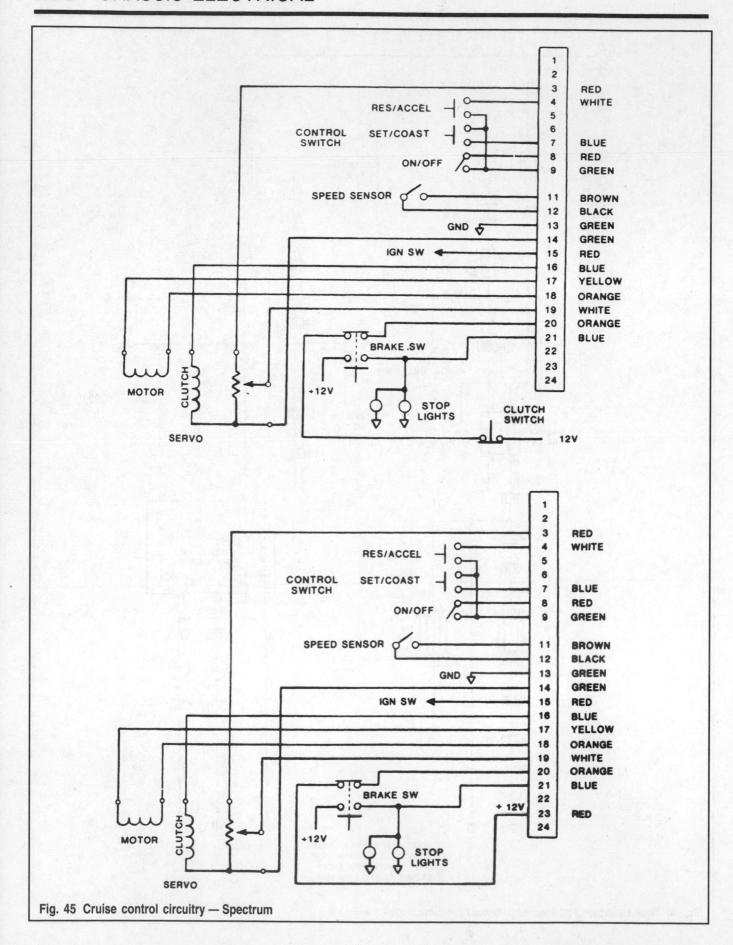

Fig. 45 Cruise control circuitry — Spectrum

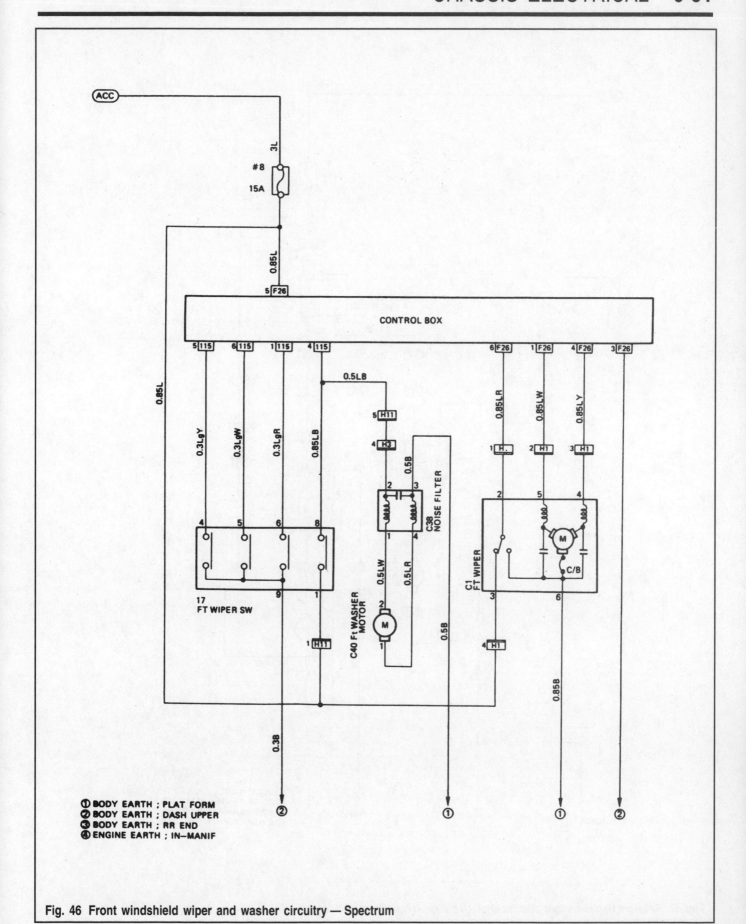

Fig. 46 Front windshield wiper and washer circuitry — Spectrum

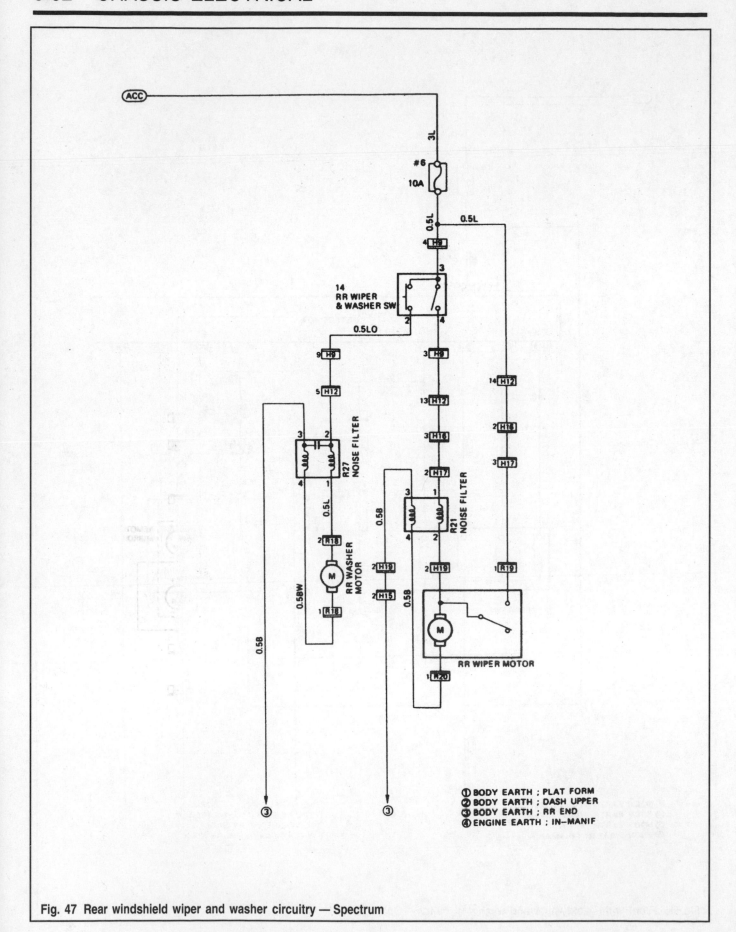

Fig. 47 Rear windshield wiper and washer circuitry — Spectrum

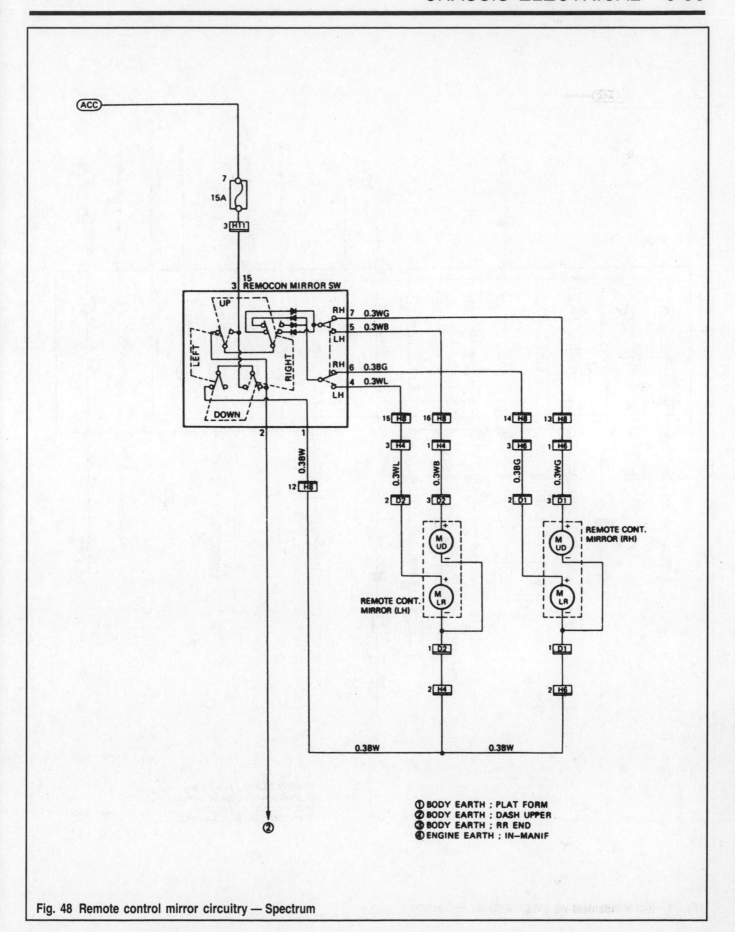

Fig. 48 Remote control mirror circuitry — Spectrum

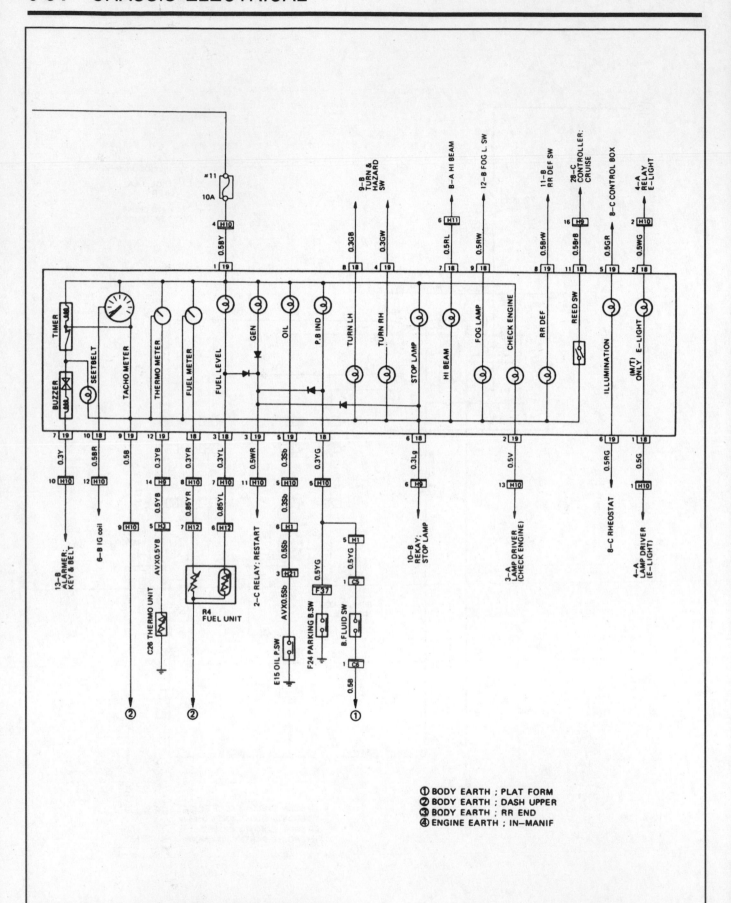

Fig. 49 Meter and warning lamps circuitry — Spectrum

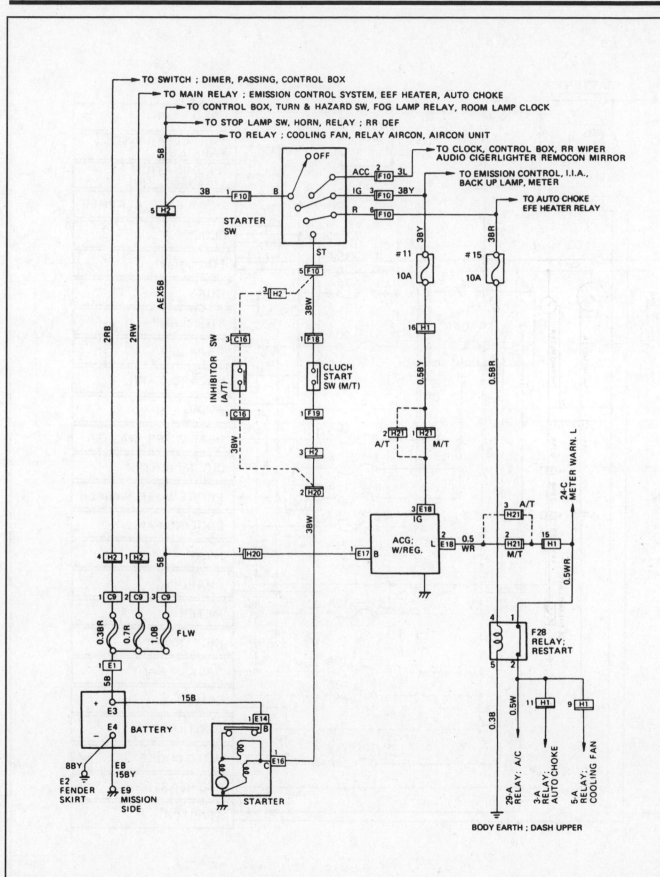

Fig. 50 Starting system circuitry — Spectrum

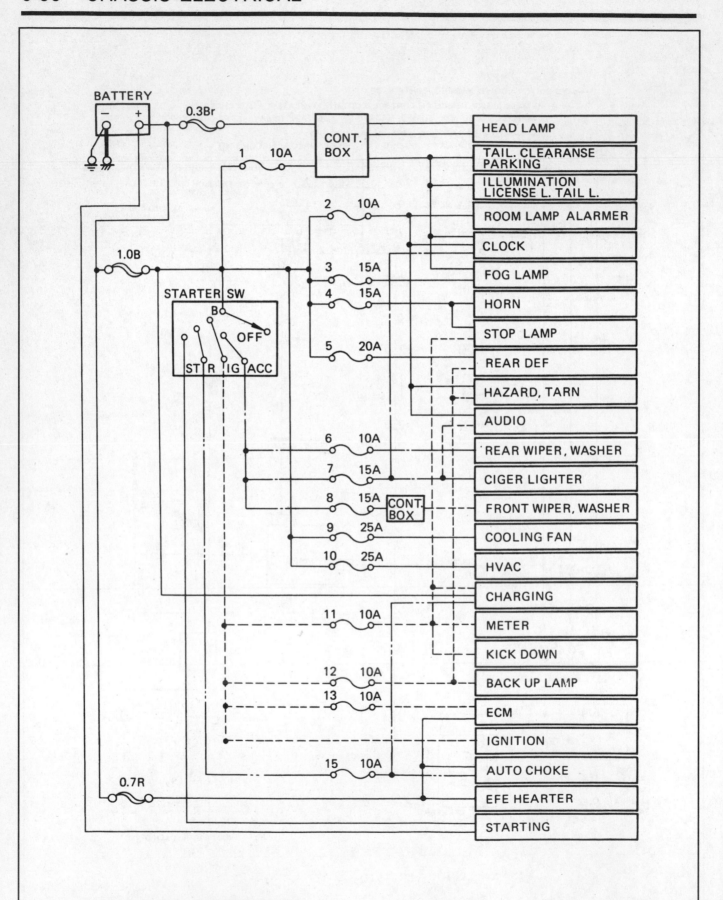

Fig. 51 Fuse block circuitry — 1987-1989 Spectrum

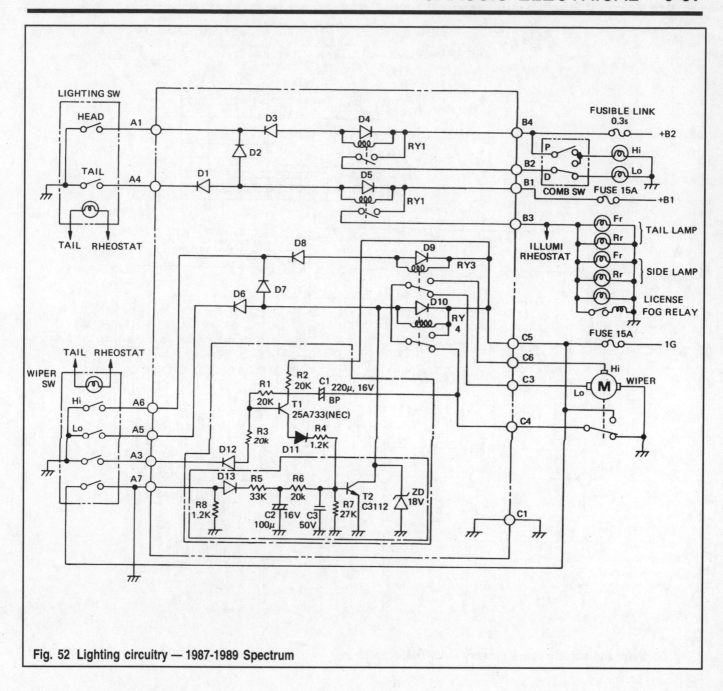

Fig. 52 Lighting circuitry — 1987-1989 Spectrum

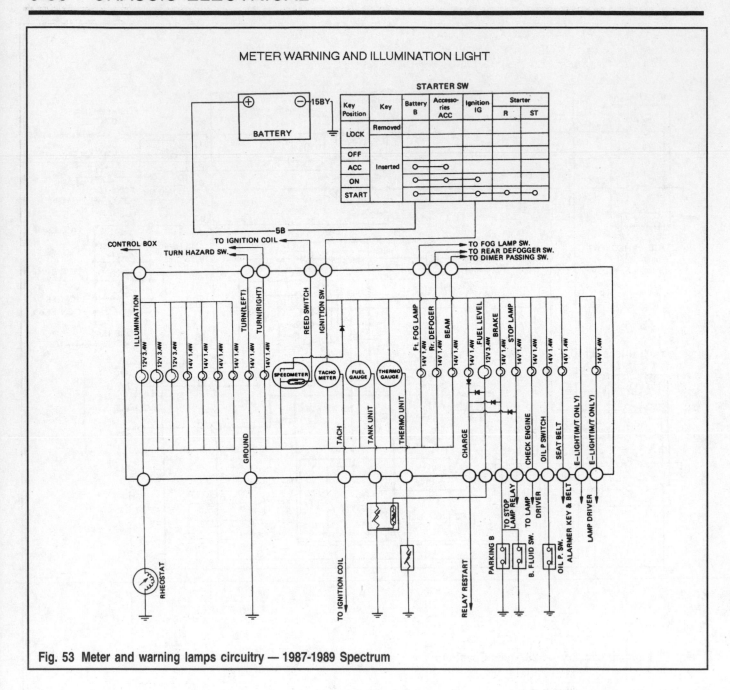

Fig. 53 Meter and warning lamps circuitry — 1987-1989 Spectrum

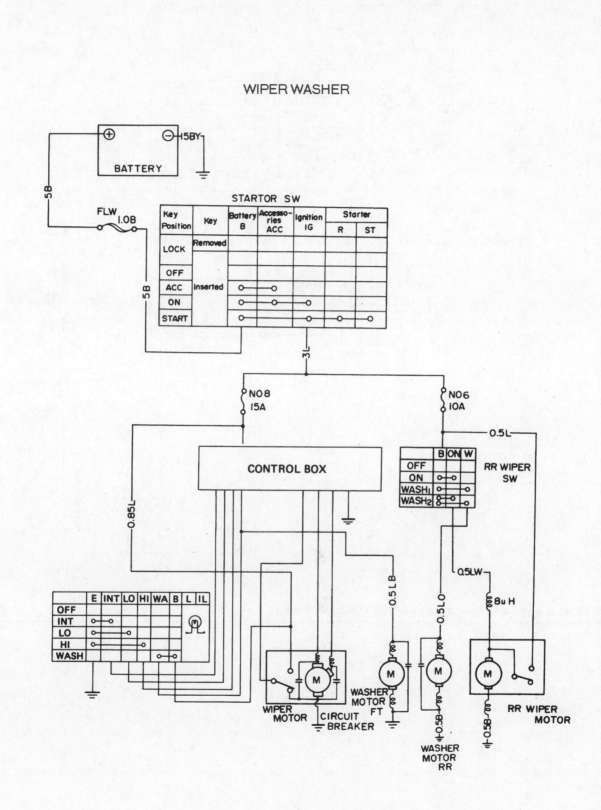

Fig. 54 Windshield wiper and washer circuitry — 1987-1989 Spectrum

HORN, STOPLIGHT, BACKUP LIGHT, TURN SIGNAL, HAZZARD

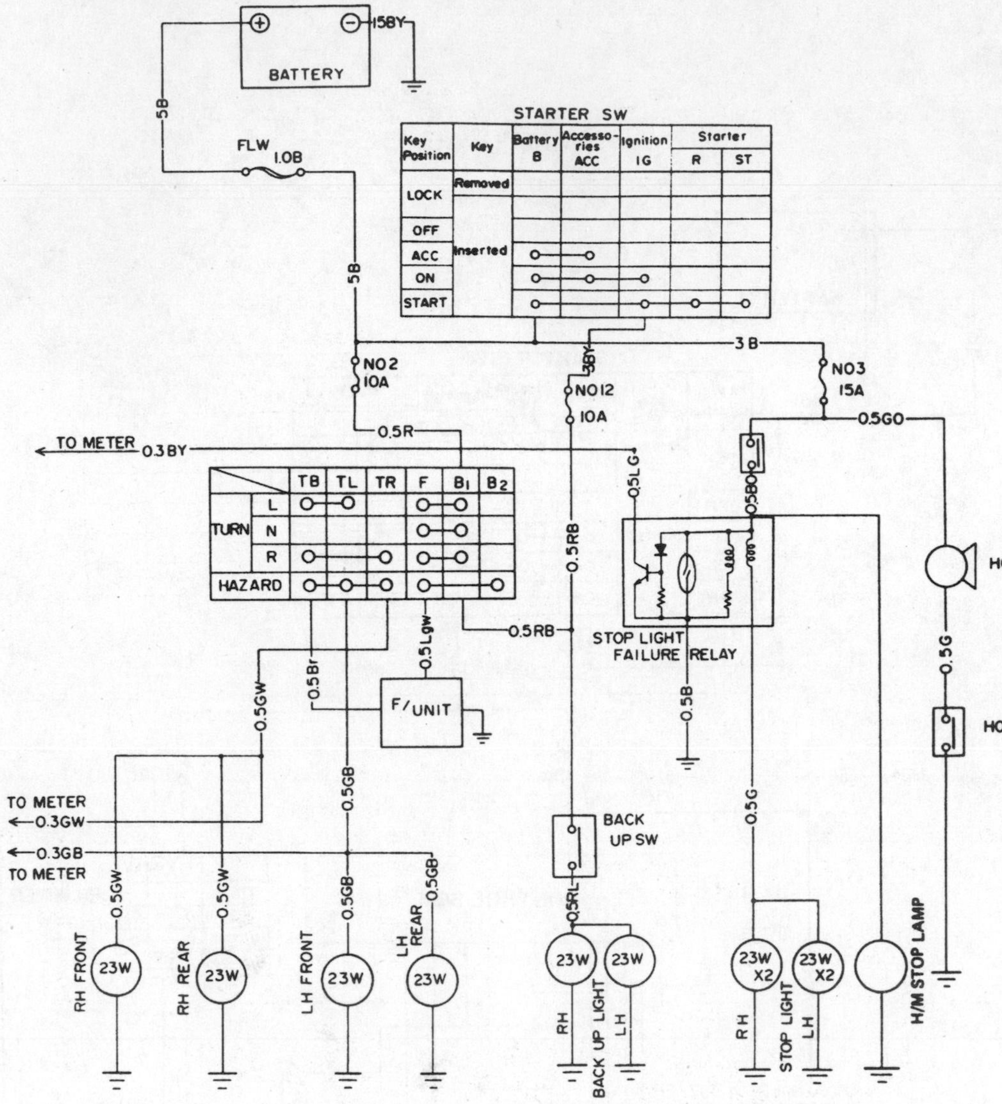

STARTER SW

Key Position	Key	Battery B	Accessories ACC	Ignition IG	Starter R	Starter ST
LOCK	Removed					
OFF						
ACC	Inserted	o——o				
ON		o——o	o			
START		o		o——o	o	

TURN

		TB	TL	TR	F	B_1	B_2
L		o——o			o——o		
N					o		
R		o		o——o	o		
HAZARD		o——o——o			o	o——o	o

F/UNIT

STOP LIGHT FAILURE RELAY

BACK UP SW

HORN

HORN SW

RH FRONT 0.5GW 23W

RH REAR 0.5GW 23W

LH FRONT 0.5GB 23W

LH REAR 0.5GB 23W

BACK UP LIGHT RH 23W LH 23W

STOP LIGHT RH 23W X2 LH 23W X2

H/M STOP LAMP

Fig. 55 External lights and horn circuitry — 1987-1989 Spectrum

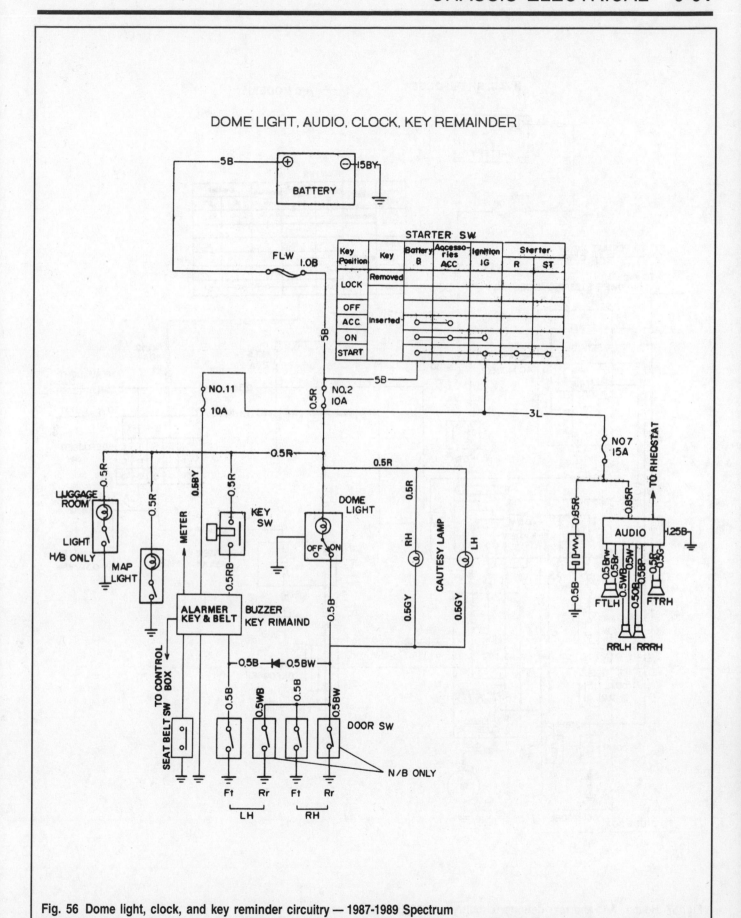

Fig. 56 Dome light, clock, and key reminder circuitry — 1987-1989 Spectrum

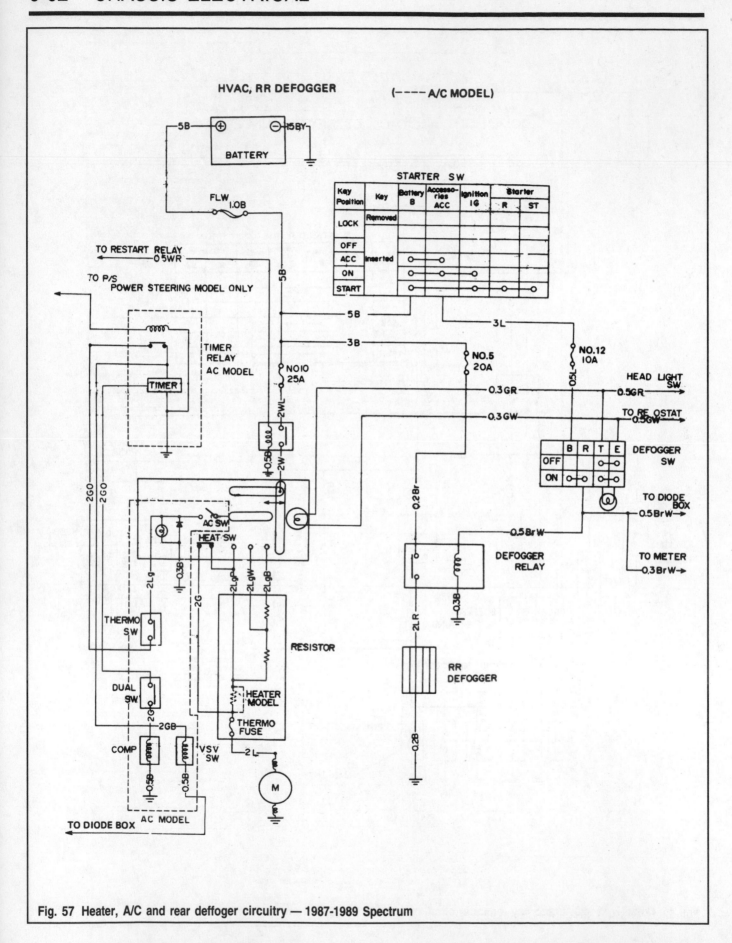

Fig. 57 Heater, A/C and rear deffoger circuitry — 1987-1989 Spectrum

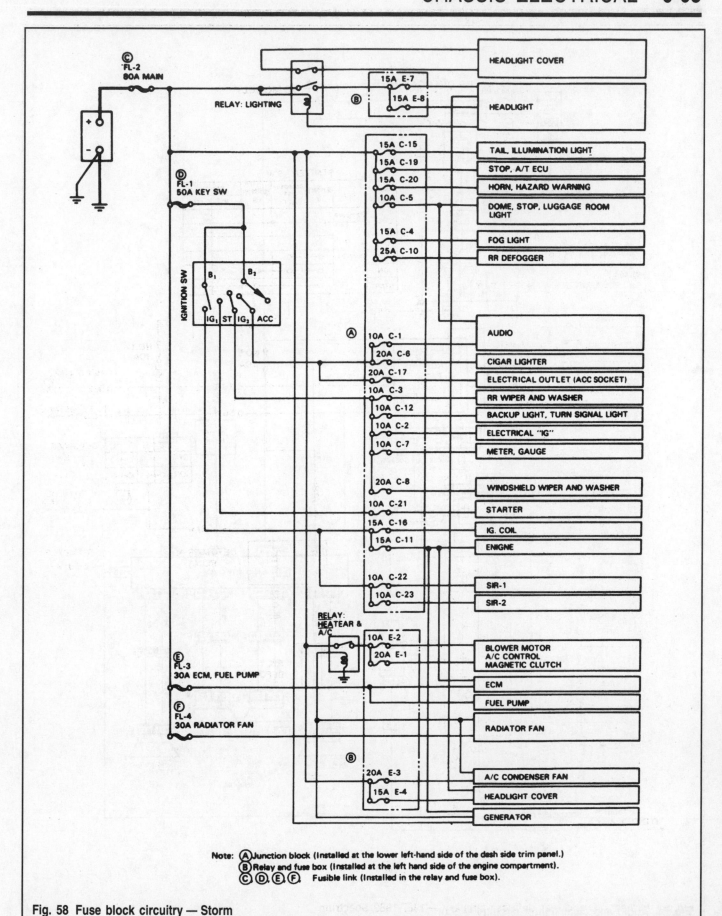

Fig. 58 Fuse block circuitry — Storm

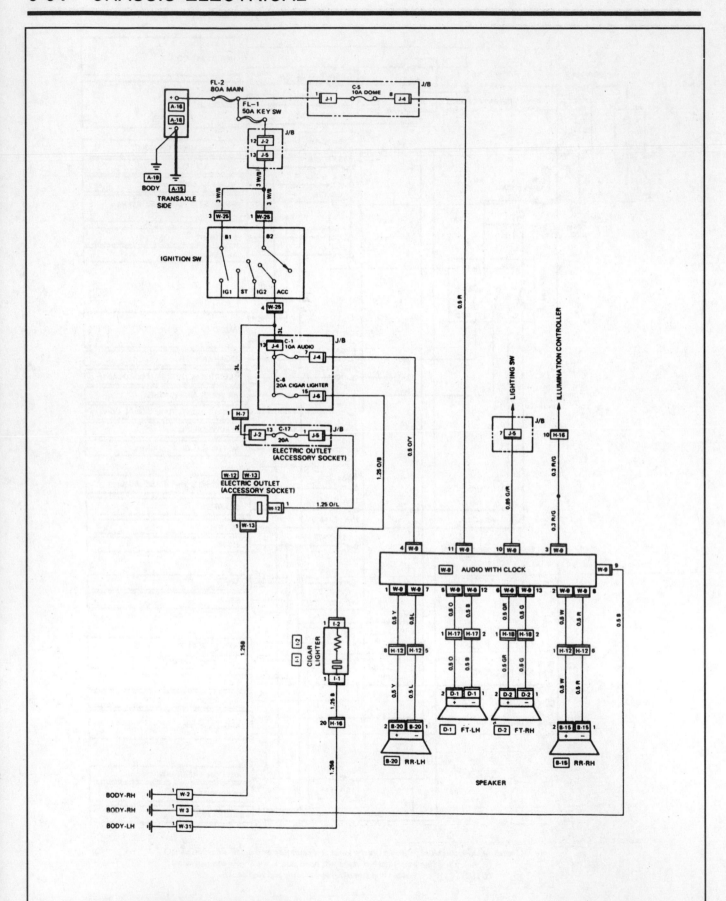

Fig. 59 Audio and cigar lighter circuitry — Storm

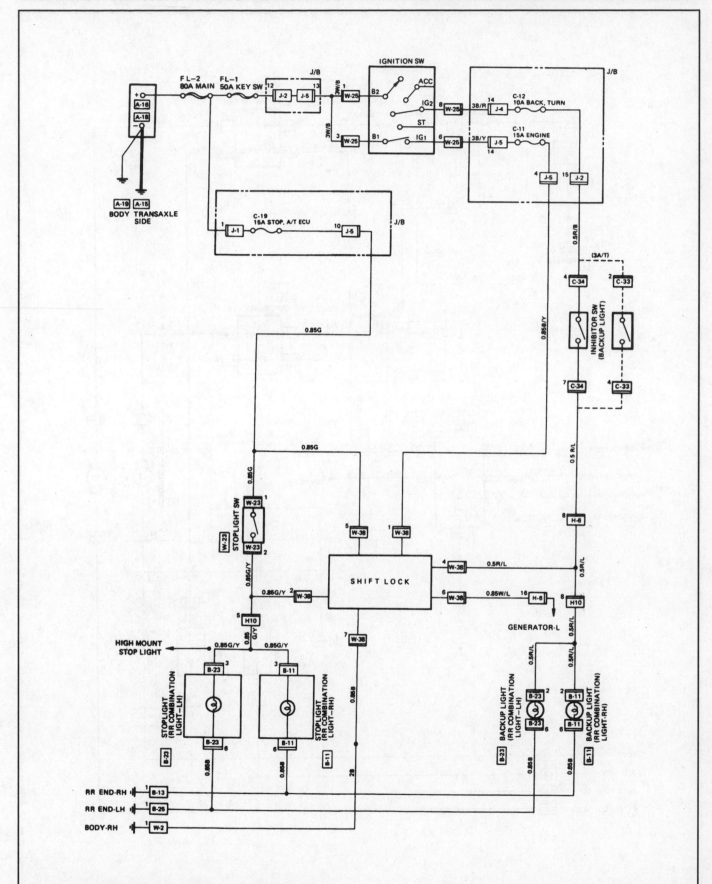

Fig. 60 Automatic transaxle shift lock circuitry — Storm

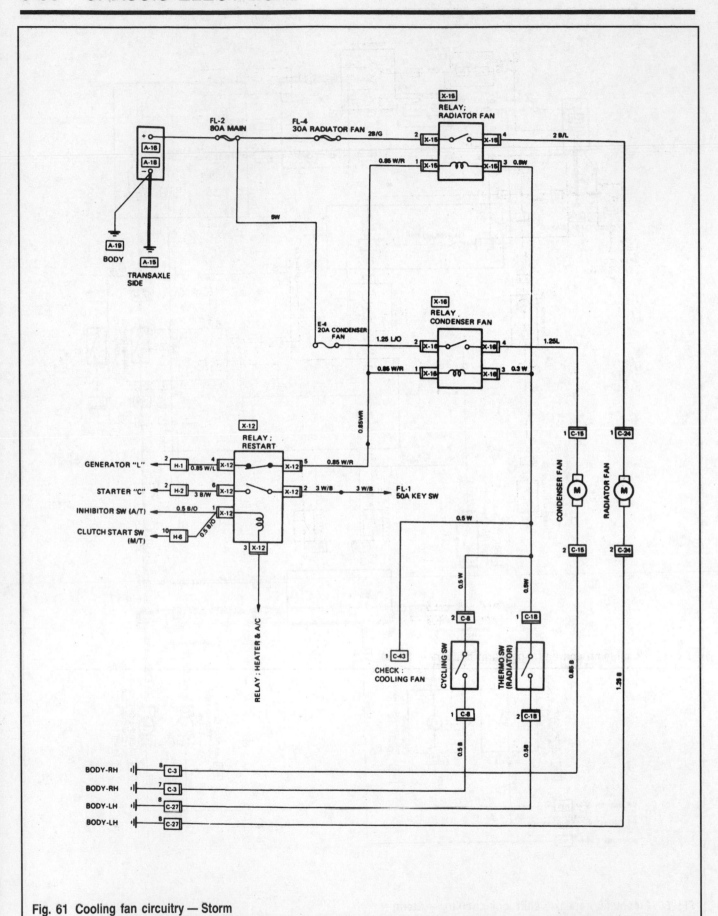

Fig. 61 Cooling fan circuitry — Storm

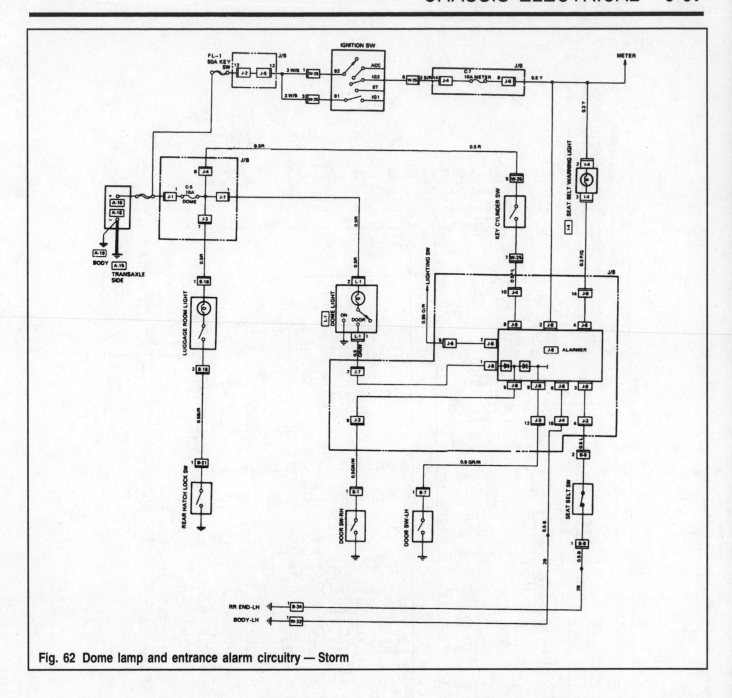

Fig. 62 Dome lamp and entrance alarm circuitry — Storm

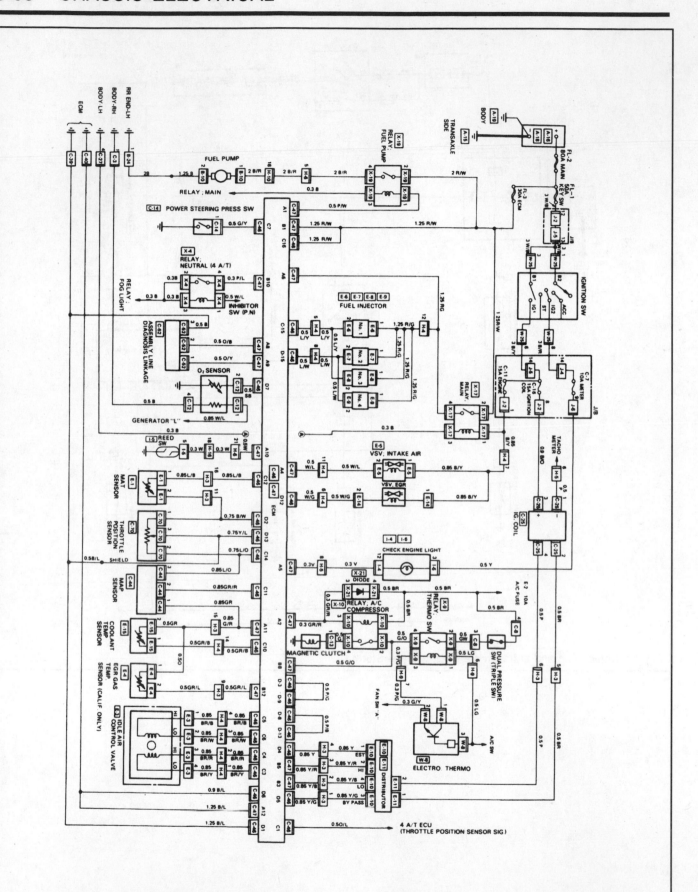

Fig. 63 DOHC engine control module circuitry — Storm

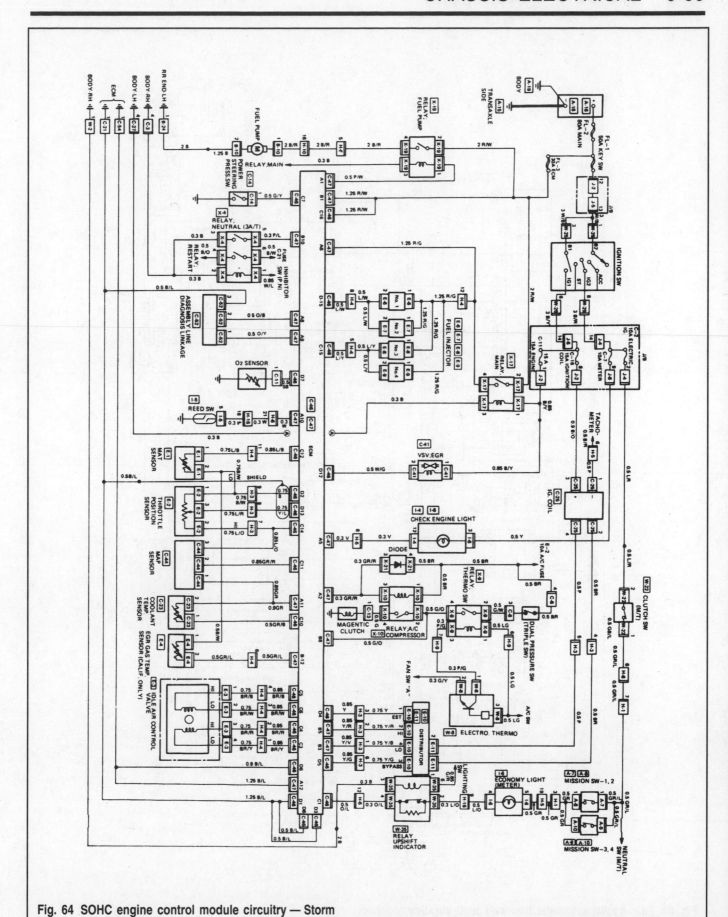

Fig. 64 SOHC engine control module circuitry — Storm

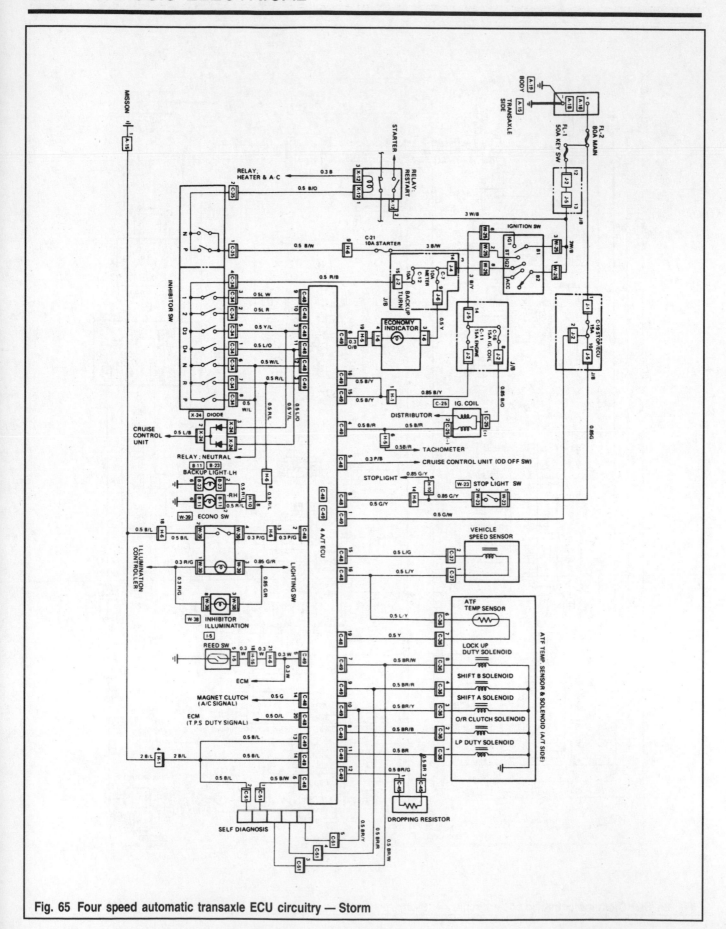

Fig. 65 Four speed automatic transaxle ECU circuitry — Storm

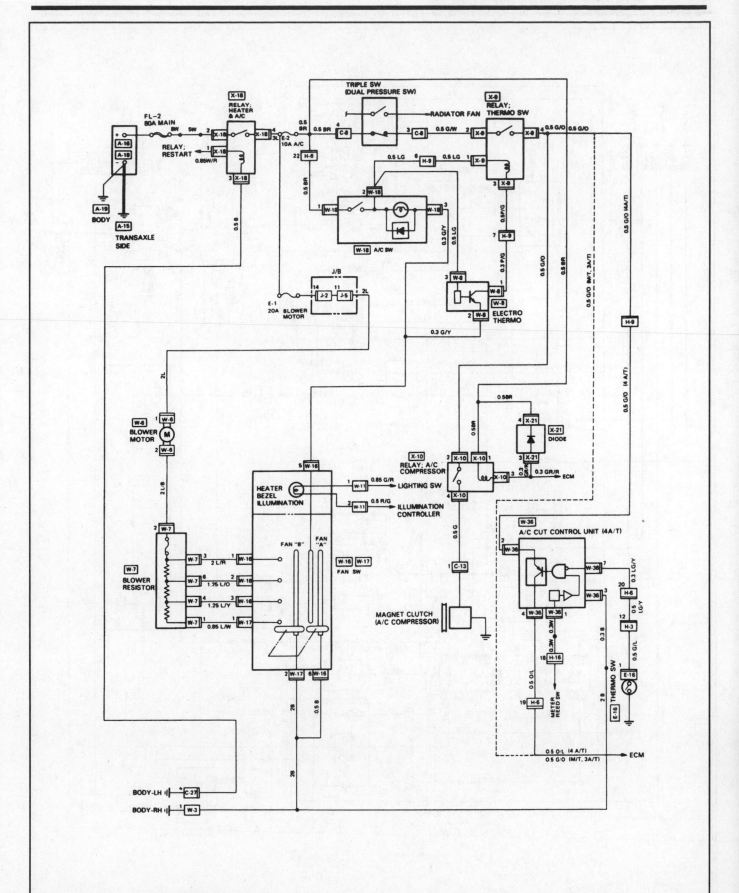

Fig. 66 Heating and A/C circuitry — Storm

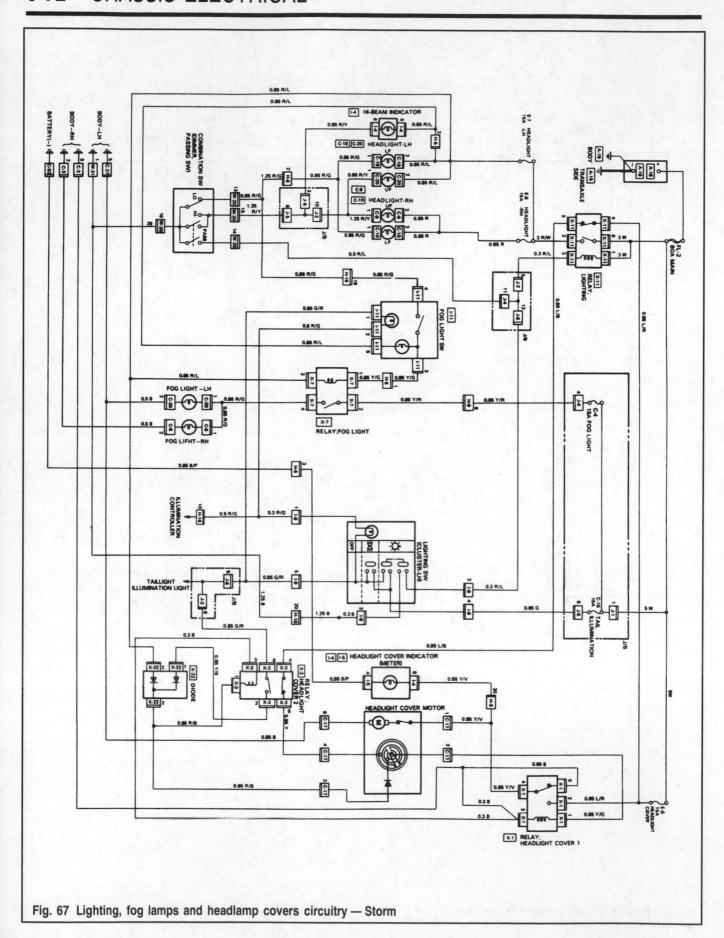

Fig. 67 Lighting, fog lamps and headlamp covers circuitry — Storm

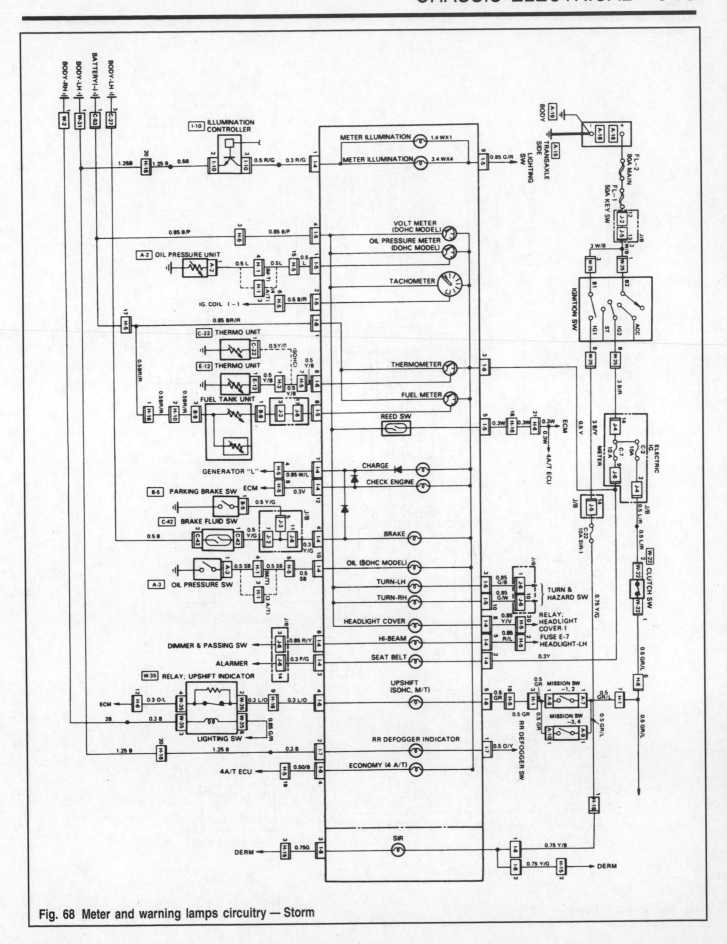

Fig. 68 Meter and warning lamps circuitry — Storm

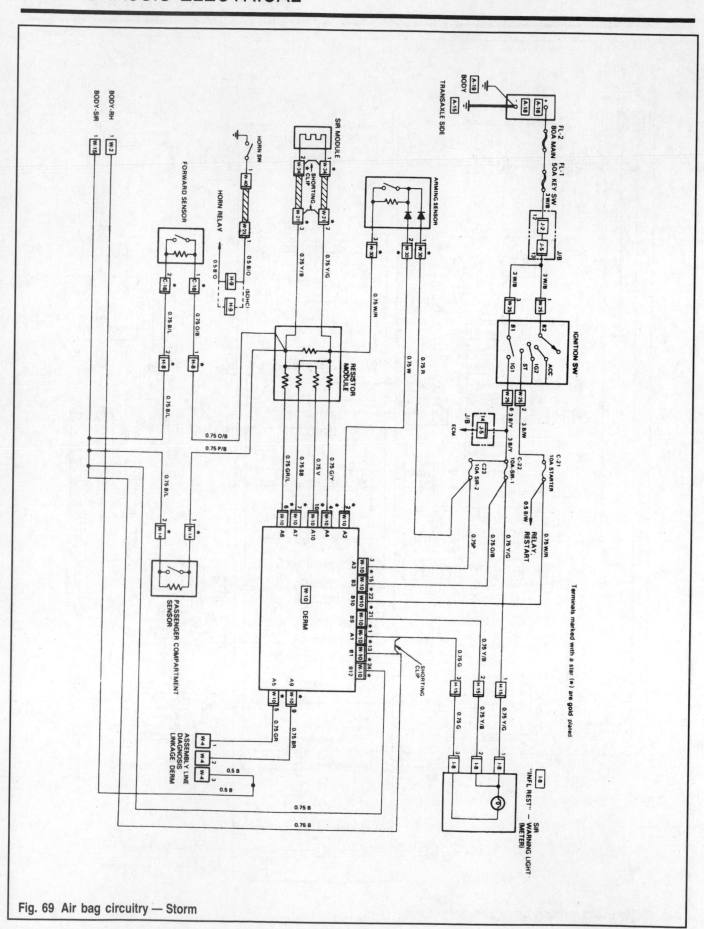

Fig. 69 Air bag circuitry — Storm

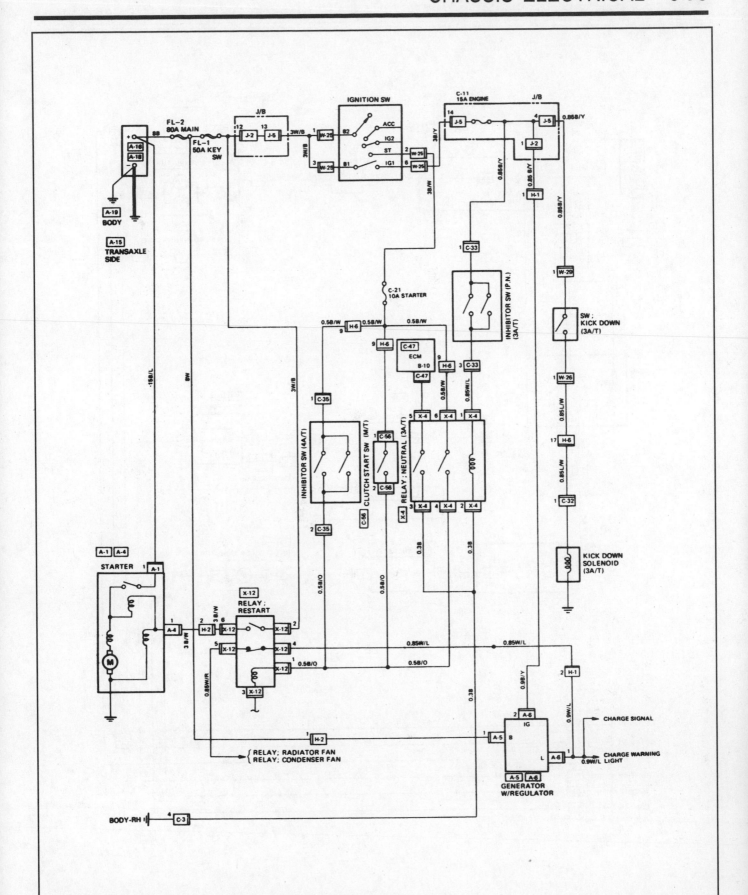

Fig. 70 Starter, generator and power source circuitry — Storm

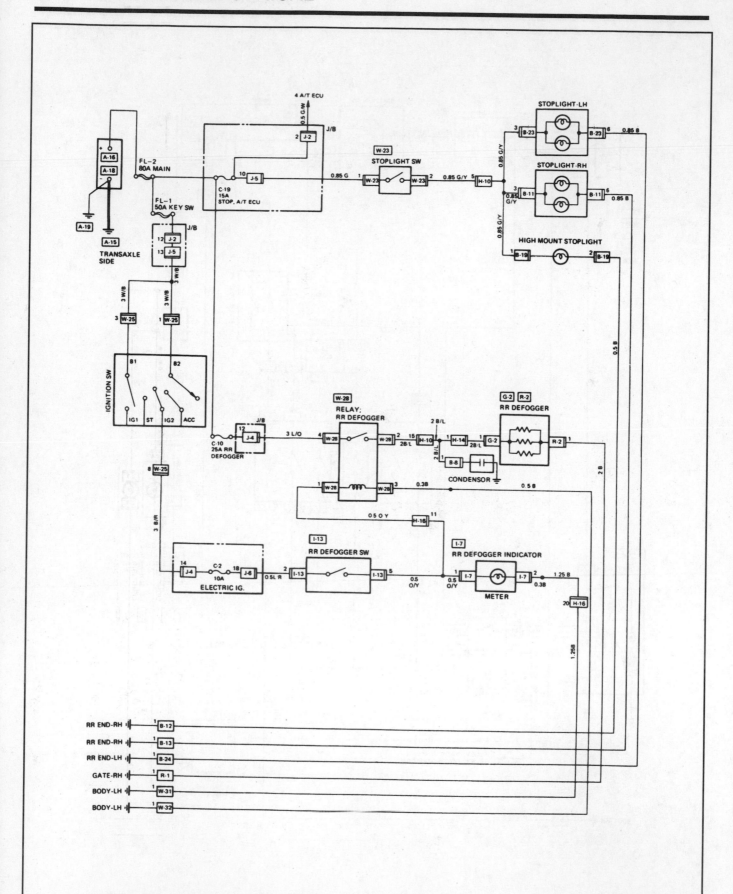

Fig. 71 Stoplamps and rear defogger circuitry — Storm

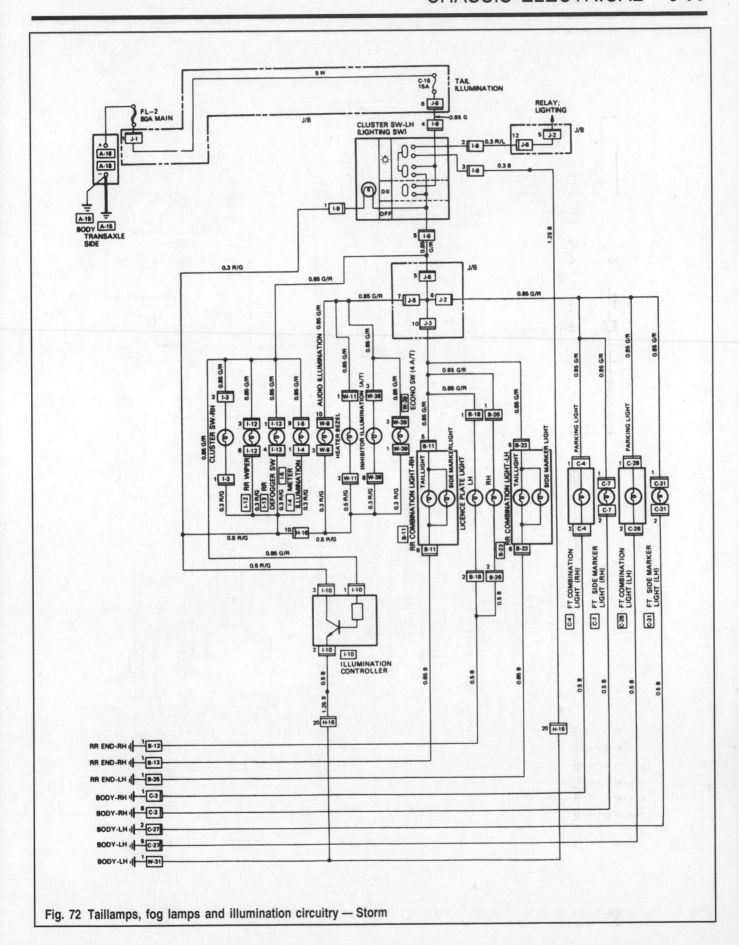

Fig. 72 Taillamps, fog lamps and illumination circuitry — Storm

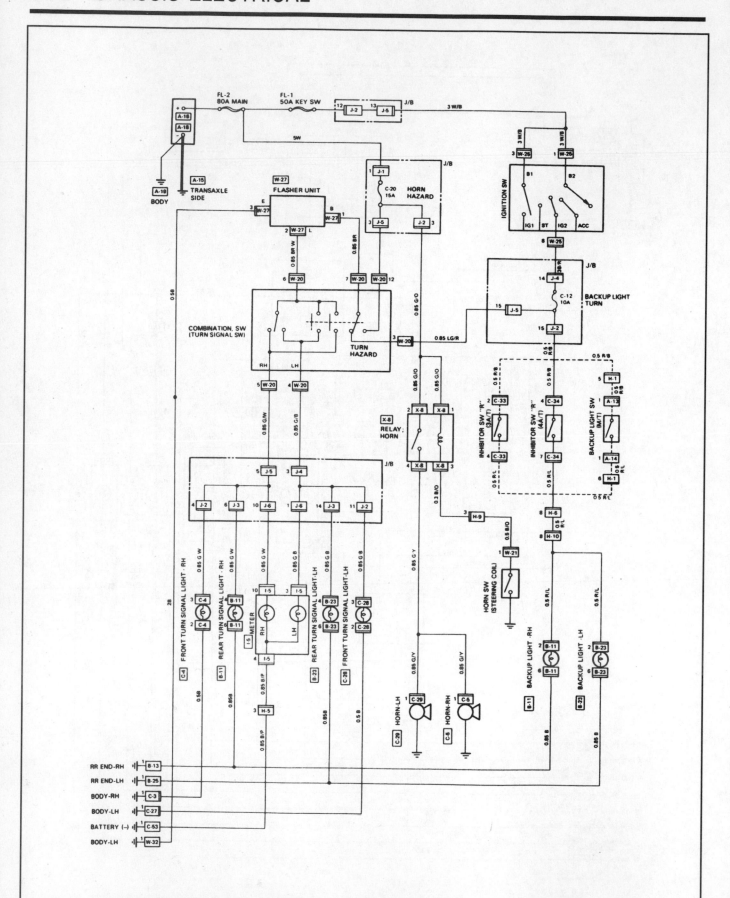

Fig. 73 Turn signals, hazard lamps, backup lamps and horn circuitry — Storm

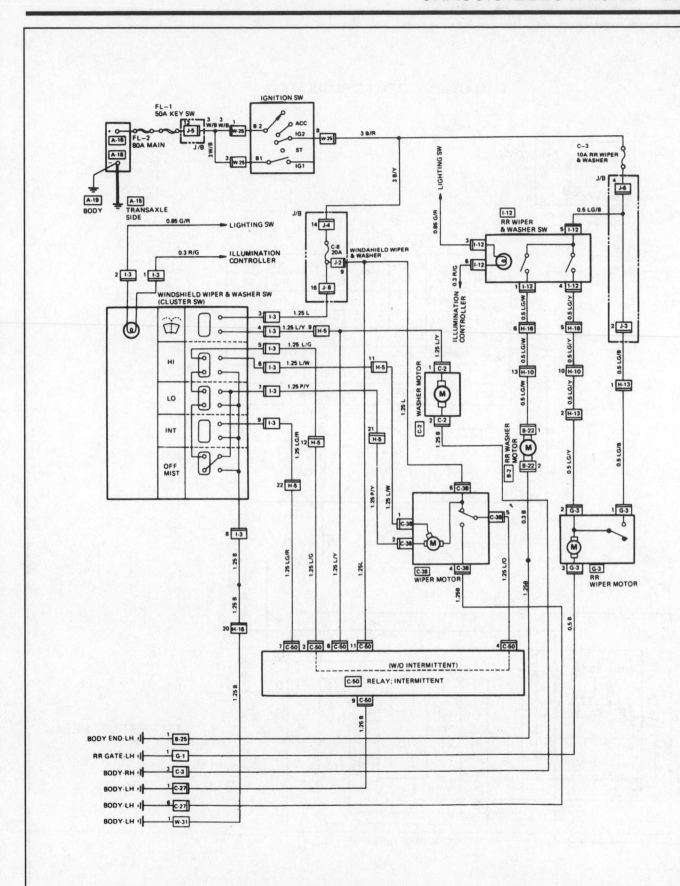

Fig. 74 Front and rear windshield wiper and washer circuitry — Storm

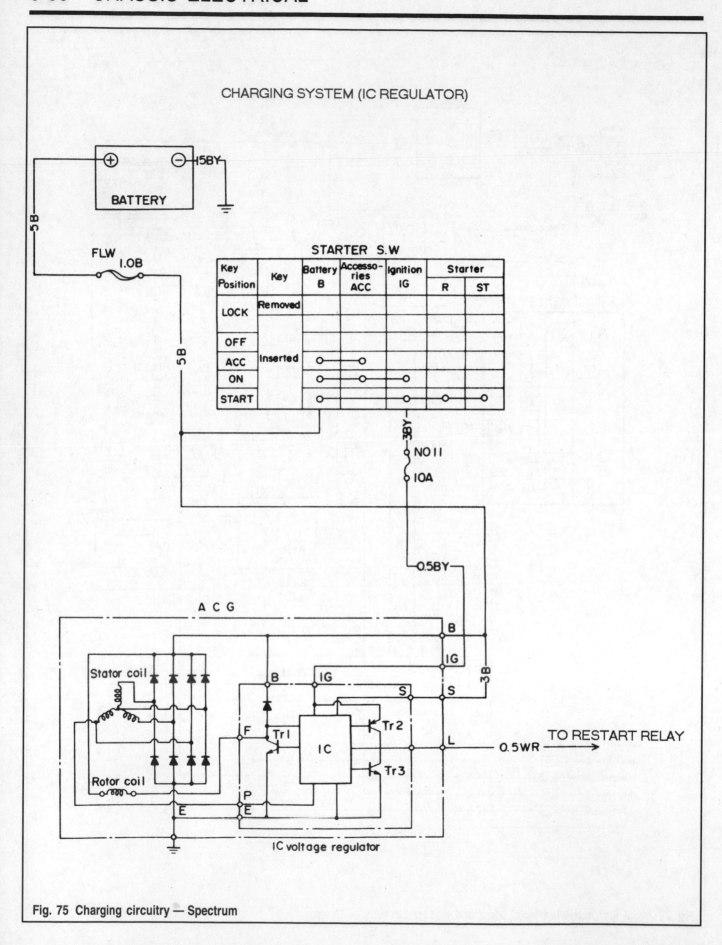

Fig. 75 Charging circuitry — Spectrum

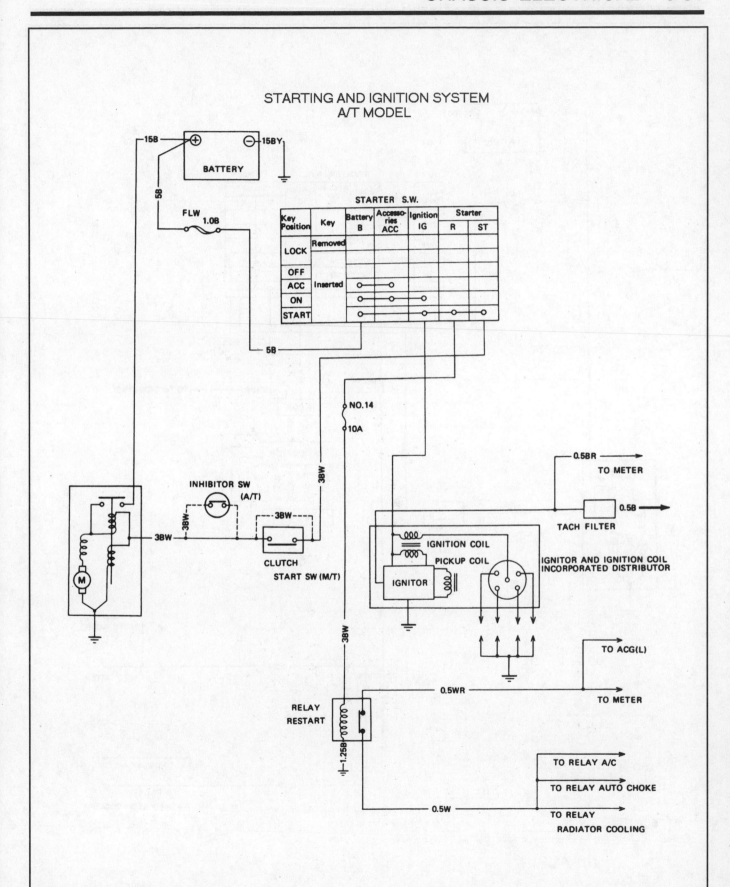

**STARTING AND IGNITION SYSTEM
A/T MODEL**

STARTER S.W.

Key Position	Key	Battery B	Accessories ACC	Ignition IG	Starter	
					R	ST
LOCK	Removed					
OFF						
ACC	Inserted	○——○				
ON		○——○	○			
START		○——○	○	○——○		

Fig. 76 Ignition circuitry — Spectrum

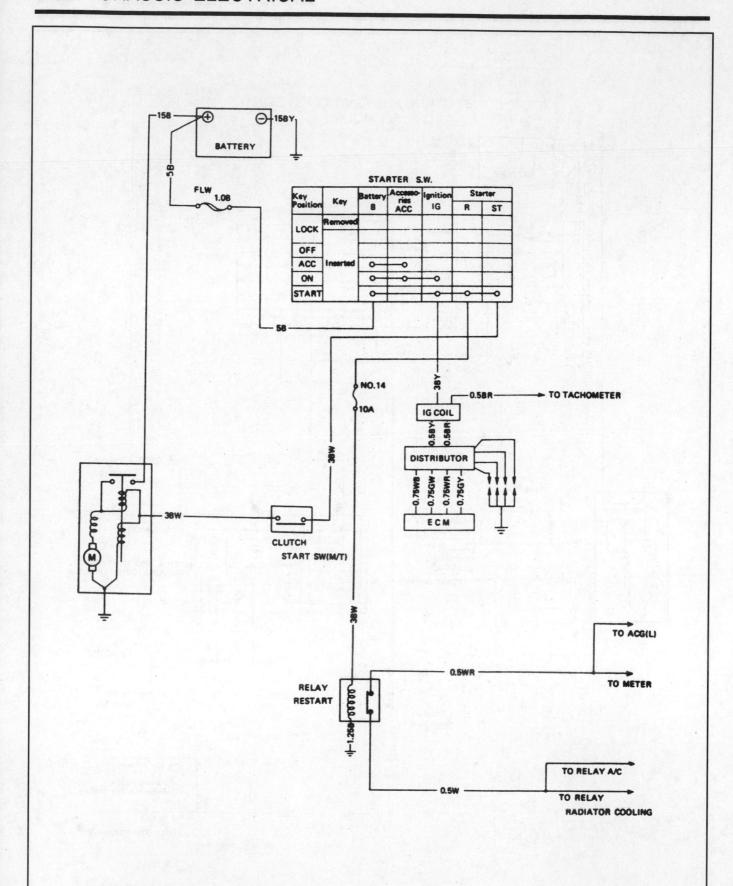

Fig. 77 Starting and ignition system circuitry — 1987-1989 Spectrum Turbo

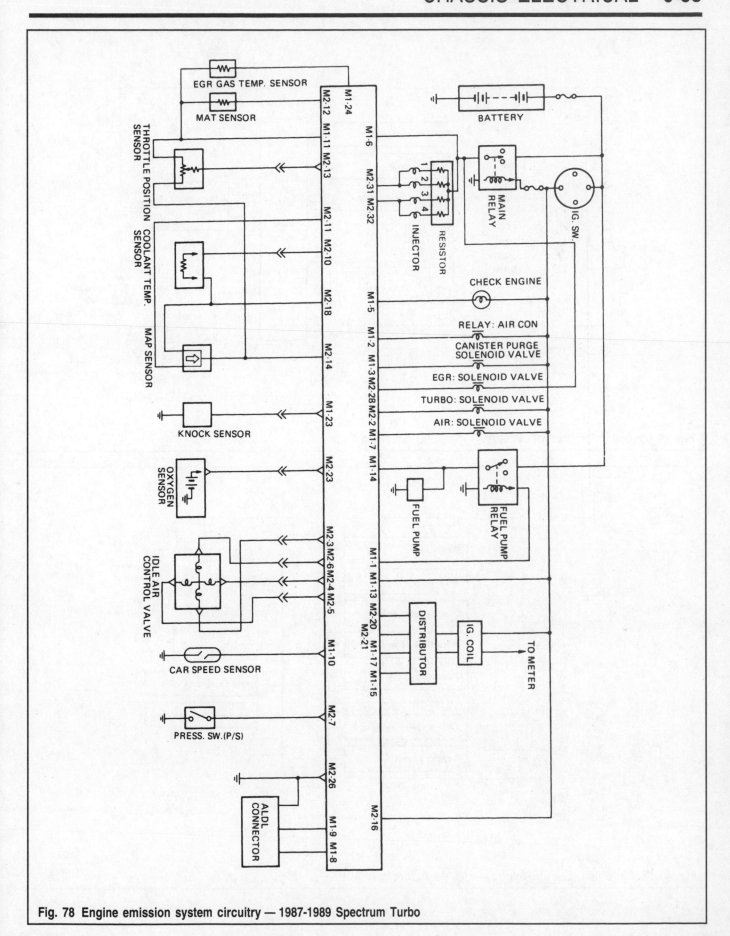

Fig. 78 Engine emission system circuitry — 1987-1989 Spectrum Turbo

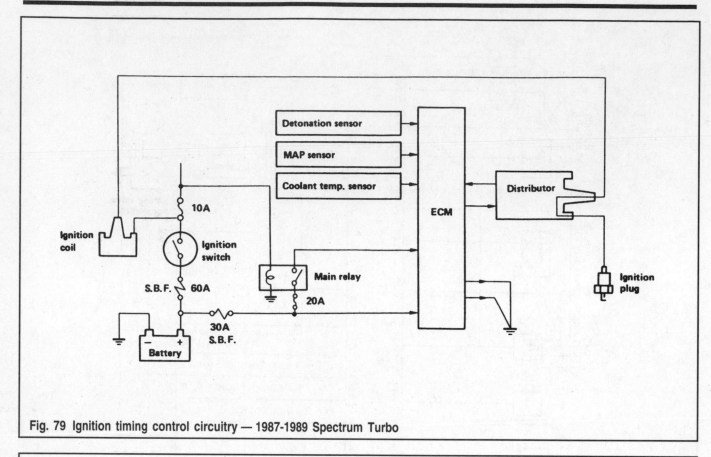

Fig. 79 Ignition timing control circuitry — 1987-1989 Spectrum Turbo

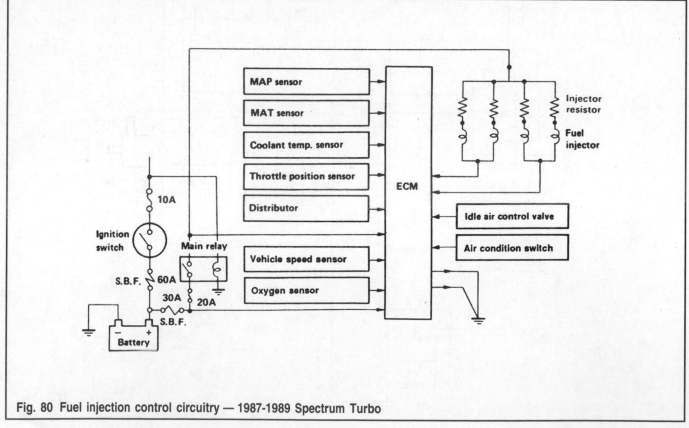

Fig. 80 Fuel injection control circuitry — 1987-1989 Spectrum Turbo

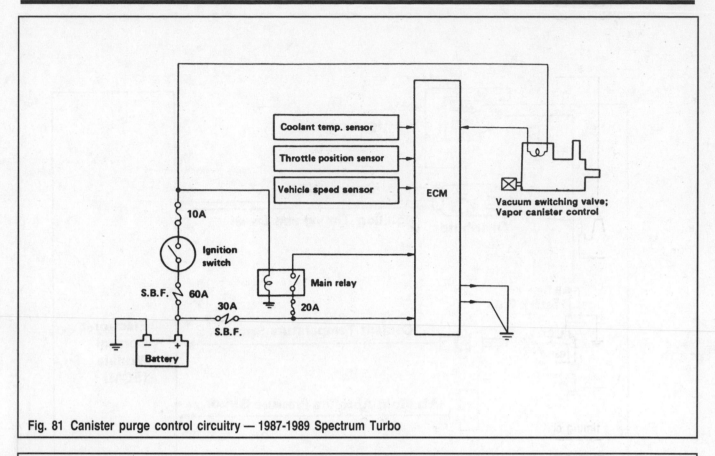

Fig. 81 Canister purge control circuitry — 1987-1989 Spectrum Turbo

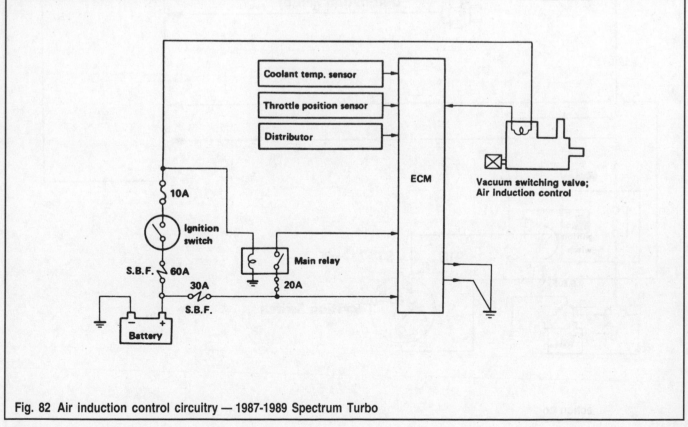

Fig. 82 Air induction control circuitry — 1987-1989 Spectrum Turbo

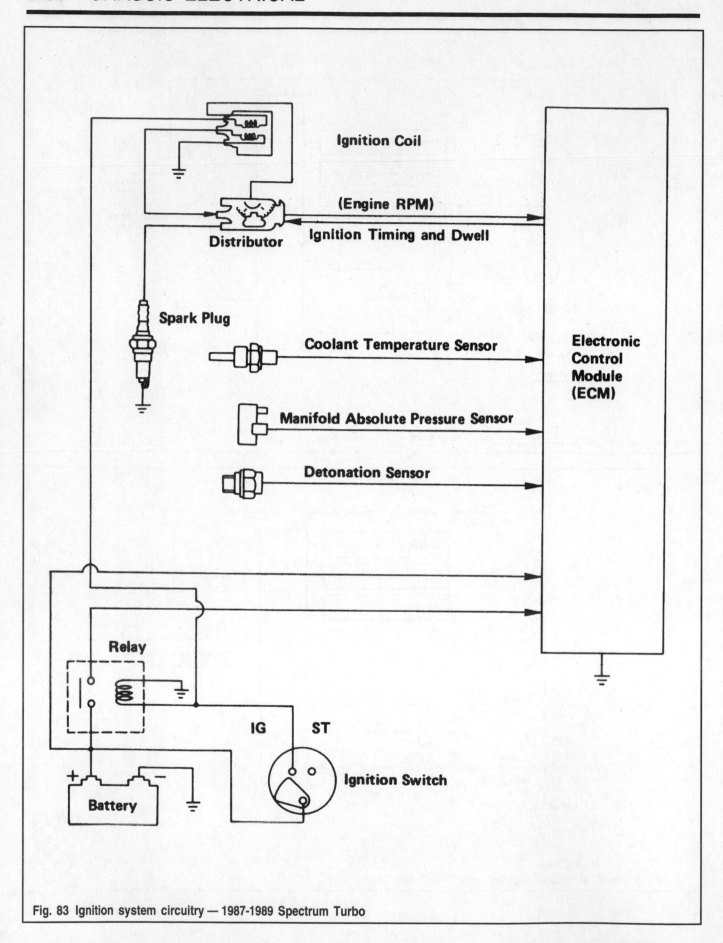

Fig. 83 Ignition system circuitry — 1987-1989 Spectrum Turbo

7

DRIVE TRAIN

MANUAL TRANSAXLE

Identification

The manual transaxle used on the Spectrum and the Storm is the Isuzu-built 76mm five speed manual unit. All forward gears on the 76mm unit are in constant mesh. The reverse gear uses a sliding idler gear arrangement. The final output gear is an integral part of the output shaft. It turns the ring gear and the differential assembly, which turns the drive axle shaft to power the front wheels.

The transaxle uses a cable to control the clutch. The cable runs from the pedal through two brackets in the rear of the engine compartment. The cable snaps into the clutch lever forward of the second bracket.

Transaxle

REMOVAL & INSTALLATION

Spectrum

1. Disconnect the negative battery cable.
2. Disconnect the wiring connectors, speedometer cable, clutch cable, ground cable and shift cables from the transaxle.
3. Remove the air cleaner heat tube.
4. Remove the upper transaxle-to-engine bolts.
5. Raise and support the vehicle safely.
6. Drain the oil from the transaxle assembly.
7. Remove the left front wheel assembly and splash shield.
8. Disconnect the left tie rod at the steering knuckle. Disconnect the left tension rod.
9. Disconnect the halfshafts and remove the shafts by pulling them straight out from the transaxle. Avoid damaging the oil seals during removal of the shafts.
10. Remove the dust cover at the clutch housing.
11. Using a floor jack, support the transaxle, then remove the transaxle-to-engine retaining bolts.
12. While sliding the transaxle away from the engine, carefully lower the jack, guiding the right halfshaft out of the transaxle.

➡The right halfshaft must be installed into the transaxle when the transaxle is being mated to the engine.

To install:
13. When installing the transaxle, guide the right halfshaft into the shaft bore as the transaxle is being raised.
14. Install the transaxle-to-engine mounting bolts. Torque bolts to 55 ft. lbs. (75 Nm).
15. Install the left halfshaft into its bore on the transaxle.
16. Install the left tension rod and torque bolts to 80 ft. lbs. (108 Nm).
17. Install the tie rod to the steering knuckle.
18. Install the clutch housing dust cover bolts and the splash shield.
19. Install the tire and wheel assembly and lower the vehicle.
20. Install the remaining transaxle-to-engine attaching bolts. Torque bolts to 55 ft. lbs. (75 Nm).

21. Connect the ground cable at transaxle, clutch cable, speedometer cable and the battery negative cable.
22. Fill the transaxle with transmission fluid. Start engine and check for leaks.

Storm

▶ See Figure 1

1. Disconnect the battery cables, then remove the battery and tray from the vehicle.
2. Drain the transaxle fluid.
3. Remove the air cleaner assembly.
4. Disconnect the electrical connectors from the transaxle.
5. Disconnect the ground cable and engine wiring harness clamp from the transaxle.
6. Disconnect the ignition coil ground cable from the engine, then the ground cable at the ignition coil.
7. Disconnect the speedometer cable, clutch cable and shifter cables.
8. Support the engine using engine support tool J-28467-A or equivalent.
9. Raise and support the vehicle safely, then remove the tire and wheel assemblies.
10. Remove the front undercovers, then the ball joints from the steering knuckles.
11. Remove the left and right halfshaft, then the front exhaust pipe.
12. Remove the torque rod and bracket, then the left transaxle mount.
13. Remove the front transaxle through bolt, then the center beam with the rear transaxle mount.
14. Remove the engine stiffener attaching bolts, then the engine stiffener from the vehicle.
15. Remove the flywheel dust cover from the clutch housing. Support the transaxle using a suitable jack.
16. Remove the transaxle-to-engine attaching bolts, then the transaxle from the vehicle.

To install:
17. Install the transaxle, then the transaxle-to-engine attaching bolts. Torque bolts to 55 ft. lbs. (75 Nm).
18. Install the flywheel dust cover, engine stiffener and center beam with the rear transaxle mount.
19. Install the left transaxle mount, then the front transaxle mount through bolt.
20. Torque the center crossmember bolts to 45 ft. lbs. (61 Nm). Torque the left transaxle mount bolts to 29 ft. lbs. (39 Nm) and the front transaxle through bolt to 64 ft. lbs. (87 Nm).
21. Install the torque rod and bracket, then the front exhaust pipe.
22. Install the right and left halfshafts, then the ball joints onto the steering knuckles.
23. Install the front undercovers, then the front tire and wheel assemblies.
24. Lower the vehicle and remove the engine support tool.
25. Connect the shift cable, clutch cable and speedometer cable.
26. Install the battery bracket and the ignition coil assembly.
27. Install the ignition coil ground cable onto the engine.

28. Install the engine harness wiring clamp, then the ground cable.

29. Connect all electrical connectors to the transaxle. Install the battery and battery tray.

30. Fill the transaxle with transmission fluid. Connect the battery cables. Adjust the shift cables, if necessary. Start engine and check for leaks.

OVERHAUL

▶ **See Figures** 2, 3, 4, 5, 6, 7, 8, 9, 10, 11, 12, 13, 14, 15, 16, 17, 18, 19, 20, 21, 22, 23, 24, 25, 26, 27, 28, 29, 30, 31, 32, 33, 34, 35, 36, 37, 38, 39, 40, 41, 42, 43, 44 and 45

1. Remove the clutch release bearing and attach the transaxle assembly to the transaxle holding fixture J 33366 or equivalent. The transaxle holding fixture J 33366 should be then attached to base plate J3289-20, or equivalent.

2. Remove the rear cover assembly together with the seven bolts from the transaxle case.

3. Remove the control box assembly along with the four bolts from the transaxle case.

4. Shift the transaxle into gear. Remove the fifth speed drive and driven gear retaining nuts from the input and output shaft and discard the retaining nuts. Shift the transaxle back into neutral, aligning the detents on the shift rails.

5. Remove the detent spring retaining bolts for 1st/2nd, 3rd/4th and 5th speeds, and remove the detent springs and the detent balls. Remove the reverse detent spring retaining bolt and remove the spring and detent ball. Remove the

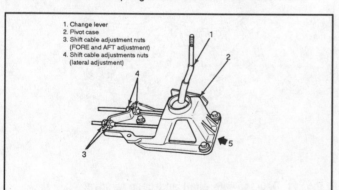

Fig. 1 Manual transaxle shift cable adjustment — Storm

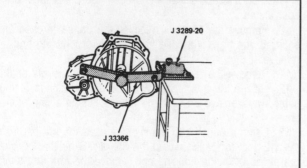

Fig. 2 Transaxle attached to workbench

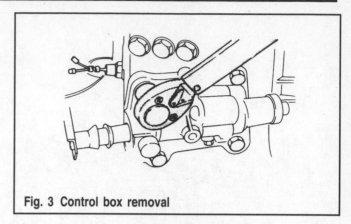

Fig. 3 Control box removal

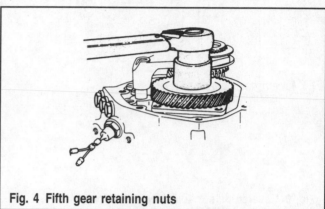

Fig. 4 Fifth gear retaining nuts

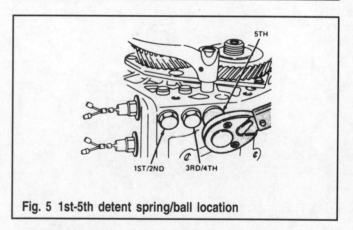

Fig. 5 1st-5th detent spring/ball location

switches for 1st/2nd and 3rd/4th gears. Use a magnet and remove the tow pins from the 3rd/4th gear switch hole.

6. Place the 5th speed synchronizer in neutral. Remove the roll pin at the 5th gear shift fork and discard the roll pin. Remove the 5th gear synchronizer hub, sleeve, roller bearing and gear with the shift fork as an assembly from the output shaft. Remove the 5th speed gear from the input shaft using the J 35274 gear puller, or equivalent.

7. Remove the seven Torx® screws from the bearing retainer. Remove the bearing retainer and shims from the input and output shafts.

8. Remove the bolt retaining the reverse idler shaft at the transaxle case.

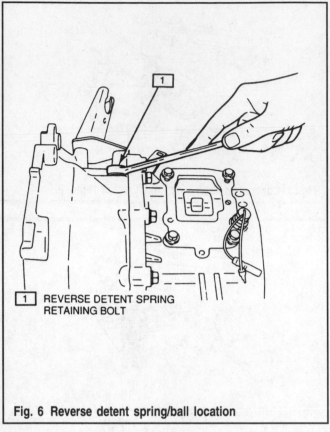

1   REVERSE DETENT SPRING
     RETAINING BOLT

Fig. 6 Reverse detent spring/ball location

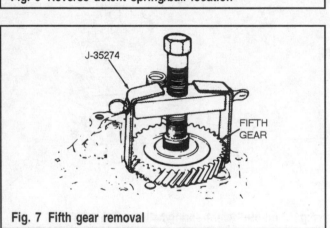

J-35274

FIFTH
GEAR

Fig. 7 Fifth gear removal

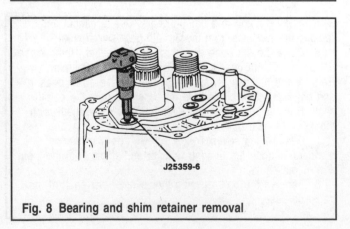

J25359-6

Fig. 8 Bearing and shim retainer removal

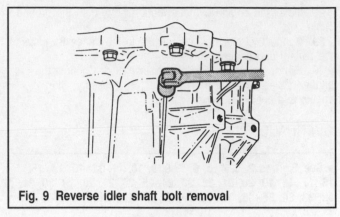

Fig. 9 Reverse idler shaft bolt removal

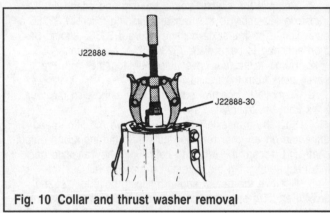

J22888

J22888-30

Fig. 10 Collar and thrust washer removal

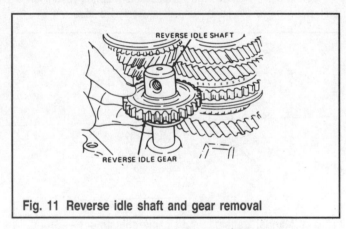

REVERSE IDLE SHAFT

REVERSE IDLE GEAR

Fig. 11 Reverse idle shaft and gear removal

9. Remove the collar and the thrust washer from the output shaft using J 22888 puller and J-22888-30 puller legs, or equivalents.

10. Remove the 14 bolts retaining the transaxle case and separate the transaxle case from the clutch housing and remove.

11. Remove the reverse idle gear and reverse idle shaft.

12. Lift the 5th gear shaft. With the detent aligned facing the same way, remove the 5th and reverse shafts at the same time.

13. Using a punch and hammer, remove the roll pin from the 1-2 shift fork and discard the roll pin. Slide the 1-2 shaft upward to clear the housing and remove the fork and shaft from the case.

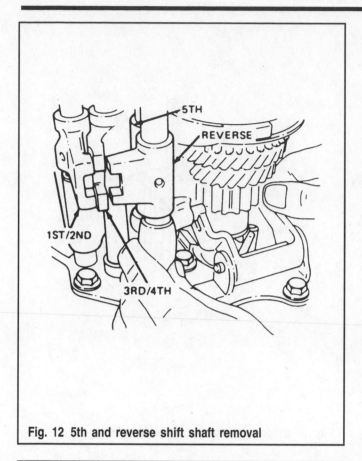

Fig. 12 5th and reverse shift shaft removal

Fig. 13 1st-2nd shift fork roll pin removal

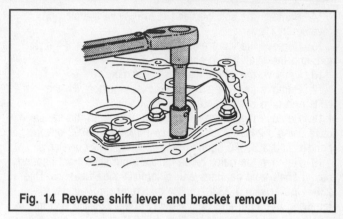

Fig. 14 Reverse shift lever and bracket removal

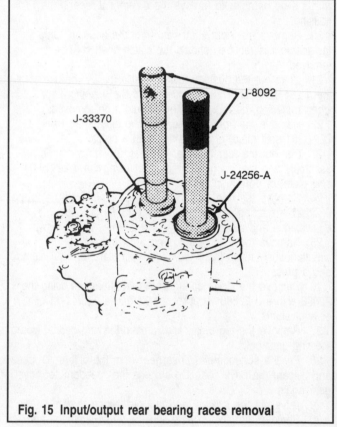

Fig. 15 Input/output rear bearing races removal

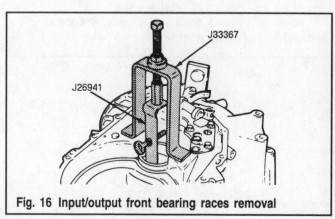

Fig. 16 Input/output front bearing races removal

14. Remove the split pin, and then remove the pin and reverse shift lever.

15. Remove the input and output shafts with the 3-4 shift fork and the shaft as an assembly.

16. Remove the differential case assembly.

17. Remove the reverse shift bracket together with the four bolts and take out the three inter lock pins.

18. Remove the rear bearing outer races from the transaxle case using J 24256-A bearing race remover, J 8092 driver handle, and J 33370 bearing race remover, or equivalents.

19. Remove the outer races for the input shaft front bearing, output shaft front bearings and differential side bearings. Use J 26941 puller with J 33367 puller bridge, or equivalents, for removing the input and output races in the housing and the differential race in the case. Use J 26941 puller, or equivalent, with a slide hammer to remove the differential race in the housing.

20. Remove the input shaft seal from the housing. Only if replacement is required should the clutch shaft seal be removed.

21. Drive out the bushing toward the inside by the use of the J 28412, or equivalent, and discard the bushing. Only when replacing the fork assembly should it be removed.

22. Remove the front bearing from the input shaft using J 22912-01 split plate, or equivalent, with a press.

23. Pull out the rear bearing 4th gear, 3rd/4th synchronizer assembly and the 3rd gear all together using the J 22912-01 split plate, or equivalent, and a press.

24. Remove the front bearing from the output shaft using the J 22227-A bearing remover with the J 33369 pilot, or equivalents, and a press.

25. Remove the rear bearing and 3rd/4th gear simultaneously using the J 22912-01 split plate, or equivalent, and a press.

26. Remove the side bearing from the differential using the J 22888 with a J 22888-30 puller leg kit and a J 2241-11 pilot, or equivalents.

27. Remove the ten bolts, and remove the ring gear. Discard the ring gear bolts.

28. Pry the speedometer drive gear from the differential case and discard the drive gear. Do not use the speedometer drive gear again.

29. Drive out the lockpin, and pull out the cross pin.

30. Remove the pinion gears and the thrust washers, and remove the side gears and thrust washers.

31. Clean and inspect all parts thoroughly. Replace any damaged or excessively worn parts.

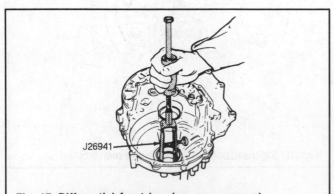

Fig. 17 Differential front bearing race removal

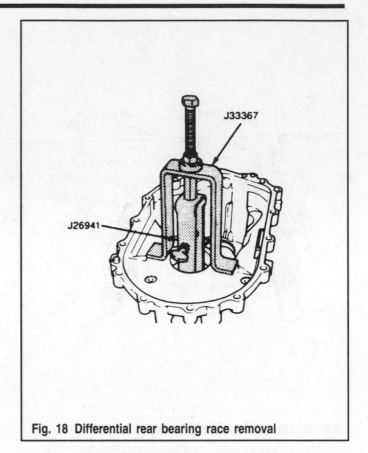

Fig. 18 Differential rear bearing race removal

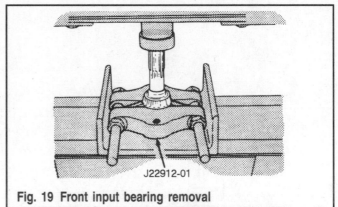

Fig. 19 Front input bearing removal

To install:

32. Apply oil to the thrust surfaces on all gears and all bearing interiors and race surfaces.

33. Install the needle bearing and 3rd gear to the input shaft. Install the block ring.

34. Match the inserts of the 3rd/4th sleeve and hub assembly with the grooves of the blocker ring and press the sleeve and hub assembly and collar, using J 33374 bearing/collar installer, or equivalent, and a press. Apply oil to the collar and hub interiors, install and apply oil to the circumference of the collar.

35. Install the blocker ring and needle bearing, and install the 4th gear and thrust washer with the recessed area facing 4th gear.

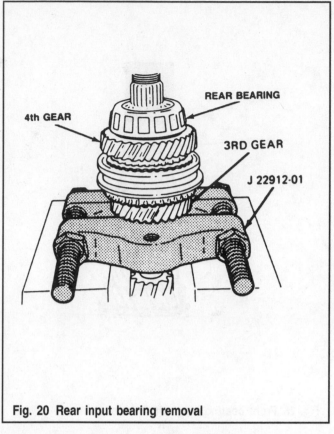

Fig. 20 Rear input bearing removal

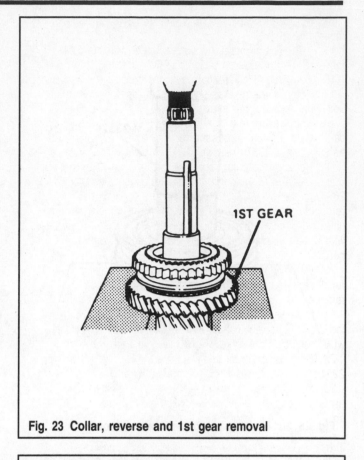

Fig. 23 Collar, reverse and 1st gear removal

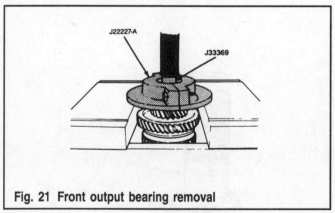

Fig. 21 Front output bearing removal

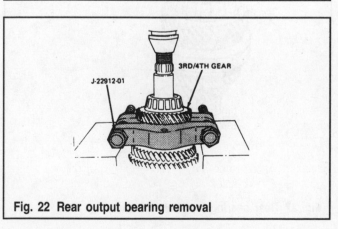

Fig. 22 Rear output bearing removal

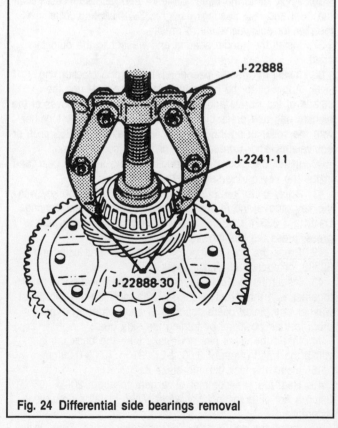

Fig. 24 Differential side bearings removal

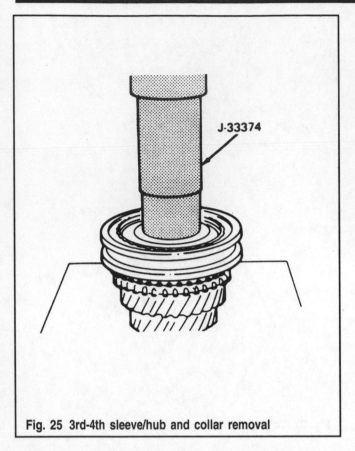

Fig. 25 3rd-4th sleeve/hub and collar removal

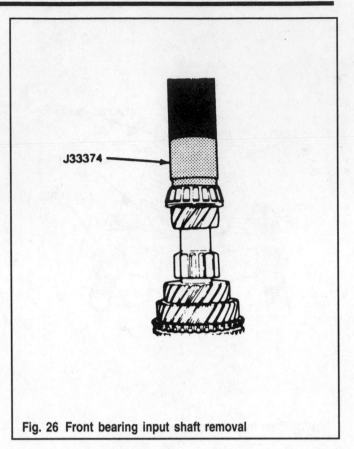

Fig. 26 Front bearing input shaft removal

36. Apply oil to the bearing interior and race surfaces. Install the front and rear bearings using J 33374 bearing/collar installer, or equivalent, and a press.

37. Install the needle bearing and washer to the output shaft.

38. Install the needle bearing, 1st gear and blocker ring.

39. Apply oil to the hub and collar interiors. Match the inserts of the sleeve and hub assembly with the grooves of the blocker ring and press the sleeve and hub assembly together with the collar using J 8853-01 collar installer, J 33369 pilot, or equivalents, and a press. Apply oil to the collar exterior.

40. Install the blocker ring needle bearing and 2nd gear, and install the key on the key groove next.

41. Apply oil to the 3rd/4th gear interior, match the key with the key groove and fit the key together with the rear bearing. Using a J 33374 bearing/collar installer, or equivalent, and a press, press the bearing on the output shaft.

42. Press the front bearing on the output shaft using a J 33368, or equivalent, and a press.

43. Install the two side gears on the differential case together with the thrust washers. Then, position the two thrust washer and pinion gears opposite of each other, and instal them in their positions by turning the side gear.

44. Insert the cross pin, and make sure the backlash is within the rated range of 0.0012-0.0031 in. (0.03-0.08mm).

45. Install the lock pin and stake it.

46. Heat the speedometer drive gear to about 200°F (95°C) using a hot oil dryer, not hot water. Then install it onto the differential.

47. Install the ring gear on the differential case. Then, install ten new bolts and then tighten them to the specified torque in a diagonal sequence. Apply oil to the surface of the ring gear,

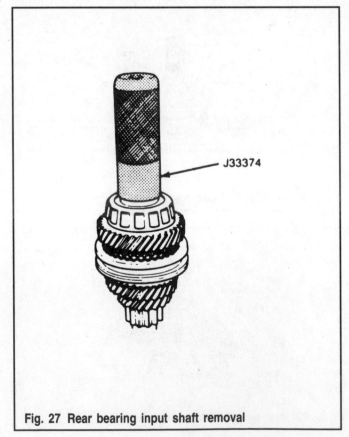

Fig. 27 Rear bearing input shaft removal

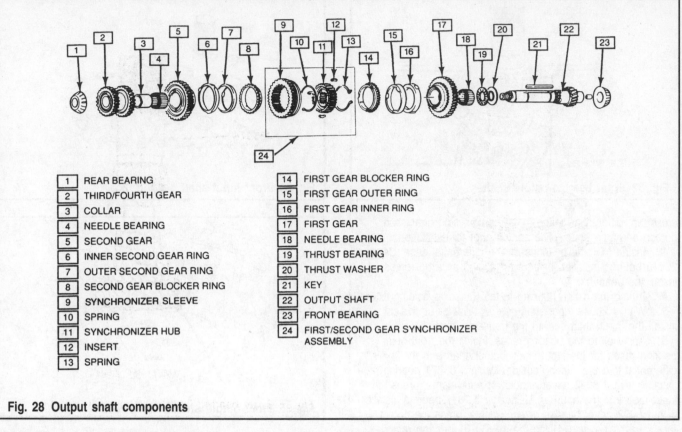

1	REAR BEARING	14	FIRST GEAR BLOCKER RING
2	THIRD/FOURTH GEAR	15	FIRST GEAR OUTER RING
3	COLLAR	16	FIRST GEAR INNER RING
4	NEEDLE BEARING	17	FIRST GEAR
5	SECOND GEAR	18	NEEDLE BEARING
6	INNER SECOND GEAR RING	19	THRUST BEARING
7	OUTER SECOND GEAR RING	20	THRUST WASHER
8	SECOND GEAR BLOCKER RING	21	KEY
9	SYNCHRONIZER SLEEVE	22	OUTPUT SHAFT
10	SPRING	23	FRONT BEARING
11	SYNCHRONIZER HUB	24	FIRST/SECOND GEAR SYNCHRONIZER ASSEMBLY
12	INSERT		
13	SPRING		

Fig. 28 Output shaft components

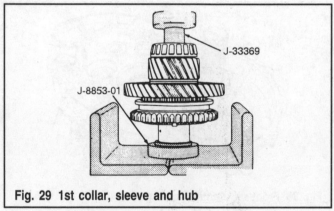

Fig. 29 1st collar, sleeve and hub

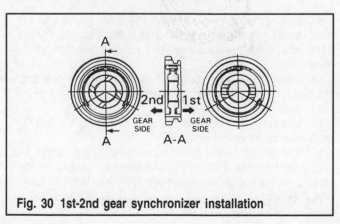

Fig. 30 1st-2nd gear synchronizer installation

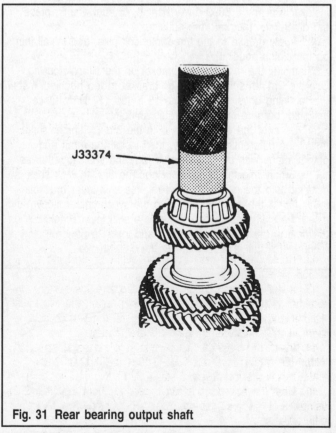

Fig. 31 Rear bearing output shaft

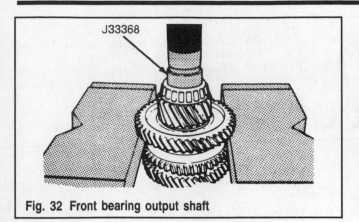

Fig. 32 Front bearing output shaft

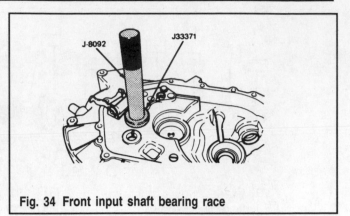

Fig. 34 Front input shaft bearing race

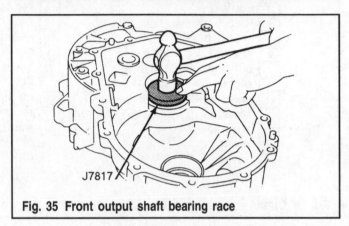

Fig. 35 Front output shaft bearing race

cross pin, differential gears, thrust portion, side gear shaft portion and side gear spline portion prior to installation.

48. Install the side bearings on the differential case. Using J 22919 bearing installer, or equivalent, and an arbor press, install the bearings.

49. Attach the clutch housing to the transaxle holding fixture.

50. With J 26540 input shaft seal installer or equivalent, install the input shaft seal to the transaxle assembly.

51. Apply oil to the bearing races. Install the front outer bearing races for the input shaft, output shaft and the differential into the clutch housing. Using J 33371 bearing race installer with J 8092 driver handle, or equivalents, press the input race into the housing. Using the J 7817 bearing installer with J 8092 driver handle, or equivalents, press the output race into the housing. Using the J 8611-01 bearing race installer with the J 8092 driver handle, or equivalents, press the differential race into the housing.

52. Apply grease to the three interlock pins, and install them on the clutch housing.

53. Install the reverse shift bracket on the clutch housing. Use the 3rd/4th shift rod to align bracket to the housing. Install the retaining bolts and torque to 13 ft. lbs. (17 Nm). Once installed, be sure the rod operates smoothly.

54. Be sure the interlock pin is in the 3rd/4th shifter shaft. Install the differential assembly, then install the input and output shafts with the 3rd/4th shift fork and shaft together as an assembly into the clutch housing. The 3rd/4th shift shaft is installed into the raised collar of reverse shift lever bracket.

55. Install the 1-2 shift fork onto the synchronizer sleeve and insert the shifter shaft into the reverse shift lever bracket. Align the hole in the fork with the shaft and install a new roll pin.

56. Install the reverse lever on the shift bracket.

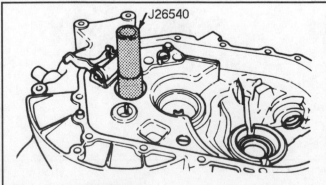

Fig. 33 Input shaft seal

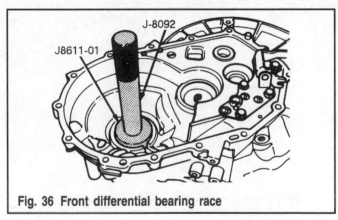

Fig. 36 Front differential bearing race

57. Make sure the interlock pin is in the 5th gear shifter shaft. Install the reverse and 5th gear shifter shaft and, at the same time, engage the reverse shaft with the reverse shift lever.

58. Install the reverse idler shaft together with the gear into the clutch housing. Make sure reverse lever is engaged in the collar gear.

59. Measure and determine the shim size using a J 33373 shim selector, or equivalent.

60. Position the outer bearing races on the input, output and differential bearings. Position the shim selector gauges on the bearing races. The three gauges are identified: Input, Output and Differential.

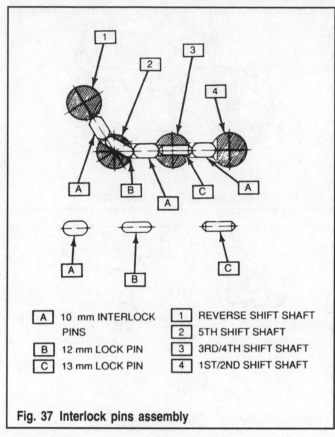

A 10 mm INTERLOCK PINS

B 12 mm LOCK PIN

C 13 mm LOCK PIN

1 REVERSE SHIFT SHAFT

2 5TH SHIFT SHAFT

3 3RD/4TH SHIFT SHAFT

4 1ST/2ND SHIFT SHAFT

Fig. 37 Interlock pins assembly

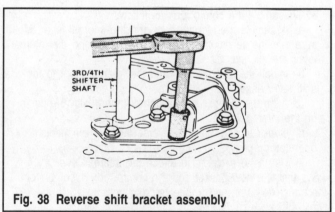

3RD/4TH SHIFTER SHAFT

Fig. 38 Reverse shift bracket assembly

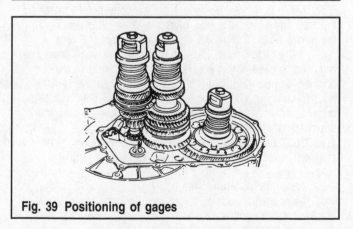

Fig. 39 Positioning of gages

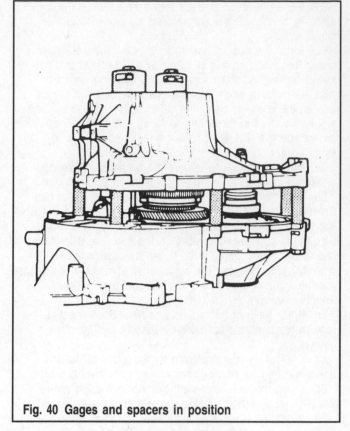

Fig. 40 Gages and spacers in position

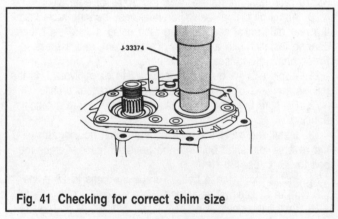

J-33374

Fig. 41 Checking for correct shim size

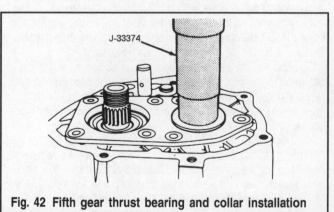

J-33374

Fig. 42 Fifth gear thrust bearing and collar installation

61. Place the seven spacers providers with J 33373 shim selector, or equivalent evenly around the perimeter of the clutch housing.

62. Install the bearing and shim retainer on the transaxle case. Torque the screws to 13 ft. lbs. (17 Nm). After final torque on screws, stake screws to the retaining plate.

63. Carefully position the transaxle case over the gauges and on the spacers. Install the seven bolts provided with the tool kit and tighten the bolts alternately until the case is seated on the spacers. The bolts should be torqued to 10 ft. lbs. (15 Nm).

64. Rotate each gauge to seat the bearings. Rotate the differential case through three revolutions in each direction.

65. With the three gauges compressed, measure the gap between the outer sleeve and the base pad using the available shim sizes. The input shaft shim should be one size smaller than the largest shim that will fit in the gap. The differential should use a shim three sizes larger than that which will smoothly fit in the gap. The output shaft should use the largest shim that can be placed into the gap and drawn through without binding.

66. When each of the three shims have been selected, remove the transaxle case, seven spacers and the three gauges.

67. Position the shim selected for the input, output and differential into the bearing race bores in the transaxle case.

68. Install the rear input shaft bearing race using a J 24256-A race bearing installer with a J 8092, or equivalent.

69. Install the rear output shaft bearing racing using a J 33370 race bearing installer with a J 8092, or equivalent.

70. Apply oil to the rear differential case bearing race. Install the rear differential case bearing race using a J 8611-01 race bearing installer with a J 8092, or equivalent, and a press. Press bearing until seated in its bore.

71. Apply a ⅛ in. bead of Loctite® 514 or equivalent, to the mating surfaces of the clutch housing and transaxle case.

72. Be sure the magnet is installed in the transaxle clutch housing.

73. Install the transaxle case on the clutch housing. Install the reverse idle shaft bolt into the transaxle case. Torque the bolt to 28 ft. lbs. (38 Nm).

74. Install the 14 case bolts. Torque the bolts to 28 ft. lbs. (38 Nm) in a diagonal sequence.

75. Install the drive axle seals using a J 26938 or J 29130 drive axle seal installers with a J 8092, or equivalents.

76. Apply oil to the thrust surfaces of the thrust washer and collar. Install the thrust washer and collar to the output shaft using a J 33374 bearing installer, or equivalent.

77. Apply oil to the output gear thrust surfaces. Install the 5th gear to the input shaft. Install the needle bearing, 5th gear, blocker ring, hub/sleeve assembly with the shift fork in its groove and back plate on the output shaft. Align the shift fork on the shifter shaft and install a new roll pin.

78. Install the detent balls and detent springs for the reverse, 1st/2nd, 3rd/4th and 5th speeds. Install the retaining bolts and torque them to 18 ft. lbs. (25 Nm). Install the 1st/2nd gear switch. Install the short pin and then the long pin into the 3rd/4th gear hole. Install the 3rd/4th gear switch.

79. Apply Loctite® 262 or equivalent to the threaded portion. Install new retaining nuts and torque them to 94 ft. lbs. (128 Nm). After reaching final torque, stake nuts.

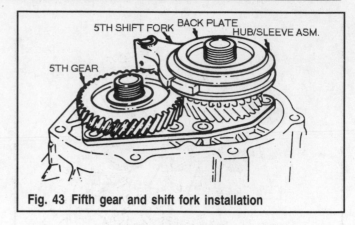

Fig. 43 Fifth gear and shift fork installation

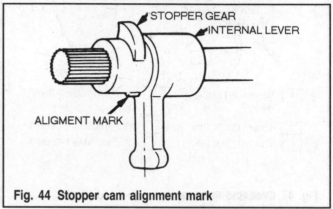

Fig. 44 Stopper cam alignment mark

80. Assemble the control box as follows:

  a. Assemble the stopper cam and the internal lever. Make sure that the serrations on the stopper cam and the internal lever are aligned.

  b. Install the stopper cam and the internal lever to the shift lever assembly.

  c. Align the stopper cam alignment mark with the center on the internal lever.

  d. Check to see that the reverse inhibitor mechanism operates properly.

  e. Use a new roll pin to attach the internal lever.

81. Install a new gasket and the control box assembly on the transaxle case, and torque the four bolts to 13 ft. lbs. (17 Nm).

82. Make sure the transaxle shifts properly before installing the rear cover. Install a new gasket and the rear cover with the seven bolts. Torque the bolts to 13 ft. lbs. (17 Nm).

83. If the clutch shaft, bushing, bearing and seals have been removed, grease both the inside and the outside of the bushing and bearing. Install a new bearing into the clutch housing using a J37159 inner bearing installer with a J 36190 driver handle, or the equivalents. Install a new oil seal, then the clutch shaft. Install a new outer bushing using a J 28412 or J 36037 outer bushing installer, or the equivalent. Drive the bushing inward until the line on the tool is flush with the housing.

84. Install the clutch release bearing.

85. Measure the rotating torque on the input shaft. When measuring, the input shaft should be to the upper side and the differential assembly to the lower side. The rotating torque should be less than 7 in. lbs. (0.8 Nm).

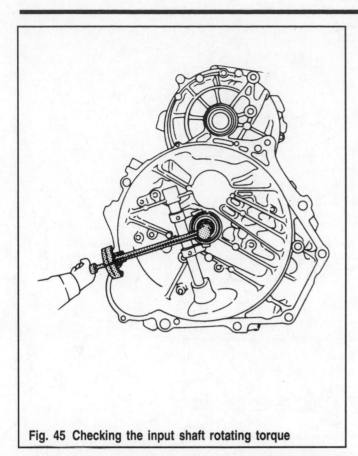

Fig. 45 Checking the input shaft rotating torque

Adjustments

LINKAGE

1. Loosen the adjusting nuts.
2. Place the transaxle and the shift lever in the **N** position.
3. Turn the adjusting nuts until the shift lever is in the vertical position.
4. Tighten the adjusting nuts.

Halfshafts

REMOVAL & INSTALLATION

Spectrum

▶ See Figure 46

1. Raise and support the vehicle safely, allowing the wheels to hang.
2. Remove the front wheel assemblies, the hub grease caps, the hub nuts and the cotter pins.
3. Install the halfshaft boot seal protector tool J-28712 or equivalent, on the outer CV-joints and the halfshaft boot seal protector tool J-34754 or equivalent, on the inner Tri-Pot joints.

➡**Clean the halfshaft threads and lubricate them with a thread lubricant.**

4. Have an assistant depress the brake pedal, then remove the hub nut and washer.
5. Remove the caliper-to-steering knuckle bolts and support the caliper, on a wire, out of the way.
6. Remove the rotor. Remove the drain plug and drain the oil from the transaxle.
7. Using a slide hammer puller and the puller attachment tool J-34866 or equivalent, pull the hub from the halfshaft.
8. Remove the tie rod-to-steering knuckle cotter pin and the nut. Using the ball joint separator tool J-21687-02 or equivalent, press the tie rod ball joint from the steering knuckle.
9. Remove the lower ball joint-to-control arm nuts/bolts.
10. Swing the steering knuckle assembly outward and slide the halfshaft from the steering knuckle.
11. Place a large prybar between the differential case and the inboard constant velocity joint. Pry the halfshaft from the differential case.
12. Remove the halfshaft assembly.

➡**When installing the halfshaft, press it into the differential case until it locks with the snapring.**

To install:

13. Use new cotter pins and reverse the removal procedures.
14. Torque the ball joint-to-control arm nuts/bolts to 80 ft. lbs. (108 Nm), the caliper-to-steering knuckle bolts to 41 ft. lbs. (55 Nm) and the halfshaft-to-hub nut to 137 ft. lbs. (186 Nm).
15. Check and/or adjust the front alignment.

Storm

▶ See Figure 47

1. Remove the wheel cover.
2. Loosen the wheel nuts.
3. Elevate and safely support the vehicle.
4. Remove the front wheel.
5. Install the halfshaft boot seal protector tool J-28712 or equivalent, on the outer CV-joints and the halfshaft boot seal protector tool J-34754 or equivalent, on the inner Tri-Pot joints.
6. Unstake the hub nut. Have an assistant depress the brake pedal, then remove the hub nut and washer.
7. Remove the lower control arm to ball joint attaching nuts and bolts.
8. Use a ball joint separator such as GM J-24319-01 or equivalent to remove the tie rod ball joint from the knuckle.
9. Remove the bolts holding the brake caliper bracket to the steering knuckle. Use stiff wire to suspend the caliper out of the way; do not let the caliper hang by its hose. Remove the brake disc.
10. Push the axle from the hub using a brass or plastic hammer.

➡**If the axle can not be separated from the hub using a brass or plastic hammer. Use a puller such as GM J-25287 or equivalent, to push the axle from the hub.**

11. Use a slide hammer and appropriate end fitting (GM J-2619-01 and J 35762 or equivalents) to pull the driveshaft from the transaxle. Remove the shaft from the vehicle.

To install:

12. Install halfshaft into transaxle.
13. Install the shaft into the wheel hub.

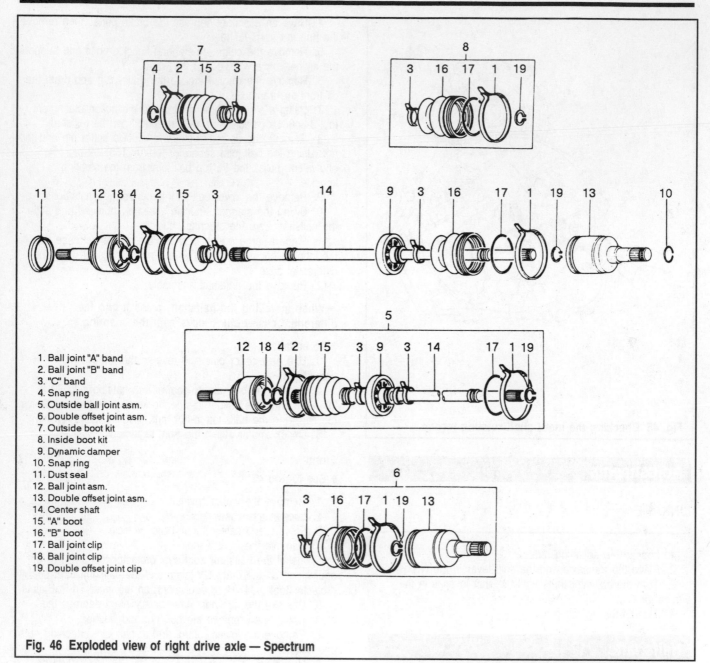

1. Ball joint "A" band
2. Ball joint "B" band
3. "C" band
4. Snap ring
5. Outside ball joint asm.
6. Double offset joint asm.
7. Outside boot kit
8. Inside boot kit
9. Dynamic damper
10. Snap ring
11. Dust seal
12. Ball joint asm.
13. Double offset joint asm.
14. Center shaft
15. "A" boot
16. "B" boot
17. Ball joint clip
18. Ball joint clip
19. Double offset joint clip

Fig. 46 Exploded view of right drive axle — Spectrum

14. Install the lower control arm to the lower ball joint. Tighten the nuts and bolts to 115 ft. lbs. (156 Nm).

15. Install the tie rod end to the steering knuckle and tighten the nut to 40 ft. lbs. (54 Nm).

16. Install the brake disc; install the brake caliper and tighten the bolts to 65 ft. lbs. (88 Nm).

17. Install the wheel.

18. Install the hub nut and washer.

19. Lower the vehicle to the ground.

20. TIghten the wheel lugs to 76 ft. lbs. (103 Nm). Tighten the hub nut to 137 ft. lbs. (186 Nm).

21. Install the nut, cap, cotter pin and washer. Install the wheel cover.

Boot and CV-Joint

REMOVAL & INSTALLATION

Storm

OUTER ASSEMBLY

1. Raise and safely support the vehicle and remove the tire and wheel assembly.

2. Remove the halfshaft.

3. Place halfshaft into a suitable vise.

4. Using a suitable prybar, remove the circlip.

5. Remove the case housing from the shaft.

6. Remove the 6 balls from the ball guide, then move ball guide towards center of shaft.

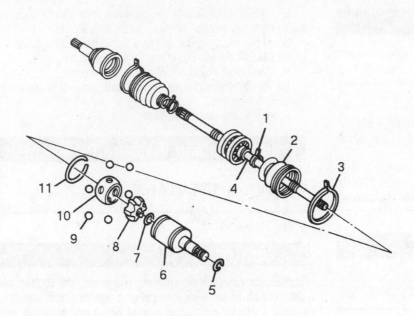

1. Differential-side shaft boot band
2. Differential-side boot
3. Differential-side boot band
4. Drive axle shaft
5. Differential-side gear snap ring
6. Differential-side joint housing
7. Roller ball guide snap ring
8. Roller ball guide
9. Roller ball
10. Roller cage
11. Differential-side joint housing snap ring

Fig. 47 Exploded view of drive axle — Storm

7. Remove the snapring from the shaft, then the ball guide and ball retainer from the shaft.

8. Remove boot from shaft. Reverse procedure to install. Pack new boot with suitable grease.

INNER ASSEMBLY

1. Raise and safely support the vehicle. Remove the tire and wheel assembly.

2. Remove halfshaft from the vehicle.

3. Place halfshaft into a suitable vise and remove the large boot clamp.

4. Remove the tri-pot housing from the drive halfshaft.

5. Using a suitable brass drift and hammer, remove the spider assembly from the halfshaft.

6. Remove the small boot clamp, then the boot from the shaft. Note the alignment marks on the spider assembly and the halfshaft and on the drive halfshaft and the tri-pot housing. If no marks are present, make alignment marks for easy installation.

7. Reverse procedure to install. Pack new boot with a suitable grease.

Spectrum

INNER ASSEMBLY

1. Disconnect the negative battery terminal from the battery.

2. Raise and support the vehicle safely, the remove the front wheels.

3. Remove the outer boot assembly.

4. Remove the boot retaining clamps and the spacer ring.

5. Slide the axle and the spider bearing assembly out of the tri-pot housing. Install the spider retainer onto the spider bearing assembly.

6. Remove the spider assembly and the boot from the axle.

7. To install, pack the new boot with grease and reverse the removal procedures.

OUTER ASSEMBLY

1. Disconnect the negative battery terminal from the battery.

2. Raise and support the vehicle safely, then remove the front wheels.

3. Remove the brake caliper and support on a wire, then remove the rotor.

4. Slide the outer CV-joint assembly off the halfshaft.

5. Remove the bearing retaining ring, the boot retainer, the clamp and the outer boot.

6. To install, pack the new boot with grease and reverse the removal procedures.

CV-JOINT INSPECTION

All Models

To inspect the inner joint, disassemble and inspect all components for pitting, damage or excess wear. If excess wear or damaged components are found, replacement of the assembly is recommended.

The outer CV joint cannot be disassembled. The outer CV joint should turn smoothly at angles of 40 degrees or less.

CLUTCH

Adjustments

PEDAL HEIGHT/FREE-PLAY

▶ **See Figure 48**

1. Disconnect the negative battery terminal from the battery.
2. Loosen the adjusting nut and pull the cable to the rear until it turns freely.
3. Adjust the cable length by turning the adjusting nut.
4. When the clutch pedal free-play travel reaches 0.39-0.79 in. for Spectrum or 0.20-0.59 in. on Storm, release the cable.
5. Tighten the locknut to secure in place.

Clutch Linkage

REMOVAL & INSTALLATION

1. Disconnect the negative battery terminal from the battery.

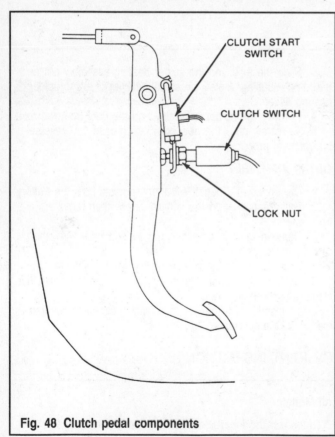

Fig. 48 Clutch pedal components

2. Loosen the clutch cable adjusting nuts. Disconnect the cable from the release arm and cable bracket.
3. At the clutch pedal, remove the cable retaining bolt.
4. Disconnect the cable from the front of the dash.
5. Remove the clutch cable from the vehicle.
6. To install, grease the clutch cable pin and reverse the removal procedures.
7. Adjust the pedal free-play.

Driven Disc and Pressure Plate

REMOVAL & INSTALLATION

▶ **See Figure 49**

❊❊CAUTION

The clutch driven disc contains asbestos, which has been determined to be a cancer causing agent. Never clean clutch surfaces with compressed air! Avoid inhaling any dust from any clutch surface! When cleaning clutch surfaces, use a commercially available brake cleaning fluid.

1. Remove the transaxle from the vehicle. Refer the procedure listed earlier in this Section.
2. Install the pilot shaft tool J-35282 or equivalent, into the pilot bearing to support the clutch assembly during the removal procedures.

➡**Observe the alignment marks on the clutch and the clutch cover and pressure plate assembly. If the markings are not present, be sure to add them.**

3. Loosen the clutch cover and pressure plate assembly retaining bolts evenly, one at a time, until the spring pressure is released.
4. Remove the clutch cover and pressure plate assembly and clutch plate.

➡**Check the clutch disc, flywheel and pressure plate for wear, damage or heat cracks. Replace all damaged parts.**

5. Before installation, lightly lubricate the pilot shaft splines, pilot bearing and pilot release bearing surface with grease.
6. To install, reverse the removal procedures. Torque the clutch cover/pressure plate-to-flywheel bolts evenly to 13 ft. lbs. (18 Nm), to avoid distortion.

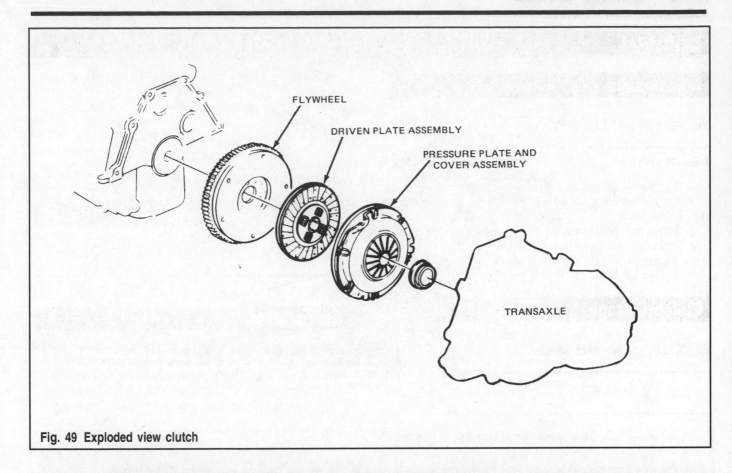

Fig. 49 Exploded view clutch

AUTOMATIC TRANSAXLE

Identification

The Spectrum is available with one automatic transaxle, the KF100 3 speed unit. The Storm is available with one of two automatic transmissions. The KF400 automatic transaxle is a 3 speed unit, and the JF403E unit is a 4 speed transaxle.

Fluid Pan

REMOVAL & INSTALLATION

▶ **See Figure 50**

1. Disconnect the negative battery cable.
2. Raise and support the vehicle safely. Place a drain pan, or suitable container under the transaxle.
3. Inspect the transaxle fluid pan for interfering components, then disconnect and reposition components as necessary for access. If equipped, remove the transaxle fluid pan guard.
4. Remove the transaxle fluid pan retaining bolts.
5. Carefully separate the fluid pan from the transaxle. If the pan is difficult to remove, tap the pan with a soft hammer to aid separation.

To install:
6. Clean the transaxle fluid pan surface and matching surface on the transaxle.
7. Install a new transaxle fluid pan gasket.
8. Be sure the fluid pan magnet is in the bottom of the fluid pan. Install the transaxle fluid pan and tighten the retaining bolts to 5 ft. lbs. (7 Nm) on the KF100 and KF400 transaxles, and 71 inch lbs. (8 Nm) on the JF403E transaxle.
9. Replace and connect all components moved to gain access to the fluid pan.
10. Safely lower the vehicle and connect the negative battery cable.
11. Fill the transaxle with Dexron®II or equivalent transmission fluid.

FILTER SERVICE

1. Disconnect the negative battery cable.
2. Raise and support the vehicle safely.
3. Remove the transaxle fluid pan.
4. Remove the filter retaining bolts.
5. Remove the filter from the transaxle.
To install:
6. Install a new filter to the transaxle.
7. Clean the transaxle fluid pan surface and matching surface on the transaxle.
8. Install a new transaxle fluid pan gasket.

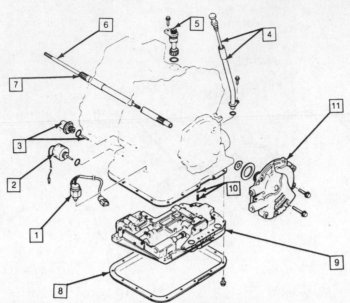

1. INHIBITOR SWITCH
2. KICKDOWN SOLENOID
3. VACUUM DIAPHRAGM AND DIAPHRAGM ROD
4. OIL LEVEL GAUGE AND TUBE
5. SPEEDOMETER DRIVEN GEAR
6. OIL PUMP SHAFT
7. TURBINE SHAFT
8. OIL PAN
9. CONTROL VALVE
10. STEEL BALL AND SPRING
11. OIL PUMP

Fig. 50 Automatic transaxle external controls — Spectrum

9. Be sure the fluid pan magnet is in the bottom of the fluid pan. Install the transaxle fluid pan and tighten the retaining bolts to 5 ft. lbs. (7 Nm) on the KF100 and KF400 transaxles, and 71 inch lbs. (8 Nm) on the JF403E transaxle.

10. Replace and connect all components moved to gain access to the fluid pan.

11. Safely lower the vehicle and connect the negative battery cable.

12. Refill the transaxle assembly to the proper level using Dexron®II transmission fluid.

Adjustments

SHIFT LINKAGE

Spectrum

1. Loosen the 2 adjusting nuts at the control rod link and connect the shift cable to the link on the transaxle.

2. Shift the transaxle into the **N** detent.

3. Place the shifter lever into the **N** position.

4. Rotate the link assembly clockwise to remove slack in the cable.

5. Tighten the rear adjusting nut until it makes contact with the link. Tighten the front adjusting nut until it makes contact with the link and tighten the adjusting nuts.

Storm

1. Place the ignition switch in the **LOCK** position.

2. Set the selector lever in the **PARK** position.

3. Loosen the adjuster nuts at the transaxle.

4. Be sure that the shift lever at the transaxle is in the **PARK** position.

5. Pull the cable forward and tighten the forward adjuster nut until it contacts the shift lever.

6. Tighten the rear nut until it comes in contact with the shift lever.

7. Tighten both adjuster nuts.

8. To adjust the brake drive cable, use the following procedure:

  a. Place the shift lever to the **PARK** position.

  b. Place the ignition switch to the **LOCK** position.

  c. Pull the cable forward at the shift lever bracket and tighten the forward adjuster nut until it makes contact with the bracket.

  d. Tighten the rear nut until it makes contact with the shift lever bracket and then tighten both the adjuster nuts.

THROTTLE LINKAGE

1. Position the ignition switch/key in the **LOCK** position.

2. Place the selector lever in the **P** position.

3. Loosen the adjuster nuts on the transaxle. Ensure that the shift lever on the transaxle is in the **P** position.

4. Pull the cable forward, then tighten the forward adjuster nut until it contacts the shift lever. Tighten the rear nut until it contacts the shift lever.

5. Tighten both adjuster nuts.

Neutral Safety Switch

REMOVAL & INSTALLATION

Spectrum

1. Disconnect the negative battery cable.
2. Disconnect the electrical connector for the switch at the left fender.
3. Raise the vehicle and support it safely.
4. Remove the switch retaining bolts and remove the switch.
5. Installation is the reverse of removal. Add transaxle fluid as necessary.
6. Check and make sure the engine starts in only the **P** and **N** detents.

Storm

WITH 4-SPEED TRANSAXLE

1. Disconnect the negative battery cable.
2. Remove the intake air duct and breather tube from the air cleaner assembly.
3. Disconnect the shift control cable from the selector cable.
4. Remove the neutral safety switch attaching screws and disconnect electrical connectors.
5. Remove the neutral safety switch.
6. Installation is the reverse of the removal procedure. Adjust the neutral safety switch after installation.
7. Check and make sure the engine starts in only the **P** and **N** detents.

WITH 3-SPEED TRANSAXLE

1. Disconnect the negative battery cable.
2. Disconnect the electrical connector at the switch.
3. Raise the vehicle and support it safely.
4. Remove the switch retaining bolts and remove the switch.
5. Installation is the reverse of removal. Align the groove and neutral basic line. Hold the switch in position and tighten the bolts to 48 inch lbs.
6. Check and make sure the engine starts in only the **P** and **N** detents.

ADJUSTMENT

1. Remove the intake air duct and air breather tube from the air cleaner assembly, as required.
2. Loosen the neutral safety switch attaching screws.
3. Place selector lever in the **N** position.
4. Install a pin into the adjustment holes in both the neutral safety switch and the switch lever.
5. Torque the retaining screws to 26 inch lbs. (3 Nm).
6. Install the air breather tube and intake air duct onto the air cleaner assembly.

Back-up Light Switch

REMOVAL & INSTALLATION

Spectrum

For removal and installation of the back-up light switch, refer to the procedures under NEUTRAL SAFETY SWITCH, in this section.

Storm

KF400 TRANSAXLE

1. Disconnect the negative and the positive battery cables.
2. Remove the nut, bolt and the battery hold down bracket.
3. Remove the battery from the vehicle.
4. Disconnect the back-up switch electrical connector. It is below the right side of the battery tray.
5. Raise the vehicle and support it safely.
6. Remove the six screws and the left splash shield from the vehicle.
7. Turn the back-up switch counterclockwise to remove it from the transaxle.
   To install:
8. Apply Loctite® pipe sealant or the equivalent, to the switch threads, and turn the switch clockwise to install it into the transaxle. Tighten it to 15 ft. lbs. (20 Nm).
9. Install the left splash shield to the vehicle and tighten the six screws.
10. Safely lower the vehicle.
11. Connect the back-up switch electrical connector to the switch.
12. Install the battery and the battery hold down bracket. Tighten the bolt to 44 inch lbs. (5 Nm) and the nut to 71 inch lbs. (8 Nm).
13. Connect the positive battery cable and tighten the terminal retainer to 11 ft. lbs. (15 Nm).
14. Connect the negative battery cable.

JF403E TRANSAXLE

1. Engage the parking brake and block the wheels. Place the manual selector in the **N** position.
2. Disconnect the negative battery cable.
3. Disconnect the intake air duct from the air cleaner assembly.
4. Disconnect the air breather tub from the air cleaner assembly.
5. Separate the air cleaner assembly halves.
6. Remove the three bolts and loosen the left half of the air cleaner assembly from the left front strut tower.
7. Remove one retaining clip and disconnect the wire harness from the left half of the air cleaner assembly. Remove the air cleaner from the vehicle.
8. Disconnect the inhibitor switch electrical connectors from the back-up/inhibitor switch.
9. Remove the manual shift shaft nut from the manual shift shaft.
10. Disconnect the transaxle shift lever with the shift select cable from the manual shift shaft.

11. Remove the three bolts and the inhibitor switch from the transaxle.

To install:

12. Install the inhibitor switch to the transaxle aligning the manual shift shaft lever pin with the slot provided in the inhibitor switch lever; securing with three bolts, but do not tighten fully.

13. Rotate the manual shift shaft lever clockwise until the manual shift shaft is in the **N** position.

14. Adjust the inhibitor switch using a standard drift punch. With the punch place through the hole in the manual shift shaft lever, align the manual shift shaft lever with the alignment cavity in the inhibitor switch.

15. Tighten the inhibitor switch mounting bolts to 26 inch lbs. (3 Nm).

16. Install the transaxle shift lever with the shift select cable onto the manual shift shaft.

17. Install the manual shift shaft nut onto the manual shift shaft and tighten it to 20 ft. lbs. (27 Nm).

18. Connect the inhibitor switch electrical connectors to the inhibitor switch.

19. Install the left half of the air cleaner assembly into the vehicle. Install the wiring harness to the left half of the air cleaner assembly and tighten the three bolts to 11 ft. lbs. (15 Nm).

20. Pair the air cleaner assembly halves.

21. Connect the air breather tube to the air cleaner assembly.

22. Connect the intake air duct to the air cleaner assembly.

23. Connect the negative battery cable.

Transaxle

REMOVAL & INSTALLATION

Storm

1. Disconnect the battery cables, then remove the battery and tray from the vehicle.

2. Remove the intake air duct and breather tube from the air cleaner assembly.

3. Disconnect the electrical connectors, shift cable, shift cable bracket, breather hose and speedometer cable from the transaxle.

4. Disconnect the vacuum diaphragm hose from the vacuum diaphragm, if equipped.

5. Install engine support tool J-28467-A or equivalent, then remove the left transaxle through bolt.

6. Remove 4 transaxle-to-engine attaching bolts, then raise and support the vehicle safely.

7. Remove the right and left undercovers, then the front wheel and tire assemblies.

8. Disconnect the left control arm from the steering knuckle, then drain the transaxle fluid.

9. Remove the halfshafts and suspend on a wire.

10. Remove the front transaxle mount through bolt, then the dampener from the rear mount through bolt.

11. Remove the rear transaxle mount through bolt, then the 2 front center crossmember mounting bolts.

12. Remove the front exhaust pipe-to-exhaust manifold attaching nuts, then 2 rear front pipe bolts. Disconnect the front pipe from the exhaust manifold.

13. Remove the 2 rear center crossmember mounting bolts, then the crossmember from the vehicle. Lower the vehicle.

14. Lower the engine slightly using engine support tool J-28467 or equivalent. Do not remove the engine support.

15. Raise and safely support the vehicle, then position a suitable jack under the transaxle.

16. Remove the rear mount to transaxle case bolt, the front mount attaching bolt.

17. Remove the front mounting bracket attaching bolts, then the front mounting bracket from the engine.

18. Remove the flywheel cover, then the flywheel-to-torque converter attaching bolts.

19. Disconnect the oil cooler lines from the transaxle, then remove the 2 rear transaxle mount bolts. Lower the transaxle from the vehicle.

To install:

20. Raise the transaxle into position, then install the 2 rear transaxle mounting bolts. Remove transaxle jack.

21. Lower the vehicle, then install the 4 transaxle-to-engine mounting bolts.

22. Using engine support tool J-28467-A or equivalent, raise the engine slightly.

23. Install the through bolt on the left transaxle mount. Torque through bolt to 64 ft. lbs. (87 Nm).

24. Raise and safely support the vehicle, then install the flywheel-to-torque converter attaching bolts. Torque converter bolts to 31 ft. lbs. (42 Nm).

25. Install the flywheel cover, then connect the oil cooler lines to the transaxle. Torque oil cooler line trunnion bolts to 10 ft. lbs. (15 Nm).

26. Install the front transaxle mount nut and bolt. Torque bolt to 45 ft. lbs. (61 Nm).

27. Install the rear mount through bolt. Torque rear transaxle mount attaching bolts to 29 ft. lbs. (39 Nm) and the rear mount through bolt to 64 ft. lbs. (87 Nm).

28. Install the center crossmember. Torque crossmember bolts to 45 ft. lbs. (61 Nm).

29. Install the front mount through bolt. Torque bolt to 64 ft. lbs. (87 Nm).

30. Install the dampener on the rear mount through bolt.

31. Install the front pipe to the exhaust manifold and secure in place.

32. Install the halfshafts into the vehicle.

33. Install the left control arm onto the steering knuckle, then the right and left under covers.

34. Install the tire and wheel assemblies, then lower the vehicle. Torque the engine-to-transaxle attaching bolts to 31 ft. lbs. (42 Nm).

35. Remove the engine support tool, then install the speedometer to the transaxle.

36. Install the breather hose, shaft cable bracket and shift cable to the transaxle.

37. Install the vacuum hose to the vacuum diaphragm, if equipped.

38. Connect the electrical connectors to the transaxle.

39. Install the air breather tube and the air intake duct onto the air cleaner assembly.

40. Install the battery and battery tray. Connect the battery cables and check transaxle fluid. Start engine and check for leaks.

Spectrum

1. Disconnect the negative battery terminal from the battery.
2. Remove the air duct tube from the air cleaner.
3. From the transaxle, disconnect the shift cable, speedometer cable, vacuum diaphragm hose, engine wiring harness clamp and the ground cable.
4. At the left-fender, disconnect the inhibitor switch and the kickdown solenoid wiring connectors.
5. Disconnect the oil cooler lines from the transaxle.
6. Remove the 3 upper transaxle-to-engine mounting bolts. Raise and support the vehicle safely.
7. Remove both front-wheels and the left-front fender splash shield.
8. Disconnect both tie rod ends at the steering knuckles.
9. Remove both front tension rod brackets and disconnect the rods from the control arms.
10. Disengage the halfshafts from the transaxle.
11. Remove the flywheel dust cover and the converter-to-flywheel attaching bolts.
12. Remove the transaxle rear mount through bolt.
13. Disconnect the starter wiring and the starter. Support the transaxle.
14. Remove the lower transaxle-to-engine mounting bolts and remove the transaxle.

To install:

15. Install transaxle to engine. Torque the converter-to-flywheel bolts to 30 ft. lbs. (41 Nm), and the transaxle-to-engine bolts to 56 ft. lbs. (76 Nm).
16. Install the flywheel dust cover.
17. Install both halfshafts into the transaxle.
18. Install the tension rod brackets and both tie rod ends to the steering knuckle.
19. Install the splash shield to the left front fender. Install the tire and wheel assemblies.
20. Connect the transaxle cooler lines.
21. Connect all electrical connectors and hoses that were disconnected during the removal.
22. Connect the speedometer cable and shift cable to the transaxle.
23. Connect the battery negative cable, adjust the shift linkage and fill the transaxle with Dexron® II automatic transaxle fluid. Start engine and check for leaks.

Halfshafts

Removal and installation, as well as CV-joint replacement, is the same for the manual and the automatic transaxles. For removal and installation of the halfshaft or CV-joint replacement procedures, refer to Manual Transaxle in this Section.

TORQUE SPECIFICATIONS

Component	U.S.	Metric
Back up light switch:		
Storm (KF400)	15 ft. lbs.	(20 Nm)
Ball joint-to-control arm nuts/bolts:		
Spectrum	80 ft. lbs.	(108 Nm)
Bearing and shim retainer screws	13 ft. lbs.	(17 Nm)
Brake caliper bolts:		
Storm	65 ft. lbs.	(88 Nm)
Caliper-to-steering knuckle bolts:		
Spectrum	41 ft. lbs.	(55 Nm)
Center crossmember bolts:		
Storm	45 ft. lbs.	(61 Nm)
Clutch cover/pressure plate-to-flywheel bolts	13 ft. lbs.	(18 Nm)
Control assembly retaining nuts	20 ft. lbs.	(28 Nm)
Control box-to-case bolts	13 ft. lbs.	(17 Nm)
Detent spring retaining bolts	18 ft. lbs.	(25 Nm)
Engine-to-transaxle attaching bolts:		
Storm	31 ft. lbs.	(42 Nm)
Filler plug	20 ft. lbs.	(28 Nm)
Flywheel-to-torque converter attaching bolts:		
Storm	31 ft. lbs.	(42 Nm)
Front transaxle mount bracket:		
Storm	45 ft. lbs.	(61 Nm)
Front transaxle mount retaining nut:		
Storm	45 ft. lbs.	(61 Nm)
Front transaxle through bolt:		
Storm	64 ft. lbs.	(87 Nm)
Halfshaft-to-hub nut:		
Spectrum	137 ft. lbs.	(186 Nm)
Hub nut:		
Storm	137 ft. lbs.	(186 Nm)
Inhibitor switch mounting bolts:		
Storm (JF403E)	26 inch lbs.	(3 Nm)
Input rotating torque	7 inch lbs.	(0.8 Nm)
Input/output shaft retaining nuts	94 ft. lbs.	(128 Nm)
Left tension rod bolts:		
Spectrum	80 ft. lbs.	(108 Nm)
Left transaxle mount bolts:		
Storm	29 ft. lbs.	(39 Nm)
Lower control arm nuts/bolts:		
Storm	115 ft. lbs.	(156 Nm)
Manual shift shaft nut:		
Storm (JF403E)	20 ft. lbs.	(27 Nm)
Neutral safety switch (automatic transaxle)	26 inch lbs.	(3 Nm)
Oil cooler line trunnion bolts:		
Storm	10 ft. lbs.	(15 Nm)
Rear cover bolts (manual transaxle)	13 ft. lbs.	(17 Nm)
Rear transaxle mount bolts:		
Storm	29 ft. lbs.	(39 Nm)
Reverse idle shaft bolt	28 ft. lbs.	(38 Nm)
Reverse shift bracket retaining bolts	13 ft. lbs.	(17 Nm)
Tie rod end to steering knuckle nut:		
Storm	40 ft. lbs.	(54 Nm)
Transaxle case-to-clutch housing bolts	28 ft. lbs.	(38 Nm)
Transaxle fluid pan retaining bolts:		
Spectrum	5 ft. lbs.	(7 Nm)
Storm (JF403E)	71 inch lbs.	(8 Nm)
Storm (KF400)	5 ft. lbs.	(7 Nm)
Transaxle-to-engine attaching bolts	55 ft. lbs.	(75 Nm)
Wheel lugs:		
Storm	76 ft. lbs.	(103 Nm)

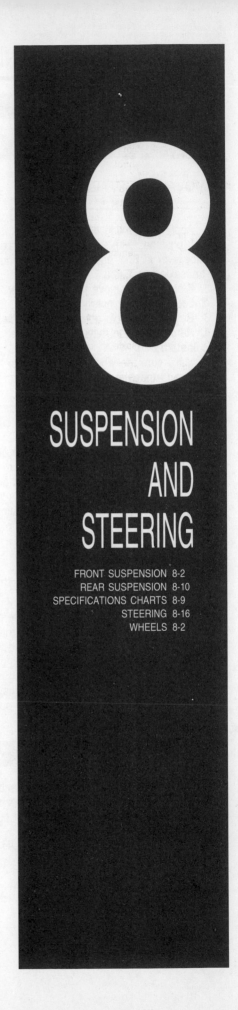

8

SUSPENSION AND STEERING

WHEELS

Wheels

REMOVAL & INSTALLATION

1. Apply the parking brake and block the opposite wheel.
2. If equipped with an automatic transaxle, place the selector lever in **P**. If equipped with a manual transaxle, place the transaxle in reverse.
3. If equipped, remove the wheel cover.
4. Loosen the lug nuts.
5. Raise the vehicle until the tire is clear of the ground.
6. Remove the lug nuts, tire and wheel assembly.

To install:

7. Make sure the wheel, brake drum or hub mating surfaces and the wheel lug studs are clean and free of all foreign material.
8. Position the wheel on the hub or drum and hand-tighten the lug nuts. Tighten all the lug nuts in a criss-cross pattern, until they are snug.
9. Lower the vehicle until the wheel touches the ground. Tighten the lug nuts in a criss-cross pattern to 65 ft. lbs. (88 Nm) on the Spectrum and 87 ft. lbs. (118 Nm) on the Storm. Always use a torque wrench to tighten the lug nuts, to prevent warping the disc brake rotors or brake drums, and to prevent stretching the wheel studs.

INSPECTION

Check the wheels for any damage. They must be replaced if they are bent, dented, heavily rusted, have elongated bolt holes, or have excessive lateral or radial run-out. Wheels with excessive run-out may cause a high-speed vehicle vibration.

Replacement wheels must be of the same load capacity, diameter, width, offset and mounting configuration as the original wheels. Using the wrong wheels may affect wheel bearing life, ground and tire clearance, or speedometer and odometer calibrations.

FRONT SUSPENSION

The front suspension on the Spectrum and the Storm consists of MacPherson struts and lower control arms. The struts are anchored to the vehicle by strut supports in the wheel wells.

The lower control arms contain a ball joint which connects to the steering knuckle. A stabilizer shaft helps to control body roll during hard cornering.

Wheel Lug Studs

REMOVAL & INSTALLATION

1. Raise and safely support the vehicle
2. If replacing the stud in a brake drum, removal of the drum is required. Refer to Section 9 of this manual for the proper procedure.
3. If replacing a wheel stud that is in the hub assembly, remove it according to the procedure outlined later in this Section.
4. Once the brake drum or hub is removed from the vehicle, drive the damaged stud from the unit using the proper equipment. If a press is not available, remove the stud using a hammer and a brass drift. Make sure to properly support the drum or hub.

➡ **When using a press, hammer and brass drift, personal injury from flying metal may result. Always were proper eye and facial protection.**

To install:

5. Line up the serrations on the replacement stud with the serrations in the hub or drum.
6. If installing the stud into a brake drum, drive into position using a press or hammer and brass drift. In order to avoid damage to the drum, support the drum carefully during installation.
7. If installing the stud into a hub, perform the following:
   a. With the stud already positioned in the hub, add enough washer to take up space while you draw the stud into its bore.
   b. Install the lug nut, flat-side facing the washers, and tighten until the stud is seated in the hub flange.
   c. Remove the nut and washers.
8. Install the hub or drum onto the vehicle as required.
9. Install the tire and wheel assembly.

MacPherson Strut

REMOVAL & INSTALLATION

▶ **See Figures 1, 2 and 3**

1. From in the engine compartment, remove the nuts attaching the strut to the strut mount.
2. Loosen the wheel nuts. Raise and support the vehicle safely. Support the vehicle so that the weight of the vehicle rests on the support and not the control arms.
3. Remove the wheel and tire assembly.
4. Remove the brake hose clip at the strut bracket.

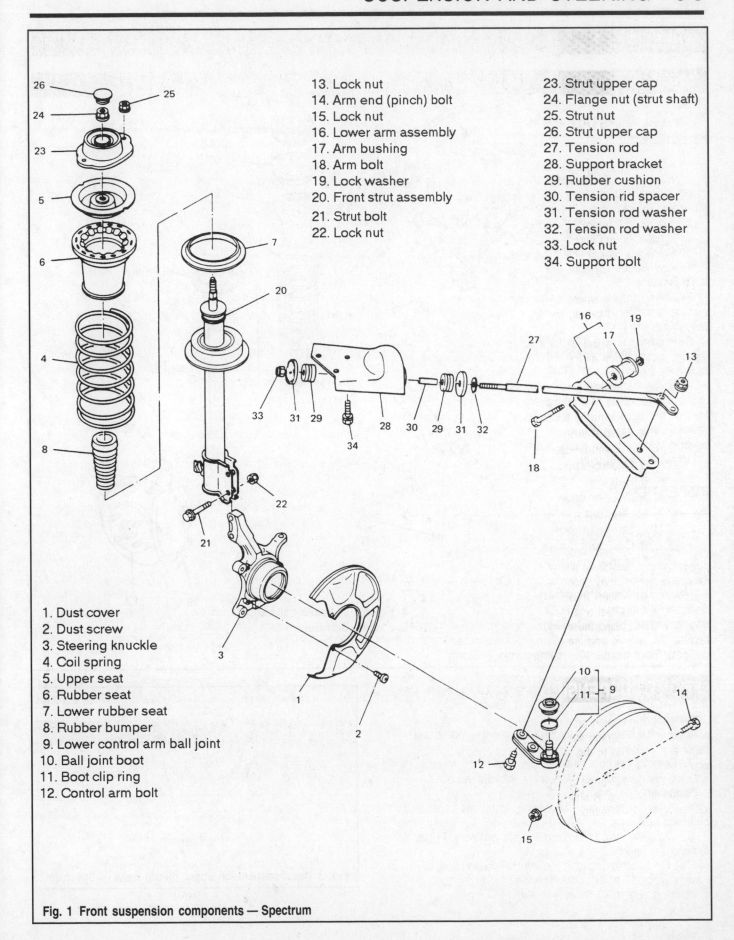

13. Lock nut
14. Arm end (pinch) bolt
15. Lock nut
16. Lower arm assembly
17. Arm bushing
18. Arm bolt
19. Lock washer
20. Front strut assembly
21. Strut bolt
22. Lock nut

23. Strut upper cap
24. Flange nut (strut shaft)
25. Strut nut
26. Strut upper cap
27. Tension rod
28. Support bracket
29. Rubber cushion
30. Tension rid spacer
31. Tension rod washer
32. Tension rod washer
33. Lock nut
34. Support bolt

1. Dust cover
2. Dust screw
3. Steering knuckle
4. Coil spring
5. Upper seat
6. Rubber seat
7. Lower rubber seat
8. Rubber bumper
9. Lower control arm ball joint
10. Ball joint boot
11. Boot clip ring
12. Control arm bolt

Fig. 1 Front suspension components — Spectrum

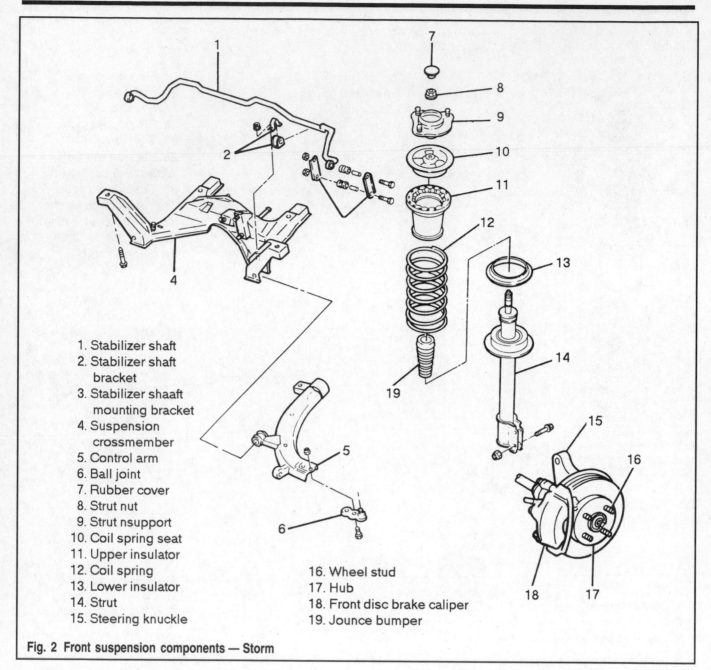

1. Stabilizer shaft
2. Stabilizer shaft bracket
3. Stabilizer shaaft mounting bracket
4. Suspension crossmember
5. Control arm
6. Ball joint
7. Rubber cover
8. Strut nut
9. Strut nsupport
10. Coil spring seat
11. Upper insulator
12. Coil spring
13. Lower insulator
14. Strut
15. Steering knuckle
16. Wheel stud
17. Hub
18. Front disc brake caliper
19. Jounce bumper

Fig. 2 Front suspension components — Storm

5. Disconnect the brake hose from the brake caliper. Cap the brake line and caliper openings to prevent system contamination.

6. Pull the brake hose through the opening in the strut bracket.

7. Remove the nuts attaching the strut to the steering knuckle. Remove the strut assembly from the vehicle.

To install:

8. Install the strut onto the vehicle. Install the upper strut mounting nuts.

9. Install the strut to steering knuckle retainers. Tighten all fasteners to specifications:

a. On Spectrum, torque the strut-to-steering knuckle retainers to 80 ft. lbs. (108 Nm), and the upper strut mounting nuts to 41 ft. lbs. (55 Nm).

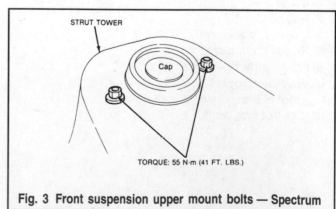

Fig. 3 Front suspension upper mount bolts — Spectrum

b. On Storm, torque the upper strut retaining nuts to 58 ft. lbs. (78 Nm). Torque the steering knuckle to strut assembly bolts to 116 ft. lbs. (157 Nm).

10. Install the brake hose through the strut bracket and onto the caliper. Install a new washer on the brake hose, if equipped, before installation.

11. Secure brake hose to strut bracket using clip.

12. Fill the master cylinder to the proper level with clean brake fluid. Bleed the brake system. Refer to Section 9 for details.

13. Install the tire and wheel assembly. Inspect the front end alignment and adjust as required.

OVERHAUL

1. Remove the strut from the vehicle.

2. Place the strut assembly into a holding fixture. Loosen, but do not remove the upper strut nut.

3. Remove the strut assembly from the vice and compress the coil spring using Strut Spring Compressor J 34013 (J 34013-B for the Storm) or equivalent. Remove the strut nut.

4. Gradually release the tension on the spring compressor.

5. Remove the coil spring seat, upper insulator, jounce bumper, lower insulator and the coil spring from the strut.

To install:

6. Install the strut into the spring compressor with the strut assembly-to-steering knuckle bolt holes facing outward.

7. Install the lower insulator and the jounce bumper to the strut. Install the coil spring onto the strut, making sure the paint marks on the spring are towards the lower insulator.

8. Install the upper insulator and the coil spring seat, with the 'IN' stamping facing outward.

9. Carefully compress the coil spring with the spring compressor.

10. Install the strut support assembly and the strut nut. Tighten the strut nut to 43 ft. lbs. (58 Nm). Install the nut cover.

11. Slowly loosen the coil spring compressor. Remove the strut assembly from the compressor.

12. Install the strut into the vehicle. Inspect the front wheel alignment.

Lower Ball Joint

INSPECTION

Raise the front of the vehicle and safely support it on stands. Do not place stands under the control arms; the arms must hang free. Grasp the tire at the top and bottom and move the top of the tire through an in-and-out motion. Look for any horizontal motion in the steering knuckle relative to the control arm. Such motion is an indication of looseness within the ball joint. If the joint is checked while disconnected from the knuckle, it should have minimal or no free-play and should

not twist in its socket under finger pressure. Replace any joint showing looseness or free-play.

REMOVAL & INSTALLATION

▶ See Figure 4

1. Raise and safely support the vehicle.
2. Remove the front tire and wheel.

➡**Care must be exercised to prevent the CV-joints from being overextended. When either end of the halfshaft is disconnected, overextension of the joint will result in separation of the internal components and possible joint failure. Drive axle joint seal protectors should be used any time service is performed on or near the drive axles. Failure to observe this could result in interior joint or seal damage and possible joint failure.**

3. Place jackstands under the suspension crossmember and lower the vehicle so the weight of the vehicle rests on the suspension crossmember and the jackstands, and not the control arms.

4. Install Inner Drive Joint Seal Protector J 34754 or the equivalent, to the drive axle boot.

5. Remove the pinch bolt and separate the ball joint from the steering knuckle.

6. Remove the two nuts, two retainer bolts and the ball joint from the control arm.

To install:

7. Install the ball joint to the control arm and secure with the two mounting bolts and nuts. Tighten the ball joint-to-control arm bolts and nuts to 80 ft. lbs. (108 Nm) on Spectrum, and 115 ft. lbs. (156 Nm) on Storm.

8. Install the ball joint to the steering knuckle and secure in place with the pinch bolt. Tighten pinch bolt to 51 ft. lbs. (69 Nm) on Spectrum or 48 ft. lbs. (65 Nm) on Storm.

9. Remove the seal protector from the axle boot.

10. Raise and safely support the vehicle. Remove the jackstands.

11. Install the tire and wheel assembly and lower the vehicle.

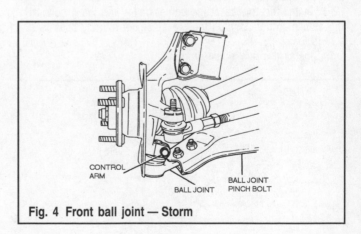

Fig. 4 Front ball joint — Storm

CONTROL ARM
BALL JOINT
BALL JOINT PINCH BOLT

Stabilizer Bar

REMOVAL & INSTALLATION

Storm

▶ See Figure 5

1. Install engine support tool J-28467-A or equivalent, onto the engine.

2. Raise the vehicle, then position suitable support under the suspension supports. Lower the vehicle onto the supports, not the control arms.

3. Remove both front tire and wheel assemblies.

4. Disconnect the front exhaust pipe from the exhaust manifold.

5. Disconnect the power steering lines from the rack and pinion gear, as required.

6. From inside the vehicle, remove the boot from the steering shaft. Remove the steering shaft pinch bolt.

7. Separate the ball joint and tie rod end at both steering knuckles.

8. Support the engine to prevent it from rotating. Remove the engine torque rod from the center beam. Remove the engine rear mount.

9. Safely support the crossmember assembly using a jack. Remove the 2 bolts from the center beam and 4 bolts from the crossmember. Lower the center beam and crossmember assembly with the rack and pinion gear and stabilizer bar attached.

10. Remove the rack and pinion assembly from the crossmember. Remove the stabilizer bar from the crossmember.

To install:

11. Install the stabilizer bar and rack and pinion assembly to the crossmember. Tighten the stabilizer bar-to-crossmember bolts to 12 ft. lbs. (16 Nm), and the rack and pinion-to-crossmember nuts to 65 ft. lbs. (88 Nm).

12. Install the center beam and crossmember assembly into the vehicle, guiding the steering shaft coupling over the pinion shaft on the steering gear.

13. Install the 2 bolts at the center beam and the 4 bolts at the crossmember. Tighten the crossmember-to-body bolts to 137 ft. lbs. (186 Nm).

14. Install the rear engine mount.

15. Install the engine torque rod at the center beam. Install the stabilizer bar to the control arm. Tighten the stabilizer bar-to-control arm bolts to 19 ft. lbs. (26 Nm).

16. Install the tie rods and ball joint to the steering knuckle and secure in place. Torque ball joint pinch bolt to 48 ft. lbs. (66 Nm), and the tie rod-to-knuckle nut to 40 ft. lbs. (54 Nm).

17. From inside the vehicle, install the steering shaft retainer bolt and boot.

18. Install the front exhaust pipe, using a new gasket as required. Install the tire and wheels.

19. Lower the vehicle and remove the engine support tool.

Tension Rods

REMOVAL & INSTALLATION

Spectrum

▶ See Figure 6

1. Raise and support the vehicle safely.

2. If equipped with a stabilizer bar, remove the nuts, bolts and insulators attaching it to the tension rod.

3. Remove the nut and washer attaching the tension rod to the body.

4. Remove the nuts and bolts attaching the tension rod to the control arm, then the tension rod from the vehicle.

5. Reverse procedure to install. Torque tension rod-to-body nuts to 72 ft. lbs. (98 Nm) and the tension rod-to-control arm nuts to 80 ft. lbs. (108 Nm).

Lower Control Arms

REMOVAL & INSTALLATION

Storm

1. Raise and support the vehicle safely.
2. Remove the tire and wheel assembly.
3. Remove the stabilizer bar from the control arm.
4. Separate the ball joint from the steering knuckle.
5. Remove the front bushing-to-body attaching bolt, then the rear bushing-to-crossmember attaching bolts.
6. Remove the control arm from the vehicle.

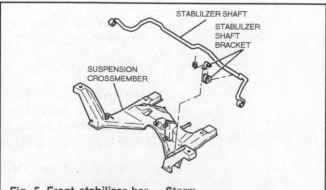

Fig. 5 Front stabilizer bar — Storm

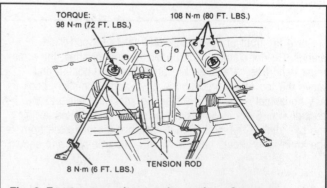

Fig. 6 Front suspension tension rods — Spectrum

To install:

7. Install the control arm onto the vehicle and secure in place. Torque the rear bushing-to-crossmember bolt to 51 ft. lbs. (69 Nm); front bushing-to-body attaching bolt to 95 ft. lbs. (129 Nm).

8. Install the ball joint to the control arm. Tighten the ball stud-to-knuckle pinch bolt to 46 ft. lbs. (62 Nm).

9. Install the stabilizer bar to the control arm.

10. Install the tire and wheel assembly.

Spectrum

1. Raise and safely support the vehicle.

2. Remove the tire and wheel assembly.

3. Remove the control arm-to-tension arm attaching nuts and bolts.

4. Remove the nut and bolt attaching the control arm to the body, then the control arm from the vehicle.

5. Reverse procedure to install.

➡**Raise the control arm to a distance of 15 inches from the top of the wheel well to the center of the hub. Retorque the control arm-to-body bolts to 41 ft. lbs. (55 Nm) and the control arm-to-tension rod bolts to 80 ft. lbs. (108 Nm). This procedure aligns the bushing arm to the body.**

Front Wheel Hub, Knuckle and Bearings

REMOVAL & INSTALLATION

▶ **See Figure 7**

1. Raise and support the vehicle safely, allowing the wheels to hang.

2. Remove the front wheel assemblies, the hub grease caps and the cotter pins.

3. Install the halfshaft boot seal protector tool No. J-28712 or equivalent, on the outer CV-joints and the halfshaft boot seal protector tool No. J-34754 or equivalent, on the inner Tri-Pot joints.

➡**Clean the halfshaft threads and lubricate them with a thread lubricant.**

4. Remove the hub nut and washer. On the Spectrum, disconnect the brake flex hose from the caliper.

5. Remove the caliper-to-steering knuckle bolts and support the caliper, on a wire, out of the way.

6. Remove the rotor.

7. Inspect the hub bearing end-play prior to removal of the hub, as follows:

   a. Mount a dial indicator with magnetic base to the strut assembly.

   b. Position the indicator so that when the hub assembly is moved in and out, the end-play will be measured.

   c. Move the hub in and out while noting the deflection of the indicator.

   d. If the end-play exceeds 0.0020 in. (0.05mm), replacement of the hub bearing assembly will be required.

8. Using a slide hammer puller and the puller attachment tool J-34866 or equivalent, pull the hub from the halfshaft.

9. Remove the tie rod-to-steering knuckle cotter pin and the nut. Using the ball joint separator tool J-21687-02 or equivalent, press the tie rod ball joint from the steering knuckle.

10. To remove the steering knuckle from the vehicle, perform the following procedures:

   a. Remove the lower ball joint-to-control arm nuts/bolts.

➡**Before separating the steering knuckle from the strut, be sure to scribe matchmarks on each component.**

   b. Remove the steering knuckle-to-strut nuts/bolts and the steering knuckle from the vehicle.

11. Using a medium prybar, pry the grease seals from the steering knuckle. Using a pair of internal snapring pliers, remove the internal snaprings from the steering knuckle.

12. Support the steering knuckle (face down) on an arbor press (on 2 press blocks). Position tool J-35301 (on Spectrum), J-22912-01 (on Storm) or equivalent, on the rear-side of the hub bearing, then, press the bearing from the steering knuckle.

13. Using an arbor press, the wheel puller tool and a piece of bar stock, press the bearing inner race from the wheel hub.

14. Clean the parts in solvent and blow dry with compressed air.

To install:

15. Using wheel bearing grease, lubricate the inside of the steering knuckle.

16. Using the internal snapring pliers, install the outer snapring into the steering knuckle.

17. Position the steering knuckle on a arbor press (outer face down), a new wheel bearing and the bearing installation tool J-35301 (on the Spectrum), J-38284 (on the Storm) or equivalent, then press the bearing inward until it stops against the snapring.

18. Using the internal snapring pliers, install the inner snapring into the steering knuckle.

19. Using the grease seal installation tool J-35303 (on the Spectrum), outer oil seal installer J-38287 (on Storm), inner oil seal installer J-38285 (on the Storm) or equivalents, drive new grease seals into both ends of the steering knuckle until they seat against the snaprings.

20. To install the hub into the steering knuckle, perform the following procedure:

   a. Position tool J-35302 (on the Spectrum), J-38287 (on the Storm) or equivalent, facing upward on a arbor press.

   b. Position the steering knuckle (facing upward) on the tool J-35302, the wheel hub and a piece of bar stock (on top).

   c. Press the assembly together until the hub bottoms out on the wheel bearing. Lubricate the new bearing seal with wheel bearing grease and install.

21. To install steering knuckle to the vehicle, perform the following procedures:

   a. Install the steering knuckle and tighten the steering knuckle-to-strut nuts/bolts. On Spectrum, torque the steering knuckle-to-strut bolts to 87 ft. lbs. (118 Nm). On Storm, torque steering knuckle nuts and bolts to 115 ft. lbs. (156 Nm).

   b. Install the lower ball joint-to-control arm nuts/bolts. On the Spectrum tighten the ball joint-to-control arm nuts/bolts to 80 ft. lbs. (108 Nm). On Storm, tighten ball joint pinch bolt to 48 ft. lbs. (66 Nm).

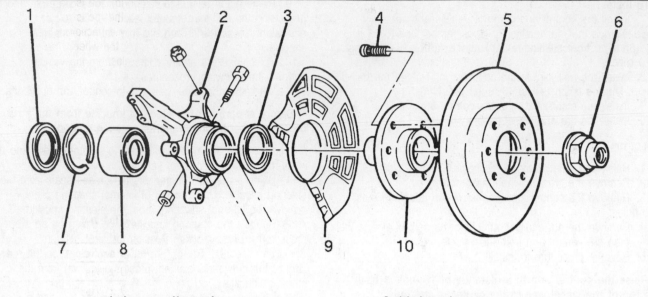

1. Inner oil seal
2. Steering knuckle
3. Outer oil seal
4. Wheel stud
5. Brake rotor
6. Hub axle nut
7. Inner snap ring
8. Bearing assembly
9. Dust cover
10. Hub

Fig. 7 Steering knuckle and hub exploded view — Storm

22. Press the tie rod ball joint to the steering knuckle. Install a new tie rod-to-steering knuckle cotter pin and tighten the nut on the Storm to 40 ft. lbs. (54 Nm),

➡**Clean the halfshaft threads and lubricate them with a thread lubricant.**

23. Install the hub to the halfshaft.
24. Install the brake rotor.
25. Install the caliper. On the Spectrum, tighten the caliper-to-steering knuckle bolts to 41 ft. lbs. (55 Nm) and connect the brake flex hose to the caliper. On the Storm, tighten the brake caliper-to-steering knuckle bolts to 72 ft. lbs. (98 Nm)
26. Install the hub nut and washer and tighten the hub nut to 137 ft. lbs. (186 Nm).
27. Grease the hub, install the hub grease caps and cotter pins. Install the front wheel assemblies.
28. Lower the vehicle. Bleed the brakes as necessary.
29. Check and/or adjust the front end alignment.

Front End Alignment

The do-it-yourself mechanic should not attempt to perform any wheel alignment procedures. Expensive, highly-specialized alignment tools are needed and making these adjustments blindly would most likely result in damage. The 4-wheel alignment should be performed by a certified alignment technician using the proper alignment tools.

CASTER

Caster is the tilting of the upper most point of the steering axis either forward or backward from the vertical (when viewed from the side of the vehicle). A backward tilt is positive and a forward tilt is negative. Caster influences directional control of the steering, but does not affect tire wear.

Caster is affected by vehicle height; therefore, it is important to keep the body at its designed height. Overloading the vehicle or a weak or sagging spring will affect the caster. When the rear of the vehicle is lower than its normal designated trim height, the front suspension moves to a more positive caster. If the rear of the vehicle is higher than its designated trim height, the front suspension moves to a less positive caster.

CAMBER

Camber is the tilting of the wheels from the vertical when viewed from the front of the vehicle. When the wheels tilt outward at the top, the camber is positive. When the wheels tilt inward, the camber is negative. The amount of tilt measured in degrees from the vertical is the camber angle. Camber influences both directional control and tire wear.

Camber and caster cannot be adjusted on these vehicles. If the camber is found to be out of specification, the cause should be located and corrected. Suspension parts may be damaged, bent, worn or loose. These parts should be replaced.

TOE-IN

Toe is a measurement of how much the front of the wheels are turned in or out from the geometric centerline/thrust line.

When the wheels are turned in (toe-in), toe is positive. When the wheels are turned out (toe-out), the toe is negative. The actual amount of toe is normally only a fraction of a degree. The purpose of toe is to ensure that the wheels roll parallel. Toe can be adjusted on these vehicles.

FRONT WHEEL ALIGNMENT

Year	Model	Caster		Camber		Toe-in (in.)	Steering Axis Inclination (deg.)
		Range (deg.)	Preferred Setting (deg.)	Range (deg.)	Preferred Setting (deg.)		
1985	Spectrum	$1\frac{3}{4}$P–$2\frac{3}{4}$P	$2\frac{1}{4}$P	$\frac{7}{16}$N–$1\frac{1}{16}$P	$\frac{11}{16}$P	$0 \pm \frac{1}{16}$	$11\frac{27}{32}$
1986	Spectrum	$1\frac{3}{4}$P–$2\frac{3}{4}$P	$2\frac{1}{4}$P	$\frac{7}{16}$N–$1\frac{1}{16}$P	$\frac{11}{16}$P	$0 \pm \frac{1}{16}$	$11\frac{27}{32}$
1987	Spectrum	$1\frac{3}{4}$P–$2\frac{3}{4}$P	$2\frac{1}{4}$P	$\frac{7}{16}$N–$1\frac{1}{16}$P	$\frac{11}{16}$P	$0 \pm \frac{1}{16}$	$11\frac{27}{32}$
1988	Spectrum	$1\frac{3}{4}$P–$2\frac{3}{4}$P	$2\frac{1}{4}$P	$\frac{7}{16}$N–$1\frac{1}{16}$P	$\frac{11}{16}$P	$0 \pm \frac{1}{16}$	$11\frac{27}{32}$
1989	Spectrum	$1\frac{3}{4}$P–$2\frac{3}{4}$P	$2\frac{1}{4}$P	$\frac{11}{16}$N–$1\frac{5}{16}$P	$\frac{5}{16}$P	$0 \pm \frac{5}{32}$	16
1990	Storm	2P–4P	3P	1N–$\frac{1}{4}$P	$\frac{1}{2}$N	$0 \pm \frac{1}{16}$	$10\frac{3}{16}$
1991	Storm	2P–4P	3P	1N–$\frac{1}{4}$P	$\frac{1}{2}$N	$0 \pm \frac{1}{16}$	$10\frac{3}{16}$
1992	Storm	$3\frac{1}{2}$P–$5\frac{1}{2}$P	$4\frac{1}{2}$P	1N–$\frac{1}{4}$P	$\frac{1}{2}$N	$0 \pm \frac{1}{16}$	$10\frac{3}{16}$
1993	Storm	$3\frac{1}{2}$P–$5\frac{1}{2}$P	$4\frac{1}{2}$P	1N–$\frac{1}{4}$P	$\frac{1}{2}$N	$0 \pm \frac{1}{16}$	$10\frac{3}{16}$

REAR SUSPENSION

Coil Springs

REMOVAL & INSTALLATION

Spectrum

▶ **See Figures 8, 9, 10, 11 and 12**

1. Raise and safely support the vehicle.
2. Remove the tire and wheel assembly. Removal of the brake assembly may aid in spring removal, remove assembly as required.
3. At the center of the rear axle , remove the brake line, retaining clip and flexible hose.
4. Remove the parking brake tension spring, located on the rear axle.
5. Disconnect the parking brake cable from the turn buckle and the cable joint.
6. Support the axle with a jack, then remove the lower shock absorber bolt and the shock absorber from the vehicle.
7. Carefully lower the rear axle assembly and remove the rear coil spring.

To install:

8. Install the coil spring in position on the rear axle and raise the axle to position.
9. Support the axle in position and install the shock absorber to the vehicle. Tighten the lower shock absorber bolt to 30 ft. lbs. (40 Nm).

➡ **Raise the axle assembly to a distance of 15.2 in. from the top of the wheel wheel to the center of the axle hub, then torque the fasteners. Always replace the lower shock absorber bolt with a new one.**

10. Connect the parking brake cable to the turn buckle and the cable joint.
11. Install the parking brake tension spring, located on the rear axle.
12. At the center of the rear axle , install the brake line, retaining clip and flexible hose.
13. Install the tire and wheel assembly.
14. Carefully lower the vehicle.

Shock Absorbers

REMOVAL & INSTALLATION

Spectrum

1. Open the trunk and lift off the trim cover, hatch back vehicles only. Remove the upper shock absorber nut and raise and safely support the vehicle.
2. Remove the shock absorber lower attaching bolt.
3. Remove the shock absorber from the vehicle.
4. Reverse procedure to install.

➡ **When replacing the shock absorber, never reuse the old lower bolt, always use a new one.**

MacPherson Strut

REMOVAL & INSTALLATION

Storm

▶ **See Figures 13, 14, 15 and 16**

1. Raise and safely support the rear of the vehicle, then place a support under the suspension support. Remove the tire and wheel assembly.
2. Lower the vehicle slightly so the weight rest on the support and not the suspension arms.
3. Remove the flexible brake hose clip at the strut and the brake hose from the brake pipe.
4. Disconnect the stabilizer bar link from the strut assembly, then the strut assembly mounting nuts and bolts.
5. Open the rear hatch, then remove the trim cover panel from the strut tower.
6. Remove the strut assembly mounting nuts holding the top of the strut support, then the strut assembly from the vehicle.

To install:

7. Install the strut assembly to the vehicle and tighten the upper strut assembly mounting nuts to 50 ft. lbs. (68 Nm).
8. Install the rear trim cover panel to the strut tower.
9. Install strut to the knuckle and tighten the nuts and bolts to 116 ft. lbs. (157 Nm).
10. Install the brake hose to the brake pipe and install the flexible brake hose clip at the strut. Bleed the brakes.
11. Install the wheels and tire assemblies.
12. Raise and safely support the rear of the vehicle. Remove the jackstands.
13. Lower the vehicle.

Rear Control Arms

REMOVAL & INSTALLATION

Storm

1. Raise and safely support the vehicle.
2. Remove the tire and wheel assembly.
3. Remove trailing control arm nuts, then the trailing control arm from the vehicle.
4. Remove the right and left lateral control arms as follows:
   a. Remove the right lateral control arm attaching bolts from the rear crossmember and the rear suspension knuckle, then the right lateral control arm from the vehicle.
   b. Remove the left lateral control arms by loosening the 2 rear crossmember-to-body attaching bolts/nuts, then push crossmember down as far as possible and support with a jack. Remove the bolt from the rear crossmember and rear suspension knuckle, then the left lateral control arms from the vehicle.

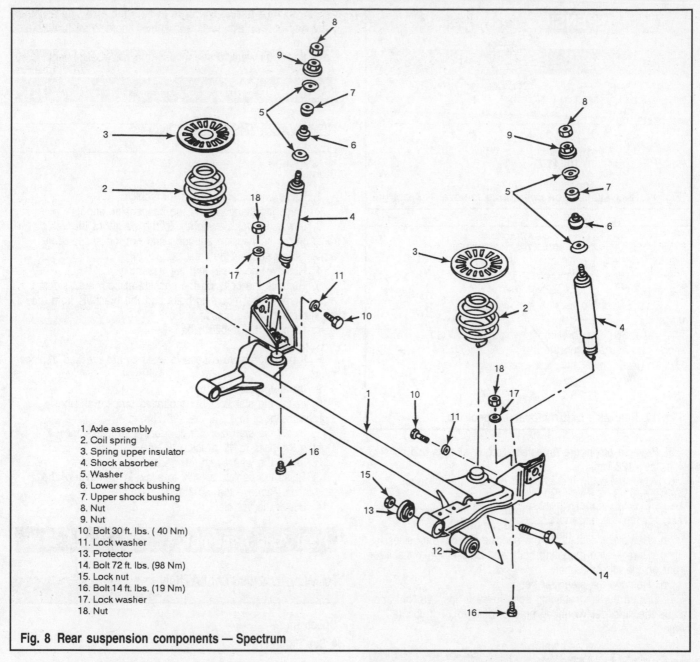

1. Axle assembly
2. Coil spring
3. Spring upper insulator
4. Shock absorber
5. Washer
6. Lower shock bushing
7. Upper shock bushing
8. Nut
9. Nut
10. Bolt 30 ft. lbs. (40 Nm)
11. Lock washer
13. Protector
14. Bolt 72 ft. lbs. (98 Nm)
15. Lock nut
16. Bolt 14 ft. lbs. (19 Nm)
17. Lock washer
18. Nut

Fig. 8 Rear suspension components — Spectrum

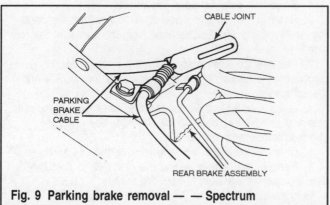

CABLE JOINT

PARKING
BRAKE
CABLE

REAR BRAKE ASSEMBLY

Fig. 9 Parking brake removal — — Spectrum

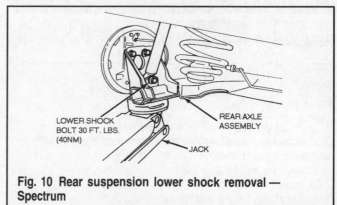

LOWER SHOCK
BOLT 30 FT. LBS.
(40NM)

REAR AXLE
ASSEMBLY

JACK

Fig. 10 Rear suspension lower shock removal — Spectrum

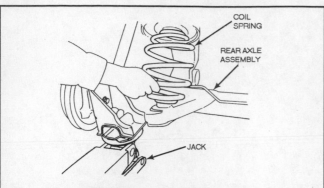

Fig. 11 Rear suspension coil spring removal — Spectrum

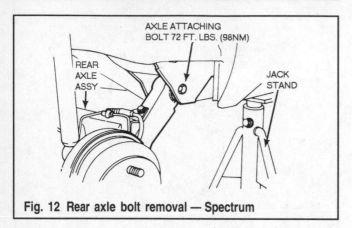

Fig. 12 Rear axle bolt removal — Spectrum

5. Reverse procedure to install. Torque all nuts and bolts to 94 ft. lbs. (128 Nm).

6. When removing the stabilizer bar use the following procedure:

    a. With the vehicle still in the raised and supported position and the wheel assemblies removed.

    b. Remove the bolts on the shackle at both strut sides.

    c. Remove the mounting bolts and brackets from stabilizer bar on the crossmember.

    d. Remove the stabilizer bar.

7. Torque the link retaining bolts to 19 ft. lbs. (26 Nm) and torque the stabilizer mounting bracket bolts to 71 ft. lbs. (96 Nm).

Trailing Links

REMOVAL & INSTALLATION

Storm

▶ See Figure 17

1. Raise and safely support the vehicle.
2. Remove the trailing link bolts from both the axle side and the body side.
3. Remove the trailing link from the vehicle.
To install:
4. Install the trailing link to the vehicle.

5. Install the trailing link bolts to both the axle side and the body side of the trailing link and tighten them to 94 ft. lbs. (128 Nm).

6. Lower the vehicle and inspect the wheel alignment.

Stabilizer Bar

REMOVAL & INSTALLATION

Storm

1. Raise and safely support the vehicle.
2. Place jackstands under the suspension support.
3. Lower the vehicle slightly so the weight of the vehicle rests on the suspension supports and not the suspension arms. Safely support the vehicle.
4. Remove the wheel and tire assembly.
5. Remove the bolts on the shackle at both strut sides.
6. Remove the mounting bolts and the brackets from the stabilizer bar on the crossmember.
7. Remove the stabilizer bar.
To install:
8. If bushings have excessive wear or are cracked, replace them.
9. Install the stabilizer bar.
10. Install the stabilizer bar mounting bracket and bolts. Tighten the bolts to 71 ft. lbs. (96 Nm).
11. Install the stabilizer bar link to the strut assemblies. Tighten the bolts to 19 ft. lbs. (26 Nm).
12. Install the wheel and tire assembly.
13. Raise the vehicle slightly to allow for removal of the jackstands. Remove the jackstands.
14. Lower the vehicle.

Rear Axle Assembly

REMOVAL & INSTALLATION

Spectrum

▶ See Figure 18

1. Raise and safely support the vehicle.
2. Remove the tire and wheel assemblies, then the brake line, retaining clip and flexible hose from the center of the rear axle.
3. Remove the tension spring from the rear axle, disconnect the parking brake cable from the turn buckle and the cable joint.
4. Using a suitable jack, support the lower side of the rear axle and remove the lower shock absorber bolt, then the shock absorber from the vehicle.
5. Carefully lower the jack and remove the coil spring.
6. Remove the bolts attaching the rear axle to the body, then the rear axle assembly from the vehicle.
To install:
7. Install the rear axle assembly to the lower part of the body and partially tighten the bolts.

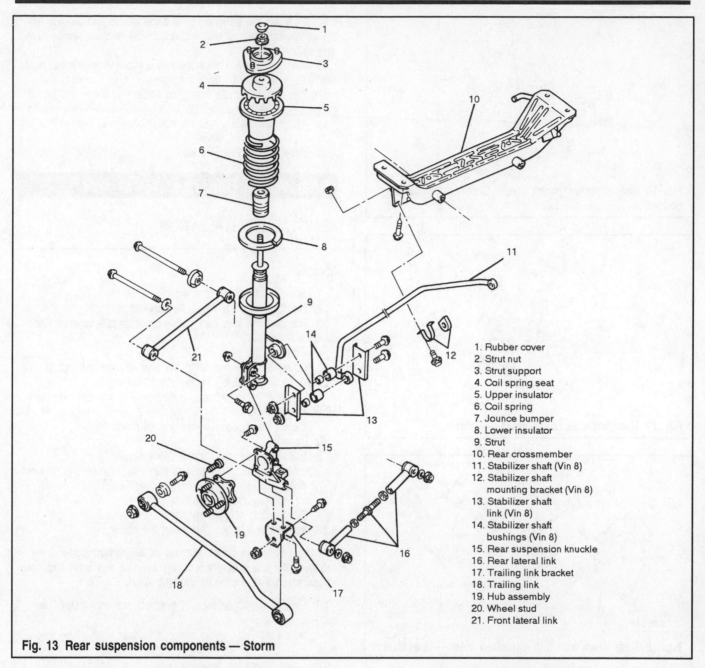

1. Rubber cover
2. Strut nut
3. Strut support
4. Coil spring seat
5. Upper insulator
6. Coil spring
7. Jounce bumper
8. Lower insulator
9. Strut
10. Rear crossmember
11. Stabilizer shaft (Vin 8)
12. Stabilizer shaft mounting bracket (Vin 8)
13. Stabilizer shaft link (Vin 8)
14. Stabilizer shaft bushings (Vin 8)
15. Rear suspension knuckle
16. Rear lateral link
17. Trailing link bracket
18. Trailing link
19. Hub assembly
20. Wheel stud
21. Front lateral link

Fig. 13 Rear suspension components — Storm

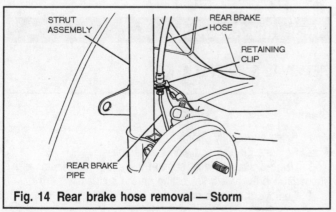

Fig. 14 Rear brake hose removal — Storm

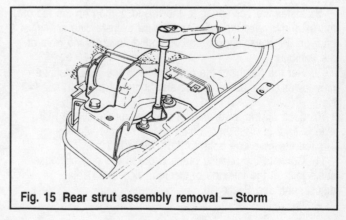

Fig. 15 Rear strut assembly removal — Storm

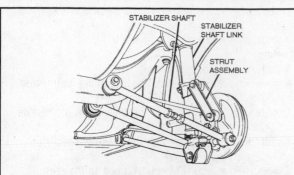

Fig. 16 Rear stabilizer shaft link — Storm with engine code 8

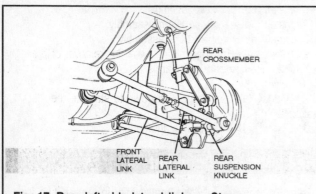

Fig. 17 Rear left side lateral links — Storm

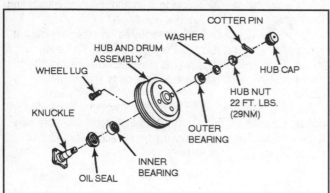

Fig. 18 Rear drum and hub exploded view — Spectrum

8. Install the coil spring to the raised portion on the top of the axle and raise the axle. Make sure to install the spring end, on the lower end of the coil spring, towards the front of the vehicle.

9. Set the height of the rear axle with the jack. Install a new lower shock absorber bolt and tighten it to 30 ft. lbs. (40 Nm).

10. Jack up the lower part of the rear axle until the rear axle is 15.2 in. (386 mm) below the top of the wheel arch. Tighten the rear axle bolts to 72 ft. lbs. (98 Nm).

11. Connect the parking brake cable to the parking brake cable joint at the left side of the rear axle. For cable adjustment, see Section 9.

12. Connect the parking brake cable to the turn buckle at the center of the rear axle and attach the tension spring to the rear axle.

13. Connect the flexible hose to the bracket at the top of the rear axle and secure it with the retaining clip. Connect the brake line to the flexible hose and tighten it. Bleed the brake system, see Section 9.

14. Attach the wheel and tire assemblies and tighten the lug nuts.

15. Safely lower the vehicle.

Rear Wheel Bearings

REMOVAL & INSTALLATION

Spectrum

1. Raise and support the vehicle safely.
2. Remove the rear wheel assemblies.
3. Remove the hub cap, cotter pin, hub nut, washer and outer bearing.
4. Remove the hub.
5. Using a slide hammer puller and attachment, pull the oil seal from the hub. Remove the inner bearing.
6. Using a brass drift and a hammer, drive both bearing races from the hub.
7. Clean, inspect and/or replace all parts.
   To install:
8. Install the hub and brake drum assembly.
9. Install the hub washer and hub nut. Tighten the hub nut to 22 ft. lbs. (29 Nm) while rotating the hub.
10. Completely loosen the hub nut.
11. Tighten the hub nut by hand.
12. Install the retainer and insert the cotter pin.

➡**If the cotter pin holes are out of alignment upon reassembly, use a wrench to tighten the nut until the hole in the shaft and a slot of the nut align.**

13. Grease the inner area of the hub cap and install the cap.
14. Install the rear wheel assemblies and tighten the wheel nuts.
15. Safely lower the vehicle.

Rear Hub Assembly

REMOVAL & INSTALLATION

Storm

1. Raise and safely support the vehicle.
2. Remove the tire and wheel assemblies.
3. Using a suitable jack, support the under suspension supports to prevent it from resting on the suspension arms.
4. Remove the brake drum, see Section 9.

5. Before removing the hub assembly, check the end-play as follows:

a. Using a suitable dial indicator tool (J-8001 or equivalent) along with the magnetic base (J-26900-1 or equivalent) measure the hub assembly end-play.

b. If the end-play exceeds 0.0020 in. (0.05mm), replace the axle hub bearing.

6. Remove the 4 retaining bolts holding the hub assembly to the knuckle.

7. Remove the hub assembly from the knuckle.

To install:

8. Install the hub assembly to the knuckle. Install the retaining bolts and torque them to 49 ft. lbs. (66 Nm).

9. Install the brake drum, see Section 9.

10. Install the tire and wheel assembly. Raise the vehicle and remove the jack. Lower the vehicle.

11. Bounce the vehicle up and down to stabilize the suspension.

12. Check the rear wheel alignment.

Rear Knuckle

REMOVAL & INSTALLATION

Storm

1. Raise and safely support the vehicle.

2. Place jackstands under the suspension support.

3. Lower the vehicle slightly so the weight of the vehicle rests on the suspension supports and not the suspension arms. Safely support the vehicle.

4. Remove the wheel and tire assembly.

5. Remove the rear hub unit assembly.

6. Remove the backing plate with the brake assembly and set aside.

7. Disconnect the through bolt from the trailing link at the axle side.

8. Disconnect the through bolt from the lateral link at the axle side.

9. Remove the knuckle from the strut.

To install:

10. Install the knuckle to the strut.

11. Connect the through bolt to the lateral link at the axle side and tighten to 94 ft. lbs. (128 Nm).

12. Connect the through bolt to the trailing link at the axle side and tighten to 94 ft. lbs. (128 Nm).

13. Install the backing plate with the brake assembly in place.

14. Connect the lateral link mounting bolt to the rear suspension knuckle and tighten.

15. Connect the trailing link mounting bolt to the rear suspension knuckle and tighten.

16. Install the rear hub assembly.

17. Install the rear brake drum assembly.

18. Install the wheel and tire assembly.

19. Raise the vehicle slightly to allow for removal of the jackstands. Remove the jackstands.

20. Lower the vehicle.

21. Bounce the vehicle up and down to stabilize the suspension.

22. Check the rear wheel alignment.

Rear Wheel Alignment

Refer to 'Front Wheel Alignment' earlier in this Section for explanations of important alignment angles, which also pertain to the rear wheels. The following is in addition to that text, and is informational only.

Camber and caster cannot be adjusted on these vehicles. If the camber is found to be out of specification, the cause should be located and corrected. Suspension parts may be damaged, bent, worn or loose. These parts should be replaced.

Rear toe cannot be adjusted on the Spectrum. If the toe is out of specification, damaged or broken suspension parts may be the cause. These parts should be replaced. The rear toe on the Storm can be adjusted.

REAR WHEEL ALIGNMENT

Year	Model	Caster Range (deg.)	Caster Preferred Setting (deg.)	Camber Range (deg.)	Camber Preferred Setting (deg.)	Toe-in (in.)	Steering Axis Inclination (deg.)
1985	Spectrum	NA	NA	$1^3/_{16}N - ^{27}/_{32}P$	$^3/_{16}N$	$^5/_{64} \pm ^5/_{64}$	NA
1986	Spectrum	NA	NA	$1^3/_{16}N - ^{27}/_{32}P$	$^3/_{16}N$	$^5/_{64} \pm ^5/_{64}$	NA
1987	Spectrum	NA	NA	$1^3/_{16}N - ^{27}/_{32}P$	$^3/_{16}N$	$^5/_{64} \pm ^5/_{64}$	NA
1988	Spectrum	NA	NA	$1^3/_{16}N - ^{27}/_{32}P$	$^3/_{16}N$	$^5/_{64} \pm ^5/_{64}$	NA
1989	Spectrum	NA	NA	$^3/_4N - ^3/_4P$	0	$^7/_{32} \pm ^7/_{32}$	NA
1990	Storm	NA	NA	$1^1/_2N - ^1/_2P$	$^1/_2N$	$^5/_{32} \pm ^1/_{32}$	NA
1991	Storm	NA	NA	$1^1/_2N - ^1/_2P$	$^1/_2N$	$^5/_{32} \pm ^1/_{32}$	NA
1992	Storm	NA	NA	$1^1/_4N - ^1/_4P$	$^1/_2N$	$^5/_{64} \pm ^3/_{64}$	NA
1993	Storm	NA	NA	$1^1/_4N - ^1/_4P$	$^1/_2N$	$^5/_{64} \pm ^3/_{64}$	NA

NA—Not available

STEERING

Steering Wheel

❊❊CAUTION

On vehicles equipped with an air bag, the air bag system must be disarmed before working around the steering wheel or instrument panel. Failure to do so may result in deployment of the air bag and possible personal injury. Refer to the Air Bag Disarming procedures later in this Section.

REMOVAL & INSTALLATION

Spectrum

▶ See Figure 19

1. Disconnect the negative battery terminal from the battery.
2. Using a suitable tool, remove the shroud screws from the rear-side of the steering wheel (Type 1) or pry the shroud from the steering wheel (Type 2).
3. Disconnect the horn connector and remove the shroud.
4. Remove the nut/washer retaining the steering wheel to the steering shaft.

5. Using a steering wheel puller, remove the steering wheel.

➡The steering shaft and the steering column are designed to absorb impact from collision. Be careful not to severely jar the steering column and shaft during removal and installation.

To install:

6. Install the steering wheel onto the steering shaft.
7. Tighten the nut/washer retaining the steering wheel to the steering shaft to 22 ft. lbs. (29 Nm).
8. Connect the horn connector.
9. Install the shroud and tighten the shroud screws from the rear-side of the steering wheel, if so equipped.
10. Connect the negative battery terminal from the battery.

Storm

▶ See Figures 20 and 21

1. If equipped, with an air bag system, disable the air bag system as follows:
   a. Turn the ignition switch to the OFF position.
   b. Disconnect the battery negative cable.
   c. Remove fuses C-22 and C-23 from the fuse box.
   d. Disconnect the orange 3-way connector at the base of the steering column.

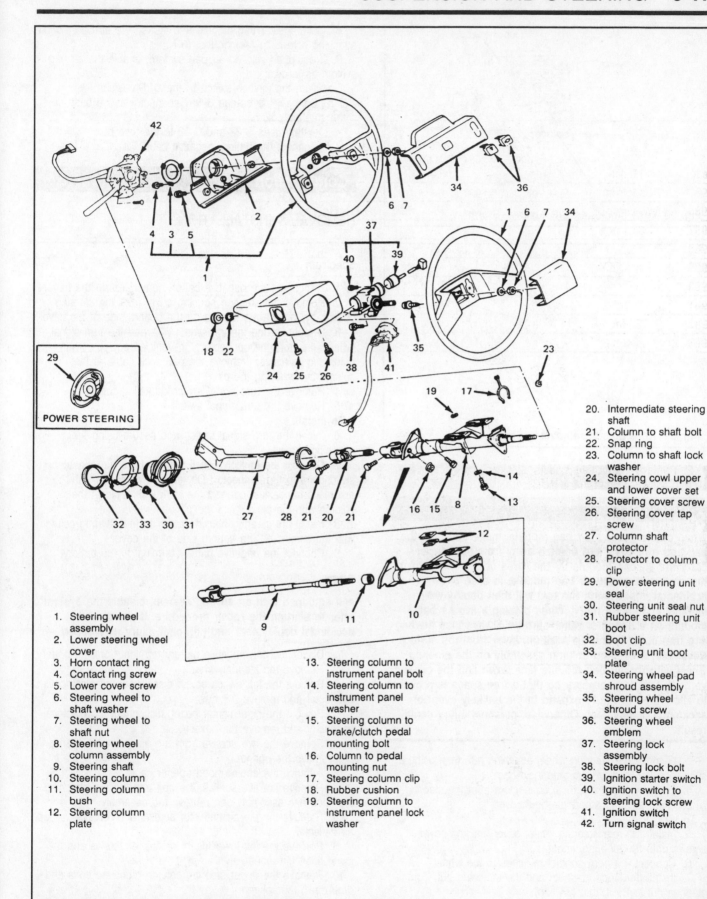

POWER STEERING

1. Steering wheel
   assembly
2. Lower steering wheel
   cover
3. Horn contact ring
4. Contact ring screw
5. Lower cover screw
6. Steering wheel to
   shaft washer
7. Steering wheel to
   shaft nut
8. Steering wheel
   column assembly
9. Steering shaft
10. Steering column
11. Steering column
    bush
12. Steering column
    plate

13. Steering column to
    instrument panel bolt
14. Steering column to
    instrument panel
    washer
15. Steering column to
    brake/clutch pedal
    mounting bolt
16. Column to pedal
    mounting nut
17. Steering column clip
18. Rubber cushion
19. Steering column to
    instrument panel lock
    washer

20. Intermediate steering
    shaft
21. Column to shaft bolt
22. Snap ring
23. Column to shaft lock
    washer
24. Steering cowl upper
    and lower cover set
25. Steering cover screw
26. Steering cover tap
    screw
27. Column shaft
    protector
28. Protector to column
    clip
29. Power steering unit
    seal
30. Steering unit seal nut
31. Rubber steering unit
    boot
32. Boot clip
33. Steering unit boot
    plate
34. Steering wheel pad
    shroud assembly
35. Steering wheel
    shroud screw
36. Steering wheel
    emblem
37. Steering lock
    assembly
38. Steering lock bolt
39. Ignition starter switch
40. Ignition switch to
    steering lock screw
41. Ignition switch
42. Turn signal switch

Fig. 19 Steering column components — Spectrum

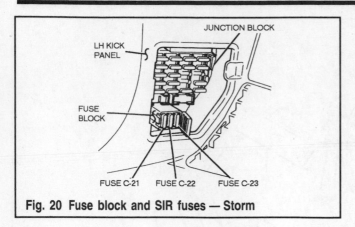

Fig. 20 Fuse block and SIR fuses — Storm

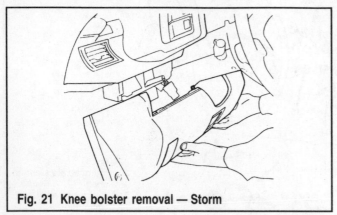

Fig. 21 Knee bolster removal — Storm

2. Remove the air bag module attaching screws, then the air bag assembly from the vehicle.

✳✳CAUTION

When carrying a live air bag module, make sure that the bag and trim cover are pointed away from you. Never carry the air bag module by the wires or the connector on the underside of the air bag module. In case of an accidental deployment, the bag will then deploy with minimal chance of injury. When placing a live air bag module on a bench or other surface, always face the bag and trim cover in the up position, away from the surface. Never rest a steering column assembly on the steering wheel with the air bag module face down and the column vertical. This is necessary so that a free space is provided to allow the air bag to expand in the unlikely event of accidental deployment. Otherwise, personal injury could result.

3. Remove the steering wheel attaching nut, then using a suitable puller, remove the steering wheel.

4. Disconnect the electrical connectors from the steering wheel, then the rear steering wheel cover.

To install:

5. Install the rear steering wheel cover and the cover screws onto the steering wheel.

6. Connect the horn contact switches to the wheel.

7. Install the steering wheel and the attaching nut. Torque steering nut to 25 ft. lbs. (34 Nm).

8. Install the air bag module and tighten the air bag module attaching screws to 44 inch lbs. (5 Nm).

9. If equipped with an air bag system, enable the air bag system as follows:

   a. Turn the ignition switch to the **OFF** position.

   b. Connect the orange 3-way connector at the base of the steering column.

   c. Install fuses C-22 and C-23 to the fuse box.

   d. Connect the battery negative cable.

Combination Switch

REMOVAL & INSTALLATION

Spectrum

1. Disconnect the negative battery terminal from the battery.

2. Remove the steering housing cover from the steering column by remove the screws on the bottom side of the cover.

3. Disconnect the ignition switch wire and the turn signal switch wire from the connector. On vehicles equipped with automatic transaxles, remove the park lock cable at the column by removing the pin.

4. Remove the turn signal switch attaching screws.

5. Remove the turn signal switch.

To install:

6. Install the turn signal switch and secure using the attaching screws.

7. Connect the ignition switch wire and the turn signal switch wire to the connector. On vehicles equipped with automatic transaxles, connect the park lock cable at the column with the pin.

8. Install the steering housing cover to the steering column with the screws on the bottom side of the cover.

9. Connect the negative battery terminal to the battery.

Storm

➡**If equipped with an air bag system, disable the system prior to starting the repair procedure. If not disabled, accidental deployment and personal injury may occur.**

1. Disconnect the negative battery terminal from the battery.

2. Remove the steering wheel.

3. Pull out the left switch bezel, disconnect the electrical connector and remove the bezel.

4. Pull out the cigar lighter bezel, disconnect the electrical connector and remove the bezel.

5. Remove the two screws from the engine hood opener and remove the opener.

6. Remove the engine hood opener cable.

7. Remove the five screws, the bolt and the nut attaching the knee pad assembly and remove the assembly.

8. Remove the lap air deflector screws and remove the lap air deflector.

9. Remove the left lower dash trim panel screws and the lower dash trim panel.

10. Remove the upper steering column mounting bolts and drop down the column.

11. Remove the two piece steering column cover screws and the two piece steering column cover.

12. Disconnect the coil assembly wiring harness from the turn signal switch.

13. Remove the four screws and the coil assembly from the turn signal switch.

14. Remove the turn signal switch screws and the turn signal switch.

To install:

15. Install the turn signal switch screws and the turn signal switch.

16. Install the four screws and the coil assembly to the turn signal switch.

17. Connect the coil assembly wiring harness to the turn signal switch.

18. Install the two piece steering column cover and the two piece steering column cover screws.

19. Raise the steering column and install the upper steering column mounting bolts. Tighten the bolts to 18 ft. lbs. (24 Nm).

20. Install the left lower dash trim panel and tighten the lower dash trim panel screws.

21. Install the lap air deflector and tighten the lap air deflector screws.

22. Install the knee pad assembly and tighten the five screws, the bolt and the nut attaching the assembly.

23. Install the engine hood opener cable.

24. Install the engine hood opener and tighten the two screws.

25. Connect the electrical connector to the cigar lighter bezel and install the bezel.

26. Connect the electrical connector to the left switch bezel and install the bezel.

27. Install the steering wheel.

28. Connect the negative battery terminal to the battery.

Ignition Switch

REMOVAL & INSTALLATION

Spectrum

1. Remove the negative battery cable.

2. Remove the steering wheel and the steering cowl by removing the screws under the cowl. Remove the combination switch.

3. Disconnect the switch wires at the connectors.

4. Remove the two screws attaching the ignition and starter switch. Remove the switch.

To install:

5. Install the starter switch and the two screws attaching the switch to the ignition.

6. Connect the switch wires at the connectors.

7. Install the combination switch.

8. Install the steering cowl and tighten the screws underneath.

9. Install the steering wheel.

Storm

➡If equipped with an air bag system, disable the system prior to starting the repair procedure. If not disabled, accidental deployment and personal injury may occur.

1. Remove the negative battery cable.

2. Remove the steering wheel.

3. Remove the combination switch assembly.

4. Turn the key to the **OFF** position, depress the retaining pin and remove the ignition lock cylinder from the switch.

5. Disconnect the electrical connector from the ignition switch.

6. Remove the snapring and spacer collar from the steering shaft.

7. Disconnect the back drive cable from the ignition switch.

8. Remove the ignition switch bolts and the ignition switch from the steering column.

To install:

9. Install the ignition switch to the steering column and tighten the bolts.

10. Connect the back drive cable to the ignition switch.

11. Install the spacer collar and the snapring to the steering shaft.

12. Connect the electrical connector to the ignition switch.

13. Install the lock cylinder into the switch.

14. Install the turn signal switch screws and the turn signal switch.

15. Install the four screws and the coil assembly to the turn signal switch.

16. Connect the coil assembly wiring harness to the turn signal switch.

17. Install the two piece steering column cover and the two piece steering column cover screws.

18. Raise the steering column and install the upper steering column mounting bolts. Tighten the bolts to 18 ft. lbs. (24 Nm).

19. Install the left lower dash trim panel and tighten the lower dash trim panel screws.

20. Install the lap air deflector and tighten the lap air deflector screws.

21. Install the knee pad assembly and tighten the five screws, the bolt and the nut attaching the assembly.

22. Install the engine hood opener cable.

23. Install the engine hood opener and tighten the two screws.

24. Connect the electrical connector to the cigar lighter bezel and install the bezel.

25. Connect the electrical connector to the left switch bezel and install the bezel.

26. Install the steering wheel.

27. Connect the negative battery terminal to the battery.

Ignition Lock Cylinder

REMOVAL & INSTALLATION

Spectrum

1. Remove the negative battery cable.

2. Remove the steering wheel and the steering cowl by removing the screws under the cowl. Remove the combination switch.

3. Disconnect the switch wires at the connectors.

4. Remove the two screws attaching the ignition and starter switch. Remove the switch.

5. Turn the key to the **OFF** position, depress the retaining pin and remove the ignition lock cylinder from the switch.

To install:

6. Install the lock cylinder into the switch.

7. Install the starter switch and the two screws attaching the switch to the ignition.

8. Connect the switch wires at the connectors.

9. Install the combination switch.

10. Install the steering cowl and tighten the screws underneath.

11. Install the steering wheel.

Storm

➡**If equipped with an air bag system, disable the system prior to starting the repair procedure. If not disabled, accidental deployment and personal injury may occur.**

1. Remove the negative battery cable.

2. Remove the steering wheel.

3. Remove the combination switch assembly.

4. Turn the key to the **OFF** position, depress the retaining pin and remove the ignition lock cylinder from the switch.

To install:

5. Install the lock cylinder into the switch.

6. Install the turn signal switch screws and the turn signal switch.

7. Install the four screws and the coil assembly to the turn signal switch.

8. Connect the coil assembly wiring harness to the turn signal switch.

9. Install the two piece steering column cover and the two piece steering column cover screws.

10. Raise the steering column and install the upper steering column mounting bolts. Tighten the bolts to 18 ft. lbs. (24 Nm).

11. Install the left lower dash trim panel and tighten the lower dash trim panel screws.

12. Install the lap air deflector and tighten the lap air deflector screws.

13. Install the knee pad assembly and tighten the five screws, the bolt and the nut attaching the assembly.

14. Install the engine hood opener cable.

15. Install the engine hood opener and tighten the two screws.

16. Connect the electrical connector to the cigar lighter bezel and install the bezel.

17. Connect the electrical connector to the left switch bezel and install the bezel.

18. Install the steering wheel.

19. Connect the negative battery terminal to the battery.

Steering Column

REMOVAL & INSTALLATION

Spectrum

▶ See Figures 22 and 23

1. Disconnect the negative battery cable.

2. From under the dash, remove the steering column protector nut, clip and protector.

3. Remove the pinch bolt between the intermediate shaft and the steering shaft.

4. Remove the mounting bracket bolts from the lower column.

5. Remove the steering column-to-instrument panel mounting bolts.

6. Remove the electrical connectors and park lock cable at the ignition switch.

➡**If equipped with an automatic transaxle, remove the park lock cable bracket.**

7. Remove the steering column assembly.

To install:

8. Install the steering column assembly.

9. Connect the electrical connectors and park lock cable at the ignition switch.

➡**If equipped with an automatic transaxle, install the park lock cable bracket.**

10. Install the steering column-to-instrument panel mounting bolts.

11. Install the mounting bracket bolts from the lower column.

12. Install the pinch bolt between the intermediate shaft and the steering shaft and tighten the bolts to 19 ft. lbs. (26 Nm).

13. Under the dash, Install the steering column protector nut, clip and protector.

14. Connect the negative battery cable.

Storm

1. If equipped, with an air bag system, disable the air bag system as follows:

   a. Turn the ignition switch to the **OFF** position.

   b. Disconnect the battery negative cable.

   c. Remove fuses C-22 and C-23 from the fuse box.

   d. Disconnect the orange 3-way connector at the base of the steering column.

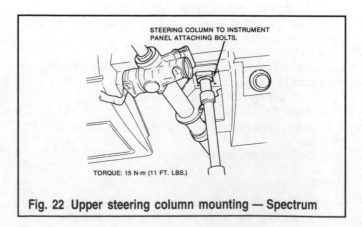

STEERING COLUMN TO INSTRUMENT PANEL ATTACHING BOLTS.

TORQUE: 15 N·m (11 FT. LBS.)

Fig. 22 Upper steering column mounting — Spectrum

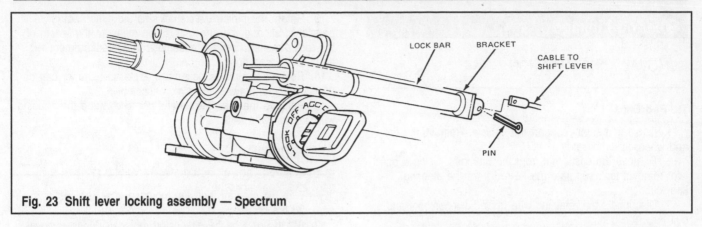

Fig. 23 Shift lever locking assembly — Spectrum

2. Remove the air bag module attaching screws, then the air bag assembly from the vehicle.

✳✳CAUTION

When carrying a live air bag module, make sure that the bag and trim cover are pointed away from you. Never carry the air bag module by the wires or the connector on the underside of the air bag module. In case of an accidental deployment, the bag will then deploy with minimal chance of injury. When placing a live air bag module on a bench or other surface, always face the bag and trim cover in the up position, away from the surface. Never rest a steering column assembly on the steering wheel with the air bag module face down and the column vertical. This is necessary so that a free space is provided to allow the air bag to expand in the unlikely event of accidental deployment. Otherwise, personal injury could result.

3. Remove the steering wheel attaching nut, then using a suitable puller, remove the steering wheel.

4. Disconnect the electrical connectors from the steering wheel, then the rear steering wheel cover.

5. Remove the lower switch panel and the dash lighter panel.

6. Disconnect the hood release cable, then remove the lap air deflector.

7. Remove the left lower trim panel, then the upper steering column attaching bolts and lower the column.

8. Remove the 2 piece steering column attaching screws, then the 2 piece steering column cover.

9. Disconnect the electrical connectors, then the back drive cable from the ignition switch.

10. Remove the pinch bolt from the steering column knuckle, then the 2 lower column mount attaching nuts. Remove the column from the vehicle.

To install:

11. Install steering column assembly, then the 2 rear column mount nuts. Torque nuts to 18 ft. lbs. (24 Nm).

12. Install intermediate shaft to column, then the pinch bolt. Torque pinch bolt to 30 ft. lbs. (40 Nm).

13. Connect the back drive cable to the ignition switch.

14. Connect all the electrical connectors, then install the 2 piece steering column cover.

15. Install the upper column bolts. Torque bolts to 18 ft. lbs. (24 Nm).

16. Install the lower dash trim panel and the air conditioning lap deflector.

17. Connect the hood release cable, then install the lighter panel and the lower switch panel.

18. Install the steering wheel. Connect the battery negative cable.

19. Reactivate the air bag system as follows:

   a. Turn the ignition switch to the **OFF** position.

   b. Connect the orange 3-way connector at the base of the steering column.

   c. Install fuses C-22 and C-23 to the fuse box.

   d. Connect the battery negative cable.

DISASSEMBLY & ASSEMBLY

1. Remove the turn signal switch to the column attaching screws and remove the switch assembly.

2. Insert the key into the ignition and turn the key to the **ON** position (with the lock bar pulled all the way in).

3. Remove the steering shaft snaping and the rubber cushion.

4. Remove the lock assembly-to-steering column attaching screws and remove the lock assembly.

5. Remove the shaft from the column.

6. On the Storm, remove the cable and guide from the column.

To assemble:

7. Slide guide onto column on the Storm.

8. Slide the steering shaft into the column.

9. Insert the key into the ignition and turn the key to the **ON** position (with the lock bar pulled all the way in). Install the lock assembly to the steering column and tighten the attaching screws.

10. Install the rubber cushion and snapring to the steering shaft. Be sure the snapring is securely seated.

11. Install the turn signal switch assembly to the column and tighten the attaching screws.

Steering Linkage

REMOVAL & INSTALLATION

Tie Rod Ends

1. Raise and safely support the vehicle. Remove the tire and wheel assemblies.
2. Remove the castle nut from the ball joint. Using a ball joint removal tool, separate the tie rod from the steering knuckle.
3. Disconnect the retaining wire from the inner boot and pull back the boot.
4. Using a chisel, straighten the staked part of the locking washer between the tie rod and the rack.
5. Remove the tie rod from the rack.
6. Reverse procedure to install.

Manual Rack and Pinion

REMOVAL & INSTALLATION

▶ See Figure 24

1. Remove the intermediate shaft cover.
2. Loosen the upper pinch bolt. Remove the lower pinch bolt at the pinion shaft.
3. Raise and safely support the vehicle. Remove the wheel assemblies.
4. Remove both tie rod ends from the steering knuckles and the left inner tie rod from the rack.
5. Remove the steering gear-to-body attaching nuts and the rack and pinion assembly from the vehicle.

To install:

6. Install the rack and pinion assembly to the vehicle and tighten the steering gear-to-body attaching nuts.
7. Install both tie rod ends to the steering knuckles and the left inner tie rod to the rack.
8. Install the wheel assemblies. Safely lower the vehicle.
9. Install the lower pinch bolt at the pinion shaft and tighten the upper pinch bolt.
10. Install the intermediate shaft cover.

DISASSEMBLY

▶ See Figures 25, 26 and 27

1. Place the steering unit a vise.
2. Remove the tie-rod end.
3. Remove the boot.
4. Straighten the bent part of the locking washer between the inner tie-rod and the rack. A new washer should be used when reassembled.
5. Remove the tie-rod from the rack.
6. Loosen the adjusting plug nut, remove the spring and plunger.
7. Remove the pinion seal.
8. Remove the snapring.

9. Rotate the pinion gear shaft until the pinion flat is parallel or aligned with the rack. Then measure the length of the rack exposed from the assembly. This measurement will be used to reassemble the unit.
10. Remove the pinion assembly. A plastic hammer can be used when withdrawing the pinion assembly.
11. Remove the rack. Be careful not to damage the housing while remove the rack.

ASSEMBLY

1. With the steering housing mounted in a vise, install the rack into the housing.
2. Set the rack to the dimension recorded during removal. Install the pinion with the flat side parallel to the rack.
3. Install the pinion retaining snapring.
4. Lubricate the plunger well and install. Install the spring, adjusting plug and the locknut.
5. Tighten the adjusting plug to 4 ft. lbs. (5 Nm).
6. Repeat step 5.
7. Back off the adjusting plug up to 25 degrees.
8. Install the pinion shaft seal. Tighten the locknut snug.
9. Measure the pinion shaft preload. If the preload is not between 0.4-0.9 ft. lbs. (0.6-1.3 Nm), loosen the locknut and readjust the plug torque. When the acceptable preload is achieved, apply liquid thread lock to the locknut and tighten the locknut to 49 ft. lbs. (66 Nm).
10. Install the inner tie rod and a new locking washer to the rack end. Tighten it to 65 ft. lbs. (88 Nm). Protect the rack from the vise. Stake the locking washer to the flat of the inner tie-rod. Apply grease to the inner surface of the small opening in the boot.
11. Install a new boot over the inner tie-rod.
12. Install the tie-rod nut and attach the tie-rod end.
13. Adjust the tie-rod so the length from the outer side of the boot clamp to the outer side of the locknut is 7.5 in. (190.4 mm).
14. Tighten the tie-rod locking nut to 40 ft. lbs. (54 Nm).
15. Install the boot clamp and wire.

Power Rack and Pinion

REMOVAL & INSTALLATION

Spectrum

1. Raise and support the vehicle safely.
2. Remove both tie rod ends from the steering knuckles and the right inner tie rod from the rack.
3. Place a drain pan under the rack assembly and clean around the pressure lines at the rack valve.
4. Cut the plastic retaining straps at the power steering lines and hose.
5. Remove the power steering pump lines, the rack valve and drain the fluid into the pan.
6. Remove the rack and pinion.
7. To install, reverse the removal procedures, add fluid, bleed the system and check the toe-in.

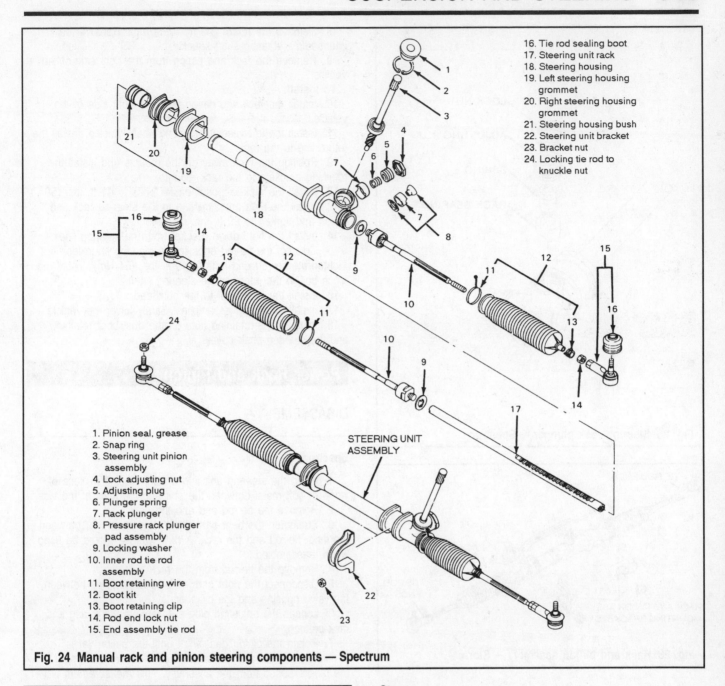

16. Tie rod sealing boot
17. Steering unit rack
18. Steering housing
19. Left steering housing grommet
20. Right steering housing grommet
21. Steering housing bush
22. Steering unit bracket
23. Bracket nut
24. Locking tie rod to knuckle nut

STEERING UNIT ASSEMBLY

1. Pinion seal, grease
2. Snap ring
3. Steering unit pinion assembly
4. Lock adjusting nut
5. Adjusting plug
6. Plunger spring
7. Rack plunger
8. Pressure rack plunger pad assembly
9. Locking washer
10. Inner rod tie rod assembly
11. Boot retaining wire
12. Boot kit
13. Boot retaining clip
14. Rod end lock nut
15. End assembly tie rod

Fig. 24 Manual rack and pinion steering components — Spectrum

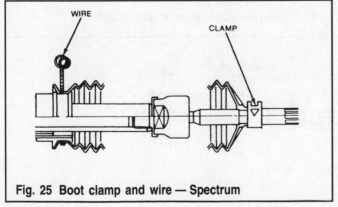

WIRE

CLAMP

Fig. 25 Boot clamp and wire — Spectrum

Storm

▶ See Figure 28

1. Remove the steering shaft cover and 3 retaining nuts on the dust boot retaining ring.

2. Raise and safely support the vehicle. Remove the tires and wheels.

3. Remove the dust boot from the bulkhead. Place a drain pan beneath the vehicle.

4. Remove the pinch bolt from the intermediate steering shaft. Disconnect the tie-rod ends from the steering knuckles.

5. Remove the hold down bracket from the steering lines.

6. Remove the high pressure line from the steering rack and pinion. Remove the rack to crossmember bolts.

7. Remove the retaining brackets from the rack mounts. Position the rack away from the mounts.

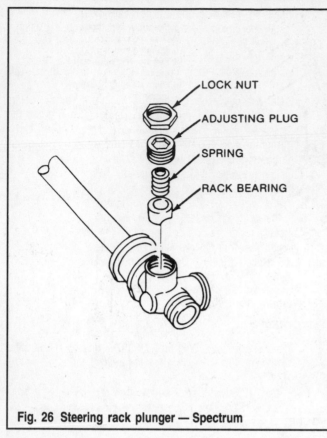

Fig. 26 Steering rack plunger — Spectrum

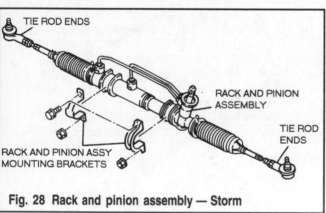

Fig. 28 Rack and pinion assembly — Storm

8. Remove the return line from the rack. Remove the intermediate steering shaft knuckle.

9. Remove the rack and pinion from the right side of the vehicle.

To install:

10. Install the rack and pinion from the right side of the vehicle.

11. Install the intermediate steering shaft knuckle. Install the return line to the rack.

12. Position the rack away on the mounts and install the retaining brackets to the rack mounts.

13. Install the rack-to-crossmember bolts to 41 ft. lbs. (59 Nm). Install the high pressure line to the steering rack and pinion and tighten to 20 ft. lbs. (27 Nm).

14. Install the hold down bracket from the steering lines.

15. Connect the tie-rod ends to the steering knuckles. Tighten the tie rod end nuts to 40 ft. lbs. (54 Nm). Install the pinch bolt to the intermediate steering shaft.

16. Install the dust boot to the bulkhead.

17. Install the wheel assemblies. Safely lower the vehicle.

18. Install the 3 retaining nuts on the dust boot retaining ring and the steering shaft cover.

Power Rack and Pinion

DISASSEMBLY

Spectrum

1. Insert the steering unit into a vise, placing a piece of wood or soft metal between the unit and the jaws of the vise.

2. Remove the tie-rod end and the boot.

3. Straighten the bent part of the locking washer between the inner tie-rod and the rack. A new washer should be used when reassembled.

4. Remove the tie-rod from the rack.

5. Disconnect the right and left pipe assemblies between the valve housing and the cylinder.

6. Loosen the adjusting plug nut, remove the spring and rack bearing.

7. Rotate the pinion gear shaft until the pinion flat is parallel or aligned with the rack. Then measure the length of the rack exposed from the assembly. This measurement will be used to reassemble the unit.

8. Remove the valve/pinion housing assembly.

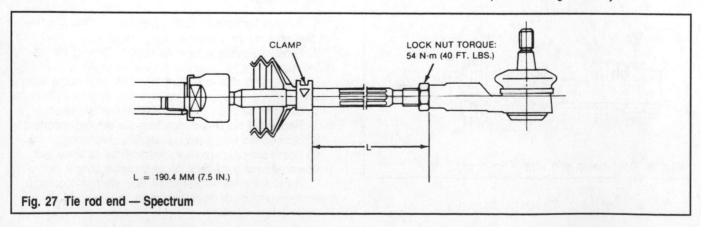

Fig. 27 Tie rod end — Spectrum

9. Remove the adjusting shims.

10. Remove retaining ring from the right side.

11. Withdraw the rack assembly, on the right side, and the seal holder together. Carefully remove the rack from the housing to avoid damaging the inner housing face.

12. Remove the inner rack seal and the shock dampener.

13. Remove the piston and the O-ring seals from the rack.

14. With a soft head hammer, drive the valve assembly from the housing.

15. Drive the bearing and seal from the valve housing with tool J 33997, or the equivalent.

16. Remove the snapring from the spool end of the valve assembly, then slide the spool, seals and spacer. Do not remove the teflon seals. The valve is serviced as an assembly.

Storm

1. Insert the steering unit into a vise, placing a piece of wood or soft metal between the unit and the jaws of the vise.

2. Retaining ring and dust boot from the rack.

3. Remove the clamps from the tie rod boots. Separate the boots from the rack and slide them down the tie rods. Unstake the locking washers between inner tie rods and the rack.

4. Remove the right tie rod assembly from the rack.

5. Remove the left tie rod assembly from the rack.

6. Loosen the adjusting plug nut, remove the spring and rack plunger.

7. Rotate the pinion gear shaft until the pinion flat is parallel or aligned with the rack. Then measure the length of the rack exposed from the assembly. This measurement will be used to reassemble the unit.

8. Remove the valve plug.

9. Remove the pinion fixing nut.

10. Remove pinion retaining snapring.

11. Remove the pinion valve assembly from the rack.

12. Remove the retaining ring from the right side of the rack housing.

13. Withdraw the rack from the housing.

14. Using the inner rack seal remover J 38304-5 or the equivalent, remove the inner rack seal and the shock dampener.

15. Remove the lower pinion bearing from the rack housing.

16. Using the J 38304-1 lower pinion valve housing seal and bearing remover or the equivalent, remove the bearing and seal from the valve housing.

ASSEMBLY

Storm

1. Install the inner rack seal onto J 33997-3 rack seal ring installer, using a J 33997-2 rack seal ring expander. Install inner rack seal into the rack, using a J 33997-3 rack seal ring installer.

2. Install the upper bearing and seal into the pinion valve housing, using a J 38304-4 lower pinion valve housing seal and bearing installer.

3. Install the rack into the housing and seat the inner rack seal, using the rack piston ring installer J 38304-7 and the inner rack seal installer J 38304-6, or equivalents.

4. Insert the seal holder into the housing.

5. Install the retaining ring on the seal holder.

6. Install the pinion valve assembly into the housing using J 38304-8 pinion ring compressor.

7. Install the lower bearing on the pinion valve.

8. Install the pinion fixed nut and tighten it to 29 ft. lbs. (39 Nm).

9. Install the cap on the bottom of the pinion valve housing.

10. Install the rack plunger and the plunger plug. Tighten the rack plunger adjusting plug to 44 in. lbs. (5 Nm). Loosen the plug and tighten again to 44 in. lbs. (5 Nm), then back the nut off 26 degrees and tighten the locking nut.

11. Install the upper pinion valve seal.

12. Install the retaining ring on the upper pinion valve seal.

13. Install the left tie rod assembly. Tighten the inner tie rod to 65 ft. lbs. (88 Nm). Peen the stake washer.

14. Install the left tie rod boot.

15. Install the right tie rod assembly. Tighten the inner tie rod to 65 ft. lbs. (88 Nm). Peen the stake washer.

16. Install the right tie rod boot.

Valve/Pinion Assembly

SPECTRUM

1. Install the spacer. With tool J 33997-7 or equivalent, slide the oil seal onto the shaft, with the flat side of the seal toward the spacer.

2. Install the valve spool. Do not force the spool onto the pinion shaft. If it does not slide onto the pinion shaft, use tool J 33997-4 or equivalent to compress the seal ring, then install the spool.

3. Install the snapring on the shaft at the spool.

4. Use a press to install the upper bearing and, using tool J 33997-4 or equivalent, install the seal into the valve housing with the flat side toward the bearing.

5. Use tool J 33997-8 or equivalent to compress the seal rings onto the spool housing and install pinion/valve assembly into the valve housing.

6. Place tool J 33997-9 on the upper pinion shaft. Install the pinion/valve assembly into the valve housing.

Rack Piston

SPECTRUM

1. Use tool J 33997-6 or equivalent to compress the seal ring. Install the seal onto the rack piston.

2. Apply grease to the rack gear surfaces. Install the seal into the seal holder with the flat end of the seal first. Install the seal holder assembly using the seal protector tool J 33997-9 or equivalent.

3. Install the shock damper ring using tools J 35527 and J 7079-2 or equivalents.

4. Install inner rack seal on the gear side of the rack. The shim stock should be used to protect the seal from the rack gear surface. The flat end of the seal should be away from the rack piston.

5. Install the rack assembly and push the seal holder into the housing. Install the retaining ring.

6. Move the rack assembly into the housing as far as possible and measure the distance between the end of the holder and the tip of the rack shaft. The seals are positioned correctly when the distance is 10mm or more.

Valve/Housing Adjustment

SPECTRUM

1. Center the rack. Measure the distance between the end of the seal holder and the end of the rack. It should be adjusted to 2.5 in. (63.5 mm).

2. Apply grease to the pinion gear teeth and the pinion ball bearings.

3. Using the valve assembly repair kit, install all seven adjusting shims.

4. Install the pinion/valve assembly to the housing and carefully snug the two bolts, 1/4 turn each until snug.

5. Using a feeler gauge, measure the clearance between the valve and gear housings. Remove one shim for each 0.002 in. (0.05 mm) of clearance. The final clearance should be less than 0.002 in. (0.05 mm).

6. Set the rack to the dimension recorded during removal. Install the pinion with the flat side parallel to the rack.

7. Use RTV No. 1052366 or equivalent to seal the mating surfaces of the valve and the steering housing, and tighten to 18 ft. lbs. (25 Nm).

8. Lubricate the rack plunger well and install. Install the spring, adjusting plug and the locknut.

9. Tighten the adjusting plug to 3.6 ft. lbs. (5.0 Nm).

10. Loosen the plug and repeat Step 9.

11. Back off the adjusting plug 30-35 degrees. Tighten the locknut.

12. Measure the pinion shaft preload. If the preload is not between 0.4-1.2 ft. lbs. (0.6-1.6 Nm), loosen the locknut and readjust the plug torque. When the acceptable preload is achieved, apply liquid thread lock to the locknut and tighten the locknut to 49 ft. lbs. (66 Nm).

Rack Unit Assembly

SPECTRUM

1. Install the right and left cylinder pipes. Tighten the fittings to 14 ft. lbs. (20 Nm).

2. Install the inner tie-rod and a new locking washer to the rack end. Tighten to 65 ft. lbs. (88 Nm). Protect the rack from the vise. Stake the locking washer to the flat of the inner tie-rod. Apply grease to the inner surface of the small opening in the boot.

3. Install a new boot over the inner tie-rod. Install a new boot clamp and wire.

4. Install the tie-rod nut and attach the tie-rod end.

5. Adjust the tie-rod so the length from the outer side of the boot clamp to the outer side of the locknut is 7.5 in. (190.4 mm).

6. Tighten the tie-rod locking nut to 40 ft. lbs. (54 Nm).

Power Steering Pump

REMOVAL & INSTALLATION

1. Disconnect the negative battery cable.

2. Place a drain pan below the pump.

3. Remove the pressure hose clamp, pressure hose and return hose. Drain the fluid from the pump and reservoir.

4. Remove the adjusting bolt, pivot bolt and drive belt.

5. Remove the pump assembly.

6. To install, reverse the removal procedures, Tighten the pressure hose to 20 ft. lbs. (27 Nm).

7. Adjust the drive belt, fill the reservoir and bleed the system.

BLEEDING

1. Turn the wheels to the extreme left.

2. With the engine stopped, add power steering fluid to the 'MIN' mark on the fluid indicator.

3. Start the engine and run it for 15 seconds at fast idle.

4. Stop the engine, recheck the fluid level and refill to the 'MIN' mark.

5. Start the engine and turn the wheels from side to side, 3 times.

6. Stop the engine check the fluid level. If air bubbles are still present in the fluid, repeat the bleeding procedure.

TORQUE SPECIFICATIONS

Component	U.S.	Metric
Air bag module attaching screws	44 inch lbs.	5 Nm
Ball joint pinch bolt:		
Storm	48 ft. lbs.	66 Nm
Ball joint-to-control arm bolts:		
Spectrum	80 ft. lbs.	108 Nm
Storm	115 ft. lbs.	156 Nm
Ball stud-to-knuckle pinch bolt:		
Storm	46 ft. lbs.	62 Nm
Brake backing plate retaining bolts:		
Storm	12 ft. lbs.	16 Nm
Brake caliper-to-steering knuckle bolts:		
Spectrum	41 ft. lbs.	55 Nm
Storm	72 ft. lbs.	98 Nm
Control arm-to-body bolts:		
Spectrum	41 ft. lbs.	55 Nm
Control arm-to-tension rod bolts:		
Spectrum	80 ft. lbs.	108 Nm
Crossmember-to-body bolts:		
Storm	137 ft. lbs.	186 Nm
Front bushing-to-body attaching bolt:		
Storm	95 ft. lbs.	129 Nm
Hub nut:	137 ft. lbs.	186 Nm
Hub assembly retaining bolts (rear):		
Storm	49 ft. lbs.	66 Nm
Lateral control arm-to-crossmember nuts:		
Storm	94 ft. lbs.	128 Nm
Lateral control arm-to-suspension knuckle nuts:		
Storm	94 ft. lbs.	128 Nm
Lateral link bolts:		
Storm	94 ft. lbs.	128 Nm
Pinch bolt:		
Spectrum	51 ft. lbs.	69 Nm
Storm	48 ft. lbs.	65 Nm
Pinion fixed nut:		
Spectrum	29 ft. lbs.	39 Nm
Pinion shaft locknut:		
Spectrum	49 ft. lbs.	66 Nm
Pinion shaft preload:		
Spectrum	0.4–1.2 ft. lbs.	0.6–1.6 Nm
Power steering adjusting bolts:		
Storm	15 ft. lbs.	20 Nm
Power steering high pressure and return lines:		
Spectrum	20 ft. lbs.	27 Nm
Storm	41 ft. lbs.	59 Nm
Power steering pivot bolt:		
Spectrum	15 ft. lbs.	20 Nm
Power steering rack adjusting plug:		
Spectrum	3.6 ft. lbs.	5.0 Nm
Power steering valve to housing nuts:		
Spectrum	18 ft. lbs.	25 Nm
Rack cylinder pipe fittings:		
Spectrum	14 ft. lbs.	20 Nm

TORQUE SPECIFICATIONS

Component	U.S.	Metric
Rack and pinion-to-crossmember nuts:		
Storm	65 ft. lbs.	88 Nm
Rear bushing-to-crossmember bolts:		
Storm	51 ft. lbs.	69 Nm
Rear link retaining bolts:		
Storm	19 ft. lbs.	26 Nm
Rear stabilizer bar mounting bracket bolts:		
Storm	71 ft. lbs.	96 Nm
Rear stabilizer bar-to-strut assembly:		
Storm	19 ft. lbs.	26 Nm
Stabilizer bar-to-control arm bolts:		
Storm	19 ft. lbs.	26 Nm
Stabilizer bar-to-crossmember bolts:		
Storm	12 ft. lbs.	16 Nm
Steering column mounting bolts (upper):		
Storm	18 ft. lbs.	24 Nm
Steering knuckle to strut assembly nuts:		
Spectrum	87 ft. lbs.	118 Nm
Storm	116 ft. lbs.	157 Nm
Steering wheel nut:		
Spectrum	22 ft. lbs.	29 Nm
Storm	25 ft. lbs.	34 Nm
Steering shaft pinch bolts:		
Spectrum	19 ft. lbs.	26 Nm
Steering shaft pinch bolts (intermediate shaft):		
Storm	30 ft. lbs.	40 Nm
Strut support nut	43 ft. lbs.	58 Nm
Strut-to-knuckle bolts (rear):		
Spectrum	80 ft. lbs.	108 Nm
Storm	116 ft. lbs.	157 Nm
Strut tower nuts:		
Storm	50 ft. lbs.	68 Nm
Tension rod-to-body bolts:		
Spectrum	72 ft. lbs.	98 Nm
Tension rod-to-control arm bolts:		
Spectrum	80 ft. lbs.	108 Nm
Tie rod locking nut:		
Spectrum	40 ft. lbs.	54 Nm
Tie rod-to-steering knuckle bolt:		
Storm	40 ft. lbs.	54 Nm
Trailing control arm nuts:		
Storm	94 ft. lbs.	128 Nm
Trailing link bolts:		
Storm	94 ft. lbs.	128 Nm
Upper strut retaining nuts:		
Spectrum	41 ft. lbs.	55 Nm
Storm	58 ft. lbs.	78 Nm
Wheel lug nuts:		
Spectrum	87 ft. lbs.	118 Nm
Storm	65 ft. lbs.	88 Nm

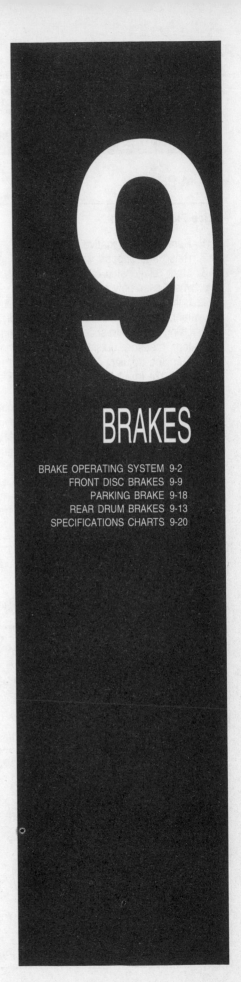

9

BRAKES

BRAKE OPERATING SYSTEM

Adjustments

DRUM BRAKES

▶ **See Figures 1 and 2**

1. Remove the negative battery cable.
2. Raise and support vehicle safely.
3. Mark relationship of wheel to axle flange. Remove wheel nuts, wheel assembly and brake drum.
4. Using a drum-to-shoe clearance gauge (J-22364-01), or equivalent, measure the inside diameter of brake drum.
5. Using a drum-to-shoe clearance gauge (J-22364-01), or equivalent, measure outside diameter of the brake shoes.
6. Turn the adjuster until the outside diameter of the brake shoes is 0.024 in. (0.6mm) less than the inside diameter of the brake drum.
7. Install brake drum and wheel assembly. Lower the vehicle.
8. Reconnect the negative battery cable.
9. Check the brake fluid and add as required.
10. Pump brake pedal to seat brake shoes before moving vehicle.

BRAKE PEDAL

▶ **See Figure 3**

1. Measure brake pedal height after engine is started and engine speed increased several times. Ensure pedal is fully returned by the pedal return spring.
2. Stop engine operation. Measure distance from floor panel to top of brake pedal (see illustration). The correct brake pedal height specification should be 6.07 in. (154mm) for Spectrum. The correct brake pedal height specification should be 6.22 in. (158mm) for Storm.
3. If the measurement is not correct, adjust brake pedal height as follows:
   a. Disconnect the negative battery cable.
   b. Disconnect brake light (stop light) switch connector.
   c. Loosen brake light switch locknut and back switch away from brake pedal.
   d. Loosen locknut on brake pedal pushrod and adjust brake pedal to the specified height.
   e. Tighten locknut to 18 ft. lbs.
   f. Adjust brake light switch — refer to the necessary service procedures.

Brake Light Switch

REMOVAL & INSTALLATION

▶ **See Figure 4**

1. Disconnect the negative battery cable.
2. Locate the brake light switch on the brake pedal bracket assembly.
3. Disconnect the electrical connection for the brake light switch.
4. Remove the locknut and the brake light switch.
To install:
5. Install brake light switch on brake pedal bracket and adjust to specification.
6. Tighten the locknut.
7. Install the connector and the negative battery cable.

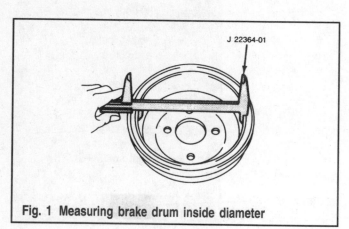

Fig. 1 Measuring brake drum inside diameter

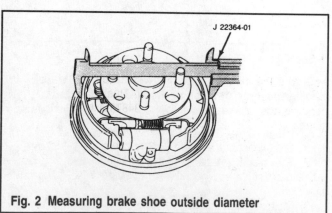

Fig. 2 Measuring brake shoe outside diameter

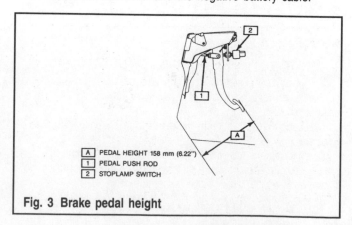

A	PEDAL HEIGHT 158 mm (6.22″)
1	PEDAL PUSH ROD
2	STOPLAMP SWITCH

Fig. 3 Brake pedal height

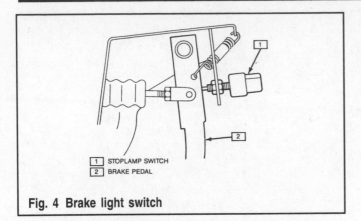

1 STOPLAMP SWITCH
2 BRAKE PEDAL

Fig. 4 Brake light switch

8. Check the operation of the brake light switch. With the engine OFF, depress the brake pedal and check that the brake lights come ON. With the brake pedal released, make sure the brake lights are OFF.

9. If operation is not as described above, repeat adjustment of the brake light switch.

➡The brake light switch is almost always the first place to look for the cause of the brake lights flickering over bumps or staying on without use of the brakes. If the brake lights fail to work with the brakes applied, check all fuses then check adjustment of the brake light switch.

ADJUSTMENT

1. Loosen locknuts on brake light switch.
2. Adjust the brake light switch so the clearance between the brake light switch housing (not plunger) and brake pedal is 0.02-0.04 in. (0.5-1.0mm). In this position, the plunger will be retracted inside the brake light switch housing.
3. Tighten locknuts to secure switch in position. Connect the electrical connector, if removed.
4. With the engine OFF, depress the brake pedal and check that the brake lights come ON. With the brake pedal released, make sure the brake lights are OFF.

Brake Pedal Assembly

REMOVAL & INSTALLATION

▶ See Figure 5

1. Disconnect the negative battery cable.
2. Remove the steering column assembly.
3. Disconnect the brake and clutch switch electrical connectors.
4. Disconnect the clutch cable from the clutch pedal, if so equipped.
5. Disconnect the fork clevis from the brake pedal.
6. Remove the brake pedal assembly-to-body mounting nuts. Remove the brake pedal assembly.
   To install:
7. Install the brake pedal assembly to the vehicle in the correct position.

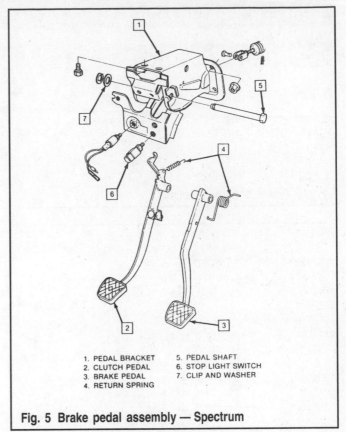

1. PEDAL BRACKET   5. PEDAL SHAFT
2. CLUTCH PEDAL   6. STOP LIGHT SWITCH
3. BRAKE PEDAL   7. CLIP AND WASHER
4. RETURN SPRING

Fig. 5 Brake pedal assembly — Spectrum

8. Tighten brake pedal assembly-to-body mounting nuts to 15 ft. lbs.
9. Connect the yoke clevis to the brake pedal.
10. Connect the clutch cable to the clutch pedal. Adjust the clutch pedal free-play, if so equipped.
11. Reconnect the brake and clutch switch electrical connectors.
12. Install the steering column assembly.
13. Check brake pedal height adjustment. Reconnect the negative battery cable.
14. Check the brake pedal, brake light switch and clutch pedal for proper operation.

Master Cylinder

REMOVAL & INSTALLATION

▶ See Figures 6 and 7

➡Before the master cylinder is reinstalled, the brake booster pushrod must be adjusted. This adjustment requires the use of special tool J-34873-A booster pushrod gauge.

1. Disconnect the negative battery cable.
2. The master cylinder is equipped with a brake fluid level warning sensor. Disconnect the sensor harness connector at this time.
3. Clean area around the reservoir and brake lines at master cylinder. Remove the cap from the master cylinder.

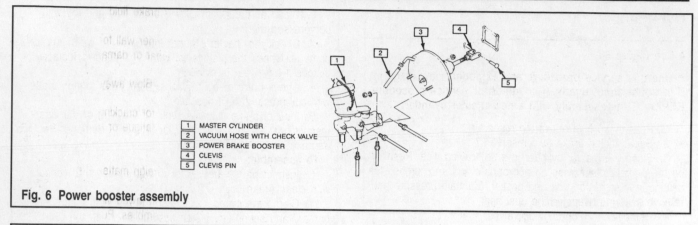

1 MASTER CYLINDER
2 VACUUM HOSE WITH CHECK VALVE
3 POWER BRAKE BOOSTER
4 CLEVIS
5 CLEVIS PIN

Fig. 6 Power booster assembly

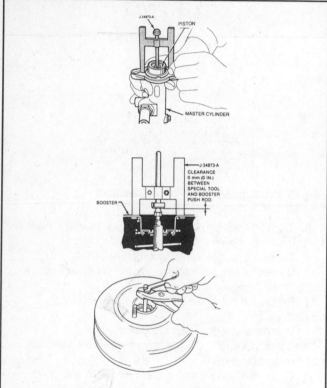

Fig. 7 Correct procedure for adjusting brake booster pushrod length

Drain the fluid out with the use a turkey baster or similar syringe. Deposit the fluid into a container.

➡**Take the proper precautions to prevent brake fluid from contacting painted surfaces. If brake fluid does come in contact with painted surfaces, the finish will be damaged.**

4. Remove the top of the air cleaner and air duct if necessary.
5. Disconnect the brake lines from the master cylinder. Drain the fluid from the lines into the container. Plug the lines to prevent fluid from leaking onto and damaging painted surfaces or the entry of moisture into the brake system.
6. Remove the 2 nuts that attach the master cylinder to the brake booster assembly. Remove the master cylinder.

To install:

7. Clean the brake booster and the master cylinder flange surfaces. Install a new gasket onto the brake booster if so equipped.
8. Adjust the length of the brake booster pushrod as follows:
   a. Set the special tool on the master cylinder with the gasket and lower the pin of the tool until it lightly contacts the piston.
   b. Turn the special tool upside-down and position it onto the booster.
   c. Measure the clearance between the booster pushrod and the pin head of the tool. There must be zero clearance. To obtain ZERO clearance, adjust the pushrod length until the pushrod just contacts the head of the pin.
9. If a new master cylinder is to be installed, bench bleed as follows:
   a. Mount the master cylinder into a vise or suitable holding fixture. Take care not to damage the cylinder.
   b. Fill the cylinder to the correct level with the specified fluid.
   c. Block off all the outer brake line holes but one, then using a long tool such as rod, position it in the cylinder to actuate the brake master cylinder.
   d. Slowly depress the piston inside the master cylinder, which will force brake fluid from the cylinder. While holding the piston in the depressed position, cover the open hole and allow the piston to return to a resting position.
   e. Repeat this procedure until the fluid exiting the master cylinder is free of air bubbles.
   f. Repeat this procedure on the remaining ports.
10. Install the master cylinder over the mounting studs and tighten the 2 mounting nuts to 9 ft. lbs. (13 Nm).
11. Reconnect the lines to the master cylinder. Use the proper tool (flare wrench or line wrench) to tighten the fittings at the master cylinder.
12. Connect the level warning switch connector.
13. Fill the brake fluid reservoir to the proper level with clean brake fluid. If air is present in the system, bleed the brake system as described in this Section.
14. Check for a firm brake pedal and for fluid leaks. Check and/or adjust the brake pedal as required.
15. Road test the vehicle for proper operation.

OVERHAUL

▶ **See Figure 8**

➡**Use this service procedure and exploded view diagram. If in doubt about overhaul condition or service procedure REPLACE the assembly with a new master cylinder.**

1. Pour brake fluid out of the reservoir.
2. Separate the brake fluid reservoir.
3. Place the master cylinder in a soft jawed vice. Push IN on the primary piston with an appropriate tool and remove the secondary piston stop bolt and gasket. Maintain pressure and remove snapring. Remove the dust seal.
4. Remove the proportioning valves.
5. Remove the primary and secondary piston assembly from the master cylinder.

6. Clean all parts with DOT-3 brake fluid and dry with compressed air.
7. Check the master cylinder inner wall for wear, rust or damage. Check the pistons for wear or damage. Replace pistons if any wear is evident.
8. Check bore for obstructions. Blow away foreign matter with compressed air if possible.
9. Inspect brake fluid reservoir for cracking or damage. Inspect gaskets and snaprings for fatigue or damage. Replace as necessary.
   To assemble:
10. Inspect parts carefully for foreign matter and lubricate with clean brake fluid.
11. Clamp the cylinder into a soft jawed vice. Install the primary and secondary piston assemblies. Push the piston in

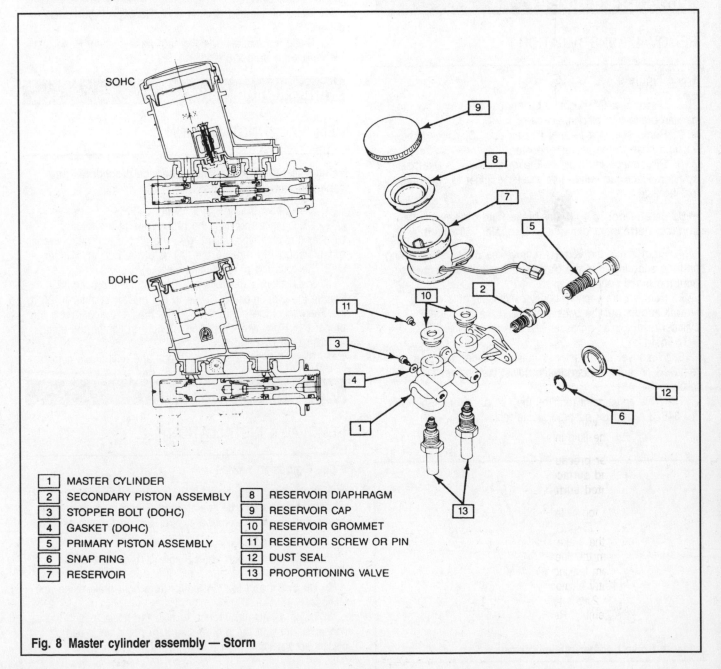

1	MASTER CYLINDER
2	SECONDARY PISTON ASSEMBLY
3	STOPPER BOLT (DOHC)
4	GASKET (DOHC)
5	PRIMARY PISTON ASSEMBLY
6	SNAP RING
7	RESERVOIR
8	RESERVOIR DIAPHRAGM
9	RESERVOIR CAP
10	RESERVOIR GROMMET
11	RESERVOIR SCREW OR PIN
12	DUST SEAL
13	PROPORTIONING VALVE

Fig. 8 Master cylinder assembly — Storm

with an appropriate tool and install the snapring. Install the dust seal--the dust seal notch must be facing downward.

➡ **Be careful not to scratch the piston cups when installing the piston assemblies.**

12. Maintain pressure on the piston an install the stopper bolt and gasket hand tight. Torque stopper bolt to 6 ft. lbs.

13. Press the piston all the way into the cylinder and release several times. Check for smooth piston return and brake fluid being forced from the front and rear outlets.

14. Install the proportioning valves. Torque valves to 33 ft. lbs.

15. Install the brake fluid reservoir.

16. Fill the reservoir with fluid and bleed the master cylinder. After installation, bleed brake system.

Power Brake Booster

REMOVAL & INSTALLATION

▶ **See Figure 9**

1. Disconnect the negative battery cable. Firmly, set the parking brake and block the wheels.

2. Remove the air cleaner and air duct. Disconnect the vacuum hose to the vacuum booster.

3. Disconnect and plug the brake fluid lines at the master cylinder. Place rags under the master cylinder to catch any leaking fluid.

➡ **Be careful not to spill any brake fluid on any painted surface. Permanent damage to the paint will result.**

4. From inside the vehicle, remove the pedal return spring and the snapring from the clevis pin. Separate the clevis pin from the brake pedal.

5. Remove the vacuum booster mounting nuts at the firewall and lift out the booster unit and master cylinder/reservoir as an assembly.

To install:

6. Whenever the booster or master cylinder has been removed or replaced, check and adjust the booster pushrod as follows:

a. This adjustment requires the use of special tool J-34873-A booster pushrod gauge tool.

b. Set the special tool on the master cylinder with the gasket and lower the pin of the tool until it lightly contacts the piston.

c. Turn the special tool upside-down and position it onto the booster.

d. Measure the clearance between the booster pushrod and the pin head of the tool. There must be zero clearance. To obtain ZERO clearance, adjust the pushrod length until the pushrod just contacts the head of the pin.

7. Install the booster assembly into the vehicle. Torque the retaining nuts evenly to 10 ft. lbs.

8. Install the clevis to the brake pedal. Install clevis pin and clip. Install brake pedal return spring.

9. Install vacuum hose to the the booster assembly.

10. Reconnect the lines to the master cylinder. Use the proper tool (flare wrench or line wrench) to tighten the fittings at the master cylinder.

11. Install air cleaner and air duct. Reconnect the battery cable.

12. Bleed the master cylinder and brake system. Road test the vehicle for proper operation.

Proportioning Valve

REMOVAL & INSTALLATION

➡ **Refer to the Master Cylinder service procedures and exploded view, if necessary.**

1. Disconnect the negative battery cable.

2. Disconnect and plug the brake lines at the master cylinder (proportioning valve). Use the proper tool (flare wrench or line wrench) to remove the fittings at the master cylinder.

3. Remove the proportioning valve(s).

4. Installation is the reverse of the removal procedure. Torque the proportioning valves to the master cylinder to 30 ft. lbs. Reconnect the brake lines to the master cylinder. Use the proper tool (flare wrench or line wrench) to tighten the fittings at the master cylinder.

5. Bleed the brake system. Check and refill brake fluid.

Brake Hoses and Lines

REMOVAL & INSTALLATION

▶ **See Figures 10 and 11**

➡ **A minimum clearance of 1 inch from all moving or vibrating parts must be maintained, when installing brake hoses and lines. Never use copper tubing for a brake line service repair.**

1. Raise and support vehicle safely. Remove wheel if necessary.

2. Clean dirt and foreign matter from both brake hose and fittings.

3. Using a back-up wrench to hold the hose, loosen the connector nut with the proper size flare nut wrench and disconnect the hose from the fitting. Remove the hose retaining clip.

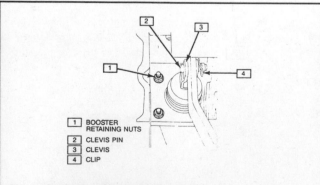

1	BOOSTER RETAINING NUTS
2	CLEVIS PIN
3	CLEVIS
4	CLIP

Fig. 9 Brake booster retaining nuts

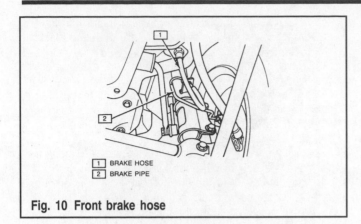

1 BRAKE HOSE
2 BRAKE PIPE

Fig. 10 Front brake hose

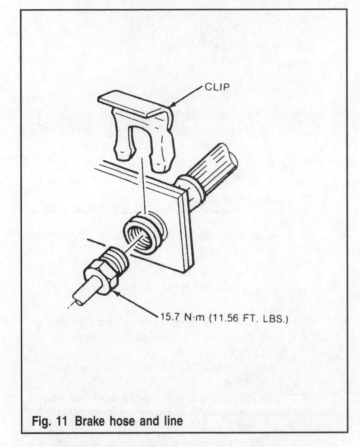

CLIP

15.7 N·m (11.56 FT. LBS.)

Fig. 11 Brake hose and line

4. Drain the hose into a container. If equipped with gaskets on either side of the hose connections, discard old gaskets and replace with new.

5. Visually inspect the brake hose for signs of cracking, damage and swelling. Inspect the fitting threads for damage. Make replacements as required. If a repair or part is questionable, replace the part.

6. Visually inspect the brake line for damage, cracks, indentations or corrosion. Inspect the threads for damage. Make replacements as required.

To install:

7. Connect the brake hose to the brake line fitting by hand making sure new gaskets are in place, if equipped. Slowly tighten (by hand) the fitting and loosen it several times to ensure the correct mating of the threads.

8. Using the flare nut and back-up wrenches, tighten the fitting. Install brake hose retaining clip.

9. Fill the master cylinder and bleed the brake system.

BRAKE PIPE FLARING

Flaring steel lines is a skill that needs to be practiced, before it should be done. Flaring steel lines should be used only as a last resort method of repair. If attempted, it is essential that the flare be done uniformly to prevent any leaks when the brake system is under pressure. It is also recommended that the flare be a 'double flare' (rolled twice). With the supply of parts available today, a preflared steel brake line should be available to fit your needs. Due to the high pressures in the brake system and the serious injuries that could occur if the brake system (flare in a brake line) should fail, it is strongly advised that preflared lines are installed when repairing the braking system. If a line were to leak brake fluid due to an defective flare, and the leak was to go undetected, brake failure would result.

The following procedure applies to most commercially available double-flaring kits. If these instructions differ in any way from those in your kit, follow the instructions in the kit.

1. Cut the brake line to the necessary length using a tubing cutter.

2. Square the end of the tube with a file and chamfer the edges.

3. Insert the tube into the proper size hole in the bar until the end of the tube sticks out the thickness of the single flare adapter. Tighten the bar wing nuts tightly so the tube cannot move.

4. Place the single flare adapter into the tube and slide the bar into the yoke.

5. Position the yoke screw over the single flare adapter and tighten it until the bar is locked in the yoke. Continue tightening the yoke screw until the adapter bottoms on the bar. This should form the single flare.

➡**Make sure the tube is not forced out of the hole in the bar during the single flare operation. If it is, the single flare will not be formed properly and the procedure must be repeated from Step 1.**

6. Loosen the yoke screw and remove the single flare adapter.

7. Position the yoke screw over the tube and tighten until the taper contacts the single flare and the bar is locked in the yoke. Continue tightening to form the double flare.

➡**Make sure the tube is not forced out of the hole in the bar during the double flare operation. If it is, the double flare will not be formed properly and the procedure must be repeated from Step 1.**

8. Loosen the screw and remove the bar from the yoke. Remove the tube from the bar.

9. Check the flare for cracks or uneven flaring. If the flare is not perfect, cut it off and begin again at Step 1.

Brake System Bleeding

♦ See Figures 12 and 13

1. Remove the vacuum reserve by applying the brakes several times with the engine OFF.

2. Remove the master cylinder reservoir cap and fill the reservoir with brake fluid. Keep the reservoir at least ½ full during the bleeding operation.

3. If the master cylinder is replaced or overhauled, first bleed the air from the master cylinder and then from each caliper or wheel cylinder. Bleed the master cylinder as follows:

   a. Disconnect the forward brake line from the master cylinder.

   b. Allow brake fluid to fill the master cylinder bore until it begins to flow from the forward connector port.

   c. Connect the forward brake line to the master cylinder and tighten.

   d. Have an assistant depress the brake pedal slowly once and hold it depressed. Loosen the forward brake line connector at the master cylinder to purge air from the bore. Tighten the connection, and then have the assistant release the brake pedal slowly. Wait 15 seconds. Repeat this sequence, including the 15 second wait, until all air is removed from the bore. Care must be taken to prevent brake fluid from contacting any painted surface.

   e. After all air has been removed at the forward connection, repeat the procedure outlined above to bleed the master cylinder at the rear connection.

4. If it is known that the calipers and wheel cylinders do not contain air, it will not be necessary to bleed them.

Fig. 12 Bleeding front brakes

Fig. 13 Bleeding rear brakes

5. If it is necessary to bleed all of the wheel cylinders and calipers, follow the sequence below:

   a. Right rear
   b. Left rear
   c. Right front
   d. Left front

6. Bleed individual wheel cylinders or calipers only after all of the air is removed from the master cylinder assembly. Follow this service procedure:

   a. Place an appropriate box end wrench or equivalent over the bleeder valve.

   b. Attach a clear tube over the bleeder valve and allow the tube to hang submerged in a clear container partially filled with clean brake fluid.

   c. Have a helper depress the brake pedal slowly one time and hold. Loosen the bleeder valve to purge air from the cylinder. Tighten the bleeder valve and have the helper slowly release the brake pedal. Wait 15 seconds. Repeat the sequence, including the 15 second wait, until all of the air is removed.

   d. It may be necessary to repeat the sequence 10 or more times to remove all of the air from the system.

   e. Rapid pumping of the brake pedal pushes the master cylinder secondary piston down the bore in a way that makes it more difficult to bleed the rear side of the system.

7. Check the brake pedal for sponginess and the brake warning lamp for an indication of uneven brake pressure. Repeat the entire bleeding procedure to correct either of these 2 conditions.

FRONT DISC BRAKES

✳✳CAUTION

Brake shoes contain asbestos, which has been determined to be a cancer causing agent. Never clean the brake surfaces with compressed air! Avoid inhaling any dust from any brake surface! When cleaning brake surfaces, use a commercially available brake cleaning fluid.

Disc Brake Pads

Most disc brake pads are equipped with wear indicators. If a squealing noise occurs from the brakes while driving, check the pad wear indicator plate. If there is evidence of the indicator plate contacting the rotor disc, the brake pad should be replaced.

REMOVAL & INSTALLATION

▶ **See Figures 14, 15, 16, 17, 18, 19, 20, 21 and 22**

1. Disconnect the negative battery cable. Raise and support the vehicle safely.
2. Remove the wheels. Reinstall 2 wheel lug nuts to retain brake rotor during service procedure.
3. Siphon a sufficient quantity of brake fluid from the master cylinder reservoir to prevent any brake fluid from overflowing the master cylinder when removing or installing new pads. This is necessary as the piston must be forced into the caliper bore to provide sufficient clearance when installing the new pads.
4. Loosen and remove the 2 caliper mounting slide pins (bolts) and then remove the caliper assembly. Position it aside. Do not disconnect the brake hose.

➡ **Support the brake caliper housing so that the brake hose is not stretched or damaged.**

5. Remove 2 brake pads (shims and spring if so equipped), 2 wear indicator plates and 4 brake pad retainers. MAKE SURE TO NOTE THE POSITION OF ALL ASSORTED BRAKE PAD HARDWARE.
   To install:
6. Check the brake disc (rotor) for thickness and run-out. Inspect the caliper and piston assembly for breaks, cracks, fluid seepage or other damage. Overhaul or replace as necessary.
7. Install 2 wear indicator plates, 4 pad retainers and 2 brake pads (shims and spring if so equipped).
8. Position the caliper back down over the pads. If it won't fit, use a caliper piston compression tool or equivalent and carefully force the piston into its bore.
9. Install caliper housing with 2 slide pin bolts to caliper mounting bracket.
10. Tighten the caliper mounting bolts (slide pin bolts) EVENLY to 36 ft. lbs.
11. Install the wheels and lower the vehicle.

12. Reconnect the battery cable. Check the brake fluid level and add as required.
13. Before moving the vehicle, make sure to pump the brake pedal a few times to seat the brake pads against the rotors. Road test the vehicle for proper operation.

INSPECTION

▶ **See Figure 23**

If you hear a squealing noise coming from the front brakes while driving, check the brake lining thickness and pad wear indicator (integral part of the brake pad) by looking into the inspection hole on the brake cylinder with the front wheels removed and the vehicle properly supported. The wear indicator is designed to emit the squealing noise when the brake pad wears down, at which time the pad wear indicator and the rotor disc rub against each other. If there are traces of the pad wear indicator contacting the rotor disc, the brake pads should be replaced.

To inspect the brake lining thickness, look through the inspection hole and measure the lining thickness using a machinists rule. Also looks for signs of uneven wear. Standard thickness is 0.386 in. (10mm). The **minimum** allowable thickness is 0.039 in. (1mm) at which time the brake pads must be replaced.

Remove the brake caliper to inspect brake pads, if necessary. Refer to necessary service procedures.

➡ **Always replace the brake pads on both front wheels as a set. When inspecting or replacing the brake pads, check the surface of the disc rotors for scoring, wear and run-out. The rotors should be resurfaced if badly scored or replaced if badly worn.**

Brake Caliper

REMOVAL & INSTALLATION

1. Raise and support the vehicle safely. Remove the front wheels.
2. Disconnect the brake hose and 2 gaskets from the brake caliper. Plug the end of the hose to prevent loss of brake fluid.
3. Remove the 2 slide pin bolts that attach the brake caliper to the bracket.
4. Lift up and remove the brake caliper assembly.
5. Installation is the reverse of the removal procedure. Always use NEW gaskets for the brake hose. Lightly grease the brake caliper bushings and slide pin bolts with Lithium grease or equivalent. Install and tighten the caliper slide pin bolts EVENLY to 36 ft. lbs.
6. Fill and bleed the system. Before moving the vehicle, make sure to pump the brake pedal a few times to seat the pads against the rotors.

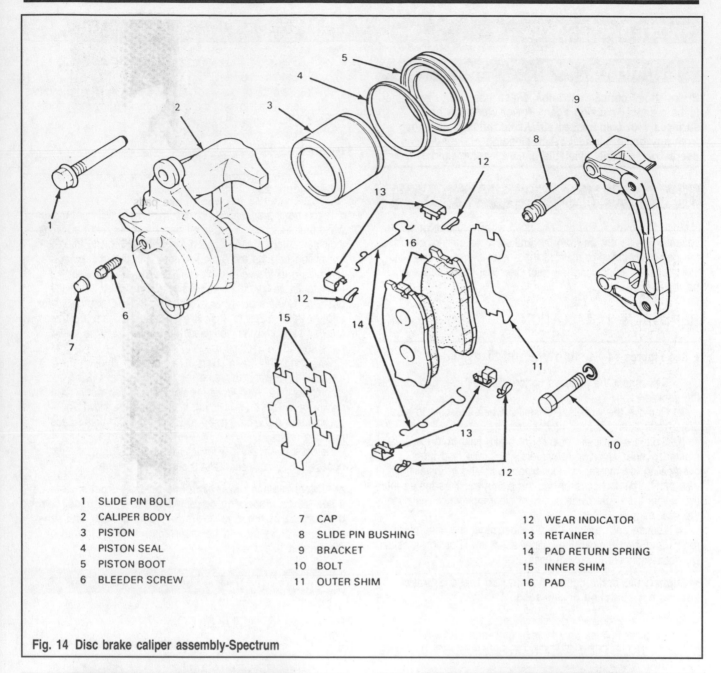

Fig. 14 Disc brake caliper assembly-Spectrum

1	SLIDE PIN BOLT				
2	CALIPER BODY	7	CAP	12	WEAR INDICATOR
3	PISTON	8	SLIDE PIN BUSHING	13	RETAINER
4	PISTON SEAL	9	BRACKET	14	PAD RETURN SPRING
5	PISTON BOOT	10	BOLT	15	INNER SHIM
6	BLEEDER SCREW	11	OUTER SHIM	16	PAD

Fig. 15 Cleaning front brake rotor

Fig. 16 Removing the caliper slide pins (bolts)

Fig. 17 Remove the brake caliper assembly

Fig. 20 Installing the front brake pads

Fig. 18 Support the brake caliper

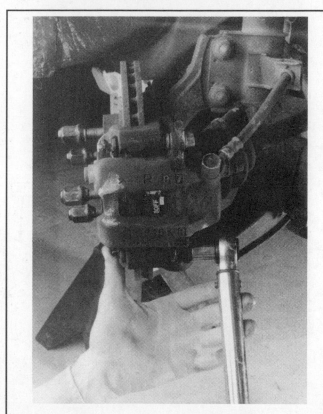

Fig. 21 Installing the caliper slide pins (bolts)

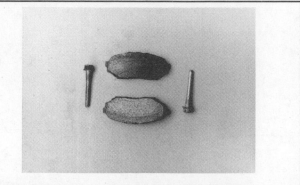

Fig. 19 Front brake pads and slide pins (bolts)

OVERHAUL

1. Remove the brake caliper from the bracket. Remove the brake pads.
2. Withdraw the 2 slide bushings from their respective bores.
3. Remove the piston boot.
4. Place a folded towel or equivalent between the piston and housing. Apply compressed air to the brake line union

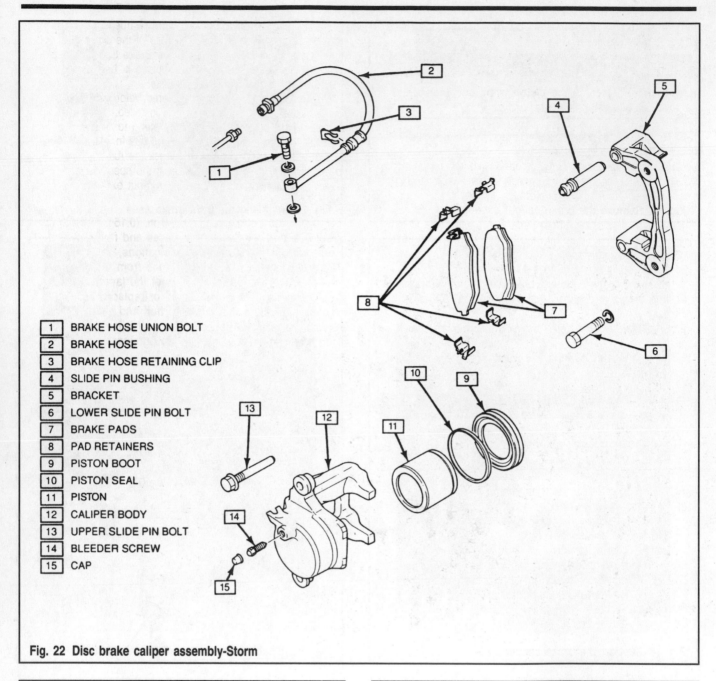

1. BRAKE HOSE UNION BOLT
2. BRAKE HOSE
3. BRAKE HOSE RETAINING CLIP
4. SLIDE PIN BUSHING
5. BRACKET
6. LOWER SLIDE PIN BOLT
7. BRAKE PADS
8. PAD RETAINERS
9. PISTON BOOT
10. PISTON SEAL
11. PISTON
12. CALIPER BODY
13. UPPER SLIDE PIN BOLT
14. BLEEDER SCREW
15. CAP

Fig. 22 Disc brake caliper assembly-Storm

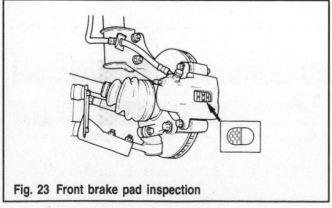

Fig. 23 Front brake pad inspection

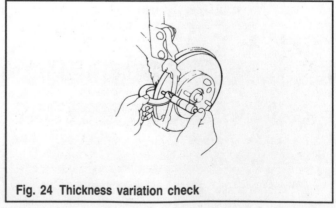

Fig. 24 Thickness variation check

fitting to force the piston out of its bore. Be careful, the piston will come out forcefully.

✳✳CAUTION

Do not attempt to catch the piston with your fingers. Let the towel or equivalent do this for you.

5. Pry the piston seal from the bore with a machinists scribe.

6. Clean all necessary components. Check the piston and cylinder bore for wear and/or corrosion. Replace components if excess wear or corrosion is present.

To assemble:

7. Coat all necessary rubber parts with clean brake fluid.
8. Install the piston seal into the bore and install the piston.
9. Install the piston boot.
10. Install sliding bushings to the brake caliper.
11. Install the brake pads and brake caliper to the bracket. Install and tighten the caliper slide pin bolts EVENLY to 36 ft. lbs.
12. Fill the master cylinder reservoir and bleed the brake system.
13. Pump the brake pedal a few times, and check the brake system for leaks.

Brake Rotor

REMOVAL & INSTALLATION

1. Raise and safely support the vehicle.
2. Remove the wheel and tire assembly.
3. Remove the brake caliper (do not disconnect brake hose) and the caliper bracket.
4. Remove the brake rotor.
5. Installation is the reverse of the removal procedure. Torque the caliper bracket bolts to 76 ft. lbs. on Storm models and 41 ft. lbs. on the Spectrum models.

INSPECTION

▶ **See Figures 24 and 25**

The brake disc rotors should be refinished on a brake lathe, when replacing the front brake pads for the brake pads to wear properly.

REAR DRUM BRAKES

✳✳CAUTION

Brake shoes contain asbestos, which has been determined to be a cancer causing agent. Never clean the brake surfaces with compressed air! Avoid inhaling any dust from any brake surface! When cleaning brake surfaces, use a commercially available brake cleaning fluid.

Examine the brake disc. If it is worn, warped or scored, it must be replaced. Check the thickness of the brake disc against the specifications given in the Brake Specifications Chart. If it is below specifications, replace it. Use a micrometer or equivalent to measure the thickness.

The disc run-out should be measured before the disc is removed and again, after the disc is installed. Use a dial indicator mounted on a magnet type stand to determine run-out. Position the dial so the stylus is 0.039 in. (10mm) from the outer edge of the rotor disc. Check the run-out specification of the brake disc against the specifications given in the Brake Specifications Chart. If run-out exceeds the specification, replace the brake disc.

➡**If lateral run-out exceeds 0.0059 in. (0.15mm) clean wheel hub and rotor mating surfaces and remeasure. If lateral run-out still exceeds specifications, index the rotor on the hub one or two bolt positions from the original position. A rotor that does not meet the lateral run-out specification should be refinished or replaced as necessary. Be sure that the front hub and bearing assembly play is with specifications. If it is not, an inaccurate run-out reading may be obtained.**

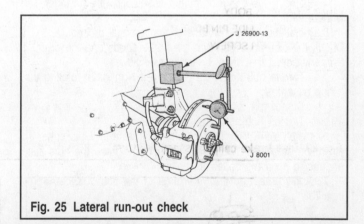

Fig. 25 Lateral run-out check

Brake Drums

REMOVAL & INSTALLATION

Spectrum
▶ **See Figure 26**

1. Raise and safely support the vehicle.

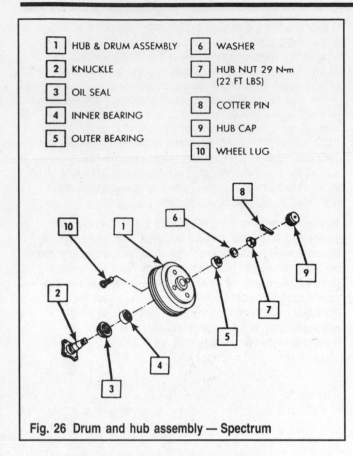

1	HUB & DRUM ASSEMBLY	6	WASHER
2	KNUCKLE	7	HUB NUT 29 N•m (22 FT LBS)
3	OIL SEAL	8	COTTER PIN
4	INNER BEARING	9	HUB CAP
5	OUTER BEARING	10	WHEEL LUG

Fig. 26 Drum and hub assembly — Spectrum

2. Remove the rear wheel and tire assembly.

3. Remove the dust cap and cotter pin. Remove the hub nut, washer and outer wheel bearing.

4. Remove the brake drum/hub assembly with the inner wheel bearing.

5. Installation is the reverse of the removal procedure. Check the clearance between the brake shoes and the drum. Properly adjust the wheel bearings as follows:

    a. Torque hub nut to 22 ft. lbs. (29 Nm) while rotating the hub assembly.

    b. Completely loosen the hub nut.

    c. Tighten hub nut finger tight.

6. Install a NEW cotter pin, after adjustment. If the cotter pin holes are out of line, use a wrench to tighten the nuts just enough to align the cotter pin holes.

7. Apply grease to the inner area of the hub dust cap and install.

Storm

1. Raise and safely support the vehicle.

2. Remove the rear wheel and tire assembly.

➡**If necessary, insert a brake spoon or equivalent through the hole in the backing plate and hold the automatic adjusting lever away from the adjusting bolt. Use another brake spoon or equivalent, and reduce the brake shoe adjustment by turning the adjusting bolt.**

3. Remove the brake drum.

4. Installation is the reverse of the removal procedure. Adjust the rear brake, if necessary.

INSPECTION

➡**Pulsation in the brake pedal is usually corrected by servicing the front brake system. Service the rear brake system only if the problem persists.**

1. Remove the brake drum and clean it thoroughly.

2. Inspect the drum for scoring, cracks, grooves and out-of-roundness. Replace or refinish the brake drum, as required. Light scoring may be removed by dressing the drum with fine grit emery cloth. Heavy scoring will require the use of a brake drum lathe to turn or refinish the brake drum.

3. Using J 22364-01 drum-to-shoe clearance gauge or equivalent, measure the inside diameter of the brake drum.

➡**Measuring a brake drum for out-of-round, taper and wear it can be accurately measured with an inside surface and at right angles to each other.**

4. On Spectrum models, the standard inside diameter is 7.09 in. (180mm). The maximum inside diameter is 7.14 in. (181.4mm). If the brake drum exceeds the maximum diameter, replace it.

5. On Storm models, the standard inside diameter is 7.87 in. (200mm). The maximum inside diameter is 7.93 in. (201.4mm). If the brake drum exceeds the maximum diameter, replace it.

6. During manufacture, weights are used to balance brake drums. These weights must not be removed. Replace the brake drum if weights are missing.

Brake Shoes

INSPECTION

1. Inspect all brake parts and springs for rust, wear and damage.

2. Measure the brake lining thickness. The minimum allowable thickness is 0.039 in. (1.0mm). If the lining does not meet the minimum specification, replace it.

➡**If one of the brake shoes needs to be replaced, replace ALL the rear shoes in order to maintain even braking.**

3. Inspect the brake drum and measure inside diameter of the drum as detailed in this section.

4. Place the shoe into the brake drum and check that the lining is in proper contact with the drum's surface. If the contact is improper, repair the lining with a brake shoe grinder or replace the shoe.

5. To measure the clearance between brake shoe and parking brake lever, temporarily install the parking brake and automatic adjusting levers onto the rear shoe, using a new C-washer. With a feeler gauge, measure the clearance between the shoe and the lever. The clearance should be within 0.0138 in. (0-0.35mm). If the clearance is not as specified, use a new washer to adjust it. When the clearance is correct, stake the C-washer with pliers.

Brake Shoes

REMOVAL & INSTALLATION

▶ **See Figures 27, 28, 29, 30, 31, 32, 33, 34, 35, 36, 37 and 38**

Spectrum

1. Disconnect the negative battery cable. Raise and safely support the vehicle.
2. Remove the rear wheel and tire assemblies.
3. Remove the brake drums.
4. Remove the brake return spring and auto adjuster spring.

5. Remove the leading shoe holding pin and spring and the leading shoe.
6. Remove the self adjuster and the adjuster lever.
7. Remove the trailing shoe holding pin and spring.
8. Disconnect the parking brake cable from the trailing shoe and remove the trailing shoe. Remove the parking brake lever from the trailing shoe.

To install:

9. Check all brake hardware-replace if necessary. Check the brake drum for scoring or other wear and machine or replace as necessary. Check the maximum brake drum diameter specification when machining. If the drum is machined, the wheel bearings must be removed and the hub thoroughly cleaned before installation.
10. Apply a thin coat of suitable high temperature grease to the shoe contact pads (and brake contact points) on the brake backing plate prior to installation.

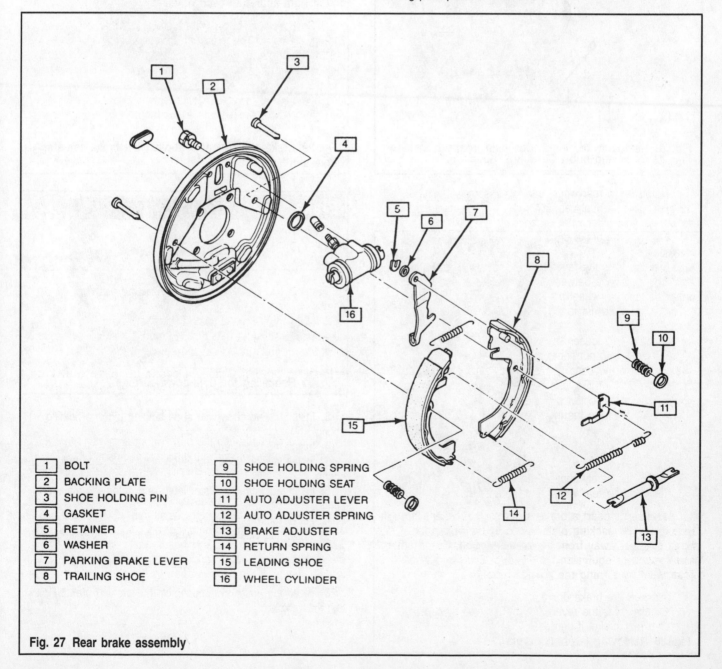

1	BOLT	9	SHOE HOLDING SPRING
2	BACKING PLATE	10	SHOE HOLDING SEAT
3	SHOE HOLDING PIN	11	AUTO ADJUSTER LEVER
4	GASKET	12	AUTO ADJUSTER SPRING
5	RETAINER	13	BRAKE ADJUSTER
6	WASHER	14	RETURN SPRING
7	PARKING BRAKE LEVER	15	LEADING SHOE
8	TRAILING SHOE	16	WHEEL CYLINDER

Fig. 27 Rear brake assembly

Fig. 28 Removing the inspection plug from the backing plate

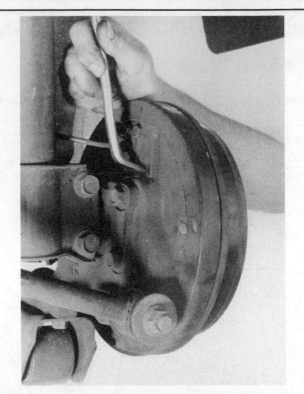

Fig. 29 Brake adjustment or loosen the brake adjuster from this hole

11. Install the parking brake lever to the trailing shoe.
12. Connect the parking brake cable to the lever.

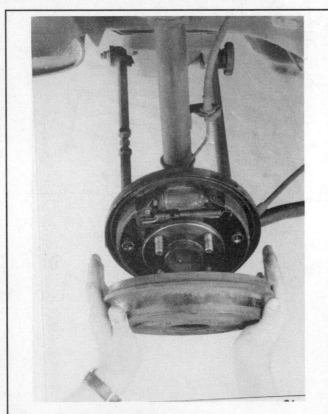

Fig. 30 Removing the brake drum

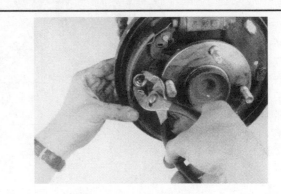

Fig. 31 Removing the hold-down springs

13. Install trailing shoe with shoe holding pin and holding spring.
14. Install the brake adjuster.
15. Install leading shoe with shoe holding pin and holding spring.
16. Install automatic adjuster lever and automatic adjuster spring.
17. Install return spring.
18. Check the clearance between the brake shoes and the drum.
19. Install brake drum and adjust preload. Install the rear wheel.
20. Bleed the brake system. Adjust the parking brake. Road test the vehicle.

Fig. 32 Removing the lower brake return springs

Fig. 33 Removing the upper brake return springs

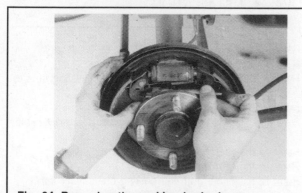

Fig. 34 Removing the parking brake lever

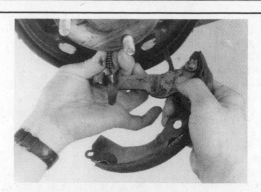

Fig. 35 Removing the brake shoe from the parking brake

Fig. 36 Lubricate the backing plate before brake shoe installation

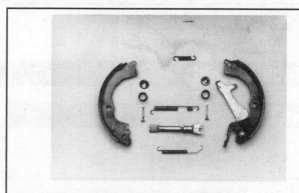

Fig. 37 Rear brake shoes and hardware

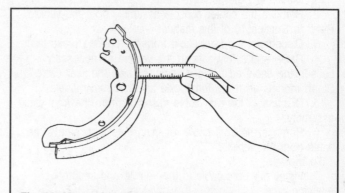

Fig. 38 Measuring the rear brake shoes

Storm

1. Disconnect the battery negative cable.
2. Raise and support the vehicle safely.
3. Remove the brake drums.
4. Remove the return spring, retainers, hold-down springs and pins.
5. Disconnect the parking brake cable from the parking brake lever.
6. Remove the adjuster spring, then the shoes and adjuster.

To install:

7. Inspect brake drums, shoes adjuster, auto adjuster lever, springs and backing plate for wear, distortion, cracks or other abnormal condition. Replace as necessary.
8. Install brake shoes and adjuster.
9. Install adjuster lever spring.
10. Connect the parking brake cable to the parking brake lever.
11. Install pins, hold down springs and retainers.
12. Install return springs.
13. Adjust brake shoes. Install drum.
14. Install the tire and wheel assembly.
15. Road test the vehicle and check for proper operation.

Wheel Cylinder

REMOVAL & INSTALLATION

1. Raise and safely support the vehicle.
2. Remove the rear wheel and tire assembly.

PARKING BRAKE

Front Cable

REMOVAL & INSTALLATION

▶ **See Figures 39 and 40**

1. Disconnect the negative battery cable.
2. Remove the center console assembly from the vehicle. Refer to Section 10 of this manual.
3. Disconnect the front cable from the parking brake lever.
4. Raise and safely support the vehicle as necessary. Loosen the cable adjusting nuts on left side the rear cable for Storm models or at the turnbuckle for Spectrum models.
5. Disconnect the rear cable assembly from the front cable assembly.
6. Remove the front cable retaining nuts and remove the cable from the vehicle.

To install:

7. Install the front cable to the vehicle and secure with retaining nuts.
8. Connect the rear cable assembly to the front cable assembly.
9. Connect the front cable to the parking brake lever.

3. Remove the brake drum and the brake shoes.
4. Disconnect and plug the brake line at the wheel cylinder.
5. Remove the wheel cylinder attaching bolts and the wheel cylinder.
6. Installation is the reverse of the removal procedure. Torque wheel cylinder retaining bolts to 7 ft. lbs. Bleed the brake system.

Brake Backing Plate

REMOVAL & INSTALLATION

1. Disconnect the negative battery cable.
2. Raise and safely support the vehicle.
3. Remove the rear wheel and tire assembly.
4. Remove the brake drum and the brake shoes (note location of all brake hardware for correct installation).
5. Remove the brake line and wheel cylinder.
6. Remove the hub from the backing plate.
7. Remove the backing plate.

To install:

8. Install the backing plate.
9. Install the hub to the backing plate. Torque the hub-to-backing plate bolts evenly to 49 ft. lbs.
10. Install the wheel cylinder and connect the brake line.
11. Install the brake shoes and install the brake drum. Adjust the bearing preload, if necessary.
12. Install the rear wheel and tire assembly.
13. Bleed and adjust the brakes. Road test the vehicle for proper operation.

10. Install the center console assembly to the vehicle. Refer to Section 10 of this manual.
11. Adjust the parking brake. Check parking brake for proper operation.

Rear Cables

REMOVAL & INSTALLATION

1. Raise and safely support the vehicle as necessary.
2. Remove the wheel and tire assembly.
3. Remove the tension spring. Loosen the adjusting nuts on left side of the rear cable for Storm models and at the turnbuckle for Spectrum models.
4. Disconnect the rear cable assembly from the front cable assembly.
5. Remove the rear cable retaining bolt.
6. Remove the rear brake drum.
7. Remove the cable from the parking brake lever inside the drum brake assembly.
8. Disconnect the cable from the backing plate.

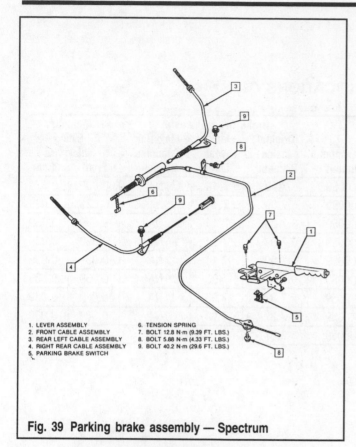

1. LEVER ASSEMBLY
2. FRONT CABLE ASSEMBLY
3. REAR LEFT CABLE ASSEMBLY
4. RIGHT REAR CABLE ASSEMBLY
5. PARKING BRAKE SWITCH
6. TENSION SPRING
7. BOLT 12.8 N·m (9.39 FT. LBS.)
8. BOLT 5.88 N·m (4.33 FT. LBS.)
9. BOLT 40.2 N·m (29.6 FT. LBS.)

Fig. 39 Parking brake assembly — Spectrum

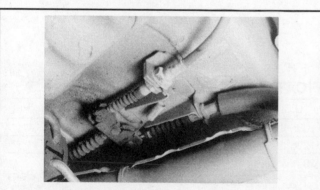

Fig. 40 Parking brake adjustment — Storm

To install:

9. Connect the cable to the backing plate. Make sure to fully seat the parking brake cable and seal if equipped in the backing plate.

10. Connect the cable to the parking brake lever inside the drum brake assembly.
11. Install the rear brake drum.
12. Install the rear cable retaining bolt.
13. Connect the rear cable assembly to the front cable assembly.
14. Install the tension spring.
15. Install the wheel and tire assembly.
16. Adjust the parking brake. Check parking brake for proper operation.

ADJUSTMENT

Before adjusting the parking brake, adjust the rear brakes and bleed the brake system, if necessary. Pull the parking brake lever all of the way up and count the number of clicks. If less than 7 or more than 8 clicks are heard, the parking brake requires adjustment. Adjustment can be made at the left parking brake cable adjuster nut on the Storm models at the turnbuckle (located at rear axle assembly) on the Spectrum models.

Brake Lever Assembly

REMOVAL & INSTALLATION

1. Disconnect the negative battery cable. Remove the center console from the vehicle.
2. Disconnect the electrical connector from the parking brake switch.
3. Loosen the parking brake cable adjuster nut or turnbuckle, if necessary.
4. Disconnect the parking brake cable from the lever assembly.
5. Remove the 2 bolts from the lever. Remove the lever assembly.
To install:
6. Connect the parking brake cable to the lever.
7. Install the lever assembly to the body with the 2 retaining bolts. Torque the retaining bolts to 10 ft. lbs.
8. Connect the electrical connector to the parking brake switch.
9. Install the center console assembly to the vehicle.
10. Adjust the parking brake. Check parking brake for proper operation.

BRAKE SPECIFICATIONS

All measurements in inches unless noted.

Year	Model	Master Cylinder Bore	Brake Disc			Brake Drum Diameter			Minimum Lining Thickness	
			Original Thickness	Minimum Thickness	Maximum Runout	Original Inside Diameter	Max. Wear Limit	Maximum Machine Diameter	Front	Rear
1985	Spectrum	0.810	0.433	0.378	0.0059	7.09	7.14	NA	0.039	0.039
1986	Spectrum	0.810	0.433	0.378	0.0059	7.09	7.14	NA	0.039	0.039
1987	Spectrum	0.810	0.433	0.378	0.0059	7.09	7.14	NA	0.039	0.039
1988	Spectrum	0.810	0.433	0.378	0.0059	7.09	7.14	NA	0.039	0.039
1989	Spectrum	0.810	0.433	0.378	0.0059	7.09	7.14	NA	0.039	0.039
1990	Storm	①	0.866	0.811	0.0059	7.87	7.93	NA	0.039	0.039
1991	Storm	①	0.866	0.811	0.0059	7.87	7.93	NA	0.039	0.039
1992	Storm	①	0.866	0.811	0.0059	7.87	7.93	NA	0.039	0.039
1993	Storm	①	0.866	0.811	0.0059	7.87	7.93	NA	0.039	0.039

NA—Not available
① SOHC engine—0.810
  DOHC engine—0.875

TORQUE SPECIFICATIONS

Component	U.S.	Metric
Master cylinder-to-booster retaining nuts	10 ft. lbs.	13 Nm
Brake line fittings	12 ft. lbs.	16 Nm
Proportioning valves-to-master cylinder	29 ft. lbs.	40 Nm
Caliper mounting bracket		
Spectrum	41 ft. lbs.	55 Nm
Storm	76 ft. lbs.	103 Nm
Caliper slide pins (bolts)	36 ft. lbs.	49 Nm
Wheel cylinder-to-backing plate	8 ft. lbs.	9 Nm
Rear wheel hub assembly retaining bolt		
Storm	49 ft. lbs.	66 Nm
Rear wheel bearing hub nut		
Spectrum	22 ft. lbs.	29 Nm
Parking brake assembly retaining bolts	10 ft. lbs.	13 Nm
Brake pedal assembly retaining bolts	15 ft. lbs.	20 Nm

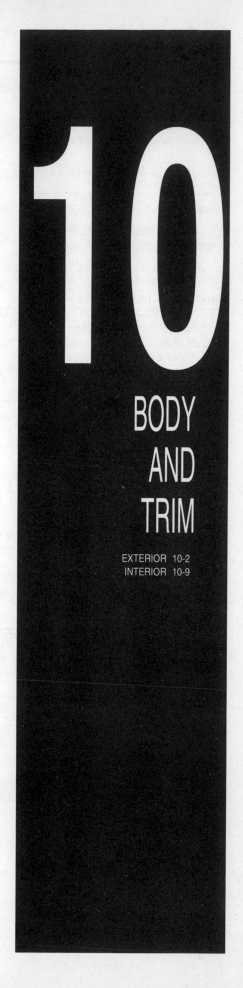

10

BODY AND TRIM

EXTERIOR

Doors

REMOVAL & INSTALLATION

▶ **See Figures 1, 2 and 3**

➡ **To prevent door glass from breaking, lower glass prior to removal or alignment of door.**

1. If door is equipped with power accessories or front door speakers, the inside door panel must be removed to disconnect the wiring harness.

2. Fully open and balance door on a floor jack (an assistant may be needed). Use a bundled rag or a block of wood to protect the painted surface of the door edge.

3. Remove the door checker pin with a hammer. Place a block of wood under the checker to prevent bending it while removing the pin.

4. Remove the door-side hinge mounting bolts

5. Slowly pull the door away from the hinges.

To install:

6. Clean and lubricate the hinges, hinge bolt holes and door checker assembly with grease.

7. Balance door on floor jack and align the door with the hinges.

8. Install door-side hinge bolts and tighten with moderate torque. DO NOT tighten down all the way.

9. Remove floor jack and close door slowly to check alignment. DO NOT slam door closed. In most cases door adjustment will be necessary.

10. Open door, loosen hinge bolts and adjust door so that all clearances are even. Hold clearance as far as possible.

➡ **It may be necessary to loosen door-side and/or body-side hinge bolts to correctly adjust door. Body shims may be necessary to adjust door or striker with the body.**

11. After alignment is satisfactory, tighten door-side hinge bolts to 18-25 ft. lbs.

12. Adjust door striker by loosening mounting screws and tapping with a plastic hammer. The striker should be parallel with the dovetail on the door latch mechanism. One or two shims are needed to control correct engagement of striker with door latch. Torque striker screws to 10 ft. lbs.

Hood

REMOVAL & INSTALLATION

1. Scribe a mark showing the location of the hinges on the hood.

2. Disconnect under hood light connector (if equipped).

3. On Storm disconnect headlight actuator terminal connector.

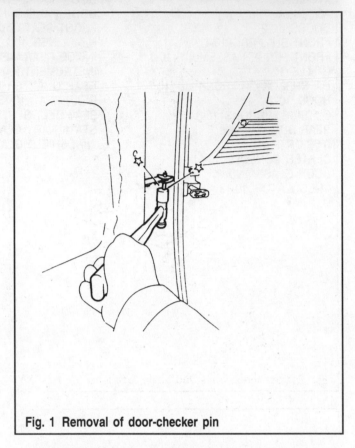

Fig. 1 Removal of door-checker pin

4. On Spectrum remove washer nozzle tubes.

5. Disconnect hood strut (if equipped) by removing bolts, or lower prop rod.

✳✳CAUTION

An assistant is needed to hold the hood in position during removal. Serious injury can result if hood should close during removal.

6. Remove hood mounting bolts and lift hood from vehicle.

To install:

7. Position hood on hinges and line up scribe line.

8. Install and tighten mounting bolts with moderate torque. DO NOT tighten down all the way.

9. Close hood slowly to check alignment. DO NOT slam hood closed. In most cases hood adjustment will be necessary.

10. Open hood, loosen hinge bolts and adjust hood so that all clearances are even and panel is flush with body. Hold clearance as far as possible.

➡ **Body shims may be necessary to adjust hood.**

11. After alignment is satisfactory, tighten hood hinge bolts to 18-25 ft. lbs.

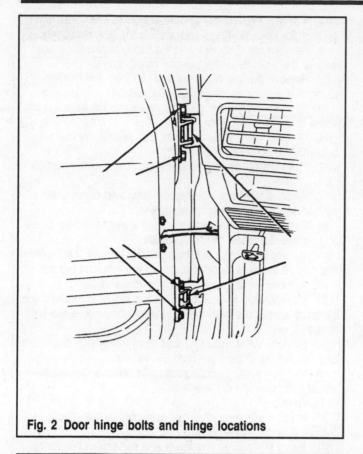

Fig. 2 Door hinge bolts and hinge locations

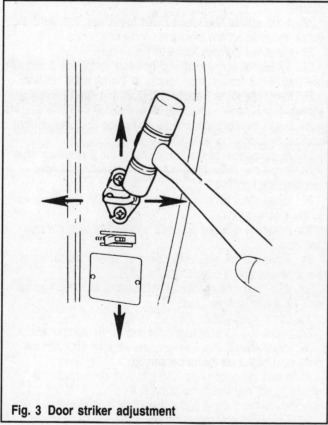

Fig. 3 Door striker adjustment

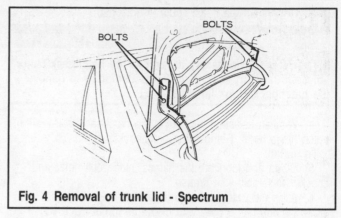

Fig. 4 Removal of trunk lid - Spectrum

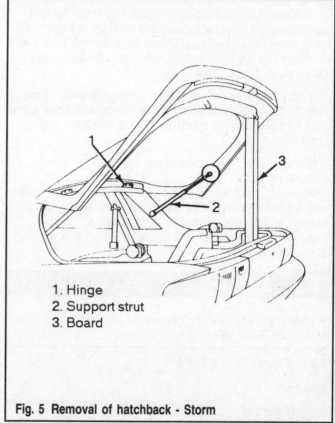

1. Hinge
2. Support strut
3. Board

Fig. 5 Removal of hatchback - Storm

Hatchback or Trunk Lid

REMOVAL & INSTALLATION

▶ See Figures 4 and 5

1. Disassemble hatch inner panel to gain access to wiring harness. Disconnect and remove tailgate harness.
2. If equipped, remove the bolt, nut and washer that attach the tailgate checker to the frame.

3. Disconnect the hatch struts (if equipped).

❋❋CAUTION

An assistant is necessary to remove the hatchback/Trunk lid. Serious injury can result from attempting to remove the hatchback/Trunk lid alone.

4. With an assistant supporting the hatchback, remove the hatch hinge bolts. Remove the hatchback/trunk lid.

To install:

5. Clean and lubricate the hinges, hinge bolt holes and checker assembly with grease.

6. Align the hatchback and install the hinge bolts.

7. Tighten hinge bolts with moderate torque. DO NOT tighten down all the way.

8. Close hatchback slowly to check alignment. DO NOT slam closed. In most cases adjustment will be necessary.

9. Open hatchback, loosen hinge bolts and adjust so that all clearances are even and panel is flush with body. Hold clearance as far as possible.

➡️**It may be necessary to loosen hatchback and/or body-side hinge bolts to correctly adjust hatchback. Body shims may be necessary to adjust hatchback or striker with body.**

10. After alignment is satisfactory, tighten hinge bolts to 18-25 ft. lbs.

11. Adjust striker by loosening mounting screws and tapping with a plastic hammer. The striker should be parallel with the dovetail on the latch mechanism. One or two shims are needed to control correct engagement of striker with the latch. Torque striker screws to 10 ft. lbs.

Front Bumpers

REMOVAL & INSTALLATION

◆ **See Figures 6, 7, 8 and 9**

Spectrum

1. Raise and support the vehicle safely (if necessary).
2. Disconnect parking light and marker light wiring harness.
3. Remove side bumpers.
4. Remove all bolts necessary to separate bumper (cover) from backing bars.
5. Remove bumper (cover) from backing bar.
6. Installation is the reverse of removal.

Storm

1. Disconnect the negative battery cable.
2. Remove the battery and battery tray from the vehicle.
3. Remove the 1 mounting nut and the 1 mounting bolt and remove the underhood fuse/relay box. Set the box aside.
4. Remove the air filter element, the air inlet duct and the remainder of the air cleaner assembly.
5. Remove the 12 bolts along the top of the bumper fascia.
6. Raise and safely support the vehicle.

7. Remove the 1 screw and 12 plastic retainer clips from each of the wheelhousings and remove the wheelhousings.

8. Remove the 2 screws and 4 plastic retainer clips and remove the left side under bumper splash shield.

9. Remove the mounting nut and clip from the bumper supports and remove the bumper supports.

10. Remove the mounting nuts that secure the bumper fascia to the side supports.

11. Remove the 2 mounting nuts that secure the bumper fascia to the front fenders.

12. From the bottom of the fascia, remove the 4 mounting clips.

13. Remove the front side marker lamp and combination light sockets from each lamp assembly.

14. Remove the 2 screws from each lower headlamp bezel and remove the bezel from the vehicle.

15. By way of each headlamp opening, remove the 2 screws that secure the front bumper fascia to the retaining bracket.

16. Remove the bumper fascia from the vehicle.

17. If the vehicle is equipped with fog lamps, disconnect the electrical connectors from the fog lamps and remove the fog lamps.

18. Remove the 4 mounting nuts from the energy absorbers and remove the impact bar from the vehicle.

19. Remove the 2 mounting nuts and remove the energy absorber assembly from the vehicle.

To install:

20. Install the energy absorber assembly to the vehicle. Secure with the mounting nuts.

21. Install the energy absorbers and the impact bar to the vehicle.

22. If the vehicle is equipped with fog lamps, install the fog lamps and connect the electrical connectors.

23. Install the bumper fascia to the vehicle.

24. By way of each headlamp opening, install the 2 screws that secure the front bumper fascia to the retaining bracket.

25. Install the lower headlamp bezels and secure with the screws.

26. Install the front side marker lamp and combination light sockets to each lamp assembly.

27. At the bottom of the fascia, install the 4 mounting clips.

28. Install the 2 mounting nuts that secure the bumper fascia to the front fenders.

29. Install the mounting nuts that secure the bumper fascia to the side supports.

30. Install the bumper supports and secure with the clips and nuts.

31. Install the left side under bumper splash shield. Install the 2 screws and 4 plastic retainer clips.

32. Install the wheelhousings and secure with the 1 screw and 12 plastic retainer clips.

33. Lower the vehicle.

34. Install the 12 bolts along the top of the bumper fascia.

35. Install the air filter element, the air inlet duct and the remainder of the air cleaner assembly.

36. Install the underhood fuse box and secure with the 1 mounting nut and the 1 mounting bolt.

37. Install the battery and battery tray to the vehicle.

38. Connect the negative battery cable.

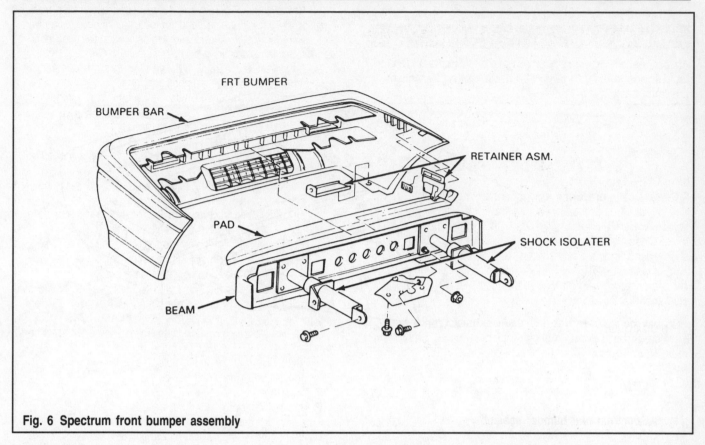

Fig. 6 Spectrum front bumper assembly

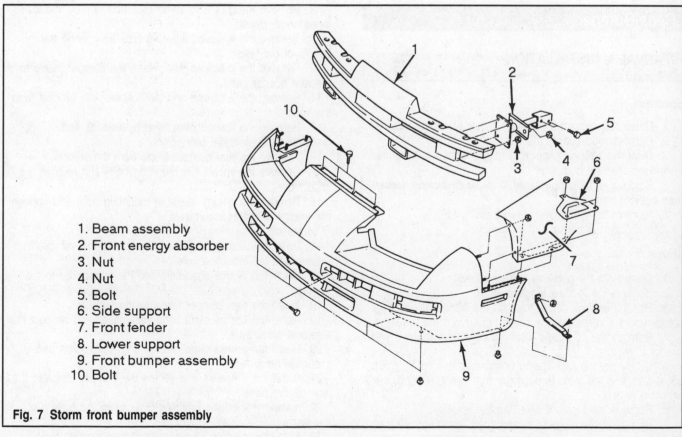

1. Beam assembly
2. Front energy absorber
3. Nut
4. Nut
5. Bolt
6. Side support
7. Front fender
8. Lower support
9. Front bumper assembly
10. Bolt

Fig. 7 Storm front bumper assembly

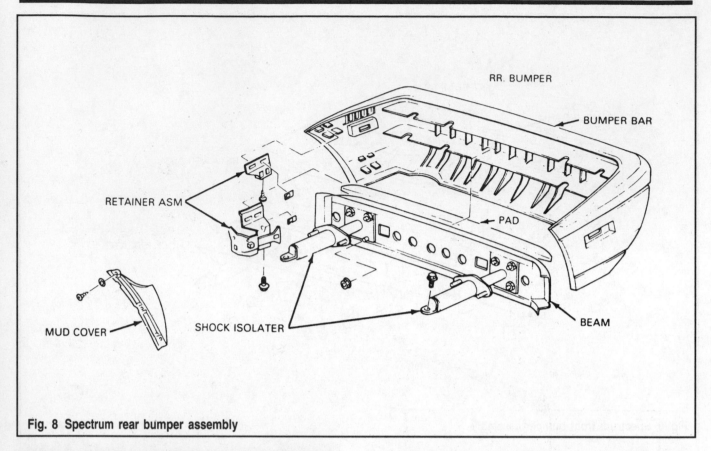

RR. BUMPER

BUMPER BAR

RETAINER ASM

PAD

MUD COVER

SHOCK ISOLATER

BEAM

Fig. 8 Spectrum rear bumper assembly

Rear Bumper

REMOVAL & INSTALLATION

Spectrum

1. Raise and support the vehicle safely (if necessary).
2. Remove mud guards (if equipped).
3. Disconnect parking light and marker light wiring harness.
4. Remove side bumpers.
5. Remove all bolts necessary to separate bumper (cover) from backing bars.
6. Remove bumper (cover) from backing bar.
7. Installation is the reverse of removal.

Storm

1. Disconnect the negative battery cable.
2. Remove the in-trunk luggage strap.
3. Roll the in-trunk carpet towards the front of the luggage compartment and remove the spare tire cover from the vehicle.
4. Remove the 10 plastic retaining clips from the rear end interior trim panel.
5. Gently pry the rear interior compartment lamp from trim panel and feed the lamp through the trim panel. Remove the 2 side trim panels.
6. Remove the 5 plastic wire harness retainers.
7. By way of the luggage compartment area, remove the 11 mounting nuts that secure the rear bumper fascia to the rear tail panel and the 2 bolts on the ends of the bumper fascia.

8. Remove the plastic retaining clips and remove the lower inner fender panels.
9. Remove the 4 plastic retaining clips from along the bottom of the fascia.
10. Remove the 2 screws that secure the bumper fascia to the rear quarter panel.
11. Remove the 2 screws and the license plate bracket from the vehicle.
12. Remove the license plate lamp assemblies and disconnect the electrical connectors.
13. Remove the rear bumper fascia from the vehicle.
14. Remove the impact bar mounting bolts and remove the impact bars.
15. Remove the energy absorber mounting bolts and remove the energy absorber assemblies.
   To install:
16. Install the energy absorber assembly to the vehicle. Secure with the mounting nuts.
17. Install the energy absorbers and the impact bar to the vehicle.
18. Install the rear bumper fascia to the vehicle.
19. Install the license plate lamp assemblies and connect the electrical connectors.
20. Install the license plate bracket onto the vehicle and secure in place.
21. Install the 2 screws that secure the bumper fascia to the rear quarter panel.
22. Install the 4 plastic retaining clips along the bottom of the fascia.
23. Install the plastic retaining clips that retain the lower inner fender panels.

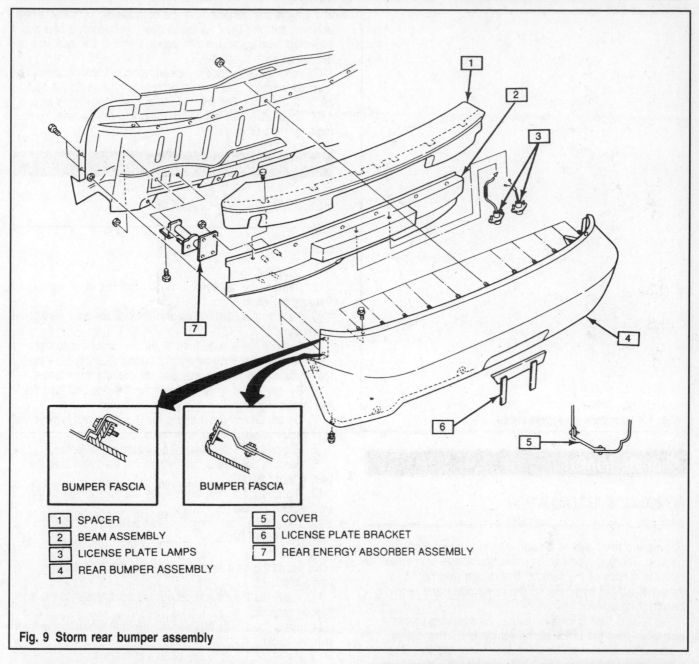

BUMPER FASCIA

BUMPER FASCIA

1	SPACER	5	COVER
2	BEAM ASSEMBLY	6	LICENSE PLATE BRACKET
3	LICENSE PLATE LAMPS	7	REAR ENERGY ABSORBER ASSEMBLY
4	REAR BUMPER ASSEMBLY		

Fig. 9 Storm rear bumper assembly

24. By way of the luggage compartment area, install the 11 mounting nuts that secure the rear bumper fascia to the rear tail panel and the 2 bolts on the ends of the bumper fascia.

25. Install plastic wire harness retainers.

26. Install the 2 side trim panels and the rear interior lamp assembly.

27. Install the 10 plastic retaining clips from the rear end interior trim panel.

28. Replace the in-trunk carpet and the spare tire cover.

29. Install the in-trunk luggage strap.

30. Connect the negative battery cable.

Grille

REMOVAL & INSTALLATION

▶ See Figure 10

1. Remove the front grille emblem.

2. Raise the setting tip of all clips holding the grille.

3. Remove all screws holding the grille.

4. Disconnect front wiring harness if parking or turn signal lights are located in grille.

5. Remove grille assembly.

6. Attaching clips must be installed into the grille prior to installation.

7. Installation is the reverse of removal.

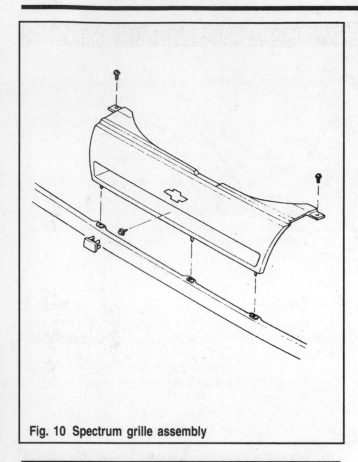

Fig. 10 Spectrum grille assembly

Outside Mirrors

REMOVAL & INSTALLATION

There are two types of outside mirrors used on Geo vehicles. The first type has the mounting screws accessible from the outside of the vehicle. This design may be removed/installed by prying off the screw cover and removing the attaching screws.

The second type of outside mirror has mounting screws accessible from the inside of the vehicle only. This design requires the removal of the inner door panel and trim. After this is removed the three mounting screws can be removed.

Antenna

REMOVAL & INSTALLATION

The antenna used on Geo vehicles is mounted in the left front pillar. To remove the antenna, simply disconnect the antenna lead wire from the radio, remove the mounting screw

and remove the antenna from the body panel. To install a new antenna, the wire must be fed through the mounting hole and pulled out from under the trim panel. Connect the lead wire to the radio.

On some models, once a new antenna is installed, the radio must be trimmed. The trim adjustment is located on the back panel of the radio. Set the radio to a weak AM station around 1400 on the dial. Use a trim adjusting tool to fine tune the radio for the best reception.

Front Fender Assembly

REMOVAL & INSTALLATION

Storm

1. Open the hood.
2. Remove the nut cover and nut from the wiper arms. Remove the wiper arms.
3. Remove the plastic clips and remove the cowl vent grille assembly.
4. Remove the 4 bolts from along the top of the fender.
5. Remove the 1 screw and 12 plastic retaining clips from the wheelhousing inner fender and remove the inner fender.
6. By way of the wheelwell, remove the one bolt from the rear of the fender.
7. On the GSi model, remove the 7 screws and remove the front rocker panel molding from below the door.
8. Remove the 1 bolt from the bottom of the fender.
9. Remove the 2 nuts that secure the front fender to the front bumper fascia.
10. Remove the 2 nuts that secure the front fender to the side support retainer.
11. Loosen the front bumper fascia bolts and remove the fender from the vehicle.
    To install:
12. Install the front fender and tighten the front bumper fascia bolts.
13. Install the 2 nuts that secure the front fender to the side support retainer.
14. Install the 2 nuts that secure the front fender to the front bumper fascia.
15. Install the 1 bolt to the bottom of the fender.
16. On the GSi model, install the front rocker panel molding to below the door.
17. By way of the wheel well, install the one bolt to the rear of the fender.
18. Install the 1 screw and 12 plastic retaining clips to the wheelhousing inner fender to secure the inner fender.
19. Install the 4 bolts to along the top of the fender.
20. Install the plastic clips and install the cowl vent grille assembly.
21. Install the nut and the nut cover to the wiper arms.

INTERIOR

Instrument Panel and Pad

REMOVAL & INSTALLATION

Spectrum
▶ See Figures 11, 12, 13 and 14

1. Disconnect the negative battery cable.
2. Remove the horn pad.
3. Remove the steering wheel nut and the steering wheel.
4. Remove the steering cowl.
5. Disconnect the electrical connectors from the combination switch and the starter switch.
6. Remove the steering column to lower dash and to pedal bracket mounting bolts.
7. Remove the steering universal joint 2nd attaching bolt. Remove the steering column assembly.
8. Remove the glove box.
9. Remove the radio bracket and disconnect the connector from the radio and the antenna cable.
10. Remove the ash tray.
11. Remove the heater/air conditioner control lever knob.
12. Remove the heater control panel and attaching screws.
13. Remove the instrument panel hood covering screws and pull the hood out away from the dash.
14. Disconnect the windshield wiper switch and lighting switch connectors.
15. Disconnect the speedometer cable. Remove the gauge assembly attaching screws and pull out the gauge assembly.
16. Remove the speedometer cable holder.
17. Remove the fuse block attaching screws.
18. Disconnect the instrument panel to chassis electrical connector.
19. Disconnect the heater/air conditioner control connector and remove the cable.
20. Remove the instrument panel attaching screw covers and remove the instrument panel attaching screws.
21. Remove the instrument panel to the heater air duct.
22. Remove the instrument panel assembly.
 To install:
23. Install the instrument panel assembly.
24. Install the instrument panel to heater air duct.
25. Install the instrument panel attaching screws and covers.
26. Connect the heater/air conditioner control connector and the cable.
27. Connect the instrument panel to chassis electrical connector.
28. Install the fuse block attaching screws.
29. Install the speedometer cable holder.
30. Connect the speedometer cable. Install the gauge assembly and the gauge assembly attaching screws.
31. Connect the windshield wiper switch and lighting switch connectors.
32. Install the hood to the dashboard and install the instrument panel hood covering screws.
33. Install the heater control panel and attaching screws.
34. Install the heater/air conditioner control lever knob.

35. Install the ash tray.
36. Install the radio bracket and connect the connector to the radio and the antenna cable.
37. Install the glove box.
38. Install the steering column assembly. Install the steering universal joint 2nd attaching bolt.
39. Install the steering column to lower dash and to pedal bracket mounting bolts.
40. Connect the electrical connectors to the combination switch and the starter switch.
41. Install the steering cowl.
42. Install the steering wheel and the steering wheel nut.
43. Install the horn pad.
44. Connect the negative battery cable.

Storm
▶ See Figure 15

1. If the vehicle is equipped with a Supplemental Inflatable Restraint (SIR) system, disable the system as described in Section 6.
2. Disconnect the negative battery cable.
3. Remove the glove box securing pins and remove the glove box assembly.
4. Remove the front console bracket.
5. Remove the 2 screws from the top of the instrument cluster cover.
6. From under the instrument cluster and remove the 4 screws securing the instrument cluster cover.

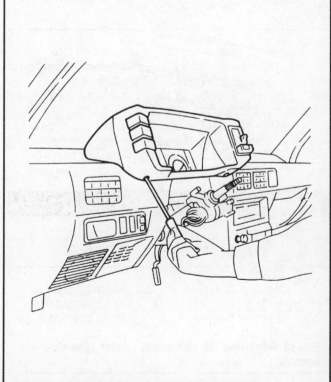

Fig. 11 Removing the instrument cluster hood — Spectrum

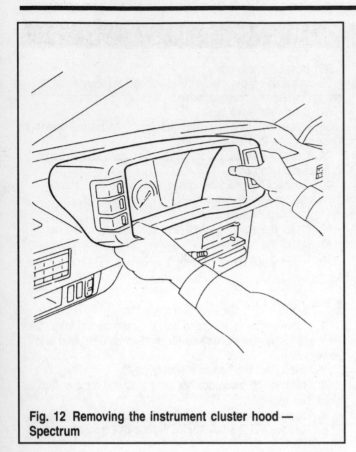

Fig. 12 Removing the instrument cluster hood — Spectrum

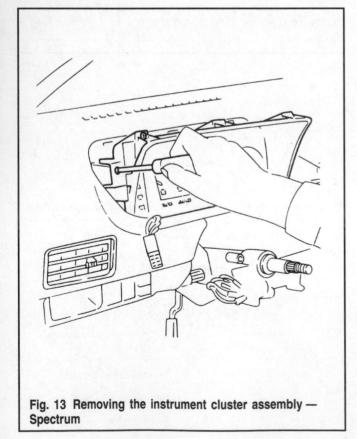

Fig. 13 Removing the instrument cluster assembly — Spectrum

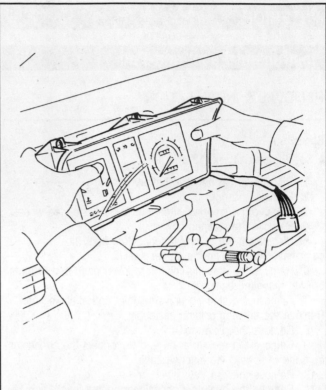

Fig. 14 Removing the instrument cluster assembly — Spectrum

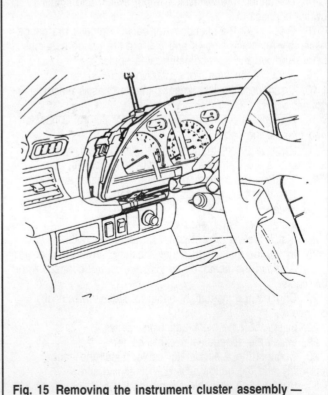

Fig. 15 Removing the instrument cluster assembly — Storm

7. Disconnect the lighting and windshield wiper/washer switches and remove the instrument cluster cover.

8. Remove the 4 screws securing the instrument cluster and pull the instrument cluster out.

9. Disconnect the electrical connectors and the speedometer cable from the back of the instrument cluster and remove the cluster from the vehicle.

10. Remove the 3 defroster grille plastic retainer covers.

11. Remove the 3 bolts and 2 screws that secure the defroster grille and remove the grille.

12. Remove the 2 screws, 4 bolts and 1 nut that secure the instrument panel assembly to the vehicle.

13. Remove the clips that secure the instrument panel wiring harness.

14. Disconnect the heater and A/C control cables and electrical connectors.

15. Remove the instrument panel from·the vehicle.

To install:

16. Install the instrument panel to the vehicle. Align the instrument panel.

17. Connect the heater and A/C control cables and electrical connectors.

18. Install the clips that secure the instrument panel wiring harness.

19. Install the 2 screws, 4 bolts and 1 nut that secure the instrument panel assembly to the vehicle.

20. Install the 3 bolts and 2 screws that secure the defroster grille.

21. Install the 3 defroster grille plastic retainer covers.

22. Connect the electrical connectors and the speedometer cable to the instrument cluster and install the mounting screws.

23. Connect the lighting and windshield wiper/washer switches to the cluster cover.

24. Install the cluster cover and install the mounting screws.

25. Connect the negative battery cable.

Center Console

REMOVAL & INSTALLATION

Storm

1. Disconnect the negative battery cable and remove the ashtray.

2. Remove the shift lever trim bezel.

3. Remove the heater control knobs.

4. Remove the radio trim bezel and remove the radio.

5. Remove the console mounting screws and pull the console away from the dashboard.

6. Disconnect the electrical connectors and remove the console.

7. Installation is the reverse of the removal procedure.

Door Panels

REMOVAL & INSTALLATION

1. Remove window crank handle with appropriate clip removal tool.

2. Remove arm rest attaching screws.

3. Remove the screw from the inside door handle. Slide the handle forward and disconnect the handle from the control rods and remove the handle.

4. Remove the mirror panel cover from inside the door.

5. Gently pry the speaker cover from the door and remove the speaker.

6. Remove the 1 screw from the door panel and gently pry the door panel away from the door to release the clips. Lift the door panel up and away from the door.

To install:

7. Install the door panel to the door. Push in on the clips to seat.

8. Connect the speaker wires to the speaker and install the speaker and speaker cover.

9. Install the interior door handle.

10. Install the arm rest screws.

11. Install the window crank handle.

Rear Quarter Trim Panel

REMOVAL & INSTALLATION

Spectrum Hatchback

▶ **See Figure 16**

1. Remove the door sill plate.

2. Remove the rear seat and the rear compartment floor carpeting.

3. Remove the rear window garnish molding and remove the rear quarter window hinge screws.

4. Remove the rear window assembly and the weatherstrip.

5. Remove the rear seat striker cover.

6. Remove the rear quarter trim panel 4 outer retainers and 6 inner retainers.

7. Remove the front seat belt.

8. Remove the rear quarter trim panel.

9. Installation is the reverse of the removal procedure.

Storm

1. Remove the retaining screw and rear seat belt trim bezel from the seat belt retractor.

2. Remove the 5 screw covers from the strut tower trim panel.

3. Remove the 6 screws from the strut tower trim panel and set the trim panel aside.

4. Remove the 2 screws that secure the luggage compartment trim panel to the rear quarter trim panel.

5. Remove the rear seat cushion.

6. Remove the 2 screws that secure the rear trim panel to the floor.

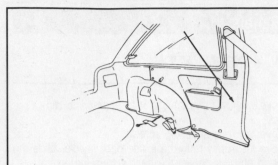

Fig. 16 Rear quarter trim panel removal — Spectrum hatchback

7. Remove the front seat belt guide loop trim cover.

8. Remove the anchor bolt and the front seat belt guide loop from the B-pillar.

9. Remove the 2 anchor bolts and the front seat belt slide bar from the floor.

10. Remove the front seat belt from the slide bar.

11. Remove the rear quarter trim panel from the vehicle while feeding the seat belt through the seat belt bezel.

To install:

12. Install the rear quarter trim panel to the vehicle. Feed the rear seat belt through the seat belt bezel.

13. Install the rear quarter trim panel screws and install the seat belt to the slide bar.

14. Install the seat belt slide bar to the floor and secure with the 2 screws.

15. Install the front seat belt guide loop to the B-pillar and install the trim cover.

16. Install the rear seat cushion and install the luggage compartment trim panel.

17. Install the strut tower trim panel and secure it with the screws. Install the screw covers.

18. Install the rear seat belt trim bezel.

Headliner

REMOVAL & INSTALLATION

Spectrum

1. Spread a protective cloth over the interior of the vehicle prior to removing the headliner assembly.

2. Remove the sun visors, rear view mirror and dome light assembly.

3. On hatchback models, remove the rear quarter glass and rear weather-stripping.

4. On the sedan model, remove the rear window glass.

5. Remove the door finisher panels and the assist grip assembly.

6. Remove the front pillar trim and rear quarter upper trim panel.

7. Roll up the peripheral sections of the headliner.

8. Remove the listing wire from the side rail.

9. Remove the headliner and the panel.

To install:

10. Install the headliner and the panel to the vehicle. Limited amounts of 2-sided tape or adhesive may be used.

11. Install the listing wire to the side rail and roll down the peripheral sections of the headliner. Make sure that there are no creases.

12. Install the trim panels and assist grips.

13. Install any glass that was previously removed.

14. Install the sun visors, rearview mirror and dome light.

Storm

▶ See Figure 17

1. Disconnect the negative battery cable.

2. Remove the rearview mirror.

3. Remove the sun visors and the dome lamp.

4. Remove the assist handles. This is done by prying off the covers and removing the 2 screws.

5. Remove the A-pillar trim panels.

6. Remove the roof side trim panels.

7. On the hatchback models, remove the rear upper quarter trim panels.

8. Remove the 3 trim clips, located at the rear of the headliner and remove the headliner from the vehicle.

To install:

9. Position the headliner in the vehicle.

10. Install the trim clips at the rear of the headliner.

11. Install all of the trim panels.

12. Install the assist handles and the dome lamp.

13. Install the rear view mirrors and the sun visors.

14. Connect the negative battery cable.

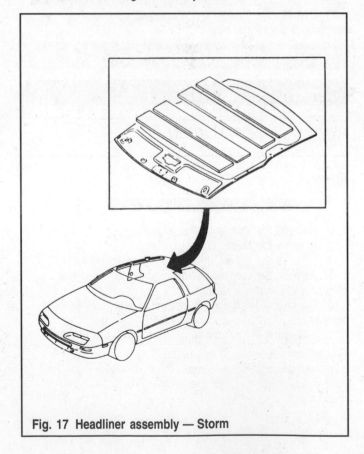

Fig. 17 Headliner assembly — Storm

Door Locks

REMOVAL & INSTALLATION

▶ **See Figure 18**

1. Remove door panel as described above. Remove water seal carefully it must be reused.

2. Disconnect the inside handle rod clips. Disconnect and remove all lock control rods, noting their position for installation.

3. Remove the door lock assembly mounting screws from the outside of the door and remove the door lock assembly.

4. Remove the key cylinder by prying the retaining clip with an appropriate tool.

5. Remove the outside door handle by loosening the two outside handle mounting bolts from inside the door.

6. Remove the inside door handle by loosening the retaining screws. Some inside handles may be attached with rivets. In this case drill the rivets out with the appropriate size drill bit.

To install:

7. Install the inside door handles and lubricate all components prior to installation.

8. Install the key cylinder to the door.

9. Connect the door lock linkage and install the outside door handle. On vehicles equipped with an adjustable lock rod, set play to zero when door lock rod is in lock position.

10. Torque door lock assembly and outside door handle mounting screws to 48 inch lbs.

11. Install the weather seal and the door panel.

Door Glass and Regulator

REMOVAL & INSTALLATION

Spectrum

FRONT GLASS

▶ **See Figure 19**

1. Remove inside door panel, weather proof sheet, waist seal and weather strip.

2. Temporarily install the inside door handle and lower window to the inside panel holes.

3. Remove window attaching screws and glass.

4. Remove window regulator mounting bolts and nuts. Remove window regulator.

5. Remove front and rear glass guide rails.

6. Lubricate operating surfaces of window regulator.

7. Check that bottom channel is properly positioned on the glass. Measure spacing from old glass.

8. Installation is the reverse of the removal procedure. When installing the window regulator bolts, torque to 48 inch lbs.

REAR GLASS

1. Remove inside door panel, weather proof sheet and door trim.

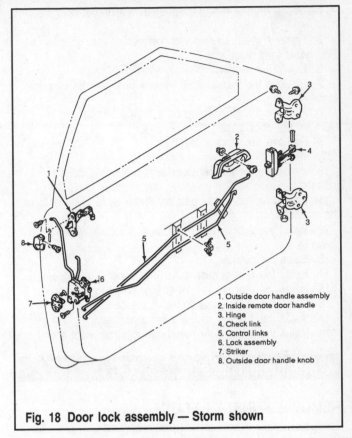

Fig. 18 Door lock assembly — Storm shown

1. Outside door handle assembly
2. Inside remote door handle
3. Hinge
4. Check link
5. Control links
6. Lock assembly
7. Striker
8. Outside door handle knob

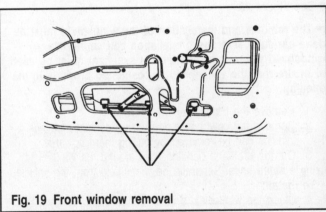

Fig. 19 Front window removal

2. Remove front guide rail, inner and outer waist seal. Then remove rear guide rail.

3. Remove door window quarter glass. Then remove door glass.

4. Remove window regulator assembly.

5. Lubricate operating surfaces of window regulator.

6. When installing window regulator bolts, torque to 48 inch lbs.

7. Installation is the reverse of removal.

Storm

DOOR GLASS

1. Remove inside door panel and weather proof sheet.

2. Remove the 1 screw from the outer sealing strip.

3. Pull the outer sealing strip from the door.

4. Gently pry the rear garnish inner filler panel from the door.

5. Remove the 3 screws and remove the rear garnish outer filler panel from the door.

6. Lower the window.

7. Remove the 2 bolts and 1 screw from the door window guide.

8. Remove the glass fixing bolts from the regulator. Remove the door glass.

9. Remove the window regulator.

To install:

10. Install the window regulator and tighten the bolts to 71 inch lbs.

11. Install the door glass and install the glass fixing bolts to the regulator.

12. Install the 2 bolts and 1 screw to the door window guide.

13. Raise the window.

14. Install the rear garnish outer filler panel to the door.

15. Install the rear garnish inner filler panel to the door.

16. Install the outer sealing strip to the door.

17. Install the 1 screw to the outer sealing strip.

18. Install the inside door panel and weather proof sheet.

Windshield Glass

REMOVAL & INSTALLATION

▶ See Figure 20

➡**The removal and installation of the windshield must be done carefully, improper installation can cause the windshield to crack or shatter. An assistant must be used to insure that the windshield is positioned properly in the opening.**

1. Remove the inside rearview mirror.

2. Remove the cowl cover and the windshield moldings. The moldings can be removed by pulling them upward.

3. Cut the urethane bonding from around the windshield using a sharp knife. Separate the windshield from the vehicle.

To install:

4. Clean the windshield area of old urethane bonding that may be loose. Clean the support spacers and reposition them on the studs.

5. With the aid of a helper, place the replacement windshield in the opening and position it in the center of the opening. Mark the glass at the supports, once it is centered, using a grease pencil or masking tape. This will help position it properly.

6. Remove the windshield from the opening and place it on a suitable support, clean the inside of the glass. Apply clear glass primer in a 1 inch path around the perimeter of the windshield and wipe with a clean cloth.

7. Apply a 15mm path of blackout primer around the top and sides of the windshield. Apply a 1 inch path to the bottom of the windshield. Allow 3 minutes drying time.

8. Position the windshield bonding compression spacers around the opening for the windshield.

9. Apply a 12mm bead of urethane around the inside of the opening.

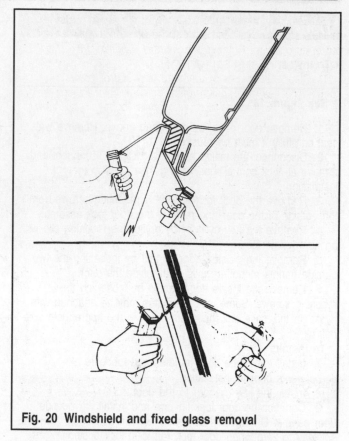

Fig. 20 Windshield and fixed glass removal

10. With the aid of a helper, install the windshield glass in position, aligning the reference marks made earlier. Push the windshield into position until it bottoms on the spacers and the top moldings is flush with the roof line.

11. Clean excess urethane from the glass using a suitable solvent. Install the moldings.

12. Use pieces of masking tape around the windshield to hold the moldings until the urethane cures.

13. Install the cowl cover and the inside mirror.

14. When the urethane cures, remove the tape and water test the windshield for leaks.

Stationary Glass

➡**To reduce the risk of injury, wear safety glasses or goggles and gloves during this entire procedure. Use the specified adhesive in order to attain original installation integrity.**

REMOVAL & INSTALLATION

1. Mask off the area around the glass to protect the painted surfaces.

2. Remove the retaining screws and remove the lock pillar molding.

3. Remove the rear seat cushion and seat back.

4. Remove the upper quarter trim, windshield trim upper garnish molding, and lower quarter trim.

5. Using a curved blade tile knife or similar item, use multiple shallow cuts, and cut out the quarter window assembly out of its opening. Remove the window assembly.

To install:

6. Clean ALL traces of urethane from the pinch weld flange. To prevent corrosion, paint damage on the pinch weld by the knife must be covered with primer before installing the window.

7. Two primers are provided in GM kit-P/N 9636067. The clear primer is used prior to the black primer. Apply primer around the entire perimeter of the assembly. Allow to dry. Then apply the black primer over the clear primer and to the pinch weld flange. Allow to dry about 5 minutes.

8. Apply a smooth continuous ⅜ in. (10mm) bead of urethane around the window assembly.

9. Install the window assembly into the opening.

10. Install the retaining clips.

11. Check the installation for water-tightness. Use a hose with warm water to duplicate rainfall. Do not use a hard stream of water on fresh urethane. Seal any leaks with additional material.

12. Install all remaining trim pieces and seat parts.

13. Allow the car to remain at room temperature for at least 6 hours to complete the curing process.

Inside Rear View Mirror

The rear view mirror on Geo vehicles is attached to the center of the windshield brace in the interior. It is removed by simply unscrewing the attaching screw(s). On some models, the attaching screw(s) may be covered with plastic trim.

Front Seats

REMOVAL & INSTALLATION

▶ **See Figure 21**

1. Remove door sill plate if necessary.

2. Remove the seat adjuster bracket cover. Loosen and remove the seat adjuster attaching bolts.

3. Remove the seat from the vehicle.

➡**Some rear seats may be attached by spring clips. To remove, push seat bench toward the rear of the car and lift up.**

4. Installation is the reverse of removal. Torque seat attaching bolts to 29 ft. lbs.

Rear Seat

REMOVAL & INSTALLATION

▶ **See Figure 22**

1. Push the lower forward edge of the seat cushion rearward.

Fig. 21 Front seat removal and installation — Storm shown

2. Lift upward and pull forward on the seat cushion frame to disengage the cushion frame wires from the retainers on the rear seat pan.

3. Remove the lower seat cushion from the vehicle.

4. At the bottom of the seat back, remove the anchor bolts securing the rear seat wire retainers.

5. Grasp the bottom of the seat back and swing it forward to disengage the offsets on the upper frame bar from the hangers.

6. Lift the seat back upward and remove from vehicle.

7. To install, reverse the above process. Torque the bolts to 31 ft. lbs.

Seat Belt System

REMOVAL & INSTALLATION

Front Seat Belt

SPECTRUM

▶ **See Figures 23 and 24**

1. Remove the rear seat cushion.

2. Remove the door sill plate.

3. Remove the door finishing panel.

4. Remove the center pillar lower trim (sedan) or the outer anchor bolts (hatchback).

5. Remove the shoulder anchor bolt covers and bolts.

6. Open the rear quarter window and remove the rear quarter trim panel.

7. Remove the seat belt retractor mounting bolts and remove the retractor assembly.

8. Remove the seat belt from the rear quarter trim panel.

9. Disconnect the seat belt electrical harness connector.

10. Remove the seat belt buckle anchor bolts and remove the buckle assembly.

To install:

11. Install the buckle portion of the seat belts and tighten the bolts to 22-49 ft. lbs. (30-67 Nm).

12. Install the seat belt retractor unit. Tighten the mounting bolts to specification.

13. Install the rear quarter interior trim panel.

14. Install the shoulder anchor bolts and tighten the bolts to 22-49 ft. lbs. (30-67 Nm).

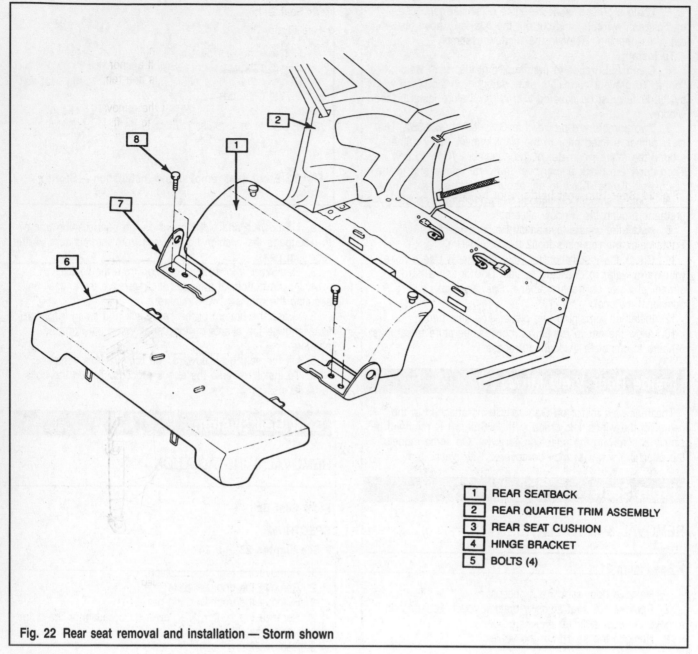

1	REAR SEATBACK
2	REAR QUARTER TRIM ASSEMBLY
3	REAR SEAT CUSHION
4	HINGE BRACKET
5	BOLTS (4)

Fig. 22 Rear seat removal and installation — Storm shown

15. Install the remaining trim panels and install the rear seat cushion.

16. Inspect the operation of the seat belt by firmly tugging on the belt. The belt should lock as it is yanked.

STORM

▶ **See Figure 25**

1. Remove the rear quarter trim panels.

2. Remove the plastic anchor cover and remove the anchor bolt.

3. Remove the 2 bolts and remove the safety belt slide bar.

4. Remove the retractor anchor bolt and remove the retractor assembly.

5. Disconnect the seat belt electrical connector and remove the seat belt assembly.

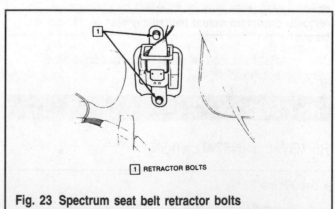

1 RETRACTOR BOLTS

Fig. 23 Spectrum seat belt retractor bolts

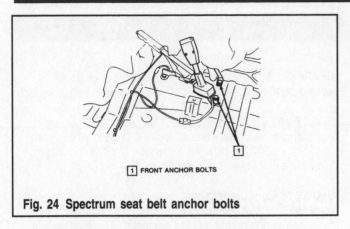

Fig. 24 Spectrum seat belt anchor bolts

6. Installation is the reverse of the removal procedure. Tighten all mounting bolts to 32 ft. lbs. (43 Nm).

Rear Seat Belt

▶ See Figure 26

1. Remove the rear seat cushion.
2. Remove the rear shoulder belt anchor bolt.
3. Remove the floor anchor bolts and remove the seat belt assembly from the vehicle.
4. Installation is the reverse of the removal procedure. Tighten all seat belt mounting bolts to 32 ft. lbs. (43 Nm).

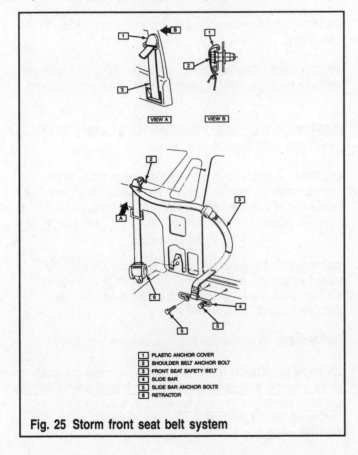

Fig. 25 Storm front seat belt system

1	PLASTIC ANCHOR COVER
2	SHOULDER BELT ANCHOR BOLT
3	FRONT SEAT SAFETY BELT
4	SLIDE BAR
5	SLIDE BAR ANCHOR BOLTS
6	RETRACTOR

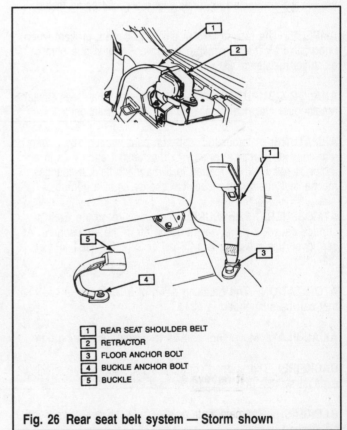

Fig. 26 Rear seat belt system — Storm shown

1	REAR SEAT SHOULDER BELT
2	RETRACTOR
3	FLOOR ANCHOR BOLT
4	BUCKLE ANCHOR BOLT
5	BUCKLE

GLOSSARY

AIR/FUEL RATIO: The ratio of air to gasoline by weight in the fuel mixture drawn into the engine.

AIR INJECTION: One method of reducing harmful exhaust emissions by injecting air into each of the exhaust ports of an engine. The fresh air entering the hot exhaust manifold causes any remaining fuel to be burned before it can exit the tailpipe.

ALTERNATOR: A device used for converting mechanical energy into electrical energy.

AMMETER: An instrument, calibrated in amperes, used to measure the flow of an electrical current in a circuit. Ammeters are always connected in series with the circuit being tested.

AMPERE: The rate of flow of electrical current present when one volt of electrical pressure is applied against one ohm of electrical resistance.

ANALOG COMPUTER: Any microprocessor that uses similar (analogous) electrical signals to make its calculations.

ARMATURE: A laminated, soft iron core wrapped by a wire that converts electrical energy to mechanical energy as in a motor or relay. When rotated in a magnetic field, it changes mechanical energy into electrical energy as in a generator.

ATMOSPHERIC PRESSURE: The pressure on the Earth's surface caused by the weight of the air in the atmosphere. At sea level, this pressure is 14.7 psi at 32{248}F (101 kPa at 0{248}C).

ATOMIZATION: The breaking down of a liquid into a fine mist that can be suspended in air.

AXIAL PLAY: Movement parallel to a shaft or bearing bore.

BACKFIRE: The sudden combustion of gases in the intake or exhaust system that results in a loud explosion.

BACKLASH: The clearance or play between two parts, such as meshed gears.

BACKPRESSURE: Restrictions in the exhaust system that slow the exit of exhaust gases from the combustion chamber.

BAKELITE: A heat resistant, plastic insulator material commonly used in printed circuit boards and transistorized components.

BALL BEARING: A bearing made up of hardened inner and outer races between which hardened steel balls roll.

BALLAST RESISTOR: A resistor in the primary ignition circuit that lowers voltage after the engine is started to reduce wear on ignition components.

BEARING: A friction reducing, supportive device usually located between a stationary part and a moving part.

BIMETAL TEMPERATURE SENSOR: Any sensor or switch made of two dissimilar types of metal that bend when heated or cooled due to the different expansion rates of the alloys. These types of sensors usually function as an on/off switch.

BLOWBY: Combustion gases, composed of water vapor and unburned fuel, that leak past the piston rings into the crankcase during normal engine operation. These gases are removed by the PCV system to prevent the buildup of harmful acids in the crankcase.

BRAKE PAD: A brake shoe and lining assembly used with disc brakes.

BRAKE SHOE: The backing for the brake lining. The term is, however, usually applied to the assembly of the brake backing and lining.

BUSHING: A liner, usually removable, for a bearing; an anti-friction liner used in place of a bearing.

CALIPER: A hydraulically activated device in a disc brake system, which is mounted straddling the brake rotor (disc). The caliper contains at least one piston and two brake pads. Hydraulic pressure on the piston(s) forces the pads against the rotor.

CAMSHAFT: A shaft in the engine on which are the lobes (cams) which operate the valves. The camshaft is driven by the crankshaft, via a belt, chain or gears, at one half the crankshaft speed.

CAPACITOR: A device which stores an electrical charge.

CARBON MONOXIDE (CO): A colorless, odorless gas given off as a normal byproduct of combustion. It is poisonous and extremely dangerous in confined areas, building up slowly to toxic levels without warning if adequate ventilation is not available.

CARBURETOR: A device, usually mounted on the intake manifold of an engine, which mixes the air and fuel in the proper proportion to allow even combustion.

CATALYTIC CONVERTER: A device installed in the exhaust system, like a muffler, that converts harmful byproducts of combustion into carbon dioxide and water vapor by means of a heat-producing chemical reaction.

CENTRIFUGAL ADVANCE: A mechanical method of advancing the spark timing by using flyweights in the distributor that react to centrifugal force generated by the distributor shaft rotation.

CHECK VALVE: Any one-way valve installed to permit the flow of air, fuel or vacuum in one direction only.

CHOKE: A device, usually a moveable valve, placed in the intake path of a carburetor to restrict the flow of air.

CIRCUIT: Any unbroken path through which an electrical current can flow. Also used to describe fuel flow in some instances.

CIRCUIT BREAKER: A switch which protects an electrical circuit from overload by opening the circuit when the current flow exceeds a predetermined level. Some circuit breakers must be reset manually, while most reset automatically

COIL (IGNITION): A transformer in the ignition circuit which steps up the voltage provided to the spark plugs.

COMBINATION MANIFOLD: An assembly which includes both the intake and exhaust manifolds in one casting.

COMBINATION VALVE: A device used in some fuel systems that routes fuel vapors to a charcoal storage canister instead of venting them into the atmosphere. The valve relieves fuel tank pressure and allows fresh air into the tank as the fuel level drops to prevent a vapor lock situation.

COMPRESSION RATIO: The comparison of the total volume of the cylinder and combustion chamber with the piston at BDC and the piston at TDC.

CONDENSER: 1. An electrical device which acts to store an electrical charge, preventing voltage surges.
2. A radiator-like device in the air conditioning system in which refrigerant gas condenses into a liquid, giving off heat.

CONDUCTOR: Any material through which an electrical current can be transmitted easily.

CONTINUITY: Continuous or complete circuit. Can be checked with an ohmmeter.

COUNTERSHAFT: An intermediate shaft which is rotated by a mainshaft and transmits, in turn, that rotation to a working part.

CRANKCASE: The lower part of an engine in which the crankshaft and related parts operate.

CRANKSHAFT: The main driving shaft of an engine which receives reciprocating motion from the pistons and converts it to rotary motion.

CYLINDER: In an engine, the round hole in the engine block in which the piston(s) ride.

CYLINDER BLOCK: The main structural member of an engine in which is found the cylinders, crankshaft and other principal parts.

CYLINDER HEAD: The detachable portion of the engine, fastened, usually, to the top of the cylinder block, containing all or most of the combustion chambers. On overhead valve engines, it contains the valves and their operating parts. On overhead cam engines, it contains the camshaft as well.

DEAD CENTER: The extreme top or bottom of the piston stroke.

DETONATION: An unwanted explosion of the air/fuel mixture in the combustion chamber caused by excess heat and compression, advanced timing, or an overly lean mixture. Also referred to as "ping".

DIAPHRAGM: A thin, flexible wall separating two cavities, such as in a vacuum advance unit.

DIESELING: A condition in which hot spots in the combustion chamber cause the engine to run on after the key is turned off.

DIFFERENTIAL: A geared assembly which allows the transmission of motion between drive axles, giving one axle the ability to turn faster than the other.

DIODE: An electrical device that will allow current to flow in one direction only.

DISC BRAKE: A hydraulic braking assembly consisting of a brake disc, or rotor, mounted on an axle, and a caliper assembly containing, usually two brake pads which are activated by hydraulic pressure. The pads are forced against the sides of the disc, creating friction which slows the vehicle.

DISTRIBUTOR: A mechanically driven device on an engine which is responsible for electrically firing the spark plug at a predetermined point of the piston stroke.

DOWEL PIN: A pin, inserted in mating holes in two different parts allowing those parts to maintain a fixed relationship.

DRUM BRAKE: A braking system which consists of two brake shoes and one or two wheel cylinders, mounted on a fixed backing plate, and a brake drum, mounted on an axle, which revolves around the assembly.

DWELL: The rate, measured in degrees of shaft rotation, at which an electrical circuit cycles on and off.

ELECTRONIC CONTROL UNIT (ECU): Ignition module, module, amplifier or igniter. See Module for definition.

ELECTRONIC IGNITION: A system in which the timing and firing of the spark plugs is controlled by an electronic control unit, usually called a module. These systems have no points or condenser.

ENDPLAY: The measured amount of axial movement in a shaft.

ENGINE: A device that converts heat into mechanical energy.

EXHAUST MANIFOLD: A set of cast passages or pipes which conduct exhaust gases from the engine.

FEELER GAUGE: A blade, usually metal, of precisely predetermined thickness, used to measure the clearance between two parts.

FIRING ORDER: The order in which combustion occurs in the cylinders of an engine. Also the order in which spark is distributed to the plugs by the distributor.

FLOODING: The presence of too much fuel in the intake manifold and combustion chamber which prevents the air/fuel mixture from firing, thereby causing a no-start situation.

FLYWHEEL: A disc shaped part bolted to the rear end of the crankshaft. Around the outer perimeter is affixed the ring gear. The starter drive engages the ring gear, turning the flywheel, which rotates the crankshaft, imparting the initial starting motion to the engine.

FOOT POUND (ft.lb. or sometimes, ft. lbs.): The amount of energy or work needed to raise an item weighing one pound, a distance of one foot.

FUSE: A protective device in a circuit which prevents circuit overload by breaking the circuit when a specific amperage is present. The device is constructed around a strip or wire of a lower amperage rating than the circuit it is designed to protect. When an amperage higher than that stamped on the fuse is present in the circuit, the strip or wire melts, opening the circuit.

GEAR RATIO: The ratio between the number of teeth on meshing gears.

GENERATOR: A device which converts mechanical energy into electrical energy.

HEAT RANGE: The measure of a spark plug's ability to dissipate heat from its firing end. The higher the heat range, the hotter the plug fires.

HUB: The center part of a wheel or gear.

HYDROCARBON (HC): Any chemical compound made up of hydrogen and carbon. A major pollutant formed by the engine as a byproduct of combustion.

HYDROMETER: An instrument used to measure the specific gravity of a solution.

INCH POUND (in.lb. or sometimes, in. lbs.): One twelfth of a foot pound.

INDUCTION: A means of transferring electrical energy in the form of a magnetic field. Principle used in the ignition coil to increase voltage.

INJECTOR: A device which receives metered fuel under relatively low pressure and is activated to inject the fuel into the engine under relatively high pressure at a predetermined time.

INPUT SHAFT: The shaft to which torque is applied, usually carrying the driving gear or gears.

INTAKE MANIFOLD: A casting of passages or pipes used to conduct air or a fuel/air mixture to the cylinders.

JOURNAL: The bearing surface within which a shaft operates.

KEY: A small block usually fitted in a notch between a shaft and a hub to prevent slippage of the two parts.

MANIFOLD: A casting of passages or set of pipes which connect the cylinders to an inlet or outlet source.

MANIFOLD VACUUM: Low pressure in an engine intake manifold formed just below the throttle plates. Manifold vacuum is highest at idle and drops under acceleration.

MASTER CYLINDER: The primary fluid pressurizing device in a hydraulic system. In automotive use, it is found in brake and hydraulic clutch systems and is pedal activated, either directly or, in a power brake system, through the power booster.

MODULE: Electronic control unit, amplifier or igniter of solid state or integrated design which controls the current flow in the ignition primary circuit based on input from the pick-up coil. When the module opens the primary circuit, the high secondary voltage is induced in the coil.

NEEDLE BEARING: A bearing which consists of a number (usually a large number) of long, thin rollers.

OHM:(Ω) The unit used to measure the resistance of conductor to electrical flow. One ohm is the amount of resistance that limits current flow to one ampere in a circuit with one volt of pressure.

OHMMETER: An instrument used for measuring the resistance, in ohms, in an electrical circuit.

OUTPUT SHAFT: The shaft which transmits torque from a device, such as a transmission.

OVERDRIVE: A gear assembly which produces more shaft revolutions than that transmitted to it.

OVERHEAD CAMSHAFT (OHC): An engine configuration in which the camshaft is mounted on top of the cylinder head and operates the valve either directly or by means of rocker arms.

OVERHEAD VALVE (OHV): An engine configuration in which all of the valves are located in the cylinder head and the camshaft is located in the cylinder block. The camshaft operates the valves via lifters and pushrods.

OXIDES OF NITROGEN (NOx): Chemical compounds of nitrogen produced as a byproduct of combustion. They combine with hydrocarbons to produce smog.

OXYGEN SENSOR: Used with the feedback system to sense the presence of oxygen in the exhaust gas and signal the computer which can reference the voltage signal to an air/fuel ratio.

PINION: The smaller of two meshing gears.

PISTON RING: An open ended ring which fits into a groove on the outer diameter of the piston. Its chief function is to form a seal between the piston and cylinder wall. Most automotive pistons have three rings: two for compression sealing; one for oil sealing.

PRELOAD: A predetermined load placed on a bearing during assembly or by adjustment.

PRIMARY CIRCUIT: Is the low voltage side of the ignition system which consists of the ignition switch, ballast resistor or resistance wire, bypass, coil, electronic control unit and pick-up coil as well as the connecting wires and harnesses.

PRESS FIT: The mating of two parts under pressure, due to the inner diameter of one being smaller than the outer diameter of the other, or vice versa; an interference fit.

RACE: The surface on the inner or outer ring of a bearing on which the balls, needles or rollers move.

REGULATOR: A device which maintains the amperage and/or voltage levels of a circuit at predetermined values.

RELAY: A switch which automatically opens and/or closes a circuit.

RESISTANCE: The opposition to the flow of current through a circuit or electrical device, and is measured in ohms. Resistance is equal to the voltage divided by the amperage.

RESISTOR: A device, usually made of wire, which offers a preset amount of resistance in an electrical circuit.

RING GEAR: The name given to a ring-shaped gear attached to a differential case, or affixed to a flywheel or as part a planetary gear set.

ROLLER BEARING: A bearing made up of hardened inner and outer races between which hardened steel rollers move.

ROTOR: 1. The disc-shaped part of a disc brake assembly, upon which the brake pads bear; also called, brake disc.
2. The device mounted atop the distributor shaft, which passes current to the distributor cap tower contacts.

SECONDARY CIRCUIT: The high voltage side of the ignition system, usually above 20,000 volts. The secondary includes the ignition coil, coil wire, distributor cap and rotor, spark plug wires and spark plugs.

SENDING UNIT: A mechanical, electrical, hydraulic or electromagnetic device which transmits information to a gauge.

SENSOR: Any device designed to measure engine operating conditions or ambient pressures and temperatures. Usually electronic in nature and designed to send a voltage signal to an on-board computer, some sensors may operate as a simple on/off switch or they may provide a variable voltage signal (like a potentiometer) as conditions or measured parameters change.

SHIM: Spacers of precise, predetermined thickness used between parts to establish a proper working relationship.

SLAVE CYLINDER: In automotive use, a device in the hydraulic clutch system which is activated by hydraulic force, disengaging the clutch.

SOLENOID: A coil used to produce a magnetic field, the effect of which is produce work.

SPARK PLUG: A device screwed into the combustion chamber of a spark ignition engine. The basic construction is a conductive core inside of a ceramic insulator, mounted in an outer conductive base. An electrical charge from the spark plug wire travels along the conductive core and jumps a preset air gap to a grounding point or points at the end of the conductive base. The resultant spark ignites the fuel/air mixture in the combustion chamber.

SPLINES: Ridges machined or cast onto the outer diameter of a shaft or inner diameter of a bore to enable parts to mate without rotation.

TACHOMETER: A device used to measure the rotary speed of an engine, shaft, gear, etc., usually in rotations per minute.

THERMOSTAT: A valve, located in the cooling system of an engine, which is closed when cold and opens gradually in response to engine heating, controlling the temperature of the coolant and rate of coolant flow.

TOP DEAD CENTER (TDC): The point at which the piston reaches the top of its travel on the compression stroke.

TORQUE: The twisting force applied to an object.

TORQUE CONVERTER: A turbine used to transmit power from a driving member to a driven member via hydraulic action, providing changes in drive ratio and torque. In automotive use, it links the driveplate at the rear of the engine to the automatic transmission.

TRANSDUCER: A device used to change a force into an electrical signal.

TRANSISTOR: A semi-conductor component which can be actuated by a small voltage to perform an electrical switching function.

TUNE-UP: A regular maintenance function, usually associated with the replacement and adjustment of parts and components in the electrical and fuel systems of a vehicle for the purpose of attaining optimum performance.

TURBOCHARGER: An exhaust driven pump which compresses intake air and forces it into the combustion chambers at higher than atmospheric pressures. The increased air pressure allows more fuel to be burned and results in increased horsepower being produced.

VACUUM ADVANCE: A device which advances the ignition timing in response to increased engine vacuum.

VACUUM GAUGE: An instrument used to measure the presence of vacuum in a chamber.

VALVE: A device which control the pressure, direction of flow or rate of flow of a liquid or gas.

VALVE CLEARANCE: The measured gap between the end of the valve stem and the rocker arm, cam lobe or follower that activates the valve.

VISCOSITY: The rating of a liquid's internal resistance to flow.

VOLTMETER: An instrument used for measuring electrical force in units called volts. Voltmeters are always connected parallel with the circuit being tested.

WHEEL CYLINDER: Found in the automotive drum brake assembly, it is a device, actuated by hydraulic pressure, which, through internal pistons, pushes the brake shoes outward against the drums.

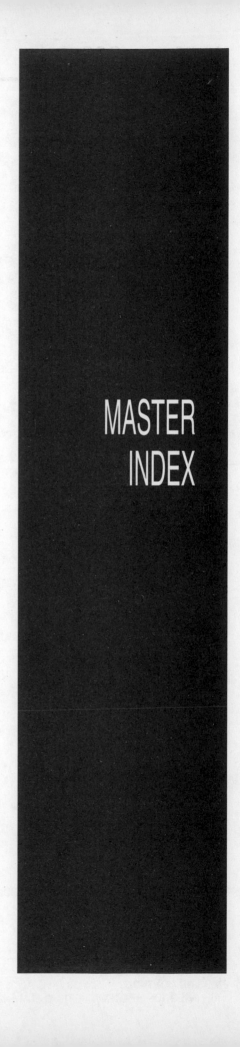

MASTER INDEX